PRAYING THE

NEW TESTAMENT

BOOKS BY THE AUTHOR

Knowing God Through Fasting

Praying the Psalms

Praying the Proverbs, Ecclesiastes, and Song of Solomon

Praying the Book of Job

Praying the Book of Revelation

Praying the Gospels

Praying the Book of Acts and the General Epistles

Praying Paul's Letters

AVAILABLE FROM DESTINY IMAGE PUBLISHERS

PRAYING THE

NEW
TESTAMENT

Elmer L. Towns

DESTINY IMAGE® PUBLISHERS, INC.
P.O. Box 310, Shippensburg, PA 17257-0310

"Speaking to the Purposes of God for this Generation and for the Generations to Come."

This book and all other Destiny Image, Revival Press, Mercy Place, Fresh Bread, Destiny Image Fiction, and Treasure House books are available at Christian bookstores and distributors worldwide.

For a U.S. bookstore nearest you, call **1-800-722-6774.**

For more information on foreign distributors, call **717-532-3040.**

Reach us on the Internet at **www.destinyimage.com.**

ISBN 10: 0-7684-2704-5

ISBN 13: 978-0-7684-2704-2

For Worldwide Distribution, Printed in the U.S.A.

1 2 3 4 5 6 7 8 9 10 11 / 11 10 09 08

CONTENTS

INTRODUCTION 13

PRAYING THE GOSPELS 15

PART ONE
Jesus—Immanuel 17

Chapter 1
The Gospel of Luke 19

Chapter 2
An Angel Speaks. 21

Chapter 3
The Birth of Jesus. 39

Chapter 4
Egypt and Beyond 55

Chapter 5
The Gospel of John 59

PART TWO
Jesus—The Son of God and Man 71

Chapter 6
Jesus, Disciples, and Miracles 73

Chapter 7
My Father's House and Kingdom 93

Chapter 8
Jesus Heals. 119

Chapter 9
The Sermons of Jesus 131

Chapter 10
John the Baptist 155

Chapter 11
Feeding His People 161

Chapter 12
The Absolute Love of Jesus 189

Chapter 13
Parables of Lost Things 215

PART THREE
Jesus—The Redeemer 237

Chapter 14
Jesus in Jerusalem 239

Chapter 15
The Prayers of Jesus 271

Chapter 16
Jesus' Last Days on Earth 277

Chapter 17
The Resurrection of Jesus Christ 301

PRAYING THE BOOK OF ACTS

Praying the Book of Acts 1:1–28:31 315

Chapter 18
The Story of Writing the Book of Acts 317

Chapter 19
The Story of the Ascension of Jesus to Heaven 321

Chapter 20
The Story of Barnabas: The Rich Young Ruler 337

Chapter 21
The Story of Choosing Seven Deacons 345

Chapter 22
The Story of Stephen 351

Chapter 23
    The Story of Saul's Rise to Power 359

Chapter 24
    The Story of Paul's Conversion 365

Chapter 25
    The Story of the Antioch Church 379

PRAYING PAUL'S LETTERS **431**

Praying With Me the Letters of Paul 433

ROMANS **435**

Chapter 26
    The Story of Writing the Book of Romans 437

Chapter 27
    Praying the Book of Romans 1:1–16:27 441

FIRST CORINTHIANS **485**

Chapter 28
    The Story of Writing the Book of First Corinthians 487

Chapter 29
    Praying the Book of First Corinthians 1:1–16:24 491

SECOND CORINTHIANS **533**

Chapter 30
    The Story of Writing the Book of Second Corinthians 535

Chapter 31
    Praying the Book of Second Corinthians 1:1–13:14 539

GALATIANS **569**

Chapter 32
    The Story of Writing the Book of Galatians 571

Chapter 33
    Praying the Book of Galatians 1:1–6:18 575

EPHESIANS **591**

Chapter 34
The Story of Writing the Book of Ephesians 593

Chapter 35
Praying the Book of Ephesians 1:1–6:24 597

PHILIPPIANS. **609**

Chapter 36
The Story of Writing the Book of Philippians. 611

Chapter 37
Praying the Book of Philippians 1:1–4:23 615

COLOSSIANS. **625**

Chapter 38
The Story of Writing the Book of Colossians 627

Chapter 39
Praying the Book of Colossians 1:1–4:18 631

FIRST THESSALONIANS **641**

Chapter 40
The Story of Writing the Book of First Thessalonians 643

Chapter 41
Praying the Book of First Thessalonians 1:1–5:28 647

SECOND THESSALONIANS **657**

Chapter 42
The Story of Writing the Book of Second Thessalonians. 659

Chapter 43
Praying the Book of Second Thessalonians 1:1–3:18 663

FIRST TIMOTHY **669**

Chapter 44
The Story of Writing the Book of First Timothy 671

Chapter 45
Praying the Book of First Timothy 1:1–6:21 675

SECOND TIMOTHY **689**

Chapter 46
    The Story of Writing the Book of Second Timothy 691

Chapter 47
    Praying the Book of Second Timothy 1:1–4:22 697

TITUS **705**

Chapter 48
    The Story of Writing the Book of Titus 707

Chapter 49
    Praying the Book of Titus 1:1–3:15 709

PHILEMON **715**

Chapter 50
    The Story of Writing the Book of Philemon 717

Chapter 51
    Praying the Book of Philemon 1:1-25 721

PRAYING THE GENERAL EPISTLES **725**

HEBREWS

Praying the Book of Hebrews 1:1–13:25 727

Chapter 52
    The Story of Writing the Book of Hebrews 729

JAMES

Praying the Book of James 1:1–5:20 759

Chapter 53
    The Story of Writing the Book of James. 761

FIRST PETER

Praying the Book of First Peter 1:1–5:14 773

Chapter 54
    The Story of Writing the Book of First Peter 775

SECOND PETER

Praying the Book of Second Peter 1:1–3:18 798

Chapter 55
    The Story of Writing the Book of Second Peter 791

FIRST JOHN

Praying the Book of First John 1:1–5:21 801

Chapter 56
    The Story of Writing the First Letter of John 803

SECOND JOHN

Praying the Book of Second John 1–13 815

Chapter 57
    The Story of Writing the Second Letter of John 817

THIRD JOHN

Praying the Book of Third John 1–14. 821

Chapter 58
    The Story of Writing the Third Letter of John. 823

JUDE

Praying the Book of Jude 1–25 827

Chapter 59
    The Story of Writing the Book of Jude. 829

PRAYING THE BOOK OF REVELATION 837

Praying the Book of Revelation 1:1–22:21. 839

Chapter 60
    Worship: When You Come to the End. 841

Chapter 61
    Worship: Waiting in Jesus' Presence for His Message 853

Chapter 62
    Worship: Immediately Upon Entering Heaven 865

Chapter 63
    Worshiping the Lamb 881

Chapter 64
    Martyrs Worship as They Enter Heaven,
    and The Seven Trumpet-Judgments 895

Chapter 65
    Worship: When We First See the Ark, and
    The Seven Personages of the Future Tribulation 915

Chapter 66
    The Unknown Song of the 144,000 933

Chapter 67
    Worshiping the Lamb 943

Chapter 68
    Worship at the Marriage Supper of the Lamb 961

Chapter 69
    Seeing the Future Heaven 975

INTRODUCTION

When you pray your way through the New Testament, you are traveling the way of Christ. As you read, you will be transported to the time when the Holy Spirit was inspiring writers to tell His story.

This book is a compilation of four of my previously published books in the series *Praying the Scriptures: Praying the Gospels, Praying the Book of Acts and the General Epistles, Praying Paul's Letter,* and *Praying the Book of Revelation.*

The first project in this series began one morning when I was translating Psalm 37 into popular, everyday English, then transposing it into the second person—a prayer to God for my own spiritual growth. It went so well that I decided to translate the entire Book of Psalms.

As with the previous seven books in this series, this book is a translation of Scripture from the original Greek into modern language—not a word-for-word translation, rather a thought-for-thought edition. It contains vivid descriptions of events and prayers that will touch your intellect, emotion, and spirit—transforming your life and growing your faith.

Why should you pray the Scriptures? Praying is a heart response to God, while reading the Bible is usually a head response to Him. Please note that this is not an inspired version of Scripture, but a human paraphrase; so read your Bible along with praying the Scriptures.

May God open your eyes as you read *Praying the New Testament,* and may Christ fill your heart and mind with His almighty love and enduring favor.

Sincerely yours in Christ,
Elmer Towns
Written at my home at the foot of the Blue Ridge Mountains
Spring 2008

PRAYING THE GOSPELS

Part One

Jesus—Immanuel

Chapter 1

THE GOSPEL OF LUKE

Luke 1:1-4

While Paul was in prison in Caesarea, Luke wrote a biography of Jesus and addressed it to a rich Christian named Theophilus (his name means "lover of wisdom"). A church probably met in Theophilus' house, and since he was rich, he probably had a library where he kept books for casual reading or serious study. Probably some Christian manuscripts were kept there also. Most wealthy men had an educated slave who could copy manuscripts for his master. Perhaps Theophilus had sent his slave to copy some of Paul's letters, to places like Colosse (the Book of Colossians) and Ephesus (the Book of Ephesians) and Galatia (the Book of Galatians).

Theophilus probably sent money to pay for Paul's expenses while he was in prison. In return, Luke sent Theophilus a complete biography of the life and works of Jesus, and explained, *"I have interviewed original eyewitnesses of the life of Christ, so I could write a complete narrative giving accurate information about the life of Christ"* (Luke 1:2-3 ELT). Luke also read all the bits and pieces of stories about Jesus and used them as sources for his biography of Jesus, *"Many have undertaken the task of writing the things we believe about Jesus...I in turn have gone over the whole course of their description..."* (Luke 1:1,3 ELT).

Like a newspaper reporter gathering all the facts before writing a story, Luke did his research in books and interviews (he did his research and writing while Paul was two years in prison). As Luke began to write, it was not the usual process of writing. Luke was inspired by the Holy Spirit so that what he wrote was accurate and without error. Luke was even aware of what was happening because he said, *"It seemed good to me also, having had perfect understanding of all things **from the very first**..."*

19

(Luke 1:3 KJV). The phrase "from the very first," is *anothen* in the original Greek which means "from above." Luke testified he had perfect understanding from above—from God. The Gospel of Luke is the authority of God because he wrote what God told him to write, and he did it with the inspirational help of God.

Introduction to Luke

Luke 1:1-4

Lord, Luke said that many others have written a biography
> Of the events of Jesus on the earth;
He researched carefully the reports they wrote
> And he interviews disciples who followed Him,
> And eyewitnesses who saw these things.
So that he would have perfect understanding
> To write an accurate account of Jesus,
Luke wrote the events in perfect sequence,
> Being inspired by God from on high.
Therefore, Theophilus had confidence in
> The things that have been taught to him.

Lord, I have confidence in the things
> *That have been taught to me from Your Word,*
> *And I will study it carefully to know what You said.*

Chapter 2

AN ANGEL SPEAKS

The Story of God Promising Zechariah a Son

Luke 1:5-25

The old man looked wistfully to the distant mountains. The leathery skin stretched over his frail bones told that he was past 60 years of age. He looked for Messiah to come each day; the One who would deliver his people from Rome's oppression. But the Messiah had not come.

"Come inside to eat," said his elderly wife who stood at the door of their home in Abia, a community that was home to Jerusalem's priests.

"I'm not hungry."

His wife asked, "Not hungry? Is it because of joy...or sadness?"

Zechariah smiled. Tomorrow would be his last day of temple duty. He was retiring. Tomorrow, when he entered the Holy Room to offer evening prayers, it would be his first and last time to pray for his nation. Priestly duties were assigned by lottery, and a priest could have the privilege of burning incense in the Holy Place usually once in his lifetime—sometimes never. If the selection had not been made for tomorrow, Zechariah would have ended his service unfulfilled.

"Don't frown," his wife, Elizabeth, told Zechariah. "You'll do fine."

Zechariah was not worried about praying.

"I'm concerned about the younger priests," he told his wife. "They do not love people, they love power. They have lost their faith."

"And why not?" Elizabeth wondered. "What is there to have faith in?"

"Hush!" Zechariah protested. "We must have faith in the Word of God; we must not look for miracles."

"I do. I do," Elizabeth declared. "But where is God? If the Almighty One loves His people, why doesn't He send Messiah to drive the Romans into the sea?"

The next day, excitement swept Zechariah and Elizabeth along the path on their short walk to Jerusalem. Friends and family accompanied them.

They entered the temple and Zechariah reached out to rub the gold on its gate one last time in his official role as a priest. Inside he glimpsed the 12 golden stairs and on a platform the Levitical choir.

Behind the choir were 12 more golden stairs. Clusters of people milled about, beginning to fill the large courtyards of the temple.

The priest in the pinnacle measured the falling shadow on the sundial, and when it was four o'clock, he put a trumpet to his lips and sounded the call for prayers. When the last note finished, the choir began to sing.

Zechariah climbed the golden stairs toward the Holy Room. Supportive eyes watched him disappear between its heavy curtains.

Zechariah stood before the Lord. He bowed his head in gratitude. I'm going to pray for myself, before I pray for Israel, he thought. "*Lord...give me a son.*"

He didn't mean to ask for a child—he blurted out the words without thinking. It was a prayer he had uttered many times. Elizabeth, his wife, was barren. Thousands of times he had asked for a son.

A cold shiver ran down Zechariah's back. There before him was a beautiful young man. He scared Zechariah because no one was supposed to be in the Holy Room except the appointed priest.

"Fear not," the young man said. "I am Gabriel. God wants you to know your prayers have been heard. Your wife will become pregnant and deliver a son."

"No!" the old priest protested. "We are too old for children."

"Your son will be special," Gabriel continued. "He will announce the Deliverer of Israel."

"The Messiah is coming?" Zechariah's eyes lit up.

"Your son will not be Messiah," the angel explained, "but your son will prepare the people for His coming."

"But I'm too old," Zechariah protested again.

Gabriel paid no attention. "Your son will have the name John," he instructed.

"Can you prove this?" Zechariah sputtered. "How will I know?"

"Because you did not believe the words of God, you will be unable to speak until the child is born." Gabriel pointed with an outstretched finger to Zechariah's mouth.

"Ugh...ugh...ugh...." Nothing came out of Zechariah's mouth.

"*Forgive me...forgive me,*" Zechariah prayed silently. Then the old man crumpled to the floor.

The crowd of worshipers outside was becoming restless. Zechariah had been in the Holy Place much longer than was usual. The other priests knew they couldn't enter the Holy Room to see what was wrong, but they had to do something. The sun was setting, and the blessing hadn't been given.

One priest spoke to quiet the crowd. "Be patient...he will come out soon."

The curtains rippled. Zechariah stepped out onto the stairs. "Give the benediction!" one of the clerics called.

Zechariah shook his head and pointed to his mouth. "Ugh...ugh...ugh..." were the only sounds he could make.

The archpriest, sensing trouble, stepped beside his old friend. Lifting his hand, he said to the people, "The Lord bless and keep you. The Lord make His face to shine upon you. The Lord lift up His countenance upon you and give you peace."

My Time To Pray

- Lord, help me to wait patiently for the events in life when I will be the most effective for you.

- Help me to be sensitive to Your inner voice when You are trying to guide my life.

- Lord, sometimes I don't believe Your Word just as Zechariah didn't believe You. Help me to see my unbelief and give me a trusting heart.

- Lord, may I be quick to act on Your promises, something Zechariah didn't do.

- Lord, I want my personal life to honor You and I want to be faithful in service to the end of my life, as was Zechariah.

God Promises Zechariah a Son

Luke 1:5-25

Lord, Luke began to describe the events
    During the reign of King Herod.
Zechariah, a priest of the Abijah corps,
    Had married Elizabeth who was from the priestly family,
    So he had impeccable qualifications to serve God.
Zechariah and Elizabeth were spiritually minded
    And they carefully obeyed every aspect of religious law,
    And because Elizabeth was barren, they had no children.
When it finally came Zechariah's turn to offer
    Evening prayers in the Holy Place for all Israel,
He also entered to burn incense,

A symbol of prayers ascending up to God.
A great multitude was outside praying
    At the tenth hour, which was 4 P.M.

Lord, may I be as faithful to You
    As were Zechariah and Elizabeth in all things.

Lord, the appearance of an angel standing by the altar of incense
    Frightened Zechariah;
    The angel said, "Do not be afraid,
God has heard your prayers,
    Your wife Elizabeth will have a son
    And you must name him John."
"Your son will give you joy and happiness
    And multitudes will rejoice with you."

Lord, help me receive Your message
    When You come to speak to me.

Lord, the angel told Zechariah, "Your son will be a great man for God,
    He must never drink intoxicating liquor,
    And the Holy Spirit will fill him for service.
"Your son will convince many to turn to God,
    He will be rugged like Elijah
    And will precede the coming Deliverer.
"He will prepare for the coming of Deliverer
    By softening the hearts of fathers to be like children,
    And convincing the disobedient to return to Your wisdom."
Zechariah objected saying he was an old man,
    And his wife was beyond child-bearing years.

Lord, when You promise to work in my life
    May I never disbelieve Your Word.

The angel Gabriel reminded Zechariah that
    He heard this good news standing in the presence of God,

And that God sent him to tell Zechariah.
Because Zechariah didn't believe God would do the things
    For which he prayed all his life,
Then the angel said that Zechariah wouldn't be able to speak
    Until the child was born.

Lord, may I be quick to believe, quick to
    Obey all You tell me to do.

The waiting crowd got anxious because Zechariah tarried
    And he couldn't speak when he appeared,
    So they realized he saw a vision.
Shortly, after Zechariah returned home, Elizabeth became pregnant
    And she hid herself from public view.
Elizabeth proclaimed, "Lord, You are gracious
    To take away the embarrassment of having no children."

The Story of Gabriel Promising Mary a Son

Mary was a pretty young woman, nearly always adorned with a smile. But today she wore a worried look as she walked toward the Nazareth Synagogue. Joseph was posting bands for their marriage.

"Suppose the elders say no?" Mary asked her mother. "They will approve," the mother assured her anxious daughter. Mary and her mother climbed the outside stairs to the synagogue loft where the women and children sat. They positioned themselves where they could see the elders when Joseph approached them.

"They must give approval to Joseph," Mary whispered to her mother.

Her mother only smiled. The people in the community knew that Mary was the most godly young woman in the synagogue. When Mary had caught Joseph's eye, all old grand mothers approved. They knew Joseph was a godly young man too.

26

Joseph rose and handed the parchment to the ruling elder. The elder nodded.

From the balcony, Mary watched without blinking. The elders, arranged in a row, were ready to make the announcement. Normally, the old men frowned when young men asked permission to marry. But for Joseph, their wrinkled, old eyes twinkled, their gray beards nodding up and down in approval.

After dinner, Mary rushed to the fig tree to pray. She loved to talk with God. It's the place where her father prayed.

O Lord God, may Your Kingdom come in our village...in our family...in my life....

Suddenly, she felt the presence of someone else under the tree; pivoting, she saw a stranger.

"Greetings," said the pleasant young man, smiling. "You who are highly favored, the Lord is with you."

Mary gasped. "Who are you?"

"Gabriel," the young man answered. "My name is Gabriel. Do not be afraid," he said. "You have found favor with God. You are to have a child. Your son shall be conceived in your womb, and when he is born, you shall give him the name Jesus."

Mary's heart leaped. In Hebrew, the language of her people, the name Jesus translated to Joshua, meaning "Jehovah saves." A little boy named Jesus would call to mind Joshua, the great leader who had defeated Israel's enemies.

Gabriel interrupted her thoughts. "God shall give your son the throne of his father, David. And His Kingdom shall never end."

The Deliverer? Mary thought. My son will be the Messiah? The coming of the Messiah had been foretold for hundreds of years. According to the prophecies, Mary was from the right family, descended from David. Her son could defeat the Romans just as the boy David had defeated Goliath, the Philistine giant. She said to the angel, "I am not yet married to

Joseph." The angel told Mary, "Joseph is not to be the father, the Holy Spirit shall come upon you and overshadow you, and the child shall be the Son of God."

Mary's thoughts tumbled one over another. How could she have a child without a father? What would people think? And what of Joseph?

As though he could read her thoughts, the angel reassured Mary. "Your cousin Elizabeth is too old to have children," he said. "She was said to be barren, but she has conceived. With God nothing is impossible."

Mary struggled briefly with her thoughts, but then she bowed her head. "Behold," she submitted, "I will be the Lord's handmaiden. Do to me what You have promised."

When she opened her eyes again, Gabriel was not there.

My Time to Pray

- Lord, may I be as submissive to Your plan for my life as Mary was to Your plan for her life.

- Please forgive me for any time in the past when I rebelled at Your plan for my life.

- May I be sensitive to Your plan when it comes to me.

Gabriel Promises Mary a Son

Luke 1:26-38

When Elizabeth was six months pregnant
    The angel Gabriel appeared to Mary
    A virgin who was engaged to Joseph;

They were both in the family line of King David.
Gabriel greeted Mary, "Rejoice, Mary,
    You are highly favored of God,
    The Lord is with you."
Mary was confused with this greeting,
    She didn't know what it meant.
Gabriel said, "Do not be afraid,
    God has decided to use you
    To be a blessing to all the world.
"You will conceive and deliver a Son,
    You must call His name Jesus.
"He will have great influence on the world
    And He will be the Son of the Most High God.
"God will give Your Son the throne of David
    And He will rule over Israel forever."
Mary replied, "How can this happen,
    I am a virgin,
    And have not known a man?"
Gabriel answered, "The Holy Spirit will come on you,
    Power from the Most High God will make it happen,
    And you'll have a child who is the Son of God."
Gabriel continued, "Your Aunt Elizabeth
    Has become pregnant with a child in her old age;
    With God, nothing is impossible."
Mary answered. "I will be the Lord's handmaiden,
    I am willing to be what the Lord wants me to be;
    Let it happen, as you said."

Lord, I believe You can do miracles in my life,
    But my doubts are always lurking;
    I believe, help Thou my unbelief.

An Angel Speaks to Joseph

Matthew 1:1-25

Matthew wrote a biography of Jesus
    Emphasizing the Kingly ancestry of Jesus the Messiah.
Matthew included a family tree that showed Jesus
    Was the son of both King David and Abraham.
Matthew included the name of each generation,
    But the Holy Spirit had him include the
    Name of three women with questionable qualifications.
Matthew included Tamar, the daughter-in-law of *Judah*
    Whose disobedience and sin would have blocked
    The line leading to the Messiah.
But Tamar's faith and persistence
    Led to her son Perez that continued the Messianic line.
Matthew included Ruth, a Gentile, an outsider to the covenant,
    But her deep faith in You, led to her salvation;
She became the great grandmother of David when she
    Married into the line of the Messiah.
Matthew included Bathsheba, a married woman
    Who committed adultery with David.
But through the repentance of both she and David,
    Solomon was born who continued the line.

Lord, You included women of sin and unbelief
    In the line that led to Your Son, Jesus.
You did this because no one lives without sin,
    And You continually extend grace to each
    Just as You did to those three women.

Lord, when I don't believe You, or sin ignorantly,
    Please forgive me and extend Your grace to me.

Lord, the genealogy of Your son, Jesus, stretched
     For 14 generations from Abraham to David,
     For 14 generations from David to the Babylon Captivity,
     And 14 generations from the Babylonian Captivity to Jesus.

Joseph was engaged to Mary when it was discovered
     Mary was pregnant, but Joseph didn't know
     The pregnancy was by the Holy Spirit.
Because Joseph was a *man of high character*,
     He decided to privately break the engagement
     And not publicly embarrass Mary.
As he was praying and thinking about this matter,
     The angel of the Lord appeared and said to him,
     "Don't hesitate to take Mary as your wife.
"Her child has been conceived by the Holy Spirit,
     She will have a Son, name Him Jesus
     For He will save His people from their sin."

Lord, all this took place to fulfill the Scripture in Israel,
     "The virgin will conceive and give birth to a Son,
And He shall be called Immanuel,
     A name that means, 'God With Us.'"
Then Joseph did what the angel told him to do,
     He took Mary to his home;
But did not have sexual intercourse with her
     Until she gave birth to her Son, Jesus.

The Story of Mary Meeting Elizabeth

Mary walked up the rough-hewn path toward the village of Abia. She was 60 miles from home. Within her body was a human being, placed there by God.

"Maybe it is best if I stay with Elizabeth for a while," she had told her mother, concerned about what people in Nazareth would say.

Mary approached Elizabeth and Zechariah's house and stood for a moment in front of the open door. Then she walked into the room.

"Hello...I am Mary of Nazareth."

"Oh...oh...oh...!" Elizabeth cried out, reaching for her midsection. "My baby just leaped in my womb!"

Then all at once Elizabeth knew what was happening. She exclaimed loudly to her uninvited guest, "Blessed are you among women, and blessed is the fruit of your womb!"

At the sound of Mary's voice, the baby in Elizabeth's womb had leaped for joy. Somehow, her unborn baby had recognized the presence of the Messiah. "Why has the mother of our Lord come to see me?" Elizabeth asked.

But Mary couldn't give an earthly answer. She lifted her voice and praised God:

"My soul magnifies the Lord,
And my spirit has rejoiced in God my Savior.
For he has regarded the lowly state of his maidservant.
From this day forward, all generations will call me blessed."

Elizabeth and Mary talked until late in the evening. All that Elizabeth had learned about living with a man of God was absorbed by young Mary.

"What about Joseph?" Elizabeth asked. "What does Joseph think?"

Mary admitted that Joseph had at first sought to break their betrothal. But before he could gather the necessary witnesses, an angel of the Lord appeared to Joseph in a dream. He had instructed Joseph to take Mary as his wife and to call the baby Jesus.

My Time to Pray

- Lord, may I be as sensitive to Your presence coming into my life as Elizabeth and John the Baptist were when You entered the room.

- May I magnify You in all things as did Mary in her worship of You.

- May others see in me a trusting heart in You as Elizabeth saw that kind of trust in Mary.

Mary Visits Elizabeth

Luke 1:39-56

Mary left her home and went to Judah
    To visit Zechariah and Elizabeth.
She greeted Elizabeth as she entered the house,
    The babe leaped in Elizabeth's womb
    Because he knew he was in the presence of the Messiah.
Elizabeth was filled with the Holy Spirit
    And said, "Blessed are you among women
    And blessed is the child you bear.
"This is an honor that the mother of our lord should visit me;
    You believed the promises of our Lord
    That's why you've been given this great privilege."

Lord, help me always rejoice
    When I'm in the presence of Jesus,
    As did the babe, John the Baptist.

Mary's Song—The Magnificat

Mary responded to the Lord, "You are great, my God,
    My spirit rejoices in You, my Savior;
"You look upon this lowly servant,
    Now all generations will call me blessed.
"For You—the Mighty God—have done great things,

Holy is Your name.
"Your mercy extends to those who reverence You
From one generation to another.
"You have done mighty works by Your arm,
You have cast down the proud of heart.
"You have brought down mighty kings from their thrones,
And you lift up the lowly.
"You have filled the hungry with good things,
And sent the arrogant away empty.
"You have come to help Israel, Your people,
And You have remembered to be merciful
To Abraham and his descendants forever."

Mary stayed with Elizabeth three months,
Then returned to her home.

Lord, may I ever praise You for using me,
As Mary magnified You in song.

The Story of the Birth of John the Baptist

Zechariah sat with friends on the bench in front of his dwelling. He could hear the moans of Elizabeth from inside. Lord, make this delivery easy, was all he could think of to pray. Then Zechariah heard the wail of new life: "Waa-aa-aah…Waa-aah…Waa-aa-ah!" The neighbors heard the cry and came running.

"It's a boy!" the midwife announced as she emerged from the house. A cheer went up from the crowd gathering in Zechariah's yard.

Eight days later, the ceremony to circumcise the baby was held. The family tried to name the child after his father. An uncle announced, "Call the baby Zechariah."

"Yes! Zechariah," the relatives agreed. "Call the baby Zechariah."

Zechariah jumped to his feet and waved his arms in protest. "Ugh...ugh...ugh...."

He reached for the slate and chalk. The boisterous crowd grew silent. With shaking hand, Zechariah wrote in large bold letters: HIS NAME IS JOHN.

At the moment Zechariah finished writing, he felt something in his throat. He rubbed his neck with both hands, then tried to say something. He looked at the words he had written and read aloud, "His name is John."

My Time to Pray

- Lord, help me to have a trusting heart in all circumstance as Zechariah had living with the consequences of his unbelief.

- Lord, when I'm pressured by relatives and friends to do something contrary to Your will, may I be as firm in obeying You as was Zechariah.

The Birth of John the Baptist

Luke 1:57-66

Elizabeth gave birth to a son at the appointed time,
    The relatives and neighbors rejoiced with the parents.
When they came to circumcise him on the eighth day,
    The relatives tried to name him after his father.
Elizabeth protested saying, "Call him John,"
    The relatives said no one in the family had that name.
When they asked the father about the child's name,
        Zechariah asked for a tablet and wrote,
        "His name is John."

Immediately, Zechariah was able to speak again,

     He praised You, and all the relatives joined him.

Everyone who heard about it wondered,

     "What will this child be?"

     For Your hand was with the child.

Lord, keep Your hand on me,

     As You kept Your hand on John the Baptist.

Zechariah's Song: The Benedictus

Luke 1:68-80

Zechariah was filled with the Holy Spirit

     And he spoke this prophecy,

"Blessed be You, Lord God of Israel,

     For You visited and rescued Your people.

"You have sent a mighty Deliverer

     To the people of Your servant, David,

     As You promised by the holy prophets.

"And the Deliverer will save us from our enemies,

     And from the hand of those who hate the Jews,

     So we can serve You all our days.

"And you my child, John, shall be called

     The prophet of the Most High God.

"John shall go before the Deliverer

     To prepare the way for His coming.

"John will tell the people about Your salvation

     And preach the forgiveness of sins,

"Showing us Your tender mercies that will

     Come to us like the rising of the sun.

"The Deliverer will give light to those living in darkness,

     And guide their feet in Your way."

And the child, John, grew strong physically and spiritually,
    And lived in the desert until
    His time to preach publicly to Israel.

Chapter 3

THE BIRTH OF JESUS

The Story of the Birth of Jesus in a Stable

"I could have made the trip without the donkey." The petite but very pregnant girl shut her eyes to the pain. "We can't afford this animal."

"The price is not important," replied her young husband. They had taken a shortcut from Jerusalem to Bethlehem and were trying to find a place to sleep before nightfall.

Bethlehem was the home of Mary's parents, and the Roman authorities had commanded everyone to return to his hometown to register for a census.

"Oh!" Mary clutched her midsection. "It's a labor pain." "Hold on," Joseph counseled. "Count the time between the pains."

Joseph was frantic as he banged at the wooden door of the inn. Mary pulled her cloak tighter against the wind. Her labor pains were closer together with every inn that turned them away. Bethlehem was swamped with pilgrims who had returned home for Rome's census.

"No room in this inn!" came a gruff voice from behind the door.

"We've got to have a place! My wife's having labor pains...a baby's coming!"

The innkeeper stepped out, closing the door behind him. Providentially, a pain hit and Mary moaned.

The innkeeper flinched. "There," he pointed to the stable. "You can deliver your baby in there."

"Thank you," was all Joseph could say as he led the donkey off.

He found some fresh hay for Mary to lie on, then he found some clean strips of white cloth. He prepared everything, then sat beside Mary to wait.

Two hours later, it happened—a healthy baby boy was born. Joseph didn't have to swat him. The baby's red face let out a bawl.

"Don't cry, Jesus," the new mother reached for her son. Baby Jesus nestled into Mary's loving arms.

My Time To Pray

- Lord, give me patience to accept Your regulations that make life difficult for me; and help me see Your plan for my life in them.

- Lord, help me joyfully accept the "closed doors" in my life. Lord, help me realize that when doors are closed to me, other opportunities will re-open to me.

The Birth of Jesus

Luke 2:1-7

Caesar Augustus commanded all people
> Had to return to their hometown to register
> For a census for tax purposes.
Then Joseph left Nazareth to return to Bethlehem
> Because he was in the royal line of David,
> His wife Mary was also in that line.
This happened when Quirinius

Became governor of Syria in 4 B.C.
Mary was pregnant and the birth imminent
So she gave birth while in Bethlehem.
The baby was born in a stable
Because there was no room in any of the inns.
Mary wrapped the baby in strips of cloths—swaddling clothes,
And laid Him in a feed trough.

The Story of Shepherds Watching Their Flocks

The breeze had died down and some of the shepherds came out of the small cave where they had taken shelter from the wind. Several others were already sleeping—waiting for their watch.

"Nothing happens this early in the evening," the younger shepherd moaned. His body was cold, his mind was cold, his world was cold.

"When nothing happens," the older shepherd said impatiently, "maybe we'll have peace." He had lost faith in God. The only thing he believed in was the tyranny of Rome because he had felt the sting of a Roman whip.

"When the Deliverer, the Son of David, comes, we'll have peace," said the younger man.

"Ha!" snorted the older shepherd. "Then I can go home, rather than hide up here in the hills." He paused, scratched his beard, and thought of a crime he committed when he was young. Hardened by years of running from the Roman authorities, he had finally taken work as a shepherd to hide.

The younger shepherd had prayed for the Messiah to come. The younger shepherd was hiding from the authorities for a different reason. He had sinned against his family and village, against God.

"When the Deliverer comes," the young man broke the silence, "He will purify my memory."

"What is that supposed to mean?" the older voice barked. "I've done something. I try to forget, but I can't."

A warm wind flushed the shepherds' faces. Then the night exploded in LIGHT!

Light from the heavens obliterated the darkness, blinding the two shepherds. With their hearts in their throats and their eyes stinging, they hid their faces.

"Do not be afraid," came a voice from the other side of the light.

"Wh-wh-what is it?" the young shepherd managed to ask.

"The voice is from Heaven. Only Heaven can be this bright," the older shepherd managed to say.

The younger shepherd shouted, "I see people in the sky!" The older man squinted toward the heavens. The glorious light appeared to be emanating from a breach in the sky. And flooding through the opening were angels. Thousands upon thousands of angels. And they were singing.

"Look…look…! There are so many I can't count them!" the youth cried.

"Do not be afraid," the voice behind the light repeated. "I have come to bring you tidings of great joy. Your Savior was born tonight in Bethlehem. He is Christ the Lord."

Then a magnificent sound flooded the night—a sound that flooded out the noise of past failures. The heavenly host praised God, singing: "Glory to God in the highest, And on earth peace, goodwill toward men!"

Then just as suddenly as the angels came, they were gone. "Let's go!" The younger shepherd leaped to his feet. "Where?" the other asked.

"Bethlehem! Didn't you hear? Our Savior was born in Bethlehem."

The shepherd in charge now spoke up. "We must bring the Savior a gift…a lamb."

"Mine," the young shepherd volunteered. "My lamb for the baby Savior."

Back in Bethlehem in the stable, Joseph bolted upright when he heard noises. Creeping to the door, he tried to be silent.

"Who is there?" Joseph spoke into the dark courtyard.

"We are shepherds," the lead shepherd replied. "Was a baby born here tonight?"

"Yes."

"We must see him. We have been told the child is the Savior sent from God."

Joseph opened the stable door wider. "Mary," he whispered. "Some shepherds want to see Jesus."

At Joseph's behest, the shepherds crowded through the door. But when the light shone upon the baby, the shepherds prostrated themselves in adoration.

Several minutes passed as the shepherds worshiped. Then one of them lifted his head and repeated the angels' song: "Glory to God in the highest, and on earth peace, goodwill toward men!"

One by one the shepherds looked up at the baby, Mary saw their eyes were streaked with tears.

The young shepherd whose secret sin had brought him to this place rose, the spotless lamb in his arms. He approached the feed trough where Jesus lay sleeping. Placing the lamb in the straw, he said simply, "For you. This lamb is in my place."

My Time To Pray

- Lord, may I worship You wholeheartedly like the shepherds. Lord, don't let any sin in my life keep me from worshiping You, as the sin of the older and younger shepherds stopped them.

- Lord, I will bring offerings with my worship, I will give You a tenth of all I have, and more importantly; I will give You myself.

Shepherds Visiting the Baby Jesus

Luke 2:8-20

The same evening the baby Jesus was born,
> Shepherds were in an open field guarding their sheep.
Suddenly the sky lit up with an overwhelming light,
> And a shining angel appeared to them;
> The shepherds were scared out of their wits.
The angel announced to them, "Don't be frightened,
> I have a wonderful message for you,
> And for everyone else in the world.
"Tonight, the Deliverer—even the Lord—was born
> In Bethlehem.
"You will recognize Him because He will be
> Wrapped in swathes of cloths,
> And will be lying in a feed trough."
Suddenly, the angel was joined by a gigantic choir
> Praising God saying, "Glory to God
> In the highest,
Peace to those who enjoy
> God's good will."
When the angelic choir returned to Heaven,
> The shepherds said to one another,
> "Let's go see this baby God told us about."
When they ran to Bethlehem, they found
> Mary, His mother, and the Babe lying in a manger.
Then the shepherds told everyone about the Babe,
> And people were astonished at what they heard.

Lord, may I embrace the story of the Baby
> *And worship Him with all my heart.*
May I tell everyone about the Baby
> *And how Jesus came to forgive their sins.*

Dedication of the Baby Jesus

Luke 2:21-39

Jesus was circumcised eight days after He was born,
    And they called His name Jesus,
    Just as the angels instructed them.
Later, they returned to the temple
    For the ritual cleansing of the mother
As was required by Moses in the Law,
    "Every male that opened the womb
    Shall be dedicated to the Lord.
"They did this with the offering of the poor,
    Two young turtledoves and two pigeons."
There was an elderly man named Simon
    Who looked for the restoration of the Kingdom.
Simeon lived blameless, and served God continually,
    And he was filled with the Holy Spirit.
The Lord had revealed to Simeon he would
    See the Deliverer before he died.
Simeon was led by the Spirit into the temple
    On the day the Baby was to be dedicated.
Simeon took Jesus into his arms and blessed Him
    Saying, "Lord, I have seen what You promised,
    Now I am ready to die.
"For my eyes have seen Your salvation
    Which all people will see one day.
"The Deliverer will be a light to the Gentiles,
    And will bring glory to Your people, Israel."
Joseph and Mary marveled at Simeon's words,
    Then Simeon said to Mary,
"This Child will be rejected by many in Israel
    And God will judge their unbelief.
"But the Child will also be received by many in Israel,

And they shall be saved and rewarded of God."
There was also a prophetess named Anna
    Who was very old and had lived with her
    Husband only seven years after they were married.
She lived in the temple, worshiping God,
    Praying, and very often fasting.
She came along as Simeon finished his blessing;
    She gave thanks to God for the Child,
    Telling everyone the Deliverer had come.
Joseph and Mary then returned to their home,
    And the Child became physically strong
    And was filled with wisdom.

The Story of the Wise Men's Visit

"This house is wonderful," Mary chirped as she tidied the table. Mary and Joseph had settled down in Bethlehem when Jesus was born. Joseph had helped build several homes for the residents of Nazareth, but he had done some of his best work here in Bethlehem for his wife and son.

"This house will do for a while," he said, continuing his work. Mary and Joseph had chosen not to return to their hometown of Nazareth, because the rumors of a pregnancy out of wedlock made them uncomfortable.

They decided to remain in Bethlehem. "We'll be close to the temple for the baby," Joseph had reasoned. "If Jesus is to be the leader of our nation, he should live near the City of God."

Mary had opened the front and back doors to allow the cool morning air to ventilate the house. Joseph sat on a stool in the corner, carving.

"Look at the camels!" a small boy yelled outside their door.

Mary gathered Jesus in her arms, and she and Joseph stepped into the street, blinking against the sunlight. A block away a large crowd of villagers were gathered about a string of camels.

The lead camel driver was talking to Melki, the boy with the loud voice. The local youth lifted his arm and pointed toward Joseph. Now all eyes stared at Joseph and Mary—and the baby.

A man on a camel in a gold turban also pointed at Joseph and his family. He whispered to a servant, and the servant ran toward Joseph. Joseph spoke quietly to Mary. "Go in the house," he said. "There may be danger."

The servant bowed to Joseph. "We are searching for the one born king of the Jews."

How do they know? Joseph thought before answering. *What do they know?*

Sensing Joseph's apprehension, the servant again bowed deeply. Joseph recognized the curled toes on the man's sandals as a Persian fashion. The servant asked, "May we visit the young king this evening?"

Joseph again nodded, almost too shocked to speak.

That evening young Jesus sat under the meal table playing quietly. As the twilight faded, the toddler grew tired. Mary lit all the candles they had in the house and sat down for the first time that evening. Jesus crawled into her lap and dozed in her arms.

"THEY'RE COMING!" Joseph heard Melki yelling from down the street. Moments later there came a rapping at the door. Opening it, Joseph was greeted by the sight of a massive camel. The driver beat a stick on the camel's knee, and it knelt.

The servant who had spoken with Joseph earlier bowed. "Why did they ride?" Joseph asked. "It's a short distance from your camp."

"Royalty does not walk in dirty streets," the servant said.

With the tapestry robe held in one hand, the camel rider stepped onto the rug. He walked halfway to the house, then turning, snapped his fingers. Two servants lifted a heavy chest and followed him into the house. The second and third camels dislodged their distinguished riders in equally elegant fashion.

"We have come to worship the king of the Jews," the first and eldest of the noblemen spoke in flawless Greek.

The other two noblemen strained forward to see the child. Jesus let out a yawn, and they smiled when they saw it.

"We study the stars," the first nobleman explained. "The stars tell us God has sent a Savior." He said they were called magi, or wise men, because their lives were dedicated to studying the scrolls of the ancients.

"How did you know where to find us?" Joseph asked.

"We studied the holy books of the Jews. Your Scriptures promise a Deliverer, saying He will come from among the Jews."

"We believe this to be true," another of the magi spoke up.

"Your Scriptures tell of a star that will be a sign of his birth, so we began searching the sky for His star. About a year ago, a star that had not been in our sky just...appeared."

"His star," the third wise man insisted.

Jesus slept, blissfully unaware of the conversation in the room.

"His star began moving; we followed," the wise man's eyes flashed. "The star moved. We obeyed its direction. It led us to Jerusalem, we went immediately to see the one called Herod the Great to inquire of this child."

Joseph listened carefully as the wise men described Herod as a fat, arrogant, greedy man.

"I AM THE ONLY KING OF THE JEWS!" Herod had blustered, and demanded they tell him where the baby king could be found.

"We do not know," was their response. "We only followed the star."

"Go then," Herod had told the wise men. "Find him and bring me the location...I will come to worship the child."

Joseph's brow furrowed. Herod was ruthlessly cruel. An unsettling fear lodged in the mind of the young father.

The wise old leader clapped his hands for his valet. A cedar chest was placed on the floor before Mary and the child. Bending, the old man opened the chest. All present saw the light from the candle flames flicker off the gold coins inside it.

"Bless the Lord, O my soul," the wise man prayed in the Hebrew tongue.

Another of the magi then brought an expensive flask filled with myrrh, a rare, aromatic sap, and the third dignitary set a cask of frankincense before Mary. He opened the top and released the fragrance into the room.

After a time, the three magi arose. The oldest glanced to his traveling companions for approval, then he asked, "May we get a closer look...? We want to learn His features."

Mary unfolded the cloth from the child's face, then Jesus smiled at His guests.

My Time To Pray

- Lord, help me see that every gift that comes into my life is from You, then help me to use it properly in Your service.

- Lord, I know hard times will come sometimes in the future, help me see the ways You prepare me for them.

- When "marginal" people come into my life—like the magi— help me learn from them and accept the contributions they make to my life.

The Wise Men Visit The Child Jesus

Matthew 2:1-12

After Jesus was born in Bethlehem,
    Wise men—astrologers—came from the East,

Looking for the baby born King of the Jews.
They told King Herod that they saw His star in the East
    And followed it so they could worship the Baby.
King Herod was disturbed because the Roman Senate
    Had declared He was King of the Jews.
Herod assembled Jewish leaders to find out
    Where the prophets predicted the Deliverer would be born.
They quoted the Scripture, "You, Bethlehem in Judah,
    Are not the least important town
Because the Deliverer will come from You
    That will rule the people of Israel."
Herod met privately with the wise men
    To find out exactly when the star appeared.
Herod then sent the wise men to search for the Baby,
    And report back to him
    So he deceptively could also worship Him.
The wise men started toward Bethlehem and the Star
    Appeared again and led them,
    Stopping where the Child was.
Going into the house, they saw the Child with His mother
    And falling to their knees,
Then they gave Him their gifts: gold,
    Frankincense, and myrrh.
The wise men were warned in a dream
    Not to return to Herod,
    So they went home a different way.

Lord, I worship You as did the wise men,
    Whereas they gave You earthly wealth.
I also surrender all my earthly stuff to Your use
    But most importantly, I give You my heart.

The Story of Danger to the Baby Jesus

The town of Bethlehem dozed beneath a blanket of stars. Mary and Jesus slept peacefully. A dog barked in the distance, then let out a whimper. Joseph was awakened, but it was not the dog that had roused him. He had been startled out of sleep by a dream. In his dream,

He was working on a table, growing frustrated with his inability to balance the table's legs which he was building. So he set it aside and instead put the finishing touches on a cradle he had fashioned for the royal family. He stood back to admire his handiwork then he realized he had mistakenly made not a cradle, but a feed trough! Terror gripped his heart as a long shadow fell across the doorway. Had the king come for his cradle?

He turned to greet his highness, but it was not the king. There stood a beautiful angel, one with familiar features.

"Get up, Joseph," the angel-visitor warned. "An enemy is coming to kill the child."

Then Joseph knew. This was the angel-messenger who had foretold the birth of Jesus.

"Hurry," the angel warned. "Death comes after sun up. Go to Egypt. Take the child and his mother and stay until I tell you to return." Joseph nodded his willingness to obey.

There was a faint light in the east when Joseph led Mary out to the donkey. He helped her up, then brought her the bundled child. He threw two sacks filled with gold, frankincense, and myrrh over the animal that was their "money" to pay for the trip. By the time they made their way out of Bethlehem, the light was beginning to reveal the road ahead.

A few miles out of Bethlehem the donkey refused to go any farther. The donkey jerked his head angrily against Joseph's direction. The donkey pulled Joseph toward a little stream at the side of the road.

"What's wrong?" Mary was concerned.

"We left so quickly. I didn't give him water."

Mary decided it was a good time to feed Jesus and found a secluded spot out of the breeze. Joseph led the animal into the stream to drink.

Moments later, Joseph heard shouts coming from the direction of Jerusalem. Then Joseph heard the unmistakable tramp of Roman soldiers.

"Stay hidden in the rocks," Joseph instructed his wife.

The troops were led by a centurion dressed in battle gear. Spotting the stream, the centurion stopped to give his horse a drink. The horse waded into the shallow water near the rocks where mother and child were hidden.

Mary prayed, *Lord, don't let Jesus cry.* The toddler closed His eyes and slept.

In the darkness, the Roman officer couldn't see into the bushes, but Joseph could see out of the bushes. He saw the centurion clearly enough. He wanted to run, but held his ground. The donkey stood silently.

The centurion jerked at his reins and the white horse ascended the bank from the stream and took up its trot beside the soldiers. With hands on their swords and death on their minds, they marched toward Bethlehem.

Quickly Joseph and Mary were back on the road. By midmorning, they had traveled far enough that their fears subsided.

Two nights later they were halfway to Egypt, and stopped for the night at an oasis. They were almost ready to go to sleep when a loud gruff voice was heard approaching.

The burly new arrival dropped his pack. Sticking his feet into the cool water, he complained of walking all day to anyone who would listen.

"I never want to see another Jew!" the voice carried over the water. "Yesterday, King Herod killed all the baby boys in Bethlehem!" The traveler went on to describe how the Roman soldiers had stacked the bodies of the babies near the well. Herod had ordered the death of all male children two years old and younger because of a rumor that a rival to his throne had been born in Bethlehem.

Mary looked at Joseph through the evening shadows. She silently wondered, *Why was our Jesus saved?*

My Time To Pray

- Lord, help me joyfully give up friends and home when it comes time for You to lead me to a new home and place to live.

- Lord, protect me from unseen dangers that I am not aware of and protect me from dangers I know.

- Lord, when I come face-to-face with danger, give me poise, courage, and show me how to react.

- Lord, I don't understand why anyone would kill another; I pray for murderers that they would repent and turn to You for forgiveness.

Slaughter of Babies in Bethlehem

Matthew 2:13-18

After the wise men left Mary and the Child,
　　　The angel of the Lord spoke to Joseph in a dream,
"Get the child and His mother and escape to Egypt,
　　　King Herod will try to kill Him;
　　　Stay there until I tell you to come back."

Joseph immediately took the child and His mother
    And left for Egypt.
Then the prophecy of the Lord was fulfilled,
    "I will call my Son out of Egypt."
When Herod realized the wise men deceived him,
    He sent soldiers to Bethlehem to kill every child
    Who was two years or younger.
Then, the prophecy of Jeremiah was fulfilled,
    "Screams and mourning were heard in Ramah,
    Rachael was sobbing for her children
    And she would not be comforted
    Because they no longer lived."

Chapter 4

EGYPT AND BEYOND

The Story of Baby Jesus in Egypt

Mary and Joseph had settled in a small Egyptian town. Joseph worked in a carpenter shop, making furniture for Egyptian customers.

One night a sudden gust of wind blew through the room and Joseph awoke in the darkness. A rooster had crowed, but dawn was not near. He prayed, *Lord, what are you trying to say to me?*

Joseph listened, but nothing came to him and he soon drifted off to sleep.

He was back in his shop in Bethlehem, working on the table...again. Two years, and he had been unable to balance the legs. Then Jesus his young son entered the shop. Little Jesus walked over to the table and, taking a saw in his small hand, shortened the errant leg. He stepped away and looked at his father for approval.

Joseph nudged the table, but it no longer wobbled. He turned to Jesus. "How did you do this, my son?"

Jesus smiled again and said, "I must be about my father's business." Joseph then looked past Jesus toward the door. There, towering above the doorway once again was the angel-messenger of God.

The angel-visitor spoke. "Take Jesus and his mother and return to the land of Israel. Herod is dead."

During the next few days, Joseph wrapped up his business. On the appointed day, the family left Egypt, never to return. Three days later they stopped at the same oasis where they had spent the night on their flight from Bethlehem. That night Joseph lay on his pallet. He soon slipped into sleep and dreamed.

The angel once again visited, *"Do not go to Jerusalem," the angel said to Joseph. "There is danger waiting there for Jesus. Return to Nazareth in Galilee."*

Joseph thought about Galilee. They had fled Nazareth because of the rumors. He was afraid they would criticize Mary. Then Joseph realized that only embarrassment faced them in Nazareth.

In Jerusalem, his son faced death. "It will be as you say," he told the messenger. "I will return to Nazareth."

My Time To Pray

- When I'm put in strange or uncomfortable situations, help me to adapt; then help me to do my business, and keep me faithful to You when I'm separated from family and friends.

- Lord, I believe there are guardian angels; I accept their protection and I thank You for them.

- May I surrender to You in all circumstances, as did Mary and Joseph.

Jesus' Exile in Egypt

Matthew 2:19-23

The Lord sent an angel to Joseph after Herod died,
>Telling him to return to the land of Israel,
>"Those who tried to kill Jesus are now dead."

So Joseph took the child and Mary and headed
>Toward the land of Israel.

Then Joseph heard that Archelaus was now king
>So he was afraid to go to Bethlehem.

So, the Lord spoke to Joseph in a dream telling him
>To go back to Galilee and his home in Nazareth.

Then the prophecy was fulfilled,
>"He (Jesus) shall be called a Nazarene."

The Story of Jesus Leaving Egypt for Nazareth

Mary and Joseph had lived in Egypt for three years. Now they were back in Nazareth. Near the back of the house, Joseph had built a carpenter shop. Mary was pregnant with their third child. She called her son into the house. "Jesus, it is time to learn how to write." Mary handed him a stylus. "Hold this pen between your fingers like this."

Within a year, he was copying his favorite psalms. "Jesus, if you're going to be a king," Mary said to him, "then you must write a complete copy of the Scriptures, just like a king. Then the thoughts of Scripture will belong to you."

So each day Jesus copied a different psalm and memorized it, repeating it flawlessly to his mother.

My Time To Pray

- Lord, help me see Your guiding hand in my life and help me follow You today.

- Lord, help me learn the Scriptures as did the young Jesus.

- Lord, I will read and study Your Word each day.

Chapter 5

THE GOSPEL OF JOHN

John 1:1-18

The first three Gospels—Matthew, Mark, and Luke—tell the human side of the birth of Jesus because Jesus was totally human. The Gospel of John tells the divine side of Jesus coming into the world because Jesus was totally God.

Lord, I worship Jesus Who is from the beginning;
>Jesus is the Word Who tells me
>All that You are.

Jesus, the Word, was face to face with You throughout eternity
>Because Jesus is God.

Lord, I worship Jesus, the mighty God Who created all things,
>And without Him was nothing created;
>Jesus does all the things that You do.

Lord, I worship Jesus who has all life in Himself
>And gives life to all His creation.

Jesus is the life of God who is the
>Light to all lost in a dark hideous world.

Jesus shines in the hostile darkness,
>But the darkness doesn't even know He exists.

Lord, John the Baptist was a prophet sent by You
>Who came to tell all about the shining Light,
>That through the Light, all might be saved.

John the Baptist was not the saving light
>But was the human sent to point everyone to the Light.

Jesus is the true saving Light
    Who offers spiritual light to all in the world.

Lord, Jesus came to the world that He created,
    But those living in the world
    Did not recognize Jesus as their Creator.
Jesus came to His own people—the Jews—
    And they refused to recognize Him.
But as many as recognize Jesus and receive Him,
    He will make them Your children,
    Simply because they believe in the authority of Jesus' name.
They will be born again by Your power,
    Which is not being born of blood,
    Or the choice of people, or of flesh.

Lord, I worship Jesus, the Word, who became flesh,
    And lived as man among men.
Jesus had all the celestial glory of Heaven
    But He clothed His heavenly glory with human flesh;
    God living in flesh was the greatest glory of all.
Jesus is Your uniquely begotten Son,
    And has all Your grace and truth.

Lord, John the Baptist said of Jesus, "This is the Messiah
    Whom I introduced to the world;
    Jesus comes after me, but is pre-eminently before me."

Lord, I received the full benefits of Jesus;
    His grace was offered and my need of grace was fulfilled.
The law of Moses condemned me to death,
    But grace and truth by Jesus gave me life.
I could never have seen You, the eternal Father,
    But Jesus Christ came from Your bosom
    To show us what You, our Father is like.

The Story of 12-year-old Jesus in the Temple

The Bar Mitzvah of Jesus

"Look, Mary!" Joseph called to his wife. "I always get a thrill when I first see the Eternal City set high on Mount Zion."

Mary and Joseph had left home three days earlier from Nazareth with a caravan of family and friends. The annual pilgrimage to Jerusalem for the Passover was a festive occasion.

Joseph and Mary were taking their 12-year-old son, Jesus, for his first visit to the temple. Jesus was now of an age to observe the requirements of Jewish law, and the Law required that Jewish men attend the feasts of Passover, Pentecost, and Tabernacles in Jerusalem.

Jesus scooted up the path ahead of his parents toward Jerusalem. He seemed pulled to the city.

The next day, they hastened through the crowded corridors of the city, the family entered the temple. The clamor of the streets died away and the sweet peace of the psalms rippled through the courtyard of the temple. Suddenly Jesus dropped to his knees beside Joseph. This experience had been a long time coming, and Jesus wanted to drink deeply from it.

Without coaxing, his childlike voice blended with the resonant sounds of mature priests as they repeated, "Hear, O Israel: The Lord our God is one Lord! You shall love the Lord with all your heart, with all your soul and strength."

The family had left Jerusalem at noon for the return home to Nazareth. Walking half a day, they reached El Birech, an oasis north of Jerusalem.

"We'll set up camp over there," Joseph pointed to a grassy place. He nodded to his son James. "Find your brother Jesus and gather some sticks for a fire."

When James returned he said, "I can't find Jesus."

Mary's heart jumped. "Run up ahead and check the campsites," Joseph commanded James. "Ask if they have seen Jesus."

Joseph left the oasis and began retracing their route back toward Jerusalem, asking anyone he met along the way about Jesus. James returned and reported that no one had seen Jesus all day. Evening was darkening when Joseph returned to camp. He had not found his son. "Pack up everything," he barked to the younger children, "Jesus must still be in Jerusalem." Within minutes, the family was back on the road.

By the next day, the parents were frantic. Joseph and Mary knew that Jesus could take care of himself in Nazareth, but this was a metropolitan city. They were at their wits' end.

Then Joseph remembered the strange look on his son's face when they worshiped at the temple. "Let's look in the temple," Joseph said. They hurried to the temple. Joseph managed to ask the first priest he saw, "Have you seen a young boy here? Beautiful olive skin? A child's white tunic, well-washed but worn?"

"All the children here look like that," the kindly priest laughed. "But there is a child sitting with the teachers of the Law; he's causing quite a commotion...."

Joseph and Mary didn't wait for him to elaborate. Dashing into a courtyard, they saw a tightly grouped crowd of people. There at the center was Jesus, standing in the midst of several bearded teachers and scholars.

"Let me put this question to you...." Jesus directed a question to the scholars. They were sitting at his feet!

Mary could not contain herself any longer. With a voice of concern mixed with relief, she called out, "Son! Why have you worried us?"

The crowd was silent. No one dared speak.

"We have searched all of Jerusalem for you..." Mary said. Twelve-year-old Jesus sensed anguish in his mother's voice. "Why didn't you look first in my Father's house?" he asked.

"Didn't you know that I would be about my Father's business?"

My Time To Pray

- Lord, give me a deeper desire to attend Your house and to join others to worship You there.

- Teach me the value of Your presence in my life. Help me to be diligent to get children into Your house to learn of You and worship You.

Twelve-year-old Jesus in Jerusalem

Luke 2:41-52

Jesus went with His parents to Jerusalem for
    The annual Passover Feast
    For He was 12 years old.
As the parents left Jerusalem for home,
    Jesus stayed in Jerusalem
    But His parents didn't know it.
After a day's journey, they went looking for Him,
    Thinking Jesus was with relatives.
When they failed to find Jesus, they returned to Jerusalem
    To search for Him.
After three days, they found Jesus sitting among the teachers,
    Listening to them and asking questions.
All who heard Jesus were greatly impressed
    At His level of comprehension
    And the difficult questions He asked them.
Joseph and Mary were astonished when they saw Him,
    And Mary asked Him,
"Son, why have You treated us like this?
    Your Father and I have been worried to death."
Jesus answered, "Why were you searching for Me?

Didn't you know that I had to
Be about My heavenly Father's business?"
Jesus returned to Nazareth with them and
Was under authority to them.
His mother didn't forget any of these incidents
And meditated on them often.
Jesus grew in mental ability and physical strength
And was respected by God and men.

Lord, I love the boy Jesus as much as
I love the Savior on the Cross;
Help me to always follow Him.

John the Baptist Begins Preaching

Matthew 3:1-12

In the 15th year of Emperor Caesar Tiberius,
Herod was the Tetrarch of Galilee and Pontius Pilate
Was governor of Judaea.
Philip ruled Ituranea and Lysanias ruled Abilene
And the High Priest was Caiaphas.
The Word of God came to John the Baptist
And he went through all Judaea
Preaching baptism of repentance for the forgiveness of sins.
John quoted the Book of Isaiah proclaiming
"I am the voice of one crying in the wilderness,
Make ready the way for the Lord,
Make straight paths for Him,
Fill in every valley
And make level the hills and mountains,
Take the curves out of crooked roads,
Smooth out rough streets,
So all mankind can receive God's Savior."

John preached to the crowds,
> "Who warned you to escape the coming wrath?
> Show good fruit if you have repented;
> Do not think you can escape judgment
> Just because you are Abraham's children.
> God can make children of Abraham
> From these stones in the desert.
> "Every tree that doesn't grow good fruit
> Will be cut down and thrown into the fire;
> The axe is ready to cut down your tree."

The crowd cried out, "What must we do?"
> John answered their questions:
> "If you have two coats, give one to the poor,
> If you have extra food, give it to the hungry."

Corrupt tax collectors asked John, "What must we do?"
> John replied, "Don't threaten or brutalize people,
> Be satisfied with your pay."

Everyone anticipated their Deliverer would soon appear,
> And many thought John was the Messiah.

John answered them, "I only baptize with water,
> The One following me will baptize with fire
> And with the Holy Spirit;
> I am not worthy to unloose his sandal straps.

"The One following me will separate real believers
> Who represent good grain
> From chaff that represent false believers.

"He will store the good grain in His barns,
> But will burn the chaff in eternal fire."

Lord, John preached the truth and I believe it,
> *I believe in Jesus the Messiah of Israel;*
> *He will protect me in the Day of Judgment.*

The Story of the Jews Questioning John the Baptist

Jesus walked through the bushes toward the Jordan River near Bethabara, a small village north of the Dead Sea. The sound of water told him the river was close.

Then he heard a voice preaching to a crowd. As Jesus stepped out of the underbrush, the piercing bass voice of John the Baptist rang out, "REPENT! Prepare the way of the Lord."

Jesus smiled when he saw John the Baptist. John stood in water ankle-deep as he spoke, wild and uncivilized in his appearance. Around him people sat on the rocks on the bank. All kinds of people had come to hear John—slaves, Roman soldiers, mothers with children.

Then Jesus noticed a cluster of men who were not enjoying the sermon. These were religious leaders, scribes and Pharisees. One of them interrupted John to ask: "Who are you?"

"I am the voice of one crying in the wilderness," John answered.

"Are you the Deliverer?" another demanded.

"No! I am here to prepare the way for Messiah." John had lived apart from the villages for many years. He subsisted on a diet of locusts and honey and had little use for the religious establishment.

"Then why are you baptizing?" one of them asked him. John was usurping the authority of the temple. He baptized people rather than sending them to the temple to offer sacrifices. Only Gentiles who wished to become Jews were required to undergo such ritual cleansing. By baptizing Jews, John made no distinction between Gentiles and God's chosen people.

One of the scribes spoke up angrily, saying, "Are we also to be baptized?"

"You brood of vipers!" John shouted, incensed. "The axe is already at the root of the trees, and every tree that does not produce good fruit will be cut down and thrown into the fire."

"What should we do then?" someone in the crowd called out.

"The man with two tunics should share with him who has none, and the one who has food should do the same."

A Roman soldier sitting with a few comrades stood up. "And what should we do?"

John replied, "Don't extort money and don't accuse the people falsely."

The people murmured, again wondering if John might be Christ, their Deliverer. John answered, saying, "I baptize you with water. But One more powerful than I will come, whose sandals I am not fit to carry. Even now He is among us."

Scandalized, the scribes and Pharisees refused to hear any more. They scooped up fistfuls of sand and threw it into the air, cursing John. Then they departed.

The following day, John again preached to the hundreds assembled at the river. When he gave his invitation to the people to be baptized, Jesus stepped into the river.

Jesus was unremarkable in appearance, his features plain. But when John saw Jesus coming to him, the Baptist stopped in mid-sentence. With the confidence of Heaven and assurance in his heart, John pointed to Jesus: "BEHOLD, THE LAMB OF GOD WHO TAKES AWAY THE SIN OF THE WORLD!"

A murmur started low but grew steadily. "Does John know this man?" "What does the Baptist mean, 'Lamb of God'?" "Surely John doesn't believe this man is the Messiah!"

Jesus splashed through the shallow water to where John was standing. Each man looked into the other's soul. Finally, Jesus broke the silence. "I am ready to be baptized," he said, smiling.

"You are the One sent by God," John said. "I need to be baptized by You."

"Allow this," Jesus said, "because it is the right and proper thing to fulfill all that God requires."

So, John the Baptist placed his hands on the chest and back of Jesus and dipped Him into the waters. When he raised Him from the river, Jesus was smiling. The crowd on the riverbank did not understand what they had just seen.

Then it happened. Silently...harmlessly...just as a dove rests on the branch of a tree, the Holy Spirit descended from Heaven and rested gently on Jesus.

Jesus stood praying there in the shallow waters when a sound came like thunder. It was a voice from Heaven. Everyone heard it, though many were unsure of what they heard. Still, those who truly believed, whose hearts swelled at this remarkable visitation, heard clearly the voice of the living God. "YOU ARE MY BELOVED SON, IN WHOM I AM WELL PLEASED."

My Time To Pray

- Lord, may I be willing to be baptized in water as was Jesus. Lord, I know when I'm dipped in water, I'm identifying with Jesus' death and burial. When I'm raised from the water, I'm identified with Jesus' resurrection. May I live by the power of the new life I get from His resurrection. I believe in the Trinity: Jesus the Son of God was baptized, the Father spoke from Heaven and the Holy Spirit descended on Jesus as a dove.

- Lord, I'm pleased with all that Jesus was and did just as the Father was pleased with Him.

Religious Leaders Question John the Baptist

John 1:9-28

The religious establishment sent delegates
>To interrogate John the Baptist, asking,
>"Who are you?"
John told them he was not the Messiah;
>Then they asked, "Are you Elijah
>Or the prophet who will come at the end of the age?"
John said, "No, I am the voice of one crying in the wilderness,
>Repent and prepare for Messiah."

Lord, may I be a clear witness to Jesus,
>*Pointing all to Christ, as did John the Baptist.*

The religious delegates asked why John was baptizing.
>He answered, "I baptize with water,
>But there is one among us who will baptize
>With the Spirit of God."

Lord, I want to be immersed into the Holy Spirit
>*As John the Baptist promised would happen.*

Part Two

Jesus—The Son of God and Man

Chapter 6

JESUS, DISCIPLES, AND MIRACLES

The Story of Jesus' First Disciples

The young fishermen had grown up together in Bethsaida. Andrew and John trusted each other. As followers of John the Baptist, they had often talked late into the night about the promised Messiah. "Get ready for His coming," the Baptist preached.

Yesterday, Andrew and John had witnessed the baptism of a man named Jesus, whom John the Baptist had declared was the "Lamb of God." Both friends had heard the voice of God from Heaven saying, "THIS IS MY BELOVED SON...."

When they saw Jesus walking among the crowds the next day, Andrew and John followed Him, at first from a distance. After a few moments, Jesus stopped and confronted them. "What do you seek?"

Andrew spoke up. "Rabbi..." he spoke the title "rabbi" with reverence, surprising his friend John with his use of the honorific word for "teacher." "Rabbi, where are You living?"

"Come and see." Jesus said, "We'll eat together."

Soon it would be dark, Jesus, Andrew, and John settled around a simple meal.

"If you are the Messiah," Andrew asked, "why did you not preach to the multitudes today?" Andrew believed the Jews would acknowledge their Deliverer and follow Him. John pointed out that more than a thousand men had been present that day at the river; they could have formed the nucleus of a formidable army.

"My Kingdom will not come by war," Jesus explained. "I must rule the hearts of people. I must rule within before I rule without."

Jesus taught them what the Messiah would do, tracing God's plan for the redemption of mankind. Beginning with the Torah—the first five books of Scripture—through the books of the prophets Jesus showed them what God had said about the coming Anointed One. And Jesus had piercing questions for these young men.

"What does God want you to do with your life?"

Neither man was sure how to answer.

"When will you begin searching for God's will?"

"Now," they promised.

"Come, follow Me." Jesus said. "Then go tell others about the Kingdom."

The next morning the young men were gone. But Jesus knew they had not rejected what He taught them; these were true seekers whose hearts were open to the things of God.

Later, as Jesus was returning on the road to Galilee, Andrew came walking swiftly from the opposite direction. Someone was with him. Andrew waved, then yelled, "This is my brother Simon. I told him you are the Messiah."

A tall man with a broad chest and a red beard, Simon was ten years older than Andrew. "Are you the Christ?" he yelled as they approached.

Jesus laughed at the boldness of the man, then looked into his eyes, "You are Simon, son of Jonah," Jesus said to him, "but from now on you shall be called Peter. You will be like a rock."

"You are a blunt speaker," Jesus continued, "I will need you to help build my Kingdom."

Turning to Andrew, Jesus said, "I will need your sensitivity and insight in the Kingdom. You are careful of people's feelings."

They walked on. Soon they met young John and his brother James. Brawny and tall, James didn't say much, though like his brother he had a fiery temperament.

"I don't like to speak," James said to Jesus, "but if You are who they say, I'll do anything You ask."

My Time To Pray

- Lord, may I follow You as did Andrew and John. Lord, help me to reach my relatives to become devoted followers of Jesus, as Andrew and John got their brothers to follow You.

- Lord, give me sensitive eyes so I can see people in the daily crowd around me who want to be Your followers.

- Lord, my talents are different than others. Use my unique gifts in Your service; just as You used the four fishermen, although each was different from the other.

Jesus Meets Six Disciples

John 1:28-51

John the Baptist said, "I saw the Spirit descend on the Messiah when He
    was baptized with water."

The next day John the Baptist told two of His disciples,
    "Behold the Lamb of God."
As Andrew and John were following Jesus, He asked,
    "What do you want?"
That evening Andrew and John talked at length to Jesus;

The next day Andrew told his brother Simon,
"We have found the Messiah,"
And Andrew brought his brother to Jesus.

Lord, may I be zealous to tell family and friends about Jesus
And may I bring them to know Jesus.

Jesus changed Simon's name to Peter
    Which meant he was firm and solid as a stone.

Lord, may I be strong and courageous in my life.

The next day when Jesus saw Philip, He said, "Follow Me";
    Philip was from the same hometown as Andrew and Peter.
Philip told his friend Nathaniel,
    "We have found the Messiah."

Lord, may I find answers to all my questions in Jesus.

Nathaniel was skeptical, "Can any good thing come out of
    Nazareth?" Philip just said, "Come and see."

Lord, help me always focus my sight on Jesus and see the
    greatness of His character.

When Jesus saw Nathaniel He said,
    "You are a sincere Israelite, you are an honest seeker,"
Nathaniel asked, "How do you know me?"
    Jesus revealed His divine omnipresence by saying, "I
    saw You talking under the fig tree to Philip when he told
    you About Me."

Nathaniel responded, "Jesus, You are the Son of God,
    You are the King of Israel."

Lord, may I worship You when I learn of Your divine Sonship;
    I yield myself to Your kingly rule.

Nathaniel believed in Jesus because of what Philip told him;
　　But Jesus said, "You'll see much greater things than this.
"You'll see Heaven opened and the angels of God going up and
　　Down upon Me, the Son of Man."

Lord, I believe what I learn of Jesus in Scripture,
　　I want to see greater things in my experience;
　　May Christ be magnified in my life.

The Story of the First Miracle—Water to Wine

"JESUS!" the feminine voice rang out. The young Galilean men gathered around Jesus turned to see a middle-aged woman waving to them.

"Jesus," she repeated the name of her oldest son. "Thank You for coming to Your cousin's wedding," Mary said.

They were interrupted by a demanding voice from the house. "Mary, the wine is running low!" Levi, the master of ceremonies, was an elderly man, short and thin. His voice was quiet, but insistent.

"JESUS!" Levi raised his voice when he recognized his nephew. Jesus introduced His disciples to His uncle, who in turn responded, "You must come and eat with us."

After meeting the guests and the families of the wedded couple, the young men took their places at the table.

"Bring them a plate of food," Mary instructed the servants. Quickly, warm bread appeared, and lamb stew.

At the head of the table, Levi told stories. There was laughter and there were more than a few red faces.

While Levi was speaking, Mary whispered to Jesus, "There's no more wine. The pitchers are empty. What am I to do?"

"Why do you come to Me? You are responsible for the food at this wedding," Jesus said to her.

"But I am not the one who will bear the shame," Mary thought aloud. "Levi and this poor young couple will suffer the humiliation of failing to provide for their guests."

Jesus left the festivities and walked outside to the back of the house. The servants followed, watching Him.

Against a corner of the house were six water pots, each of a different size and color. Jesus turned to the servants and said, "Fill each one to the top with water. Then take the wine to Levi."

The servants quickly took small vessels and filled the larger pots. Then, picking up the pots, they started toward the door.

"Attention, everyone!" Levi managed to conceal his relief at the arrival of additional wine. "Let's have a toast to the bride and groom."

The table grew silent. Panic flashed in the servants' faces. They placed a large pot on the floor on either side of Levi. Levi took his cup and dipped into the water pot. Since it was customary for the master to drink first, he put the cup to his lips.

"Ah-h-h," he sighed. Then Levi's crinkled eyes and deep smile suddenly vanished. He stared unbelievingly into his cup. "Why have you hidden the best wine until now? Every man sets out the good wine first. But you have saved the best for last!"

Levi laughed. The groom laughed. The guests all laughed. But the servants began jabbering among themselves. John turned to his brother James and whispered, "The servants claim Jesus turned water into wine."

The disciples talked excitedly between themselves. Was this possible?

"*Tell us what you are saying!*" Levi called loudly to James and John.

John spoke carefully. "The vintage you are drinking came from the pots that catch rain. An hour ago, it was not wine, but water."

Levi commanded that the servants be brought to him. "Where did you get this wine?" he demanded.

The head servant spoke with his eyes downcast. "Your nephew, the son of Mary, commanded us to fill the pots to the brim with water. We do not know how He did it, but the water became wine!"

The room fell silent. All eyes turned to Jesus, but Jesus was not there. He had departed before the wine was served.

My Time To Pray

- Lord, You have many ways to supply my needs, thank You for them all.

- Lord, thank You for going beyond supplying my basic necessities; thank You for supplying wine that is better than that which was served at first.

- Lord, I'm glad You recognized the institution of marriage by attending a wedding and blessing it with Your provision.

- Lord, help me reverence my parents—or their memory—as Jesus who had a proper relationship to His mother.

- Lord, help me see and act on the importance family has in my life.

- Lord, I believe in the miraculous, help me accept it when You send it into my life.

Jesus' First Miracle

John 2:1-11

On the seventh day after His baptism,
>Jesus was in Cana where a marriage ceremony was held;
>His mother was also there.

Jesus and His six disciples were invited to the meal
    When the wine ran out; the mother of Jesus
    Said to Him, "There is no more wine."
Jesus answered, "Why do you turn to me for help?
    It is not the time to reveal who I am."
Jesus' mother told the servants,
    "Do whatever He tells you."
There were six stone water pots available to them,
    Each one held 20 to 30 gallons.
Jesus said to the servants, "Fill them to the brim with water."
    Then He said, "Take them to the master of ceremonies."
The servants carried the water to the one in charge;
    When they arrived the water had turned to wine,
    Then the master of ceremonies toasted the wine.
He called the bridegroom to ask, "Why have you
    Kept back the best wine until now?
"People usually serve their best wine first?
    When the guests have drunk a lot
    Then a poorer quality is served."
The servants who carried the water pots
    Knew what happened.
This was the first miracle that Jesus did
    And His disciples believed in Him.

Lord, I believe in You for who You are,
    Not for the things You do for me.

The Temptation of Jesus

Matthew 4:1-11; Mark 1:12; Luke 4:1-13

Jesus was led by the Holy Spirit into the wilderness
    To be tempted by satan.
Jesus fasted for 40 days and He was hungry,

Then in His hour of physical weakness
The tempter came tempting Him, saying,
"If You are the Son of God,
Turn these stones into bread."
But Jesus answered the tempter by quoting Scripture,
"Man shall not live by bread alone,
But by every Word that comes out of the mouth of God."
Next, the tempter took Jesus into Jerusalem
And they stood on its highest pinnacle.
The temper said, "If You are the Son of God,
Throw Yourself down." Then the tempter
Quoted Scriptures to entice Jesus,
"God will put You in charge of His holy angels;
They will catch You in their hands
So You will not be smashed on the stones."
Jesus answered the tempter by quoting Scripture,
"Do not put the Lord your God to a test."
Next, the tempter took Jesus to a high mountain
And showed Him the kingdoms of the world.
The tempter said, "I will give You all of these
If You will prostrate Yourself to worship me."
Then Jesus answered, "Get away from Me."
Jesus quoted Scripture, "You must worship
The Lord Your God, and serve Him only."
Then the tempter left Jesus alone
And angels came to meet His needs.

Lord Jesus, I praise You for overcoming temptation
So You remained the perfect Lamb of God
To die for my sins.
Help me overcome temptation when I'm tempted,
So I can be victorious for You.

So Jesus began preaching everywhere, "Repent,
>> For the kingdom of Heaven is at hand."
Thus Jesus fulfilled the prophecy about His ministry:

> *Land of Zebulum and Naphtali,*
> *The way to the sea from the far side of Jordan,*
> *Called Galilee of the nations,*
> *The people that live in darkness*
> *Will see a great light.*
> *Those who live in the land of His shadow of death*
> *Will be illuminated by the Light.*

Jesus Calls Fishermen

Matthew 4:18-21; Mark 1:16-20

Then Jesus returned to Capernaum after the temptation;
>> As He walked by the Sea of Galilee He saw
>> Peter and Andrew casting their nets into the sea.
Jesus called out to them, "Come, be my disciples,
>> I'll teach you how to catch people";
>> Immediately they left their nets and followed Jesus.
A little farther, Jesus saw two more fishermen, James and John;
>> They were mending their nets
>> With their father Zebedee and the servants.
Jesus called them also to be His disciples;
>> Immediately they left their nets
>> To follow Jesus.

Lord, teach me instant obedience
>> *So I can serve You better.*

Jesus Attends Sabbath Services

Mark 1:21-28

It was the Sabbath so Jesus went into the synagogue
    As was His custom every Saturday.
Because Jesus was a visiting rabbi, the elders
    Gave Him an opportunity to teach the people.
They were amazed at what Jesus said
    And the way He said it;
    Jesus' words were authoritative, not like the others.
There was a demon-possessed man in the congregation,
    He screamed out to Jesus.
"Jesus of Nazareth, what do you want with me?
    Have you come to destroy me?"
    This was the demon speaking through the man.
The demon said to Jesus, "I know who you are,
    You are the Holy One of God;
    You are El Elyon, the possessor of Heaven and earth."
Jesus commanded the demon, "Be quiet!"
    Then Jesus said, "Come out of the man."
The demon screamed loudly,
    Then the man shook uncontrollably
    With convulsions,
    And the demon came out of the man.
The crowd was amazed saying, "What is this new teaching,
    Even demonic spirits obey Him?"
The people went back to their homes telling everyone
    About the mighty power and message of Jesus Christ.

Lord, I bow before Your omnipotent power.

Jesus Heals Peter's Mother-in-law and Others

Mark 1:29-45

Jesus left the synagogue and went to Peter's house
  Where his mother-in-law was sick with a fever.
When Jesus heard about it, He took her by the hand,
  Helped her up and the fever went away;
  She got up and prepared a meal for them.
At sundown the sick and demon-possessed
  Were brought to Peter's house for healing;
  The whole town crowded in to see what would happen.
Jesus cured many of them and cast demons out of others,
  But He wouldn't permit demons to speak
  Because they knew who He was.
In the morning, Jesus woke up before anyone else,
  And went into a private place to pray.
Simon and the others searched until they found Him,
  Then Peter said,
  "Master, everyone is looking for You."
Jesus told them He couldn't stay in Capernaum,
  But He said, "Let us go to the towns of Galilee
So I can preach to people there,
  That is why I came into the world."
As Jesus went through Galilee, a leper pleaded with Him,
  "If You are willing, You can heal me."
Because Jesus was moved with love for him, He touched the leper
  And said to him, "Be healed!"
  Immediately, his leprosy was healed.
Then Jesus sent him to be examined by a priest, and
  To make an offering that was required by Moses.
Jesus also told him not to tell anyone
  But the man told everyone what happened.
As a result, Jesus could no longer enter any town,

But even when He stayed in the fields,
    People came to Him from all around.

Lord, I want You to touch me today,
    To heal me of my sin and failure;
Then let me touch You today
    To experience Your victorious power.

The Story of Getting a Friend to Jesus

Unbeknownst to the disciples of Jesus, more than just large crowds awaited them in the city. Religious authorities in Jerusalem had sent representatives to observe Jesus of Nazareth and report on his activities and teachings to the Sanhedrin. If possible, they were to entrap Jesus, to find something they could use to discredit Him as a teacher or even have Him arrested by the civil magistrates. So Pharisees and scribes of the Law had come to Capernaum from the neighboring towns of Galilee and from Jerusalem to scrutinize the so-called Messiah.

Early one morning, Jesus knocked at Peter's door, even though his friends knew that Simon Peter was a sound sleeper and a late riser. But this morning, Peter was up, sitting at the breakfast table with Andrew.

"Come in," Peter motioned to Jesus. "Sit down and eat with us."

In short order, the room was filled with disciples. James and John had come from their father's home, telling people along the way that Jesus would be teaching this day. One by one, neighbors came to Peter's door asking, "May we come in? We want to hear what the rabbi says...."

The priest from the synagogue came to the house, and with him came visiting rabbis from Jerusalem and doctors of the Law from local villages. Because rabbis always occupied the places of honor, they sat near to Jesus, while everyone else was left to the other places in the room.

As usual, the majority of the listeners were responsive to Jesus' teaching. Some were just curious; others were hungry to know God. The religious leaders were not warm and responsive; doubt hung on their faces for all to see.

About the third hour of the day, down the main street of Capernaum came four men carrying a stretcher between them. On the stretcher was a friend, a paralytic man. They had started out before dawn from a town seven miles away, bringing their crippled friend to see Jesus. But when they reached the home of Peter and Andrew, they were unable to get to the front door. People were blocking the doorway.

"Please," the spokesman pleaded. "Let us through to see Jesus."

"Sh-h-h!" someone hushed them.

Picking up the bed with their friend, they went around to the back door, but again a crowd of people blocked the way into the building.

The four men lifted their paralytic friend and carried him up the stone stairs that led to the roof. No one took notice of them as they mounted the stairs; all attention was focused on what was going on inside the house. On the roof they found hard-packed dirt covering the flat stone tiles underneath. The four men began digging at the dirt with their hands. With a stick, they pried up a covering tile above the family room, and sunlight poured into the home of Peter.

"What are you doing?" Peter hollered, while his visitors shouted in protest against the loose dirt and pebbles raining down on them. Jesus raised a hand to hush the crowd.

The crowd was stunned to see the form of a man in a large blanket being lowered through the hole in the ceiling. Several men seated nearby stood to grab the pallet and assisted in lowering it slowly to the floor. The feverish face and glistening eyes of the paralyzed man turned up to Jesus.

Jesus said to the man, "Your sins are forgiven."

The Scribes and Pharisees in the room dared say nothing; they exchanged contemptuous looks, asking the same questions in their hearts and minds: Why does this man speak blasphemy? *Who can forgive sins but God?*

Then Jesus turned to the scribes and Pharisees and said to them, "Why are you thinking these things? Which is easier: To say to the paralytic, 'Your sins are forgiven,' or to say, 'Get up, take your bed and walk'?"

Peter suppressed a laugh. Jesus smiled and said, "But that you may know that the Son of Man has authority on earth to forgive sins...." Jesus then turned to the paralyzed man and said to him, "I tell you, get up, take your blanket and go home."

Immediately, the man stood up, gathered up his pallet and walked through the crowd and out the front door to the accompaniment of unabashed cheers and praises to God.

My Time To Pray

- Lord, I want to be a "helper" of needy people, getting them to Jesus.

- Lord, give me tenacity to seek Your presence when people or things block my access to You.

- Lord, give me faith to pray for sick people so they can get well.

Getting a Friend to Jesus

Matthew 9:1-8; Mark 2:1-12; Luke 5:18-20

Jesus was in Peter's house in Capernaum
>   When a crowd gathered to hear Him teach,
>   So that the house was packed with people.
Four men brought a man with palsy to Jesus
>   But they could not get in the house
>   Because there were so many people.

They took the sick man up to the roof,
    Then removed tiles in the roof,
    And let down the palsied man in front of Jesus.
Jesus knew they had faith for healing
    So He said, "Son, your sins are forgiven."
There were some Jewish leaders in the crowd
    Who criticized Jesus in their hearts, saying,
    "Who can forgive sins but God?
"This man is blaspheming God,
    Does He think He is God?"
Jesus knew their thoughts and said to them,
    "Why are you criticizing in your mind?
"What is easier to say, 'Your sins are forgiven';
    Or 'arise, pick up your bedroll and walk?'"
Then Jesus told them He would prove
    That He was the Messiah—the Son of Man,
    Who could forgive sins.
Jesus then told the man, "Get up, pick up
    Your bedroll and walk."
The man jumped to his feet, took his bedroll,
    And everyone saw him walk.
They were astounded and praised God saying,
    "We have never seen anything like this."

Lord, I praise You for the way
    Jesus handled those who criticized Him.
Lord, I am astounded at everything You do.

A Story of the Call to Matthew

The road from Damascus to Egypt ran outside the outer wall of Capernaum. Jesus and his disciples exited Capernaum through the city gate, turned left on the Roman road and began walking south in the direction of Judea.

Almost immediately, they encountered the customs booth where taxes were collected. Capernaum was the convergence of most traveled roads in Galilee, so that's where taxes were collected.

Everything that went through customs was taxed—grain, wine, cloth, produce of all kinds. To add to the burden, Levi, the chief tax collector for King Herod, collected *ad valorem* on everything that passed his table: axles, wheels, pack animals, and anything else he could think of to tax. Thus he had become extremely wealthy.

Because tax collectors ruled over everything that passed through their domains, they were thought to be oppressors. Rabbis expelled at once any Jew who accepted a job collecting taxes for the Romans.

Levi was philosophical about his ejection from the synagogue in Capernaum. But deep down he knew he was a sinful man. Levi had paid attention to the crowds listening intently to this new teacher.

When he looked up to see Jesus in the tax line, Levi wanted to say something to Him, but he didn't know how to greet Him. As Jesus stepped to Levi's table, Jesus said to him simply, "Follow Me."

With this simple invitation from Jesus, Levi saw his past swallowed up. And an overwhelming sense of relief washed over him.

Levi left the booth to follow Jesus.

Jesus looked behind him and smiled, saying, "You will be called Matthew, for you are a gift of God."

My Time To Pray

- Lord, may I instantaneously obey when Jesus enters my life and calls me to do a job.

- Lord, keep reminding me that there is no sinner who is too hardened to follow You as a dedicated disciple.

- Lord, teach me to love the unsaved, as You loved Matthew.

The Call to Matthew

Matthew 9:9-17; Mark 2:13-22; Luke 5:27-39

Jesus left Capernaum and followed the road
    That ran along side of the Sea of Galilee.
When Jesus came to the customs office,
    He saw Levi sitting there calculating taxes.
Jesus said to Him, "Follow me,"
    And to everyone's amazement,
    Levi left the tax office to follow Jesus.
That evening, Levi gathered a number of his friends
    To hear Jesus—politicians and tax collectors.
When the Jewish leaders saw Jesus eating with the crowd,
    They called His disciples,
"Why does your master eat with questionable characters?"
When Jesus knew what the religious leaders asked,
    He asked a question to get His point across,
"Do the healthy need a doctor, or
    Is it the sick who need help?
"I did not come to offer salvation to people
    Who think they are good enough,
    But I offer salvation to sinners."
The disciples of John the Baptist and the Jewish leaders fasted
    As part of their religious activities.
They approached Jesus, asking,
    "Why do these disciples of John the Baptist and Pharisees fast
    But Your disciples do not?"
Jesus answered, "Do you expect wedding guests to fast
    When they are at the wedding feast?

"They eat as long as they are with the bridegroom,
>But they will fast when the bridegroom
>Is taken from them."
Jesus continued, "No one sews a patch of unshrunken cloth
>On an old coat.
"If he does, the new patch will shrink and tear the old coat
>And it will be worse than ever.
"No one puts new wine into an old wineskin,
>As the new wine ferments, it will burst
>The old wine skin.
"The wine will be lost and the wineskin ruined."
>New challenges need new solutions.

Lord, teach me when to embrace the new,
>*Guide me when to leave the old.*

Chapter 7

MY FATHER'S HOUSE AND KINGDOM

The Story of Jesus Cleansing the Temple

When it was nearly time for the Jewish Passover, Jesus and his disciples made the journey to Jerusalem. Inside the temple, loud voices filled the courtyard. The Galileans had expected to hear Levites singing psalms. But instead of reverence, they saw a tumultuous crowd. People were buying and selling in the outer courtyard. Moneychangers were negotiating with worshipers to change foreign coins into Hebrew currency for temple offerings.

One farmer held several oxen by a harness. Another had a small pen for lambs. Still another had a gigantic bull he was trying to sell. "If you have a big sin, I have a big bull," he hollered.

Jesus' nostrils flared, He picked up three leather cords laying near Him on the ground. He walked up the stairs and out onto a small wall where He could be seen. Then, lifting His voice, He cried, *"How dare you turn my Father's house into a market! This is not a house of merchandise!"*

Laughter erupted from the businessmen.

"Stop!" Jesus yelled out over the crowd. Silence began to ripple out to the edges of the courtyard.

"This is a house of prayer," Jesus' voice echoed. "Take your business outside the temple. Now!"

There was absolute silence. No one moved.

The owner of the bull pointed at Jesus and shouted, "Why don't you take your business outside." He laughed at Jesus. The crowd that had been given over to unrestrained haggling now united in scorn.

Leaping down, Jesus kicked a table over with a thunderous crash. He unleashed His wrath on the moneychangers' tables, overturning each of them in succession. Coins flew every which way. Cages crashed to the ground as Jesus stormed through the courtyard, turtledoves and pigeons fluttering free.

With His makeshift whip in hand and His face flushed with anger, Jesus stepped toward the man with the bull. The man stumbled backward and the bull bolted toward the exit. Merchants and customers scattered like leaves.

The businessmen had escaped, but many honest worshipers were still there. They were stunned yet scared, not knowing what Jesus would do to them.

"My Father's house is to be a house of prayer," Jesus announced to them.

Slowly, priests began appearing in the courtyard. One by one they appeared. They surveyed the coins on the floor, the broken pens and the overturned tables.

One of the priests walked over to Jesus. "By what authority do you clear the temple?" he asked.

"The priests are the keepers of the temple," he said. The other priests nodded.

Jesus ignored them.

"Are you not Jesus of Nazareth?" he asked. Word had reached Jerusalem of a Galilean doing miracles with wine. "What miraculous sign can you show us to prove your authority to do this?" the priest asked.

"If you destroy this temple," Jesus said in answer, "I will raise it again in three days."

"It has taken 46 years to build this temple," the priest mockingly answered, "and you think you can rebuild it in three days?"

No one fully understood what Jesus meant. But Jesus spoke of His own death and resurrection, which He knew was coming. Jesus remained in Jerusalem for Passover. He continued teaching and performing miracles. The temple merchants stayed out of His way and for the rest of the week they kept their merchandise out of the temple.

My Time To Pray

- Lord, may I always be angry at religious hypocrisy and those who practice Christianity to make money.

- Lord, keep my motives pure when I enter a church-house of worship.

- Lord, it's easy for me to get angry; help me control my temper and to only be angry against the inappropriate things people do at inappropriate times.

- Lord, I accept the centrality of Your resurrection as the validity of my faith. That's because I know Christ is alive in my heart.

Jesus Cleanses the Temple

John 2:13-25

Lord, when the Passover came in the spring of A.D. 26,
    Jesus went up to Jerusalem with His disciples.
Jesus found people in the temple selling animals and birds
    For sacrifice—cattle, sheep and pigeons.
Money changers had set up tables to exchange foreign coins
    Into Hebrew money
    Because they had images of false gods.

Jesus made a whip out of some rope and
>> Drove the animals out of the temple
>> And overturned the tables of the moneychangers.
Jesus commanded, "Stop turning my Father's House
>> Into a market to sell your sacrifices."
The disciples were amazed at His anger and said,
>> "His devotion to the Lord's House'
>> Burns in Him like a fire."
The Jewish leaders challenged Jesus,
>> "What miracle can You show us
>> That gives You authority to do this?"
Jesus replied, "Destroy this temple,
>> And I will raise it up in three days."
They said, "It has taken 46 years to build this temple,
>> Do You think You can rebuild it in three days?"
After the resurrection His disciples remembered this event
>> And realized Jesus was referring to
>> Raising up His body, not rebuilding the temple.
While Jesus was in Jerusalem for the Passover,
>> Many believed in Him because they saw
>> The miracles He did.
But Jesus did not entrust Himself to them,
>> Because He knew what was in their hearts.

Lord, come cleanse the temple of my heart,
>> *Just as You cleansed Herod's temple.*

The Story of a Night Interview with Nicodemus

A cool breeze rustled the palm branches at the edge of the flat-roofed house. April was hot in the daytime but chilly at night. The Passover moon was so bright that the Torah could be read by its light. With no clouds in the sky, the stars created a perfect canopy for the evening discussion.

Jesus sat with John, James, and Peter on the rooftop, waiting for Nicodemus. A Jewish leader among the most influential in Jerusalem, Nicodemus would be severely censured by the Sanhedrin if they knew of this meeting. The other 69 members of the council did not consider Jesus to be a legitimate teacher. After all, Jesus had expelled the merchants from the temple; He was considered a menace.

But the taciturn shadows would hide all, the outside stairway allowing Nicodemus to slip upstairs unnoticed for his meeting with Jesus.

Passover week was a festive week for celebration. Many banquets were held during Passover. People got together to discuss current events, family matters, or just to renew old friendships. New friendships were also begun in this festive atmosphere. What began as a formal discussion would often end up in intimate conversation. This discussion between Jesus and Nicodemus was such an appointment, but Nicodemus wasn't ready to let his peers know about it, and Jesus understood this. Power...position...prestige...Nicodemus was a man with much to lose.

Young John had not said anything all evening. He was suspicious of priests, scribes, anyone who represented the religious establishment. Nicodemus was a Pharisee and a respected member of the Sanhedrin, the ruling council that exercised authority in all Jewish religious matters. The Roman governor was the final authority in Judean civil matters, but as part of the occupational agreement, the Romans allowed the Jews to take charge over their own religious and civil affairs—as long as they didn't interfere with the Roman government.

James gave voice to his brother's concerns. "Nicodemus is the most influential teacher in Jerusalem," he said. "He may have been sent here to spy on us."

But Jesus said nothing, and they waited.

When Nicodemus arrived with his academic attachés, he found two prominent chairs set on the roof, the first an ornate oak chair, padded with blue leather. This was the taller chair. Nicodemus would sit in the exalted chair, surrounded by his lieutenants. Across from him, a stool, lower in height, had been placed for Jesus. Behind Jesus was a bench set against the wall. On the bench sat John, the impulsive youth. Next to him was Peter, the stubborn, outspoken fisherman. Beside Peter sat James, the quiet but fiery one.

According to custom, it was the privilege of the elder Nicodemus to choose the topic of the evening. By all standards, it would have been inappropriate for Jesus to set the agenda for discussion. Nicodemus had a reputation for arguing the significance of historical events in the Talmud, those areas in which he excelled. Sometimes the discussions were nothing more than monologues, with Nicodemus discoursing all evening on a particularly fascinating topic. He was a brilliant scholar, and people invited him to their evening feasts just to glean something of his magnificent wisdom and understanding.

As they took their seats under the stars, Nicodemus and his three fellow scholars presented a formidable challenge for anyone wishing to engage in a religious debate. They held within their grasp a world of knowledge and learning that was feared by most illiterate people. Before them was Jesus, an itinerant teacher with no formal education, and three unlearned fishermen.

The disciples fully expected that the Pharisee would try to intimidate Jesus. But the shadows hid the face of Nicodemus, and his intentions were unclear. When at last he spoke, he did not attack Jesus, nor did he challenge Him with a question. Nicodemus leaned forward into the light, lowering his own head in clear deference to Jesus.

"We know about the miracles you have been doing in Jerusalem. We know about the miracle of turning water into wine…." Nicodemus' eyes were soft and pleading. They did not flash hot, nor were they ready for academic battle. "Rabbi, we know that you have come from God," he said, "because no one could perform these signs if God were not with Him."

To the disciples' surprise, Nicodemus had spoken to Jesus as an equal. Nicodemus, as the first to speak, had complimented Jesus. It was customary among such men that the compliment be returned.

Nicodemus waited for Jesus' reply. All eyes on the rooftop turned to Jesus who was sitting in the full moonlight. There were no shadows to hide

Jesus' reaction. Jesus waited for a few seconds to make sure it was His turn to speak. But rather than return the compliment, Jesus bypassed the niceties of rhetoric and went straight to the heart of the issue—the reason Nicodemus had come. Jesus told him, "Unless a man is born again, he cannot see the kingdom of Heaven."

The body language of three scholars-in-tow stiffened; they didn't like what they heard. They expected Jesus to compliment Nicodemus on his wisdom or his influence with the Sanhedrin. But Jesus was blunt.

Nicodemus did not take offense at the slight. It was as if Jesus had known what the Pharisee had come seeking, so He answered his unspoken question. But Nicodemus was puzzled by the logical impossibility. "How can a man be born when he is old?" he asked. "Surely he cannot enter a second time into his mother's womb to be born!"

"I tell you the truth, unless a person is born of water and of the Spirit, that person cannot enter the kingdom of God."

The three lieutenants to Nicodemus were disarmed by the intimacy of the discussion. Though offended when Jesus didn't compliment their leader, the warm, inquisitive response of Nicodemus told them the discussion was going well.

"Flesh gives birth to flesh, but the Spirit gives birth to spirit." Jesus explained, "When a man is born into this world that man is flesh, like the parents who gave him birth. But when a man is born of the Spirit, his life will be rooted in the spiritual."

Nicodemus understood the simplicity of Jesus' logic; there was a profundity in its simplicity. *But what does it mean to be "born again,"* he wondered silently.

Jesus looked deep into the eyes of Nicodemus. "You shouldn't be surprised when I tell you, 'You must be born again.'"

A swift evening breeze swept up the street and over the house. "Being born again is like the blowing of the wind," Jesus said to help Nicodemus. "You hear the sound of the wind, but you cannot tell where it comes from or where it is going. So it is with everyone born of the Spirit."

Nicodemus' eyes were still searching. Jesus continued. "Sometimes the wind stops blowing. Other times it blows briskly. No one can tell the wind where to blow, or when to blow. The wind blows wherever it pleases. So the world cannot fathom a man born of the Spirit."

"How can this be?" Nicodemus asked.

"You are Israel's teacher," Jesus said to Nicodemus. "You claim to know about God, and yet you have difficulty understanding the simplest teachings of the Kingdom."

Jesus arose from his stool and walked to the wall. Nicodemus followed him, listening as they walked. The others remained seated. Jesus looked out on the people in the street below. People were still walking, returning home from work or an evening meal. From the house next door there came the sound of congenial laughter. Everywhere Jesus looked, there were people who needed to hear about the kingdom of God.

Jesus turned to Nicodemus and said, "I have spoken to you of earthly things and you do not believe. Then how will you believe if I speak to you of heavenly things?"

Jesus folded His robe over His arm and returned to His stool. Beckoning to Nicodemus, He motioned for him to sit with the others. This was no longer a discussion between two great scholars, but a lesson from a master teacher.

"As Moses lifted up the serpent in the wilderness, so must the Son of Man be lifted up. Whoever looked at the snake on the pole, did not die of poison, and whoever believes in the Son of Man will live forever.

"For God so loved the world that He sent His only Son, that whoever believes in Him will not perish, but have everlasting life.

"For God did not send His Son into the world to condemn the world, but to save the world through Him. But whoever does not believe stands condemned already because he has not believed in the name of God's one and only Son."

Nicodemus did not know what to say to this.

"God has sent His Son as a light into the world..., Jesus explained. Just then a cloud covered the moon. The rooftop went black, as though a cosmic hand had extinguished its light. Almost immediately with the blackness, they heard a wicked laugh from the shadows in the street below...a chilling laughter.

The scholars and the disciples traded glances. Jesus, sensing the moment, said, "Men love darkness rather than light because their deeds are evil and the darkness hides what they are doing. But he who lives according to the truth will come into the light, that his deeds may be clearly seen, that they have been done in the name of God."

Nicodemus nodded. A spark had been touched in his own soul, and he determined to do whatever he could within the Sanhedrin to allow Jesus to teach openly. And Nicodemus himself would watch...and listen.

My Time To Pray

- Lord, come into my heart and save me, I want to be born again (pray this if you are not a Christian).

- Lord, help me be an example to my family and friends who are not born again so they can become Christians.

- Lord, take away any blindness that keeps me from seeing the truth of the new birth.

A Night Interview With Nicodemus

John 3:1-21

Nicodemus was a Jewish leader who observed the Law;
     He came to Jesus at night to compliment Him, saying,
"Jesus, You are a Teacher who comes from God

Because You perform miracles
That couldn't be done without God's help."
Jesus told him, "Verily, verily, I say to you,
You must be born again
To see the kingdom of God."
Nicodemus replied, "How can a man be born
When he is old? Can he go back
Into his mother's womb to be born again?"
Jesus answered, "Verily, verily, I say to you,
Unless you are born again of water and the Spirit,
You will not enter the kingdom of God.
"That which is born of flesh is flesh,
That which is born of Spirit is Spirit.
"Do not be surprised when I tell you,
'You must be born again.'
"The wind blows anywhere it pleases;
You can hear its sound, but you
Cannot tell where it comes from or goes.
"That describes those who are born of the Spirit,
And how the Spirit bestows life on them."
Nicodemus asked, "How can this happen?"
Jesus answered, "You are a respected teacher,
Yet you do not understand these things."
Jesus continued, "Verily, verily, I say to you,
I am telling you what I know,
But you will not believe me."
"If you do not believe what I say about this world,
How can you believe heavenly things?
"Since I have come to earth from Heaven,
I can explain heavenly things to you.
"As Moses lifted up the serpent in the wilderness,
So people could repent by looking to the serpent.
"In the same way the Son of Man will be lifted up

So that everyone who believes in Him will be saved.
"The Father loved everyone in the world so much
>> That He gave His only begotten Son
>> To die for each of them.
"So that everyone who believes in the Son
>> Will not perish in hell,
>> But will have eternal life.
"For the Father did not send His Son
>> To condemn the people of the world
>> But that they might be saved through Him.
"No one who believes in the Son will be condemned,
>> But those who refuse to believe in the name
>> Of God's only Son are condemned already."

The verdict of death is handed down because light
>> Has shined to the people of the world,
But people love darkness more than light
>> Because of their love of evil things.
Everyone who continually does evil things
>> Hates the light and rejects it
>> Because it exposes their motives and actions.

Lord, I want everyone to know that You offer eternal life
>> *When Jesus told Nicodemus, "You can be born again."*

Lord, I want to live by Your truth
>> *So I will come into the light*
>> *So everyone can see what I do for You.*

Jesus and John the Baptist

John 3:22-36

Jesus and His disciples left Jerusalem for the countryside
>> Where many people were baptized by His disciples.

103

John the Baptist was baptizing nearby at Aenon;
>   Many also came there for baptism.
The Jewish leaders tried to tell the disciples of John the Baptist
>   That the baptism of Jesus
>   Was better than their baptism.
John's disciples came to tell Him, "The man
>   You baptized—the one you called Messiah—
>   He is baptizing more than you are."
John the Baptist answered, "God in Heaven
>   Gives each man the work he is to do,
I told you I am not the Messiah, I am sent
>   To prepare the way for Messiah.
"The crowds—the Bride of Christ—will naturally
>   Go where Christ the Bridegroom is located.
"I am a friend of the bridegroom, I rejoiced
>   When I answered His voice calling to me.
"He—Jesus—must increase,
>   I—John the Baptist—must decrease.
"He comes from Heaven, and He is greater than all;
>   We who are born on this earth
>   Only understand the things of earth."
"Those who believe in Jesus have discovered
>   The truth of God that has come from Heaven.
"He speaks the words of God
>   Because He has the Spirit of God on Him.
"The Father loves Jesus, the Son,
>   And has given everything to Him."

Lord, I believe in the Son, I have eternal life;
>   *Those who refuse to believe in the Son,*
Will never have eternal life;
>   *But Your punishment rests on them.*

The Story of the Samaritan Woman

John 4:1-42

As the scorching April sun neared its zenith, the disciples trudged up yet another charred Samaritan hill. Jesus had been led by the Holy Spirit to make the difficult trek through Samaria on their return home from Jerusalem.

"If we had gone by way of the Jordan Valley," young John complained, "we could have avoided these hills and saved ourselves a few blisters."

"Ha!" Peter laughed. With his lighter complexion, his red eyebrows were beginning to blend into a sunburned face. "I don't mind how we get there, as long as we're heading home," he said, keeping in mind that his Master had chosen this route. "Let's not complain...."

John pointed to the sun directly overhead. "It's nearly noon. We need to stop and let Jesus rest."

"The village of Sychar is up ahead."

"Jacob's Well is closer," John reminded him. "Let's stop there."

Jesus looked to John as though he could go no farther. Several days of intense ministry to the people in Jerusalem had seemed to drain Him. Peter gave Jesus a needed shoulder to lean on. The small olive trees surrounding the well were in sight just a few paces up the road.

Jacob's Well was located in the middle of the broad, flat valley with wheat growing in the fields on either side of the road. The fields were flanked by two mountains rising several hundred feet from the desert floor, forming a beautiful backdrop. To the disciples' left was Mount Ebal, the Mount of Blessings, where Joshua had once sacrificed to the Lord for the great victory over the northern kingdom. To their right was Mount Gerizim, the Mount of Cursing. The mountains stood like sentinels guarding the deep well that had been dug by Jacob, the father of the 12 tribes of Israel.

Now the area was populated with Samaritans, and most Jews had very little to do with the Samaritans because of their apostate faith. Still, the Jews revered the well of their forefather and would make the pilgrimage to this place just to drink from the well and pray to the God of Jacob.

Jesus wearily collapsed onto the stone wall next to the well, under the shade of a small olive tree, where He promptly fell asleep.

"Let's go into town and get something to eat," Andrew said to John. "No one will bother Jesus. It's too hot to come for water at this hour of the day." So the disciples left their Master sleeping by the well, and they made their way to Sychar.

Jesus was dozing in the shade and didn't hear the bare feet coming down the powdery road toward the well. He sat up when he heard the squeak of a leather bucket being lowered into the well. A Samaritan woman was there. She wore dark clothes—a black robe similar to that of a widow or an unmarried woman. A dark blue shawl protected her from the sun.

"Oh...," she said, startled by the presence of a stranger at the well. She let go of the rope and her bucket fell with a distant splash a moment later. "I didn't see you resting in the shade."

Jesus greeted her kindly, then seeing her jar asked, "Could you give Me something to drink? I am very thirsty."

"But you are a Jew and I am a Samaritan woman," the woman said, her curiosity winning out over fear and hatred. Looking past their cultural differences, she knew it was highly unusual for a Jewish man to talk alone with a woman. And yet there was something different about this man.

"How can you ask me for a drink?" she demanded.

Jesus did not immediately answer.

"Jews have no dealings with the Samaritans," she reminded Him.

Jesus was not interested in such distinctions. He was, however, interested in the life of this woman. He knew she was why the Holy Spirit had led Him and His disciples into the hills of Samaria.

"If only you knew the gift of God," He said, smiling at her reluctance. "If you knew who it was that asked you for a drink, you would ask for water from Me. Anyone who drinks from My living water will never thirst again."

"Where would you get this 'living water'? Sir, you have no bucket. You have no rope, and the well is deep."

Jesus continued to smile at her.

"Who are you?" the woman asked. "Are you greater than our father Jacob who gave us this well and drank from it, as did his sons, his flock and his herds?"

"Everyone who drinks this water will be thirsty again," Jesus answered, "but whoever drinks the water I offer will never thirst. Indeed, the water I give you will become in you a spring of water filling your heart and over-flowing into eternal life."

"I want this water," the woman said, "so that I don't have to come to this well to draw water again. I want eternal water."

"Go call your husband," Jesus said to the woman. "Tell your husband about the water of eternal life, then bring your husband here to see Me."

"I don't have a husband."

"I know you are telling me the truth," Jesus said to her, "for you have had five husbands in your lifetime, and the man you are now living with is not your husband."

Stunned, she said nothing for a moment. She had never met this man. How could He know all about her life? Her closest friends in Sychar did not know of her five marriages. She blurted out, "Sir, you must be a prophet of God. You know the secret things about me."

So she tested Him to learn whether he was indeed a prophet. "The Samaritans worship on Mount Gerizim where Joshua worshiped," she said, "but the Jews say we should worship in Jerusalem...."

Jesus had not come to argue religion with the Samaritan woman, so He didn't answer her.

"Where should we worship?" she asked.

"Woman, the hour is coming when you will not worship on a mountain or in Jerusalem. A time is coming when true worshipers will worship the Father in Spirit and in truth.... These are the kind of people the Father seeks to worship Him."

She did not have an answer for this, but said to Jesus, "I know the Messiah is coming. When He comes, He will explain everything to us."

"I who speak to you am the Messiah."

When the disciples returned with food and found Jesus talking with the Samaritan woman, they were taken aback but said nothing out of respect for their teacher. Nevertheless, the woman turned and ran swiftly away, leaving behind her water jar, rope, and bucket.

"Wait...!" Peter yelled after her, but she continued running.

The disciples drew water for Jesus and gave Him a drink from Jacob's Well. Unfolding their food cloth, they began distributing bread and dried lamb for lunch. But Jesus didn't eat.

Finally, Peter spoke. "Take some bread, Rabbi."

But Jesus shook His head and said, "I have food that you know nothing about."

The disciples looked at one another, wondering who could have brought Jesus food while they were gone.

When He saw His disciples wondering at His words, Jesus said to them, "My food is to do the will of my Father who sent Me and to finish His work." Jesus drew His strength from feeding others, as He had done for the Samaritan woman.

"Don't say there are yet four months until harvest," He said to them, pointing. "Lift up your eyes and look on the fields now." But Jesus wasn't pointing toward the wheat fields.

The disciples looked toward the village. Coming down the road from Sychar were dozens of men—all in white turbans—walking fast toward the well, looking like a field of whitened wheat waving in the wind.

Jesus said, "The field is white for harvest."

The woman had gone back to the city, babbling to everyone she knew, "Come see a man who told me everything I ever did." She ran from one group of men to another. To each group she said the same thing: "This man is from God."

Upon hearing about the man who knew the secrets of the heart, many Samaritans quickly ran out of Sychar toward Jacob's Well. They listened to Jesus and urged Him to stay with them. So Jesus and His disciples departed the well and went into Sychar.

That evening in the town piazza, Jesus taught the crowd from the Scriptures concerning himself. Many believed that He was the Christ. As He finished speaking, an elderly man stood, his stringy beard bouncing from his chin as he talked, "Now we believe You are the Messiah. We have heard for ourselves, and we believe You are the Savior of the world."

My Time To Pray

- Lord, make me thirsty for a drink from You.

- Lord, give me a passion to share my testimony with needy people like the Samaritan woman.

- Lord, I will tell my non-Christian friends, "Come see a Man who knows everything about me."

The Samaritan Woman

John 4:1-42

When Jesus left the Passover at Jerusalem,
  He surprisingly went home through Samaria
  Because the Jews have no dealings with the Samaritans.
When He came near Sychar, He sat on Jacob's well

Because He was worn out from the hot journey
    And it was 12 noon.
The disciples went into the town to get food;
        Jesus was sitting there when a Samaritan woman
        Came to draw water from the well.
Jesus said, "Give me a drink";
        She was surprised that a Jew
        Would ask because the Jews despised the Samaritans.
She said, "Why would you—a Jew—ask water
        From me, a Samaritan?"
Jesus said, "If you only knew God's gift
        And Who it is that offers you water,
You would have asked Me for a drink,
        And I would have given you living water.
The woman replied, "You do not have a bucket;
        How could You get water from this deep well?"
She continued, "Are You greater than Jacob who drank
        From this well with his family and cattle
        Then gave us this well?"
Jesus answered, "Whoever drinks this water
        Will get thirsty again,
But those who drink of the water that I give
        Will never be thirsty again.
"The water I give will be an artesian well inside them
        That gushes up into eternal life."
The woman said, "Give me some of that water
        So I will never get thirsty again,
        And have to come to this well for water."
Jesus abruptly said, "Go call your husband!"
        She answered, "I have no husband."
Jesus replied, "You have correctly answered
        Because you have had five husbands."
"And now you're not married

To the one you're living with."
    She exclaimed, "You must be a prophet to know this";
        Then she argued, "Our fathers worshiped here.
        The Jews say Jerusalem is the place to worship."
Jesus interrupted to say, "The hour is coming when no one will
        Worship on this mountain or in Jerusalem.
"You don't know whom you worship;
        The Jews know whom they worship.
"In fact, the hour is already here when true worshipers
        Will worship the Father in Spirit and truth.
"God is Spirit, and those who worship Him
        Must worship in spirit and truth."
The woman said, "I know that Messiah is coming;
        He will tell us everything when He comes";
        Jesus answered, "I am the Messiah."

Lord, the disciples were surprised when they returned
    Because Jesus was talking to a Samaritan woman.

The woman left her water pot and hurried off
        To tell the men in the village,
"Come see a man who told me
        Everything I've ever done."
She asked, "Could this man be the Messiah?"
        They left the town to go meet Jesus.
Meanwhile, the disciples told Jesus to eat
        But He said, "I have food to eat
        That you don't know about."
The disciples thought somene else had
        Brought Him food.
Jesus said, "My food is doing the will of the Father
        And completing His work.
"People say, 'Harvest comes four months after planting,'
        "But I say, 'Look around at the fields

They are already ripe for harvest.'
"Everything is ready for the reaper to go to work
　　To bring in the 'grain' of eternal life;
　　Then sower and reaper will rejoice together."
Then Jesus explained, "One sows, another reaps;
　　I send you to reap where you didn't sow,
　　And you get rewards for their effort."

Many Samaritans believed in Jesus
　　Because the woman said, "Come see a man who
　　Told me everything I have ever done."
The Samaritans begged Jesus to stay with them
　　And He stayed two days,
　　And many got saved.
The Samaritan men told the woman, "Now we believe
　　Because of what we have heard for ourselves,
　　Not just because of what you said."

Lord, thank You for saving the woman at the well,
　　And thank You for saving me.

Healing the Nobleman's Son

John 4:43-54

Jesus returned to Cana where He turned water to wine,
　　There an official from Herod's court
　　Came begging Jesus to heal his son.
The official had sought to find Jesus in the area
　　Because his son was very, very sick.
Jesus said, "Why is it that none
　　Will believe in Me unless they see miracles?"
The official answered, "Come down to Capernaum
　　And heal my son before he dies."

Jesus answered, "Go home, your son will live";
>> The official believed the words of Jesus
>> And turned to start his journey home.
While he was on the road, his servants met him
>> To say, his son recovered.
The official asked what time had the fever broke;
>> The servant told him, "4 P.M."
The father realized that was the same hour
>> When Jesus said, "Your son will live."
This was the second sign-miracle Jesus did in Cana
>> And the official and his family believed in Jesus.

The Story of Jesus Facing Unbelief in Nazareth

Word had spread quickly through the small village. The son of Mary and Joseph had returned to Nazareth and had been asked to speak at the synagogue.

Jesus entered the synagogue and took a seat reserved for visiting speakers. When the time came for Him to speak, the leader of the synagogue selected the writings of Isaiah, and handed the scroll to Jesus. Jesus carefully unrolled the scroll to where Isaiah prophesied concerning the Messiah, then read aloud:

> *"The Spirit of the Lord is upon Me, because He has anointed Me to preach the gospel to the poor; He has sent Me to heal the broken-hearted, to proclaim liberty to the captives and recovery of sight to the blind, to set at liberty those who are oppressed; to proclaim the acceptable year of the Lord."*

Jesus rolled the scroll back into place and returned it to the leader. Then He sat down. Every eye in the room looked at Him. They were waiting for His sermon.

But all Jesus said was, "Today this Scripture is fulfilled in your hearing."

The elders began to shake their heads in disapproval. The passage Jesus had read referred to the coming Messiah. The word that jumped to their minds was blasphemy, but no one wanted to say that word. This was Joseph's son.

"No!" one of the elders dared to say out loud. "You may be a worker of miracles, but You cannot call Yourself Messiah!" Jesus knew they came to see miracles but they did not believe in Him.

He said, "Many of you want Me to do miracles here in Nazareth as I have done at Capernaum and at Jerusalem. But I say to you, no prophet is accepted in his hometown."

The minister of the synagogue asked, "Why will You not show us what You can do? If You are the Messiah, give us a sign."

Jesus didn't answer him directly, but spoke to the congregation: "*In the time of Elisha, there were many lepers in Israel, but none of them were cleansed except Naaman, a Syrian. I cannot do miracles in my hometown because of your unbelief. You will not believe that I am who I say I am.*"

The synagogue erupted in indignation. Jesus had told them they were not fit for miracles.

Voices began to swell like thunder, and the Nazarenes drove Jesus out of their synagogue. They cursed Him and forced Him to the outskirts of town.

Just outside Nazareth, the road to Capernaum passed dangerously close to a 40-foot cliff. They pushed Jesus up the hill toward the cliff, determined to throw Him off. Jesus allowed Himself to be pressed forward until they reached the brow of the hill.

Then He turned and looked upon His pursuers, and the mob was silenced. They held their collective breath, waiting for Jesus to speak. But Jesus said nothing. He walked back down the hill toward Capernaum, His new home.

My Time To Pray

- Lord, may I be a good testimony to those who grew up with me.

- Lord, teach me how to properly react to those who are blinded with unbelief.

- Lord, there are people in this world who hate You and reject You; protect me when they attack me.

- Lord, I'm willing to be a martyr and die for You because You died for me.

- Lord, give me faith to pray for spiritual insight for those who are spiritually blinded.

Jesus Facing Unbelief in Nazareth

Luke 4:14-30

Jesus came back to minister in His home region, Galilee,
     And the power of the Holy Spirit was on Him.
Everyone in the region heard about Jesus
     And when He preached in the synagogues,
     Everyone was glad to hear Him.
Then Jesus went to Nazareth, His boyhood home,
     Because it was His custom on the Sabbath
     He went to the synagogue.
An elder handed Jesus the scroll of Isaiah,
     He unrolled it to a certain place and read,
"The Spirit of the Lord is upon Me,
     Because the Lord has anointed Me
     To preach the Gospel to the poor.
"The Lord has sent Me to preach prisoners shall be free,

And the blind shall see,
And the oppressed shall be released.
"To proclaim, God will bless
        Those who come to Him."
Then Jesus rolled up the scroll
        And returned it to its place
        And took His seat.
Every eye in the synagogue stared at Him,
        Then Jesus spoke,
"This Scripture was fulfilled today."
        And everyone was amazed at what He said,
        They said, "Is not this Joseph's Son?"
Jesus told them, "You will probably want me
        To prove Myself, like the proverb,
        'Physician, heal yourself.'
"You want Me to do miracles here in Nazareth
        Like I have done in Capernaum
"But I know your unbelief,
        You have not accepted Me,
        But rather you have rejected Me.
"Verily, I say that no prophet
        Is accepted in His hometown.
"Remember how Elijah did a miracle
        To help the widow of Zerephath,
        Even though she was a foreigner?
"There were many needy widows in Israel
        Because there was a famine.
"It hadn't rained for three and a half years,
        Yet, Elijah was not sent to them.
"Elijah also healed Naaman of leprosy
        Even though there were many lepers in Israel."
The people in the synagogue were furious
        When they heard what Jesus said.

The people mobbed Jesus and pushed Him outside
　　　Toward the edge of the cliff near town.
But He walked through the midst of the mob
　　　And returned to Capernaum.

Lord, give me the boldness of Jesus to face unbelief,
　　　And give me the wisdom of Jesus to do what is right.

Chapter 8

JESUS HEALS

The Story of Healing at the Pool of Bethesda

When Jesus returned to Jerusalem to observe the Feast of Passover, He had gained popularity with the people. His reputation with the religious authorities had worsened, however.

Slowly Jesus eased through the crowd at the Pool of Bethesda, looking from one face to the next. Then, seeing a man against a wall, Jesus walked straight toward him.

The poor man's worn pallet showed the wear and tear of being rolled and unrolled every day for 38 years. Each day during that time, the lame man had waited in vain for the moving of the waters, knowing full well that when the waters were stirred he could not be first in.

The man slumped against the wall, his hope long depleted. In an act of rebellion against God nearly four decades earlier, the lame man had done something to make him crippled. Because of one act of rebellion, he had never walked again.

"Do you want to be healed?" Jesus asked.

"Sir, I don't have anyone to help me into the pool."

Jesus commanded the lame man, "Rise! Pick up your mat and walk."

Instantly, the man felt sensations he hadn't felt for 38 years. He stood! No one around him noticed, and he did not yell, scream, or dance. He had been told to take up his mat and walk, so he obeyed.

Jesus continued walking through the crowd. Because all eyes were fixed on the water, none had seen the miracle.

But a pair of Jewish leaders walking to the temple immediately spotted the healed man. "THIS IS THE SABBATH DAY!" they shouted. "PUT THAT MAT DOWN!"

The Sabbath day had been instituted as a sign of God's covenant with His people. Just as God rested from His work on the seventh day, so the Jews were to work six days and rest on the seventh. But through the years Jewish leaders had developed so many regulations, the meaning of the Sabbath had become hopelessly obscured.

Now inside the temple, the lame man who was healed wanted to say to God, "Thank you for healing me."

Suddenly, Jesus was there. "God has heard your prayers," Jesus said.

The healed man's eyes welled up with tears of gratitude.

But Jesus did not seek the man's gratitude, He sought his heart. He searched the man's eyes. "Do not go back to the sin that crippled you."

Then Jesus turned and melted into the crowd.

Unknown to the man, the Pharisees had been watching. They had recognized Jesus, and approached the man.

"Was that the man who healed you?" they demanded. The healed man nodded.

"Did He tell you to pick up your bed and walk?" "Yes."

Immediately the priests stormed through the crowds after Jesus. Not only had He healed the lame man but He had incited the man to break the Sabbath! They finally caught up to Jesus near the Gate Beautiful. "Why do You violate the Sabbath?"

Jesus smiled a knowing smile and nodded His head. He said to them, "My Father is always ready to work on the Sabbath day, and so the Son must work while He is on earth."

"Blasphemy!" a priest shouted. Jesus had proclaimed himself the Son of God.

By now a large crowd was gathering, drawn by the shouting. If they had been outside the temple, the crowd would have stoned Jesus. Jesus saw the rage in their hearts, but said,

"I tell you the truth, the Son can do nothing by Himself. He can do only what He sees His Father doing. For the Father loves the Son and shows Him all things. You have never heard His voice nor seen His form, nor does His Word dwell in you, for you do not believe the One He sent."

The priests retired to discuss what they had just heard, and to plot how they could put Jesus to death.

My Time To Pray

- Lord, help me not give excuses as the lame man.

- Lord, see me in the middle of a crowd as You saw the lame man and come help me today.

- Lord, take away any hardness of my heart as the Jewish leaders rejected You. Help me respond positively to Your direction for my life.

The Lame Man at Bethesda

John 5:1-17

Jesus obeyed the Old Testament command to attend
    The Feast of Passover at Jerusalem
      At the end of His first full year of ministry.
Jesus went by the pool of Bethesda, a name

That meant "House of Mercy."
There were five porches where a great number
    Of sick invalids were waiting
    For an angel to come stir the waters in the pool.
The sick believed that the first one into the water
    Would automatically get healed.
There was a man who had waited unsuccessfully for 38 years;
    Jesus went only to him because
    He had been there a long time.
Jesus asked, "Would you like to be healed?"
    The lame man answered, "I don't have anyone
    To put me in the waters after it is stirred up.
"When I am going to the water,
    Someone jumps in before me."
Jesus said, "Take up your bedroll and walk";
    Immediately, the man was healed
    And he picked up his bedroll and walked.
The healed man walked through the crowd to the temple;
    The Jews told him it was wrong
    To carry any burden—a bedroll—on the Sabbath.
The lame man answered that the One who healed him
    Also told him to pick up his bedroll.
Later Jesus found the healed man in the temple
    And told him, "Go and don't do the sin any more
That was responsible for this lame condition; because
    A worse thing will happen if you do."
The healed man went and told the Jews
    That it was Jesus who healed him.

Equal in Nature, Power, and Authority

John 5:18-30

The Jews confronted Jesus
        Because He told the healed man
        To carry his bedroll on the Sabbath.
Jesus answered the Jewish leaders, "My Father
        Has worked up until now, now I work."
The Jewish leaders sought to kill Jesus because
        Jesus said He was just like the Father,
        And because He had broken their law,
        And He said the Father and Son are equal in nature.

Jesus answered the Jewish leaders, "Verily, verily,
        I say to you, the Son does nothing by Himself.
"But when the Son sees the things the Father does,
        He does the same things."
        The Father and Son are equal in power.

Then Jesus said, "The Father loves the son
        And shows the Son everything He does.
"The Father will do greater miracles
        Than healing the lame so you'll marvel.
"As the Father raises the dead and gives them life,
        So the Son will also raise the dead."
        The Father and Son are equal in authority.

"The Father does not judge the sins of everyone,
        All judgment is given to the Son;
        He that honors not the Son, honors not the Father."
"Verily, verily," Jesus said, "he that receives My Word,
        And believes on Me, has eternal life.
"That one will not be judged for his sins
        But has passed from death unto eternal life."

"Verily, verily," Jesus said, "the time is coming
  When all dead will hear My voice
  And be raised to eternal life.
"The Father has given Me the authority to execute judgment;
  Therefore, the time is coming when all in the grave
  Will hear My voice and be raised.
"They who have obeyed the Father will be raised
  To the resurrection of life.
"They who have disobeyed the Father will be raised
  To the resurrection of the damned."
Jesus told them, "I can do nothing by Myself,
  But I do the will of the Father who sent Me."

Four Witnesses: John the Baptist, Jesus' Miracles, the Father's Voice, and the Scriptures

John 5:31-47

Jesus said, "No one can bear witness of themselves
  And have other people believe them.
"The Old Testament said at the mouth of two witnesses
  Shall every testimony be established.
"The testimony of John the Baptist was a light
  That shined so people believed what he said about Me."

"But the testimony of My miracles was even greater;
  They proved the Father sent Me into the world."

"A third testimony is the voice of the Father that
  Thundered at My baptism. No one has seen God,
  But you heard His voice but didn't believe it.
"Because you do not have the Word of God dwelling in you,
  You do not believe the words the Father said."

Jesus told them, "Search the Scriptures, these words
     Testify of Me that I am from the Father.
"You think you have eternal life but you don't
     Because you refuse to believe in Me;
     You do not have the love of God in you."
Jesus said, "I have come in the Father's name,
     And you will not receive Me
     Yet you receive others coming in their own name.
"You seek glory from other Jewish leaders
     And do not seek the glory that comes
     From the heavenly Father.
"I will not accuse you in the final judgment
     Moses whom you revere;
     He will accuse you in the judgment.
"If you believe Moses—and you don't—then
     You would believe Me
     Because Moses predicted my coming."

"The Lord your God will raise up to you a prophet
From your brothers who will be like me (Moses). *Listen to Him"*
(Deut. 18:15).

Lord, I receive the four testimonies and believe them.
     Jesus, You are God and I worship You.

Debate About the Sabbath

Matthew 12:1-8; Mark 2:23-28; Luke 6:1-5

As Jesus journeyed home from the Passover at Jerusalem
     He went past the corn fields on the Sabbath
     And His disciples picked the grain and ate it.
The Pharisees criticized them because
     They broke the Sabbath Law.

Jesus answered that David went into the Tabernacle
>   To eat the shewbread when he was hungry
>   And those with him also ate it.
Jesus also mentioned the priest ate shewbread
>   On the Sabbath day which outwardly broke the Law.
Then Jesus added Hosea the prophet said,
>   "God wants us to be merciful,
>   He doesn't want us to just to keep the Law.
"God wants us to know Him,
>   Not just bring in burnt sacrifices to Him."
Finally Jesus noted, "The Sabbath was made
>   To serve man, not for man to just keep its law."
Jesus proclaimed, "Therefore the Son of Man
>   Is master of the Sabbath, not the reverse."

Lord, help me properly observe Your Lord's Day,
>   *Not as the religious leaders legalistically observed it.*
>   *Lord, I will worship You properly on Sunday.*

The Shriveled Hand Healed

Matthew 12:10-14; Mark 3:1-5; Luke 6:6-11

When Jesus got to Capernaum He entered the synagogue,
>   And a man was there with a shriveled up hand.
The Jewish leaders watched Jesus closely
>   Whether He would heal on the Sabbath day
>   So they could charge Him with breaking the Law.
Jesus said to the man with the shriveled up hand,
>   "STAND IN THE MIDDLE OF PEOPLE."
Then Jesus asked, "Is it right to
>   Help or hurt on the Sabbath Day?
>   To kill or save lives?"
Jesus continued, "If a man's sheep fall into a pit,

126

Isn't it proper to rescue the sheep on a Sabbath day?
Isn't a man worth more than a sheep?"
But the Pharisees wouldn't answer Jesus,
He looked at them with anger,
Being grieved for their hardness of heart.
Jesus then said to the man,
"STRETCH OUT YOUR HAND."
The man held out this withered hand
And it was completely restored.
And the Jewish leaders refused to believe in Him,
But began making plans to destroy Jesus.

Lord, I don't want to be critical of anyone
Who comes to You for help or healing
Like the Jewish leaders criticized You.

Lord, I marvel at Your compassion on
Those who hurt or need Your help;
And at Your patience with those who reject You.

Multitudes Healed

Matthew 12:15-16; Mark 3:7-12; Luke 6:17-19

Jesus and His disciples left to go to the seaside;
Multitudes followed Him from Galilee, Judea,
Jerusalem, Idumea, Tyre, and Sidon.
Because they heard about His miracles.
Jesus told His disciples to have a boat ready,
Because the crowds were crushing Him.
Jesus had cured so many people that anyone
With an ailment crowded in to touch Him.
When people possessed with demons encountered Jesus,
They fell down at His feet screaming,

"You are the Son of God."
But Jesus warned them repeatedly
    That they should not make Him known.

Lord, Your healing power demonstrates
    You are a powerful God,
    Your tenderness demonstrates You are a loving God.

The Story of Choosing the Twelve Apostles

Knowing the religious authorities plotted against His life, Jesus withdrew with His disciples to the Sea of Galilee. A great multitude followed.

The crowds pressed in on Jesus so much, He was unable to talk with His disciples. He asked that a small boat be kept ready to take Him across the sea should the crowd grow unruly.

Jesus climbed into the boat and sailed away, leaving the crowd on shore. Arriving near Magdala, He left the craft on the beach and climbed a steep hill, looking for a place where He could be alone. Tonight, Jesus would ask His heavenly Father for guidance to appoint 12 as His followers or apostles.

All those who faithfully followed Him were known as His "disciples," but Jesus would call His chosen 12 "apostles," a Greek word that meant "sent ones." The 12 apostles would be the ones He would send to carry the Gospel, or good news, to the entire earth.

Jesus prayed all night. When the sun peeked over the eastern mountains, He came down from the hill to where the disciples were waiting.

Jesus said to them. "All of you will continue to follow Me. You will all be called disciples. But only 12 will be apostles. They will preach and be given power to heal sickness and cast out demons."

Jesus looked from face to face. "Simon will be first," Jesus nodded to the strapping fisherman. "Simon will be called Peter, for he will be strong."

His next choice was James. Everyone was surprised by this choice, because James was so quick to anger. The third choice was his brother John, the youngest of all the disciples.

Jesus said, "James and John are as thunder; they will roar like the thunderstorm at sin or iniquity."

Jesus selected Andrew as his fourth apostle. Once a follower of John the Baptist, Andrew was sensitive to the needs of people. "Philip, you too will be an apostle. Philip will be in charge of the next three apostles and will supervise the crowds, arrange accommodations, and other details."

Jesus appointed three other apostles to serve with Philip: his friend Nathanael; Matthew, the former tax collector; and Thomas, who was known for his pragmatism.

"The ninth apostle will be James, son of Alphaeus," Jesus nodded to the shortest of His disciples. "Your group will be in charge of our money."

To work with James, Jesus called Thaddeus and Simon the Zealot.

The first 11 men Jesus chose were from Galilee. They spoke with a Galilean accent, and understood the area from which Jesus came.

Then Jesus announced, "Judas Iscariot will be my twelfth apostle. He is the one especially chosen by My Father." He assigned Judas to carry the money bag.

Choosing the Twelve

Matthew 10:1-4; Mark 3:13-20; Luke 6:12-16

Jesus went up into the hill country
    And He continued all night in prayer.
The next day He called certain men to be His apostles
    So they would be with Him to learn,
Then they would be sent forth to preach,
    Heal and cast out demons.

Simon was the first whom He called Peter,
    He was the leader of the first group of four.
That included James and John
    Whom Jesus named the Sons of Thunder
    And Andrew was in that group.
The second group of four apostles was led by Philip,
    And included, Bartholomew, Matthew
    And Thomas, the one with a twin brother.
The third group of four was led by James the short one,
    And included, Thaddeus and Simon
The former terrorist fighter and Judas Iscariot,
    The one who betrayed Jesus.

Lord, teach me to pray about important decisions,
    As You prayed before choosing the 12 disciples.

Chapter 9

THE SERMONS OF JESUS

The Story of the Sermon on the Mount

The morning broke softly over the hills around Tiberias. Jesus left the highway and began to climb. He pointed to the top of a small hill.

"Up there," he said.

At the pinnacle of the hill, the mount flattened out and Jesus sat on a rock with His disciples. This was the place Jesus would hold His first staff meeting. Jesus would use this sermon to instruct His disciples about their attitude and actions as they served Him.

But they were not alone. The multitudes had followed Jesus. Every day, more and more people were coming to be near Him. They wanted to know what Jesus would do about re-establishing David's earthly kingdom. So the disciples sat close to Jesus as the multitude spread out on the mountain to hear this, "The Sermon on the Mount."

The Sermon on the Mount

Matthew 5:1–7:29; Luke 6:20-49

When Jesus saw the multitudes following Him,
    He went to the top of a hill to teach
    His disciples and the multitudes.

Lord, thank You for blessing me:
> When I am poor in spirit—totally dependent on You—
> The kingdom of Heaven is mine.

When I mourn—broken over sin in my life,
> You will give me consolation.

When I am meek—willing to set aside my rights—
> You will give me possession of the earth.

When I hunger and thirst after righteousness,
> Having a desire for outward holiness,
> I will be satisfied by Your presence.

When I am merciful—looking on others,
> Mercy will be shown to me.

When I am pure—a desire for inward holiness—
> Then I shall see You.

When I am a peacemaker—building
> Relationship in others,
> I will be called a child of God.

When I am persecuted for righteousness' sake—
> Suffering for You,
> Mine will be the kingdom of Heaven.

When I am persecuted falsely—because of
> My loyalty to the person of Christ,
> I will accept it as a rich reward

Because this is what the enemies of God
> Did to the prophets and to Jesus Christ.

Lord, I want to be like the salt of the earth
> So I can make people thirsty for Jesus.

If I lose my ability to influence people,
> I might as well be thrown away
> Like salt that has lost its saltiness.

I want to be a light to the world
> So people will know how to
> Find their way to Jesus.

People don't put a candle under a bucket,
>>They put it in a candle-holder
>>So it can light a whole room.

I want to shine before You so
>>*People can see my good works*
>>*And glorify You, the heavenly Father.*

Lord, I know Jesus didn't come to do away with
>>The teachings of the Old Testament
>>But to fulfill the prophecies about Him.
I know not one dot and comma can be changed
>>In the Old Testament Scriptures;
Everything it promised will come to pass,
>>Just the way it was predicted.
Any one who breaks one commandment of the Law,
>>Or teaches people to break them,
>>Will be last in the Kingdom.
When I keep or teach others to keep the commandments,
>>I will be great in the Kingdom.
I accept Your imputed righteousness to me
>>Which is greater than the self-righteousness
>>Of the scribes and Pharisees.
I know You said whoever kills
>>Will be in danger of eternal judgment,
May I never become so angry with anyone
>>That I condemn them to hell
Because You said I would be in danger
>>Of going to hell myself.
As I begin to pray and remember
>>Someone who is mad at me,
I will stop praying and go reconcile
>>Myself with that offended person,
>>Then I will pray to You.

I will come to terms with those who sue me
    Before I meet them in court,
Lest the judge agree with my opponent
      And they put me in jail
      Or make me pay the full cost.

Lord, I know You said for us not to commit adultery,
      I won't even have impure intentions,
      Lest I commit adultery in my heart.
If anything entices me to sin,
      I will rid it from my life.
It's best for me to get rid of a stumbling block
      Than to lose my testimony or life.
If part of my body is a snare to me,
      I will ignore it, as though it's not there.
It's best to lose the use of part of my body
      Than to destroy the whole body
      And perhaps even the soul.

Jesus quoted the Old Testament that a notice of divorce
      Must be given before putting away a spouse.
Then Jesus said, "If you put away a wife for any reason,
      Other than unfaithfulness,
      Both you and she have become adulterers."
Jesus said, "You have been taught not to break an oath
      By the Old Testament standards."
But Jesus said don't even swear by anything
      Because you can't make one hair black or white.
Jesus commanded us to tell people what we will do,
      But, we should do what we say;
      Our word of promise should be enough.
Jesus quoted the ancients, "An eye for an eye
      And a tooth for a tooth"
      But that principle is not our standard.

Jesus also said don't take revenge;
>   If someone hits you on the right cheek,
>   Offer them the left cheek.
If a man asks to take away your coat,
>   Give him your overcoat also.
If anyone orders you to go one mile,
>   Go two miles with him.
If anyone wants to borrow something,
>   Do not turn that person down.

Lord, You said to love my enemies,
>   I will do good to those who hate me.
You said to bless those who hate me;
>   I will pray for those who despitefully use me,
>   I will treat them as I want to be treated.
Jesus said, "If you love only those who love you,
>   There is no spiritual reward in that,
>   Even sinners love those who love them."
I will love my enemies
>   And do good things to those who hate me,
Because You said, "I would receive a rich reward,
>   And show everyone that I am a child of the Most High."

Lord, I will not practice my piety before people,
>   To be "holy" in their eyes,
>   Because You will not reward it.
I won't show off when I give money
>   Because that would be hypocritical,
>   Recognition is the only reward a hypocrite gets.
When I give my money secretly,
>   I won't let my left hand know
>   What my right hand is doing.
Lord, You know all intentions, and see all gifts,
>   And will reward me if I give humbly and honestly.

Lord, I will not be like the hypocrites when I pray,
> Because they love to pray before people to get attention
> And that's all the reward they'll get.
I will go to my prayer closet
> Where no one can see or hear me,
> Then I'll pray to You, my Father, in secret.
Then you'll see my sincerity in private
> And reward me openly.
I'll not rattle off long prayers like the unsaved,
> Who think they'll be heard
> Because they pray a long time.
I realize You know everything in my heart,
> You know my needs before I pray.

Lord, when I pray, I'll follow this pattern:
> My Father in Heaven, may Your name be holy,
> In my life on earth as Your name is holy in Heaven.
May Your Kingdom come in my life
> On earth as Your Kingdom rules in Heaven.
May Your will be done in my life
> On earth as Your will is done in Heaven.
Give me daily bread for this day
> And forgive the consequences my sin,
> As I forgive the sins of those who hurt me.
Do not let me be tempted to do evil
> And protect me from the evil one,
For You have the ability to answer this prayer.
> Let Your Kingdom rule my life,
> May You get credit when these prayers are answered.

Lord, if I forgive the failings of others,
> You will forgive my faults.
But if I refuse to forgive others
> You will not forgive me.

Lord, I will not fast with an outward "religious" face,
> For that is just to get attention from others,
> The "attention" they get is their reward.
I will dress my normal way when I fast
> So no one will know I'm fasting.
My fast will be a secret between You and me
> And You will reward me with the answers I seek.

Lord, I'll not pile up wealth on earth
> Where inflation or corruption will destroy it.
I'll deposit my wealth in Your heavenly bank,
> Where nothing can destroy it.
Therefore, I will put my treasure
> Where I make a heart commitment.

Lord, may I see things clearly,
> Give me light and understanding in my heart
Because when my eye is clouded with lust and evil thoughts,
> My heart will be blinded by darkness;
> I'll not understand or seek spiritual things.
I'll not serve two masters—God and money,
> Because I'll naturally love one and reject the other.
So Lord, what must I do?
> I won't worry about clothes, entertainment or food.
My life is far more important than
> What I eat, or wear.
The birds will be my example, they don't worry,
> About sowing, reaping or eating food.

Lord, I'm more important to You than birds,
> I know worry will not give me anything I need.
I'll let the lilies of the field be my example for clothing
> They don't worry about their appearance.
Yet Solomon in all his glory
> Is not as beautiful as the lilies.

So Lord, since You wonderfully care for the flowers
    That are here today, and gone tomorrow,
    I know You can take care of me.
Lord, forgive me when I have so little faith,
    About the necessities of life.

Lord, I'll not worry about having enough food and clothing
    Because You know I need them;
    These are the things unsaved people worry about.
I'll seek first Your Kingdom and righteousness,
    Then all these things will be added to me.
I'll not be anxious about tomorrow
    Since You'll take care of tomorrow's needs;
    I'll live one day at a time.

Lord, I'll not criticize others, so they won't criticize me,
    Because the way I treat others
    Is the way they will treat me.
What I give to others is what they'll give me,
    So Lord make me a gracious giver.

Lord, I'll not criticize the small trash in another's eye,
    When my eye is full of garbage.
I can't say, "Let me clean out Your eye,"
    When my eye is full of dirt and filth.
I must first cleanse my eyes
    Before I can help anyone see more clearly.

Lord, I will not give beautiful pearls to pigs,
    They will stomp them into the mud
And then they will turn to attack me,
    So I'll not give "holy things" to evil people.

Lord, I will ask in prayer for the things You can do,
    For You give to those who ask.

I will seek for the things I need,
    For You supply those who seek.
When a door is closed for the things I need,
    I will constantly knock
    For You will open and allow me to find.
I would never give anyone a stone
    When they need bread to eat.
I would never give anyone a snake
    When they ask for a fish to eat.
Since hard-hearted people give good things to their children
    Then I know that You the Heavenly Father will give
    Good gifts to Your children when they ask.

Lord, I will do good things for other people
    That I want them to do for me.

Lord, I will enter Your presence by the narrow door
    Since the road to hell is wide and inviting,
    And most of the crowd takes this road.
But the door to Your presence is small
    And the path to eternal life is narrow.
    So only a few find it.

Lord, I will watch out for false preachers disguised as sheep,
    Because they are ravenous wolves
    Who will eat up young Christians.
I can tell people by their fruit
    Just as I can't pick good fruit from weeds,
    So false preachers are known by their evil deeds.
A good tree cannot grow bad fruit,
    And an evil tree can't grow good fruit.
A tree that produces bad fruit is cut down
    And thrown in the fire,
    That's what'll happen to false preachers.

Lord, those who cry publicly "Lord, Lord"
    Will not enter the kingdom of Heaven.
But those who do Your will
    Will be able to enter Your presence.
Others will cry out "Lord, Lord, I preached in Your name
    And cast out demons and did miracles."
Then You'll say to them, "I never knew you,
    Get out of my sight."

Lord, those who listen to this sermon and obey Your words,
    Will be like a sensible man
    Who builds his house on a rock foundation.
The rains came, floods swirled, and the wind
    Blew upon this house but it didn't fall,
    Because it was founded on a rock.
But those who hear this sermon and reject Your words,
    Are like a stupid man
    Who built his house on sand.
The rains came, floods rose and gale winds blew,
    And it collapsed with a mighty crash.

When Jesus finished this sermon,
    The people were amazed at its content
Because Jesus taught them with authority
    Not like the scribes and other religious preachers.

The Story of the Long Day

The long day is included in Scripture to show how busy Jesus was on this particular day in July, A.D. 27. It began at the breakfast table in Peter's house in Capernaum where Jesus taught, healed a demon-possessed boy, and explained the unpardonable sin. Then Jesus went outside by the lake to deliver an extremely long sermon. (This sermon by the sea is not printed in the action-events of the Long Day. It appears at the conclusion of the Long Day Scripture). Then Jesus sailed across the lake with the apostles where a storm threatened their lives, but Jesus calmed the storm. On the other side, Jesus cast 2,000 demons out of a man and they entered hogs, which rushed down a cliff and drowned in the sea. The owner of the hogs and the people insisted that Jesus leave. He returned to Capernaum that evening and healed a woman who touched the hem of His robe, then he raised Jairus' daughter from the dead.

The Long Day

Matthew 12:24–13:52; Mark 3:20–5:43; Luke 11:14-32

Jesus was eating breakfast at Peter's house,
> When a blind mute was brought to Him
> Who was also demon possessed.

Jesus cast out the demon so that
> The man both spoke and saw,

The crowd shouted with wild enthusiasm,
> "IS THIS MAN DAVID'S SON?"

But the Jewish leaders rejected the crowd saying;
> "This man cast out demons by the
> Power of Beelzebub, the ruler of demons."

Jesus knew their malicious thoughts and answered,
> "If satan casts out satan,
> He has an internal fight with himself."

Then Jesus continued, "When part of a kingdom fights
> Against itself, it will destroy itself."

Every city or house that fights against itself,
> Will collapse."

Jesus said, "If I cast out devils by Beelzebub,
> Then you and your sons can do the same thing."
> Jesus was suggesting they were sons of the devil.

Jesus then said, "If I cast out demons by the Spirit of God,
> Then the King of God's kingdom is here.

141

"You can't steal the things of a strong man's house,
      Unless you first tie up the strong man.
"Those who do not follow Me and My principles
      Are against Me.
"Every sin and blasphemy you commit will be forgiven
      But when you blaspheme the work of the Holy Spirit,
      You will not be forgiven because it's the Holy Spirit
      Who delivers salvation into your heart.
"Those who speak against Christ will be forgiven,
      Those who reject the Holy Spirit and speak against Him
      Shall not be forgiven in this world or the next."
Jesus told the religious leaders, "You are snakes, how can you
      Speak good things when your hearts are evil?
      You speak what's in your heart.
"Good people out of their good heart do good things;
      Evil men out of their evil heart do evil things.
"Every word you say—including casual words—will be
      Used to judge you in the final judgment.
"By your words, you will enter eternal life,
      And by your words, you will be punished."

Lord, I believe every word You've spoken and I will welcome the Holy
      Spirit to come and work in my heart.

The religious leaders asked Jesus to do a miracle for them;
      He answered, "You are an evil and selfish generation that
      Seeks miracles.
"I will only give you the sign of Jonah the prophet who was
      Three days and three nights in the belly of the great fish;
      So, I'll be three days and three nights in the heart of the earth.
"The people of Nineveh will condemn you because they repented
      Because of the preaching of Jonah, but you haven't repented;
      Behold, one greater than Jonah is here.
"The queen of Ethiopia will condemn you because she believed

All she heard and saw about King Solomon;
 Behold, one greater than Solomon is here.
"When a demon is cast out of a person—as I did earlier—
 The demon wandered aimlessly looking for a place to live.
"If the life from which the demon is cast out is not filled
  With the presence of God, the demon will return
  And bring with him seven demons worse than him.
"Then the lost state of the cleansed person becomes more evil
  Than the first state. That's what will happen
  To this present evil generation."

Lord, transform me, give me a new heart so I'll always do your will.
 May everything that comes out of my heart bring praise to You.

Then Mary, the mother of Jesus, came to the edge of the crowd
  And called for Jesus;
  Someone told Jesus, "Your mother and brother are calling for you."
Jesus answered, "Who is my mother and brother but those who
  Follow Me and obey My teaching." Then Jesus stretched His
  hands to His disciples, "Behold my mother and brethren. They
  who do The will of God are My family."
Jesus went out of the house and sat by the Sea of Galilee;
  A great crowd followed Him and overwhelmed Him;
  He got into a boat—pushed out a little from the beach—
  And taught the multitude.

Lord, I count it a privilege to be a member of your family.
 May I be worthy of this great honor.

The sermon by the seaside was preached at this time. It appears at the end of the long day, so the reader can follow the events of this day.

Jesus Calms the Storm

Matthew 8:23-27; Mark 4:35-41; Luke 8:22-25

Just after noon Jesus said to the disciples,
> "Cross over to the other side of the lake";
> So Jesus dismissed the crowd.
The small boat in which He taught began sailing across the sea,
> And because Jesus was tired, He went to sleep.
A violent storm arose and waves broke into the boat,
> Almost swamping the boat.
The disciples woke up Jesus and said, "Master,
> Get up quick, we're about to drown."
Then Jesus rebuked the storm, "Be still" and
> There was a great calm.
Jesus asked His disciples, "Why were you scared?
> Don't you trust Me yet?"
The disciples were filled with awe and said,
> "Who really is Jesus that even a storm obeys Him?"

Lord, teach me to trust You
> *When the storms of this life beat on me.*

Jesus Heals a Violent Demon-Stricken Man

Matthew 8:28-34; Mark 5:1-20; Luke 8:26-37

After the storm they reached the other side of the lake;
> As Jesus got out of the boat He was met by a demon-possessed man.
The surrounding neighbors tried to chain the man,
> But he broke the chain because he was so powerful
> No one was able to control him.
At night he howled in the surrounding tombs

And cut himself with sharp stones.
When the demon-possessed man saw Jesus at a distance,
    He ran and fell at Jesus' feet,
Shouting at the top of his voice,
    "WHAT DO YOU WANT ME TO DO,
    SON OF THE MOST HIGH GOD?"
He cried, "DON'T TORTURE ME!"
    But Jesus said, "Demon, come out of the man."
Then Jesus asked the demon, "What is your name?"
    The demon answered "My name is Legion,
    For we are many."
The demon begged Jesus, "Don't send us away,
    Send us into those hogs."
There was a huge herd of hogs rooting
    In the field above the lake.
Jesus allowed them to enter the hogs
    And the whole herd of 2,000 hogs
    Stampeded into the lake and drowned.
The herdsmen ran to the neighboring towns
    To tell the people what happened to the hogs.
When the people came to investigate, they found the man
    Who had been demon possessed properly clothed,
    Perfectly sane, sitting at the feet of Jesus.
Then the people demanded that Jesus go away
    And leave them alone.
As Jesus got back in the boat, the healed man
    Begged Jesus to let him go with them.
Jesus said, "No...go home to tell your family and friends
    What wonderful things God has done for you."
The healed man visited ten towns in that area
    To relate the story of what Jesus did,
    And the people were simply amazed at his testimony.

The Woman and the 12-year-old Little Girl

Matthew 9:18-26; Mark 5:21-43; Luke 8:41-56

Jesus got back in the boat and returned across the sea to Capernaum,
    A great crowd surrounded Him when He disembarked.
Jairus, the leader of the synagogue, met him begging,
    "My little girl is desperately sick
    Come lay Your hands on her to heal her."
Jesus and the large crowd followed Jairus,
    People pressed on Jesus from all sides.
A woman who had been hemorrhaging blood
    For 12 years came behind Jesus in the crowd for healing.
She had seen many doctors, spending all her money
    And had not gotten better, but worse,
She kept saying in her heart, "If I can touch Jesus,
    I will be healed."
She barely touched the hem of His robe,
    When she felt that she was healed.
Jesus hadn't seen the woman, but He was aware
    That healing power flowed from Him.
So He turned to the crowd to ask,
    "Who touched Me?"
The disciples didn't understand what was happening,
    They said, "A large crowd is pressing on You,
    Yet You said, 'Who touched Me?'"
As Jesus looked around, the woman came forward
    Frightened and shaking, she fell at His feet
    And told Jesus the whole story.
Jesus said, "Daughter, your faith—not your touch—
    Has healed you."
While Jesus was speaking to the woman,
    A messenger arrived to tell Jairus,
    "Your daughter has just died."

But when Jesus heard the message, He said to Jairus,
    "Don't give up, just trust Me."
Then Jesus would not let anyone follow Him except
    Peter, James, and John.
When they arrived at Jairus' home, they confronted
    A commotion of professional mourners who were
    Weeping and wailing unrestrainedly.
Jesus announced to them, "Why this commotion?
    The little girl is not dead, she's asleep."
The mourners laughed at Jesus, so He went
    Into the house with only Peter, James, and John.
Taking the little girl by the hand, Jesus said,
    "Talitha, cumi" which is translated,
    "By the power of My Word, get up."
Immediately, the 12-year-old girl jumped to her feet,
    And walked about the room
    So Jesus said, "Give her something to eat."
Everyone was completely amazed,
    But Jesus said to them not to tell anyone.

Lord, give me faith like the woman You healed,
    Teach me to trust You for all things.

The Sermon by the Sea

Matthew 13:1-52; Mark 4:1-25; Luke 8:4-18

Jesus had taught in Peter's house early on the Long Day. He then left the house and sat in a boat near the seashore where He taught the multitudes. This sermon emphasizes the ministry that His disciples would do. It is included here after the Long Day rather than inserting it in its proper sequence in the day's action. This way the reader can see the sequence of events and how busy Jesus was on this Long Day which is symbolic of all His days.

Lord, be my teacher in all things,
I want to learn from You.

Jesus left Peter's house to teach the multitude
From a boat beside the shore of the Sea of Galilee.
"Look," Jesus said pointing to a farmer sowing seed
In his field which was nearby.
Jesus said, "Some seed fell on the path next to the field;
Birds quickly came to eat up the seeds."
Jesus noted next, "Other seed fell among the rocks
And because there was little dirt,
The grain sprang up fast,
But withered when the hot sun beat upon it,
Because the roots had little nourishment."
Jesus continued, "Other seed fell among thorns
And the thorns choked their growth."
Jesus told, "Still other seed fell on rich soil
And produced a crop, some places a hundredfold,
Some other places sixty, and some places thirty."
Finally Jesus said, "If you have ears to hear,
Then you will understand the spiritual application of
This parable."
The disciples asked, "Why do You use stories to teach?"
Jesus replied, "Because you have the privilege
Of understanding the secrets of the Kingdom,
But the unbelievers don't understand spiritual truth."
Jesus continued, "When a person does something for Me,
He will be given more till he has plenty."
"If a person does nothing for Me,
What he has will be taken away."

Jesus quoted Isaiah to describe three who rejected Him,
"They listen with their ears,
But they don't understand what God says.

"They see with their eyes, but don't perceive
    Because their heart is hardened to God.
"So they hear the good news, but don't understand
    What God wants them to do,
    So they won't believe and become converted."

Jesus then interpreted the story for the disciples
    Because they had a believing heart
    To understand what the story meant.
"When a person hears the message of the Kingdom
    And does not respond, the devil comes to snatch the message,
    As the birds take the seed from the path.
"When a person receives the message but doesn't understand,
    He gives up when trouble or persecution comes;
    He is just like the grain sown in the rocks.
"When a person hears the message but gives up
    Because of worldly things or pursuit of money,
    It is like the seed sown among the thorns.
"But when someone hears and believes the message,
    He brings forth fruit: thirty, sixty, or a hundredfold,
    It is like seed sown on rich soil."

Lord, may my heart be good soil to receive and believe;
    Take away the thorns of sin, and the
    Stubbornness of unbelief.

Jesus then told another story of a farmer who
    Planted seed in his field.
"While he slept the enemy sowed weeds among the good seed;
    The workers told the owner what the enemy did.
"The workers asked, 'Do you want us to pull up
    All the weeds right now?'
"'No,' the farmer said, 'If you pull up the weeds,
    You'll also pull up the good grain.'"

"'Let them both grow till harvest, then burn the weeds
    But put the grain in the barn.'"

Lord, I know there are unsaved in our churches,
    I will leave them alone and
    Let You handle them at the judgment seat.

Jesus then told another story that His Kingdom
    Was like a tiny mustard seed sown in a field.
While it is the smallest of things, it grows into the largest of trees,
    And many birds rest in its branches.

Lord, I know Your message seems weak to the unsaved,
    But it is the power of God to salvation
    That will attract many to You.

Jesus then told a story that His Kingdom is like yeast,
    When put in flour, the bread swells up much larger.

Lord, I know when I humble myself
    I become strong to accomplish much for You.

When Jesus continued to speak to the crowd with stories,
    The disciples asked why He used parables.
Jesus told them He was fulfilling the prophecy of Israel,
    "I will open my mouth with parables
    To explain God's eternal mysteries."

Again, Jesus told a story that His Kingdom was
    Like a treasure that was buried in a field.
Someone found the treasure, then went to sell
    Everything to get money to buy the field.

Lord, I will sacrifice everything—including my life—
    To obtain the treasure of eternal life.

Again, Jesus told the story of someone searching for pearls to buy;
>When he found the greatest pearl ever,
>He sold everything to buy it.

Lord, You are the pearl of infinite price,
>*I will give up everything to have You.*

Jesus told the final story of a big net
>That was thrown into the sea.
When it was full, the fisherman pulled it to shore;
>They put the good fish in a barrel
>But threw away the bad ones.

Lord, I know at the end of the age
>*You will separate the righteous from the evil ones*
>*Who will be thrown into the flames of hell.*
Those who are righteous will go to Heaven,
>*Because Jesus died for them.*

The Twelve Sent Two by Two

Matthew 9:35–11:1; Mark 6:6-13; Luke 9:1-9

Lord, send me where You want me to go,
>*I'll follow You anywhere You send me*
>*Just as the disciples followed You.*

Jesus went through the villages and cities of Galilee
>Preaching the Kingdom in their synagogues
>And healing all manner of sicknesses.
But Jesus was deeply moved when He saw the multitudes
>Because they didn't know where to turn,
>Like sheep without a shepherd.
Jesus said, "The harvest is extremely great,
>And there are not enough workers,

"So pray for the Lord of the harvest to recruit
    More workers to work in the harvest fields."

Lord, I will work diligently in Your fields;
    I will use my efforts to reach lost people.

Then Jesus sent the Twelve out with these instructions,
    "Don't go to the Gentiles or Samaritans,
    But only go to the lost people of Israel.
"As you go preach the Kingdom is here,
    Heal the sick, raise the dead
    Cure the lepers and cast out demons.
"Freely you have received your ministry from Me,
    Now freely give it out to the people."

"Don't take any money in your wallets, nor a suitcase,
    Nor a change of clothes or extra shoes;
    Give as you have received, without charge.
"As you go, stay with someone who believes,
    Give the home your blessings if it deserves it.
"If the people will not listen to you, or receive you,
    Shake the dust off of that place from your shoes.
"God will be easier on Sodom and Gomorrah
    Than on that place in the judgment."

Lord, help me be a courageous witness
    In the face of opposition and persecution.

Jesus told them, "I am sending you as sheep among wolves,
    Be as cunning as serpents,
    And as harmless as doves.
"Be on your guard at all times, your enemies
    Will take you to court or whip you.
"When you stand before religious leaders,
    Testify what God has done for you.

"When you are arrested and stand before judges,
    The Holy Spirit will tell you what to say
    For the Spirit will speak through you.
"When they persecute you in one town,
    Escape to the next place of ministry;
    Your enemies will search for you everywhere.
"People reject Me and call Me 'the prince of evil';
    What sort of name will they call you?
"The disciple is not superior to his teacher,
    And the servant is not better than his master;
    What they do to Me, they will do to you."
Jesus said, "Never be afraid of them who
    Kill the body, but can't harm the soul.
"But be afraid of Him who can destroy
    Both body and soul in hell."

Lord, I want to be Your servant to follow You;
    I will accept what Your enemies do to me.

Jesus continued, "Two sparrows are sold for
    A farthing, but not one falls to the ground
    Without the heavenly Father knowing it."
"The Father even numbers the hairs on your head,

    So Lord, I know I am valuable to You.

"Everyone who acknowledges Me before people,
    I will acknowledge before My Father.
"Everyone who disowns Me before people,
    I will deny before My Father.
"I did not come to bring millennial peace to earth,
    But I have brought a sword of division.
"A son will be against his father, and a daughter
    Will be against her mother.
"A believer's worst enemy may be right

In his own home.
"If anyone puts father or mother before Me,
    They are not worthy of Me.
"If anyone puts son or daughter before Me,
    They are not worthy of Me.
"If you do not take up your cross to follow Me,
    You are not worthy of Me.
"Anyone who prizes their life more than Me,
    They will lose it.
"Anyone who loses his life for My sake
    Will find eternal life.
"Those who welcome you, are welcoming Me;
    And those who welcome Me,
    Welcome the Father who sent Me.
"If you welcome the servants of God,
    You will get the same reward they get.
"If you give a cup of cold water in My name,
    You will not lose Your reward."

Chapter 10

JOHN THE BAPTIST

The Doubts of John the Baptist

Matthew 11:2-19; Luke 7:18-35

John the Baptist called two of his disciples to his prison cell
  Because Herod had arrested him for preaching;
  John sent them to ask Jesus a question.
"Are You the Messiah, or should we look for another?"
  John's disciples arrived as Jesus was healing the sick,
  Casting out evil spirits, and giving sight to the blind.
Then Jesus told the disciples, "Go tell John
  What you have seen and heard.
"The blind see, the lame walk, lepers are healed,
  The deaf hear, and the dead are raised.
"The good news of the Gospel is proclaimed,
  Happy is the man who doesn't lose faith in Me."

Lord, increase my faith; I want unquestioning allegiance.

When the disciples left to return to John the Baptist,
  Jesus asked the crowd,
"When you went to the desert to hear John,
  Did you see a reed shaken in the wind?
"No, you saw a prophet, but he was more than that,
  John was My forerunner, as predicted by God,
  'I will send My messenger before Messiah comes.'"
Then Jesus said, "There is not a man born

Of woman who is greater than John the Baptist,
And anyone who considers himself least in the Kingdom
        Is greater than John the Baptist."

Lord, I want to be that person.

Jesus said, "Everyone—even tax-collectors—
        Believed and were baptized by John,
But the Jewish leaders rejected God's plan
        So they refused John's baptism."
Jesus asked, "What is this generation like?"
        Then He answered, "You are like children
        Complaining about the games they play.
"John the Baptist came first and didn't drink wine;
        So you said, 'He is crazy.'
"Then I, the Son of Man, come enjoying food and drink,
        And you call Me a glutton and drunkard.
"Make up your minds what you want;
        You are a generation that rejects God,
        You always justify what you think is right."

Lord, I accept Jesus for who He is;
        Jesus is the Son of God, my Savior.

The Story of John the Baptist's Murder

On an early, cool spring evening, one week before Passover, the palace at Machaerus was brilliantly lit up like a torch on the hill. The people in the town below could smell the tempting aromas and hear the drunken laughter from the festive banquet. The meal was extensive; one course of food followed another. Wine and alcohol were abundant. Finally, Herod Antipas called for his thoroughly drunken guests to be entertained. Clapping his hands, he commanded the dancers to commence.

To the surprise of everyone, Salome, the alluring young daughter of Herodias, danced into the light of the room. Salome danced magnificently, tempting and taunting the men with provocative movements and gestures. Herodias recognized the burgeoning charms of her young daughter—her husband was clearly attracted to the young girl—so the mother coaxed her into this wretched, fleshly amusement to achieve her own ends. When Salome reached the end of her spectacle, the entire audience erupted into applause. Antipas jumped to his feet, wildly cheering. Then, with his guests as witnesses, he made a drunken vow to Salome: "You shall have anything you want, even half of my kingdom."

Salome smiled, her mother's words leaping out of her mouth like the fangs of a cobra. "Give me the head of John the Baptist here on a silver platter."

Silence fell across the drunken assembly. The shock of her request sobered men who previously in the evening had willingly given their sense of morality over to wine. Herod's countenance dropped. Anger gripped his heart, but having been put on the spot, he could not rescind his offer to Salome in front of his guests.

Antipas ordered his guards, "Go immediately and bring me the head of the Baptist."

The appointed executioner stepped out of the banquet hall into the cold spring night, walking up the steps from the palace to the prison. When he opened the rusty doors to enter with a torch, John the Baptist knew that his end was at hand. He knew he was to be sacrificed on the altar of Herod Antipas.

Within a few minutes, the guard came dashing down the stairs to the banquet hall, the silver platter in hand, the gory head of John the Baptist held high for all to see. The piercing eyes of the dead Baptist were open, accusing the man to whom the head was delivered. As the platter was offered up to Herod Antipas, John preached his final message: "REPENT."

Young Salome eagerly received the silver platter, then ran through the night to her mother Herodias, delivering to her the ghastly prize for which she had asked.

My Time To Pray

- Lord, if I have to die a martyr's death, help me to die like John the Baptist.

- Lord, help me to live as though each breath were my last.

The Murder of John the Baptist

Matthew 14:1-12; Mark 6:14-29; Luke 9:7-9

Lord, John the Baptist was the greatest man to ever live,
  May I be as humble as he,
  And fill me with the Spirit as You did Him.

Then Herod the Tetrarch said about the fame of Jesus,
  "This is John the Baptist risen from the dead,"
For Herod had arrested John and chained him in prison
  Because John had preached that it was against
  Scripture for Herod to marry his brother's wife.
Herod wanted to execute John but was afraid
  Because the people regarded John as a prophet.
His wife, Herodias, also wanted to kill John
  Because he had embarrassed her,
  But she couldn't arrange for it to happen.
During Herod's birthday, the daughter of Herodias
  Danced before the guests at the party.
Herod was so delighted with her that he
  Made an oath to give her anything she asked.
Her mother Herodias told her to ask for
  The head of John the Baptist on a platter.
Herod sent immediately and beheaded John;
  The head was brought in on a platter

And given to the girl who gave it to her mother.
John's disciple's came and took the body
    And buried it; then they told Jesus.

Lord, if I have to die a martyr's death,
    May I accept my martyrdom as did John.

Chapter 11

FEEDING HIS PEOPLE

The Story of Feeding the Five Thousand

Jesus was angered and heartbroken over the death of the prophet. The apostles encouraged Him to speak against this atrocity. The youngest apostle John agreed with Simon that this might be the catalyst that would stir the Jews to war. But Jesus did not want a confrontation with Herod Antipas. This was not the battle He came to fight.

The roads were filled with pilgrims on their way to Jerusalem for Passover. Wanting to avoid the crowds and any speculation about what He would do, Jesus got into a boat with His apostles and headed north.

When men and women on the highway along the lake saw Jesus leave, many abandoned their pilgrimage and began following Him along the shore. Jesus' boat landed near a large expanse of grass. He went to the top of a small hill to pray. But soon the multitudes gathered at the hill. When Jesus saw the people, as always His heart was moved. He began teaching them.

Because only men were required to attend Passover, many of their wives and children had stayed home. Jesus looked out to see thousands of strong men. If ever a dictator wanted an army to recruit and train for his purposes, this was the occasion. Jesus had only to proclaim Himself their leader.

Jesus ministered all day. The apostle Philip was the first to notice the shadows falling over the crowd.

Philip spoke to Jesus. "Lord, this is a deserted place, and the hour is late. Send the multitudes away, so they may buy food." Since Philip was in charge of food and provisions, Jesus asked him, "Where can we buy bread so that these people may eat?" Jesus was testing Philip; He already knew what He would do.

Philip had already counted the crowd. He knew there were about 5,000 men there, plus a few hundred women and children. Philip answered, "Why, eight months of wages wouldn't feed this many!"

Philip sent the apostles into the crowd to inventory what food was available. Only Andrew found food. Andrew said to Jesus, "There is a little boy here. He has five barley loaves and two small fish, but what are they among so many?"

Jesus said to Philip, "Make the people sit down, and bring the loaves and fish to Me."

The apostles followed Jesus' directions.

Jesus took the loaves, held them to Heaven and gave thanks: "Blessed are you, our God, who calls this bread to come forth from the earth."

He directed the Twelve to gather some baskets, then began breaking the loaves of bread, placing the morsels in a basket. He repeated the practice until the baskets were filled.

"Give this food to the people to eat," he said to Philip, who had watched the process. Then the apostles fanned out into the crowd. The baskets were never emptied, yet each person ate as much as he needed.

As the sun set, Jesus said to his apostles, "Gather up the fragments."

When the apostles had gathered up the fragments, there were 12 baskets left, one for each apostle—enough food for three or four days.

My Time To Pray

- Lord, I'm hungry today; feed me with Your presence.

- Lord, help me know that people are hungry who I meet in life, and help me feed them with Your Word.

- Lord, I pray for a great revival in the world, there are so many people who are hungry for something, and they don't know they are hungry for You.

Feeding the Five Thousand

Matthew 14:13-23; Mark 6:30-46; Luke 9:10-17; John 6:1-15

There was a great multitude following Jesus
    So He went up into a mountain near Tiberius.
The multitude followed Him because of His miracles
    And because He healed the sick.
They were on their way to Jerusalem to celebrate
    The springtime feast of Passover.
Jesus surveyed the multitude, then said to Philip,
    "Where can we buy food for them?"
Jesus knew He would feed them with a miracle;
    He was testing Philip's faith in Him.

Lord, may I be faithful when tested.

Philip answered, "If we had the wages of 200 servants
    There would only be a little bit for each one."
Andrew heard the conversation and found a young boy
    With five loaves of bread and two small fishes;
    Then Andrew said, "This isn't enough for all the crowd."
Jesus said, "Make the men sit down in groups of
    Fifty and 100 to make distribution easy";
    They sat on grass in the area.
Jesus looked to Heaven to bless the food,

Then He gave it to the disciples
And they distributed it to the multitude.
Everyone had as much as they could eat
Then Jesus said to His disciples,
"Gather the food that is left over";
So they gathered up 12 baskets full.
After the people saw the miracle, they said,
"This is the One who the prophet Jeremiah
Predicted was coming into the world to feed us bread."
The multitude rushed toward Jesus;
They wanted to make Him King.

Lord, feed me when I'm spiritually hungry
Just as You fed the 5,000 by the sea.

The Story of Jesus Walking on Water

By the estimation of anyone in Palestine—Roman or Jew—5,000 well-fed men was a potential army. Here were 5,000 men who wouldn't be distracted by hunger. Jesus could feed them miraculously. If they were wounded in battle, Jesus could heal them. Surely these men could be motivated to follow the Messiah in a campaign to liberate the Holy Land.

The same thoughts occurred to a number of the 5,000. The men were carried away with their potential and talked about making Jesus their king—by force if necessary.

Jesus directed the apostles toward the boat, then pointing across the sea, He instructed them, "Go to Capernaum."

Jesus walked swiftly through several clusters of excited men, then slipped between some high rocks into the hills. He needed to be alone, to pray and commune with the Father.

A desert storm rolled into the Sea of Galilee, and the hot air mixing with cool breezes off the cold water unleashed a torrential rain.

As Jesus was praying, He looked out and saw the disciples caught in the storm. If they tried to make it to shore, the boat would be pounded to pieces. If they stayed on the lake, the boat would capsize. Immediately, Jesus left His place of prayer and went to them—walking across the water.

The waves grew higher; even the apostles who were hardened fishermen were frightened.

"YE-E-E-A-A-A-I-I-I!" one of the apostles screamed when he saw Jesus. "It's a ghost!" The scream startled the other apostles, who caught sight of the apparition walking on the water. They stopped pulling on the oars and stared, dumbstruck.

Another one of them yelled again, "It's a ghost!"

Peter didn't believe it. He knew this was no spirit, but someone dear. The stout, red-bearded fisherman yelled, "It's the Lord!" Jesus called out, "It is I! Do not be afraid."

Ever impetuous, Peter shouted out over the water, "Lord…if it is You, tell me to come to You, and I will walk to You on the water."

This was the kind of faith Jesus had been waiting to see in His disciples. He said to Peter, "Come…."

Instinctively, Peter leaped from the boat. He began walking toward his Master on the water.

At first, the eyes of Peter were riveted on Jesus. In faith, the big fisherman was doing something no man had ever done. But when Peter saw the waves swirling around him, he became afraid and began to sink. Peter looked to Jesus with beseeching eyes. He cried out, "Lord, save me!"

Jesus stretched out a hand and caught him, asking, "O you of little faith, why did you doubt?"

When Jesus and Peter got into the boat, Jesus commanded the raging waves, "Peace…be still." And the wind ceased.

My Time To Pray

- Lord, thank You for coming to me in the past when I had storms in my life. I know You will come to help me in future storms.

- Lord, I know You send me into the storm, as You sent the disciples into the storm. Help me to learn Your purpose for storms in my life.

- Lord, I worship You for helping me through my storms, just as You delivered the disciples from their storms.

Jesus Walks on the Water

Matthew 14:24-33; Mark 6:47-51

Jesus sent His disciples across the sea
    In a boat to Capernaum.
He then went to an isolated area
    In the mountains to pray.
A storm broke over the sea and the disciples
    Were afraid because they couldn't
    Control the boat in the massive waves.
About 3 A.M. Jesus saw their distress
    And went to them, walking on the water.

Lord, when I am distressed because of problems,
    Come to meet my needs and help me get through
    The problems of my life.

The disciples were frightened when they saw Jesus
    Because they thought He was a ghost.
Jesus made as if He would pass them by,
    So they cried out to Him.

Jesus answered, "It is I, do not be afraid";
       Then Peter yelled to Jesus,
"Lord, if this is You, let me
       Come to You, walking on the water."
Jesus answered with one word, "Come!"
       Peter jumped out of the boat
       And walked on the water to Jesus.
But then he looked at the waves
       And began to sink into the sea.
Peter yelled to Jesus, "Save me";
       Jesus stretched out His hand to him
       And lifted Peter up.
Jesus told Peter, "Why do you have such
       Little faith? Why do you doubt Me?"

Lord, may I yell out a desperate prayer
       When an emergency threatens me?"

When they got into the boat, the winds ceased
       And they worshiped Jesus, saying,
       "Truly, You are the Son of God."

Sermon on the Bread of Life

John 6:22-71

The next day the crowd walked around the sea toward Capernaum
       And they only saw one boat there.
And they knew Jesus didn't get into the boat
       With the disciples to cross the sea.
So they asked Him, "Rabbi, how did You get here?" Jesus didn't answer.
He said, "You seek Me because you saw the miracles;
       Yesterday, you ate of the bread and fishes."
Jesus told them, "Don't work for food that perishes,

But work for the bread of eternal life
Which the Son of Man offers you."
The crowd asked, "What must we do to perform
The works of God which You do?"
Jesus answered, "The work of God is to believe
On the Son whom the Father has sent."
The crowd answered, "Do a miracle for us
So we can believe in You and follow You.
"Our fathers ate the manna in the wilderness that Moses
Gave to them during the 40 years of wilderness wanderings."
Then Jesus said to them, "Verily, verily, I say to you,
It was not Moses who gave you bread from Heaven.
My Father gives true bread out of Heaven;
The bread of God is He who comes
From Heaven to give life to the world."
The crowd said, "Please give us this bread";
Jesus said, "I am the Bread of Life.
"He who comes to Me will never hunger;
He who believes in Me will never thirst,
But you don't believe in Me.
"All the Father gives Me shall come to Me,
And I will not turn them away
"Because I come from Heaven to do the will
Of the Father, and not My will.
"And this is the will of the Father that
Everyone who believes in the Father will have eternal life
And that I will raise Him up in the last day."

The Jewish leaders complained because Jesus said,
"I am the Bread who comes from Heaven."
They argued, "Is not this Jesus the Son of Joseph;
We know His father and mother,
How can He say, 'I come from Heaven?'"
Jesus answered, "Don't complain! No one comes

To Me except the Father draw him,
        And I will raise him up in the last day.
"It is written in Isaiah, 'All will be taught by God,
        Everyone who believes what I say will come to Me.'
"No one has seen the Father except the One
        Who comes to you from the Father;
        He has seen the Father.
"The Jewish forefathers ate manna
        In the wilderness, and they died.
"I am the Bread who comes from Heaven
        That you may eat and not die.
"If you eat of this Bread, you will live forever
        And the Bread I give you is Myself,
        It is given for the world.
"Verily, verily, I say to you, the one who
        Believes has eternal life;
        I am the Bread of Life."

The Jewish leaders argued among themselves saying,
        "How can this man give us Himself to eat?"
Jesus answered them, "Verily, verily, I say to you,
        Except you eat the Son of Man, you will not have eternal life
"He who eats and drinks has eternal life
        And I will raise Him up in the last day
"For I am meat to eat and water to drink,
        And the one who eats Me will abide in Me
        And I will abide in Him.
"I live because the living Father sent Me,
        And the one who eats Me will live because of Me.
"This is the Bread who comes from Heaven,
        It's not like the bread the forefathers ate and died;
        He that eats this Bread will live forever."

When Jesus ended His sermon in Capernaum,
    Many of Jesus' disciples said this sermon
    Was too hard to believe.
But Jesus knew they were complaining, so He said,
    "If this sermon causes you problems,
What will you think when you see Me
    Ascending back to Heaven where I was previously?
"The words I spoke are Spirit and life;
    The Spirit will give you eternal life,
    The flesh cannot help you.
"Some of you have not put your faith in Me."
    Jesus knew from the beginning those
    Who believed in Him, and who would betray Him.
So Jesus said, "No one can come to Me
    Except the Father draw Him."
    Therefore, many disciples stopped following Jesus.
Then Jesus said to the Twelve,
    "Will you also stop following Me?"
Peter answered, "Who else can we follow?
    You have the words of eternal life;
    We believe and know You are the Messiah."
Jesus answered them, "I chose all 12 of you
    Yet one of you is a devil."
Jesus was referring to Judas Iscariot
    The one who would betray Him.

Lord, I will eat the Bread of Life
    To satisfy my spiritual hunger.

Questions About Ceremonial Cleansing

Matthew 15:1-20; Mark 7:1-23; John 7:1

Lord, teach me the right way to observe
  Church traditions, just as You taught Your disciples.

Jewish leaders came from Jerusalem to Capernaum,
  To find fault with Jesus' religious practices.
They were angry because Jesus' disciples ate bread
  With defiled hands; they didn't wash
  Their hands ceremonially before eating.
The leaders cleansed themselves ceremonially,
  When they came from the market place,
  They did the same to all eating utensils.
The leaders asked Jesus why His disciples
  Didn't keep the tradition of the elders?
Jesus answered by quoting Isaiah, "This people
  Honors Me in outward ways,
  But their heart is far from Me."
"They vainly worship Me, teaching
  Their doctrine as the Word of God."
Jesus told the Jewish leaders, "You leave
  The Word of God and hold to your traditions.
"Moses told you to honor your father and mother;
  The one who speaks evil of
  Father and mother shall be put to death.
"But you say, 'My mother and father are
  Better off because they gave birth to me.'
"This statement does not honor your parents,
  You deny Scriptures by saying that."

Lord, may I be careful to always honor
  My mother and father.

Jesus then spoke to the crowd, "A person
        Is not defiled by what goes in the mouth,
        But by what comes out of the heart.
"What goes into the mouth, enters the stomach,
        And finally is discharged from the body,
"But things that come out of the heart,
        Defile a person,
"For out of the heart come evil thoughts,
        Murders, adulteries, sexual perversions,
        Thefts, lying, pride, and anger.
"The things that come out of the heart defile a person,
        Not eating with unwashed hands."

Lord, forgive the sinful desires of my heart
        And keep me from all outward transgression.

Jesus Visits Lebanon

Matthew 15:21-28; Mark 7:24-30

Lord, give me faith to persevere in prayer
        When it seems You are reluctant to answer
        As was the case of the Syria-Lebanon woman.

Jesus left Galilee and went to Tyre and Sidon,
        And slipped quietly into a house for rest
        Where the crowd wouldn't exhaust Him.
But the crowds found out where He was,
        Then a Greek woman from Syria-Lebanon
        Came and fell down before Jesus.
Her daughter was possessed with a demon
        And she begged Jesus to cast the demon out.
Jesus said, "No one takes bread from the children,
        And gives it to the dogs under the table."

So, Jesus didn't respond in a positive way
      But referred to her as a dog,
      The Jewish word for Gentile.
But the woman showed faith by replying,
      "Yes, Lord, but the dogs under the table
      Get to eat the crumbs."
Jesus answered, "Woman you have great faith,
      You will get what you asked";
      And the daughter was healed.

Jesus Visits Caesarea Philippi

Mark 8:27–9:1; Matthew 16:18-28; Luke 9:18-27

Lord, instruct me how to love Your church
      Just as You instructed Your disciples.

Next, Jesus went to the village of Caesarea Philippi,
      And as they were walking, Jesus asked,
      "Who do the people say that I am?"
The disciples answered, "Some say You are John the Baptist,
      Others say You are Elijah, or Jeremiah
      Or one of the prophets."
Jesus then asked, "But who do you say that I am?"
      Simon Peter answered, "You are the Christ,
      The Son of the Living God."
Jesus answered, "Simon Peter, son of Jonah, you are blessed,
      You didn't think this up,
      My Father in Heaven gave you this revelation.
"Peter, you have faith like a rock,
      And I will build My church on
      The solid rock statement of My deity that you spoke."
"The gates of hell cannot stop My followers
      When they go preaching who I am."

Jesus then replied, "I will give you the keys
    To the kingdom of Heaven."
"Whatever you bound on earth will not enter Heaven,
    Whatever you lose on earth, will enter Heaven."
Jesus then instructed them not to tell anyone
    He was the Messiah, the anointed of God.

Then Jesus told His disciples that He
    Must go to Jerusalem to suffer
    Many things from the Chief Priest and the Scribes
And be killed by them, but He would
    Rise from the dead on the third day.
Peter rebuked Jesus saying, "This will never happen to You."
    Jesus turned and said to Peter,
    "Get behind Me, you are a stumbling block.
"You are not concerned with the things of God,
    But with the things of men."
Then Jesus said, "If any person will follow Me,
    Let him take up his cross daily and follow Me."

Lord, I don't want to save my life, then lose it;
    I will give my life for You
    And find Your purpose for my life.
What shall it profit me if I gain
    The whole world but lose my own soul?
    I will not sell my soul to satan.

Then Jesus added, "Whoever will be ashamed
    Of Me and My words,
I will be ashamed of them when
    I come into the glory of My Father.
"Some of you standing here will not taste death,
    Till they see Me coming in glory."

Lord, I will not be ashamed of You
But will follow You to death.

The Story of the Transfiguration of Jesus

Jesus spoke privately to the three men closest to Him. "Peter, James, and John," He said, "come with Me." He pointed to the peak of Mount Hermon.

They climbed all that day toward the snowcapped summit; Jesus climbing ahead of the them.

As John and his fellow apostles crested a plateau in the side of the mountain, the breeze picked up speed, blowing a cloud rapidly toward the plateau, where Jesus now stood about 50 paces away. John saw there was something unusual about this cloud. Rather than absorbing light, sunbeams danced off the cloud.

The cloud settled over the plateau, covering them as a warm blanket. Peter, James, and John looked for their Master through the mist and then saw Jesus as they had never seen Him.

He appeared opalescent, as though reflecting the light from the sun. He glistened.

Through the mist, two men appeared to talk with Him. He conversed amiably with the men as though they were long-lost friends.

"That's...that's Elijah," sputtered Peter. "And the other one is Moses. I'm certain of it."

Peter felt a need to celebrate. He jumped to his feet, calling out to Jesus, "Lord, it is good for us to be here! If you wish, let us make three tabernacles. One for You, one for Moses and one for Elijah."

Suddenly, the shining cloud grew a hundred times brighter. A commanding voice spoke.

"This is my beloved Son, in whom I am well pleased. Listen to him!"

This was too much for the apostles. Terrified, they fell to the ground.

Then Jesus knelt beside them, saying, "Get up. Don't be afraid."

My Time To Pray

- Lord, I worship You now because of what I know of You in Scripture. I look forward to worshiping You in Heaven when You are glorified and transformed.

- Lord, teach me how to worship better than I now do.

The Transfiguration of Jesus

Mark 9:2-13; Matthew 17:1-13; Luke 9:28-36

Lord, help me see Your glory
And worship You as the disciples did.

Six days after Jesus spoke at Caesarea Philippi
     He took with Him Peter, James, and John
     And climbed up into the heights of Mount Hermon.
Jesus was transfigured before them,
     His face glistened as the sun,
     His clothes were sparkling white.
Then Moses and Elijah appeared
     And talked with Jesus
     About His coming death.
When Moses and Elijah departed from the Lord,
     Peter said to Jesus,
"Master, it is good for us to be here,
     Let's make three tents, one for You,

One for Moses, and one for Elijah."
While Peter was speaking, a cloud covered them
    And the three disciples were afraid.
Then a voice spoke from the cloud,
    "This is my beloved Son,
    In whom I am well pleased; hear Him."
The disciples fell to the ground in fear,
    Then Jesus touched them saying, "Don't be afraid."
Then as they were going down the mountain,
    Jesus said to them "Don't tell anyone about this,
    Until I am raised from the dead."
The disciples asked Jesus, "Why do the Scribes say
    Elijah must come before Messiah comes?"
Jesus answered, "It is true that Elijah
    Must come to restore all things.
"But I'm telling you that the Messiah has already come
    But the Scribes didn't know it
    And unsaved people will do to him as they want.
"In the same way I, the Son of Man,
    Will suffer because of them."
The disciples understood that Jesus meant
    John the Baptist was Elijah.

The Disciples Can't Heal

Mark 9:14-29; Matthew 17:14-20; Luke 9:37-43

Lord, teach me what to do
    When my prayers are not answered.

The next day Jesus returned from the Mount of Transfiguration
    And saw a large crowd listening
    As they questioned the nine disciples.
When they saw Jesus, they ran and greeted Him

Jesus asked, "What are you discussing?"
A man spoke up, "I brought my epileptic son
    To Your disciples who is deaf and unable to speak,
    But they couldn't heal him.
"My son foams at the mouth, and falls
    In the fire or water.
"He has an evil spirit—a demon—
    And when You were coming, it
    Threw him to the ground and wounded him."
Jesus answered, "O faithless and evil generation,
    How long must I put up with your unbelief?"
Then Jesus challenged them, "If you believe,
    All things are possible to the one who believes."
The father cried out, "I believe,
    Help me overcome my unbelief."
Then Jesus rebuked the evil spirit,
    "You deaf and dumb spirit, come out of him."
The evil spirit cried out and came out of the boy,
    Who dropped to the ground as though he were dead.
Jesus raised His hand and the boy arose;
    Everyone was astonished.
When they entered a house, the disciples asked privately
    Why they couldn't cast the demon out.
Jesus answered, "This kind comes out
    By continued fasting and prayer."

Paying the Temple Tax

Matthew 17:24-27

When they came to Capernaum, those who collected
    The temple tax asked Peter,
    "Why doesn't your Master pay the half-sheckle tax?"

Jesus asked Simon, "Do the kings receive taxes
    From his son or from citizens?"
    Peter answered, "From citizens."
Since Jesus is the Son of the Father in Heaven,
    And the temple belongs to His Father,
    Jesus doesn't need to pay temple taxes.
Then Jesus explained to Peter, "Lest
    We become a stumbling block to them,
Go to the sea, cast a hook, and
    Take a coin out of the mouth of
    The first fish you catch.
"Take that coin and pay the temple tax
    So they are not offended."

Lord, teach me how not to offend people
    So I can reach them with salvation.

Childlike Faith

Matthew 18:1-5; Mark 9:33-37; Luke 9:46-48

Lord, give me childlike faith
    To believe every word You've said.

As Jesus and the disciples were in Peter's house
    In Capernaum, Jesus asked them,
"What were you talking about as you
    Were walking here?"
The disciples didn't say anything because
    They were embarrassed.
They had been arguing which of them
    Was the greatest.
Jesus sat down and said, "If any would
    Be first, he must become last."

Jesus called a little child and set him
 In the middle of the disciples, and said,
"Verily I say to you, except you become as little children,
 You will not enter the kingdom of Heaven."
Jesus took the little child in His arms, and said,
 "Those who receive such little children
 In my name, receive Me."
"And those who receive Me, do not just receive Me,
 But they receive the Father who sent Me."

Lord, I'm like a child, not very smart
 And not very talented to serve You;
 I trust You as a child trusts his father.

Mistaken Zeal of John the Apostle

Matthew 18:6-14; Mark 9:38-50; Luke 9:49-50

Lord, help me be tolerant of believers
 Who are not members of my church,
 Just as You taught John to be tolerant.

John said to Jesus, "We saw a person
 Casting out demons in Your name
And we forbid him because
 He didn't follow You."
Jesus said, "Don't forbid him, one cannot do mighty works
 In My name or speak evil of me and be against Me;
 He who is not against us, is for us.
"Those who give you a cup of water because
 You serve Me, will be rewarded."
Then returning to the children, Jesus said,
 "Whoever causes one of these little ones to stumble
 A great mill stone should be hung

About his neck and be cast into the sea.
"There will be many who cause children to stumble,
But woe to the one who does it."

A Sinful Woman Anoints Jesus' Feet

Luke 7:36-50

Lord, may I worship You with my tears
And the sacrifice of things precious to me,
Just as the sinful woman worshiped You.

A Pharisee invited Jesus to eat in his house,
So Jesus entered the home and sat down to eat.
A sinful woman heard that Jesus was there,
So she came and stood behind Him crying.
When her tears wet the feet of Jesus,
She dried them with the hair of her head,
And kissed His feet, then anointed them
With the cruse of alabaster oil she brought.

Lord, may I love You so much
That I worship You with the perfume of my praise.

The Pharisee was incensed and thought, "If Jesus
Were a prophet, He would know the kind
Of woman that touched Him, and kissed His feet."
Jesus knew the Pharisees' thought, and said,
"Simon, listen to this story;
A certain leader had two debtors, one owed him
$500, the other owed him $50.
"Because they didn't have anything to pay him,
The leader forgave both debts."
Then Jesus asked, "Which will love him the most?"

Lord, thank You for forgiving all my sin-debts.

Simon answered, "The one who was forgiven the most."
  Jesus replied, "You are right."
Turning to the woman, Jesus said, "See this woman?
    You did not wash My feet,
    But this woman has washed them with her tears.
"You did not give Me a towel to dry my feet,
    But this woman has dried them with her hair.
"You did not give me a kiss of common hospitality,
    But she continued to kiss My feet.
"You did not anoint Me with oil as a courtesy,
    But she has anointed My feet with oil."
Again turning to the woman Jesus said, "Her sins,
    Which are many are forgiven her
    Because she loves much.
"Those who are forgiven little, love little;
    Those who are forgiven much, love much."
Then Jesus said to the woman, "Your sins are forgiven!"
    The Pharisees at the table inwardly criticized,
    "Who does Jesus think He is—God?"
    For only God can forgive sin.
Finally Jesus said to the woman, "Go in peace,
    Your faith has saved you."

Lord, I rest in the peace you've given
  Because I asked You to forgive my sins.

Giving Up Everything

Matthew 8:19-22; Luke 9:57-62

Lord, I will give up everything for You
  Because You ask for complete dedication.

As Jesus was traveling, a man told Him,
  "I will follow You wherever You go."
Jesus told him, "The foxes live in holes,
  And birds have a nest for their home,
  But the son of Man doesn't have a home."
Jesus said to another man, "Follow Me!" But the man said
  He had to go arrange for the burial of his aged father.
Jesus said, "Let the dead bury the dead
  But you go preach the Gospel of the Kingdom."
Another man said he would follow Jesus
  But he first had to arrange things
  At home before following Jesus.
Jesus said, "No man who puts his hand to the plough
  And looks back is fit for the kingdom of God."

Lord, I want to give You everything;
  Forgive me for my ignorant lapses.

Jesus and His Unbelieving Brothers

John 7:1-10

Lord, help me know when to take the advice
  Of my unsaved relatives.

Jesus' unsaved brothers counseled Him to go
  To the Feast of Tabernacles at Jerusalem.
They said, "Go do miracles so the multitude
  Will believe You and follow You.
"A person who wants to be known
  Doesn't do things in secret,
  But he manifests himself to the world."
Jesus told them, "The hour for me to manifest
  Myself is not here yet.

"The world does not hate you, but it hates Me
     Because I tell them their works are evil.
"It's not time for Me to manifest Myself";
     So He didn't do what they suggested.
After Jesus' brethren went to the feast in Jerusalem
     Jesus privately went on an out-of-the-way road,
     Arriving in the middle of the week.

Jesus at the Feast of Tabernacles

John 7:11-52

Lord, protect me when I'm in danger
     As You protected Jesus from danger at Jerusalem.

The Jewish leaders were looking everywhere
     Saying, "Where is Jesus?"
The crowd was confused, some said,
     "Jesus was a good man,"
     Others said, "He leads the multitude astray."
Yet no one supported Jesus publicly
     Because they were afraid of the Jewish leaders.
Jesus went into the temple on Wednesday and taught,
     Everyone marveled at His knowledge
     Because Jesus hadn't graduated from the best schools.
Jesus answered, "I don't think up the things I teach,
     This doctrine comes from my heavenly Father."
"If anyone is yielded to do the Father's will,
     He shall understand this doctrine
     Whether this is my idea or the Father's.
"He who does his own will, also seeks his own glory
     But he who seeks to glorify the Father
     There is no unrighteousness in Him.

"Moses gave you the Law, but none of you keep it;
        None of you are righteous before God."

Jesus said, "Why do you want to kill Me?"
        The Jewish leaders said, "You have a demon
        Because You think someone is trying to kill You."
Jesus said, "I healed a lame man on the Sabbath
        Eighteen months ago, and you hate me for it."
"Moses gave you the Law to circumcise a boy
        And you circumcise on the Sabbath."
"Yet you are angry with Me because I healed
        On the Sabbath day,
        Aren't healing and circumcision both a work of God?"
"Let's judge according to God's perfect judgment,
        Did we not both do right on the Sabbath?"

The crowd began talking among themselves,
        "Isn't this the man the leaders want to kill
        Yet they say nothing when He speaks openly?"
"Maybe they think He is our Messianic Deliverer
        So they don't do anything to Him."
Jesus preached loudly to the crowd, "You think you know Me,
        And you think you know where I come from,
But you don't really know Me;
        The Father who sent Me, knows Me
        And I know Him, because I come from Him."
The crowd wanted to take Jesus to the Jewish leaders
        But no one laid a hand on Him
        Because His hour was not come.
Yet, many in the crowd believed on Jesus
        Saying, "Messiah won't do more miracles
        Than this Man has done."
When the Jewish leaders heard Jesus was preaching
        To the multitude, they sent officers to arrest Him.

Jesus responded, "I will be with you for only a little while,
    Then I'll go to the One who sent Me."
"You will look for Me, but not find Me
    Because I'm going where You can't come."
The crowd talked among themselves asking,
    "Where is He going that we can't find Him,
Is He going to the Jews in the dispersion
    Or is He going to teach Gentiles?"

On Sunday, the last day of the Feast of Tabernacles
    When thousands of priests were parading with
    Pots of water to pour out as a drink offering to God,
Jesus shouted to the crowd, "If anyone is thirsty,
    Come to Me for satisfaction."
"He that believes on Me, will have living water
    Flowing out of his inner being."
Jesus was referring to the indwelling Holy Spirit
    But the Holy Spirit had not yet been given
    Because Jesus had not yet gone to glory.
Someone who had been in the crowd, said, "Jesus is a true prophet!"
    Others said, "He is the Messiah!"
But the crowd argued, "The Messiah doesn't come
    From Gentiles, but from Bethlehem,
    The village where David was born."
The crowd was divided because of Jesus,
    And no one laid a hand on Him.
The Jewish leaders asked the officers
    Why they didn't arrest Jesus;
    They answered, "No one speaks like Him."
Some said, "This man is not the Messiah;
    We know this man comes from Nazareth,
    We don't know where Messiah comes from."
The leaders rebuked them, "Are you also
    Deceived by this Man?

Have any of our leaders believed Him?"
Nicodemus (by this time a believer) said to them,
"Does our Law judge a man before we hear Him?"
The leaders ridiculed Nicodemus, "Search the
Record, no prophet comes out of Galilee."

Lord, thank You that I understand spiritual truth,
And I'm not spiritually blind like the Jewish leaders.

Chapter 12

THE ABSOLUTE LOVE OF JESUS

The Story of the Woman Taken in Adultery

On the Monday after the Feast of Tabernacles, the fields around Jerusalem were littered with branches and leaves from the discarded booths where people had slept. Before the sun came up, Jesus was in the temple to worship, but even at daybreak the people were drawn to Him. A few hundred gathered around Him as He sat to teach. The Pharisees and priests remained at a distance, with a conspiratorial air.

Then a woman's cry was heard outside the gates.

"*No! No!*" The protests and shouts grew louder until two Pharisees appeared, dragging a disheveled woman. A pack of scribes and Sadducees followed, barking, "*Guilty! Guilty!*" The woman's eyes were wide with panic. She was thrown onto the pavement in front of Jesus.

One of the Pharisees announced smugly to Jesus, "This woman was caught in adultery. The Law of Moses commands that we stone her." He looked about him with a sneer. "But what do you say?"

The authorities were well aware of this woman's affair and had been waiting for just the right moment to serve her up to the healer from Nazareth. With a crowd of witnesses present, her sin would pose a prickly dilemma for Jesus.

"Everyone knows the Law," an elder Pharisee had reasoned. "If a man and woman lie together in adultery, they are to be stoned. If this Jesus is from God, He cannot deny God's Law."

"But Rome has taken away our authority to stone sinners," said another, "Only a Roman court can condemn a person to death."

"Precisely!" said another. "If Jesus says, 'Stone her,' He will be arrested for murder and inciting a riot. Then He will be Rome's problem. And if He says, 'Stone her,' where then is His Gospel of forgiveness?"

The woman wondered...the Pharisees wondered...the people wondered: What will Jesus say?

But Jesus said nothing. Instead, He bent to scribble in the dust with His finger.

The Pharisees began to grow uncomfortable. They demanded of Jesus, "Moses commanded that we stone adulterers. What is Your verdict?"

Jesus looked into the faces of the Pharisees. His quiet pronouncement was heard by all: "Let he among you who has never committed this type of sin, throw the first stone."

The silent crowd refused to move. Jesus stooped to continue writing.

After a few moments of embarrassment, the oldest Pharisee turned to leave. One by one, the Pharisees slipped away. Jesus stood to look around. Seeing none of the religious leaders, He said to the woman, "Where are the people who accuse you? Has no one condemned you?"

"No one, sir," she said. "They've all gone."

"Then neither do I condemn you," Jesus said. "Go and sin no more."

My Time To Pray

- Lord, keep me from being hypocritical like the religious leaders who only want to criticize.

- Lord, help me to show compassion to sinning people as You did to the woman.

- Lord, forgive any hidden sin.

The Woman Taken in Adultery

John 8:1-11

Jesus went early on the following morning
      And sat down in the middle
      Of the multitude to teach in the temple.
The religious leaders put a woman in the
      Middle of the crowd who was caught
      In the very act of adultery.
The leaders said to Jesus, "This woman was
      Caught in the very act of adultery,
The Law demands that she be stoned,
      But what do You say we do?"
The Jews used this occasion to try and trap Jesus
      So they would have an accusation against Him.
Jesus stooped to write with His finger in the ground,
      But the leaders continued to question Jesus.
Then Jesus stopped to say, "He who has not
      Committed this self-same sin,
      Let him cast the first stone."
Again Jesus stooped to write on the ground,
      Then the eldest leader left first,
      And eventually all the other leaders left.
Then Jesus said to the woman, "Where are those
      Who accuse you of sin?"
She answered, "They are not here to accuse me";
      Jesus said, "Neither do I accuse you,
      Go from here and sin no more."

Jesus Argues With the Religious Leaders

John 8:12-59

Lord, I need the light of Your guidance in my trouble,
There are always some who try to trip me up.

Jesus said, "I am the light of the world,
Those following Me shall not walk in darkness,
But shall have the light of life."
The religious leaders snarled, "You bear witness
To Yourself, You are bragging and lying."
Jesus answered them, "My claim is true,
I know where I come from,
And I know where I am going.
"But you don't know anything about Me,
You don't know the facts.
"I will not judge you now,
But will do it in the future.
"The Law says to accept a statement
If two agree about what happened
"Then I am one witness to My claims,
And My Father is the other witness."
"Where is the Father?" they asked.
Jesus answered, "If you knew who I am,
You would have known the Father."

Later, Jesus was sitting where money was received
But the officials didn't arrest Him
Because His hour was not yet come.
Jesus said to the crowd, "I am going away,
You will search and not find Me
Because You can't come to where I'm going."
The Jews didn't understand, so they asked rhetorically:
"Will He commit suicide?"

Then Jesus said to them, "I am from above,
>You are from this world
>And you shall die in your sins
>Unless you believe that I AM the Messiah."
The Jews asked again, "Who are You?"
>Jesus answered, "I AM the One I claim to be,
I could teach you much, but that would condemn you;
>I AM the One the Father sent to you,
>The One who sent Me is true."
But the Jews still didn't understand He was
>Telling them He came from God,
>And that He was the Son of God.

Then Jesus said, "When you have lifted up
>The Son of God, then you will realize
>I AM the Messiah from Heaven."
"The One who sent Me is with Me,
>He has not deserted Me;
"I do always the things that please
>The One who sent Me into the world."
Many people believed the words Jesus spoke,
>Then Jesus explained to them,
"If you abide in My words,
>Then You are truly My disciples,
"And You shall know the truth,
>And the truth will set you free."

Then the Jewish leaders answered, "We are Abraham's descendents,
>We have never been slaves to anyone;
>How can You make us free?"
Jesus answered, "Verily, verily, I say to you,
>Everyone who commits sin is a bond slave to sin.
"If the Son shall make you free,
>You shall be truly free."

"Yes, you are descendents of Abraham,
>But some of you are trying to kill Me
>Because My words have not set you free."
"I speak what My Father tells Me to say,
>But you speak what your father tells you."
The Jews answered, "Our father is Abraham."
>Jesus answered, "No, if Abraham were your father,
>You would do what Abraham told you to do.
"Instead, you are planning on killing Me
>Just because I told you the truth."
The Jews said, "We were not born out of wedlock,"
>Suggesting Jesus didn't have a father.
The Jews bragged, "Our Father is God;
>Jesus answered, "If God were your father,
>You would love Me, because I come from the Father."
Then Jesus told them plainly, "Your father is the devil,
>And you do the lustful sins of the devil."
"The devil is a murderer from the beginning,
>And doesn't have any truth in him;
>The devil is a liar, and doesn't speak the truth.
"I tell you the truth and you do not believe Me,
>None of you can point out any sin
>That I have ever done.
"If you were of God, you would listen to My words,
>But you don't understand them
>Because you are not of God."
The Jews accused Jesus of being a Samaritan
>And being possessed with a demon.
Jesus answered, "I have not a demon
>And I honor the heavenly Father.
"I have no desire to make Myself great,
>The Father will do this for Me."
Then Jesus said, "Verily, verily I say to you,

If you will obey My words,
    You will never taste death."
"Now we know you have a demon," the Jews answered,
    "Even Abraham died, and You claim
    If a man obeys Your words he shall never die."
The Jews asked, "Who do You think You are—God?"

Then Jesus answered them, "If I am just bragging,
    It doesn't mean anything;
    It is the Father who will glorify Me.
"But you do not know the heavenly Father,
    If I said you knew the Father,
    I'd be lying like you lie.
"Your father Abraham rejoiced to see My day,
    He knew I would come into the world
    And Abraham rejoiced in My day."
The Jewish leaders said, "You aren't even 50 years old,
    And You said You've seen Abraham."
Jesus answered, "You're right, I existed
    Before Abraham was even born,
    I AM."
The Jewish leaders picked up stones to kill Him
    But Jesus hid Himself and
    Walked past them out of the temple.

The Story of the Man Born Blind

John 9:7-41

John was puzzled by the instructions that Jesus gave to the blind man.
Jesus told him to go wash in the pool of Siloam and he would see. The
pool of Bethesda was only a half a block away. Why hadn't Jesus sent the
blind man to wash in Bethesda? Across the street, a donkey drank from
a feed trough; it had water with which the blind man could wash the clay

from his eyes. But the pool of Siloam was all the way down the Tyropoeon Valley on the other end of Jerusalem. It was a long, tedious walk through many narrow arches, across shopping bazaars and down terraced steps.

The raggedly dressed blind man seemed to know the way to Siloam. He had not hesitated, but at Jesus' command had struggled to his feet, propping himself on a gnarled walking cane, and immediately set out for the pool as Jesus had instructed him. In fact, it was a trip the blind man had taken many times. *Tap...tap...tap...*, he instinctively began tapping his cane on the cobblestones, searching for a passage through the crowds. His steps were unsure on the uneven pavement, yet his feet had direction. He began walking toward Siloam.

Near the pool of Siloam, the steps narrowed and descended steeply. The flow of water emerged from Hezekiah's Tunnel and, with a friendly gurgle, emptied into a larger pool. Palms and a large eucalyptus shaded the gardenlike setting tucked away under the shadow of the outer wall of Jerusalem. The freshwater usually attracted a large crowd, most of who came to fill their water pots. But on the Sabbath, only a few moved about the pool enjoying a relatively cool autumn day. Slowly, step by step, the blind man descended.

Tap, tap, tap, the blind man stumbled toward the edge of the pool. *Tap...tap...SPLASH*. He found the water's edge. Dropping his walking stick to the ground, he bent over to lie flat on his belly at the pool's edge. Dipping his hands into the water, he splashed clear liquid into his muddied eyes. Then he splashed another handful of water into his face. Then he repeated the process again...and again.

Finally, he dried his eyes with the sleeve of his robe, then stopped suddenly, realizing he could see the fibers of his tunic. He jerked his head backward when he spotted his reflection in the water for the first time. He stared steadfastly at his face in the water, puzzled every time the waves of the pool distorted his vision. He lay on his stomach for a long time trying to match the image he saw in the pool with his previous self-perception.

"Aren't you the blind man that begs at the temple gate?" someone asked, surprised that a blind man's sight had been restored.

The healed man nodded vigorously. "I was blind, but now I see!"

"How were your eyes opened?" the stranger asked.

"A man called Jesus put clay on my eyes then He told me to wash in the pool of Siloam." He pointed to the waters of the pool. "When I washed, I could see!"

The blind man walked back to the temple where a group of religious leaders were gathered at the gate in heated debate about the morning's events involving Jesus of Nazareth. The once-blind man, waving his arms at the priests and Pharisees, shouted to get their attention. He told them of the miraculous healing. The eyes of the priests widened at the mention of Jesus' name. One of the Pharisees went to the healed man and callously pulled his eyelids apart to inspect his eyes.

"Where do you live?" the Pharisee asked.

"Get this man's parents," a priest demanded, and a young temple guard ran off on the errand.

The Pharisees asked how he had received his sight. He said, "Jesus put clay on my eyes, and I washed, and I see. It is a miracle from God!"

One of the Pharisees protested, "This man Jesus is not from God, because He does not keep the Sabbath."

But others had their doubts. "How then can a man who is a sinner perform such signs?"

One of the Pharisees confronted him, booming in rage, "I don't believe you were ever blind! You are a liar!"

"But...my parents will tell you I was born blind," the frustrated beggar pleaded, as a crowd began to gather, drawn by the dispute.

"You are one of the disciples of this rabble-rouser from Nazareth," the Pharisee accused him. "We will not allow anyone who follows Jesus to worship in the temple."

The healed man gazed once more upon the splendor of this place dedicated to praising the Lord, looking upward to the dome on the engineering marvel that towered a hundred feet above him. If he told these men he believed in Jesus, these things would be taken away from him. *I see this exquisite temple because of Jesus, he thought. How can I deny the One who gave me my sight?*

"Are you the parents of this man?" one of the Pharisees pointed to the healed man.

Both man and wife nodded, afraid to speak before the assembly of threatening faces.

"He claims to have been born blind," the Pharisee continued, "but clearly he is able to see. How is this possible?"

The mother's eyes were downcast in shame; she felt guilty for not running to embrace her son who had somehow been healed.

"We will deny you entrance to the temple," the Pharisee threw down the challenge, "If I do not get the truth, you will never return to this temple to make sacrifice to God."

Then turning to the parents, he snapped, "Is this your son?"

"Yes," they whimpered.

"Was he born blind?"

"Yes," the mother nodded more vigorously than the father.

"How then does he now see?"

"Speak up!" the Pharisee was shouting now. "How did he get his sight?"

"We know that this is our son," the father fumbled for the correct answer, a reply that would not incriminate them, "and that he was born blind. But how he now sees or who opened his eyes, we do not know." The father spoke clearly, "Ask him! He is of legal age. Let him speak for himself."

The healed man could contain himself no longer. He blurted out, "This is a miracle! Jesus is indeed a prophet."

"Jesus is a sinner," the Pharisee yelled at him. "Give glory to God."

"Whether Jesus is a sinner I do not know," the blind man answered, "but one thing I do know: I was blind, but now I see! I already told you, but you wouldn't listen," he retorted in exasperation. "Why do you want to hear it again? Do you want to become His disciples, too?"

The crowd roared in laughter. This uneducated man was making fools of the religious scholars, his pragmatism confounding them.

"We are disciples of Moses!" the Pharisee proclaimed. He pulled his elegant robe around his bulging midsection, showing disdain for the simple man. "We know that God spoke to Moses, but as for this fellow Jesus, we don't even know where He comes from."

Jesus soon heard that the healed man had been barred from temple worship. He found the healed man talking to a crowd of people; he was still telling the story of going to the pool of Siloam.

Jesus smiled inwardly at the man's faith. Then He interrupted him to ask, "Do you believe in the Son of God?"

"Who is He, sir?" he asked. "Tell me so that I may believe in Him."

"I AM He." Jesus looked deep into the eyes He had healed. The eyes were no longer blinded, but were alive with love and faith.

"Lord, I believe," he said. He knelt and worshiped Jesus.

My Time To Pray

- Lord, thank You for giving me spiritual sight when I was blinded by sin.

- Lord, remove any spiritual blindness that remains from my unsaved days.

- Lord, You are the light of the world, guide me this day.

The Man Born Blind

John 9:1-41

Lord, take away my blindness and help me see
Your perfect will for my life.

As Jesus left the temple, He saw a blind man
  And His disciples asked, "Who sinned,
   His parents or this man that he was born blind?"
Jesus answered, "Neither did this man nor his parents,
  But to demonstrate the power of God."
"Each of us is given a task in life,
  We must do it in the daylight
  Because the night comes when work ends.
"While I'm still in this dark world,
  I am the light of the world."
Then Jesus spat on the ground to make clay
  And then rubbed it in the blind man's eyes
And told him, "Go wash in the Pool of Siloam";
  So he went and washed, and came back seeing.
The neighbors who knew he was blind were dumbfounded,
  "Is this the same one we knew who begged?"
  Others said, "It just looks just like him."
The healed man said, "I'm the one who was blind!"
  They said, "How were you healed?"
He answered, "A man named Jesus made clay and
  Rubbed it in my eyes and said, 'Go
  Wash in Siloam.' I did and now I see."
They asked, "Where is this Jesus fellow?"
  He answered, "I don't know!"
The crowd brought the healed man to the religious leaders;
  They also asked how he was healed.
The healed man answered, "Jesus put clay

On my eyes, and now I see."
The religious leaders criticized, "This Jesus
  Is not from God because He breaks the Sabbath."
But someone in the crowd answered, "How can a sinner
  Do such a great miracle?"
The religious leaders asked the healed man
  What he thought of Jesus;
  He answered, "Jesus is a prophet!"
The religious leaders said, "This man wasn't blind."
  So they asked his parents
  If the man was born blind.
The parents answered them, "We know that he is
  Our son, and that he was born blind,
"But we don't know what happened to him;
  Ask him, he is old enough to speak for himself."
The parents were afraid of the Jewish leaders
  Because anyone saying Jesus was the Messiah
  Would be excommunicated from the temple.
Then the Jewish leaders asked the man a second time,
  "Give glory to God, not to this Jesus fellow,
  We know He is a sinner."
The healed man said, "I don't know if Jesus is evil,
  All I know is that I was blind, now I see."
The religious leaders kept demanding,
  "How did Jesus heal you?"
The healed man became exasperated, "I told you once,
  Do you want to hear it again?
  Do you want to become Jesus' disciple?"
They cursed him, "You are His disciple
  But we are Moses' disciples."
The healed man was incredulous, "Why, here is a miracle
  And you don't realize Jesus opened my eyes."
"We know God does not hear the prayer of sinners,

But He hears those who worship Him and do His will."
"Since the world began, no one has opened the eyes
Of a blind man. If this Jesus
Is not of God, He could do nothing."
The religious leaders shouted, "You were born in sin
Are you trying to teach us anything?"
They excommunicated him also from the temple.

Lord, I will testify what You've done for Me
Just as the healed man told what You did for him,
No matter what the consequence.

Jesus heard they excommunicated him so He found him
And asked, "Do you believe in the Son of God?"
The healed man answered, "Who is He?"
Jesus answered, "You are looking at Him,
I am the One who healed you."
The blind man said, "Lord, I believe";
And then he worshiped Jesus.

I too worship Jesus because I was blind
But now since my conversion I see.

Then Jesus announced to the crowd, "I come to judge
So that those who think they see will become blind,
And those who are blind will see."
The religious leaders asked, "Do you think we are blind?"
Jesus answered, "If you were blind,
You would want Me to heal you.
"But because you don't understand who I am,
You are blinded to the truth of God."

The Good Shepherd

John 10:1-42

Lord, because You are my Shepherd, I will follow You
And trust You for everything.

Jesus said, "Verily, verily, those who don't follow Me
But climb over the wall into the sheepfold are thieves;
My sheep enter by the door because I am the
Shepherd of the sheep."

"Lord, I am Your sheep, I hear You call my name,
And I follow You because I recognize Your voice.
"You go before me each day of my life,
So I will follow You because I know You are good.
"I will not follow a stranger, but run from him
Because the stranger does not have Your voice."
When Jesus used this extended metaphor,
The crowd didn't understand what He meant.

So Jesus said, "Verily, verily, I am the door for the sheep,
Those who come before are thieves and robbers
But My sheep didn't obey their voice."
Jesus repeated Himself, "I am the Door,
All who come by Me will be saved;
They shall go in and out to find pasture.
"The thief comes to kill and destroy the sheep,
I come to give sheep the fullness of life."

Jesus said, "I am the Good Shepherd
Who will die for His sheep."
"A hired man will run away when the wolf attacks
Because the sheep don't belong to him
And he isn't their shepherd.

"The wolf attacks the sheep and scatters the flock;
      The hired man runs away because he is hired,
      He doesn't really care about the sheep."

Jesus said, "I am the Good Shepherd and know My sheep
      And my sheep know Me and follow Me.
"Just as the Father knows Me, and I know the Father,
      I know My sheep and will lay down My life for them."
"I have other sheep who are not in this fold,
      They are the Gentiles who will believe on Me;
      I will lead them also."
"These other sheep will listen to My voice
      And then all My sheep will be one flock
      And all will live in one sheepfold—Heaven."

    Lord, I know You because I am Your sheep.

Jesus said, "The Father loves Me because I lay down My life,
      But I will take back My life.
"No one can take My life from Me; I willingly die
      And I have power to raise Myself from the dead,
      This is the assignment I was given by the Father."

The crowd was divided over what Jesus said,
      Some said, "He raves like a man possessed by a demon,
      Why should we listen to Him?"
Others said, "Can a demon-possessed man cause the blind to see;
      He doesn't sound like one possessed by a demon?"

When winter settled on Jerusalem, it was time for Hanukkah;
      Jesus returned to the temple near Solomon's Porch.
The crowd surrounded Him, asking, "How long will You
      Keep us in suspense? Tell us if You are Messiah."
Jesus answered, "I did tell you, but you didn't listen;
      I did miracles but you wouldn't believe them."

"You didn't believe because you are not sheep of My flock,
  My sheep know My voice and obey Me;
  I know them and they know Me and follow Me.
"I give My sheep eternal life and they shall never perish,
  No one can snatch them from Me.
"My Father has given them to Me
  And He is more powerful than anything else,
  So no one can steal them from Me."

Then Jesus said, "I and the Father are One."
  The Jewish leaders picked up stones to kill Him.
Jesus responded, "The Father has directed Me to do many miracles,
  To help people who are hurting,
  For which one of these miracles do you stone Me?"
They answered, "Not for works of mercy, but for blasphemy;
  You are a mere man like us
  But You have said You are God."
Jesus quoted Scripture, "Your Law says men are gods,
  So if the Scripture is always right,
  Why did it call mere men gods?
"How can You say I blasphemed God when the
  Father who sent Me said I am the Son of God?"

"Even if you refuse to believe who I am,
  At least believe the miracles I do.
"Then you will realize the Father is in Me,
  And I am in the Father."

They tried to arrest Jesus but He walked away from them
  And crossed over the Jordan to stay near the place
  Where John the Baptist first baptized.
His disciples said, "John didn't do miracles, but everything
  He said about Jesus is true";
  So many people believed in Jesus.

Lord, I can be faithful without doing miracles
*   Like John the Baptist who didn't do miracles;*
I can pray for miracles and they will happen
*   Because I follow Jesus who did miracles.*

The Good Samaritan

Luke 10:25-37

Lord, may I love all people regardless of color or race,
*   Just because all are made in Your image*
*   And You love all the people of the world.*

A lawyer stood up to test Jesus with questions,
        Asking, "What must I do to inherit eternal life?"
Jesus responded, "You must love the Lord your God,
        With all your heart, soul, strength and might."
        Then Jesus added, "And love your neighbor as yourself."
Then Jesus concluded, "Do this, and you will live";
        But the lawyer tried to justify himself asking,
        "And who is my neighbor?"
Jesus answered with a parable, "A Jewish man
        Went down from Jerusalem to Jericho.
"He was attacked by bandits who beat him, and
        Stripped him of his clothes and money,
        And left him half dead in the road.
"A Jewish priest came down the road
        And passed by the wounded man.
"Next a temple assistant passed by on the other side of the road,
        Looked at the man and did nothing.
"When a despised Samaritan saw the man,
        He knelt beside him, cleansed the wounds with oil,
        And bandaged them up.
"Then the Samaritan put the man on his donkey,

Took him to an inn and took care of him.
"The next day the Samaritan gave the inn keeper
Money to take care of the man, and promised;
'If you need more, I'll pay next time I'm here.'"
Then Jesus asked the lawyer, "Which of these three was a neighbor
To the one who was attacked by the thieves?"
The lawyer answered, "The one who showed mercy."
Jesus said, "Yes, now go do the same thing."

Lord, make me sensitive to the needs of people,
Then give me initiative to do something about it.

Mary and Martha

Luke 10:38-42

Lord, may I know when to work with my hands
And when to sit at Your feet to learn from You.

When Jesus entered a village near Ephraim
Martha received Him into her house.
Her sister Mary sat at Jesus' feet
To listen to the things Jesus said.
But Martha was busy working in the kitchen,
So she told Jesus, "It's unfair for Mary
To listen to You, when I'm doing all the work."
Martha asked, "Tell her to help me in the kitchen"
But Jesus answered, "Martha, Martha,
You are upset over these trivial things.
"There is only one thing to be concerned with,
Mary has found the main thing
And it can't be taken from her."

Lord, may I always make Your main thing
My priority in life.

The Lord's Prayer

Luke 11:1-13

After a few days Jesus prayed all night and when He finished,
　　　The disciples asked, "Lord, teach us to pray!"
Jesus gave them the Lord's Prayer as their example,
As He had previously given it in the Sermon on the Mount.
He said, "When you pray say, 'Our Father, who is in Heaven,
　　　Holy be Your name
　　　Your Kingdom come
　　　Your will be done,
　　　In Heaven, as on earth.
　　　Give us day by day, our daily bread,
　　　And forgive us our sins, as we forgive everyone
　　　Who is indebted to us;
　　　And don't allow us to be overcome by temptation.'"
The Lord did not finish the prayer
　　　As He did on the previous occasion.
Jesus said, "What if you went to a neighbor's house
　　　In the middle of the night to borrow bread."
"You would yell to wake up your neighbor, saying,
　　　'A friend has just arrived for a visit,
　　　And I don't have any bread to eat.'
"Suppose your neighbor yelled back, 'I am in bed,
　　　My family is asleep, I can't help you.'"
Jesus said, "Though he won't do it as a friend,
　　　If the man kept asking and knocking,
　　　His neighbor would get up and give him bread,
　　　Just because of his persistence."
"So you can do the same with prayer, keep on asking,
　　　And you will receive.
"Keep on seeking, and you will find,
　　　Keep on knocking and the door will open.

"For everyone who keeps on asking—receives,
>Everyone who keeps on seeking—finds,
>Everyone who keeps on knocking—the door opens.
"If your son asks for bread,
>Will you give him a stone—No!
"If he asks you for a fish,
>Will you give him a serpent—No!
"If he asks for an egg,
>Will you give him a scorpion—No!
"If fallen people like yourselves give good gifts to your children,
>How much more will the Heavenly Father give you?"

Lord, give me faith to believe You for the things I need;
>*So teach me to pray.*

Woe to the Pharisees

Luke 11:37-54

The Pharisees asked Jesus to eat with them,
>So Jesus went to the table and sat down.
The Pharisees were angered because Jesus didn't practice
>The ceremonial cleansing of the hands as they did.
Jesus, knowing their thoughts replied, "You Pharisees,
>Wash the outside of the cup,
>But the inside is full of evil and greed."
"You're foolish, God made both the inside and the outside
>If you are righteous on the inside,
>You'd be clean on the outside also.
"But woe to you Pharisees. You pay tithes on the
>Mint that grows at your back doors,
>But you forget about justice and the love of God.
"Woe to you Pharisees because you love the front seats,
>And you demand people address you by a title.

"Woe to you Pharisees, because your hearts are like a grave;
      People don't know there's death inside your body
      So they walk by you, not smelling your death stench."

A lawyer asked, "Why are you reproaching them?"
      Jesus said, "Woe to you lawyers, you strangle
      People with religious demands
      But you don't do what you require of others.
"Woe to you lawyers; you'd kill the prophets of God,
      Just as your fathers did long ago.
"The Scriptures teach, 'God will send prophets and apostles
      But you will kill and persecute them.'
"And this generation will kill God's servants,
      Just as your fathers killed them in the past,
      From the blood of Abel to the blood of Zechariah.
"Woe to you lawyers, you hide God's truth from the people,
      You won't believe it yourself
      And prevent others from believing it."

Lord, open my spiritual eyes.
      I don't want to be blinded like these religious leaders.

Current Events in Jerusalem

Luke 13:1-9

Lord, help me see Your hand in the current events
      That influence my life and service for You.

Some in the crowd told Jesus about the rebellious Galileans
      Who Pilate executed and mixed their blood
      With the sacrificial blood that was offered in the temple.
Jesus answered "Were these men the greatest sinners
      Among all the Galileans because of their crimes?"
Then Jesus explained, "No, they were not!

All men are sinners, and all must repent
    Or they will likewise perish."
Then Jesus referred to the tower in Siloam that fell
    And killed 18 people. "Were they greater
    Sinners than these who live in Jerusalem?"
Again Jesus answered, "No, they were not!
    All men are sinners, so all must repent
    Or they will likewise perish."
Then Jesus told a parable, "A man planted a fig tree in his garden,
    Then came looking for fruit, but he found none."
The man said to his gardener, "I have been looking for figs on this
    Tree for three years, but haven't found any;
    Cut it down, why should it take up valuable space?"
The gardener answered, "Leave it alone for a year;
    I will dig around its roots and use fertilizer."
"If it bears figs next year, fine!" If not,
    Then we will cut it down."

Lord, in the same way You give people an opportunity to get saved;
    The Holy Spirit "digs" away at their hardened sin,
And He adds the nourishment of the Word of God and Christian Witness,
    But each person must eventually repent or
    Suffer the consequences.

Lord, I will pray for the salvation of my hardened friends.

Jesus Heals a Cripple on the Sabbath

Luke 13:10-17

Lord, help me keep my eyes on Your ministry to people,
    And help me overlook religious traditions that don't matter.

As Jesus was teaching in the synagogue on the Sabbath
    There was a severely crippled woman present who

Had been bent over double and for 18 years could not Stand straight.
When Jesus saw her, He called out, "Woman you are healed!"
    Then Jesus laid His hands on her and she immediately stood Up
    straight and began glorifying God.
The leader of the synagogue got mad because it was the Sabbath,
    And said to the crowd, "There are six days for work,
    And men ought to work during the work week.
"People ought to come get healing during the week,
    But not on the Sabbath day."
The Lord answered, "You are a hypocrite! Everyone on the Sabbath
    looses their ox from the stall and leads the animal to water.
"Ought not this Jewish woman who has been bound
    For 18 years be loosed from her bondage on the Sabbath?"
The leader and his fellow Jewish officials were put to shame,
    And the crowd shouted for joy.

Jesus Heals Again on the Sabbath

Matthew 22:1-14; Luke 14:1-24

Later Jesus went to the house of a religious leader for a meal;
    There was a man there with greatly swollen arms and legs.
The leaders watched Jesus closely to see what He would do;
    Jesus said to a lawyer, "Is it lawful to heal on the Sabbath?"
    But the lawyer and the leaders refused to answer Jesus.
So Jesus took the man by the hand and healed him, then sent him away;
    Then Jesus asked, "If your ox falls into a well on the Sabbath,
    Will you not get him out immediately?"
The religious leaders had no answer for Jesus,
    So He gave them three parables to explain God's attitude
    Toward needy people.
"When you are invited to a wedding banquet, don't sit
    In the best seats, lest someone who is more important

Be given those seats and you are moved lower;
> You will be embarrassed because you must take a lower seat.
But when you go to the banquet, take the lower seat
>> Then your host will see you and move you to a higher seat;
>> As a result, you will be honored in front of the guests.
Those who try to honor themselves will be humbled,
> And those who humble themselves will be honored.

Jesus told a second parable of a man planning a banquet,
>> "Don't invite your friends, relatives, or rich neighbors,
>> Thinking they will invite you to their banquet.
"But invite the poor, the sick, and the disenfranchised
>> And God will bless you because these people can't return the favor,
>> And God will remember when He passes out rewards."

A Jewish leader thought Jesus had a good point, so he said,
>> "I would consider it an honor to eat in the kingdom of God."
But Jesus answered him with a parable, "A man prepared
>> A great banquet and sent out many invitations."
"When the banquet was ready, he sent a servant to get the guests,
>> But everyone began making excuses; one man said
>> He bought a field and had to go inspect it.
"Another man said he just bought a pair of oxen,
>> And had to go try them out.
"Still a third man said he just got married,
>> So he explained, 'I'm sure you'll understand.'
"The host was extremely angry and said to his servant,
>> 'Go quickly into the streets and back roads and invite
>> The poor, the sick, and the disenfranchised.'
"Even then there was more room, so the host said,
>> 'Go into the rural roads and look in the woods
>> And urge as many as you can find to come to the banquet.'
"'I want my house full. None of those I first invited came,
>> So they won't even taste the meal I prepared for them.'"

Lord, this is a picture of your invitation to Heaven. Many will
Reject Your invitation to enter Heaven and eat at Your table
But I will come and fellowship with You.

Count the Cost

Luke 14:25-35

Lord, I will follow You no matter how hard,
I will not turn back when the way is hard.

Lord, a great crowd was following Jesus, so He challenged them
To follow Him even though it is difficult and tiring.
"Those who follow Me must love Me more than he loves
His father, mother, sister or brothers, even his own life.
"Otherwise, You cannot be My disciples, but
You must pick up your own cross and follow Me.
"Don't begin following Me until you have counted the cost;
No one begins building a house but first determines the cost
Of materials and labor and if he has enough to complete the Project,
"Otherwise, when you lay the foundation, you find out
You don't have enough money to complete the project
Then you are embarrassed because you can't complete the house.
"Any general planning a battle will first determine if his
10,000 soldiers can win a battle against 20,000 soldiers.
"If a general doesn't plan well, he will have to send a team
To arrange conditions of peace or surrender.
"So living for me is a battle you must fight
Or you will give up and surrender to the world,
The flesh and the devil;
So you must renounce all that you have to be My disciple."

Lord, I renounce all.

Chapter 13

Parables of Lost Things

Lost Sheep, Lost Coin, Lost Prodigal

Luke 15:1-32

Lord, the religious leaders were complaining about Jesus
    Because He received sinners, and ate with them.
Jesus answered them with a parable, "If you had 100 sheep,
      And one of them were lost, wouldn't you leave the 99
      And go search for the one lost sheep till you found it?
"When you found it, wouldn't you carry it home in your arms,
      And tell everyone to celebrate with you
      Because you found the one lost sheep?
"Even so, there will be more rejoicing in Heaven
      Over one sinner who repents, than over 99 self-righteous people
      Who think they don't need to repent."

Lord, I repent of my sins and come humbly to You.

Jesus told a second parable of a woman who had
      10 pieces of silver that was part of her marriage vow.
"If she loses one piece of silver, doesn't she search for it with a lamp
      And sweep the house till she finds it?
"Then she calls her friends to rejoice with her because she found it.
      There is joy by God in the presence of angels,
      Over one sinner who repents and turns to God."

Jesus told a third parable of a man who had two sons and
      The younger son demanded his portion of the inheritance,
      So the father divided the inheritance between the two sons.
"The younger son took his money and went to a distant country,
      There he wasted his money on sinful and luxuriant living,
      Spending everything he had.
"When a famine came, the boy was hungry, so he took a job
      Feeding pigs. No one gave him anything to eat,
      And he decided to eat the pig's husks because he was starving.
"The young man came to his senses when he realized his father's
      Servants had more to eat than he had.
"He decided, 'I will go to my father and tell him I have
      Sinned against Heaven and against you. I am no longer
      Worthy of being called your son. Will you hire me as a servant?'
"The young man returned home to his father. While he was
      A great distance away, his father saw him coming;
      He loved him, ran to hug him, and kissed him.
"The son said, 'Father, I have sinned against Heaven and you,
      I am no longer worthy to be called your son!'
"But the father told the servants, 'Bring the family robe and put it on him,
      Put the signet ring on his finger, and shoes on his feet;
      Kill the fatted calf, let's have a feast.'
"'This my son was dead, but now he is alive;
      He was lost, but now is found,'
      And they began a family banquet celebration.
"The older son was working in the field. When he approached
      The house, he heard music, laughter and rejoicing;
      He found out from a servant they were celebrating
      His brother's return.
"The older son was angry and would not go into the banquet,
      So his father came out to invite him in.
"The older son said angrily, 'I have served you many years,
      I have never disobeyed you, yet you never killed

A fatted calf for me or had a party for me.'
"'Yet, my younger brother squandered his inheritance in sinful living
And you throw him a big celebration.'
"The father said, 'You are always with me, and
Everything I have is yours.'
"'It is right to celebrate because he is your brother,
For he was dead, but now is alive;
He was lost, but now he is found.'"

Lord, help me never leave You as did the younger son,
Help me never be bitter over Your forgiveness of anyone;
Help me rejoice with You over the salvation of all.

Three Stories

To the Disciples—the Unjust Manager

To the Pharisees—the Rich Man and Lazarus

To the Disciples—an Unprofitable Worker

Luke 16:1–17:10

Lord, help me be a good manager of all You've given me,
And help me serve You with great integrity.

Jesus told the disciples a story of a rich man and
His unjust manager who was stealing from him.
The rich man told his manager that he learned
He had wasted his goods, and was fired,
So the manager had to get the books in order.
The manager thought about where he would work next;
He said, "I am not strong enough to dig,
And I'm too ashamed to beg."
The manager then planned to adjust the books of those

Who owed money to the rich man
So they would take care of him.
The manager called the first, "How much do you owe?"
He answered, "One hundred barrels of oil";
The manager said, "Write on the debit 50 barrels."
The manager asked the second, "How much do you owe?"
He answered, "One thousand bushels of wheat";
The manager said, "Write on the debit 800 bushels."
The rich man commended the fired manager for such a shrewd act,
Because the people of the world are more shrewd,
In dishonesty than the people of the light.
Jesus said, "Shall I teach you to act that way—to buy
Friendship dishonestly? No! If you are not honest
In small things, you won't be honest in larger matters.
"If you have not been faithful in handling the money of others,
You will not be entrusted with your own.
"And if you are unfaithful in handling worldly wealth,
Who would trust you in the eternal wealth of Heaven?
"No one can serve two masters. Either you will love the first,
And hate the second, or you will love the second and hate
The first. You cannot serve God and money."

Lord, help me manage everything honestly that You've entrusted to me;
Help me serve You with financial integrity.

The Pharisees who loved to make money laughed at Jesus
When they heard the Lord's principles about finances.
Jesus answered, "You make people think you are honest,
But God knows your greedy hearts.
"You pretend to be honest and humble before others,
But you are despicable in God's sight.
"The law of Moses and the messages of the prophets have been
Your guides in the former dispensation.
"Now the Good News preached by John the Baptist that

The kingdom of God is ushering in a new dispensation
    Is now your guide.
"That doesn't mean the force of the law has changed,
    For it is easier for Heaven and earth to pass away
    Then for one dot of an 'i' of the law to change.
"That means the marriage law remains the same;
    Anyone who divorces and marries another commits adultery,
    Anyone who marries a divorced woman commits adultery."

Jesus then told of a rich man who wore expensive clothes
    And lived in great luxury every day.
"A poor man named Lazarus was lying in the street outside his gate,
    Covered with sores and the dogs came to lick them;
    He yearned to eat the leftovers from the rich man's table.
"The beggar died and the angels carried him to be with Abraham
    Where those who died in faith were located.
"The rich man also died, and was buried, but went to hell;
    As he was in torment, he saw Lazarus far off
    In the company of Abraham.
"The rich man shouted, 'Father Abraham, have pity on me;
    Send Lazarus to come dip his finger in water
    And cool my tongue, for I am tormented by these flames.'
"But Abraham said, 'Son, remember on earth you had everything,
    And Lazarus had nothing. Now he is comforted,
    And you are in pain.'
"'Besides, there is a great pit between us so that those
    Who want to come here from your side can't cross over,
    And those on this side can't come to you.'
"The rich man begged Abraham, 'Send Lazarus to my home on earth,
    To warn my five brothers so they don't come here.'
"Abraham answered, 'Your brothers have Moses and the prophets
    To warn them, let them listen to the Scriptures.'
"The rich man answered, 'That is not enough. If someone
    Were to rise from the dead and tell them,

They would turn from their sins.'
"Then Abraham replied, 'If they will not listen to
 Moses and the prophets, they will not repent,
 Even though one returns from the dead to tell them.'"

Then Jesus said to the disciples, "It is impossible
 To keep people from being tempted to sin
 But woe to those who tempt others to sin.
"He would be better off if a huge stone were tied
 Around his neck and he were thrown into the sea,
"Then he is facing punishment for tempting
 A little one to sin!
"Rebuke your brother when he sins,
 And forgive him when he repents;
"If he sins seven times in a day,
 You must forgive him each time he repents."

The disciples asked, "Lord, help us have more faith";
 The Lord answered, "If you had the smallest amount of faith,
 The size of a mustard seed, which is the smallest of seeds,
"Then you could say to a mulberry tree, 'Be uprooted
 And be cast into the sea,' and it would happen."
Jesus told His disciples another parable, "Suppose you were a servant
 Who plowed in the field or shepherded the sheep,
 Would you just return home, sit down and eat?
"No! First you prepare your master's meal and then
 Serve it to him before you eat your own meal.
"The servant does not deserve thanks,
 He does what he is supposed to do;
 Those who follow the Lord should have the same response.
"We do not consider ourselves worthy of praise,
 We have simply done what we were supposed to do."

The Story of Raising Lazarus

John 11:1-54

Flames crackled from the small fire. Jesus and the Twelve huddled around the flame for warmth. They had tarried in the cold highlands of the Moab hills for what seemed all winter, though they had been there but a few weeks.

"Someone is coming!" James the Less whispered. The apostles stood to meet the stranger.

Jesus immediately recognized him as the servant of Mary, Martha, and Lazarus, their brother. "Lazarus is sick." The servant spoke anxiously to Jesus. "Mary and Martha ask that you come immediately."

The Twelve glanced nervously at one another. The apostles knew and loved Lazarus and his sisters, but a return to Judea was ill advised. The people of Jerusalem had tried to stone Jesus the last time He was there. If the Jewish leaders caught wind of the fact that He was within their borders, they would likely try to arrest Him.

"This sickness will not end in death," Jesus told the servant. "Lazarus is sick for the glory of God."

"What shall I tell Mary and Martha?" the servant inquired.

"Tell them that God's Son will be glorified through this."

During the next two days, Jesus did not mention Lazarus but explained to His apostles that soon it would be necessary for Him to go to Jerusalem. There He would suffer at the hands of the authorities, be crucified, and on the third day rise again. Even though Jesus constantly predicted His death, the apostles did not understand it.

After the two days had passed, Jesus awakened the Twelve early in the morning. "Get up," He urged. "We are going to Bethany."

Nearly every Jew experienced some level of holy excitement when approaching Jerusalem, but there was no excitement in the hearts of the

Twelve this day. As they drew near Bethany, one of the apostles instructed a boy to run ahead to Mary's house to tell them Jesus was coming.

Shortly, Martha came running and fell at Jesus' feet. Without greeting Him, she blurted out, "Oh, Lord! If only you had been here my brother would not have died."

Lazarus had already been dead four days.

Jesus, smiling, said, "Your brother will rise again."

Martha stood, trying to muster her strength, and said, "I know he shall rise again in the resurrection at the last day."

But Jesus had more immediate plans. "I am the resurrection and the life," he said to her. "Whoever lives and believes in Me will never die."

He placed His hands on her shoulders to ask, "Do you believe this?"

Martha answered him, saying, "I believe that you are the Christ...the Son of God, who was to come into the world." Jesus smiled and nodded, as Martha ran off to tell her sister. Soon Mary came hurrying down the path toward Jesus.

Mary said the same thing as her sister, "Lord, if you had been here my brother would not have died," Mary fell at Jesus' feet and began to weep.

Jesus, deeply moved by her grief, asked, "Where have you laid him?"

They walked into a narrow valley with limestone caves. Many of these caves had been fashioned into tombs. As Jesus approached the tomb of Lazarus, a crowd convened. As Jesus surveyed those gathered, he realized that no one there truly understood He held life in His hands.

Jesus wept.

Someone in the crowd saw His tears and said, "See how Jesus loved Lazarus!"

"Take away the stone," Jesus commanded, and four young men quickly rolled it away. Through the dark shadows, the corpse could be seen.

Then Jesus lifted His face to pray, "Father, I pray for the benefit of the people standing here, that they may believe you sent me."

Then with a loud voice, Jesus shouted: "LAZARUS...COME FORTH!"

The body wrapped in linen sat up. Quickly, several young men and apostles ran to Lazarus, unwrapping the cloths that had been wound about his body.

My Time To Pray

- Lord, help me understand Your patience when You delayed, or when You didn't come when Mary and Martha expected You.

- Lord, when my saved relatives die, help me look beyond the grave to the resurrection.

- Lord, thank You for eternal life now that I am saved and thank You for heavenly life beyond the grave.

The Raising of Lazarus

John 11:1-54

Lord, one day I'll die if You don't come back first,
I look forward to my bodily resurrection from the grave
Just as You raised Lazarus.

Jesus was sent a message from Mary and Martha
    Telling Him that Lazarus was sick.
This is the same Mary that anointed Jesus with oil
    And wiped His feet with the hair of her head.
The sisters reminded Jesus that He loved Lazarus;
    Technically, Jesus loved all three of them.

When Jesus received the message He told His disciples,
This sickness will not end in death
But the Son of God will be glorified through it.
Jesus stayed where He was for two more days
Then He told His disciples, "Let's go to Judea."
They cautioned Him against making the trip because
The Jews tried to stone Him the last time He was there.
Jesus replied, "There are 12 hours of daylight for walking
So you won't stumble when there is light to see by."
Those who walk in darkness stumble because
There is no light to guide them.

Jesus then said, "Our friend Lazarus sleeps, I go to awaken him";
The disciples answered, "It's good if he sleeps."
They didn't understand what Jesus meant,
So He said plainly, "Lazarus is dead."
"Now I'm glad I wasn't there when he died
Because now you will believe completely in Me."
Then Thomas—the twin—said to the other disciples,
"Let us go with Him, and die with Him."

When Jesus arrived, He found out Lazarus had been dead four days;
Bethany was about two miles from Jerusalem,
So many Jews had come to sympathize with Mary and Martha.
When Martha heard that Jesus had arrived,
She went out to the graveyard to meet Him;
Mary stayed in the house grieving.
Martha accused Jesus, "If You would have been here,
My brother would not have died."
"But now I know that whatever You ask from God,
He will give it to You."
Jesus told Martha, "Your brother will rise again."
Martha said, "I know he'll arise in
The resurrection at the last day."

Jesus said to her, "I am the resurrection and the life,
　　And those who believe in Me will never die."
Martha answered, "Yes, I believe You are the Deliverer-Messiah,
　　The Son of God Who was sent into the world."
Martha ran to whisper to Mary in a low voice,
　　"The Master is here and wants to see you."
Mary immediately got up and went to Jesus;
　　When the Jews who were mourning saw Mary leave,
They followed her thinking she was visiting the cemetery.
As soon as Mary saw Jesus, she threw herself at His feet
　　Saying the same thing as her sister, "Lord,
　　If You had been here my brother would not have died."
Jesus saw Mary's tears and the mourning Jews following her,
　　He said with a deep sigh, "Where is the body?"
　　Then Jesus wept.
The Jews responded, "Behold how much Jesus loved Lazarus";
　　Other Jews said, "This man makes the blind see,
　　Why couldn't He keep Lazarus from dying?"
Jesus sighed deeply. When He got to the tomb—a
　　Cave—with a stone closing the opening
　　He said, "Take away the stone."
Martha protested, "Lord, the body stinks
　　He's been dead four days."
Jesus answered, "Have I not told you that if
　　You will believe, you'll see the glory of God."
They rolled the stone away, then Jesus looked into Heaven,
　　"Father, I thank You for hearing Me before
　　I pray, so that the people here will believe in Me."
Then Jesus yelled with a strong voice, "*Lazarus come out!*"
　　Lazarus came bound, hands and feet with swaths of cloth,
　　And a cloth wrapped around his face.
Jesus cried, "Unwrap him and free him";
　　Then some of the Jewish leaders saw it happen, and believed.

Results from Raising Lazarus

John 11:45-54

Lord, I know Jesus raised the dead, because
>   *He gave me new life and new desires to worship You.*

Therefore, many Jews believed in Jesus because
>   He raised Lazarus from the dead,
>   But others ran to tell the religious rulers what happened.

They gathered in council to decide what to do;
>   One said, "What can we do, this man does miracles?"

Another said, "If we don't do something, the Romans
>   Will come punish us and the nation because they will think
>   Jesus is fermenting a revolution."

Caiaphas the High Priest said "You're all dumb!
>   Let this man die instead of people;
>   Why should our whole nation perish?

"This prophecy that Jesus should die for everyone
>   Came from Caiaphas the High Priest,
>   When He was inspired by God to make this prediction."

So from that time on the religious leaders were convinced,
>   That it was right to plan the death of Jesus.

Jesus stopped preaching to the multitudes and went to the desert
>   And stayed on the border of Ephraim and Samaria.

People were journeying to Jerusalem for the Passover,
>   They were curious to see Jesus and kept asking,
>   "Do you think Jesus will come to this Passover?"

Meanwhile the religious leaders had announced that
>   Anyone seeing Jesus must report it to the authorities
>   So He could be arrested.

Lord, people hate Jesus because they love their sin
>   *And they do not want to repent and follow Him.*

Healing Ten Lepers

Luke 17:11-37

As Jesus was heading back toward Jerusalem, He
  Came to the boundary between Samaria and Galilee.
Ten lepers stood off at a distance as Jesus approached a village,
  They shouted out to Him, "Jesus, Master, have mercy on us."
Jesus answered "Go show yourself to the priest,
  Just as it is commanded in the Scripture."
As they obeyed Jesus and began the journey, they were healed;
  One came back shouting, "Glory to God for healing me,"
  He threw himself at Jesus' feet and thanked Him.
The healed man was a despised Samaritan;
  Jesus asked, "Did I not heal ten lepers?
  Where are the other nine?"
The only one who has come back to praise God
  Is this foreigner.
Then Jesus said to the man, "Stand up,
  And go home; your faith has healed you."

One day a religious leader asked Jesus, "When will the kingdom of God
  begin?" Jesus answered,
The kingdom of God won't come with outward signs,
  So you can't say it began here or there;
The kingdom of God stands among you";
  Jesus was referring to Himself as the King.

Lord, I don't just live for the day of the rapture
  Rather, I live today for You—Lord Jesus—the coming One.

Later Jesus talked about this with His disciples,
  "There is coming a time when you will look for Me
  To be with you, but I won't come to you physically."
"Some will proclaim I have returned either here or there,

Don't believe the report, nor go out looking for Me.
"Everyone will see Me when I return. It will be
    As bright as lightning flashing across the heavens;
    But first I must suffer grievously and be rejected.
"When I return the people will be just like those in Noah's days,
    They ate, got drunk, married and ignored Noah's warning
"Right up to the day when Noah entered the ark,
    Then the flood came to destroy them.
"My coming will be the same as it was in Lot's day,
    They were eating, getting drunk, buying, and selling,
    Planting and building right up till Lot left Sodom,
Then God rained fire and brimstone from Heaven
    To destroy them all.
"The same will happen when the Son of Man is revealed
    From Heaven to those on earth who reject Him."

"When the day of judgment comes, those on the house top
    Must not go in the house for possessions,
    Neither shall those in the field try to retrieve their things.
"Remember Lot's wife, anyone who holds on to the things of this life
    Will lose his life and those who give up their life for Me,
    They will save their life.
"At that hour, two will be sleeping in the bed,
    One shall be taken, the other left behind.
"Two women will be grinding corn, one will be taken
    The other one will be left behind."
The disciples asked, "What will happen to them?"
    Jesus didn't fully answer them, but said,
    "Wherever there are dead bodies, the buzzards gather."

Two Parables on Prayer

Luke 18:1-14

Lord, I know that prayer makes a difference in my life,
  Forgive me for spending so little time praying.

Jesus used a parable to teach we should always pray and not give up.
  There was a judge who was godless, and
  Despised those who came before him for judgments.
A widow kept coming to the judge demanding justice
  Against her enemy. The judge kept refusing her.
Finally he reasoned, "I don't fear God or people, but
  This woman is pestering me to death with her
  Continual begging for me to do something.
"I will give her justice because she continually asks for it."
  Jesus said, "God will see that justice is done
  To those who continually pray to Him,
  Just as the widow got justice.
"Even when God seems to delay, He will answer persistent prayer,
  And when I—the Messiah—return, will I find
  People of faith on earth who continually pray?"

Then Jesus gave the following parable to those who considered
  Themselves righteous, but they hated others.
"Two men went into the temple to pray, one a self-righteous Pharisee,
  And the other one was a sinner.
"The Pharisee boasted in his prayer that he was not a
  Cheating, adulterous law breaker; but he fasted
  Twice a week and gave a tithe to God of all he possessed.
"The cheating tax collector did not lift his eyes to Heaven,
  But beat upon his chest to express
  His sorrow for his sin; then prayed,
  'God be merciful to me a sinner.'
Jesus said, "This sinful tax collector—not the Pharisee—was forgiven,

Those who exalt themselves will be humbled
And those who humble themselves will be exalted."

Jesus Teaches About Divorce

Matthew 19:1-12; Mark 10:1-12

Jesus left Galilee and came into the edge of Judea
    On the other side of the river Jordan;
    There He healed great multitudes that followed Him.
A Pharisee tempted Jesus, "Is it lawful for a man
    To divorce his wife for any cause?"
Jesus answered, "Have you not read what God said who made
    Them male and female; 'A man shall
    Leave his father and mother and cleave to his wife,
They shall be one flesh, so what God puts together
    No one should separate them.'"
The Pharisee asked "Why then did Moses say
    A man may divorce his wife by simply
    Giving her a writ of dismissal?"
Jesus answered, "Moses did it because of your hard
    And wicked heart. But that was not what God
    Originally intended for marriage.
"Anyone who divorces his wife and marries another,
    Except for fornication; commits adultery."
Jesus' disciple answered, "If that is the case then
    It is better not to marry!"
Jesus answered, "Some are born with the ability not to marry,
    Some are made eunuchs by others,
    And some became eunuchs for the kingdom of God."
Then people brought little children for Jesus to lay hands on them,
    And bless them, but the disciples turned them away.
Jesus said, "Let the children come to Me, and do not

Prevent them from coming to Me,
For of such is the kingdom of God,"
And Jesus put His hands on them and blessed them.

The Rich Young Ruler

Matthew 19:16–20:16; Mark 10:17-31; Luke 18:18-30

A rich young ruler asked, "Good Master, what must I do
To get eternal life?" Jesus answered,
"Why are you calling Me good, only God is good,
But if you wish eternal life, keep the commandments."
The young man answered, "Which should I keep?"
Jesus said, "Do not kill, and do not commit adultery,
Do not steal; do not bear false witness,
Honor your father and mother
And love your neighbor as yourself."
The young man said, "I have kept all these";
Jesus said, "If you would be perfect,
Go sell all you have and gave it to the poor,
You will have treasure in Heaven, and then follow Me."
The young man was sad when he heard this,
For he had great wealth.

Then Jesus told His disciples, "Verily, I say to you
It is hard for a rich man to enter Heaven,
It is easier for a camel to go through a needle's eye
Than a rich man to enter Heaven."
The amazed disciples said, "Who then can be saved?"
Jesus answered, "No one from a human perspective,
But all things are possible with God."
Then Peter added, "We have left all to follow You,
What will be our reward?"
Jesus answered, "In the next world when I sit on My throne,

You—my disciples—will sit on twelve thrones,
>   Ruling the twelve tribes of Israel.
"Everyone who has left housing, brothers, sisters, father,
>   Mother, children or land for My sake,
>   Will receive 100 times more when he receives eternal life.
"Those who are first will be last, and the last first."

Lord, I will be last in this life to be rewarded in Heaven.

The Selfish Ambition of James and John

Matthew 20:17-28; Mark 10:32-45; Luke 18:31-34

As Jesus was heading toward Jerusalem, He said to His disciples,
>   "I will be betrayed to the religious leaders in Jerusalem,
>   They will condemn Me and crucify Me,
>   But on the third day I will rise again to life."
The mother of James and John came to Jesus with her sons
>   And knelt in front of Jesus with a request.
"What do you want?" Jesus asked her;
>   "Let my sons sit at Your left hand and right hand,
>   When You come into Your Kingdom."
"You don't know what you're asking," Jesus answered;
>   "Can they drink the cup of suffering that I'll drink?"
>   The brothers answered, "Yes, we can."
Jesus answered, "Very well, you will suffer with Me.
>   But as for the seats on my left and right,
>   They are not for Me to give out;
>   My Father in Heaven will assign them."
When the other ten heard about the request,
>   They were angry at the two brothers.
Jesus called them together and said, "Earthly rulers have
>   Authority over those they lead.
"However, this is not the way I do things;

If you want to be great, you must serve others,
    If you want to be first, you must be a slave.
"The Son of Man did not come to be served, but to serve,
    And give His life as a ransom for many."

Jesus Heals Blind Bartimaeus

Matthew 20:29-34; Mark 10:46-52; Luke 18:35-43

A large crowd followed Jesus to the gate of the city Jericho,
    Two blind men were sitting there
    One man was Bartimaeus, a blind beggar.
When they heard Jesus was passing by they shouted,
    "Have pity on us, Son of David."
The crowd scolded them, telling them, "Keep quiet";
    But they shouted even louder,
    "HAVE PITY ON US, SON OF DAVID."
Jesus stopped and called for them, asking,
    "What do you want Me to do for you?"
    They answered, "Give us our sight."
Jesus said, "Receive your sight, your faith has healed you";
    Immediately, they saw. They glorified God and followed Jesus,
    All the people praised God.

Lord, give me spiritual sight so I can see Kingdom things,
    Help me to praise You in all I do.

Zacchaeus

Luke 19:1-28

As Jesus was walking through Jericho,
    Zacchaeus, an extremely rich and influential tax collector,
    Tried to get a look at Jesus, but he couldn't

See over the crowds on the road side.
Zacchaeus ran ahead and climbed up into a sycamore tree;
> When Jesus passed that way, He looked at him and said,
> "Zacchaeus, come down, I'm going to eat at your home."
Zacchaeus hurriedly came down and prepared a banquet for Jesus,
> But the crowd disapproved because Zacchaeus was a
> Backslidden Jewish tax collector.
Zacchaeus told Jesus, "I will give half my wealth
> To the poor, and those I've cheated; I will restore
> Four times what I took from them."
Jesus said, "Today salvation has come to this house
> Because he is a son of Abraham.
"The Son of Man has come to seek and save
> Those who are lost, such as Zacchaeus."

Some thought the Kingdom would come immediately,
> So Jesus told a parable to correct that wrong impression.
"A noble man was called to a distant place,
> To be crowned king of that province.
"Before he left, he called his ten workers and gave them
> Each $2,000 to invest while he was gone.
"But some of the workers rebelled and sent the nobleman
> Word that he was no longer their lord and king.
"When the nobleman returned, he called the workers
> To whom he had given money to find out their profit.
"The first man reported his $2,000 had made a profit
> Of $20,000, ten times the original amount.
"'Wonderful,' responded the nobleman, 'you have been faithful;
> You will be ruler of 10 cities.'
"The second worker reported he had turned his $2,000
> Into $10,000, five times the original amount;
> The nobleman made him ruler of five cities.
"The third man had only the original $2,000, so he explained,
> 'Because you are an exacting man, reaping

Where you don't sow, I was afraid.
    I hid it safely in linen cloth.'
"The nobleman called him a 'wicked worker,' saying,
    'You are condemned by your own words.
"'You knew I reaped where I didn't sow, therefore,
    Why didn't you deposit my money in a bank,
    So I could have drawn interest from it?'"
"The nobleman said to those standing near, 'Take the $2,000
    From him and give it to the man with $20,000';
    They answered the nobleman, 'He already has $20,000.'"
Jesus answered, "Those who do more with more, will get even more,
    And those who do little with little, it shall be taken from him."

Lord, make me faithful with what I have
    Use me even in a greater way in the future.

The Anointing at Bethany

Matthew 26:6-13; Mark 14:3-9; John 12:1-9

Lord, I worship Jesus for His death for my sins,
    Just as Mary worshiped Him at the feast at Bethany.

Six days before the Passover meal, Jesus attended a banquet
    At the home of Martha in Bethany;
    Lazarus her brother sat with Jesus at the head of the table.
Mary poured a jar of costly spikard perfume
    Over the feet of Jesus and wiped them with her hair;
    The house filled with the beautiful smell.
Judas Iscariot complained that the perfume could be sold
    And the fortune given to care for the poor.
Not that he cared for the poor, but he was a thief
    Who was in charge of the money given to Jesus.
Jesus answered, "Let her alone, she is preparing me

For burial. You can help the poor later,
　But you won't have Me very long."
When the crowds heard that Jesus had come to Jerusalem,
　　They came eagerly to see Him and Lazarus;
　　The one who Jesus raised from the dead.
Then the religious leaders decided to kill Lazarus also,
　　Because many believed on Jesus because of Lazarus.

Lord, because I believe Jesus is the Son of God
　　I give to Him the perfume of my worship.

Part Three

Jesus—The Redeemer

Chapter 14

JESUS IN JERUSALEM

The Story of the Triumphant Entry into Jerusalem

In the days leading to the feast of Passover, the word on the streets was that the chief priest planned to arrest Jesus if He dared to show Himself in Jerusalem. Because of this, many said, "Jesus will not come to Jerusalem. It is too dangerous for Him here." Others argued that if Jesus were truly the Messiah, He had nothing to fear.

The Pharisees and priests fully expected the Nazarene to come, and were prepared to seize Him before He could enter the temple. "If anyone knows where He is staying," the priests told their spies, "report it immediately so that we might arrest Him."

Early Sunday morning, the day after the Sabbath, many of His followers went ahead of Jesus into Jerusalem to spread news of His coming. Thousands gathered at the city gate to see if the one they called Messiah would indeed come to the city.

Jesus and the Twelve departed Bethany. As they came near to a village, Jesus instructed Peter and John, saying, "Go to the village ahead of you. Just as you enter, you will find a donkey with a colt which no one has ever ridden. Untie it and bring it here."

Jesus said to them, "If anyone asks you, 'Why are you taking this animal?' tell him, 'The Lord has need of the donkey and will send it back.'"

As Peter and John entered the village, they spotted a young donkey. Without hesitation, they began to lead it away. The owner of the donkey ran after them, shouting, "Where are you going with my colt?"

Peter said, "The Lord has need of the donkey and will send it back shortly."

Leading the donkey to Jesus, Peter and John removed their tunics to drape them over the animal for Jesus to ride upon. Jesus sat upon the colt. Resuming their ascent of Olivet, the apostles broke into a psalm of praise. "Open to me the gates of righteousness. I will go through them and praise the Lord," they sang.

The apostles marched victoriously, moved by the excitement of the crowd. When the procession swept over the ridge, the city of Jerusalem loomed before them.

Thousands of people had lined the road leading into Jerusalem to greet Jesus. Many had spread their cloaks on the road, while others cut palm branches for the festive occasion.

The crowds ahead of Him picked up the refrain of those who followed, shouting, "Hosanna to the Son of David! Blessed is He who comes in the name of the Lord!"

The apostles were caught up in the excitement and did not notice that Jesus was untouched by the enthusiasm. A single tear fell down His face as He stared at the city that had rejected Him. Jesus said quietly, "O Jerusalem, if you only knew…. The day will come when your enemies will trample down your walls, because you did not recognize the time of God's coming to you."

There was no chance the religious leaders could arrest Jesus when He was surrounded by so many supporters. Still, one of them forced his way into the road to confront Jesus. With agitation in his voice, he said, "Teacher, rebuke Your disciples! They are out of control!"

Jesus now turned from His disciples and smiled broadly. He looked down on the Pharisee and said, laughing, "If they were to keep quiet, the stones would cry out in their place."

Jesus rode the donkey through the gate and into the narrow streets of the city. There He dismounted and looked about Him as the people cheered ever louder. Within days, these who worshiped Him would turn fickle and shout for His death. But today their voices would not be silenced.

The Triumphant Entry

Matthew 21:4-9; Mark 11:7-10; Luke 19:35-38; John 12:12-19

Lord, I gladly receive the presence of Jesus into my life
Just as the crowds received Jesus on Palm Sunday.

The next day—Sunday—news that Jesus was coming to Jerusalem
    Swept through the crowds of Passover pilgrims.
As Jesus came to Bethpage, He sent two disciples
    Into the village, telling them they would find
    A donkey with her young colt tied there.
"If any one asks why you are taking the donkey,
    Tell them the Master needs it to ride into Jerusalem."
This act fulfilled Scripture, "Tell the people of Zion,
    Your king is coming to you, humbly riding on a donkey,
    Even on a young colt."
The disciples did as instructed and found the donkey as Jesus said,
    They put their coats on the donkey and Jesus rode on him,
    On a colt that had never been ridden by anyone.
Great crowds spread their coats on the road,
    Others waved their palm branches as they went to meet Him.
The crowds who marched in front of Jesus shouted,
    "Hosanna to the Son of David,
    Blessing on Him who comes in the Lord's name,
    Hosanna in the highest Heaven."
The religious ruler said to Jesus, "Rebuke Your followers,
    For they are blaspheming God and the Scriptures."

Jesus answered them, "If they stopped praising God,

    The rocks would immediately cry out praise to God."

The religious rulers said among themselves,

    "The whole world is following Him."

When Jesus entered the city, people everywhere were asking,

    "Who is this?"

The multitude answered, "This is Jesus, the prophet from Nazareth."

Cursing the Barren Fig Tree and Cleansing the Temple

Matthew 21:12-19; Mark 11:12-18; Luke 19:45-48

    The following morning, Jesus left Bethany and was hungry,

    He saw a fig tree with leaves but

    There were no figs for Him to eat.

Jesus said, "You'll never bear fruit again";

    The disciples heard and made a mental note of it.

When Jesus got to the temple, He began cleansing it;

    He forced the merchants and their customers to leave,

    Then He upset the tables of those selling pigeons,

    And stopped workers from bringing in their merchandise.

Jesus said, "Do not the Scriptures teach, 'My house

    Shall be called a house of prayer for all people,

    But it's become a den of thieves?'"

The religious leaders heard what Jesus said

    But they were afraid to do anything against Jesus,

Because the people were listening intently to His teaching.

Lord I love You for the truth You teach me

    Even when the world hates You and Your truth.

The Greeks Want To See Jesus

John 12:20-50

There were some Greeks worshiping in the temple;
>They approached Philip asking, "We would like
>To see Jesus," Philip told Andrew and they told Jesus.

Jesus didn't answer directly but said,
>"The hour has come
>For the Son of Man to return to Heaven and be glorified.

"A grain of wheat must die when it falls to the ground,
>Otherwise it will remain only one grain of wheat.

"But if it dies, it yields a rich harvest of food,
>Those who love their life will lose it
>And those who don't live for this life
>Will exchange it for eternal life.

"If anyone wants to be My disciples, including the Greeks,
>They must follow Me, then they will be where I am
>And the Father will honor them when they follow Me.

"Now my soul is greatly troubled. Shall I ask
>My Father to deliver Me from the house of suffering?

"No! That is the purpose why I came to earth;
>Father, glorify Your name through My coming death."

Then they heard a voice from Heaven, "I have glorified it, and
>I will glorify it again."

Some who heard it thought it was thunder,
>Others thought it was an angel speaking.

Jesus answered, "This sound was for your sake, not Mine,
>The time for judgment of sin has come,
>Satan—the prince of the world—will be cast out.

"When I am lifted up—on the Cross—I will draw all to Me";
>Jesus said this to predict the way He would die.

The crowd was astonished answering, "We thought
>The Scriptures taught Messiah would live forever.

"Why are You saying the Son of Man must be lifted up in death?
        Are You talking about the Messiah?"
Jesus said, "My light will illuminate you only a short time,
        Learn from the light while you can
        Or else darkness will fall and you'll be lost in it.
"While you have the light, believe the light.
        And you'll become children of the light";
        Then Jesus left and they couldn't find Him.

Despite all the miracles Jesus did, most of the people
        Did not believe Jesus was the predicted Messiah.
This fulfilled the prediction of Isaiah who said,
        "Lord they don't believe, they don't accept Your miracles."
Indeed, they couldn't believe, as Isaiah said in another place,
        "God has blinded their eyes and hardened their hearts,
        Lest they should see with their eyes and understand with their
        Hearts, and turn to God and He saves them."

Nevertheless, many leading citizens believed on Jesus,
        But they didn't confess Him openly for fear of social pressure.
They were afraid of being excommunicated from the temple
        For they desired acceptance by people, more than from God.

Jesus proclaimed loudly in the temple, "Those believing in Me,
        Also believe in the Father who sent Me.
"And those who understand what I am saying,
        Also understand what the Father wants them to know.
"I have come as a light to all people,
        And those who believe in Me will not live in darkness.
"If anyone hears and understands My teachings, but rejects them,
        I will not judge them for I come to save all people.
"But those who do not accept my teachings and reject Me,
        Will be judged in the last day by what I've said;
        The Father will judge him.
"Because the Father who sent Me told Me what to say

And His words give life eternal.
"Therefore everything I am saying to you
    Comes from the Father in Heaven."

Lord, I believe in You and will obey Your words,
    For I know they give me eternal life.

The Withered Fig Tree

Matthew 21:19-22; Mark 11:19-25; Luke 21:37-38

During the Passover week Jesus stayed in Bethany;
    On Tuesday morning Jesus and the disciples saw that the fig tree
    He had cursed the previous day was dead and withered.
Peter was amazed that the tree had withered to its roots;
    Jesus answered, "Let God's faith control you.
"Verily, if you will say to a mountain,
    'Be removed and thrown in the sea' and you don't doubt,
But believe that you will receive what you ask,
    You shall have it."
Jesus then explained, "You shall have all things for which you ask
    If you believe before you receive them."

Jesus then instructed, "When you begin to pray,
    You must forgive those you have an issue with,
    So that yoru Father may forgive your sin,
    Then you have a basis for getting an answer to your prayer."

Lord, I forgive those who sin against me and I want You
    To forgive me for my wrong feelings against any.
Forgive me of all my sins so You can
    Answer my prayers.

A Day of Controversy in the Temple

Matthew 21:23–22:14; Mark 11:27–12:12; Luke 20:1-19

As Jesus entered the temple, the chief priest and scribe
      Asked Him, "By what authority are you doing these things?"
Jesus responded, "I will ask you one question, and what you say
      Will answer your question to Me.
"Did John the Baptist get his authority from Heaven or men?"
      They realized that if they said, "From God"
      Jesus would ask why they didn't receive Him.
They also realized that if they said "From men,"
      They would upset the multitude
      For they believed John the Baptist was from God.
So the religious leaders answered Jesus, "We don't know";
      Then Jesus said, "Neither will I answer you
      Where I get My authority."

Jesus told a parable of a Father who had two sons,
      He said to the first, "Son, go work today in the vineyard,
      The son said, "I will not go," but later repented and went.
The father said the same thing to the second son,
      He answered, "I will go," but he didn't do it, and
Then Jesus asked, "Which son did the Father's will?"
      The leaders answered, "The first." Jesus answered,
      "Sinners and rebels who repent will go into the Kingdom
      Before you because they do the will of the Father.
"John the Baptist preached the way of righteousness,
      But you did not believe him, so you rebelled against the Father,
      Yet sinners responded to his message and entered the Kingdom."

Then Jesus told them another parable of a landowner
      Who planted a vineyard, planted a hedge to protect it,
      Built a tower and winepress, then rented it out
      To renters and moved away.

When the harvest of grapes came, the landowner sent for the rent
    That would come from the harvest.
The renters beat the first to collect the rent,
    Stoned another, and killed the next one;
    When the landowner sent more to collect, they did the same
Then the landowner said, "The renters will reverence my son,"
    But the renters conspired, "The son will get
    The vineyard as an inheritance. Let's kill him
    So we will get the vineyard." And they did it.
When the owner heard what the renters did, he
    Destroyed the miserable renters
    Then he rented out the vineyard to other renters.
This is a picture of the Father giving the Promised Land
    To the Jews, but they rejected the prophets
    So the Jews were punished by God.
The Father then turned His attention to different people,
    The Gospel was presented to the Gentiles.
Jesus said, "The stone which the builders rejected
    Became the most useful and prominent stone of all;
    Then you'll marvel at what God does."

Jesus told yet another parable that the kingdom of God
    Was likened to a king planning a marriage feast for his son;
    He sent messengers to call those who were invited,
    But they wouldn't come.
Again, the king sent messengers telling them the best beef
    Is being cooked, and everything is on the table
    But they made light of the king's invitation.
One guest went to his farm, another opened his store for business,
    The other guest beat the king's messengers, killing some.
The king was angry and sent his army to kill the murderers
    And destroy their cities.
The king told his messengers, "The marriage feast is ready
    And those I invited were not worthy to attend.

"Go to the country roads, and invite everyone that you see
    To come to the marriage feast for my son."
The servants did as the king commanded and invited
    Both the good and the bad and the wedding was filled.
But when the king entered the banquet hall,
    He saw a man without wedding garments.
The king said, "Why aren't you wearing wedding clothes?"
    The man couldn't answer the king.
The king told his servants to bind the man and
    Cast him into outer darkness where
    There is weeping, wailing, and gnashing of teeth.
This means the Jews who were originally God's people,
    Like the invited guests, refused God's invitation
    So He aggressively punished them.
Those who came from the country roads are the Gentiles
    Who responded to God's grace.
The man without wedding garments represents those
    Who know about God's offer, but haven't received Christ,
    So they are not dressed in the garments of righteousness.

Lord, I believe You and have been justified by faith;
    I look forward to the marriage supper of the Lamb.

The Pharisees' and Herodians' Question

Matthew 22:15-22; Mark 12:13-17; Luke 20:20-26

Still in the temple, some Pharisees and Herodians tried to
    Trip up Jesus with the issue of bringing Roman coins
    Into the temple with an image of Caesar.
Since Caesar considered himself God, this broke the
    Law about possessing images of a god.
They said, "Master, we know You stand for the truth,
    And you teach the truth, no matter who is listening to You,

Should we pay taxes to Caesar?"
If Jesus said "no," they'd accuse Him of insurrection.
Jesus knew their evil plan, so He said, "Show me a coin";
They had broken the law by having a coin in the temple.
Jesus said, "Hypocrites, whose image is on this coin?"
They answered, "Caesar's."
Jesus answered them, "Give to Caesar the things that are Caesar's,
And give to God the things that are God's";
They marveled at Jesus' wisdom, and left Him alone.

The Sadducees' Question

Matthew 22:23-33; Mark 12:18-27; Luke 20:27-40

The Sadducees, who deny the resurrection, came to Jesus
With a question about the resurrection.
"Master, a man married a woman and they had no children,
If he dies and his brother marries her,
So that the legal line continues...
"Then the same thing happens seven more times, so that
She has had seven husbands...in the resurrection,
Whose wife of the seven shall she be?"
Jesus answered, "You are basically wrong in your understanding
Of the Scriptures and the power of God.
"In the resurrection, people are not married nor do they get married;
And they won't die again, but they are like angels
They possess eternal life.
"When Moses met God at the burning bush, God said
'I am the God of Abraham, Isaac, and Jacob.'
"If there were no resurrection, God would have said,
I was their God. But because they had a future hope,
Even though dead, God was their God at that time."

Some other religious leaders told Jesus He gave
    A good answer to the Sadducees.

Lord, I believe in the resurrection and I know I
    Will be raised because I now live in Jesus Christ.

A Legal Question

Matthew 22:34-40; Mark 12:28-34

A lawyer next tried to trip up Jesus, asking, "Master
    What is the greatest law in the commandments?"
Jesus answered, "You shall love the Lord your God,
    With all your heart, with all your soul,
    With all your mind, and with all your strength.
"The second which is like unto it, 'You shall love
    Your neighbor as yourself.'"
The lawyer replied, "Master, You spoke correctly,
    There is only one God, and none other than He;
    And that we should love Him with all our hearts,
    With all our understanding, with all our strength."
"And to love our neighbors as ourselves. All this is greater
    Than offering burnt offerings and sacrifices."
Jesus noticed he answered sincerely and said,
    "You are not far from the kingdom of God."
As a result, no other religious leaders questioned Jesus
    Because they were afraid of being embarrassed by Him.

Lord, I trust every answer You have to all my questions.

Now Jesus Asks a Question

Matthew 22:41-46; Mark 12:35-37; Luke 20:41-44

Since the religious leaders had no more questions,
>   Jesus then asked them, "You scribes say that
>   Messiah—Christ—is the son of David.
"Yet David himself said, 'The Lord said to my Lord,
>   Sit on my right hand till I make
>   Your enemies a foot stool for Your feet.'
"Since David called Messiah his Lord
>   How can Messiah be His son?"
No one was able to answer Jesus and
>   No one wanted to debate Him.

Jesus Denounces Scribes and Pharisees

Matthew 23:1-39; Mark 12:38-40; Luke 20:45-47

After a while, Jesus went into the courtyard
>   Of the temple to teach the multitudes,
"Beware of the scribes, who like to sit in Moses' seat
>   They make rules for you to obey, but they themselves
>   Do not obey their own rules.
"They put heavy and grievous burdens on your shoulders,
>   But they will not bear them, nor
>   Will they lift one finger to help you.
"They love to wear long robes to get greetings from everyone,
>   They love the best seats at the feast and in the synagogues."

"Woe to you scribes and Pharisees—hypocrites—because
>   You shut the door to the kingdom of God
>   And you yourselves will not enter,
>   Nor will you let anyone else enter.

"Woe to you scribes and Pharisees—hypocrites—because
  You go everywhere to make people your proselyte,
  Yet you make him a two-fold son of hell.
"Because he was originally on his way to hell,
  Now as your proselyte he is doubly directed to hell.
"Woe to you blind guides, you say it is alright
  To swear by the temple, but not by the gold on the temple;
  You're fools, what is greater, the temple or the gold?
"You say it is alright to swear by the altar,
  But it's not right to swear by the gift on the altar;
  You're blind, what is greater the altar or the sacrifice?
"If you swear by the heavens, you also swear by
  The throne of God, and by Him who sits on the throne.
"Woe to you scribes and Pharisees—hypocrites—you are careful to
  Tithe the mint that grows out your back door, but
  You've left undone the weightier things of the law
  Which is judgment, and self-control, and faith.
"It's right to tithe everything God gives to you,
  But it's wrong to ignore those greater things;
  You strain at a gnat and swallow a camel.
"Woe to you scribes and Pharisees—hypocrites—because
  You clean the outside of the cup, but leave the inside filthy.
"Woe to you scribes and Pharisees—hypocrites—because
  You're like a freshly painted grave that looks beautiful,
  But inwardly you're dead, rotting, stinking corpses.
"Outwardly, you appear to people to be righteous,
  But inwardly, you're full of sin and hypocrisy."
"Woe to you scribes and Pharisees—hypocrites—because
  You build monuments at the tombs of the prophets,
  And you make a big spectacle of putting flowers on their graves.
"Yet if you lived in their day, you'd be
  Part of those who killed them.
"You are serpents and children of snakes,

How will you escape the punishment of hell?"
"You are just like those to whom the Father sent prophets
    To preach to them. Yet you would scourge them,
    Persecute them and crucify them.
"And on your hands is the blood of all righteous martyrs,
    From the blood of Abel to the blood of Zechariah
    Who was killed in the temple next to the altar."

"O Jerusalem, Jerusalem who killed the prophets and
    Stoned those who were sent to you from the Father.
"How often would I have gathered you to Me, as a hen gathers her chicks,
    But you would not come to Me.
"You will not see Me or understand what I am doing in the world,
    Till I come again in the name of the Lord."

Then Jesus went to sit by the place where
    Money offerings were made to God.
The rich poured in much money, and the people applauded;
    No one noticed a poor widow giving two small coins.
Jesus said to His disciples, "Verily, this woman
    Has given more than all the others
    Because they gave out of their abundance,
    But she gave all that she had."

Lord, I give You all that I have, not for the applause of people,
    But because You gave all that You had—Your life—for me.

The Mount of Olives Discourse

Matthew 24 and 25; Mark 13:1-37; Luke 21:5-36

Later in the day—Tuesday—Jesus sat
    With His disciples on the Mount of Olives
    To look at the city of Jerusalem and the temple.
Jesus said, "You see the city and temple, verily not one stone

Will be left on another, but shall be thrown down."
His disciples asked Jesus privately, "Tell us when this
  Will happen? And what shall be the sign of Your coming?
  And what shall be the sign of the end of the world?"
Jesus answered, "Don't let anyone lead you astray, because
  Many will come in my name, saying, 'I am the Christ!'
"You will hear of wars and rumors of wars, but don't worry
  Because these things must happen before the end."
"Nation will fight nation, and alliances of nations will fight
  Other alliances; and there will be earthquakes;
  These are the beginning of hard tribulations.
"Your enemy will arrest you, persecute you, and kill you,
  All nations will hate the nation of Israel for my sake.
"Many false prophets will lead astray many, and the influence
  Of sin will influence every area of life
  And love for Me will become cold.
"But those followers of Mine who endure tribulation to the end,
  They shall be finally saved.
"The Gospel of the Kingdom will be preached to the whole world
  Then the end shall come."

"When you see the abomination of desolation—a pig
  Sacrificed on the altar—which was predicted by Daniel,
  Realize this is the beginning of the Great Tribulation.
"Then let my people flee to the mountains for protection,
  Let those on the roof top not go in their house
  To take anything with them.
"Let those working in the field not return home for clothes,
  And those with child will suffer the most;
  And pray your escape is not in winter or on the Sabbath.
"This will be the Great Tribulation which is greater than any
  Since the beginning of the world and greater than any after it.
"Except God shortening these days, no one can live through it,
  And for God's people, those days will be shortened.

"If anyone tells you, 'Here is the Messiah, or there is the Messiah,'
  Don't believe it, because many false Messiahs
  Will come and perform miracles to lead away God's people.
"If anyone tells you Messiah is in the wilderness,
  Don't go out there to check it out. And if they say
  Messiah is in an inner room, don't believe it either.
"Because the coming of the Son of Man will be as spectacular
  As lightening flashing from the East to the West.
"And there'll be so many slain by His coming, that the buzzard
  Will gather to eat their flesh.
"The sun will be darkened and the moon won't shine,
  And stars will fall from the sky, and Heaven itself
  Will be shaken as the Son of Man makes
  His appearance in Heaven.
"Then shall all ethnic tribes mourn when they see Him,
  Coming with great power and glory through the clouds.
"He will send His angels with the sound of a trumpet
  To gather His people from the four corners of the earth."

"Learn from the parable of the fig tree, when new growth
  Appears and the leaves are growing, realize it is summer;
  So when you see these signs happening, Messiah is at the door.
"This generation of Jewish believers will not pass away
  Until all these signs have appeared.
"Heaven and earth shall pass away, but My Word—which I promise—
  shall not pass away, but these things will happen as promised.
"But no one knows the hour when Messiah will come, not
  You, nor anyone else, or even the angels in Heaven, neither
  The Son of Man, but only the Father knows the hour.
"It will be like the days of Noah. He warned everyone that
  Judgment was coming. But no one believed him, they went on
  Eating, getting drunk, getting married until the flood came.
"Two will be working in the field, one will be taken, the other left.

Two women will be grinding meal, one will be taken, the other left;
Watch because you don't know when He will return."

Lord, I expect You to come at any minute.

"If the owner of the house knew when a thief would
Break into his home, he would have been constantly vigilant.
"Therefore, be ready for in just the hour you think He won't return,
He will come.
"If the owner made a faithful worker supervisor
Of all his businesses while he was gone, that worker is blessed
If the owner returns to find everything in order.
"Verily, the owner would give him a promotion,
But if the servant is lazy and spends his time eating and drinking
Because he thinks the owner is tarrying,
"The owner will come back at a time the worker doesn't expect him,
And will fire the worker and give his job to someone else;
The worker will suffer with those who weep and gnash
Their Teeth."

Jesus spoke a parable that the coming of the Kingdom is likened to
"Ten bridesmaids with ten lamps
Who were waiting for the coming of the bridegroom.
"Five foolish bridesmaids didn't take oil with them
But five wise bridesmaids took oil in addition to their lamps.
"The bridegroom was late and all the bridesmaids slept;
At midnight there was a shout, 'He's coming!
Let all the bridesmaids come meet him.'
"When the ten lit their lamps, the five foolish asked the wise,
'Give us some oil because our lamps are going out.'
"But the wise answered, 'If we give you some of ours,.
We won't have enough to light the bridegroom's way';
They told the foolish virgins to go buy some for themselves.
"The five wise virgins went into the feast, with
The bridegroom and the door was shut.

"Afterward the five foolish virgins came asking, 'Open the door,'
   But the bridegroom answered, "I don't know you.""

Lord, I will watch constantly for Your return, because
   I don't know the day or hour that You're coming.

Jesus spoke another parable about His returning, saying,
      "A businessman planned to take a long trip,
      And delegated to various workers, different jobs in the company.
"He gave one worker $500,000, another $200,000
      And the third $100,000; each according to his ability
      To manage money.
"The one with $500,000 invested wisely and doubled his money;
      The one with $200,000 also invested prudently and doubled his money.
"The worker with $100,000 hid his money carefully so it wouldn't be lost;
      After a long time, the boss returned and
      Asked his workers to report what they had done.
"The one who had $500,000 brought in another $500,000,
      The boss said, 'You've done well because you were faithful,
      I'm going to promote you to a larger responsibility.'"

Lord, like this worker I want Your approval.

"The one with $200,000 gave the owner an additional $200,000;
      The boss also said congratulations and promoted the second Worker.
"The worker with $100,000 said, 'I know you are a hard man,
      Reaping where you don't sow, and I was afraid
      So I safely hid your money, and here it is!'
"The owner said, 'You're a lazy worker. You know I expected
      Profit from my investment. You should have put it
      In a bank where it would earn interest.'
"The owner took away the $100,000 and gave it to the
      Worker that now had a million dollars."
Jesus said, "If you have gathered much for the Kingdom
      You'll be given more. If you've done little

> For the Kingdom, it'll be taken from you.
"The owner said, 'Cast the unprofitable servant into outer darkness,
> Where there is weeping and gnashing of teeth.'"

Jesus explained, "When you see the Son of Man come
> In His glory, you'll see before Him all the
> Nations of the earth.
"The Son of Man will sit on His throne to divide them
> As a shepherd divides his flock;
> Sheep will be separated to His right hand, and goats to the left.
"Then the king will say to those on the right, 'Come in
> Because you are blessed, inherit the Kingdom prepared for you.'"
Then Jesus will say to them, "You are blessed because I was
> Hungry and you fed Me. I was thirsty and you gave Me drink.
> I was naked and you took Me in. I was in prison
> And you came and visited Me.
"Those on the right said, 'When did we see You hungry,
> Or thirsty, or naked, or in prison?'
"The king shall answer, 'Inasmuch as you did it
> To my brethren and the poor, you did it to Me.'
"Then the king will say to those on the left, 'Depart
> From Me into eternal fire prepared for the devil and his demons.'"

Lord, give me a compassion for needy brethren and the poor,
> *May I do good works in service to You.*

Events on Wednesday

Matthew 26:1-16; Mark 14:1-11; Luke 22:1-6

On Wednesday Jesus said to His disciples,
> "In two days the Son of Man will be delivered up to be crucified."

The religious leaders with Caiaphas the High Priest came together
> To discuss how to arrest Jesus and kill Him.

But they decided not to do it during Passover,
>   Lest there be an uprising among the people.

That night Jesus attended a feast in Bethany in the home
>   Of Simon the leper.
A woman poured a pound of alabaster from a jar
>   On Jesus' head. The oil was very costly.
Some in the crowd were indignant, thinking the ointment
>   Was wasted. They wanted to sell it and give
>   The money to the poor.
Jesus understood what they were saying, so He answered,
>   "Why are you criticizing the woman? She has done
>   A good work on Me.
"You always will have the poor, and you can do for them
>   What you want to do. But you won't always have Me;
>   She has anointed My body for its burial.
"Wherever the Gospel is preached in the world,
>   She will be remembered for her act of worship."

One of the Twelve—Judas Iscariot—went to the chief priest
>   And asked, "What will you give me if I deliver Jesus to you?"
>   The religious rulers gave him 30 pieces of silver,
>   So Judas looked for an opportunity to deliver Jesus to them.

Events on Thursday

Matthew 26:17-19; Mark 14:12-16; Luke 22:7-13

On Thursday, the day when the Passover lamb was killed,
>   The disciples asked Jesus, "Where do You want to celebrate Passover?"
>   Jesus told Peter and John to go in the city and find a man
>   With a pitcher on his head. "Follow him to a house,
>   And ask the owner for a room where I can celebrate Passover.
"He will show you a larger upper room, get it ready

For Me to celebrate the Passover."
And they went and found the man just as Jesus said,
    And they prepared it for the Passover meal.

The Last Supper

Matthew 26:20-30; Mark 14:17-26; Luke 22:14-30; John 13:1-29

And when evening was come, Jesus sat with His disciples and said
    "I have a great desire to eat this meal with you before I suffer.
    I will not eat with you again until we eat in the kingdom of God."

The disciples began arguing who was the greatest. Jesus said,
    "The Gentiles have kings who exercise authority over them
    But you should not be like them.
"He that is greatest, let him be the servant of them;
    Who is greater, those who sit to eat, or those who serve?
    I am among you as One who serves.
"But you are those who have been with me since my temptation,
    I will give you part of the Kingdom My Father gives me.
"You will sit to eat and drink at my table in the Kingdom,
    And sit on twelve thrones ruling the twelve tribes of Israel."

Jesus knew that His time had come to leave the world
    Because Judas Iscariot had already betrayed Him
    And having loved His own, He loved them to the end.
Knowing that the Father had put all things into His hand
    That He had come from the Father and would return to Him,
He arose from the table, laid aside His tunic, and
    Wrapped a towel around Himself as a servant.
He poured water into the basin, began washing the disciples' feet
    And wiping them dry with the towel.

When Jesus came to Peter, the fisherman asked, "Will You
      Wash my feet?" Jesus answered, "You don't
      Understand now, but you'll understand in the future.
"If I don't wash you,
      You'll have no part with Me."
But Peter answered the Lord, "If that's the case, then
      Not only my feet, but my hands and head."
Jesus answered, "He that is bathed all over,
      Need only to have his feet washed;
      Now you are clean, but not all of you."
For Jesus knew who would betray him, therefore He said,
      "You are not all clean."

When Jesus finished washing their feet, He put His tunic back on
      And sat down with them and said, "Do you know
      What I have done for you?
"You call Me Master and Lord, and so I am. If I then
      Your Lord and Master have washed your feet,
      Then you ought to be willing to wash one another's feet.
"I have given you the example to do to others
      What I have done for you."

"Verily, verily I say to you, a servant is not greater than his master,
      Neither is the one sent greater than the one who sent him;
      If you know these things, happy are you if you do them.
"I have chosen all of you, but not all are of Me,
      That the Scriptures may be fulfilled, 'He that eats
      With Me, lifts up his heel against Me.'
"I'm telling you before it happens, so when it comes to pass,
      You will know I am your Messiah."

Jesus was obviously troubled, then he said, "Verily, verily
      I say to you, one of you will betray me."
The disciples looked at one another, not completely
      Understanding what Jesus meant. Then each one

Said, "Lord, is it I?"
Jesus answered, "He that dips his hand in the same dish
    That I dip, he is the one who will betray me;
    It is good if that man were never born."
John was reclining on Jesus' shoulder. Peter beckoned
    For John to find out who Jesus meant.
Jesus answered, "When I dip the bread into the lamb stew,
    The one to whom I give it is the one."
Then Jesus dipped the bread into the stew and gave it to Judas,
    But the disciples didn't understand
    Because Judas was the honored guest,
    And it was the custom to give it to that person first.
After Judas received the bread, satan entered in him;
    Jesus said to him, "Do quickly what you are going to do."
None of the disciples understood what happened because they
    Thought Jesus said, "Buy what is needed
    For the Passover feast."
When Judas received the bread, he went out into the darkness;
    The night was truly black.

Lord, may I never betray You with any deeds,
    Thought or attitudes.

Jesus and Peter

Matthew 26:31-35; Mark 14:27-31; Luke 22:31-38: John 13:30-38

When Judas left, Jesus was relieved saying, "Now is
    The Son of Man glorified and God is glorified.
"Children, I am going to be with you only a short time;
    You'll look for Me and can't find Me because where I'm going
    You cannot follow Me now."
"So, I'm giving you a new commandment that you

Love one another as I have loved you."
Peter asked, "Where are you going?" The Lord answered, "You cannot
    Now go where I am going,
    But later you can follow Me."
Peter answered, "Why can I not follow You?
    I will lay down my life for Your sake."
Jesus replied, "You only think you'll die for Me. Verily, verily,
    I say to you, you will deny Me three times
    Before the rooster crows."

Institution of the Lord's Table

Matthew 26:26-29; Mark 14:22-25; Luke 22:12-20; 1 Corinthians 11:23-26

As they were eating, Jesus took bread, blessed it and said,
    "This is my body which is broken for you,
    Eat this in remembrance of Me."
And Jesus took the cup and gave thanks and said,
    "This cup symbolizes the new agreement by God
    To forgive your sins by My blood.
"For as often as you eat this bread and drink this
    Cup, you are demonstrating your salvation
    And you should do it till I come again."

The Upper Room Discourse

John 14:1-31

Jesus told the eleven, "Do not let your heart be troubled,
    Hold on to your faith in God and your faith in Me.
"There are many rooms in my Father's house,
    If it were not true, I would have told you.

"I am going to prepare a place there for you,
  And when I get it ready, I will come back for you,
  Then I'll take you to be with Me.
"You know the way to the place I am going,
  But Thomas responded, "No! We don't know where
  You are going, nor do we know how to get there."
Jesus said, "I am the way to Heaven, also the
  Truth and eternal life. You must come through
  Me to go to the Father.
"Since you know Me, you should also know the Father,
  And from now on you'll know the Father."
Philip disagreed, "We don't know what the Father looks like,
  Show us the Father so we can believe."
Jesus answered, "I have been with you all this time,
  And you don't know Me;
  He who has seen Me has seen the Father.
"What I say are not My words, but
  They are from the Father who lives in Me;
  The Father also does the miracles that I do.
"Believe that I am in the Father, and He is in Me,
  Or else, believe it because you have seen My miracles.
"Verily, verily, I say to you, he that believeth in Me shall do
  The works that I do, and even greater ones,
  Because I am going to the Father.
"Whatever you pray in My name, I'll do it
  So that the Father will be glorified in Me;
  If you pray for anything in My name, I'll do it."

Lord, give me faith to pray for greater miracles
  Than I'll ever expect and I'll give You the glory.

Jesus told them, "If you love Me, obey the commandments,
  And I will ask the Father to send you
  Another person in My place. He will live in you forever.

"This other person is the Holy Spirit, the third person of the Trinity,
> The unsaved cannot receive Him, because they
> Do not believe in Him or know anything about Him.
"But you will know the Holy Spirit because you believe in Me;
> He will dwell in you and be with you.
"I will not leave you alone in the world, I will come to you;
> Shortly I will leave you because I'm leaving the world
But you will see Me when I'm gone;
> Because I live, you shall live also.
"At that time you'll know I'm with the Father in Heaven,
> But I'll be in you and you'll be in Me."

"Those who have and keep my commandments are the ones loving Me,
> And those who love Me will be loved by the Father
> And I will love them and I'll show Myself to them."

Lord, I love You will all my heart, take away all blindness
> *Help me to see You completely and obey You.*

Judas—not Iscariot—but another disciple with that name
> Asked, "How can You show Yourself to us
> And not to the world?"
Jesus answered, "Those who love me will obey My commandments,
> And my Father will love them, and
> We will come to live in them.
"Those who don't obey My commandments don't love Me.
> It's not just my Word they reject; it's the Father's Word.
"I am explaining these things to you while I'm with you,
> But the Holy Spirit, whom the Father will send in My place,
> He'll explain all spiritual things to you,
> And will remind you of the things I said to you.
"I am leaving My peace with you, not as the world gives,
> So don't be afraid of anything."

"Previously, I told you I am going away but I'm coming back.
Because you love Me, rejoice that I'm going to the Father;
I tell you this before it happens,
So you'll believe in Me when it happens.
"I will not be able to talk with you much more,
The evil prince of this world is coming to try Me
But don't worry, he has no authority over Me.
"I am going to do the thing the Father wants me to do,
That will show my love to Him.
"Now, let's leave this upper room."

Lord, I need the Holy Spirit to make me spiritual and I need Him to
Make me holy.

On the Street

John 15 and 16

Jesus said, "I am the true vine, my Father is the gardener,
He cuts away any branches not growing fruit
And prunes back every branch that has fruit."
Lord, I am a healthy plant by Your words;
I will settle down in Christ as He abides in me.
Just as the branch can't bear fruit except it's attached
To the vine, so I can't produce anything
Unless I'm attached to Christ.
Jesus, you are the vine, I am a branch;
As long as I remain attached to You, and You abide in me,
I will bear plenty of fruit.
Anyone who will not remain attached to Jesus,
Will be collected like dead branches
And thrown into the fire to be burned.
Jesus, when I remain settled in You, and Your words

Remain in me, I can ask what I want
And You'll give it to me.

Father, I want to glorify You by bearing much fruit,
Then everyone will know I'm Your disciple.

As the Father has loved Jesus, so He loves me,
    So I'll settle down to rest in His love to me.
I will obey the commandments of Jesus to remain in His love
    Just as Jesus kept the Father's love to remain in His love.
Jesus, you told me this so Your joy would rest in me
    And my joy would then be perfect.
Jesus, you've commanded me to love one another
    Just as You've loved us.
I can't have greater love for others than
    To lay down my life for them.
I am a friend of Jesus when I obey His commands;
    He no longer calls me His servant
    Because a servant doesn't know what his master does.
But I am Jesus' friend because I know what He's doing,
    He's doing what the Father told Him to do.
I did not choose Jesus, but He chose me
    And commissioned me to go bear fruit.
Now whatever I ask You—Father—in Jesus' name,
    You gladly give to me.

Lord Jesus, again You command me to love one another,
    Because the world will hate me,
    But it hated You long before it hated me.
I do not belong to this world and have separated from it,
    Therefore, the world hates me.
I remember what You said, "A servant is not greater
    Than his master, since they persecute Jesus,
    The world will persecute Me."
They will hate me and persecute me because I'm Jesus' disciple

Because they do not know the Father who sent Jesus.
If Jesus hadn't given the truth, the world wouldn't experience
        The guilt of their sin, but now they have no excuse.
If Jesus hadn't done miracles among them, they
Would have been blinded in their sins. Now they see
And hate both Jesus and the Father. As written
In Scriptures, "They hated Jesus without a cause."

Lord, when the Holy Spirit comes—the Spirit of truth—who
        Comes from the Father, He will speak plainly
        To their hearts about Jesus Christ.
Then I can also speak plainly about Jesus for He will
        Speak through me and remove their blindness.
Jesus told us about coming persecution so our faith
        Wouldn't be shaken. They will excommunicate me
        From their assemblies.
There is coming a time when they will kill people like me,
        Thinking they have served God. They'll do this
        Because they don't have true knowledge of Jesus or the Father.
Jesus did not originally tell His disciples about persecution
        Because He was walking among them.
But now that He is going away, they needed to be
        Reinforced, so they wouldn't be shaken when it happened.
Yet, none of His disciples asked, "Where are you going?"
        Because they were distressed that He was leaving.
But it was a good thing for Jesus to go away, because
        If He hadn't left, the Holy Spirit would not have come.
But because Jesus left, He sent the Holy Spirit
        To convict the world of sin, righteousness, and judgment.
He will convict—cause people to see—their sin
        Because they do not believe in Jesus.
He will convict—cause people to see—their lack of righteousness,
        Which will keep them out of Heaven.
He will convict—cause people to see—coming judgment

Because Jesus suffered for them on the Cross.
Then Jesus told what the Holy Spirit will do for believers;
      When He comes—The Spirit of truth—He will reveal
      To us everything that is truth. Then He'll
      Guide us to understand truth.
The Holy Spirit will not be concerned with His own agenda,
      But He will bring glory to Jesus Christ,
      And He will reveal to us things to come.
All the Father's glory also belongs to Jesus,
      This is the glory the Holy Spirit will reveal.

In a little while Jesus will leave His disciples and they will
      See Him no longer in the flesh. But a short time
      Later they will see Him.
The disciples did not understand what Jesus meant
      About leaving them and then coming back to them.
Jesus knew they wanted to question Him, so He said
      Plainly, "In a short time you'll see Me no longer;
      Then a short time later, you'll see Me."
Then Jesus explained, "You will weep when I'm gone,
      But the world will rejoice. But your weeping
      Will be turned to rejoicing.
"It'll be like a woman suffering in childbirth so that
      When the child is born, she forgets about her suffering."
Jesus explained they would be sad, but when they see
      Him again, they would be full of joy,
      A joy that no one could take from them.
When that day comes, they won't have any questions
      They can go directly to the Father with their questions.
Jesus then promised, whatever We ask in His name,
      The Father will give it to us.
Up until then the disciples hadn't prayed in Jesus' name,
      Now we can ask in Jesus' name and we receive
      So that our joy will overflow.

Up until that time Jesus used metaphors and parables
      But the time is coming when He'll speak plainly.
When that day comes—and now is—we can ask the Father
      In Jesus' name, and Jesus will pray to the Father for us.
The Father loves us because we have loved Jesus and
      We know that Jesus came to the world from the Father.
The disciples said, "Now we believe You came from the Father,
      You are not using metaphors. Now we understand."
Jesus said, "You only think you understand. The time is
      Coming when you will be scattered to your homes,
      Leaving Me alone."
Jesus said, "I have told you this so you will have peace;
      In the world you will have trials, but have faith
      I have conquered the world."

Chapter 15

THE PRAYERS OF JESUS

A Prayer to be Glorified

John 17:1-26

After Jesus left the Upper Room, tradition says
    He slipped in the Holy of Holies to pray;
    Since Jesus was God, He would know how to get there.
Jesus lifted His eyes to Heaven and prayed, "Father,
    My hour is come. Glorify Thy Son so I can glorify You.
"That those you have given Me should have eternal life;
    Eternal life is You, the only true God,
    And in Jesus Christ, the One You sent to earth."
Jesus said, "I have glorified You on earth
    And accomplished the work You sent Me to do.
"Now Father, glorify Me with the glory I had in Heaven
    Which I had with You before the world was created."

Lord Jesus, I hear Your passion for Your glory to return.
    Now that You're in Heaven,
    I glorify You for all You are and all You've done.

A Prayer to Keep the Disciples Safe

"I have given Your name to the men You gave me;
    They were Your men and You gave them to Me,
    They have faithfully kept Your Word.

"They know the things You told Me to do
> Because I told them what You said to Me.
"They have received Your Word and they believe it
> And they believe I came from Heaven to do Your will.
"I pray for these disciples, I do not pray for the world;
> I pray for those You have given Me.
"All things that are mine are Yours,
> And I am glorified in these disciples.
"I am no longer in the world, but they are in the world,
> So I pray for them.
"I pray—Holy Father—that You would keep them safe,
> That they may be one, as We are One.
"While I was with them, I kept them—guarded them,
> And not one of them is missing, except the son of perdition who
> Fulfilled Scripture by betraying Me.
"Now I come to You, Father, that they may have joy;
> I have given them Your Word, and the world hates them
> Because they reject the world, even as I am not of the world.
"I am not praying for You to take them out of the world,
> But that You would keep them from the evil one.
"Make them holy by Your Word, Your word is truth;
> I am sending them into the world,
Even as I was sent into the world.
"I set Myself apart from Heaven for them,
> Now may they be set apart to reach others.
"I am not praying for these disciples only,
> I am praying for those who will believe because of their word."

A Prayer To Be One

Jesus prayed that all believers may be one
As He and the Father are One;
> "I am in them, as You in Me."

"So that the world may realize You sent Me,
    And You love Me and You love them,
"Father, I want them to be with Me in Heaven,
    That they may see My glory
    That I've had before the foundations of the earth.
"O Father, the world does not know You,
    But I have known You and made You known to these disciples
"That the love You have for Me may be in them,
    And I in them, and they in Me."

Lord, I want to be one with You, You in me and I in You.
    May the world see my love and
    May the world become believers in You.

Jesus' Prayer in Gethsemane

Matthew 26:30-46; Mark 14:26-42; Luke 22:39-46

Jesus crossed over the brook Kidron into the Garden of Gethsemane
    Where He often went to pray. His disciples followed Him;
    He told them, "Sit here while I go elsewhere to pray."

Jesus took with Him Peter, James, and John. He said to them,
    "My soul is worried and sorrowful to death;
    "Watch and pray, I will go a little farther to pray."
Jesus bowed to the ground and prayed, "O Father if possible,
    I don't want to drink this cup of suffering. Let it pass Me by,
    Nevertheless, it's not what I want that matters; I will do Your
    will."
An angel was sent to strengthen Him, so Jesus
    Prayed more fervently with agony,
    And great drops of blood—as sweat—fell to the ground.
Jesus got up from His knees and came to the disciples
    But found them sleeping. He said to them,

"Could you not pray with Me one hour?"
Then Jesus challenged them, "Watch with Me in prayer,
     The Spirit is willing but the flesh is weak."
Jesus went back to pray a second time saying, "O Father,
     If this cup cannot pass away except I drink it,
     Then Your will be done."
Jesus came a second time to find His disciples sleeping
     Because they couldn't keep their eyes open;
     So He went back and prayed the same words a third time.
He said, "Sleep on, you need your rest";
     The hour is now that I'll be delivered to the betrayer."

Lord, forgive my prayerlessness; help me to be faithful in prayer
     Interceding for the things You want done.

Jesus Betrayed, Arrested, and Forsaken

Matthew 26:47-56; Mark 14:43-52; Luke 22:47-53; John 18:2-12

Judas knew the place where Jesus often went to prayer
     So he led Roman soldiers and officers from the religious leaders
     With lanterns, torches and weapons to arrest Jesus.
Jesus knew what was happening so He met them and asked,
     "Who are you looking for?" They answered, "Jesus of Nazareth."
Jesus responded, "I am He," His statement of deity;
     Then the Roman soldiers and Jewish guards
     Were driven backward to the ground.
Again Jesus asked, "Who are you looking for?"
     They said, "Jesus of Nazareth."
Jesus answered, "I told you, I am He." Since you want Me,
     Let these go." Thus prophecy was fulfilled,
     "I lost none of those that You gave Me."
Judas had given them a sign that Jesus would be the one whom he kissed;

"Arrest Him!" So Judas kissed Jesus, and the Master answered,
  "Are you betraying the Son of Man with a kiss?"
As the guards moved forward to take Jesus, Simon Peter, having a sword,
  Cut off the right ear of Malchus, the High Priest's servant.
Jesus answered, "Put up your sword, I must drink the cup of suffering
  The Father has for Me"; then Jesus touched him and healed him.
They grabbed Jesus and bound Him, but He responded,
  "Have you come out in the middle of the night to arrest a thief?
"I sat daily in the temple, but you didn't arrest Me,"
  But this came to pass because it was predicted in Scripture;
  Then the disciples left Jesus and fled into the night.

Lord, may I always stand courageously for You
  And not run away as the disciples.

Chapter 16

JESUS' LAST DAYS ON EARTH

The Story of Jesus' Arrest and Interrogation

The tramp of Roman troops echoed through the streets of Jerusalem in the early morning hours of Friday, just after midnight. Levitical guards from the temple followed after the soldiers.

Annas was the power behind the office of the high priest, even though Rome had removed him from office because he would not fully cooperate with them. In Annas' place, Rome had appointed his son-in-law, Caiaphas. But the Jews still considered Annas God's instrument.

Dawn was coming, and Annas and the priests needed to agree on a legal charge that would be lodged against Jesus. Because the Romans did not allow Jewish officials to exercise capital punishment, only the Romans could execute Jesus. Therefore, the charge must be worthy of swift execution. But when Annas interrogated Jesus regarding His teachings, Jesus would not answer his questions.

"I have spoken openly to the world," Jesus replied. "Ask those who heard Me. Surely they know what I said."

When Jesus said this, one of the temple guards struck Him in the face. "Is this the way You answer a high priest?"

"If I have said something evil," Jesus said, "then tell Me what evil I have spoken. But if I spoke the truth, then why do you strike Me?"

Annas had heard enough. Any official charges would have to be made by his son-in-law Caiaphas and the Sanhedrin anyway, so Annas sent Jesus to Caiaphas' palace.

As the temple guard led Jesus, bound, toward Caiaphas' quarters, Peter and the youngest apostle John fell in behind the procession. At Caiaphas' house, the temple guard entered with Jesus, but the woman at the door kept the others out.

John recognized the girl and approached her, saying, "You know me. My father is Zebedee who sells fish to Caiaphas." She allowed John to enter the courtyard, while Peter waited outside.

Caiaphas was jittery, high-strung, explosive. As Jesus was brought in, the high priest babbled, "I have You now, Galilean! Your fate is in my hands."

But although Caiaphas wanted to summarily order an execution, Rome had taken the death penalty from the Jews. He could excommunicate Jesus, but what good was that? He would gladly kill Jesus with his bare hands, but his position wouldn't allow him.

John got Peter into the courtyard; Peter gravitated toward the red glow of a charcoal fire. Several bearded men huddled around it to warm their faces. Peter attempted to blend in with the men, appearing to be indifferent to what was going on. Then he was spotted by the young woman at the door. "You were with Jesus of Nazareth, the man they have on trial upstairs."

"Not me," Peter protested. "I don't know Him."

Confusion reigned upstairs in the palace. Dawn was rapidly approaching, and those gathered in the second-floor chamber couldn't agree on a charge to bring against Jesus.

Proof was needed if any charge was to hold water with the Roman governor, Pontius Pilate. Many council members knew someone who could bring charges against Jesus, some of whom would accept payment to make false accusations. Quickly, servants were dispatched to find those witnesses.

Members of the Sanhedrin tried to coerce their servants to give testimony. But it didn't work. First one man would speak out against Jesus, then another would contradict his story.

Jesus stood in silence. Caiaphas fidgeted in his seat.

Since the servants and false witnesses could not get their stories straight, some of the members of the Sanhedrin brought charges against Jesus. One of the council members stepped forward, charging, "This fellow said that He was able to destroy the temple and build it again within three days."

Nervous laughter filled the room. They all had heard about this claim.

"His violent hands have been raised against the temple of God!" the council member continued.

Caiaphas seized the opportunity to cross-examine Jesus. "What do You say to this charge?"

When Jesus did not answer, Caiaphas demanded: "Tell me who You are!"

Jesus answered, "Ask your witnesses. They know what I said."

Caiaphas jumped to his feet, waving frantically. "I demand by the Living God: Tell us whether You are the Christ, the Son of God!"

As the echoes died, Jesus responded, "Yes, it is as you say. One day you will see the Son of Man sitting at the right hand of the Mighty One on the clouds of Heaven."

"Blasphemy!" the high priest cried. "This is blasphemy!" The Sanhedrin knew the law, that if one were pronounced guilty he could be tried on the same day, but not punished on that same day. However, in the case of blasphemy, the offender could be judged immediately.

"Put Him to death!" the high priest screamed at the top of his voice. "We'll charge Him with blasphemy before Pilate."

The crowd muttered their agreement, and Caiaphas asked, "What think you, gentlemen? For life?"

Silence.

"For death?"

"For death!" the priests cried.

"Then we shall recommend this sentence to our friend Pilate." Peter sat by the wall, despairing. He had heard the cry "For death!" from the upper chamber.

Then out of the darkness stepped a temple guard, a cousin to Malchus, the young priest whose ear Peter had cut off. He challenged Peter. "Didn't I see you with Jesus in the olive grove?"

"You are mistaken, sir," Peter said nervously. "I do not know the man."

Within the same hour, another guard stood with Peter by the fire, saying to his comrades, "Certainly this fellow was with him, for he is a Galilean." Then he said to Peter, "You are a Galilean. Your accent gives you away!"

"I tell you, I do not know the man!" Peter blurted out. He vowed an oath to God that he did not know Jesus.

At that moment, Jesus was led down the stairs and into the courtyard. Jesus glanced over at Peter, and their eyes met. Even before the tears came to Peter's eyes, a heaving sob welled up within him. He rushed out the front gate and into the darkness.

In the distance, a rooster crowed.

The First Trial—Before Annas, the Former High Priest

John 18:12-24

The soldiers and guards led Jesus bound to Annas
     The former High Priest who was deposed for his corruption
     And put Caiaphas his son-in-law into that office.
Annas asked Jesus about His disciples and what He taught;
     Jesus answered, "I spoke openly in synagogues and

The temple and I kept back nothing secretly.
"Ask those who heard Me what I taught";
    When Jesus answered this way, an officer struck Jesus
    With his hand saying, "Why do You answer the High Priest so?"
Jesus replied, "Tell me if I have spoken evil;
If not, then don't strike Me."

Lord, thank You for being faithful at Your trial;
    Though You never sinned, you died for my sin.

The Second Trial—Before Caiaphas

Matthew 26:57-68; Mark 14:53-65; Luke 22:54-65; John 18:15-27

Annas sent Jesus bound to Caiaphas to determine the indictment;
    Simon Peter and John followed Jesus, only John was known
    By the gate keeper so he entered the compound, but not Peter.
John spoke to the maid and she let Peter into the yard;
    She said to Peter, "You're a disciple of Jesus";
    Peter answered, "I am not"!
The servants were warming themselves at a fire
    For it was cold and Peter also warmed himself.
The religious leaders had gotten false witnesses against Jesus
    Because they had agreed Jesus must die.
But the false witnesses didn't agree. One witness said,
    "I heard Jesus say He would destroy the temple
    And rebuild it in three days without hands."
The High Priest asked Jesus why He didn't answer them,
    But Jesus held His peace and didn't answer them.
The High Priest then demanded, "Tell us if you're
    The Messiah, the Son of the Blessed."
Jesus answered, "I am, and you shall see the Son of Man
    Sitting next to the Father, when He'll come

With the clouds of Heaven."
The High Priest ripped his official robe in disgust saying,
    "We don't need witnesses, He has spoken blasphemy";
    The crowd shouted, "He is worthy of death!"
Then they spit in His face and slapped Him around;
    They covered His eyes and said, "Prophesy...who hit You?"

Peter was standing to warm himself when one asked,
    "Are you one of Jesus' disciples?"
    Peter answered, "I am not!"
One of the servants of the High Priest—a relative of the one whose ear
    Peter cut off—also said, "Didn't I see you in the garden with
    Jesus?"
Peter cursed and said, "I swear, I don't know Him";
    Knowing all things, Jesus turned to look out the
    Window at Peter and Peter saw his Lord looking at him.
The rooster crowed and Peter remembered what Jesus said,
    And he left the house and wept bitterly.

Lord, help me to be faithful to You and never deny You
    As Peter denied You.

The Third Trial—Before the Sanhedrin

Matthew 27:1; Mark 15:1; Luke 22:66-71

As soon as it was day, the Sanhedrin assembled
    At the directives of the High Priest who led Jesus there.
They asked, "Tell us if You are the Messiah-Deliver;
    Jesus answered, "You won't believe if I tell you
    But you will see Me seated at the right hand of God."
Then they asked, "Are You the Son of God?"
    Jesus answered, "I am what you ask."

Then the council concluded, "We don't need witnesses,
 He is guilty of blasphemy as we thought."

*Lord, even though the elected leaders spoke for all Israel
when they rejected Jesus,
 I have received Him and will follow Him.*

The Story of Judas' Suicide

The well-dressed man was frantic. He pushed his way through the crowd streaming out of the temple.

"I have sinned…," Judas panted in a low voice. "Get out of my way!"

I have sinned! he thought. *I must see the priests now!*

One of the priests recognized Judas and opened a side door to him. Judas fought his way in and ran toward the caucus room where he had made his deal with the enemies of Jesus. He came face to face with a knot of laughing priests.

"You must stop this execution!" Judas demanded.

But they laughed all the harder. "You have your money. Take your silver and go."

But Judas had to cleanse his soul. With a hoarse cry, he sobbed, "I have sinned…I am doomed to hell!"

The priests laughed. They had no words of mercy for Judas. Judas glared wildly, his chest heaving with anger and sorrow. Then he untied the bag holding the 30 pieces of silver, removed a coin and turned it over in his hand. He ran out the door toward the sanctuary of the temple.

"Wait!" the priests shouted. They could not allow him to do what it appeared he might do.

Judas ran wildly toward the Court of Israel. It was there that penitent worshipers would wait while the priests offered sacrifice of forgiveness for them. With a mad cry, he hurled the 30 pieces of silver onto the marble pavement, yelling, "I have sinned! I need forgiveness!"

Before the priests could reach him, Judas fled the temple and ran down into the valley.

Judas crossed the valley, frantically climbing up the steep ascent to the place called Potter's Field. Around its edge, cliffs dropped into the valley. The cliffs were lined with jagged rocks.

Judas was heading to a gnarled tree that grew there—a tree that extended from the cliff out over the valley. There Judas knelt to untie his sash.

For the past day, his mind had been in a storm. Now he grew calm. He had returned the silver and had asked for forgiveness. He couldn't believe it was forthcoming, however, and he knew what he must do.

Judas tied one end of the sash around his neck. Then he climbed the tree, leaning out over the precipice to attach the sash to the tree limb. The tree was visible across the Hinnom Valley, so those in the city would be able to see what he was about to do. Judas wanted his death to send a message.

Returning to the ground, Judas was ready. He stood at the edge of the cliff, looking across the valley to Jerusalem.

Then Judas jumped out over the precipice. He swung for a moment, but the knot in his sash loosened under his weight. Judas fell onto the jagged rocks beneath. His intestines spilled out as the body bounced to the bottom of the gorge.

Remorse and Suicide of Judas

Matthew 27:3-10; Acts 1:18,19

Judas was guilty because he betrayed Jesus;
>He repented and brought the 30 pieces of silver
>Back to the religious rulers saying,

"I have sinned because I betrayed an innocent man."
The religious rulers laughed at him saying, "We don't care";
    Judas threw the 30 pieces on the sanctuary floor
    And went to the land that he bought with
    The money he stole from the bag.
Judas hanged himself out over a cliff, but the
    Knot broke and he fell into a ravine;
    His intestines burst out and he died.
The religious leaders would not accept the 30 pieces
    Because it was blood money so they
    Bought a burial ground for the poor who
    Can't afford a grave, thus fulfilling the
    Prophecy of Jeremiah (Jer. 18:2; 19:2; 32:6-15).

The Fourth Trial—Before Pilate

Matthew 27:11-14; Mark 15:1-5; Luke 23:1-7; John 18:19-38

And they bound Jesus again and led Him to Pilate's palace
    After the sun was up, but the Jewish leaders wouldn't enter
    Because they didn't want to defile themselves for the Passover.
Pilate went out to them and asked, "What is the legal indictment?"
    They answered, "If this man were not guilty,
    We wouldn't have brought Him to you."
Pilate said, "Then judge Him according to your law";
    They answered, "We do not have the authority to execute anyone."
The religious rulers said Jesus was against paying taxes to Caesar
    And called Him the Messiah-King.
Pilate went inside to Jesus and asked Him, "Are You the King of the
    Jews?" Jesus answered, "Did you think up this question, or
    Did someone plant it in your mind?"
Pilate answered, "I am not a Jew. Your religious leaders

Brought You to me; what have You done?"
Jesus answered, "My Kingdom is not of this world. If it were,
    My followers would fight to rescue Me. Since they
    Haven't come for Me, then My Kingdom is different."
Pilate answered, "Then You are a King!"
    Jesus replied, "You said it. That's the reason
    I was born that I should reveal this truth
    And everyone who follows truth, would follow Me."
Pilate questioned, "What is truth?" He didn't wait for an answer
    But went out to the Jewish leaders and concluded,
    "I find no crime in this man!"

Lord, even though Pilate rejected the kingship of Jesus,
    I crown Him as King of my life and obey Him.

The Fifth Trial of Jesus

Luke 23:6-12

When Pilate heard the continuous yelling of the Jewish leaders,
    He asked if Jesus were a Galilean.
    So then Pilate sent Jesus to King Herod who was over Galilee;
    Herod was in Jerusalem for the Passover.
Herod was glad to see Jesus because of the Miracle-worker's reputation;
    Herod wanted to see Jesus perform a miracle.
The Galilean king asked questions
    But Jesus didn't answer any of them.
The religious leaders kept repeating their accusations against Jesus,
    So Herod mocked Jesus and dressed Him in kingly apparel
    And sent Jesus back to Pilate.
Herod and Pilate became friends that day, previously they were
    Political rivals and hated each other.

Lord, it's amazing how hatred for Jesus brings enemies together,
   And how love for Jesus brings me closer to
   Others who also love Him.

The Sixth Trial of Jesus

Matthew 27:15-26; Mark 15:6-15; Luke 23:13-25; John 18:39–19:16

Pilate was reluctant to give in to the demands of the religious leaders
   So he planned to release a criminal which was the custom at
   Passover.
Pilate asked, "Should I release the King of the Jews, or should I release
   Barabbas who is a lawless man and a murderer?"
The religious leaders stirred up the crowd to demand Barabbas' release
   So Pilate asked, "What shall I do with the one called 'King of
   the Jews?'"
   The crowd yelled "Crucify Him."
Pilate answered, "What evil has Jesus done?
   I find no cause to execute Him."
The crowd yelled louder, "Crucify Him!"
   Pilate was afraid of the consequences, so he re-entered
   The palace and said to Jesus, "Who are You?"
   But Jesus didn't answer Him.
Pilate rebuked Jesus, "Why are You silent? I have the authority to
   Release You or to crucify You."
Jesus said, "You have no authority that's not given to you from above;
   The Jews who brought Me to you have the greater sin."
Pilate made plans to release Jesus, but the Jews cried even louder,
   "Crucify Him. If you release Him you are not Caesar's friend;
   Everyone who calls Himself a king is Caesar's enemy."

Lord, I like that Barabbas goes free while Jesus is crucified in my place.
   Thank You for dying for me.

The Story of Jesus Being Whipped

Jesus was dragged into the belly of Antonia. The Roman guards hooked the thongs binding His wrists to a beating post, extending His arms above his head. They ripped His tunic to the waist, and the olive skin of His back was revealed.

A soldier took hold of a cat-o'-nine-tails, a leather whip of nine thongs.

"ONE!" A centurion yelled out as the guard laid the first stripes on Jesus' back. But there was no sound from Jesus.

"TWO!" came the second command. No sound from Jesus.

"THREE!" Still no sound from Jesus.

The lashes reached 39. "If He dies with 39 stripes," was the common refrain, "then it proves He was guilty." But the scourging didn't kill Jesus. It merely humiliated and tortured Him.

The soldiers loosed the knot in the straps about His wrists, and Jesus crumbled in a heap. One of the soldiers draped a scarlet robe across His swollen back. Then they twisted together a crown of thorns and set it on His head. They placed a reed in His right hand, pretending it was a royal scepter. Then, bowing before Him in mockery, one of the soldiers said, "Hail, king of the Jews," and the others laughed.

Dragging Jesus up the stairs into the judgment hall, the soldiers threw Him onto the floor before Pilate. Rising from his breakfast, Pilate walked around Jesus, who was a pitiful sight.

Perhaps, Pilate thought, the indignities this man had suffered would appease the priests. So he took Jesus by the arm and drew Him to the porch.

"*Behold the man*," Pilate called for all to hear. "I have brought Him out to show you what you have done and to let you know once more that I find no basis for a charge against Him."

And the chief priests and Pharisees took up the shout once more: "Crucify Him! Nail Him to the cross!"

Pilate said to them, "You crucify Him! I find no fault in Him." The Jewish leaders had not expected the Roman governor to be so squeamish. Frustrated, the priests announced, "We have a law, and according to that law He must die, because He claimed to be the Son of God."

But this did not move Pilate. Jesus had not broken any Roman law, only their Jewish traditions. Pilate pondered his dilemma. He took Jesus inside and demanded of Him, "Don't you realize I have the power either to free You or to crucify You?" Then Jesus answered him, saying, "You would have no power over Me if it were not given to you from above."

When Pilate returned to the porch, the spokesman for the chief priests shouted, "If you let this man go, you are no friend of Caesar. Anyone who claims to be a king opposes Caesar. Jesus of Nazareth has set himself to be king, and that is treason!" Pilate could not ignore this line of reasoning.

"Shall I then crucify your king?" Pilate cried out to the leaders.

"We have no king but Caesar," they answered.

Pilate knew the Jews' long-standing hatred of Roman rule. Their hatred for this Galilean must run even deeper. He handed Jesus over to be crucified.

Jesus is Mocked

Matthew 27:27-34; Mark 15:16-23; Luke 23:26-36; John 19:17-29

Pilate released Barabbas, but he had Jesus scourged;
>The soldiers then led Jesus to the dungeon
>Where they stripped Him and beat Him mercilessly.
The soldiers mocked Jesus and put a purple robe on Him
>And made a crown of thorns and jammed it on His head;
>They put a stick in His right hand and bowed in mock worship
>Saying, "Hail, King of the Jews."
Then the soldiers took the stick and beat Him on the head,
>And spit on Him.

289

Finally, the soldiers took the purple robe off Him
    And put His robe back on Jesus
    And led Him back to Pilate.

Lord, I was "In Christ" when He suffered for me,
    I will always be grateful that He was punished in my place.

So Pilate had Jesus brought out and placed on the judgment tribunal
    And pronounced, "Behold Your King;
    It was six o'clock in the morning
    When the Passover Lamb was sacrificed.

Lord, I accepted Jesus when He was presented to me,
    I did not reject Him as did the Jews.

The crowd seeing Jesus cried again, "Crucify Him."
    Pilate answered, "Shall I crucify your King?"
    The crowd answered, "We have no king but Caesar."
Then Pilate took water and washed his hands saying, "I am
    Innocent of the blood of this righteous man."
    The Jews said, "His blood be on us and our children."
The soldiers then led Jesus away to be crucified;
    They made Jesus carry His cross to Calvary.

Jesus was exhausted and weakened so He fell under the load of the cross,
    The soldiers made Simeon from North Africa carry the cross.
A large crowd followed Jesus, including many weeping women
    But Jesus told them, "Daughters of Jerusalem, don't weep for Me,
    But shed your tears for yourselves and your children;
For there is coming tribulation when people will pray
    For the mountains to fall on them."

Lord, the Jews have suffered because they rejected their Messiah-Deliver;
    I have accepted Jesus and He has blessed my life.

And when they came to Golgotha—the place of a skull—
>They offered Him wine as an anesthesia to block the pain,
>But Jesus would not drink it.

The Story of Jesus on the Cross

The scarlet robe was torn off Jesus' body, causing His wounds to bleed afresh. He was led out of the fortress toward the hill called Golgotha—Calvary in Greek—which means the Place of the Skull.

A centurion led a detachment of four men, a hammer swinging menacingly from his belt. The soldiers made sure the victim carried His own instrument of execution—a wooden cross. But after the scourging, Jesus was too weak to carry His load. He continually fell. "Up!" one of the soldiers cried again and again, each time beating Jesus with a rope.

Behind Jesus came two thieves, each carrying his own cross. Following close behind was John, the only apostle who hadn't run away.

Word of these happenings had reached many who believed Jesus' teaching. Hundreds of weeping men and women now lined the street, mingling with His detractors.

A wooden shingle was placed around Jesus' neck; later it would be nailed to the top of the cross. On the shingle Pilate had written, "JESUS OF NAZARETH, THE KING OF THE JEWS."

After Jesus had fallen several times along the route, the Roman soldiers didn't waste time beating Him again.

"You!" the centurion yelled to a man in the crowd.

Simon, a pilgrim from the land of Cyrene, was dressed differently; his dark-green robe and red tunic stood out in the crowd of white and brown tunics. "Pick up that cross and follow us."

So Simon the Cyrenian hefted the cross onto his shoulder and carried it for Jesus to the place called Golgotha.

The heavy timbers made a cracking sound as Simon dropped the cross at the top of the hill. Calloused hands stripped the sandals, cloak, and tunic from Jesus and stretched Him on the timbers. Ropes tied His hands and feet to the cross. Then a Roman soldier, swinging a large wooden mallet, approached Jesus. This muscular man took a black iron spike, placed it in the palm of Jesus' right hand and with a mighty swing of his hammer, began driving the spike into the timber.

THWAPPP..., the sound rang out. THWAPPP...THWAPPP... The soldiers didn't pay any attention—they had heard the sound many times.

Next, the executioner turned to Jesus' other hand, repeating the process. He lifted the hammer. THWAPPP...THWAPPP...THWAPPP...

He did the same to the feet of Jesus.

A hole almost two feet deep had been chiseled out of the limestone. With Jesus nailed to the cross, the soldiers put their huge shoulders to the weight. Slowly they lifted the cross skyward. The weight of Jesus' body caused the nails in His hands and feet to rip His flesh. His body screamed in agony, but he said nothing. The soldiers raised the cross until it was nearly upright. Then the executioner kicked it so that the base of the cross dropped into the hole.

THUMP...Jesus shut His eyes as His body shook with pain, but He said nothing for a moment. Then He lifted His eyes to Heaven in prayer, "Father, forgive them, for they know not what they do." It was nine o'clock in the morning.

On the Cross
9 A.M. to 12 Noon

Matthew 27:35-44; Mark 15:24-32; Luke 23:33-43; John 19:18-27

They nailed Jesus to the cross and lifted it up
> Then they crucified two thieves, one on each side of Jesus.
The four soldiers divided His possessions, each one taking a fourth;

Because His robe didn't have a seam, they didn't rip it up
But cast dice for it, thus fulfilling Scripture.
"They divided My clothes and cast lots for My robe" (Ps. 22:18).

Jesus' First Statement From the Cross

Luke 23:34-42

And Jesus cried with a loud voice so everyone heard,
"Father, forgive them, they don't know what they've done."

Lord, thank You for forgiving me all my sins,
Especially when I didn't know what I was doing.

Pilate had written the indictment for which Jesus was executed
On a shingle and it was nailed on the cross over His head,
JESUS OF NAZARETH, KING OF THE JEWS.
The indictment was written in Latin, Greek, and Hebrew and
Everyone could read it from the nearby roadway.
The Jewish leaders asked Pilate to change the wording because
It embarrassed them. But Pilate answered,
"No, what I have written will remain on the cross."

Lord, even though Jesus died as the rejected King of Israel,
I recognize His authority and role in my life.

Then travelers on the road laughed at Jesus saying, "You claim
To destroy the temple in three days and rebuild it,
Why can't You come down from the cross?"
The religious leaders mocked Jesus saying, "You saved others,
Why can't You save Yourself?"
"If You are the Messiah-Deliverer, come down from Your cross
So we can see and believe in You";
Both thieves on either side also mocked Jesus.
One thief repeated the mockery, "If You are Messiah,

Save Yourself and us";
    The other thief rebuked him saying, "We deserve to die
    Because we are thieves, but this man doesn't deserve this."
Then he said, "Jesus, remember me when You
    Come into Your Kingdom."

Jesus' Second Statement From the Cross

Luke 23:43

Jesus answered, "Today, you shall be with Me in paradise."

Lord, I'm glad You remembered me when You hung on the cross,
    I will live with You forever because You forgave my sin.

John returned to the Cross with Mary, Jesus' mother,
    And Mary the wife of Cleophus and Mary Magdalene.

Jesus' Third Statement From the Cross

John 19:25-27

When Jesus saw His mother, He said, "Woman, behold your son";
    Then nodding to John—the disciple who loved Him—Jesus said,
    "Son, behold your mother." They left as John took Mary
    To his own home.

From Noon Until 3 P.M.

Matthew 27:45-50; Mark 15:33-37; Luke 23:44-46; John 19:28-30

When high noon came, darkness covered the land
    Till 3 P.M. and the sunlight failed.

Jesus' Fourth Statement From the Cross

Matthew 27:45-49; Mark 15:33-36

Then Jesus cried with a loud voice, *Eli, Eli, toma sabachthani,*
    "My God, My God, why have You forsaken Me?"
    Some thought Jesus was calling for Elijah.

One ran to fill a sponge with vinegar and
    Put it on a reed, then gave Him to drink saying,
    "Let's see if Elijah comes to take Him down."

Jesus' Fifth Statement From the Cross

John 19:28

Jesus realized He was going to die, knowing all things
    Were accomplished that were required for a substitutionary death,
    Said, "I thirst."

Lord, I identify with the humanity of Jesus, and
    I realize my limitations and my thirst,
    Just as Jesus realized His physical need.

Jesus' Sixth Statement From the Cross

John 19:29-30

When Jesus received the vinegar, he again shouted,
    "It is finished."

Lord, thank You that Jesus finished my salvation
    And there is nothing left for Him to do
    To save me from my sin.

Jesus' Seventh Statement From the Cross

Luke 23:46

When three o'clock came, Jesus again shouted,
    "Father, into Your hands I commend My Spirit."
Then Jesus in one final act of humanity, bowed His head
    And gave up the ghost. No one took His life from Him,
    He gave it freely for the world.

Lord, when it comes time for me to die,
    What else can I do but commend my Spirit to you,
    Then wait for You to receive me into Heaven.

The Accompanying Phenomena

Matthew 27:51-56; Mark 15:38-41; Luke 23:45-49

When the Centurion, who commanded the soldiers,
    Saw that Jesus gave up the ghost he said,
    "Truly, this man was the righteous Son of God."
The veil in the temple that concealed the Holy of Holies
    Was ripped from top to bottom.
An earthquake shook the area, and rocks tumbled to the ground
    And tore open the graves, then
    Many bodies of the Saints in the graves were raised.
They came out of the tombs after Jesus' resurrection
    And appeared to many who saw them.
There was a group of women watching from a distant hill
    Made up of Mary Magdalene; Mary, the mother of James the Less,
    And Joseph, the mother of James and John and Salome.
These were the women who followed Jesus in Galilee and paid for
    The expenses. They had followed Him to Jerusalem.

Lord, I was there when Jesus died, for I was
"In Christ," being baptized into His death;
I know my sins were forgiven when He died.

The Burial of Jesus' Body

Matthew 27:57-60; Mark 15:42-46; Luke 23:50-54; John 19:31-42

The Jewish leaders asked Pilate to take down the three bodies
> Because they didn't want them on the crosses on the Passover.

They asked Pilate to break their legs to kill them
> If they were not already dead.

When the soldiers came to Jesus, they didn't
> Break His legs because He was already dead,
> Fulfilling the Scripture, "Not a bone of Him was broken."

But a soldier pierced the side of Jesus with his spear;
> Immediately, blood and water came out of the wound.

John the apostle saw this happen and witnessed in
> His Gospel that these things happened, so that
> Readers may believe in Jesus and be saved.

Finally, the crowd that came to see the crucifixion
> Returned to the city in a somber mood, again fulfilling Scripture,
> "They looked on Him whom they pierced."

As the evening approached, Joseph of Arimathea,
> A member of the Sanhedrin, went to ask Pilate for the body of Jesus
> To give it a proper burial.

Pilate was surprised that Jesus was already dead,
> So he called the Centurion who supervised the crucifixion
> To verify that Jesus was actually dead.

When Pilate found out Jesus was in fact dead,
> He gave Joseph the authority to bury the body.

Joseph was a believer who looked for the coming Kingdom,
>> Who was a member of the Sanhedrin,
>> But he was not there to vote for the death of Jesus.
Nicodemus joined him, who also was a member of the Sanhedrin,
>> And a secret believer in Jesus Christ,
>> But for fear of the Jews didn't tell anyone.
Joseph took the body down from the cross, and wrapped it
>> In clean linen cloths and anointed it
>> With 75 pounds of myrrh and aloes which was Jewish custom.
Near Golgotha was a garden in which was located
>> A tomb where no one had been buried.
It had been newly carved out of rock
>> And was intended to bury Joseph of Arimathea.
They buried Jesus just as the Jewish ritual demanded
>> Because the Passover was celebrated at sundown.

Lord, I was buried with Jesus because the Bible says,
>> *"Buried with Him by baptism unto death,*
>> *To be raised to newness of life."*

Friday Until Sunday Morning

Matthew 27:61-66; Mark 15:47; Luke 23:55-56

The women continued their watch from a distance,
>> Mary Magdalene, Mary the mother of Joseph,
>> And the other women who followed Jesus from Galilee.
On Saturday, the religious leaders went to see Pilate
>> Saying, "When the deceiver was alive, He
>> Claimed He would rise from the dead on the third day."
So they asked Pilate to secure the grave with
>> Soldiers until after the third day to make sure
>> The disciples didn't come steal the body and claim,
"He is risen from the dead, and the last error becomes

Greater than the first."
Pilate said, "Take guards and go make the grave
As secure as you are able to do."
So they took guards and a Roman seal secured
The tomb.

Lord, the world will do anything to deny Your resurrection,
But I know You were raised from the dead,
Because You live within my heart.

Chapter 17

THE RESURRECTION OF JESUS CHRIST

At the Tomb Early Sunday Morning

Matthew 28:2-4;11-15

Behold there was a great earthquake when the angel of the Lord
    Descended from Heaven to roll away the stone
    From the grave and he sat on it.
He was bright as lightning and his clothes were
    As white as snow. The guards fainted dead away.
Some of the guards went into the city and told the religious leaders
    What happened at the tomb.
The Sanhedrin assembled to discuss the matter, then they
    Gave money to the soldiers to bribe them to say,
    "The disciples came while we slept and stole His body."
The religious leaders told the soldiers if this gets
    To your superiors, we will persuade them to
    Look the other way.
The soldiers took the money and did as they were told,
    So the rumor spread throughout the city that
    The disciples stole the body. The Jews believed
    This explanation until this day.

The Visit of the Women to the Tomb

Matthew 28:1-8; Mark 16:1-8; Luke 24:1-8; John 20:1

Early on Sunday morning, Mary Magdalene, Mary the
    Mother of James, Salome and the other women,
    Went to the tomb before the sun came up.
They said among themselves, "Who will roll away the stone?"
    They brought spices to anoint the body of Jesus.
Because Mary Magdalene was more courageous, she left them
    And went ahead to spy at the soldiers' camp.
When she saw the stone rolled from the tomb,
    She left and ran to tell Peter and John;
    She didn't return to the women she left behind.
She told the two disciples, "They have taken away the Lord
Out of the tomb, and I don't know where He is."

Lord, I admire the ignorant zeal of Mary Magdalene;,
    May I always serve You zealously
    Whether I know or don't know what I'm doing.

The other women were concerned when Mary didn't return,
    They went to the tomb and saw the stone rolled away.
They entered the tomb and were shocked to see a young man
    Sitting there in a dazzling white robe.
He said, "Don't be shocked, you seek Jesus of Nazareth;
    He is risen. Look at the place where they laid Him.
"Go tell His disciples and Peter, He will go before
    You to Galilee."
The women were overjoyed, so they ran to
    Tell His disciples, but Jesus met them in the way;
    They held Jesus by the feet, worshiping Him.
Jesus told them, "Don't fear, tell My followers to go
    To Galilee where they will see Me."

Peter and John Visit the Tomb

John 20:2-10

On a separate road, Peter and John ran to the tomb;
> The younger John outran Peter.
John looked inside the tomb and saw the linen clothes
> Still wrapped together, but he didn't go in.

Peter didn't stop, but ran straight into the tomb
> And also saw the linen clothes together and the death mask
> Lying at another place.
Next, John entered the tomb—examined everything—then
> He believed that Jesus had risen from the dead;
> They returned to their house.

Lord, I believe You arose physically from the dead,
> *I don't need the proof of an empty tomb*
> *Because I have You in my heart.*

Mary Returns to the Tomb

John 20:11-18

Later that morning, Mary Magdalene returned to the tomb,
> She wept as she looked into the tomb.
Then she saw two angels—clothed in white—sitting
> At the head and feet where the body had been laid.
"Woman, why are you crying," the angels asked.
> She answered, "Because they have taken away
> My Lord and I don't know where He is located."
Someone was standing in back of her, but she didn't
> Know who it was. She thought he was a gardener
> So she asked,

"If you have taken away His body, tell me where it is
> And I will take Him away."
It was Jesus who said, "Mary." Her blindness
> Was taken away and she called Him, "Rabboni,"
> An old Hebrew word for "respected master."
Jesus said, "Quit clinging to Me as though things
> Will continue in the future as they were in the past."
Jesus explained, "I must go to My Father in Heaven,
> He is also your Father. He is My God and your God."
Mary returned to Jerusalem to tell the brethren,
> "I have seen the Lord." Then she told them
> All the things Jesus said to her.

Lord, may I be a witness to You of all I've experienced.
Use me to tell others of Your death and resurrection.

Jesus Appears on the Road to Emmaus

Luke 24:13-32

Sunday afternoon, Cleophus and his wife were walking
> Home from Jerusalem, talking about all the things
> That happened over the weekend.
Jesus joined them but they didn't know it was Jesus;
> He said to them, because they looked so sad,
> "What are you talking about?"
They answered, "Are You the only one in Jerusalem
> Who doesn't know what happened this weekend?"
Jesus answered, "What things?" They answered,
> "The things that happened to Jesus of Nazareth."
They explained Jesus was a prophet who did mighty miracles
> But the religious leaders delivered Him to Pilate
> Who condemned Him to death and crucified Him.
The couple said, "We hoped He would have delivered Israel

But today—the third day—some women went
>To the tomb early and found it empty.
"Then the women claimed to have seen angels, and
>That Jesus was alive.
"Some men also went to the tomb and found it empty, as
>The women said, but they didn't see Him."
Then Jesus said, "You are foolish not to believe all
>The prophets have predicted. They said the Messiah
>Must suffer before entering His glory."
Jesus began at the books of Moses and covered the Scriptures
>To the prophets, explaining to them
>All the Scriptures said about Himself.
As they drew near their home in Emmaus, Jesus
>Pretended He was going farther.
They invited Him into their home saying, "Abide
>With us, because it is toward the evening."
Jesus went into the house with them and as they
>Sat down to eat, Jesus took bread and blessed it
>And gave it to them to eat.
Their eyes were opened and He vanished out of their sight;
>They said to each other, "Didn't our hearts burn
>Within us as He explained to us the Scriptures?"
Immediately, they returned to Jerusalem and found the disciples
>Gathered together, and told them, "The Lord
>Has arisen indeed and has appeared to us."
They rehearsed the things that happened that day,
>Including the fact the Lord had appeared to Peter.

The Upper Room on Sunday Evening

Luke 24:36,37; John 20:19-25

When the evening came, ten disciples gathered in the Upper Room,
> The doors were locked for fear of the Jews;
> Jesus came to stand among them, and said, "Peace to you."

Jesus said, "Why are you afraid, and why are you
> So confused over what has happened?"

Jesus showed them His hands and feet, then said,
> "Handle Me, a Spirit doesn't have flesh
> And bones like this."

They were deliriously happy, yet still they had
> A hard time believing what they were seeing.

Jesus said, "What do you have to eat?" They gave
> Him some broiled fish and He ate it before them.

Lord, I believe You are totally human,
> *But I also believe You are totally divine.*

The disciples were glad to see and experience the presence
> Of the Lord. Then Jesus said again, "Peace to you.
> As the Father has sent Me into the world,
> So, I am sending you into the world."

Jesus breathed on them and said, "Receive the Holy Spirit
> To teach you and use you, just as He has done
> Throughout the past dispensation. He will be
> With you until you are endued with His power."

"Those you lead to faith will have their sins forgiven,
> Those who reject will retain their sins."

Lord, I need the ministry of the Holy Spirit in all I do,
> *I cannot serve You without His enablement;*
> *I yield to You, come fill me now.*

Thomas, the disciple called Didymas—a twin—was not there;
  The disciples told him, "We have seen the Lord."
He said, "I must see the nail prints in His hands, and
  Put my hand into the wound in His side;
  Otherwise, I will not believe."

Lord, I'll not demand physical assurances to believe,
  I believe You are the crucified Son of God who died for me.

The Upper Room One Week Later

Mark 16:14-18; John 20:26-31

Eight days after Passover, the disciples gathered again
  In the Upper Room on a Sunday evening;
  Thomas was with them this time.
The doors were locked but Jesus again stood among them
  And said what He said last Sunday, "Peace to you."
Jesus spoke first to Thomas, "Reach your finger to touch
  My wounds and place your hand in the wound
  In My side. Don't doubt, but believe."
But Thomas didn't do it, he answered, "You are my Lord
  And my God."
Jesus said, "God will bless you because you have
  Seen Me and believed. But God will also bless
  Those who haven't seen Me, yet they believe."
Jesus did many miracles that were not written in the Gospels,
  But these miracles are written that people will believe
  That Jesus is the Messiah, the Son of God.

I will believe that Jesus is the Son of God,
  And when I believe, I'll have eternal life.

Then Jesus repeated to them the commission,
  "Go into all the world and preach the Gospel to every person;

Baptize those who believe, and those who won't believe
Will be condemned."

"You will do miracles, speak in tongues, miraculously survive
Poisonous snake bites, and when men try to poison you;
You shall lay hands on the sick and they'll recover."

Jesus Appears on the Lake Shore

John 21

A week later, Jesus appeared to seven disciples
 On the shore of the Sea of Galilee.
Simon Peter had announced, "I am going fishing";
  There went with him Thomas, Nathaniel, James
  And John, Andrew, and Phillip.
They got into a boat and fished all night, but caught nothing;
  When the day was breaking, Jesus stood on the beach,
  But the disciples didn't know it was Jesus.
Jesus yelled to them, "Have you caught any fish?"
  They answered Him, "No!" Jesus answered, "Cast the net
  On the other side of the boat and you will catch fish."
They cast on the right side and couldn't draw in the fish,
  So John said to Peter, "It's the Lord."
Peter put on his tunic and dove into the water
  To swim to Jesus. The other disciples came in a
  Little boat, for they were 100 yards from the beach.
When they got to shore, they saw a charcoal fire cooking fish,
  There was also bread;
  Jesus said, "Add the fish you've caught to these."
Simon Peter went and pulled the net to land, it had 153 fish
  In it, yet the net didn't break.
Jesus said, "Come eat, break your fast." No one asked
  Who it was, for they all knew it was Jesus;

Jesus served all of them breakfast.
This was the third Sunday that Jesus appeared to them.

Lord, I can't see You physically, yet I see
You in the pages of Scripture.

After breakfast, Jesus said, "Simon, Son of Jonah,
Do you love Me more deeply than you love these nets?"
Peter answered, "Lord, You know that I like and admire You."
Jesus answered, "Feed My lambs."
Jesus said to him a second time, "Simon, do you
Deeply love Me?" Peter answered, "Lord, You know
That I like and admire You." Jesus answered, "Tend My sheep."
Jesus said a third time, "Simon, do you really
Like and admire Me?" Peter was ashamed the Lord
Asked him three times, because he denied the Lord
Three times, and because he only said he liked and admired the
Lord.
So Peter answered, "Lord, You omnisciently know everything,
You know I can only say I really like and admire You."
Jesus said, "Feed My sheep."
Then Jesus predicted, "When you were young,
You were able to dress yourself, and go where you wanted."
"But when you get old, they will stretch your hands
Out on a cross and they will clothe you with
What they choose, and lead you where they want to go."
This spoke Jesus indicating Peter would die as a martyr;
Then Jesus concluded, "Follow Me."
Peter turned to John and asked Jesus, "What about him?"
Jesus said, "If he lives till I return, how does
That concern you? You must follow Me."
This statement made many think John would live until
Jesus' return. But Jesus didn't say John wouldn't die,
Only, "If he lives till I return, how does that concern you?"

Jesus did many other things; if they were all written
   The world couldn't contain the books that could be written.

Lord, I really love You with all my heart,
   Give me courage to tell everyone of my devotion to You.

The Appearance on a Mountain

Matthew 28:16-20; 1 Corinthians 15:6,7

On the fourth Sunday, Jesus appeared to approximately 500 people,
   Many were still alive when Paul wrote the letter to the Corinthians.
They worshiped when they saw Him, but some still doubted.
   Jesus said, "All authority in Heaven is given to Me,
   Go make disciples of all people groups in the world,
   Baptizing them in the name of the Father, Son, and Holy Spirit,
   Teaching them to obey all I command you.
"And lo, I will be with you everywhere you go,
   Even to the ends of this age."

Lord, you've given the Great Commission to the church generally,
   And to me specifically.
   Help me do my part to obey Your command.

Jesus appears to His half-brother James
   Who was to become the leader of the church in Jerusalem,
   And He appeared privately to Peter.

Lord, I don't expect to see an appearance of You in the flesh,
   But I know You are real because You live in my heart
   And that is just as real as if I saw you physically.

Jesus' Appearance on the Fifth Sunday
And His Ascension Back to Heaven

Luke 24:44-53; Acts 1:3-12

Jesus appeared to His disciples in the city of Jerusalem
      On the fifth Sunday after His resurrection.
He said, "Remember the things I said before I died,
         That the things of Calvary must be completed because
         They were predicted in Moses, the prophets, and the Psalms.
Then Jesus opened their spiritual eyes to understand these things,
         Jesus said, "This is the Gospel that the Christ should suffer for
      sins,
         Be raised from the dead on the third day,
         And that repentance and remission of sins be preached
         In My name, in all the world, beginning at Jerusalem.
"You will have everything the Father promised
         That He will give to you, but tarry in
         Jerusalem and pray for power to do these things."

Lord, I want power to fulfill the Great Commission,
         Give me supernatural results to my ministry.

During the 40 days since His death at Passover,
         Jesus had been teaching His disciples
         The things about God's plan for the Kingdom.
Jesus charged them to pray in Jerusalem after His departure
         Until the Holy Spirit came upon them, even
         As John the Baptist had promised, "You will be
         Baptized with the Holy Spirit."
But the disciples asked, "Will You at this time usher
         In the millennial kingdom and restore Israel as a
         Sovereign nation?"
Jesus answered, "It is not for you to know the dates when
         The Father will do all these things,

"But you will receive spiritual power when the Holy Spirit
      Comes upon you, and you'll be My witnesses in
      Jerusalem, Judea, Samaria, and throughout the whole world."

Then Jesus led them out of the city to the Mount of Olives,
      He lifted His hands and blessed them.
While He was blessing them, Jesus was lifted into the heavens,
      The disciples watched Him ascend into Heaven
      And a cloud blocked their sight, so they saw Him no more.
The disciples continued staring into the sky until
      Two angels in white robes stood by them saying,
"Why are you staring into the sky? Jesus will
      Come again just as you have seen Him go."
The disciples worshiped Jesus and returned into the city
      With abundant joy, where they waited in prayer
      As Jesus had commanded them.
When Jesus returned to Heaven, He ascended the heights
      To sit down at the right hand of God, the Father.

Lord, because You're in Heaven as my intercessor,
      I come to the Father through Your prayers.
      I am as close to the Father as You are to the heart of God.

The Sixth Sunday After Pentecost

Acts 1:13-26

(See next volume—*Praying the Book of Acts*—of the series *Praying the Scripture* for a transliteration of the sixth and seventh Lord's Days after Pentecost. The following is a summary of what happened on the sixth and seventh Sundays after Pentecost.)

There were approximately 120 praying constantly in the Upper Room, doing exactly what Jesus commanded. He said, "I will return," so they probably expected Him on this Sunday, but Jesus didn't come, and the

Holy Spirit didn't come. So, they examined themselves to see what else they had to do to be in the perfect will of God. Since the number eleven was a foreign number to Jews, and there were only eleven disciples, they decided to complete their number to twelve. They elected Matthias who had followed Jesus since John the Baptist had preached and he had seen a physical resurrection appearance of Jesus. I believe they should have waited for Paul, an apostle born out of due season.

The Seventh Sunday After Pentecost

Acts 2:1-4

The Holy Spirit came on Pentecost (the Latin word for 50), 50 days after Passover. The disciples were still praying in the Upper Room on Sunday morning when the Holy Spirit was poured out on them in revival (revival means God's presence was manifested among them). There were three outward supernatural signs: (1) the followers of Jesus spoke in other languages, (2) there was the sound of a mighty rushing wind, and (3) cloven flames of fire came on them. After Pentecost, God's people were never the same again, the Church took the place of Israel, and the world was never the same again.

THE END OF THE PHYSICAL LIFE OF JESUS IS THE BEGINNING OF THE CHURCH.

The thrilling work of Jesus Christ continues in *Praying the Book of Acts*— the next book in the series, *Praying the Scriptures*.

PRAYING THE BOOK OF ACTS
1:1–28:31

Chapter 18

THE STORY OF WRITING
THE BOOK OF ACTS

Luke was the medical doctor who traveled with Paul the apostle, and took care of Paul's medical needs. But he was more than a physician, Luke was a co-minister with Paul. He could preach, but only when Paul wasn't present. But Luke's most enduring ministry was writing—he wrote the Gospel of Luke, the Book of Acts, and the Book of Hebrews.

Today we catch Luke on an important mission for the welfare of Paul and the evangelistic team that traveled with the apostles.

Because Luke was over 60 years old, he puffed as he walked up the steep incline to the large villa on the top of the hill. A very strong but little church met in the villa. It was a small church because not many people lived in the high plains region. It was a strong, well-taught church, because the owner of the villa—Theophilus—was well read. He had many books in his personal library; several of them were copies of Scripture. He used these to teach his small flock.

Theophilus was the owner of the surrounding fields that could be seen in the distance. Theophilus had servants working in the fields to fill his barns with grain. Other servants delivered his produce in wagons to nearby towns, and some even delivered goods to ships in the harbor. Theophilus was a wealthy businessman with many business connections.

"I hope he is as generous this time as last time," Luke thought to himself.

Three years ago Luke had approached Theophilus for a gift—a large one—to support Paul who was then imprisoned in Caesarea, a fortress in the Holy Land. Paul and his team needed money to pay for essentials because they weren't receiving offerings while Paul was in prison. Paul wasn't preaching where gifts were given to him. Paul had been in jail for two years and it cost almost 10,000 pieces of silver to live.

"Of course I'll give some money to support Paul," was Theophilus' response last time Luke asked him for a gift. "But, I'm a wise business-man," Theophilus told Luke. Theophilus wanted to help Paul, but he also wanted something in return.

The last time Luke came to see Theophilus he said, "I'll give you all the money you need but I want you to write a book for me while Paul is in prison." Theophilus wanted Luke to travel the Holy Land to interview people who talked to Jesus or were healed by Jesus, and write it all down in a book.

During the last trip, Theophilus walked Luke into his large library. Every wealthy person had a room where they kept books. Some rich people just showed off their books as a matter of pride. Many others allowed their servants to read their books when their daily tasks were over. But books were a passion for Theophilus, his parents loved to read so they named him Theophilus which means, "lover of wisdom."

"Ha," he laughed loudly, "I've read some of these books a dozen times."

Then Theophilus got serious, "After I became a follower of Jesus Christ, I invited Matthew the apostle to come visit my villa. I gathered all my servants in my great courtyard. The apostle Matthew preached and many of my servants began following Jesus Christ."

Theophilus told how the following evening he invited the owners and slaves from other estates to come to his courtyard to hear the message of Jesus Christ. Many became followers of Jesus Christ and the spacious courtyard became a church.

The villa was built in a large U shape, with a wall protecting the open end. The three spacious porches were perfect for protection from the hot sun or cold rain of winter. The protected courtyard gave the church privacy.

Theophilus told how each evening Matthew read from a manuscript he was writing on the life of Christ. "I had a servant who is my scribe copy Matthew's Gospel for me."

Then Theophilus told how blind Bartimaeus visited the church to tell of his healing; he had written an accurate account of his healing. The scribe copied the story to keep it in the library for the church.

Luke thought fondly of his first conversation with Theophilus because the rich land owner gave him copies of all his accounts of Jesus with the instruction, "Go write a complete record of the life of Jesus in perfect sequence so I can use it for preaching in my church."

Theophilus gave him 10,000 talents of silver to take care of Paul. Luke determined to write an account of Jesus' life and ministry that would be the most accurate and complete book available to the church. As Luke began writing, God added His Holy Spirit to Luke's efforts so that the book Luke wrote was described as Anothem which meant "from above."[1]

God's Holy Spirit had used Luke to write an inspired and inerrant Gospel that became part of the canon.

As Luke knocked on the front gate of the villa, he thought, "I wonder what Theophilus will want me to do this time?" Luke didn't ask for money right away. Like old friends, Luke and Theophilus reviewed their times together and Theophilus asked Luke to preach to his servants that evening. When most of the people in the villa had gone to sleep, Luke and Theophilus sat by a flickering candle in the library discussing things. Finally Theophilus asked, "Why have you come?"

Luke began to tell of the voyage of Paul from Caesarea to Rome. The Jews in Jerusalem had plotted to assassinate Paul, so the apostle had appealed to Caesar. Luke told all the details of the trip...Paul's sickness...the storm...the shipwreck...and Publius' father's healing and conversion. Then Luke turned his attention to Paul's condition.

"We must rent an apartment in Rome and feed the companions of Paul. Paul is chained to a guard and it will be two years before Caesar will hear his case."

"Ho, ho, ho," Theophilus laughed heartily. Not a skeptical laugh but a knowing laugh. Then he repeated himself from two years ago.

"You know I'm a careful businessman..." He paused long. Then looking into the physician's eyes said, "I want you to write a book, everything you just told me. My church needs to hear these stories of the church from the beginning. Begin the book with the Great Commission and Jesus' return to Heaven. Begin the book, "This is a continuation of all that Jesus began to do and teach. This book is the story of the Acts of the Apostles."

"I'll do that," Luke answered.

"Good..." Theophilus answered. "I'll use it in my preaching to my church. And who knows, maybe the Holy Spirit will inspire this one just like the first one.

Theophilus then winked at Luke, "Then I'll have my scribe make copies of it for the other churches."

Endnote

1. Luke 1:1-4.

Chapter 19

THE STORY OF THE ASCENSION OF JESUS TO HEAVEN

Jesus Ascended Into Heaven

Acts 1:1-11

Lord, help me understand Your plan for my life
As I pray through the Book of Acts.
Fill me with the Holy Spirit so I can
Minister in resurrection power as did the early church.

Luke reminded Theophilus that his first letter
Told all what the human Jesus began to do and teach
While He was alive on earth.
This second letter would tell of the acts of the Holy Spirit
Through the disciples as they planted the early church.

After His death, Jesus returned to Heaven,
But during the 40 days after His crucifixion,
He appeared to the disciples from time to time
Where He prepared them for life-long ministry
And He demonstrated to them proofs of His deity.

In His last meeting with them in Jerusalem,
Jesus told them not to leave Jerusalem, but to
Pray until the Holy Spirit came upon them in power.
Jesus reminded them, "John the Baptist baptized with water,
In a few days I will baptize you with the Holy Spirit."

But the disciples didn't understand; they asked, "Lord,
  Will You now restore the kingdom to free us from Rome?"
Jesus answered, "The Father has set that date, and
  It's not for you to know."
Jesus said, "But take the Gospel into all the world when
  The Holy Spirit is come upon you. Tell them about Me;
Beginning in Jerusalem, then Judaea, next Samaria, and finally
  To the ends of the earth."
When Jesus finished, He was lifted into the sky
  And disappeared into a cloud, leaving the disciples
  Staring into the sky looking for Him.
Suddenly, two men in glistening white robes said to them,
  "Why are you staring into the sky? Jesus has
  Returned to Heaven, and one day He will return just as He left."

Lord, while Your glorified body is at the right hand
  Of the throne of God in Heaven,
I know You are in my heart. Help me live
  For You until You return.

Amen.

The Story of the Ascension of Jesus to Heaven

The upper room was silent of everything except the voice of Jesus Christ. The eleven disciples sat motionlessly listening to Jesus. They couldn't take their eyes off Him. Jesus was the same human man they followed through the dusty roads of Galilee, yet He was the LORD God. He just appeared supernaturally among them when the doors were locked. Yet no one asked, "How did You get in?"

Jesus earlier had told them to go into all the world, not just to the land of Israel. Jesus had told them to preach to every one—not just the Jews. Jesus previously told them to baptize and teach all new converts.

Peter's red eyebrows reflected a questioning look. Then he blurted out, "What is our message? Should we tell people to 'follow You' just as we followed You?"

"You will preach to people the message of good news," Jesus explained. "Previously, people had to take a lamb to be sacrificed for forgiveness of their sins...I am the Lamb of God who takes away the sins of the world." The disciples remembered John the Baptist announcing Jesus was the Lamb of God.

At first the disciples did not understand the meaning of Jesus' death on the Cross. None expected Jesus to rise from the dead, so they didn't understand what the resurrection meant. Jesus explained, "Just as the lamb was the substitute for the sins of Israel, so I am the substitute for the sins of the world. Everyone should die under the judgment of God because of their sins, but I died in their place."

Jesus waited for His message to sink in, then He explained further, "When people accept Me as their Savior, I will forgive their sins."

Jesus stood to leave the upper room, the eleven also got to their feet. He told them, "As you go into all the world, preach the good news to everyone that I have died for their sins, and that I arose from the dead to give them new life—eternal life."

The piercing eyes of Jesus gazed from one disciple to another, "You have witnessed My death and resurrection, now tell everyone."

As they left the room Jesus added, "Announce to everyone they must repent from their sins and believe in Me to have their sins forgiven."

The disciples nodded that they understood.

Walking through the streets of Jerusalem, Jesus said to them, "Tarry here in Jerusalem and pray till the Holy Spirit comes on you."

The disciples understood Moses, Gideon, and Jeremiah—their heroes ministered with power when the Spirit of the Lord came upon them. They anticipated the same power.

"But you must pray to get power."

Jesus led them out of the city, walking toward the Mount of Olives. They walked passed the Temple and remembered when Jesus had cleansed it of moneychangers.

They shuttered when they walked passed Gethsemane, remembering this garden was the place where Jesus was arrested.

When they got to the top of the Mount of Olives, Peter asked the questions, "Will the kingdom be restored *now*?"

For 40 days Jesus had been teaching them about their ministry in all the world. Jesus had taught them what to preach. But the disciples were still confused. Their minds echoed Peter's question, "Lord, will You set up the kingdom now? Will You drive the Romans into the sea? Will the lion lay down with the lamb? Will righteousness roll down the hills as God's refreshing dew?"

Jesus stopped at the top of the mount to answer, "It is not for you to know when My Father will set up the kingdom—the 1,000 years of peace—it's for a future time."

Jesus explained, "I didn't come this time to sit on David's throne in Jerusalem," Jesus could still see disappointment in their eyes. They wanted to help drive the Romans out of the Holy Land. "I've come to sit on the throne of people's hearts." Jesus reminded them that was His message for the past three and a half years.

Jesus continued speaking, "Now here is your present focus, you will receive power when the Holy Spirit comes on you—after you pray 10 days—then you will be witnesses of My Gospel—first in Jerusalem, then in Judea, next in Samaria, and finally into all the world."

When Jesus finished speaking, He was lifted up into the sky. The disciples stood speechless. They saw Him going up as Elijah must have gone to Heaven. They were too speechless to yell...or ask if He was coming back...or what they should do now. They were transfixed at what they were seeing.

A cloud floated between them and Jesus. They no longer saw Him. Jesus was gone. "Why are you standing here?" two men in dazzling white robes asked them. They were angels who said, "He will return just as you have seen Him go."

The disciples remembered the last command of Jesus was to tarry in prayer in Jerusalem until the Holy Spirit came on them. They headed toward the city and to the upper room. They would wait and pray.

Praying in the Upper Room

Acts 1:12-26

Lord, it must have been perplexing to other disciples when Jesus left them.
Be with me, let me always feel Your presence.

The disciples walked a half mile back into Jerusalem
    And began praying in the upper room as Jesus instructed.
The disciples present were Peter, John, James, Andrew,
    Philip, Thomas, Bartholomew, Matthew, James, the son of
    Alphaeus, Simon the Zealot and Judas, son of James.
Several women were there, including Mary the mother of Jesus;
    There were 120 present and
    They prayed for 10 days.

Finally, Peter stood to address the group, "Brothers, it is necessary
    For us to fulfill the scriptures about Judas
    Who betrayed Jesus by guiding the mob to arrest Him."
It was predicted what we should do by the Holy Spirit through David,
    "He (Judas) was chosen just as we were, and had part
    In our ministry, but he lifted up his heel against us."
Judas purchased a field with the money he stole from us
    And he plunged to his death in that field;
    All his bowels spilled on the ground.
The news of his death circulated among the people, and
    They called it the Field of Blood.
King David also predicted in Psalms, "Let his home

Be desolate, and let no one live there, and
  Let his work be given to someone else."
Peter said they should choose someone to take Judas' place
  And join them as witnesses of Jesus' resurrection.
"Let us choose someone who has been with us since
  The baptism of John and must have seen
  The physically resurrected Jesus
  And been with us since the ascension."
They nominated two men: Joseph Justus (also called Barsabbas) and
Matthias;
  Then they prayed that the right man would be chosen, saying,
"O Lord, You know their hearts, show us which of these
  Men you have chosen as an apostle to replace
  Judas, the traitor, who has gone to his place."
Then they cast lots and Matthias' lot was chosen,
  And he was numbered with the eleven.

Lord, I want to follow You; keep me close to Your side.
  May I never betray You as did Judas, nor may I
  Embarrass You as did Peter by denying You.

Amen.

The Coming of the Holy Spirit

Acts 2:1-13

Lord, when I read of the Holy Spirit empowering the disciples,
  I want the same Holy Spirit in my life;
  I want His power in my service for You.

When the day of Pentecost had come—seven weeks and one day
  Since the Passover when Jesus died—
  They were still praying in unity in the upper room.
Suddenly they heard a great noise that sounded like a wind storm

That filled the room where they were praying;
>But they were not blown about, nor was the room disrupted.
They saw flames of fire in the air, and it settled
>On each of them, but no one was burned.
And they were all filled with the Holy Spirit and
>All began to speak in foreign languages they didn't know;
>The Holy Spirit gave them this miraculous ability.
Many obedient Jews were in Jerusalem for Pentecost,
>Having come from many nations of the earth.
When they heard the noise of the mighty wind,
>They came to see what was going on.
They were surprised to hear their own tongue
>Being spoken by the disciples.
"How can this be," they asked, "these men are from Galilee,
>Yet we hear them speaking fluently in our language?"
They were Parthians, and Medes, and Elamites, and those who
>Live in Mesopotamia and Judea, and Cappadocia,
In Pontus and Asia, Phrygia and Pamphylia,
>In Egypt, and in parts of Libya near Cyrene,
And visitors from Rome, both Jews and Jewish converts, Cretans and
Arabians.
They exclaimed, "We hear them tell the wonderful works of God
>In our mother tongue."
They were amazed and asked one another, "What does this mean?"
>Others in the crowd mocked the disciples, saying,
>"They are drunk with new wine."

Lord, help me to tell everyone what You've
>*Done for me, just as the disciples did.*
May I never keep silent because I'm afraid
>*What the crowd will think or say.*

Amen.

Peter Preaching at Pentecost

Acts 2:14-39

Peter with the eleven disciples stood before the crowd to answer them,
    "Listen you people of Judah, and all who live in Jerusalem,
These are not drunk as you suppose,
    It is too early, it's only 9 o'clock in the morning."
"What you see is what was predicted by Joel the prophet,
    'In the last days,' God said,
'I will pour out my Spirit on all mankind
    And your sons and daughters shall prophesy,
    And your young men shall see visions,
    And your old men shall dream dreams.'
    'And I will cause miracles in Heaven and earth,
    The sun shall become black, and the moon blood red
    Before the awesome Day of the Lord arrives.'
    'And all who call on the name of the Lord
    Shall be saved.'"

"Listen, men of Israel! You know God publicly endorsed
    Jesus of Nazareth by doing miracles through Him."
    "God pre-determined for you to deliver Jesus
    To the Roman government to murder Him
    By nailing Him to a cross,
    Then God released Him from the grip of death
    And brought Him back to life again
    Because death could not keep Jesus in the grave."

"David predicted this resurrection when he said,
    'I saw the LORD before me, He is always
    By my side, so that I shall not be shaken.'
'Therefore, my heart is filled with rejoicing and
    My tongue shouts praise to God because I
    Know God will take care of me in death.'

'You will not leave my soul in Hell, neither will
You let Your Holy Son decay in the grave.'
'You will give me back my physical life
And fill me with joy as I stand in Your presence.'"

Peter continued preaching saying David was dead
And buried and his tomb was in Jerusalem, yet
David was a prophet who said,
"God has sworn in an oath that Messiah would be
His descendent and sit on the throne." Seeing the future,
David said, "Messiah would not be abandoned to the grave,
Even His body would not suffer decay. We are witnesses,
That God has raised Jesus to new life,
Then He was exalted to the right hand of God and
Received by the Father."
"Then God poured out the promised Holy Spirit as
Evidenced by what you see and hear among His followers."

Then Peter referred to David again "For David did not ascend
To Heaven, yet he quoted the Messiah Who said,
'The Lord said to my Lord,
Sit at My right hand until I make Your enemies Your footstool.
"Therefore, all Israel should realize God the Father
Has made Jesus—whom you crucified—both Lord and Messiah."

The people were cut to the heart when they heard this
And asked, "What shall we do?"
Peter answered, "Repent, so your sins will be forgiven and be baptized
Every one of you in the name of the Lord, Jesus Christ,
And you will receive the gift of the Holy Spirit;
This promise is for you, your children, and those in distant lands
Who will call upon the Lord our God."

Lord, Peter preached a powerful sermon at Pentecost;
Help me witness for You according to my ability,
And according to my opportunity.

Amen.

The New Church Was Born

Acts 2:40-47

Peter preached a long sermon featuring Jesus, urging
All of his listeners to, "Save yourself from the
Punishment that's coming upon this nation."
And approximately 3,000 were baptized and joined them;
They regularly attended the apostle's teachings, and
The Lord's Table, and prayer meetings.
A deep awe came on them as many miracles
Were done by the apostles.
The believers had everything in common,
Selling their possessions to give to anyone who had need.
They met together everyday in the Temple courtyards
And broke bread together in homes and shared meals
With great joy and thankfulness, praising God.
The unsaved were favorable to the believers, and daily God added
To the church as people were being saved.

Lord, thank You for the outpouring of the Holy Spirit that draws
Unsaved people to Jesus Christ. Thank You for saving me.
Continue pouring Your Holy Spirit on me so others can be saved.

Amen.

Healing a Man Born Crippled

Acts 3:1-11

Lord, give me a passion to pray at all times,
    With all people, at all places, for all requests,
    In all the various ways You've taught us to pray.

Peter and John went into the Temple at 3:00 P.M. to
    Pray with all those seeking to call on Your name.
They encountered a lame man at the gate who had
    Never walked in his life, friends brought him there daily.
He was begging for alms from worshipers so he asked
    Peter and John for a gift of charity.
Peter looked directly at him and said, "Look at us!"
    So the lame man looked at them,
    Expecting to receive some money.
Then Peter said, "I don't have any silver or gold,
    But I'll give you what I have. In the name of
    Jesus Christ of Nazareth, rise up and walk."
Then Peter grabbed him by the hand and pulled him
    To his feet. Immediately his feet and ankles were strengthened.
He leaped up and walked into the Temple with them;
    He was leaping and dancing and shouting praises to God.
The worshipers saw him walking and leaping and
    Recognized he was the lame man who begged at the gate,
    So the crowd was surprised and curious.
The other worshipers rushed into Solomon's porch to see the healed man;
    They stood in awe at the miracle that just happened.

Lord, I stand in awe of Your miracle-working power;
    Thank You for healing the crippled man at the Temple gate.
Help me believe You today for other healing events
    And give me the prayer of faith to pray for those who are sick.

Amen.

Peter's Sermon in Response

Acts 3:12-26

Peter realized it was an opportunity to preach, so he said,
     "Men of Israel, why are you surprised and why are you
     Staring at us as though we did this?"
     "The God of our fathers has done this miracle, the God of Abraham,
     Isaac and Jacob has done this to honor His servant, Jesus."
     "You betrayed Jesus and denied Him before Pilate,
     Even when Pilate decided to let Him go."
Peter preached straight at them, "You disowned the righteous Jesus
     And begged for Pilate to give you a murderer instead."
     "You were responsible for the death of Christ, but God
     Raised Him from the dead. John and I
     Are witnesses of this truth, we saw Him alive."
     "This man was healed in the name of Jesus.
     It was faith in Christ Jesus that gave this man
     His health and healing, and all of you can see it."
     "I realize that you had no idea what
     The Jewish leaders were doing to Jesus Christ,
     But the prophets foretold that Messiah would suffer,
     And through your blindness this came about."
     "Now you must repent and turn to God so that your sins
     Can be forgiven, and so God can send to you
     Times of refreshing that come from the presence of God."
     "Then God will send Jesus Your Messiah back to you;
     But for now, He must remain in Heaven
     Until the final restoration of all things."
     "This is the prediction of Moses who said, 'The Lord God
     Will raise up a prophet like me; listen to all His messages.'
     'Every soul that will not listen to that prophet
     Shall be utterly destroyed.'"
Peter continued preaching, "All the prophets from Samuel

Onward have predicted these days."
"You are the sons of the prophets who have predicted these
Things, and heirs of the covenant that God made with
        Abraham that
'Through you shall all the families of the earth be blessed.'"
"It was you who God first wanted to bless through His Son Jesus
After He had raised Him from the dead
By forgiving the sins of every one of you."
But many believed who heard what they said,
    So that about 5,000 men now believed.

Lord, I'm encouraged when lives are changed with the Gospel
    And the outward number of believers grows.

            Amen.

The Apostles Arrested

Acts 4:1-3

While Peter and John were talking to the people, the chief priest,
    Captain of the Temple Guard, and some Sadducees
    Were disturbed that they preached Jesus had risen from the dead,
    So they arrested them and put them in jail for the night.

Lord, I know You came first for the salvation of the Jews,
    But I'm glad You provide salvation for all Gentiles...
    But most of all for me.

            Amen.

Peter and John Before the Jewish Leaders

Acts 4:5-12

The next day, the council of Jewish leaders convened in Jerusalem
    With Annas the High Priest, Caiaphas, John, Alexander
    And others of the high priest's relatives.
Then the two disciples were brought in before them
    And were asked, "By what name or authority have you done this?"
Peter, filled with the Holy Spirit, answered, "Leaders and Elders,
    Are you questioning us about the kindness
    Done to a crippled man, and how he was healed?"
    "It is high time that you leaders and all Israel realize this miracle
    Was done in the name of Jesus Christ of Nazareth!"
    "He is the One you crucified, but God raised Him from the dead;
    And by the power of Jesus this man stands here healed."
    "Jesus is the Stone which you builders rejected, but now
    He has become the Cornerstone of the building."
    "Neither is there salvation in any other;
    There is no other name
    Under Heaven given among people, whereby we must be saved."

Lord, give me boldness like Peter to witness for Jesus,
    Especially to those who don't believe in Him.

Amen.

The Jewish Leaders Forbid Preaching in Jesus' Name

Acts 4:13-22

The Jewish leaders were amazed at the boldness of Peter and John
    Because they were uneducated and ignorant men;
    The leaders realized they had been with Jesus

But they could not say anything against the disciples
      Because the healed man was standing with them.
So the leaders ordered the disciples to leave the council
      So they could discuss the issue among themselves saying,
"What are we going to do with these men?"
      "It is evident to everyone in Jerusalem that an outstanding
      Miracle has been done by these men, and we can't deny it."
"Nevertheless, to prevent this thing from spreading, let's
      Command them not to speak in His name again."
So they called Peter and John and commanded them not to
      Speak anymore in the name of Jesus.
Peter and John answered them, "We have to decide whether
      God wants us to listen to you, more than to Him;
      We cannot stop telling everyone what we have seen and heard."
After more threats, they let Peter and John go
      Because they didn't know how to punish them any further.
The people supported them wholeheartedly, glorifying God
      For the miracle on the man who was over 40 years old.

Lord, all life is in Your hands, I praise You for good health;
      I praise You for times when You heal and times when You don't.

Amen.

The Church Prays

Acts 4:23-31

When the apostles were released, they went back to the believers
      And reported what the chief priest and elders said to them;
      The Christians raised their voices to God in praise,
"Almighty Lord, You have made Heaven and earth, the seas and
      Everything in them; You spoke by the Holy Spirit through David,

'Why do the heathen rage,
And the people imagine sinful things,
The kings of the earth unite to fight You,
And oppose the Messiah, Your Son?'"

"For in this city of Jerusalem, the rulers have united to fight
    Against your holy servant, Jesus, the Anointed One."
"Herod, and Pontius Pilate, and the Roman soldiers, and the people of Israel,
    Have gathered together to carry out what You
    Had previously planned to happen."
"Now Lord, listen to their threats and give to us, Your servants,
    Boldness to speak your Word courageously."
"Continue to stretch out Your hand to heal and do miracles
    In the name of Your Holy Servant, Jesus."
When they had finished praying, the room was shaken
    And they were all filled with the Holy Spirit
    And they spoke the Word of God boldly.

Lord, I want to speak boldly for You;
    Fill me with the Holy Spirit and courage.

Amen.

Chapter 20

THE STORY OF BARNABAS: THE RICH YOUNG RULER

A man with a smile as big as his frame walked among the Christians as they waited for a prayer meeting to start. He was tall, huge-shouldered, and heavy, but not fat. He was always well dressed in the finest of clothing and his beard was immaculately manicured.

No one in the church knew when Barnabas was converted. He didn't follow Jesus before the cross and he wasn't one of those who was converted and baptized on the day of Pentecost. Then one day his story came out.

This man was the rich young ruler who had gone to Jesus to ask, "Good Master, what shall I do to inherit eternal life?"

At first, Jesus corrected him saying, "Why are you calling Me good? There is none good but God." But the rich young ruler would not back off, he kept asking, "What must I do to go to Heaven?"

Jesus answered, "You know the commandments, obey them and you shall live. Do not commit adultery, do not kill, do not steal, do not lie, and honor your father and mother."

But there was something in this big man's eyes. The rich young ruler knew that he had kept all the commandments outwardly, but his heart betrayed him; he knew he was not right with God. He answered, "I have done all these things since I was a child, but I am not sure I am going to Heaven."

Jesus looked on him and loved him; then answered, "You only lack one thing, sell all that you have, give to the poor, and come and follow Me."

When the young ruler heard this he nodded only because he understood what Jesus meant. But the more he thought about his money, and his real estate holdings, and all of his clothing, he knew that is was impossible to give them up. Then he began slowly shaking his head "no."

"I can't do it," his eyes were sad. He turned and began walking away.

Jesus commented to the crowd, "It's hard for rich people to enter the kingdom of Heaven, it's easier for a camel to go through the eye of a needle than for a rich man to enter into Heaven."

The big man was a Levite, this was the Jewish tribe set aside to serve God in the Temple. Some Levites were priests who offered animal sacrifices, other Levites were teachers, and still others took care of the physical things of the Temple. God had commanded that the Levites could not own property or acquire wealth; they were to live off the tithes and offerings that worshipers brought to the Temple.[1] And when Levites brought their animals to sacrifice, parts of the animals were given to the Levites to feed their families. God didn't want the greed of riches to choke the ministry of those who serve Him in the Temple.

The rich young ruler owned property. He knew that money deprived him of fellowship with God. His love of money deprived him of entrance into the kingdom of Heaven.

Sometime after meeting Jesus and after the birth of the church, the rich young ruler—named Barnabas—made a decision to sell everything and follow Jesus. It wasn't a dramatic decision, nor did he make it in front of the new growing community called the church. It was a decision made deep in the recesses of his heart.

When the church people gathered to listen to the Word of God, Barnabas came into the assembly with a large sack. No one paid much attention to the sack.

"Is there anything anyone else wants to say?" the red-headed Peter asked the young congregation before dismissing them. It was then when Barnabas made his way to the front of the meeting, and then kneeling before the apostles, laid a large sack of money on the floor at their feet.

"What is this?" Peter, speaking for the crowd, wondering, "What's in the bag?"

"The fruit of my repentance," was all Barnabas could say. Then he confessed that he was a Levite who had illegally owned property on the Island of Cyprus. "I sold it, and I want to give the money to Jesus Christ."

Without asking the other apostles or the congregation, Peter spoke for them all, "The money will go to take care of the widows who are among us." Everyone shook their head in agreement.

Peter walked over to a table with the heavy sack and poured the money out and the clatter could be heard by all as the coins fell on the top of the table.

"OOh-OOh-OOh," the people marveled at the amount of money. It was a lot more than most of the poor people had ever seen in one place. Then they broke into a cheer and applauded loudly. It was both an appreciation to Barnabas for giving the money as well as an applause to God who had provided resources for the young church.

Ananias was sitting on the first row—seats reserved for spiritual leaders—and when he saw all the money, he immediately thought of what he could do with that money, if it were his. Then he thought of buying large quantities of olive oil from the outlying districts and bringing it to Jerusalem for quite a profit.

Later that night, Ananias and Sapphira talked about the public response to the gift of Barnabas. After the meeting was over, the men patted Barnabas on the back, congratulating him. Then they gave Barnabas a seat of honor among the elders; they advanced Barnabas ahead of Ananias. It was a seat Ananias wanted. Sapphira commented, "If you have the seat where Barnabas is now sitting, all the other women would look up to me..." Ananias and Sapphira wanted to give to the church but in return they wanted Christians to "pat" them on the back as they had done Barnabas. Then they hatched a plan.

"I am going to sell all my fields up in Ramar," Ananias said to his wife, "then I'll place the money at the elders' feet just as Barnabas did. My sack of money will be just as big as his sack of money and the church will rejoice in that gift, and they'll appreciate us."

Then Ananias thought of those flasks of olive oil and how he could make money selling them in Jerusalem. Then he suggested an idea to his wife, "I'll keep back a little money to buy some olive oil up in Ramar, and bring it down to Jerusalem to sell it and make a profit." Sapphira nodded her head in approval. Then Ananias added, "For a short period of time we could make enough money to replenish what we gave away and then sometime in the future, we can give that amount of money a second time." Again, Sapphira nodded her head.

Endnote

1. Deuteronomy 18:1-2.

The Church Prospers

Acts 4:32-37

All of the believers were one heart and mind and
>> No one was selfish with their possessions, but
>> Shared freely, as though their things belonged to all.
The apostles continued witnessing boldly the resurrection of the Lord Jesus,
>> And there was a wonderful spirit of fellowship among them all,
>> And there was not a single believer in need of anything.
Those who owned property, sold it and brought the proceeds
>> And placed them at the apostles' feet; then
>> Distribution was made to all in need.
Joseph was given the name Barnabas by the apostles
>>> (a name meaning exhorter);
>> Barnabas was a Levite who broke the Mosaic Law by owning land,
>> So he sold his farm in Cyprus and gave it to the church.
Lord, teach me to be unselfish with all I own. I give it to You.
>> *Guide me how I should spend all my money*
>> *Because everything belongs to You.*

> Amen.

The Sin and Judgment of Ananias and Sapphira

Acts 5:1-11

Another man who owned property named Ananias
    Agreed with his wife Sapphira to sell it
    But they kept back part of the price for themselves.
Ananias placed the remaining money at the apostles' feet,
    But Peter said, "Why have you let satan fill
    Your heart to cheat the Holy Spirit?"
"Why have you kept part of the price for the land?"
    "...The land didn't need to be sold, it was yours;
    The price for the land was also yours."
"Why have you thought you could deceive God?
    You have not lied to the church, you've lied to God!"
When Ananias heard this condemnation, he collapsed and died;
    All who heard it were terrified. The young men
    Covered him with a sheet, and then buried him.
About three hours later, his wife came into the assembly
    Not knowing what happened to her husband.
Peter asked her, "Did you sell your land for so much?"
    "Yes," she answered, "that was the price."
Peter asked, "Why did you agree to cheat the Holy Spirit?
    The young men who buried your husband are at the door";
    Immediately, she collapsed and died.
The young men buried her next to her husband;
    Terror gripped the young church and no one
    Was tempted to lie or cheat God in any way.

Lord, give me a godly fear of telling a lie or
    Doing anything to cheat the Holy Spirit. Keep me honest.

Amen.

Victory in the Early Church

Acts 5:12-16

The apostles were meeting regularly at Solomon's porch
 In the Temple, doing miracles among the people.
But some were afraid to join them for the wrong reasons.
 The believers were well respected by people in general.
As a result more and more became believers
 In growing numbers, men and women.
Many signs and wonders were being done by the apostles;
 As a result, people brought the sick to the streets
 And laid them down so Peter's shadow might fall on them.
A large crowd of people came from other cities,
 Bringing their sick and those who were demon possessed,
 So they could be healed by the apostles.

Lord, keep me excited with the work of evangelism
 So that many people become Christians by my ministry.

Amen.

The Second Persecution

Acts 5:17-42

The high priest and the Sadducees reacted to the
 Work of the apostles, and in jealousy, had the apostles
 Arrested and put in a common prison.
But an angel of the Lord came at night and opened the door
 And led them out, telling them; "Go stand in the
 Temple and tell people about the Christian life."
About sun up they went into the Temple and began to preach;
 Later the members of the Sanhedrin arrived, and gathered the
 Senate and sent for the apostles to come from the jail.
The officers could not find them in the prison. They reported,

"We found the jail locked, and guards on duty, but when
　We opened the door, no one was there."
The Sanhedrin was mystified, wondering what happened to
　　Their prisoners. Then someone arrived to announce that the
　　Prisoners were preaching in the Temple.
The captain went with guards to get them, but didn't
　　Use any violence because they feared the crowd,
　　So they brought them to the Sanhedrin.
The high priest said, "We gave you strict orders not to teach
　　In this name, but you have filled Jerusalem with your
　　Teaching, and accused us of the death of Jesus."
Peter replied, "We must obey God and not men. The
　　God of our fathers raised up Jesus from the dead because
　　You had Him executed on a wooden Roman cross."
"God has exalted this man to His own right hand
　　As Prince and Savior, for the forgiveness of Israel's sin."
"We are witnesses of the resurrection and so is the Holy Spirit
　　Whom God has given to those who obey Him."

When the Sanhedrin heard this, they were furious and wanted to
　　　　execute them
　　But Gamaliel, a Pharisee and teacher greatly respected by all,
　　Stood and gave orders for the apostles to be taken outside.
Gamaliel said, "Men and brethren, be careful what action you take
　　Against these men. Remember, a man named Theudus who
　　Claimed to be something great? He had a following of 400 men."
"When Theudus was killed, his followers were dispersed and the threat
　　　　was gone;
　　Also remember Judas who had a great following. When Judas
　　　　was killed,
　　His followers dispersed."
"I suggest you leave the apostles alone;
　　If their movement is of men, it will break up of its own accord."
"If their movement is of God, you can't do anything about it,

And you may find yourself fighting against God";
    The advice of Gamaliel was accepted.
They called in the apostles and warned them not to preach in this name;
    Then they flogged them and let them go.
The apostles left the Sanhedrin rejoicing, because
    They had been counted worthy to suffer for the name of Jesus.
Day after day, they did not cease preaching and teaching Jesus Christ
    From house to house and in the Temple courts.

Lord, thank You for the courage and boldness of the early church.
    May I always live for You with the same level of courage.
Thank You for using the early church to reach people for Jesus;
    Use me as a witness in the lives of lost people.

Amen.

Chapter 21

THE STORY OF CHOOSING
SEVEN DEACONS

The young church was growing rapidly. Every day people were being converted to Jesus Christ and added to the young church. The apostles were going house to house praying with family groups and celebrating the Lord's Table. Every time a new family came to know Christ, it expanded the work of the apostles.

As more families became Christians, more widows were added to the church roll. The compassionate church wanted to do something for the widows. People were selling everything they had and donating it to the church. The young church had all things in common. So, the young church began feeding their widows every day. Families would cook extra food for them, along with their meals. Clothing was bought for the widows as well as provision for their needs.

Around noon each day in Hezekiah's court, many of the apostles came together to dispense to the widows the food that was brought for them. Several tables were set up and different kinds of food were placed on each table. Some had large pots of food, others had sacks of bread, and other tables held clothing for the widows.

"Line up!" Peter yelled to all the ladies who were crowding up to the tables. Then he yelled louder, "LINE UP." Peter had to yell over the crowd. He wanted to restore order before distributing the food. He began praying, "Let's pray." And every head quickly was bowed in silent reverence. Peter prayed, "*Blessed are You, Lord, our God, King of the Universe....*" These are the beginning words of prayer a Jewish male would have used to thank God for the food.

As quickly as Peter said "AMEN," the ladies erupted into a hub-bub of conversation, and they began pushing to the head of the line. They knew that certain pots of food were better than others. Most knew that Sarah used more roasted lamb in her stew than others. So every woman elbowed her way toward Sarah's stew.

Other women elbowed their way toward certain breads that were baked with a hard crust and still warm from the oven. No one wanted bread that was sometimes two or three days old, and a little stale. Even before lining up, women began to "eye" the food on the tables. Some women tried to touch the breads to find out which ones were still warm.

"KEEP BACK, STAY IN LINE…" Peter again yelled to the women. Some of the other disciples had to stand in a row to keep the women in line.

It took almost an hour of the apostles' time to gather the food, guard the table, and guide the widows through the line. It was so frustrating that Peter asked, "Who wants to try to control crabby women?" Young John wanted to spend more time in prayer noting, "It's not right that we have to come away from our prayers and preaching the Word of God to serve the widows their daily food."

"Yes!" the other disciples nodded in agreement.

Then one of the widows complicated the problem. She yelled out—this complaining Jewish widow who was born outside the Holy Land, "We have to stand in the back of the line because the "holy" widows from the Holy Land get first place in line." The other Hellenistic widows—those from outside the Holy Land—murmured in agreement. It was easy to identify the Hellenistic widows by their dialect and the clothing they wore.

The Hellenistic widows glared at the "holy" widows from the Holy Land, and they glared back. A few mean words were spoken under their breath and both sides could be seen turning their shoulders away from the others in disgust.

"The 'holy' women from the Holy Land are not so 'holy,'" was heard from the criticizing Hellenistic widows.

In that moment, Peter realized there was a problem in the early church. The harmony in the young Body of Christ was broken. Peter could hear it in the tone of their voices, and could see it in some "mean-spirited" eyes. Peter didn't like what he saw. He knew he had to do something because this new "Body of Christ" had been characterized by harmony and unity. Peter remembered how they prayed together earnestly in the upper room for the Holy Spirit to come upon them. Originally, they had only one voice before God, now they were divided with criticism.

Turning to the others, Peter asked, "What are we going to do about this problem?" Peter motioned for them to come with him to pray for an answer from the Holy Spirit. They had to do something before this festering sore contaminated the whole body.

The disciples found a room to pray and fell on their faces, confessing the sins of early greed and selfishness. Philip voiced their concern, "Oh, Lord, what can we do...how can we repent...how can we become unified before an unbelieving world?"

"That's it," Peter announced to the other men who still had their heads bowed in prayer. Peter said that Philip's prayer was the answer to their problem. "We must repent of our sin," Peter announced to the other disciples.

"We must repent by not only telling God we're sorry, but by telling the Hellenistic widows we're sorry." Peter suggested that they appoint seven Hellenistic servants to daily supervise giving food to the widows. Peter explained that these Hellenistic servants should not be from the Holy Land, but rather, these seven servants must be Hellenistic Jews since it was the Hellenistic widows who were complaining.

"If we bend over backward to satisfy this criticism," Peter noted, "then we'll make sure that everyone gets an equal share every day."

Internal Problems in the Early Church

Acts 6:1-7

Even though believers were multiplying in the early church,
>   There were rumblings of discontent among them.
The Hellenistic widows born outside the Holy Land
>   Were complaining about the Jewish widows born in the Holy
>   Land,
Because they were being discriminated against,
>   When food was daily passed out to those in need.
The twelve apostles called the multitude of Christians together
>   And explained that it was not appropriate for them
>   To spend their time supervising a humanitarian hot food
>   kitchen.
They explained, "Look around and pick seven men
>   Of good reputation, practical minded, and filled with
>   The Holy Spirit and faith who can administer this program."
"We will spend our time in prayer
>   And preaching the Word of God."
There was unanimous approval from the multitude
>   So they bent over backward and chose seven Hellenistic men
>   Beginning with Stephen because he was filled with the Holy Spirit.
They also chose Philip, Prochorus, Nicanor, Timon,
>   Parmenas, and Nicholas of Antioch who had
>   Just become a Christian.
These seven men were brought before the apostles
>   Who laid their hands upon them and committed them to God.
As a result, the Word of God reached a larger circle of listeners
>   And the number of disciples multiplied greatly.
Also, a number of priests—those who hated Christianity—were saved
>   When they saw how the early church handled
>   Its money problems and internal griping.

Lord, thank You that the early church repented
    And bent over backward to deal with criticism.
May I always go-the-extra-mile when criticized
    To show others the spirit of forgiveness and compassion.

Amen

The Ministry of Stephen the Deacon

Acts 6:8-15

Stephen, a deacon filled with the Holy Spirit and power,
    Worked miracles and signs among the masses.
He got opposition from the synagogues of freemen,
    Hellenistic Jews from Cyrene, Alexandria, Cilicia and Asia.
They debated with Stephen, but couldn't answer his
    Wisdom and spirit. So the freemen brought in
    Men to lie, saying Stephen cursed Moses and God.
This stirred up the people and elders and teachers of the law
    So they seized Stephen and brought him
    Before the Sanhedrin to face false witnesses,
Who said Stephen spoke against the Holy Spirit and the law,
    Also claiming Stephen said, "Jesus will destroy the Temple
    And change the customs handed down by Moses."
The members of the Sanhedrin saw Stephen's face
    Become as radiant as an angel's face.

Lord, when I take a bold stand against Your enemies,
    May they experience Your love flowing through my life
    And may they see Your beauty in my countenance.

Amen

349

Chapter 22

THE STORY OF STEPHEN

The scene was chaotic. Curious spectators came running to see him die, young zealous Levites quickly picked up rocks to join the fracas; the crowd was screaming for blood. The women were chanting,

"STONE HIM...STONE HIM...STONE HIM...."

Stephen, a leader in the new sect of the way, was a follower of Jesus. Blood trickled from his mouth. His arms were raised to ward off the rocks. An open gash on the back of his head was throbbing.

The crowd was not punishing him because he was a follower of Jesus Christ, they hated him because he had debated the Jewish teachers of the law and won. Stephen was a Jew from outside the Holy Land where he was learned in Gentile logic. The Sanhedrin had not previously faced the arguments of Stephen who interpreted the Old Testament from a Gentile point of view. So the defeated Levites beat him with their fists as they were dragging him out of the Temple.

"DRAG HIM TO THE VALLEY OF HINNON AND STONE HIM!"

"YES...," was the mob's reply.

At first they were just going to punish him, but the smell of blood in the nose of a predator spurs it to the kill. By the time they yelled to stone him, murder was the assumed conclusion in the minds of everyone.

Saul, a young member of the Sanhedrin, was not at the debate. He, like Stephen, was born outside the Holy Land. He could have answered the logic of Stephen. Saul was a Jew from Tarsus in Asia, a city of liberal education and a center of the arts. Saul was brilliant in debate because he brought a fresh interpretation to the Law. When Saul heard the clamor of the crowd; he came running.

"HERE…" Saul yelled to the stone-throwers, "I'll hold your tunics."

Saul watched the punishing stones, some missing. But no one defended the martyr, no one quieted the crowd, no one came to his rescue. The leader of the Sanhedrin arrived; the action stopped momentarily when the elderly entourage got there. Everyone looked to the leader for permission to continue, the old Jewish leader had been hastily summoned; he did not have on his official garments. He asked those assembled, "Has this man done something worthy of death?"

It was a question that would not be answered, at least not out loud. Saul thought, "Kill these Christians because they blaspheme God…because they won't bring a sacrificial lamb…because they say Jesus is God…because they do miracles by magic…because they claim Jesus arose from the dead."

Saul wanted Stephen to die, just as Jesus was killed; but no cross to make Stephen a hero, as the Christians made Jesus a legend.

The crowd stood sober…waiting…ready. Then the leader of the Sanhedrin asked again,

"Has this man done anything worthy of death?"

"YES!" the old members of the Sanhedrin yelled first.

"YES!" the other members joined in the vote.

"YES!" shouted young Saul who was glad to see a Christian die.

One stone was thrown, Stephen put up a hand to divert it away. Then three or four stones were thrown at the same time, he couldn't divert them all. A rock thrown from the rear hit Stephen in the head.

THUD.

Stephen knew it was over. Already on his knees, he looked to Heaven to pray,

"Lord Jesus…" peace came over his face, "Lord, forgive their sin…I pray for them…save them."

Even those who hated him most, momentarily stopped their assault to hear what he was saying. Stephen looked into the sky...he saw Jesus, but the crowd thought he was just looking up. Saul didn't see anything but he was just interested in the last words of this man before he died. Most historians analyze the last words before death, for they usually reveal what a man truly believes, and how he lived.

Stephen looked into Heaven. He saw Jesus sitting at the right hand of the throne of God, and Stephen recognized Jesus. Although he had not seen the Master with his physical eyes, he recognized Him in death because he had prayed to Him so many times. Jesus began walking toward Stephen as a person goes to meet a friend, Stephen reached out to Jesus. Saul heard his prayer, so did everyone in the rock quarry, although no one saw Jesus but Stephen. Saul looked up to see what Stephen was staring at, he saw nothing. Stephen cried out,

"Lord Jesus...receive my spirit."

Stephen died a martyr's death, but rocks did not smash the breath from his lungs. The Lord Jesus took him.

The Sermon by Stephen

Acts 7:1-52

The high priest asked if the charges against Stephen were true;
    Stephen answered, "My brother and father listen to me,
The God of glory appeared to Abraham while he was in Mesopotamia,
    Before Abraham went to Haran God said,
'Leave your country and family and go to a land I will show you;'
    So Abraham left Chaldea and settled in Haran,
    Staying there until his father died."
"Then Abraham left to come to this land where we now live today
    But God did not give him the land while he was alive,
But promised to give it to him and his descendents,
    Even though he was childless when the promise was made."

"Then God told him, 'Your descendents will be strangers
    In a foreign country, where they will become slaves
    And be oppressed for 400 years.'"
"God promised to judge the nation that enslaved them, then
    God promised His people would worship Him in this land."

Lord, Stephen thought it was important to show
    That You spoke to people who were not in the Promised Land.
Since You spoke to people before they entered the Promised Land,
    That meant now You could offer salvation to Gentiles outside
    The Promised Land.
Stephen was laying a foundation to prove You would bless
    The apostles as they went to preach to every person,
    Beginning at Jerusalem, then going to Judea, Samaria, and the world.

Stephen continued preaching,
    "God made a covenant of circumcision with them, so Isaac
    Was circumcised on the eighth day."
    "Isaac did the same for Jacob, and Jacob did it
    For his twelve sons who became the twelve patriarchs."
    "The patriarchs were jealous of Joseph and sold him
    Into slavery in Egypt, but God was with him."
    "God rescued Joseph and made him wise enough to get
    Pharaoh's attention who then made him governor of Egypt."

Lord, You called Your servant Joseph to serve You but
    The Jewish establishment rejected Him,
    Just as they rejected Jesus.
Lord, this helps me understand why
    The religious establishment
    Rejects Jesus today.

Stephen continued preaching,
    "When famine caused suffering and devastation throughout
    Egypt and Canaan, our ancestors had nothing to eat."

"When Jacob heard there was grain for sale in Egypt, he sent his
Ten sons there on their first visit to buy food."
"On the second visit, Joseph made himself known
To his brothers, and then told Pharaoh about his family."
"Jacob went to live in Egypt, where he and his family died;
Their bones were brought back and buried at Shechem
In the tomb Abraham purchased from Hamor, the father of
Shechem."

Lord, when I read how enemies persecuted Your people in Scripture,
It helps me understand why the world
Persecutes Your people today.

Stephen continued preaching,
"The nation of Israel grew larger in Egypt. A new king
Took the throne who didn't know Joseph. He oppressed
Our people and victimized our ancestors,
Forcing parents to abandon their babies."
"During this time Moses was born, he was no ordinary child;
For three months he was cared for at home."
"But when Moses was exposed to Pharaoh's daughter
She adopted him and raised him as her own child."
"Moses was taught all the wisdom of the Egyptians
And became mighty in speech and actions."
"At the age of forty he decided to visit his Jewish people;
He saw one of his fellow countrymen being abused
And defended him by killing the Egyptian."
"Moses thought the Jews would understand that
God would use him to deliver them;
But they didn't understand, nor respond positively to him."
"The next day Moses saw two Israelites fighting and He
separated them;
The attacker said, 'Who made you our leader and judge?
Will you kill me as you did the Egyptian yesterday?'"

"Moses fled when he heard the accusations, realizing his actions
Were known. He fled to the land of Midian
Where he became father of two sons."
"Forty years later in the desert near Mount Sinai,
An angel appeared to him in the flames of
A burning bush and he was curious."
"As he drew closer to the bush, a voice said,
'I am the God of your ancestors,
The God of Abraham, Isaac, and Jacob.'"
"Moses trembled and couldn't look at the fire;
The LORD said, 'Take off your shoes, you
Are standing on holy ground.'"
"The LORD also said, 'I have seen the suffering of My people,
And I have heard their cries for deliverance,
And I have come down to deliver them.'"
"Come do My command, go deliver My people from Egypt."
"'This was the same Moses they rejected saying,
'Who made you our leader and judge?'"
"Now Moses was sent by God to be both leader and judge;
He performed miracles and signs in Egypt, then led them
Through the Red Sea and through the desert forty years."
"Moses told the people, 'God will raise up a prophet for you,
Like myself, from among your people.'"
"Moses was the mediator between the people and God;
He gave them the living law of God from Mount Sinai."
"But the people rejected Moses, and wanted to return to Egypt;
They asked Aaron to make idols for them so
They could have gods to lead them back to Egypt."
"They made a golden calf and offered sacrifices to it
And were happy in what they were doing."
"God gave them up and let them worship the sun
The moon, and the stars as their gods."
"In the Book of Amos, the LORD God asks,

'Were you sacrificing to Me forty years in the wilderness?'
'No! You carried the sanctuary of Moloch on your backs
You carried the star-God of Rephen in your hearts.'
'You worshiped idols that you made
So I will exile you to Babylon.'"
"While in the desert, our forefathers carried the Tabernacle
With them that Moses had them construct
From the pattern that God gave him."

Stephen continued preaching,
    "It was handed down from one generation to another
    Until Joshua conquered the nations and drove them out
    And the Tabernacle was set up in the new territory."
    "Israel worshiped in the Tabernacle until the time of David,
    Then he asked for permission to build a Temple for Israel,
    Though Solomon actually built the house of God."
    "Even so, the Most High does not live in a house
    Built by human hands, as the prophet quoted You, saying;
    'Heaven is My home, the earth is My footstool,
    What kind of home could you build for Me?
    Didn't I make the heavens and the earth?'"

Lord, so many people are turning to sin,
    Turning from You and turning to the world.
Also, people with a hardened heart are persecuting
    The preachers that You send to call Your people back to You.
Lord, may I never be a persecutor of others.

Stephen continued preaching,
    "You are stiff-necked with a heathen heart; you are
    Resisting the Holy Spirit, just as your ancestors;
    Name one prophet your ancestors didn't persecute."
    "In the past they killed the prophets who predicted
    The coming of the Just One;
    The One you betrayed and murdered."

"You had the Law given to you by angels, but
You have deliberately destroyed it."

They were outraged when they heard these stinging
Accusations against themselves.
Stephen was filled with the Holy Spirit, looked into Heaven
And saw the glory of God and Jesus standing at God's right hand.
He said, "I see the heavens opened and the Son of Man
Standing at the right hand of God."
But they covered their ears with their hands and furiously
Yelled at him, and rushed at him and carried him
Out of the city and stoned him.
They dropped their coats at the feet of a young man named Saul
And stoned Stephen who called on God saying,
"Lord Jesus, receive my spirit."
Then kneeling, Stephen cried out to God;
"Lord, forgive their sin,"
And with these words, he died and Saul approved of his death.

Amen.

Chapter 23

THE STORY OF SAUL'S
RISE TO POWER

Saul went to the Sanhedrin. He had a plan to stop the spread of Christianity. When they stoned Stephen, they had stopped the street preaching of Christians; they no longer gathered publicly for prayer. Jewish spies reported Christians were leaving Jerusalem for other cities—Alexandria, Babylon, and Damascus. They chose these cities because of the large Jewish populations there. Saul was furious,

"Christians are going to proselytize their relatives…," he announced to the Sanhedrin. Saul spoke from the back row to the assembly of 70 men. Paul was in the back row because he was not yet 30 years of age. He was a youngster among the ancient elders.

With his fist clenched, the blood vessels on his temple popped out and the tempo of his voice rose to a speedier pitch.

Paul reasoned, "We must stop the spread of Christianity…," he paused to look from face to face, they agreed. "We MUST stop them." They all nodded approval, anticipating his plan.

"I'll go to Damascus," Saul suggested, "arrest the Christians, then get a letter of extradition to bring them to Jerusalem."

"You can't do that," an old Rabbi stroked his beard to embarrass young Saul. "We have no legal rights in Damascus." Several of the older members of the Sanhedrin muttered their agreement. Another member spoke against Saul, "We have no legal authority outside the Holy Land."

"Yes we do," Saul snapped at the old man. Saul was a student of Gamaliel, which meant he did his research well before speaking. "Yes, we have legal authority…in Damascus…in Alexandria…in Babylon." Saul stopped to make his point, then continued, "We have a legal authority over Jews anywhere in the Roman Empire."

Saul explained some history to the hushed assembly. He revealed how the High Priest supported Julius Caesar in his battle to defeat Pompeii in Egypt in 68 B.C. In return, Caesar gave to Hyreanus II, the High Priest and all succeeding High Priests, spiritual authority over all Jews in the Roman Empire.

Then Saul concluded, "These Christians are Jews…legal-born Jews…." The group of men smiled at the brilliance of the young Saul. Then Saul smiled back at the Sanhedrin when he saw they were on his side. Then Saul said, "This is a spiritual matter of the highest urgency. It threatens the faith of Jews everywhere."

The group broke out into applause to show appreciation and agreement. But Saul didn't want their gratitude yet. He had one last thing to add, "We can't let the authorities in these other towns deal with these Christians. They won't stop the Christians. They won't punish them as we dealt with Stephen. We must arrest the Christian leaders, bring them back to Jerusalem, and let them feel the fury of the stones."

"YES," the Sanhedrin shouted. "Yes. Yes."

Saul had not gone to the High Priest privately with his plan for fear of rejection, rejection because he was so young. So Saul used the public platform of the Sanhedrin to intimidate the High Priest. Saul wanted the Sanhedrin to pressure the High Priest. Saul carried the day, the Sanhedrin agreed; now would the High Priest agree? All eyes looked way from Saul to the High Priest.

The room sensed tension between young Saul and the old High Priest. It was a generation gap between a young hot head and the older, wiser leader. The eyes of the Sanhedrin darted from Saul's face to the High Priest's eyes. Would the old man approve the bold initiative? He slowly opened his lips to speak,

"I will give Saul a letter of authority."

With one ingenious plan, young Saul—not yet 30 years old—became one of the leading forces in the Sanhedrin. Saul achieved authority that some members never get in a lifetime. Saul became the representative of the High Priest and a powerful voice of the Sanhedrin.

Christians Leave Jerusalem

Acts 8:1-4

Saul approved of the death of Stephen
      And immediately that day a storm of persecution
      Erupted in Jerusalem against the church
And believers fled into the countrysides of Judea and Samaria
      To escape persecution, except the apostles;
      However, some reverently buried Stephen and mourned for him.
Saul then worked feverishly to destroy all remains of the church,
      Going house to house, he dragged men and women to prison;
      Christians who were scattered went everywhere preaching the Word.

Lord, thank You for the example of martyrs who gave all in death;
      Others were willing to suffer or go to prison for You.
I'll give You everything in life, and if I have to suffer or die,
      Give me the spirit to do all for Your glory.

Philip Ministers in Samaria

Acts 8:5-25

So Philip the deacon went to Samaria to preach Christ;
      The crowds paid close attention to what Philip preached
      Because they heard about what he did and saw His miracles.
Evil spirits screamed as they were cast out of their victims
      And the paralyzed and lame were healed;
      As a result, there was great joy in the city.

A man named Simon had formerly been practicing magic
      And amazed crowds by the mystifying things he did,
      The people said, "Simon must be sent by God."
Previously, the people had listened to him because of his magic
      But Simon became a believer when Philip preached.
Many men and women were converted and baptized because of Philip
      Who preached the Kingdom of God and the name of Jesus Christ;
      Simon also was baptized because he believed.
Simon followed Philip everywhere he went
      Because he was astonished at the miracles he saw.

When the apostles in Jerusalem heard all that was happening
      In Samaria, they sent Peter and John to check it out.
Peter and John prayed for the Samaritans to receive the Holy Spirit;
      They had been baptized in the name of the Lord Jesus,
      But they had not received the Holy Spirit.

So the apostles laid hands on the people and prayed for them,
      And they received the Holy Spirit.
When Simon saw that the people received the Holy Spirit
      He wanted the same power in his hands.
So Simon offered them money saying,
      "Give me this power so I can lay hands on people
      So they can receive the Holy Spirit."
Peter erupted, "Your money will go to hell, and you with it,
      Because you think money can buy what God gives for free."
"You have no part in this ministry,
      Because your heart is not right with God."
"Turn from your wickedness and pray to God. Perhaps
      He will forgive your sin for thinking this evil."
"It is plain that you are a prisoner of greed;" Simon cried out,
      "Pray for me that nothing you said will happen to me."
The apostles preached in that city and many other Samaritan villages
      Then returned to Jerusalem.

Lord, there are some in the church who don't possess eternal life,
   They only pretend to be Christians, but they're really lost.
Help me to realize who they are, and may I help them
   Come to know You as Lord and Savior of their life.

Philip Ministers to the Ethiopian Eunuch

Acts 8:26-40

The angel of the Lord then spoke to Philip,
   "Go south to the route through the desert from Jerusalem to Gaza."
There Philip saw an important Ethiopian official who was returning
   From worshiping in Jerusalem.
This Ethiopian was the country's treasurer, who was
   Reading the Book of Isaiah out loud to his entourage
   As he rode along in his chariot.
The Holy Spirit told Philip, "Go meet this man;"
   As Philip approached, he heard the man reading from Isaiah;
   Philip asked, "Do you understand what you're reading?"
"How can I," the man answered, "unless someone helps me;"
   So the Ethiopian invited Philip to ride with him.
He was reading, "We are like sheep that are led to the slaughter,
   Like a lamb that says nothing before its shearers,
   He never opened His mouth."
"He was humiliated, but no one defended Him;
   Who will ever talk about his descendents,
   Since His life is cut short on earth?"
The Eunuch asked Philip, "Is this passage a reference
   To the prophet who wrote it, or to someone else?"
Beginning with this text, Philip explained to him
   The Good News of Jesus Christ.
A little farther they came to a pool of water. The Eunuch said,
   "Look at the water, is there any reason why I can't

Be baptized right here, right now?"
The Eunuch ordered the chariot to stop, then the Eunuch
    And Philip went down into the water and Philip baptized him.
After they came out of the water, the Holy Spirit
    Caught away Philip. The Eunuch never saw him again,
    Then the treasurer went on his way rejoicing.
Philip found himself in Azotus, and continued preaching
    The Good News in every town until he got to Caesarea.

Lord, may I always rejoice when someone gets saved and baptized;
    Help me be a faithful witness to lost people.
Lord, there are many religious people who are blinded to the truth,
    Even as the Eunuch who didn't understand the Scriptures he read.
May I be able to help them understand Your truth,
    And lead them to a saving knowledge of Jesus Christ.

Amen.

Chapter 24

THE STORY OF PAUL'S CONVERSION

Several weeks later, Paul was part of a caravan of camels, donkeys, and weary travelers who reached the mountain of balsam trees west of the Baca Valley. They could see Damascus in the distance from the top of the hills. Looking back they could see the cedars of Lebanon across the Baca Valley and to the south they could see Mt. Hermon, the snow-covered mountain of the Holy Land.

Saul not only had a letter form the High Priest to arrest and extradite Jews to Jerusalem, he had a letter of credit to pay his expenses. Saul was riding a horse, the most luxurious of all ways to travel. He was not being bounced on the back of a donkey, nor was he being jerked about on camel back. Rich people rode horses, as did army officers, so Saul used his letter of credit to secure a fine horse, one that called attention to the importance that he thought his new office demanded. His luggage was being brought by porters, again an opulent show of wealth. From time to time, Saul would ride out to high observation points, there he sat like a Roman Army officer surveying a battlefield. It gave Saul a sense of self-worth.

The caravan descended the green fertile hills onto the flat plain of Ghuta. Shortly, they would drink from the Barada River, then follow the river to the city of Damascus. They would enter the "East Gate" to the city. Saul planned to ride his steed triumphantly down the street called Straight that ran east and west, straight through the city. They would reach the city at high noon, the time to make the greatest entrance.

Saul's horse drank deeply in the Barada River, he paused for a rest while the caravan went before him. When he finally caught up to the caravan, his luggage handlers were walking at the rear of the caravan. It wasn't a place Saul wanted to ride for very long, he was eating the dust of the other animals.

Saul took a white cloth to wipe the perspiration from his face and neck. He tilted his head back and looked into the sun, directly into its blinding rays. The light of the sun exploded brighter than any sun Saul had ever seen. He was blinded with its brilliance, but it was not the noon sun that blinded Saul. The intense light—the light that blinded Saul—was the Lord Jesus Christ Himself.

The horse, sensing fear, began kicking wildly. Saul was not a trained horseman; he couldn't handle a kicking horse. Blinded by the searing light and losing his equilibrium, he fell to the ground. The light was so intense, Saul covered his face with both hands; sandy hands he had used to break his fall. Covering his face with his dirty hands, he couldn't look at the sun; he couldn't look at Jesus Christ. Saul couldn't see anything.

Saul was blind.

The luggage handlers saw the intense light. They dropped their burden to the ground, and cowered in fear. They didn't know what was happening, but they knew it was supernatural. They heard a voice from Heaven, it was noise to them; they couldn't make out the words. But they knew someone was speaking to Saul. A voice spoke to Saul in the Hebrew language,

"Saul…," his blinded eyes looked skyward, but were unable to see, "Saul, why are you persecuting Me?"

"Who are You?" Saul stammered an answer.

"I am Jesus…," the voice from Heaven answered. "You think you are persecuting Christians, but you are persecuting Me."

Saul quickly processed everything in his mind. He hated Christians and was willing to kill them, just as other Jewish leaders killed Jesus. He knew Christians claimed Jesus was not dead, but was alive. Now Jesus was talking to him. Saul heard the voice,

"I am Jesus...it is hard to kick against the truth." Saul lay groveling in the dirt, thrown by a kicking horse. Instantly, Saul knew his whole legalistic approach to God was wrong. Christians didn't just have a better system of religion, they believed in a person. They followed Christ. Saul answered,

"Lord...," it was the first time Saul acknowledged the deity of Jesus Christ. "Lord..., what do you want me to do?"

In that statement, Saul yielded himself to a person. It would take awhile to sort out his theology, and he would have to think his way through all the changes that would be required in his lifestyle. But lying on the ground, Saul made one monumental change—he recognized the person of Jesus Christ. Even though blinded, Saul had seen the light. Even though blinded by the light, Saul had seen the brilliance of Jesus Christ. In yieldedness, Saul asked,

"What do you want me to do?"

The Lord gave him instructions, "Arise," Saul was to get up off the ground. "Get up, go into the city; you will be told what to do."

The horse had run away, the luggage carriers didn't go after it for the horse was not their concern. They had seen the blinding light and heard a voice speaking from Heaven. Now working for a blinded employer, they had to get him to the city if they wanted their money. The city gate was right ahead. Taking Saul by the arm, they led him on the street called Straight, to a house of a Jewish man named Judah. What a spectacle, Saul did not have a triumphant entrance upon a fine white horse. Saul was being led by his luggage handlers, he had blinded eyes and dirty robes— God had humbled Saul.

Saul was ugly, because his eyes were ugly. Not only was he blinded, but also rubbing sand into his eyes had irritated them and bloodied them. The more he tried to open his eyes, the more intense his pain, like needles piercing his eyeballs. Any light was unbearable. Saul squeezed them to shut out any light, then rubbed them until they bled. The more his eyes bled, the more Saul rubbed them creating huge ugly blood-crusted scabs in place of eyes. Saul had been spiritually blind, now he was also physically blind.

The Conversion of Saul

Acts 9:1-19

Meanwhile, Saul was still threatening to destroy every Christian;
> He had a letter from the High Priest that gave him authority
> To arrest Christians in Damascus and bring them to Jerusalem.
Suddenly, as he almost reached Damascus, a blinding light
> From Heaven shone all about him.
Saul fell to the ground and heard a voice saying,
> "Saul, Saul, why are you persecuting Me?"
Saul answered, "Who are you, Lord?" The voice answered,
> "I am Jesus whom you are persecuting."
"Now get up and go into the city, and
> You will be told what you must do."
The men traveling with Saul stood speechless.
> They heard the sound, but didn't see anyone.
Saul got up from the ground, but when he opened his eyes,
> He could see nothing. He was blind,
> So they led him into the city of Damascus.
There he remained blind for three days;
> During that time, he ate and drank nothing.

Lord, I've met You and was saved. While my conversion
> *Was not as dramatic as Saul's, I nevertheless know You are real;*
I once was blind in my sin, but now I see.

In Damascus there was a follower of Christ named Ananias.
> The Lord called him by name in a dream. He responded,
> "Here am I, Lord."
"Go to the street called Straight" the Lord said, "to the

House of Judah and ask for Saul from Tarsus. He is
    Praying. Saul knows you are coming
    To lay hands upon his eyes to restore his sight."
But Ananias replied, "Lord, I have heard evil reports
    About this man. He has done terrible things to Your servants;
    He has come with authority to arrest those who call on Your name."
The Lord said to Ananias, "Go pray for him, because I have chosen
    Saul as an instrument to preach My name before Gentiles and Kings
    And he will suffer much for My name's sake."
So Ananias found Saul, and laid hands on him, and said, "Brother
    Saul, the Lord Jesus who appeared to you on the road sent me
    So you will be filled with the Holy Spirit and get your sight back."
Instantly, the scales fell from his eyes and Saul could see;
    Then he was baptized, and ate and was strengthened;
    Saul stayed with Christians in Damascus for a while.

Lord, Saul began serving You immediately after he was saved,
    Help me be diligent in serving You, as did Saul.
Lead me today to people and places where I can serve You,
    I want to be busy in the work of Your Kingdom.

Saul Begins Preaching the Gospel

Acts 9:20-31

Immediately Saul went to the Synagogues to preach the Good News
    That Jesus was indeed the Son of God.
All who heard Saul were amazed, and asked, "Isn't this the man
    Who arrested Christians in Jerusalem
    And came here to do the same thing?"
Saul became more fervent in preaching;
    The Damascus Synagogue was silenced
    By the strength of Saul's preaching that Jesus was the Christ.

After a time, the Jews plotted to kill Saul, but he heard about it;
      The assassins waited at the gate night and day, but at night the
      Believers helped Saul escape over the wall in a basket.
When Saul got to Jerusalem, he tried to join the Christians
      But they were afraid of him.
      They were not sure Saul was a true believer.
Barnabas received Saul and introduced him to the apostles,
      And explained how the Lord appeared to Saul, and
      What the Lord had said to him, and how Saul had preached
      In the name of Jesus boldly in the Synagogue in Damascus.
Then the believers accepted Saul and he preached boldly among them,
      Some Greek-speaking Jews to whom Saul preached
      Then plotted to murder him.
The believers heard about it and took Saul to Caesarea,
      And then sent him to his hometown in Tarsus.

Lord, although the church was no longer threatened by persecution;
      They grew in number, and spiritual maturity.
They no longer worried about persecution, but they feared the Lord
      Because the Holy Spirit was their Comforter.

Lord, help me to be a persistent witness to You
      Even when people refuse to believe and reject my message.
May opposition make me stronger in my faith, and
      More determined to serve You.

          Amen.

Ministry of Peter

Acts 9:32-43

Lord, Peter was traveling to evangelize the lost
      And encourage the churches. When he came to Lydda,
      He found Aeneas who had been paralyzed eight years.
Peter said, "Aeneas, Jesus Christ heals you, get up; and
      Fold your mat." He was healed instantly.

Everyone living in the area turned to the Lord
    When they saw Aeneas walking.

A woman named Dorcas who lived in Joppa, died;
    She was a believer who always did kind things for
    Others, especially the poor. Her friends prepared the body
    For burial and placed it in an upstairs room.
When the people learned Peter was nearby, they sent two men
    To bring him to Joppa. When Peter arrived,
    He went upstairs to where Dorcas lay.
The room was filled with widows who showed Peter
    The clothes Dorcas had made for them. Peter
    Sent them out of the room, and knelt to pray.
Peter turned to the dead body and said, "Tabitha, stand up;"
    She opened her eyes, looked at Peter, and sat up;
    Peter helped her to her feet and presented her to the believers.
When the people of Joppa heard of the miracle,
    Many of them believed in the Lord.
Peter stayed there for some time,
    Living with Simon, the Tanner.

Lord, I know You can do all things, I praise You
    That You hold life and health in Your hands.
Give me faith to trust You to do miracles;
    When I don't know how to pray, teach me how,
    And show me the things for which I must pray.

Amen.

God Sends a Message to Cornelius

Acts 10:1-8

A captain in the Italian regiment of the Roman Army
    Was stationed at the military fortress in Caesarea, named

Cornelius.
He was a religious man who led his whole family
 To worship God, give to the poor and prayed constantly.
About 3:00 P.M. Cornelius saw an angel come to him in a vision
 As he stared at the angel in fear, Cornelius said,
 "What do you want with me?"
The angel answered, "God has heard your prayers, and seen
 Your works for the poor, so now He will answer you."
"Send some men to Joppa to get Simon Peter,
 Who is a guest in the home of Simon the Tanner,
 Who lives by the sea."
When the angel went away, Cornelius told what happened to two
 Of his servants and a soldier who was religious;
 He then sent them to Joppa to get Peter.

Lord, I'm glad You have compassion on extremely religious people
 Who seek You, but have never heard the Gospel.
Thank You for making a way for people like Cornelius to hear the Gospel;
 I pray for the billions of unsaved who have never heard,
 Stir their hearts to seek salvation in Christ, as you did Cornelius.

Peter's Vision and His Response

Acts 10:9-23

As they approached Joppa the next day about noon, Peter
 Was praying up on the roof top while the others were
 Preparing lunch; Peter was ready to eat.
It was then Peter had a vision where he saw Heaven opened
 And a large sheet being lowered by the four corners.
In it were all kinds of animals, reptiles and wild birds;
 He heard a voice say, "Get up, Peter, kill and eat."
Peter answered, "I can't do that Lord."
 "I have never eaten anything that was unclean or defiled."

The voice spoke again, "Do not call anything unclean
> That God has cleansed." This happened three times,
> Then the sheet was taken back to Heaven.
As Peter was thinking about what just happened,
> The men sent by Cornelius arrived at the gate to house.
They called out, "Is there a guest here by the name of Simon Peter?"
> Peter was still trying to understand what he saw
> When the Spirit of God said, "Three men are looking for you."
"Do not hesitate to go with them for I have sent them;"
> Then Peter went down and told them, "I am Peter,
> Why have you come looking for me?"
They told Peter, "Our leader, Cornelius, sent us to invite you
> To come to his house so he could hear what you have to say."
They also told Peter that Cornelius was a good man, who
> Worshiped God, and the Jewish people respected him.
Peter invited the men into the house,
> And they stayed the night with Peter.

Lord, I'm grateful for those who go to the billions who have never heard,
> *Some go to dangerous situations, some give up riches and positions.*
Bless those who preach the Gospel to those who have never heard,
> *May many hear and believe and be saved.*
Lord, I'm willing to go where You send me, and I'm willing to do
> *Anything You want me to do, just guide me today.*

Amen.

Peter and Cornelius Exchange Greetings

Acts 10:24-33

The following day Peter arrived in Caesarea at Cornelius' house
> Where he was waiting for Peter with all his relations and
> friends.

As Peter was about to enter, Cornelius met him and
Bowed at his feet saying he was unworthy to receive Peter.
But Peter made him rise saying, "Stand up, I am only a man;"
And Peter went inside with Cornelius, where he found a crowd
And said, "You know that a Jew can't associate with Gentiles."
Peter explained, "God has shown me that
I must not consider any person ritually unclean or defiled."
"Therefore, I came without objection.
Now, why did you send for me?"
Cornelius explained, "About this time three days ago
I was praying in my house when suddenly
A man in shining garments appeared to me, saying,
'God has heard your prayers, and seen your charity, send
Your servants to Joppa for a man named Peter,
He is a guest at the home of Simon a Tanner.'"
"So I sent for you at once—thank you for coming;
Now we are all here in the presence of God
Waiting to hear anything God has told you to say to us."

Lord, there are many who are hungry to hear the Good News,
May I always be willing and ready to tell them about Jesus.

Amen.

Peter's Sermon in Cornelius' Home

Acts 10:34-43

Then Peter spoke to the gathering, "God does not play favorites
But He accepts people from any nation who do the right things."
"God sent His message of peace through Jesus Christ to Israel
Because Jesus is Lord of all."
"You know what happened throughout Judea, beginning in Galilee,
After the Baptism of John, how God anointed Jesus of Nazareth

With the Holy Spirit and power,
"He went about doing good, healing all under the devil's power,
Because God was with Him."
"We are witnesses of everything Jesus did in Judea and Jerusalem,
And we saw they killed Him by hanging Jesus on a tree."
"Yet three days later God raised Him from the dead,
And He was seen by witnesses God had chosen."
"Now we are those witnesses, we have eaten and drank with Him,
After He was raised from the dead."
"Now God has commanded us to tell people everywhere,
That He has appointed Jesus to judge everyone, alive or dead,
And the prophets witness to this fact, that all who believe in Jesus
Will have their sin forgiven through His name."

Lord, remind me how simple is the plan of salvation;
People only have to believe in Jesus to be saved.
I praise You that Peter went to people of different cultures and customs;
May I always be willing to share the Gospel with all people,
No matter if they are different from me or not.

Amen.

Gentiles Are Baptized With the Holy Spirit and Water

Acts 10:44-48

While Peter was speaking, the Holy Spirit was poured out
On those who were listening to Peter's sermon.
The Jewish Christians who came with Peter were astonished
That the Holy Spirit was poured out on Gentiles
Because they were speaking in unknown languages and praising God.
Peter said, "Can anyone refuse water baptism to these
Who have received the Holy Spirit just as we did on Pentecost?"

He then gave instructions to baptize them in the name of Jesus Christ;
    Cornelius asked Peter to stay a few days.

Lord, I want the Holy Spirit to fill me with His presence;
    I want Your power and joy in my life and service.
May I never be scared or intimidated by unsaved people,
    May I always be open to the Holy Spirit and His blessing.

Amen.

Peter Explains His Actions to the Jerusalem Church

Acts 11:1-18

The apostles and brethren in Judea were critical when they heard
    That Gentiles had accepted the Word of God and been baptized.
When Peter visited Jerusalem, those who still demanded circumcision
    Were critical because Peter visited and ate with Gentiles.
Peter gave them a whole background of how it happened;
    He said, "I was praying in Joppa when I had a vision
Of a big sheet let down from Heaven by its four corners;
    I saw in it all types of beasts, reptiles, and birds,
Then I heard a voice from Heaven, 'Get up Peter, kill and eat;'
    But I answered, 'I can't do that Lord, I have never
    Eaten anything that was unclean or defiled.'"
"Then I heard the voice a second time saying, 'Do not call anything
    Unclean that God has cleansed.' This happened three times
    Then the sheet was taken back to Heaven."
"Just as that happened, three men sent by Cornelius arrived at the gate;
    They said they were sent from Caesarea to get me,
    The Holy Spirit told me not to hesitate to go with them."
Then Peter explained, "These six brothers standing here went with me
    And we went into Cornelius' home."
"He told us that he had seen an angel when he was praying

That told him 'Send to Joppa to get Simon Peter
Who will give you a message that will save you and your
household.'"
Peter continued, "While I was preaching the Holy Spirit fell on them,
As it had fallen on us at Pentecost."
"Then I remembered the promise of Jesus, 'John indeed baptized with
Water, but you will be baptized by the Holy Spirit.'"
"Since God has done for Gentiles the exact same gift
He did for us when we believed on Him,
Who was I to stand in God's way of doing things?"
Peter's explanation satisfied them and they glorified God;
They concluded, "Evidently, God has given to the Gentiles,
Repentance to eternal life."

Lord, I'm grateful when Christians work out their misunderstandings;
I'm especially thankful when they listen to one another
Before criticizing them.
Give me patience when I disagree with others and help me
Listen to people before I criticize them.

Amen.

Chapter 25

THE STORY OF THE ANTIOCH CHURCH

Barnabas stood on the Amanus Mountain range overlooking the ancient Syrian city of Antioch. From his vantage point he could see the small winding Orontes River as it made its way down to the Mediterranean Sea.

Antioch was a massive city of 800,000 people. It was called the crossroads of the Roman Empire. Huge camel trains trudged the desert sands from the East and the Euphrates River, crossing the black Ural Mountains, bringing Persian silk, spices, and all of the products that sophisticated Romans wanted. After the camel train arrived in Antioch, the goods were transferred into Roman galleons that spread out over the Mediterranean world bringing Eastern goods to Athens, Rome, Carthage, Alexandria, and the other civilized cities of the Roman Empire.

Just about every ethnic group of people was located in Antioch. Travelers got stuck there all the time, and since money was to be made, they stayed and settled down.

News of a church in Antioch got back to Jerusalem. Since there was not a Synagogue in Antioch, many wondered if there could be a church without Jews as its foundation. Many wondered what kind of mixed up group of people this could be who called themselves "Christians."

James, the leading elder in Jerusalem decided, "I'll send Barnabas to check out this group." James gave specific orders to find out if the new church believed the right things, and were they living the right way, and did they really understand the forgiveness of sins that Jesus offered to the world.

"How did they become Christians?" was a natural question that Barnabas asked.

"We don't know, but some claim to be converted on the day of Pentecost, when the Holy Spirit fell on us. Some were from Antioch. They went home and began telling others about Jesus, the Messiah."

James added a warning, "The young church in Antioch has many non-Jews who are believing; these are uncircumcised people who have put their trust in Jesus Christ." James was not sure if they understood the foundations of the faith that come from a Jewish understanding of the Old Testament.

James had a specific reason for sending Barnabas. James remembered that Barnabas had sold all the land he possessed and gave the money to the church. The property was in Cyprus and James responded that Barnabas had been to Antioch on many occasions. Most people went to Cyprus by boat from Antioch; it was approximately 60 miles by water.

When Barnabas arrived at Antioch, he sat on a hill overlooking the city, wondering, "What kind of a church will I see; what kind of Christians will I meet; what will happen to me?"

It only took Barnabas two or three days to size up the church in Antioch. The Christians represented almost every ethnic group—there were Synthians, Arabs, Greeks, Turks, and Europeans, all believed in Jesus Christ, and none of them were circumcised according to Jewish law.

The more Barnabas talked to the believers, the more he realized that they needed grounding in the Old Testament Scriptures. Barnabas was an exhorter; his primary spiritual gift was motivating people to serve God. The church in Antioch already served God. They didn't need him, they needed solid teaching.

It was then when Barnabas thought of Paul. A few years earlier when Saul, the hated persecutor of the Jews had come to Jerusalem, no one would believe that he had been converted. Many Christians were afraid that Saul's conversion was a trick so he could infiltrate the church and arrest them.

But Barnabas understood rejection. He was the rich young ruler who rejected Jesus Christ. So Barnabas went to Saul and determined that he really was saved, Saul was "pure gold." It was then when Barnabas took Saul and introduced him to James and Peter.

So, it was only natural for Barnabas to be sent to this young "rejected" church in Antioch to find out if they were "pure gold."

Barnabas thought, "Saul is a teacher trained in the law who knows the Word of God." It was then when Barnabas determined to travel some 150 miles overland to Tarsus in Asia Minor to Saul's home. Saul had been ministering to his people when he left Jerusalem.

The journey to Tarsus took a week, but it only took a few minutes for Barnabas to convince Saul to return with him to teach the Word of God to the young Christians at Antioch.

While in Tarsus, Barnabas met some of the young converts from the university that Paul had led to Christ. Most notable among them was a medical student named Luke. Paul had some problems with asthma and Luke had been treating him. When Luke gave medical permission for Paul to leave, it was only a day later they left for Antioch.

For the next year, Paul gave the young church at Antioch a full Bible education. Beginning at Moses and the first five books of the Bible, he surveyed the foundations of the Hebrew faith. Then Paul taught them what each of the prophets believed. Finally, covering the Psalms and the historical books, the Christians in Antioch learned the Word of God completely, memorizing many of its great texts.

Barnabas said, "I can almost see Christians growing spiritually, night by night, as Saul explained the Word of God." After a year of Bible study, Barnabas observed, "The Christians here in Antioch are as strong as I've seen back in Jerusalem." Barnabas realized that this was a strong church that could do much to carry out the Great Commission in all the world.

The Church at Antioch

Acts 11:19-26

Those who fled Jerusalem when Saul persecuted Christians
>   Had traveled as far as Phoenicia, Cyprus, and Antioch.
At Antioch, they shared the Gospel with Greeks,
>   Giving the Good News of Jesus Christ to them as well as Jews;
>   God worked powerfully and a large number of Gentiles
>   Turned to the Lord.
When this news reached the church in Jerusalem,
>   They sent Barnabas to check out the church in Antioch;
>   Barnabas was a good man, full of the Holy Spirit and Faith.
When Barnabas arrived, he saw what God was doing and rejoiced;
>   Then he encouraged them to be strong in the faith;
>   As a result, a number of people became Christians.
Then Barnabas went to Tarsus to find Saul, and brought
>   Saul back to Antioch where he taught the believers for a year;
>   In Antioch believers were first called Christians.

Lord, I rejoice when the Gospel is spread
>   *To places where people don't know You.*
May I do all I can to help plant new churches,
>   *To evangelize areas that need the good news.*

Amen.

Help for the Jerusalem Church

Acts 11:27-30

Some prophets came down to Antioch from Jerusalem; one of them,
>   Agabus, predicted that a great famine was coming
>   Before the end of the reign of Claudius.

The believers at Antioch decided to send supplies to the church in
    Jerusalem
    So each believer gave what they could afford;
    Barnabas and Saul delivered the supplies to Jerusalem.

Lord, You have given to Your followers a spirit of Charity;
    Thank You for those who gave to me when I was in need.
Now, I determine to give to those in need. I will give what I can give;
    I will be charitable and giving with what You give me.

Amen.

James Killed—Peter Imprisoned

Acts 12:1-17

About this time King Herod began persecuting the church in Jerusalem,
    He had James, the brother of John, put to death with the sword;
    When he saw it pleased the Jews, he arrested Peter.
He imprisoned Peter because it was the high feast of Passover, and Herod
    Intended to bring Peter to trial after Passover.
Peter was guarded by four squads of four soldiers;
    As Peter was in prison, the church prayed earnestly for him.
Peter was chained to two soldiers, sleeping between them;
    And there were two guards at the entrance.
Suddenly, there was a light in the cell and an angel stood next to Peter,
    He had to shake Peter to awaken him;
    The angel said, "Get up quickly," and the chains fell off Peter.
Then the angel said, "Get dressed—don't forget your shoes—
    And follow me." Peter thought it was a dream,
    And he didn't believe it was happening.
They passed the first and second cell, then came to the iron gate
    That led to the city. It opened by itself.
They walked out into the street, and as they were walking,

The angel disappeared. Finally Peter realized, "This is happening!"
"The Lord has sent an angel to rescue me from Herod
>   And all that the Jewish leaders wanted to do to me."

Peter went to the home of Mary, the mother of John Mark,
>   Where Christians had gathered to pray for him.
When Peter knocked at the outer gate, Rhoda, a servant girl,
>   Looked out and recognized him. She got so excited she
>   Didn't open the gate, but ran to tell everyone.
They said, "You're out of your mind," but Rhoda kept saying
>   Peter was at the gate. They thought Peter had been executed
>   And that his angel was at the gate.
Peter kept knocking, and when they opened the gate,
>   They were amazed that it was really Peter.
Peter raised his hand to stop their talking, then he told them
>   How the Lord had led him out of the prison.
Peter instructed them to tell James the Lord's brother and others,
>   Then he went to a place where Herod couldn't find him.
At dawn, there was a great commotion at the jail over
>   The disappearance of Peter. They searched thoroughly for Peter
>   And when he couldn't be found, Herod ordered the guards executed.

Lord, some of your servants are martyred like James
>   *If that's my lot, have Your way in my life.*
Lord, if you deliver me from persecution, like Peter,
>   *I'll praise You for an easy life;*
>   *May I always serve You, no matter what happens to me.*

Amen.

Herod Judged

Acts 12:18-25

Herod lived at Caesarea in the summer time. While there the
    People of Tyre and Sidon sought an audience with the king
    Because there was a quarrel between them and Herod.
Blastus, a trusted servant of Herod, worked out a compromise
    Because the people needed Herod's permission for their food supply.
When the day came for the people to meet Herod, he delivered an address
    To them wearing his crown and royal regalia.
The people shouted, "This is the voice of god, not of man,"
    And they gave him a rousing ovation.
Instantly, an angel from God struck him with a disease,
    And he was filled with maggots and died—
    Because he accepted the people's worship instead of giving it
        to God.

The Good News was spreading rapidly and many people were saved;
    Barnabas and Saul returned from Jerusalem when they finished
    Their ministry and returned to Antioch,
    Taking John Mark with them.

Lord, what a terrible sin for anyone to receive Your worship;
    Help me deal properly with pride and give You glory for everything.
I want to be more godly and I want to walk humbly with You;
    Help me say with believers, "Not I, but Christ."

Amen.

God Called Barnabas and Saul to be Missionaries

Acts 13:1-3

The church at Antioch had prophets and teachers: Barnabas,
    Simeon called Niger, Lucius of Cyrene, Manaen,
    Who was raised with Herod, and Saul.
While they were worshiping God and fasting, the Holy Spirit said,
    "Send Barnabas and Saul to a special ministry,
    To which I have called them."
So after more fasting and prayer, they laid their hands on them,
    And sent them out to minister.

Lord, teach me to listen to Your voice for direction to my life,
    Just as the leaders in Antioch sought Your will for their life and
        ministry.
I will seek Your will in my life. When You speak
    Give me ears to hear what You want me to do
    And give me strength to choose to do Your will.

Amen.

Ministry in Cyprus

Acts 13:4-12

These two men—sent by the Holy Spirit—went to Selucia,
    And sailed to the island of Cyprus.
When they landed in Salamis, they preached the Word of the Lord
    In the Synagogue of the Jews. John went along to look after details.
They traveled the whole length of the island, and came in contact
    With a Jewish magician named Bar-Jesus.
This false prophet was an attendant of Sergius Paulus,
    The Roman governor of the island, who was extremely intelligent.
The governor called for Barnabas and Saul because he wanted to hear
    The Word of God. The Jewish magician, Elymas Magos,

The Greek name for Bar-Jesus,
Tried to stop Barnabas and Saul because it looked like the governor
    Would be converted to the Christian faith.
Saul, whose name was changed to Paul at this time,
    Was filled with the Holy Spirit to stop the magician;
    Paul stared angrily at him and said,
"You son of the devil...you enemy of God...you are opposing God,
    Now God's hand will judge you, you will be blind!"
Instantly his eyes became misty and then everything went dark;
    He groped about, seeking someone to lead him by the hand.
The governor who was watching became a believer, for he was
    Astonished by what he saw and what he heard.

Lord, I want to be as courageous in witnessing for You
    As Paul was when he boldly faced opposition.
Teach me how to react when people oppose me for my faith;
    I want to react properly to attacks and I want people
    To get saved, as the governor was converted.

Amen.

Ministry in Turkey

Acts 13:13-52

Paul and his companions sailed from Paphos to Pergia in modern day
    Turkey,
    Here John Mark left them to go back home to Jerusalem;
    They went from Pergia to Antioch of Pisidia.
On the Sabbath day they went to the Synagogue and took a seat;
    After the lesson from the Law and the prophets were read,
    The president of the Synagogue asked Paul,
"Would you like to give some words of encouragement to the congregation?"
    Paul stood, held up his hand for silence, then spoke,
"Listen, men of Israel and you Gentiles who worship the God of our

nation Israel,
God chose us and made us a large nation when we lived
As foreigners in Egypt. Then by supernatural power,
God led Israel out of Egypt, and took care of them
For 40 years in the wilderness; then God destroyed seven nations
As He put Israel in the Holy Land as their inheritance.
They lived there 450 years."
"After that God gave them judges until the coming of the prophet Samuel;
When our people begged for a king, God gave them Saul,
Of the tribe of Benjamin. He was their king for 40 years."
"After God disposed of Saul, He raised up David to the throne
Whom God Himself said, 'A man after My own heart,
Who shall do all My will.'"

"To keep His promise, God brought forth Jesus from the descendents of
David
To be the Savior of Israel."
"John the Baptist came before Him to prepare the way of Jesus,
Preaching the baptism of repentance for all the people of Israel."
"John said, 'I am not the Messiah, but the One coming
After Me is so great, I'm not fit to loose his shoe strings.'"
"Saul preached, 'Men and brethren, Sons of Abraham, and
Gentiles who fear God, God has sent you this message of salvation.'
"The people of Jerusalem and their leaders refused to recognize Jesus
Even though they read the prophets every Sabbath day
That predicts His coming as Messiah."
"Even though there was nothing to justify the death of Jesus,
They asked Pilate to execute Him."
"When they did everything to Jesus that the Scriptures foretold,
They took Him down from the tree and buried Him in a tomb."
"But God raised Jesus up from the dead, and for many days
He appeared to His followers from Galilee,
These are now His witnesses before the world."

"We have come here to tell you the Good News. God made the promises
To our ancestors, but it is to us—their children—
That He has fulfilled these promises by raising Jesus from the dead;
As the psalms say, 'You are my Son, today I have become Your
Father.'
"This Psalm means that God raised Jesus from the dead,
Never to return to corruption."
"God has given to Jesus the wonderful things
He promised David, 'He will not let his Holy One decay.'"
"This was not a reference to David because after he lived seventy years,
And served his generation, David died and his body decayed."
"This was a reference to another person whom God
Brought back to life, whose body was not touched
By the ravages of death. This was a reference to Jesus."
"Brothers, listen, there is forgiveness for your sins in this man Jesus;
Everyone who trusts in Him is free from all guilt,
He will declare you righteous, something the Law cannot do."
"Be careful brothers, because the words of the prophets apply to you,
Cast your eyes around you mockers,
Be amazed before you perish,
For I work a work in your days,
A work that you absolutely will not believe
If you were to be told of it."

As Paul and Barnabas left, many Jews and Gentile converts insisted
They return the next Sabbath to speak on this topic.

Lord, help me realize many people are hungry for the Good News
That Jesus forgives sins, gives eternal life, and gives abundant
Satisfaction.

The next Sabbath, almost the whole city assembled to hear
The Word of the Lord. When the Jews saw the multitude,
They were envious, and debated the things Paul said.
Then Paul and Barnabas boldly answered them,

"It was our duty to speak the Good News to you Jews
     Who have demonstrated yourselves unworthy of eternal life."
"So now we are turning to the Gentiles, as the Lord has instructed us to do;
     'I have set you as a light to the Gentiles
     So my salvation will reach to the end of the earth.'"

The Gentiles were glad to hear this message, and
     Thanked God for it. Many of them believed.
The Word of the Lord spread throughout the region,
     But the Jews stirred up the women and civic leaders
     Against Paul and Barnabas, and threw them out of town.
But the missionaries shook the dust of that town off their feet
     And went to the next city of Iconium;
     The converts were filled with joy and the Holy Spirit.

Lord, thank You for the spread of the Gospel to those
     Who have never heard, and thank You for new converts.
If Paul and Barnabas had not gone with the Gospel
     To the Gentiles, I would not be converted today.

Amen.

In Antioch

Acts 14:1-6

At Iconium, Paul and Barnabas went into the Jewish Synagogue
     As they did in Antioch and spoke so effectively
     That a great number of Jews became followers of Jesus Christ.
But the Jews who refused to believe, stirred up the Gentiles against them
     But Paul and Barnabas stayed there to preach fearlessly.
The Lord confirmed the message of grace and allowed
     Signs and wonders to be done by them.
The people of the city were divided, some siding with the apostles,
     Others supported the Jews. But a conspiracy was

Made by the unbelievers to stone them.
Paul and Barnabas heard their plot and left for safety reasons;
> Leaving, they preached the Gospel in Lystra and Derbe in the
> surrounding Mountains.

Lord, thank You for every missionary who has gone
> *To dangerous places to preach the Gospel.*
Give me courage to stand against criticism and ridicule
> *When I share the Gospel.*

Amen.

In Derbe and Lystra

Acts 14:7-18

A man crippled from birth sat at the city gate listening to Paul;
> Paul saw him and realized he had faith to be healed.
Then Paul said in a loud voice, "Stand up straight on your feet!"
> The man jumped up and began to walk.
When the crowd saw what happened, they shouted in their language,
> "The gods have come down to us dressed like men."
They called Barnabas Zeus, and Paul they called Hermes
> Since he was the spokesman.
The priest of Jupiter, whose temple was outside the gate
>> Brought oxen and flowers to sacrifice to
>> Paul and Barnabas at the city gate in front of the crowd.
But Paul and Barnabas ripped their clothes and ran into the crowd,
> Shouting, "Friends, why are you doing this?"
> "We are human beings with feelings just as you."
"We are here to tell you the good news that you
> Should turn from idols to the living God
> Who made Heaven and earth, and the sea and everything in it."
> "In the past, he let the nations go their own way,

But there was always a witness to them;
    The earth, Heaven and the seas."
"He sent rain giving you crops and food to eat."
This speech barely restrained the crowd from
    Offering sacrifices to them.

The Stoning of Paul

Acts 14:19-28

Then Jews arrived from Antioch and Iconium and turned the people
    Against the apostles. They stoned Paul and dragged him
    Outside the city, thinking he was dead.
The Christians gathered around him, but as they did,
    Paul stood up and went back into the town;
    The next day, Paul and Barnabas departed to Derbe.

Lord, thank You that Paul was faithful to death;
    Give me courage to face death if it ever comes my way.
Thank You that Timothy became a follower because of this experience;
    May this story of Paul strengthen the faith of many.

The next day Paul and Barnabas departed for Derbe;
    They preached the Gospel and many became Christians.
They turned back and revisited Lystra, Iconium, and Antioch of Turkey
    Where they strengthened the disciples of Christ in those cities,
    Exhorting them to be strong in the faith and endure many
        tribulations.
After prayer and fasting, they appointed church leaders in every church
    Commending these men to the Lord for their new ministry.
They then crossed over the mountains to Pisidia, going to Pamphylia;
    After preaching the Word of God in Pergia, they went
    To Attalia and then sailed back to Antioch of Syria.
They arrived back at the church that originally commissioned them

Because they had completed the work they intended to do.
They assembled the church together and reported all that God had done
Especially how He had opened the door of faith to the Gentiles;
　　　They stayed in Antioch a long time.

Lord, I thank You for every missionary who has gone to unreached
　　　Places to preach the Gospel to those who have never head it.
Thank You for those who brought the Gospel to my nation and my people;
　　　Please call more missionaries so every place and
　　　Ethnic group on earth can hear the Gospel at least once.

Amen.

The First Church Council

Acts 15:1-41

Some men came to Antioch from Judaea teaching,
　　　"You are not saved unless you have been circumcised
　　　According to the practice of Moses."
A long fierce argument broke out between Paul and Barnabas
　　　And those who wanted to add "good works" to salvation.
It was arranged for Paul, Barnabas, and others to go to Jerusalem
　　　To discuss this issue with the apostles and elders.
The church gathered to see them off, and they traveled through
　　　Lebanon and Samaria telling how Gentiles were saved;
　　　Christians everywhere rejoiced when they heard this.
They were welcomed in Jerusalem by the apostles, elders, and the church,
　　　And they told them what God had done among the Gentiles.
Some of the converted Pharisees came forward to say the Gentiles
　　　Must be circumcised and keep the Law of Moses.
The apostles and elders called a meeting to discuss the issues,
　　　And after a long debate; Peter stood to address the council.
"My friends," he said, "you remember God chose me to preach

The Gospel to the Gentiles at Cornelius' house so they
     could believe."
"God knows who is genuinely converted,
So He gave them the Holy Spirit, just as He gave to us."
"God made no distinction between Jew and Gentile, because
He forgave them by faith, just as He did for us."
"Now we are trying to correct God and impose on the Gentiles
A burden that we nor our fathers were able to obey;
No one has ever kept the law to be saved."
"We are saved the same way Gentiles are saved,
   Through faith in our Lord Jesus Christ."
Peter's argument silenced the assembly, no one could say anything;
   Then Paul and Barnabas described all the signs and miracles
God had done though them among the Gentiles.

Finally, James concluded what was said, "My brothers,
    Simon Peter has described how God worked to call to Himself
Those who were saved among the Gentiles."
"This agrees with the words of the prophets, since the Scriptures say,
    'After that I will return and rebuild the
Fallen house of David.'
    'I shall rebuild it from its ruins and restore it;
Then the rest of the world—the Gentiles—
May seek the Lord to be saved.'"
James stated, "The Lord said this long ago,"
So he ruled that they should not make
Things more difficult for Gentiles to be saved.
James proposed they send a letter telling Gentile Christians,
    "To abstain from anything polluted by idols
From fornication, from meat of strangled animals and blood."
James reasoned, "Because there are disciples of Moses in every place,
They read Moses every week and faithfully obey him."

Then the apostles and elders decided to choose and send delegates
      To Antioch with Paul and Barnabas to read this letter to them.
They chose Judas known as Barnabas, and Silas;
      Both men were leaders in the Jerusalem church.
"The apostles and elders, your brothers in Christ, send greetings
      To the Gentile brothers in Antioch, Syria, and Cilicia."
      "We have heard that some of our members have upset you
      By demanding that you all be circumcised to be saved."
      "They did not have our authorization, so we have
      Unanimously elected these delegates to go with
      Paul and Barnabas to deliver this letter to you."
      "We respect highly Paul and Barnabas who have risked
      Their lives for the name of the Lord Jesus Christ."
      "Therefore we are sending Judas and Silas who will re-enforce
      What this letter says,
      The Holy Spirit has led us to conclude
      Not to burden Gentile believers with keeping the Law,
      But we want you to abstain from food sacrificed to idols,
      From blood, and the meat of strangled animals and from fornication;
      You will do right to avoid them."
      'Farewell.'"

The group left and went to Antioch where they gathered the church
      And delivered the letter to them. The church read it
      And was delighted with its conclusions.
Judas and Silas stayed preaching to the Christians in Antioch
      Then the church sent them back to their homes in Jerusalem.
Paul and Barnabas stayed in Antioch to help
      The others who were preaching and teaching to the church.
Paul said to Barnabas, "Let's go back to visit the churches
      We planted where we preached the Word of God
      So we can see how they are doing."
Barnabas wanted to take John Mark with them, but Paul
      Was not in favor of it because he had deserted

Them in Pamphylia and refused to go on with them.
Because they disagreed, they parted ways;
    Barnabas took John Mark with him to Cyprus.
Paul chose Silas to go with him
    And the church commended them to God;
    They traveled through Syria and Turkey visiting the churches.

Paul Recruits Timothy

Acts 16:1-8

When Paul and Silas reached Derbe and Lystra, they met Timothy
    Whose mother was a Jewess but his father was a Greek.
Because Timothy was an outstanding Christian, the church
    recommended him
    To travel with Paul and Barnabas, but Paul had him circumcised
    Because of the Jews who knew his father was a Greek.

Lord, thank You for the faithfulness of Timothy;
    May I have a good testimony
    So that the church would recommend me for Your work.

Amen.

The Spirit Guides Their Ministry

Acts 16:4-11

They visited many towns, delivering the decision reached
    By the apostles and elders in Jerusalem,
So the churches were strengthened in the faith
    As well as growing daily in numbers.
The Holy Spirit told them not to preach in Asia, so they
    Traveled in Galatia. The Holy Spirit wouldn't let

Them go to the north or south, so they kept going west
     Till they came to the port city of Troas on the Aegean Sea.

That night Paul had a vision of a Macedonian man
     Who said to him, "Come to Macedonia and help us."

Almost immediately they arranged passage to Macedonia
     Convinced God had called them to preach there.

Lord, You guide many ways,
     Thank You for guiding Paul by a vision.
May I always follow Your directions,
     No matter how You speak to me.

Amen.

First Mission in Europe

Acts 16:12-40

Luke joined them and they sailed to Philippi, a Roman city
     That was the major city of that district.
After several days they went to the river's edge where women
     Met for prayer on the Sabbath day. There Paul preached to the
          women.
One of them was Lydia, a worshiper of God who
     Had a business selling purple dye. She opened her heart
     To believe all that Paul was saying.
Lydia was baptized along with all her household, and
     She asked Paul and his companions to be her guests, saying,
"If you think I am a true believer, then come
     Stay in my home," and they did.

Lord, thank You that Paul came west with the Gospel
     For it finally came to America and reached me.

May I be as faithful in telling others about Jesus
As was Paul in his missionary ministry.

As Paul was going to the place of prayer,
He met a slave girl who predicted the future by demon possession;
She earned a lot of money for her master this way.
The girl followed Paul and his companions, shouting,
"These men are servants of the Most High God,
They tell us how to be saved."
She kept this up until Paul became so irritated that he turned,
Spoke to the demon, "I command you in the
Name of Jesus Christ to come out of her."
The demon came out of her immediately, and when her owner
Saw that his hope of making more money was gone,
Seized Paul and Silas and dragged them before the authorities
In the market square, where they charged them,
"These men are Jews who are advocating practices which
Are unlawful for us as Romans to accept or follow."
A crowd quickly formed and began yelling against them,
So the magistrates had them stripped and flogged.
They were given many lashes, then thrown in prison and
Told the jailer to keep a close watch on them.
He followed the instructions, threw them into the inner prison,
And locked their feet in stocks.
That night, Paul and Silas were praying and singing
Psalms to God while the other prisoners listened.
Suddenly, an earthquake shook the prison; the doors flew open
And the chains fell off all the prisoners.

Lord, as Paul and Silas fellowshipped with You in prayer,
And worshiped You with psalms,
The doors were opened and the chains fell off their hands.
I know this was Your miracle for You came to receive
Their worship. Jesus said, "You seek worship."

I know You don't need doors to open for Your entrance,
But it was a nice touch in this situation.

The jailer awakened and saw the doors open, so he drew his sword
And was about to commit suicide, thinking his prisoners had escaped.
Paul shouted, "Don't harm yourself, we are all here";
The jailer got a light and rushed in to fall at the feet
Of Paul and Silas, asking, "What must I do to be saved?"
They replied, "Believe in Jesus Christ and you will be saved,
You and your household." Then Paul explained
The Word of the Lord to him and all those in the house.
The jailer washed their wounds, then he and his family
Were baptized. He brought them into his house
And fed them a meal.
The whole family celebrated their conversion and
Belief in God.
When morning came, the magistrates sent a message
To the jailers to release them.
Paul said, "No! They have beaten us publicly without a trial,
Despite the fact we are Roman citizens. They can't get rid of us
quietly;
Let them come and release us themselves."
The magistrates were frightened when they heard they were Romans,
So they came to the jail and begged them to leave the city.
Paul and Silas returned to Lydia's home and preached words
Of encouragement to them before they left the city.

Lord, thank You for providentially protecting Paul's life;
I know a child of God is immortal and death can't touch them
Until You have finished Your will for them on earth.

Amen.

The New Church at Thessalonica and Berea

Acts 17:1-14

Lord, Paul traveled to Thessalonica and entered the Synagogue
>As was his custom. He debated with the Jews for three weeks
>Explaining and proving the Messiah must suffer and be resurrected.

Paul explained the Messiah is Jesus. Some were convinced and
>Joined Paul and Silas, as well as many God-fearing Gentiles,
>Many of these where rich women.

The unbelieving Jews resented Paul and recruited a gang of thugs
>From the marketplace to riot against Christians in the city.

They ran to Jason's home hoping to find Paul and Silas,
>And bring them before the city officials.

When they didn't find them, they dragged Jason
>And another person to court charging, "These men
>Who have turned the world upside down, have come here now."

"They defy Caesar's decree, saying, 'There is another King called Jesus;'"
>When they heard this, the crowd and city officials were alarmed;
>They made Jason post a bond before releasing them.

Lord, help me be faithful in the face of opposition.
>*You've turned my private world upside down.*
>*May I become a witness to those I meet in life.*

The Christians immediately sent Paul and Silas inland to Berea,
>There Paul went into the Jewish Synagogue and spoke.

The Bereans were more fair-minded than the Thessalonians
>In that they gave an example how to listen to the Word of God.

Lord, I will receive the word of God with an open mind,
>*I will search—daily—every part of Scripture*
>*To determine what You have said for me to believe and live.*

The Jews from Thessalonica heard that Paul was preaching in Berea,
>   So they went there to stir up a riot.
The Christians arranged for Paul to leave immediately,
>   Silas and Timothy were left to build up the church;
>   An escort went with Paul to Athens, the capitol city.

Lord, give me a love and reverence for Your Word.
>   *May I study it carefully—every word—to know what you've said.*
Give me a passion to live a holy productive life for You.
>   *May my life be based on the principles I've learned from Your*
>   *Word.*

Amen.

Paul Preaching in Athens

Acts 17:15-34

While waiting for Silas and Timothy, Paul was upset
>   Because the whole city of Athens was worshiping idols.
Paul debated in the Synagogue with the Jews and God-fearing Gentiles
>   As well as in the city market with those gathered there.
While speaking, some Epicurean and stoic philosophers listened to him
>   And they remarked, "What is this babbler trying to say?"
They accused Paul of advocating a foreign God
>   Because he was preaching Jesus and the resurrection.
They brought Paul to the forum at Mars Hill, asking,
>   "Tell us more about this religion that you're preaching."
They accused Paul of saying startling things
>   And they wanted to find out more about it.
(The Athenians and foreigners who lived there spent their time
>   Discussing the latest new ideas),
>   So Paul stood to address the whole forum.
"Men of Athens, I see that you are very religious,

Because as I walked about this place, I saw many idols."
"I even saw one with the inscription, 'TO AN UNKNOWN GOD,'
The God I worship, is the One you don't know.
"This is the God who created the world and everything in it;
He does not make His home in shrines built by humans,
Nor does He need anything humans can do for Him
Because He is the One who gives everything to everyone,
Including their life and breath."
"God created one ancestor, the whole human race comes from
        one man
And they scattered over the whole face of the earth."
"God has determined the times of their existence
And the limits where they lived."
"God wants all to search for Him so they might find Him
Because God is not far from each one of us,
For in Him we live and move and exist."

"Some of your writers have said, 'We are all His children';
Since we are the children of God, we should not think
Of deity in terms of gold, silver or a carved statue."
"God overlooks this sort of mistake when we are ignorant,
But now He tells everyone everywhere to repent
Because God has set a date when He will judge the world."
"God appointed a Man to judge rightly,
And proved this to us by raising that man from the dead."
When they heard about the resurrection of the dead, some laughed,
        Others said, "We would like to hear about this again."
At this time, Paul left the forum, but some joined him
        And became believers, among them Dionysius
        The Acropagite, a woman named Damaris, and some others.

May I have opportunities to tell people what You've done for me.
        I want to tell people the Gospel who've never heard it correctly;
        I want to be used by You, as You used Paul.

Amen.

Paul at Corinth

Acts 18:1-17

Lord, Paul left Athens and went to Corinth
> Where he stayed in the home of Aquila, the tent maker.

Aquila with his wife, Priscilla, were originally from Turkey,
> But recently they were thrown out of Rome because
> All Jews were expelled by Claudius the Emperor.

Paul worked for them for he was a tentmaker.
> Every Sabbath Paul debated in the Synagogue
> Trying to convert Jews as well as Gentiles who attended.

After Silas and Timothy came from Macedonia,
> Paul spent his full time testifying to the Jews
> That Jesus was the Messiah.

When the Jews threatened Paul, he shook the dust off of his robe and said,
> "Your blood be upon your own hands. From now on
> I will preach the gospel to the Gentiles with a clear conscience."

Paul then moved the church into the house of Justus,
> A believer who lived next to the Synagogue.

Crispus, the leader of the Synagogue, became a believer
> And a great many Corinthians also believed and were baptized.

Therefore the Lord spoke to Paul in a vision at night saying,
> "Don't be afraid of leaving the Synagogue to worship in a house;

Continue speaking because I'll be with you, no one will harm you,
> I have many in this city who will become believers."

So Paul stayed in Corinth for eighteen months, preaching the Scriptures.

Lord, thank You for my church that nourishes me.
> *I'm glad you approved the example of separating*
> *The church from the Jewish Synagogue.*

When Gallio became governor of the region, the Jews banned together
    To bring Paul before him for trial, accusing him,
"This man persuades people to worship God that break our law";
    Before Paul could speak, Gallio said,
"Listen you Jews! If this were a matter of breaking the law,
    I would not hesitate to listen to your charges,
But you are bickering about words and your religious laws,
    Settle the matter outside the court room;
    I do not intend to make a legal decision about religious matters."
Gallio sent them out of the court room, and a crowd
    Jumped on Sosthenes, the leader of the Synagogue, and beat him
    In front of the court house;
    But Gallio paid no attention to it.

Lord, thank You for living in a country that
    Has separation of church and state.
I will fully support my state as You command;
    I will fully support my church
    Which is my Christian duty.

          Amen.

Paul's Trip to Jerusalem

Acts 18:18-28

After this, Paul left Corinth and sailed for Syria
    Accompanied by Aquila and Priscilla.
Paul shaved his hair according to Jewish custom
    Because his long hair represented a vow he had made.
When they arrived at Ephesus, Paul went into the Synagogue
    To debate with the Jews about Jesus the Messiah.
They asked Paul to stay a few days, but he declined
    Because of his travel schedule.

However he promised, "I will come back if God allows me to do it";
 Paul left Aquila and Priscilla there before sailing away.
When Paul landed at Caesarea, he went up to Jerusalem
 To greet the saints there, then he returned to Antioch at Syria
 The church that sent him on the missionary trip.
After spending some time in Antioch, Paul began his third
 Missionary trip through Turkey, strengthening
 The churches he had established on the two preceding trips.

Lord, help me be sensitive to the leading of the Holy Spirit
 To follow You obediently, as did Paul.

An Alexandrian Jew named Apollos came to preach in Ephesus;
 He was exceptionally eloquent with a firm grasp of Scripture.
Apollos preached boldly and enthusiastically in the Synagogue
 But he only knew what John the Baptist said about the coming
  Christ.
When Priscilla and Aquila heard Apollos preach, they invited him
 To their home to explain to him
 The way of salvation more fully.
When Apollos left for Turkey, the brethren wrote a
 Letter of introduction to the churches, asking them to receive him.
When Apollos arrived, he strengthened the Christians there,
 And vigorously refuted the Jews in public debate,
 Proving from Scripture that Jesus was the Messiah.

Lord, thank You for lay people like Aquila and Priscilla
 Who know the Scriptures, and teach others.
May I be a faithful teacher like them.

Amen.

Paul's Ministry in Ephesus

Acts 19:1-41

Lord, while Apollos continued ministering at Corinth,
     Paul traveled through Turkey to arrive at Ephesus
Where he found 12 followers of John the Baptist
     Who were still preaching baptism of repentance,
     Looking forward to the coming of Messiah.
Paul asked them, "Did you receive the Holy Spirit when you believed?"
     They answered "No, we don't know anything about the Holy Spirit."
Then Paul asked, "What did you confess when you were baptized?"
     They answered, "Belief in the Messiah who is coming."
When Paul pointed out Jesus the Messiah had come,
     They were baptized immediately in the name of Jesus.
When Paul laid his hands on them,
     The Holy Spirit came on them, and they spoke in tongues.

Lord, I thank You for zealous people like these 12 men
     Who are willing to go anywhere to serve You,
     Even when they don't have the full truth.
Because you have given me spiritual insight and I know the truth,
     May I always be willing to serve You that zealously.

Lord, Paul spoke for three months in the Synagogue,
     Debating about Jesus and the Kingdom of God.
When the attitude of the congregation hardened
     And they began attacking the Way publicly,
     Paul took believers out of the Synagogue.
They met daily in the school of Tyrannus,
     Where believers were instructed in the Word of God
     And the gospel was spread throughout the region.

Lord, I thank You for the church where I heard the Word,
     And thank You for the church that spreads the gospel.

Lord, Paul's ministry included healing the sick through prayer;
    His handkerchiefs were taken to the sick
    And they were healed because of their faith.
Some itinerant Jewish evangelist who cast out demons came to Ephesus
    And spoke the name of "Jesus as preached by Paul."
The man Sceva, a Jewish chief priest, and his seven sons,
    Tried to cast out a demon who answered,
    "Jesus I know, and Paul I know; but who are you?"
The demon-possessed man attacked them and beat them mercilessly,
    He ripped their clothes off them,
    So that they ran out of the house, naked.
When people in Ephesus heard about the episode,
    Both Jews and Gentiles were impressed, and they were
    Afraid to attack Christianity; so the gospel spread everywhere.
Many new believers came forward to repent of their evil deeds;
    Those who practiced magic and sorcery
    Burned their incantation books and charms in a big public fire.
Someone estimated their value at 10,000 pieces of silver;
    As a result the Word of God became more influential
    And its message was spread widely.

Lord, I will always be willing to rid my life of anything
    That is used by satan to deceive and destroy people.

After this happened, Paul decided to visit Greece
    On his way to Rome, so he sent
    Timothy and Erastus to prepare the way.
About this time a riot broke out against Christianity in Ephesus;
    It began when Demetrius a silversmith called together
    Many of the craftsmen who made silver idols of Diana.
He said, "Paul has persuaded many that our idols are not gods,
    And our sales are going down. Not only here but in all Turkey,
    Paul is destroying the idol trade market."
"Paul is also desecrating our Temple dedicated to Diana

And reducing worship of Diana over the whole world."
They began to chant, "Great is Diana of the Ephesians"
    And the whole town rushed into the amphitheater
    Dragging along the believers, Gaius and Aristarchus.
Paul wanted to go make an appeal to the crowd,
    But for safety sake the Christians wouldn't let him enter;
    Roman officers also sent messages telling Paul not to go there.
The crowd was confused, some shouting one thing, others another;
    Most didn't even know about the "silversmith" controversy.
A Jew named Alexander was pushed to the front
    But the crowd wouldn't let him speak;
    They shouted, for two hours, "Great is Diana of the Ephesians."
The town clerk eventually quieted the crowd and told them,
    "Everyone knows the greatness of Diana who guards our Temple,
    We all know she fell from Heaven."
"If Demetrius and the craftsmen want to complain,
    Let them take their case to court."
"We must raise our questions in a regular city council,
    Otherwise, Rome will charge us with rioting
    And send soldiers to investigate or punish us."
The clerk then dismissed the crowd and they left.

Lord, help me see Your plan for my life when there is civic turmoil,
    May I always trust You to protect me in strife.

Amen.

Paul's Last Trip to Ephesus

Acts 20:1-38

Lord, thank You for protecting Paul's life and giving him wisdom
    When to be bold, and in this case, to avoid confrontation.

After Paul encouraged the Christians in Ephesus, he said goodbye,
      And set sail for Greece. He stayed there three months.
As Paul was planning to leave by ship, he discovered a
      Plot to kill him by the Jews. So he went by land
      Through northern Greece.
Paul had many traveling with him for protection; Sopater,
      Aristarchus, Secundus, Gaius, Timothy, Tychicus,
      And Trophimus.
After celebrating the Passover, Paul left Philippi and
      Boarded a ship for Troas in Turkey.
On Sunday, Paul observed the Lord's Table, then preached
      A long sermon that went on into the night.
The room was hot because a large number of lamps were burning;
      Eutychus, a young man sitting on the window sill,
      Fell asleep and then fell three stories to the ground.
He was picked up dead, but Paul went down and embraced him
      Saying, "Don't worry, there is life in him."
Paul went back upstairs where he ate a meal, then
      He talked until daybreak and Paul left.
They took the boy home alive, and all praised God.

Lord, thank You for healing the young man;
      Now I know You will take care of me physically.

Paul visited several cities as he traveled toward Jerusalem;
      He decided not to visit Ephesus, but had the elders
      Come meet him at the ship in Miletus.
Paul told them, "You know how honestly I lived since I came here,
      How I served the Lord in all humility,
      How I remained faithful, even when the Jews plotted against me."
      "I never hesitated to tell you the truth,
      Both publicly and in your homes."
      "I have declared to both Jews and Gentiles
      That they must repent and put their faith in our Lord Jesus."

"Now you know the Holy Spirit is leading me to Jerusalem,
But I don't know what will happen to me there;
Except that the Holy Spirit in city after city has let me know
That persecution and imprisonment await me in Rome."
"But my life will be spent finishing the race
That I have been running in the mission the Lord Jesus gave me,
And that is spreading the Good News of God's grace."
"Now I feel sure that none of you will see me again;
My conscience is clear concerning my work among you
For I have declared the whole Gospel among you."
"Guard yourselves and the flock that the Holy Spirit has given you;
Be a good example in leading them in godliness
And feed the church which is bought with Christ's blood."
"I know when I have gone, false teachers will come
Who will not have compassion on the flock."
"Also, men from among yourselves will distort the truth
To draw away disciples to follow them."
"So be on your guard, remember that night and day
I kept constant watchcare over the flock,
Shedding many tears for you in prayer."
"Now I commit you to God and the word of His grace
Which will give you an inheritance among the saints."
"I never asked anyone for money or clothes;
You know I worked to earn money to meet my needs."
"I did this to be a constant example to the church
To help the poor, for I remember the words of Jesus,
'It is more blessed to give than to receive.'"
When Paul finished speaking, they knelt on the beach and prayed;
Then they wept and embraced Paul because
He said they wouldn't see him again.

Lord, thank You for friends who pray for me
As the elders prayed for the apostle Paul.

Raise up my prayer supporters who will intercede
For me as I live and serve You.

Amen.

Paul Goes to Jerusalem

Acts 21:1-40

Lord, I see how You protected Paul in many small ways,
Do the same for me, protecting me through the hum-drum of life.

Paul sailed from Troas to Lebanon, stopping at several places,
    The ship landed at Tyre, there Paul stayed a week;
    The Christians kept telling Paul not to go to Jerusalem.
Paul then sailed to Caesarea, and stayed with Phillip the evangelist
    Who had four daughters in ministry;
    He was one of the original seven deacons.
After several days, Agabus the prophet arrived to see Paul;
    He took the belt on Paul's tunic and tied his hands and feet
Saying, "The owner of this belt will be bound hand and foot in
    Jerusalem and then handed over to the Gentiles."
Everyone who heard this begged Paul not to go to Jerusalem
    But he replied, "Why are you crying to change my mind?"
"I am ready not only to be bound in Jerusalem, but to die
    For the name of the Lord Jesus."
When the crowd saw they couldn't change Paul's mind, they said,
    "The will of the Lord be done."

Lord, give me resolute determination to follow You,
Even when it seems dangerous and life threatening.

Paul left to go up to Jerusalem, Christians from Caesarea
    Went with him to the home of Mnason from Cyprus
    Who had been one of the earliest disciples.

The brothers gave Paul a warm welcome when Paul arrived in Jerusalem:
> The next day Paul visited James and the elders.

Then Paul gave them a detailed account of what God had done
> Among the Gentiles through his ministry;
> The brothers gave glory to God when they heard it.

Then the elders told Paul, "There are thousands of Jews
> Who have been saved, who staunchly uphold the law."

"They have heard that you tell Jewish Christians to break with Moses,
> And you authorize them not to circumcise their children."

"They will certainly hear that you are here and
> Will want a meeting with you."

"Here is what we suggest you do. We have four men who
> Have taken a Nazarite vow. You go with them
> To the Temple to be purified with them."

"You pay the Temple expenses connected with shaving their heads;
> This will let everyone know you keep the Law
> And that there is no truth in the rumors about you."

"As for Gentile believers, we aren't asking them to observe
> These Temple customs. The only thing they must do is,

Not eat food offered to idols, and not eat unbled meat
> From animals that are strangled, and avoid fornication."

The next day Paul went with the four men to the ceremony
> To be purified, and announced that in seven days
> They would offer sacrifices to end the vow.

When the seven days were almost over, some Jews from Asia,
> Saw Paul in the Temple and began a riot, shouting,

"Men of Israel! This man preaches to everyone, everywhere
> That it is wrong to keep the Law and worship in the Temple."

"He has profaned the Holy Place by bringing Gentiles here."
> But they were wrong; they had seen Trophimus from Ephesus
> With Paul in the city and thought he brought him into the Temple.

People came running from every direction, they grabbed Paul
> And dragged him out of the Temple;

The gates were closed behind them.
The crowd would have killed Paul, but Roman soldiers intervened
    Because their officer heard there was rioting in the city.
The soldiers stopped the crowd from beating Paul;
    The Roman officer arrested Paul and chained his hands and feet;
    Then he asked Paul to identify himself.
The crowd called out different things and made it impossible
    For the officer to get a positive identification of Paul.
Paul was carried by the soldiers to the stairs because
    The crowd was so violent. They were shouting, "Kill him."
When Paul spoke to the officer, he was surprised Paul spoke Greek;
    Then the officer said, "You're not the Egyptian who led
    An insurrection of 4,000 cut throats."

Lord, thank You for physical protection of Paul
    In the middle of chaos and hostility.
Protect me as You did Paul when danger comes;
    I will trust You in all things.

Amen.

Paul Speaks to a Crowd in Jerusalem

Acts 22:1-30

Paul answered, "I am a Jew, a citizen of Tarsus in Turkey;
    Give me permission to speak to the people."
Paul stood at the top of the stairs and gestured to the crowd,
    And when they became quiet, he spoke in Hebrew,
"My brothers, and fathers, listen to my defense;"
    When the crowd heard him speaking in Hebrew,
    They became still, even more quiet than before.
"I am a Jew, and was born in Tarsus of Turkey. In this city
    I studied under Gamaliel and was taught to obey

Every Jewish law and custom."
"In fact, I was so devoted—as you are today—I even
Persecuted Christians, binding them to death,
Delivering both men and women in chains to prison."
"The High priest or any member of the Sanhedrin
Will testify to these facts."
"I ask a letter from them to their brothers in Damascus
To do the same there. I set off to go to Damascus
To bring back prisoners to Jerusalem for punishment."
"I was nearly to Damascus when at noon a bright light
From Heaven blinded me. I fell to the ground and heard a voice,
'Saul, Saul, why are you persecuting Me?' I answered,
"Who are You, Lord?" He answered,
'I am Jesus of Nazareth, whom you are persecuting.'"
"The people with me saw the light, but didn't understand the voice,"
I said, 'What do you want me to do?' The Lord answered,
"Stand up, go to Damascus, it will be told you what to do."
"The light was so blinding my companions
Had to lead me to Damascus by the hand."

Lord, I cannot deny the experiences of life.
Thank You for those who brought the Gospel to me,
Thank You for events that led to my conversion.

"A man named Ananias, a devout follower of the Law,
And highly respected by the Jewish community,
Came to pray beside me and said, 'Brother Saul, receive your sight.'"
"Then he said, 'God has chosen you
To do His will, to see the Messiah, and to carry out His message;
You will be a witness to all people what you have seen and heard.'
'Why delay? It's time to be baptized as a sign your
Sins are forgiven.'
"When I got back to Jerusalem, I was praying in the Temple,
In a trance, I saw the Lord who said, 'Hurry

Leave Jerusalem, they will not receive your testimony.'"
"Lord," I prayed, "is it because I arrested and beat those who
Believed in You?"
"When Stephen's blood was being shed, I gave consent
And watched the coats of those who stoned him."
"Then the Lord said to me, 'Go, I will send you to the Gentiles'";
The crowd listened to Paul until he said the word *Gentiles*,
Then they shouted, 'Away with him, he is not fit to live.'"
The Jews yelled, threw dust into the air, and waved their coats;
So the officer took Paul into the fortress.

Lord, thank You for Paul's witness in the face of opposition;
Give me boldness to testify for You when danger comes.

He ordered Paul to be examined under the whip to find out the truth;
When they strapped Paul down, he said to the Centurion,
"Is it legal for you to scourge an uncondemned Roman citizen?"
The Centurion told his superior, "This man is a Roman citizen;"
The commander asked if Paul were a Roman citizen;
"I am," was Paul's reply.
The commander replied, "It cost me a large amount of money to become
A citizen." Paul replied, "I was free born";
The soldiers who were going to flog Paul quickly left.
The commander was frightened because he could have been punished
For scourging a Roman citizen.
The next day the commander took off
Paul's chains;
He ordered the Sanhedrin to meet with the Chief Priest,
Then brought Paul to stand before them.

Lord, Paul used a legal means to escape punishment;
Give me wisdom not to be punished needlessly for Your sake,
And give me courage to accept punishment when need be.

Amen.

Paul Before the Jewish Council

Acts 23:1-35

Lord, Paul looked intently at the Sanhedrin, then spoke,
 "My brothers, I have always lived with a perfectly clear conscience."
Immediately, Ananias the High Priest ordered those near Paul
 To slap him on the mouth. Paul responded, "God strike you,
 You filthy wall that's been whitewashed."
Paul asked, "How can you break the Law striking me
 Before I am found guilty?"
The men close to Paul said, "You're insulting God's High Priest;"
 Paul answered, "I did not realize it was the High Priest,
 Because Scripture says, 'Don't curse the ruler of the people.'"
Paul became aware that the Sanhedrin was split between
 The Sadducees and the Pharisees, so he called out,
 "I am on trial for the hope of the resurrection."
Instantly, a debate broke out between the two opposing factions
 And the assembly was evenly split.
The Sadducees don't believe in the resurrection, angels, or eternal spirits
 In people, but Pharisees believe all these.
They shouted loudly at each other, and the Pharisees said,
 "We find nothing wrong with this man;
 Perhaps a spirit or angel spoke to him at his conversion."
The Roman commander fearing they would physically beat Paul,
 Ordered his troops to enter and take Paul to the fortress.
That night the Lord stood by Paul saying, "Be courageous,
 You have witnessed for Me in Jerusalem
 Now you must witness for Me in Rome."

Lord, help me to be more courageous as was Paul
 Because I don't witness for You as did Paul,
 Even when I find myself in peaceful surroundings.

Early in the morning, about 40 Jews held a secret meeting
     And vowed an oath not to eat until they killed Paul.
They told the Chief Priest and elders, "We have vowed to fast
     Until we kill Paul, now it is your responsibility to ask
     The commander to return Paul so you can examine him closely."
"It is our responsibility to kill him in the streets
     As they bring him to you."
The son of Paul's sister heard their plans of ambush
     And came to the fortress to tell Paul;
     He immediately had the boy taken to the commander.
When the boy was brought to the commander, they went privately
     Where the boy said, "There are 40 Jews who have vowed
     Not to eat until they have killed Paul."
"These Jews will get the Sanhedrin to request you to bring Paul
     To be questioned more closely, they plan to kill him in the streets;
     They are waiting your order to deliver Paul."
The commander let the boy go, warning him, "Don't tell anyone
     You've given me this information."
The commander commanded two of his centurions, "Get 200
     Soldiers ready immediately. Leave now in the dark with
     200 spearmen and 70 mounted cavalry. Put Paul on a horse,
     Get him safely to Caesarea and Governor Felix."
The commander wrote a letter,
     This man was seized by the Jews as they were
     Attempting to kill him, so I commanded my troops
     To arrest him. Then I discovered he was a Roman citizen.
     I took him to their Sanhedrin to find out what charge
     Could be brought against him. I discovered it was about
     Their Jewish doctrine, nothing worthy of imprisonment.
     When I was informed of a plot to assassinate him,
     I decided to send him to you and tell his accusers
     To bring their charge before you.
The soldiers carried out their orders and took Paul down from

Jerusalem to the Mediterranean Sea. Then the mounted soldiers
      Took Paul the rest of the way to Caesarea, and then returned.
When Felix got the letter, he asked Paul where he was born,
      Then hearing it was Turkey said, "I will hear your case,
      As soon as your accusers come from Jerusalem."
Then Felix ordered Paul held in prison in Herod's Palace.

Lord, I marvel at the way You work in small details,
      You allowed the nephew to warn the Roman Commander.
Lord, I thank You that the total might of the Roman Empire was used
      To protect Your servant so he could preach the Gospel in Rome.
      Thank You for working in little and big ways.

Amen.

Paul Before Felix

Acts 24:1-27

Lord, I see Your hand working through politics and big government.
      After five days, the High Priest, Ananias, some elders,
      And the lawyer named Tertullus appeared in court in Caesarea.
When Tertullus was called, he brought their case before Felix,
      "Your Excellency, you have given peace and protection
      To the Jews and changed bad laws that persecuted us.
      "At all times, and in all places, we acknowledge
      What you've done for all Jews—with our gratitude."
      "I don't want to take up too much of your time,
      So let me tell you briefly what this man—Paul—has done."
      "He is a trouble-maker, stirring up trouble among the Jews
      Worldwide, and is the ring leader of the sect of the Nazarenes."
      "He attempted to profane the Temple. We placed him
      Under arrest by the Temple guards and planned to judge
      Him by our laws, but the Roman Commander Lysias intervened

And used force to take him out of our hands, then ordered
Him to appear before you. Ask him, he will tell you the truth."
The Jews who came with their lawyer agreed to the charges,
So Felix motioned Paul to speak.
Paul answered, "I know you have been a fair judge over the Jews
For many years. Therefore, I defend myself with confidence."
"Only 12 days ago I made my pilgrimage to Jerusalem,
I was not arguing with anyone in the Temple
Or their synagogues throughout town, neither can they
Prove their accusations they made against me."

"I will admit that I worship the God of my ancestors,
According to the Way which they call a sect."
"I firmly believe in Jewish law and everything written in the
Prophets. I believe, just as my accusers, that there
Will be a resurrection of the righteous and wicked. I strive
To keep my conscience clear before God and man."

"After several years of absence, I came bringing alms for the
Poor and to present offerings to God; it was in this connection
That the Jews found me in the Temple. I was purified
And there was no crowd with me and no disturbance."
"Some Jews from Turkey saw me there—these are the ones
Who should testify against me—because they said I desecrated
The Temple by bringing in Gentiles; but the Gentiles were not
with me." "Therefore, I am not guilty of causing a riot.
If anything, these
Jews were the ones who caused the riot."

"I am guilty of one thing. When I was brought before the
Sanhedrin, I called out about the resurrection which caused a
Great argument."

Felix, who knew more about the Way than most people,
Adjourned the proceedings saying, "When Lysias
Comes, I will decide this case."

Felix ordered the Roman commander to keep Paul under guard,
>   But gave him some freedom and allowed his friends to come to him.
A few days later, Felix and his wife Drusilla, who was Jewish,
>   Sent for Paul for a hearing on the subject of faith in Christ.
As Paul spoke about righteousness and self-discipline
>   And judgment to come, Felix was terrified, saying,
"You may go for now. When I have a more convenient time,
>   I'll call for you." He hoped Paul would pay him money
>   So Felix frequently summoned Paul to talk with him.
Felix wanted to gain favor with the Jews, so he left Paul in prison;
>   Two years went by and Felix was replaced by Festus.

Lord, thank You for Paul's positive witness before government officials;
>   *May I always give a clear witness to Your faithfulness.*

Amen.

Paul Before Festus

Acts 25:1-27

Lord, I understand government officials represent Your power,
>   *Thank You for Your law and order that gives security to my culture.*

When Festus took up his appointment, he visited Jerusalem
>   Where the Chief Priest and Jewish leaders asked him
>   To do something immediately about the case of Paul.
They wanted Festus to side with them and asked for Paul
>   To be transferred back to Jerusalem, because they planned
>   To ambush and murder him on the highway.
Festus told them Paul would remain in custody in Caesarea
>   And that he would hold court there shortly.
Festus said, "Send your authorities to Caesarea with me,
>   And if Paul is guilty, you can bring charges against him."
Festus stayed in Jerusalem for about 10 days, then returned to Caesarea;

The next day he had Paul brought before the tribunal.
Almost immediately the Jews surrounded Paul and brought
 Accusations against him, but didn't have any proof.
Paul defended himself, "I have committed no offense against
 The Temple or against Caesar."
Festus was anxious to please the Jews, so he asked Paul,
 "Are you willing to go to Jerusalem to stand trial?"
But Paul answered, "No! I am standing before the tribunal of Caesar,
 Where I should be tried. I demand my hearing
 Before Caesar himself. I have done the Jews no wrong,
 As you very well know. I am not guilty of any civil
 Crime. I do not ask to be spared from death, but
 Since there is no substance to their charges, no one has
 The right to surrender me to them. I appeal to Caesar."
Then Festus conferred with his legal advisors and concluded,
 "You have appealed to Caesar, to Caesar you should go."

Lord, I thank You that the government protected Paul from death,
 Thank You for the protection I have by my government.

A few days later, King Agrippa and Bernice arrived in Caesarea
 To pay a visit to Festus. They stayed several days.
Festus explained Paul's case to them,
 "I have a man in prison that Felix left there."
 "While I was in Jerusalem, the Chief Priest and the leader of the
  Jews
 Demanded his condemnation. I told them Roman law does
 Not surrender a prisoner, until the accused has an opportunity
 To confront his accusers and is given an opportunity to
 Defend himself. So they came here to Caesarea and I
 Took the tribunal seat and brought the man before me."
 "The accusers did not charge him with any crime."
 "They argued religious doctrine and about a dead man called Jesus
 Whom Paul alleged to be alive. Not feeling qualified to deal with

This question, I asked if he would be willing to go to Jerusalem
To be tried on this issue. Paul appealed his case
To the judgment seat of Caesar, so I have held him
Until I could send him to Rome."
Agrippa said, "I would like to hear the man myself." Festus
Answered, "Tomorrow you shall hear him."
The next day Agrippa and Bernice arrived in great ceremony
Entering the court room with the officials of the city;
Then Festus ordered Paul to be brought in.
Festus said, "King Agrippa and all who are present today,
See this man. The whole Jewish community has
Petitioned me that he should not live. For my part,
I'm satisfied he hasn't committed a capital crime."
"But he appealed to Caesar, so I decided to send him there."
"Since I have no definite crime that I can write to Caesar,
I am presenting him here before you,
King Agrippa, and all these officials so that after you examine him,
I will have an accusation against him."
"It seems pointless to send a prisoner to Caesar without
Charges against him."

Paul Before King Agrippa

Acts 26:1-32

Lord, I'll be grateful for opportunities to witness in official places for You;
If I'm ever given the opportunity,
May I do it with power.

King Agrippa said to Paul, "You may speak in Your defense";
Paul gestured for silence, then spoke,
"I am fortunate to be able to defend myself before you, King
Agrippa,
Because I know you are an expert on Jewish customs and law."

"So please listen to my whole defense."
"Everyone knows I was trained from my childhood in Jewish
Tradition and completed my education in Jerusalem."
"The Jews have known that I lived in the strictest way among them
As a Pharisee. But the reason the Jews have charged me is
Something else. It is for the promise made to the fathers.
"It is for the promise that the 12 tribes worship God."
"It is the promise of the resurrection from the dead and eternal life,
This is why I have been put on trial by the Jews."
"Does it seem incredible that God can raise the dead?"

"I did all I could to oppose the name of Jesus of Nazareth,
That is how I spent my time in Jerusalem. I put many
Saints into prison on the authority of the Chief Priest."
"When they voted to stone Stephen, I voted with them."
"Many times I visited synagogues to punish Christians
Trying to force them to renounce their faith. I was
So angry against Christians that I pursued them to foreign cities."

"I was on one of these journeys to Damascus with authority
From the Chief Priest. About mid-day on the road
I saw a light—brighter than the sun—from Heaven."
"It shone brilliantly around me and my fellow travelers, so that
We fell to the ground. I heard a voice saying to me
In Hebrew, 'Saul, Saul, why are you persecuting me?
Your kicking is only hurting yourself.'"
"Then I answered, 'Who are you Lord?'"
"The Lord answered me, 'I am Jesus whom you are persecuting.
Get up and stand on your feet, for I have a reason
For appearing to you—to appoint you to be my servant,
And be a witness to tell everyone you have seen Me,
I will protect you from your people."
"I will send you to the Gentiles, to open their eyes
To their blinded condition, so they may turn from darkness

To light, from satan's control to God's service; so their
Sins can be forgiven, and they can receive the inheritance
Of eternal life."
"After that, King Agrippa, I was not disobedient to the
Heavenly vision. I began immediately preaching to the people
Of Damascus, then to those in Jerusalem, and all the countryside
Of Judea, and also to Gentiles; urging them to repent
And turn to God; then prove their repentance by doing good works."

"The Jews arrested me in the Temple for doing this, and
Tried to kill me, but God has protected me to this very hour."

"Therefore, I stand before you to testify to both high officials
And the lowest of people alike; the same thing the prophets
And Moses said would happen; that Christ would first suffer,
And then rise from the dead to proclaim the light of salvation
To the Jews and also to the Gentiles."
Festus jumped to his feet and shouted, "Paul you're mad, your learning
Has made you insane."

Paul answered, "Festus, Your Excellency, I am not mad, I
Am speaking the truth." Then Paul turned to King Agrippa,
"The King understands these matters. I appeal to him in these
Matters, knowing he understands these issues, because none
Of these things were done in secret."
"King Agrippa, do you believe the things the prophets said?"
"I know you do!"
Then King Agrippa replied, "Almost you convinced me to become
A Christian."
Then Paul replied, "I wish you were a Christian, both you and
Everyone who hears these words. I wish you were the
Same as I—except these chains."
At this point in Paul's speech, the king arose and with the governor
And Bernice and other government officials left the room;
They talked among themselves, saying,

"This man has done nothing that deserves death or imprisonment."
Agrippa said to Festus, "You should release this man,
Except he appealed to Caesar."

Lord, thank You for the boldness of Paul's testimony,
If he had not been faithful, I might not be saved;
Help me be as faithful as Paul.

Amen.

Paul's Trip to Rome

Acts 27:1-44

Lord, they finally made arrangements to sail for Italy,
So they handed Paul and other prisoners over to a Centurion
Named Julius, of the Augustine regiment.
They boarded a ship that was scheduled to make several stops
Along the coast of Turkey.
When they reached Lebanon, Julius let Paul go ashore to visit
Christians and receive hospitality from them.
From there, they put out to sea, but because of stormy winds,
Sailed north of Cyprus near the coast of Turkey;
At Myra, they changed ships for one heading to Rome.
The winds were still strong so they sailed under Crete;
They struggled in the wind until they came to Fair Havens,
Near the town of Lasea, near Rhodes.
They stayed there several days, because sailing was hazardous
Because it was winter. So Paul warned the commander,
"Friends, this is going to be a dangerous voyage and there is a risk
That we will lose the cargo, the ship, and also our lives."
But the Centurion listened more to the captain and owner than
to Paul.
Since Fair Havens was an exposed harbor that was a dangerous place

To spend the winter, they decided to go further;
Then they decided to winter in Phoenix because it was a
protected harbor.
Just then a light wind blew from the south that was perfect for sailing;
They took in the anchor and sailed past Crete, but before long
A hurricane caught them in open waters.
It was impossible to keep the ship headed into the wind,
So they gave up and let it run with the wind;
It was a continual struggle to keep the boat under control.
They hoisted the small life boat being towed behind them,
Then wrapped ropes around the hull to strengthen it,
So they dropped a sea anchor and let the ship drift.
The next day when the waves grew higher, they threw
Cargo overboard. The following day they threw out
The tackle and ship's gear.
They couldn't see the sun or moon for several days,
So everyone gave up hope of surviving.
When they hadn't eaten for several days, Paul addressed everyone,
"If you had listened to me, we wouldn't have this damage."
"Now I ask you don't give up hope. No one will die,
Only the ship will be lost. Last night God, to whom
I belong and whom I serve; He sent an angel to tell me
'Fear not Paul, you will appear before Caesar, therefore all
Who are sailing with you will be safe.' So be courageous,
It will happen just as God told me. We will be stranded
On some island."
On the 14th night the ship was still drifting
When the sailors felt land was near. They sounded
And found it was 120 feet of water.
A little later they sounded again and found 90 feet of water;
They realized they would be driven into rocks, so they
Threw out four anchors, and prayed for daylight.
Then the sailors planned to abandon the ship, so they lowered

An emergency boat as though they were putting out anchors.
Paul said to the Centurion, "We will all die unless the sailors
> Stay aboard." The soldiers cut the rope to let the small boat drift
> away.

As it began to get light, Paul urged everyone to eat something
> So they would have strength for the coming emergency.

Paul said, "There's no safety in fasting, not one of you
> Will lose a hair of your head."

Then Paul took bread, gave thanks, broke it, and began to eat;
> Everyone was encouraged and they ate.

There were a total of 276 on board, so then they
> Threw the grain into the sea.

When daybreak gave some light, no one recognized the island,
> But they saw a bay with a beach. They planned
> To run the ship aground on the beach if possible.

They cut the anchors, lowered the rudders, hoisted the top sail,
> And headed ashore, but the ship hit a sand bar.

The bow of the boat stuck in the sand and the pounding waves began to
> Break up the stern.

The soldiers planned to kill the prisoners because they were afraid
> They would escape. But the Centurion was determined to
> Deliver Paul safely to Rome. He wouldn't let them do it.

He gave orders for those who could swim to swim to shore,
> He then directed the others to follow on planks or pieces of
> wreckage;
> All escaped safely to the beach.

Lord, You allow your children to be tested in the storms of life,
> *Help me be courageous when I'm tested,*
> *Help me get through storms as did Paul.*

Amen.

From Malta to Rome

Acts 28:1-31

Lord, when I get through the storms of life,
I know You'll soothe and comfort me from my pain;
But help me remember to praise You for deliverance.

When they got on the beach, they discovered it was
The island of Malta. The inhabitants welcomed them and
Built a huge fire to warm them.
Paul had collected a bundle of sticks, and as he
Placed them in the fire, a viper bit him in the hand.
When the inhabitants saw the snake hanging onto Paul's hand,
They waited for him to die, saying, "He's a
Terrible sinner, the storm didn't kill him but the snake will."
Paul shook the snake into the fire, but his hand didn't swell up,
Nor did he drop dead. They changed their minds and said,
"Paul's a god."
They were near an estate belonging to Publius, the governor of the island;
He fed the survivors for three days.
Publuis' father was in bed suffering from high fever and dysentery,
Paul laid his hand on him and prayed for him and the man was
healed;
When this happened, other sick came and were cured as well.
After three months the winter was over; Paul was ready to leave.
He set sail for Italy, and the people of the island
Put provisions on board for Paul and his companions.

When the believers in Rome heard about Paul's arrival,
They came to meet Paul at the Forum of Appius and the Three
Taverns;
Paul thanked God and was encouraged when he saw them.
When Paul arrived in Rome, he was allowed to stay
In his own rented apartment where soldiers guarded him.

After three days, Paul called the leading Jews for a day's discussion;
      Paul said, "Brothers, although I have done nothing against
      Our people or our customs, I was arrested in Jerusalem,
      And delivered over to the Romans."
"They examined me and would have set me free because they found
      I was not guilty of any crime. But the Jews
      Filed an objection, and I was forced to appeal to Caesar."
"That is why I asked to see you and talk to you about this matter.
      It is for the hope of Israel that I wear these chains."
The Jews answered, "We haven't heard anything against you,
      We haven't received a letter from Jerusalem, nor have
      Any who have arrived here from Judea said anything about you."
"But we want to hear what you believe. All we know
      About Christians is that they are hated everywhere."

Lord, help me have a positive attitude in life
      Even when I know there are many with negative thoughts about You."

They set a time so that a large number of Jews
      Could visit Paul at his apartment to discuss Christianity.
Paul told them that Jesus came to sit on the throne of David,
      And he argued from the Law of Moses and the Prophet,
      Trying to persuade them about Jesus.
They began early in the morning and continued until the evening;
      Some were convinced, but others were skeptical;
      So the Jews disagreed among themselves.
Paul had one last thing to say to the Jews,
      "You Jews will hear the Gospel, but not understand,
      You will see the truth of Jesus, but are spiritually blinded,
      For your heart is hardened,
      And your spiritual ears are shut up,
      And your spiritual eyes are blinded,
      Because you refuse to believe what is presented
      Lest your heart receive the Gospel

And you become convicted and are healed."
Paul understood from that experience that salvation
    Was to be sent to the Gentiles, because they will listen to God.

Paul spent two years in this rented apartment
    Welcoming all who came to see him,
Proclaiming the Kingdom of God to all,
    Teaching the truth about the Lord Jesus Christ
    With complete freedom and no hindrance.

Lord, thank You for the great influential life of the apostle Paul;
    I cannot do all Paul could do,
    So help me to do all that I can do.
You don't ask that I do the great accomplishments of others
    You only ask me to be faithful to my gifts
    And obey your commands. I'll do that.

Amen.

PRAYING PAUL'S LETTERS

PRAYING WITH ME
THE LETTERS OF PAUL

This project began four years ago when one morning I began translating Psalm 37 into popular everyday English, then transposing it into the second person—a prayer to God. Psalm 37 went well, so I translated Psalm 34. Then I decided to translate the whole book of Psalms, not for a book for other people, but for my own spiritual growth. I wanted to pray the Psalms.

When I mentioned the project to Don Milam, editor at Destiny Image Publishers, he said, "I want to publish that book." And so in 2004, I released *Praying the Psalms.* Since that time, five other books have been released in the series *Praying the Scriptures*.

Now I invite you to join me in *Praying Paul's Letters.* If you do more than read the words of Paul—if you pray them from your heart—they will transform your life. The Bible does that.

Praying the Scriptures is superior to *reading* the Scriptures, because normal reading of the Bible deals with the intellect—you pass the message through your mind. But when you *Pray the Scriptures*, you go to a deeper level—to the heart. Your emotions become involved in the message, and then you move your will; for when you talk to God through the Scriptures, you have chosen to worship God and obey Him. *Praying Paul's Letters* will touch your intellect, emotion, and will. That's how your life will be transformed.

Rather than including dictionary facts as an introduction to each of Paul's letters, I have written a story to incorporate the facts about Paul's writings—where he was when he was writing a particular letter, why he wrote, what he wanted to say, and what he wanted to accomplish in the lives of those who received his letters. The stories are the way I think it happened, including the way I think Paul felt when he wrote each letter. Obviously the stories are not inspired. But basic facts are included to help give you insight into each letter and help you apply it to your life.

As you are *Praying Paul's Letters*, may you touch God in a new way—but in a greater way, may God touch you.

Sincerely yours in Christ,
Elmer L. Towns
Written at my home at the foot of
the Blue Ridge Mountains

ROMANS

Chapter 26

The Story of Writing the Book of Romans

Date: A.D. 60 ⌒ Written in: Corinth, Greece ⌒ Written by: Paul

I was sitting with several of my followers in a home in Corinth. The room was stuffy, but we were out of the sun. We were watching the long shadows of the afternoon darken the house.

I told the group that I had a great desire to preach the Gospel in Rome. I told them when we preach in Rome, we are reaching the world. I reminded them all the roads of the world lead to Rome, which means we can use them to travel the opposite way into all the world.

One of my followers said, "Paul, you can't go to Rome, the city is too big, sin is too rampant. The city is given to idolatry because Caesar Augustus recently built or restored 82 temples. Don't forget the politics; the Senate has just built a new forum. The city is given over to the sins of the flesh and to pleasure. The new coliseum has free admission for chariot races, gladiatorial contests, and theatrical performances. They would like nothing more than to throw you to the lions in the middle of that massive arena."

The rest of the followers said nothing, but their eyes darted from one to another to see the reaction of the others. Then they all looked at me, I was their leader. I had never backed down from a challenge, and I never went to a city that I did not evangelize.

The room was silent, an ordinary house fly, oblivious to imminent eternal decision, buzzed around the room. The only other thing heard was the deep breaths of some of the followers.

I did not say anything, but rose slowly, walked to an open window and looked down the street of Corinth. "There was not one Christian when I came to this town; Corinth was known as the most sinful harbor town on the Mediterranean Sea."

I looked around the room, then pointed down the street, "There is the place where I made tents for Aquila and Pricilla, and over there"—pointing across the street—"is where they lived. It was around their evening meal when they came to believe in Jesus Christ as their personal Messiah. From them the Gospel spread to the synagogue and many Jews believed."

I walked to the other side of the room and pushed open a door. Immediately, the evening breeze stirred the room. From the door we could see the Aegean Sea. Again I pointed, "There is the synagogue and next to it is the home of Justice. Remember, we led all the Christians out of the synagogue, and they began holding church service in Justice House. I want all my followers to remember what God did in Corinth."

I looked around the room. "This was one of the most wicked cities in Greece, yet the Gospel captured the hearts of many. Yes, and Rome is just as wicked and I am committed to preaching the Gospel in every wicked place where Christ is not known."

I moved around the room vigorously returning to the door that overlooked the sea and pointing out to the railway. "There is the railway where boats are put on railcars and pulled over the isthmus. They do that to save five or six sailing days to Rome. Every hour a boat is pulled over the narrow strip of ground, and every hour a ship leaves—taking the Gospel with them."

I reminded them that many Christians worked on the railway pulling railcars over that small strip of land. While sailors were waiting for the boats to be pulled over, they visited taverns and houses of prostitution. But Christians met their ship, and witnessed to them that Jesus the Messiah died for their sins. Many times when a ship sailed from Corinth they had Christians on board who would carry the Gospel to ports throughout the Mediterranean Sea.

Then I told them, "Where one ship may leave the harbor of Corinth every hour, there could be thousands of people leaving Rome every day on the Appian Way, going around the world with the Gospel."

That was the end of the conversation. Before the men left, I told Tertius I had a job for him. I asked him to meet me early the next morning.

The next morning I rose early and met Tertius on the back patio of the home. I explained to him that in the coming weeks I would be writing the most important letter of my life to the people in Rome. Because Rome was the center of the world, I felt they needed a letter that explained Christianity from beginning to end, from Alpha to Omega.

I laid out my project, then said to Tertius, "Get ink, pen, and paper, for you must write this epistle for me. My eyes are too weak to do it—but I will read carefully every word that you write and sign it with my signature." I explained that the letter needed authority, it needed my signature as an apostle of grace.

I could read, but not very clearly and not very fast. Sometimes it took a little while for the letters on the page to form in my mind. Ever since I had been stoned in Lystra, I had problems with my eyes. I've often thought that a stone probably damaged a nerve or maybe even a sharp stone punctured the retina.

In the early days I had written every word of my letters with my own hands. I had written to the Galatians—my first letter—"See how I have written such large letters."

But this letter to the Romans would be much longer, and if I used giant block letters, it would probably take several large scrolls. I wanted this letter to be on one scroll, because I knew it would be copied by the church in Rome and sent to all other churches. Also, itinerate preachers coming through Rome would make a copy to take this letter to other outlying churches. This letter would be circulated throughout the Mediterranean world. If there were two or three scrolls, one may be lost, and then people would not have a complete copy of God's magnificent plan of salvation.

Tertius returned with the writing box, took a scroll and unrolled it. Tertius had made a new batch of ink for this special project. He crushed the black coals from the fire into powder, and then mixed it with olive oil. Tertius stirred the mixture into ink, then inserted the quill in the ink, pressed the barrel of the feather so that it would drink up ink, and he was ready to write. Tertius ask, "What will be the first word?"

I smiled, then spoke slowly, "Paul, a bondservant of Jesus Christ, called to be an apostle, separated to the Gospel of God which the Father promised through His prophets." Nothing could be heard on the back patio except the scratching of the quill on the parchment.

Sincerely yours in Christ,
The apostle Paul

Sitting there on the patio in Corinth, the two men wrote the greatest explanation of the Gospel ever penned by humans. Why the greatest? Because Paul was inspired by the Holy Spirit to write accurately what God wanted Him to write.

Chapter 27

PRAYING THE BOOK OF ROMANS

Introduction and the Guilt of the Heathen

Romans 1:1-32

Lord, the apostle Paul wrote to the Christians in Rome telling them he was a
servant who was chosen to preach the Good News,
which You promised in the Old Testament through the prophets.

May I always be faithful to my calling,
As Paul was to his task.

Lord, thank You for the Gospel about Your Son, the Lord Jesus Christ.
Who came as a baby though King David's line, who was raised
from the dead by the Spirit of Holiness to demonstrate that He
was the mighty Son of God.

Lord, thank You that through Christ all your mercy has been poured out
on me to be a witness to everyone, everywhere about Your grace;
so they too can believe and become a Christ follower.

Lord, Paul told his dear friends in Rome that You loved them and called them;
Paul prayed for grace and peace to rest on them from You—God the
Father—and from the Lord Jesus Christ.

May Your grace and peace fill my life,
As I walk in Your love and calling.

Lord, Paul told everyone about the faith of the Roman believers, and
that it was

his duty to serve You by continually praying for them.
Paul specifically prayed that he would have the opportunity to
have a safe trip to come see them. He wanted to strengthen their
spiritual gifts so their church would grow strong spiritually.

Lord, Paul wanted to bless the Roman church by sharing his faith with
them, and allow them to be a blessing to him.

Lord, Paul told the Romans that he planned many times before to visit
them, but was prevented. He wanted to minister to them just as
he had ministered in other Gentile churches.

Lord, I have a debt to carry the Gospel to both civilized people, and to
unreached people groups who have never heard the Gospel.

Lord, I am ready to preach to any or to all, just as Paul was ready to
preach the Gospel to those in Rome and to everyone in the world.

Lord, I am not ashamed of the Good News of Christ, for it is powerful
to get people to believe so they can be saved.

Lord, I agree with the priority that Paul gave, that the Gospel must first be
preached to the Jews, then to Gentiles. When a person puts his
personal trust in the Gospel, You declare them righteous—fit for Heaven.
This is what the Old Testament teaches, "The just shall live by
expressing faith."

Why the Heathen Are Lost

Romans 1:18-32

Lord, You have revealed that You will punish everyone who trespasses Your
commandments because they reject the truth given them. You have
revealed Yourself to everyone's conscience. Also, everyone
can plainly learn from nature that it took a powerful Creator to create

this vast universe, and that it took an intelligent Creator to put the laws of nature in place to control everything.

Lord, now no one can give an excuse when they are judged and condemned because everyone knows You exist and You have eternal power.

Lord, everyone knows You exist, but they won't acknowledge You, or thank You for natural blessings, or even worship You. They are controlled by illogical thought patterns because they reject the logic of Your existence.

Their minds are blinded and confused. When they think they are wise, they actually are foolish. Instead of worshiping Your glorious presence, they worship gods made out of wood, or stone that look like birds, or animals, or snakes, or corrupt people.

Lord, You allowed those who reject You to do all types of sexual sins, so that they can fulfill their lust, degrading their bodies with one another. Instead of believing the truth they knew about You, they deliberately rejected You, choosing to worship and serve created idols rather than You, the Creator, who could bless them.

Lord, You abandoned them to their passions because their woman turned from natural sexual practices to abnormal acts. Their men turned from normal relations with women and turned to lustful sexual practices with one another, men behaving indecently with men, so that they pay a penalty with their souls for their perversion.

Lord, since they refused to acknowledge You—You gave them up to their own irrational and corrupt ideas. Now they continually try to think up new and sexually stimulating ideas that the depraved mind conceives. They are controlled by all sorts of evil and greed, and hatred, and fightings, bitterness, and lies; so that they even want to kill those who mistreat them. They quarrel, hate You, are proud, braggardly and continually think of new ways to sin, and hate their parents. They don't understand what is right, nor do they know how to do right. They break their promises, are mean and have no feelings for others. They know in their hearts You will judge them, but they deny it outwardly. They go ahead and do all these things in rebellion against You, and seek friendship with others who are also against You.

Lord, I know that You alone are God and that sin
    is denial of Your existence and rejection of Your Laws.

Give me faith to always trust You,
    And give me courage to always follow Your plan of living.

Amen.

The Guilt of Religious People

Romans 2:1-29

Lord, people have no excuse for their personal sin,
    Because they criticize others who do the same sin.
In judging others, they condemn themselves
    Because they behave no differently than those they condemn.

Lord, You condemn all who rebel against Your Laws,
    And you punish law-breakers impartially.
Those who pass judgment on other people
    Will be judged because they do the exact same things.

Lord, You are patient with those who sin against You,
    You wait a long time before punishing them.
You are giving them an opportunity to repent
    And turn to You from their sins;
    Your goodness should lead them to repentance.

But no, their stubborn refusal only adds
    To Your anger toward them.
Then one day they will suffer punishment
    When You punish everyone for their sins
Just as the Scriptures teach,
    "God will repay each as their works deserve."

Lord, those who seek Your honor and immortality
    Will earn eternal life from You.
Those who refuse Your truth and do evil,
    You will punish in Your anger and fury.
They will suffer pain and suffering
    Because they rebelled against You and chased evil,
    This includes both Jews and Gentiles as well.
But, there will be glory, honor, and peace,
    To those who seek Your salvation,
    Including both Jews and Gentiles as well.

Lord, there is no favoritism of persons with You,
    You will punish Gentiles when they sin
    Even if they never heard of Your written Law.
You will punish those who have access to Your Law,
    They will be judged by what's in the Law.

But I realize it is not knowing the Law,
    But, keeping the Law that makes anyone holy.
Gentiles who have never heard the Law
    Know by their conscience what the Law requires.
They know by their reason to obey the Law,
    Even when they don't "possess" copies of the Law.
The substance of the Law is written in their hearts,
    They know right from wrong.
Their conscience accuses them when they sin,
    Or it excuses them when they do right.

Lord, You will punish the Jews when they sin,
>Because they disobey the written Law that they possess;
>They know what is right, but don't do it.
No one is saved because they know what is right,
>They are saved when they do it.

Lord, the day is coming when Jesus Christ
>Will judge the secrets of all people.
I will be ready to meet You in judgment
>For I have been saved and I live for You.

Lord, those who called themselves Jews
>Should walk according to the Law of God,
>And honor You with their lives.
The Jews should know Your will because they know Your Law,
>And they should know what is right and wrong.
The Jews should be guides to the blind,
>And they should be a beacon to those in the dark.
They should teach the ignorant and unlearned,
>Because they embody all knowledge and truth.
But the Jews do not live by the Law,
>They should teach themselves what they teach others.
They preach against stealing, yet they steal;
>They forbid adultery, yet they commit adultery.
They despise idols, yet they make money off idol making;
>They boast about the Law, yet they break it
>And thereby dishonor You who gave the Law.
As the Scriptures teach, "It is your fault, Jews,
>That God's name is despised by the Gentiles."

Amen.

All Are Lost in Sin

Romans 3:1-31

Lord, Paul asked if there is an advantage of being Jewish,
>Does circumcision mean any thing?
Paul answers "Yes, being a Jew has many advantages,
>They received Your message in the Old Testament.
Yet, even when some Jews were unfaithful,
>Their lack of faith didn't cancel Your promises.
God, You will always keep Your Word
>Even when everyone else is unfaithful.
The Book of Psalms says, "The Word of God,
>Will always prove to be right,
>No matter who questions God."
Some point out that the sins of the Jews
>Make You demonstrate Your holiness,
>Because You always judge sin.
The Jews justify their sin
>Claiming people will say, You—God—are good
>When they see You punishing our sin.
Then the Jews ask, "Is it fair for You to punish us
>When our sin helps others recognize You?"
Paul answers, "That is absurd thinking,
>It means God could never judge sin
>If God didn't judge rebellious Jews."
Paul continues, "That's like saying my lying
>Makes You demonstrate Your truthfulness."
"When You judge the Jews' sin,
>You thus bring glory to Yourself."
That's like saying, "We do evil
>To bring about good."

Lord, Paul asked again, "Are Jews better off than Gentiles?"
     He answers, "No, both are under sin's control."
The Scriptures teach
     There is no good person left in the world,
     No not one.
There is no one who understands You
     And no one is seeking You.
All have turned from doing right,
     There is no good person on earth, no not one.
Their speech is rebellious and filthy,
     Just like an open grave.
Their tongue is full of deceit,
     Bitter curses fill their mouth, and
     Their words are deadly like a snake's poison.
They are quick to stab people in the back,
     Creating misery and strife wherever they go.
They know nothing of Your blessing
     And they don't care what You think of them.

Lord, the Jews should know what the Law says,
     And they are responsible to obey what You say.
Therefore the Jews stand guilty before You
     When they see clearly they aren't obeying You,
     So they know they are sinners.

Lord, You have spoken to silence every mouth,
     Now the whole world is guilty before You.
Therefore, no one can be justified
     By keeping the Law;
     Rather the Law makes us conscious of our sin.

Lord, I thank You that Your righteousness is made known
     Apart from knowing the Law,
     It is made known through the Gospel.
Now there is a way to Heaven for all sinners,

You will declare us "not guilty"
    When we trust Christ for salvation.
    All can be saved—Jews and Gentiles—alike,
    By believing in Jesus Christ.

Lord, I know I am a sinner, because You said
    All have sinned,
    And come short of Your glorious benefits.
But both Jew and Gentile are declared righteous
    Through Your free gift of grace
    When they are redeemed by Jesus Christ.

Lord, you sent Jesus to take the punishment for our sins,
    And reconciled us to You.
You declared that sins committed before the Cross
    Are forgiven by the blood of Christ
And declared that all sins committed,
    At this time are forgiven.
In this way You make Your righteousness known;
    Therefore, Your wrath against sin is justified,
    And You become the Justifier for sinners.

Lord, I realize I can't boast about anything
    That has to do with my salvation,
Because my forgiveness is not based on what I do,
    But is based on what Christ has done for me.

Therefore, all Christians are justified by faith
    Without keeping the Law.
You are not saving only Jews—no,
    You treat everyone the same way,
    Whether they are Jew or Gentile.
This does not undermine the Law—no!
    When we realize salvation is by faith alone,

This places the Law in its proper place.
Amen.

Justification by Faith

Romans 4:1-25

Lord, Paul points out Abraham is the founder
From which all Jews descended.
If Abraham were justified by doing something good,
He would have had something to boast about.
But the Scriptures teach, "Abraham believed God,
And God declared him as righteous."
When someone works, they get wages;
They get what's due to them.
However, when a man gets salvation free,
He has not worked for it;
You have justified him because of faith.

Lord, David said the same thing,
"A man is happy when he is forgiven
Without doing good works."
That man is blessed because his sins
Are no longer written in Your book.
Is this a blessedness only for the circumcised Jews?
Or can Gentiles be justified before You?
Look again at Abraham, he was justified
By You before he was circumcised.
When Abraham was later circumcised,
It was an outer sign of faith within his heart.
In this way, Abraham became the spiritual father
Of all the uncircumcised believers
So they might also be justified by God.
Your promise to Abraham that he would be

The spiritual father to all believers, of all times,
Was based on his faith, not his works.
If unsaved people can receive Your forgiveness
By keeping the Law,
Then our faith is pointless and empty.
The Law teaches we are punished for breaking the Law
But Christ has fulfilled the Law in His death;
He has taken it out of the way.
So, we get Your blessings by faith,
Whether we keep the Law or not.
You will bless those who belong to the Law
As well as Gentiles who weren't given the Law,
As long as we all come to You by faith.
We come like Abraham, who is the father of us all;
The Scriptures promise, "I have made Abraham
The ancestor of many nations."
God called those things that are not, i.e.,
The salvation of the Gentiles
As though it had already happened.

Lord, when You told Abraham he would have a son,
And be the father of many nations,
Abraham believed Your promises to him;
He hoped against any hope of his present circumstances.
Abraham did not have weak faith
Even though his body couldn't reproduce
And he was 100 years old.
Also, Abraham realized Sarah was barren and old, but
He staggered not at Your promises through unbelief,
But was strong in faith giving glory to You.
Abraham was convinced You had all power
To do what You promised.
Because of Abraham's faith, You forgave his sins,
And declared him righteous.

Lord, I know this kind of faith wasn't for Abraham alone,
    But it is for me also;
    You will accept me as You accepted Abraham.
I too believe Your promises
    That just as You brought Jesus back from the dead,
You will forgive all my sins
    And declare me righteous before You.
                    Amen.

The Results of Justification by Faith

Romans 5:1-21

Lord, now that I'm declared right with You by faith,
    I can experience lasting peace.
Since my faith in Jesus, I can enter Your grace,
    I can boast of looking forward to Your glory.
Also, I can rejoice in my sufferings,
    Knowing they work patience in my life.
And patience produces endurance and when I endure,
    I get Your approval which gives me hope.
My hope does not disappoint me, because You
    Have poured Your love into my heart
    By the Holy Spirit whom You gave me.

Lord, at the moment when I was helpless,
    I realized Christ died for sinful people, such as me.
I wouldn't expect anyone to die for a good person,
    Even though that is possible,
But You demonstrated Your great love for me
    By sending Christ to die for me,
    While I was a great sinner.
Since His blood has done all this for me,
    He will also declare me completely righteous.

Lord, when Jesus' death reconciled me to You,
      I was still not saved,
      I was still Your enemy.
Now that I am reconciled
      Surely I can count on Your blessings
      By the life of Your Son living in me.
I rejoice in this wonderful new relationship
      With the Lord Jesus Christ
      Based on what He did in saving me.

Lord, I know when Adam sinned, sin entered the world
      Then all people sinned
      And death spread throughout the human race.
Sin existed in the world
      Long before the written Law was given.
No one could be accused of breaking the Law,
      When there was no written Law.
Yet, all people died from Adam to Moses;
      It was their sin that led to their death,
      It was not a matter of their breaking the written Law.

Lord, Adam was a contrast to Christ,
      So the gift of Christ outweighed the fall of Adam.
Through one man—Adam—many died,
      Through the gift of one man—Christ— many lived.
The results of the gift of Christ
      Outweigh the results of Adam's fall.
For after the Fall came the judgment of condemnation,
      And many committed trespasses because of the Fall,
      But by the one Man—Jesus Christ—came abundant life.
For it is certain that death reigned
      Over everyone because of one man's fall.
It is even more certain that life reigns
      Because of one man—Jesus Christ—who gives

The free gift to those who don't deserve it.
Again, Adam's sin brought punishment on all,
>But Christ made it possible for all to be declared righteous.
By one man's disobedience, many were made sinners;
>By one man's obedience, many will be declared righteous.

Lord, the Law was given to show all
>How far short they come in obeying You.
The more we see our sins and failures,
>The more we realize how much You have forgiven us.
Before, sin reigned over all, bringing death;
>Now grace reigns to deliver eternal life
>To those who are in Christ Jesus our Lord.
>>Amen.

Deliverance From Sin in the Believer's Life

Romans 6:1-23

Lord, should I keep sinning
>So you can keep showing Your grace?
>Absolutely not!
Sin's power over me is broken;
>Should I keep sinning
>When I don't have to? Again, no!
When I was placed into Christ by Spiritual baptism,
>I was placed into His death;
>The control of my sin nature over me
>was broken by His death.
In other words, when I was baptized into Christ,
>I died when He died.
When Christ was raised up from the dead,
>I was given new life to live for Him.

Lord, I have been united with Christ in death.
>That I might share His new life.
My old lustful nature was nailed to the Cross,
>It received a death-blow
>So that I might not serve sin in the future.
For when I am dead to sin,
>I am free from all its power over me.
I believe that having died with Christ,
>I now share my new life with Him.

Lord, since Christ has been raised from the dead,
>He will never again die;
>Death has no power over Him.
Christ died once for all to end sin's control,
>Now He lives in Heaven with You.
So, I look on myself as dead to sin's control,
>But alive to Your will through Jesus Christ.
I will not let sin control my physical body
>And I will not obey its sinful lust.
I will not let any part of my body
>Become an evil tool to be used for sinning.
I give myself to you as one who is alive from the dead,
>And I give all parts of my body to you,
>As an instrument of righteousness.
I will not let sin control me,
>I will not be controlled by the Law, but by grace.

Lord, shall I continue to sin because
>I am not under the law?
>Absolutely not!
If I give myself to sin,
>I become a slave to the one I obey.
I cannot be a slave to sin and death,
>And at the same time be a slave to Christ and life.

Lord, thank You that I'm no longer a slave to sin,
> But I'm your slave,
> Having believed Your principles from my heart.
I am free from the mastery of my old nature
> And I am a slave to righteousness.

Lord, once I was a slave to uncleanliness and self-gratification,
> Now I am a slave to righteousness and holiness.
When I was a slave to sin,
> I felt no obligation to obey Your will.
I got nothing from serving sin,
> And now I am ashamed of what I did,
> Because those things lead to death.
But now I have been set free from sin,
> I have become Your slave
> That will lead to holiness and eternal life.
When I serve sin, I earn the wages of death,
> But You gave me eternal life through Christ Jesus, my Lord.
> > Amen.

The Struggle of the Old and New Nature

Romans 7:1-25

Lord, Paul told his saved Jewish brethren
> When they died to the Law,
> It no longer held them in its power.
A married woman has legal obligations
> To the husband while he is alive.
All obligations came to an end,
> When the husband dies.
But if she gives herself to another man,
> While her husband is still alive,
> She is legally an adulteress.

Nevertheless, her legal obligations cease
    When her husband dies,
    And she can legally marry another.

Lord, Paul said that is why Christians
    Who died to the Law in Christ's death,
Can now give themselves to Christ
    Who arose from the dead
    That they might bring fruit to You.
But when they give themselves to their sinful nature,
    Their lustful passions controlled their bodies
    So they bear fruit to death.
But now when we die to our lust that once controlled us,
    We are released from the Law
So we can serve You in a new way,
    Not by legalistically obeying rules and traditions
    But by the power of new life.

Lord, Paul told them the Law was not evil,
    Except that no one would have known what sin is
    Except that the Law told them.
I would have not known that "coveting" was evil,
    Except the Law said, "Thou shalt not covet."
The Law stirred up my evil desires
    By reminding me these desires were wrong.
Does that mean if there were no laws to break,
    There would be no sinning? No!
I felt OK as long as I was ignorant of the Law,
    But when I learned what the Law meant,
    I realized I was a sinner, I learned I was a slave doomed to die.
The Law was supposed to lead me to life,
    But instead it led me to death.
Sin took advantage of me by using the Law
    To give me a death sentence.

Lord, I know the Law is holy,
> And the Ten Commands are good and just.
Does that mean that something that was good
>> Was responsible for my death?
>> Absolutely not!
But sin is treacherous and deceitful,
> It used something good for evil purposes,
>> Thus sin exercised all its lustful powers over me.

Lord, I know the Law is spiritual
> But I am unspiritual, sold as a slave to sin.
I cannot understand my reaction to things;
> What I am supposed to do,
> I don't do.
What I hate to do,
> I continually go back to do it.
When I act against what I want to do,
> That means the Law is good.
When I rebel against the Law,
> It is not me that's doing it,
> But sin that dwells in me.
I know that nothing good lives in me,
> It's my sinful nature that controls my life.
I have a desire to do good things, but
> I cannot carry it out.
When I try not to do wrong things,
> I do them anyway.
So when I do the things I don't want to do,
> Then it is not my true self doing them;
> Sin still controls my life.

Lord, I've discovered a new law in me,
> Every time I want to do good,
> I do wrong, intentionally.

I love to keep the Law of God,
>   But I see another law working in me.
It fights the logic of my mind,
>   Making me a prisoner of the Law,
>   Working in my body to make me sin, it's my old nature.
What a miserable person I am.
>   Who can rescue me from my slavery to sin?
Thank You, Lord, that You will deliver me
>   Through Jesus Christ my Lord.

Lord, what is the result of all of this?
>   In my lower nature I am a slave of sin,
>   But in my mind I am Your slave.
>   Amen.

The Power of the Holy Spirit in the Believer

Romans 8:1-39

Lord, now there is no condemnation against me,
>   Because I am in Christ Jesus.
The power of the life-giving Holy Spirit
>   Is mine through Christ Jesus.
He has released me from the compulsive cycle
>   Of sin and lust of my old nature.
For the Law was powerless to help me obey,
>   Because I was a slave to my old nature.
But You sent Your Son in a human body
>   To be a sacrificial offering for my sin
>   To destroy sin's domination over me.
Now I can obey Your laws
>   By following the leading of the Holy Spirit,
>   And refusing the lust of my old nature.

Lord, those who are dominated by their sinful nature
    Have made up their minds to sin,
But I am dominated by the Holy Spirit,
    Because I have made up my mind
    To do what He desires of me.
If I follow the dictates of my old nature,
    It will lead to death.
When I obey the Holy Spirit,
    He leads me to life and peace.
As a result, when I only obey my old nature,
    I have made myself Your enemy.
My old nature has never been Your friend,
    And I can never make it obey You.
Those who only please their old nature,
    Never please You.

Lord, I am not interested in pleasing the old nature,
    I am interested in spiritual things,
    Because the Holy Spirit lives in my life.
And I know I am Your child,
    Because I possess the Holy Spirit.

Lord, even when my body is dead because of sin,
    My spirit is alive because I was declared righteous,
And the Holy Spirit who raised Jesus from the dead
    Lives in me to give me life.
Therefore, after this body is dead,
    I will live again by the same Holy Spirit
    Who is living within me.

Lord, I know it is not necessary for me
    To obey the lust of my old nature.
If I died physically obeying my old nature,
    I'd be doomed to death.
But Your Holy Spirit can stop my rebellion,

By His power that indwells me.
Therefore, I will be led by the Spirit of God,
    I will be Your child.

Lord, I am not just a slave who cowers in fear
    Of breaking laws or displeasing You,
But I received the Holy Spirit, who made me Your child,
    So I cry to you, "Papa, Father."
The Holy Spirit constantly tells my spirit
    That I am Your child;
Now if I am Your child, I am also an heir,
    Your heir, and co-heir with Christ.
Because I suffer as a Christian,
    I will also share in His glory in Heaven.

Lord, my present sufferings are nothing
    When compared with the glories
    That are waiting for me in Heaven.
As a matter of fact, all Creation groans,
    Waiting for the glorification of Your children
Because Creation will lose its thorns, thistles,
    And the curse you put upon it
    When You send Jesus at the end of time.
Creation will be liberated from its corruption
    To enjoy the same magnificent redemption
    You will give to all of Your children.
From the beginning until now, animals and plants groan,
    Expecting to be redeemed from the bondage of decadence
    To enjoy the same redemption as Your children.
I too groan while I wait for my body to be transformed,
    For that is my inward hope.
By trusting You, I'm looking forward to getting a new body;
    Those who are already in Heaven don't need hope
    They have already received their reward.

I continue to trust for something I don't have yet,
>   But I wait patiently and confidently for it.

Lord, thank You for the help of the Holy Spirit
>   Who comes to assist me in my weakness.
I don't know how I ought to pray
>   But the Holy Spirit intercedes for me,
>   He prays with words I can't understand or express.
What the Holy Spirit prays for me
>   Is in agreement with You, my Heavenly Father.
Therefore, the things that will happen to me
>   Are for my good because He prays for me.
For when You foreknew me, You predestinated me
>   To be confirmed to the image of Your Son,
>   So Your Son will be the first born among many children.

Lord, You predestined me and called me,
>   Because You called me, You also justified me,
>   And those You justified, You will glorify.

Lord, how shall I respond to Your great plan?
>   If You are for me, who can be against me?
Since You did not hold back Your only Son,
>   But You gave Him for us all,
>   I know You will freely give me all things.
Who can bring any charge against Your children?
>   Since You justify me, who can condemn me?
Christ Jesus who died for me and was raised,
>   Stands at Your right hand to intercede for me.
Who can separate me from Your love?
>   Not trouble, hardship, or persecutors,
>   Hunger, nakedness, or danger.
The Scriptures teach, "I must be ready
>   To die at any time, I am like sheep
>   Awaiting slaughter."

These are all trials over which I must triumph
 By the power of Christ who loves me,
 And died for me.

Lord, I am positive nothing can separate me
 From Your love for me.
Death can't separate me from You, also
 Angels can't to it;
Neither can the satanic power of hell,
 Nor things present, or things to come.

Nothing can separate me from Your love,
 Not height, nor depth, nor any other creature,
 For I am safe in Christ Jesus my Lord.
       Amen.

Continuing Jewish Unbelief

Romans 9:1-33

Lord, Paul's conscience made him tell everyone that he had a deep desire that his Jewish relatives might be saved. He was willing to be cut off from Christ for their salvation. Paul had deep sorrow and mental anguish because the Jewish people rejected Christ.

Lord, give me a burden for the salvation of my lost relatives and friends, that Paul had for the Jews who represented his flesh and blood.

Lord, the Jewish people were adopted by You, and given Your covenants, and Your glory visited them. You gave them the Law and principles how to worship You. They had everything, but rejected You.

Lord, the Jewish people descended from the patriarch's and Christ came from their flesh and blood. Christ is the One whom they should worship above all, He is the One they should bless.

Lord, does this mean You have failed to keep your promises because the
Jews refused to recognize Christ? Absolutely not! Not all physical
Jews are spiritual Jews, and not all the physical descendants of
Abraham have the faith of Abraham. You promised that through
Isaac the spiritual promises would be carried out, which means
other physical children of Abraham didn't get the privilege of being
in the line of Christ. That means not all the physical children of
Abraham are his spiritual descendents, only those who are the
children of promise.

Lord, I believe Your promises to Abraham apply to me,
    I have acted on the promises You made.
I recognized Jesus is the Messiah, the Son of God,
    I have received Him by faith and I am saved.

Lord, Paul quoted your promise, "I will visit you and Sarah will have a son."
    Then later you promised to Rebecca when she was pregnant by
    Isaac, before her twin sons were born, and before either of them did
    good or evil, that "The elder shall serve the younger." You chose
    Jacob before he was born—because your choice is free—and it didn't
    depend on human merit. The Scripture said, "Jacob I love, because
    he is the child of promise." Does this make You unjust? No!
    Remember what You said to Moses, "I will have mercy on whom I will
    have mercy, and I will have compassion on whom I please."

Lord, I know the only thing that counts is Your mercy, not what people
    desire or try to do. I am saved by Your grace.

Lord, thank You for having mercy on me.
    I didn't deserve salvation and eternal life,
But you saved me by Your grace,
    And made me a member of Your family.

Lord, You said to Pharaoh, "For this purpose I raised you up, so I might
    show my great power and that my name may be known throughout

the world." Therefore, God shows mercy when He wants to show mercy, and He hardens those He wants to harden.

Lord, thank You for sending the Holy Spirit
  To soften my heart to spiritual things.
Thank You for opening my blind eyes,
  And giving me a desire to know You.

Lord, many will ask, "How can You ever punish anyone since no one can reject Your will?" Therefore You answer them, "What right has any human to question Me?" You created everyone. "The pot has no right to question the potter, 'Why have you made me this shape?'" Every potter—or craftsman—can do what he wills with the clay. He decides whether a lump of clay should be used for an extraordinary pot or an average pot.

Lord, I thank You for making me who I am,
  And thank You for my special gifts.
Help me glorify You through my unique calling,
  And help me fulfill Your purpose for my life.

Lord, You have a perfect right to show Your anger, at any time against those who rebel against You, even when You were originally patient with them. You put up with rebels so you can show Your mercy and richness of grace.

Lord, You are patient with us—both Jews and Gentiles—to reveal Your grace and kindness to us. You said in Scripture, "I will say to a people who are not my people, that you will be Mine. You are my people, I will say to a nation that I have not loved, I love you." They will be called the sons of the Living God.

Lord, You said "Though Israel should have as many descendants as there are grains of sand on the seashore, only a remnant will be saved. For You will swiftly carry out Your punishment once and for all. For the Scriptures said 'Unless You—the all-powerful Lord—show Your mercy, all Jews would be destroyed, just as You destroyed Sodom and Gomorrah."'

Lord, then the Gentiles who were not looking for Your righteousness found it, they found Your righteousness that came by faith. The Jews who were trying to find Your righteousness by keeping the Law did not keep the Law and did not find righteousness. Why? Because they relied on their legalism, and not on faith. In other words, they stumbled over the Law and it became a stumbling stone to them. The Scriptures say, "You lay in Zion a stumbling stone—a rock to trip people up—that Rock was Jesus Christ. Those who believe in Him will not stumble or fall."

Amen.

Salvation Is for Everyone

Romans 10:1-21

Lord, Paul told the Romans that the longing of his heart was for Jewish people to be saved. Paul knows the enthusiasm they have for You, but it is misdirected zeal. Their passion is based on wrong knowledge. They have never realized Your demands of them for perfect righteousness, all the while they were trying to keep the Law to demonstrate their own righteousness. Therefore, all Jews, along with all Gentiles, are not perfect, but sinners in Your sight.

Lord, when I received Christ as my Savior,
It was the end of my struggle
To be righteous by keeping the Law.

Moses wrote that if anyone could keep the Law perfectly,
And hold out against temptation,
And never break one Law,
They could be saved and appear before God,
But I could never reach that standard.

I found salvation without searching Heaven
    To bring the physical Jesus down to me,
Nor did I descend into death to find Jesus
    And raise Him from the dead
    To give me eternal life.

I was saved by trusting Christ
    And He is within reach of any who look for Him.
Everyone can have this salvation,
    It is as easy as opening one's mouth to call for it,
    And opening their heart to You.
Salvation is obtained by the Word of faith,
    Which I received when I believed;
That was when I confessed with my mouth
    That Jesus is Lord,
And believed in my heart that You raised Him from the dead;
    I was saved!
For with my heart, I believed unto righteousness,
    And with my mouth
    Confession was made to salvation.

The Scriptures promise that when I believed in Christ,
    I would not be disappointed,
    And that is surely true.

Lord, Paul said Jews and Gentiles are the same, all must call upon You for
    Salvation; You are the same Lord who gives generously to those
    who call upon You. Paul quoted the Old Testament, "Whoever calls
    upon the Lord will be saved."

Lord, Paul reasoned, "How can anyone ask You to save them, unless they
    believe in You? How can they believe if they have never heard?
    How can they hear unless someone tells them? And how will
    anyone go preach the Gospel unless someone else sends them?"

Paul quotes the Old Testament to prove his point, "How beautiful are the feet of those who bring good tidings of good things!"

Lord, Paul was concerned that not everyone was responding to the Gospel. He quoted Isaiah, "Lord, who will believe?" Then Paul concluded, faith comes from hearing the Gospel—the Good News of Jesus' death, burial, and resurrection.

Lord, Paul was concerned about the Jews being saved; they have heard Your Word—yes—it is preached wherever the Jews live. Paul asked, "Do they understand?" Even back in Moses' time, God told the Jews, "I will use a nation—Gentiles—that is devoid of spiritual understanding to provoke you to action." Because Israel refused to preach to non-Jews, You told them, "I will be found by people who weren't looking for Me."

Lord, even while Gentiles are being saved, You still reach out Your hands to the Jews—a disobedient people—who refuse to come to You.
Amen.

God's Mercy on the Jews

Romans 11:1-36

Lord, Paul asked, "Has God rejected His people?" Absolutely not! Paul was a Jew, an Israelite, a descendant of Abraham, from the tribe of Benjamin. No, it is unthinkable that God has repudiated His unique people, whom He originally chose. Remember what Elijah said in the Scriptures when interceding to You for Israel, "Lord, they have killed your prophets and broken down your altars. I am the only one faithful to You, and they seek to kill me." You answered, "No, you are not the only one, I have 7,000 left who have not bowed to Baal."

Lord, in the same way, there was a remnant in Paul's day chosen by Your grace. So it was not the Jews' legalism but Your kindness that made them follow You. For if You recognized them for good works, Your grace would no longer be free.

Lord, Paul came to this conclusion, most of the Jews have not been saved— a few have found salvation—but the rest are judicially blinded, so they don't understand the Gospel. The Scriptures teach, "God has given Israel a blinded heart to this day, so that their eyes see not, and their ears hear not." David said, "The food God has provided for them has become a trap so that they think everything is well between them and God. Let their eyes be blinded to God's goodness and let them serve sin."

Lord, I realize the Jews lost their divine privileges
     Because of their sin and rejection of Your plan for them.
May I ever follow closely Your leading in my life
     And may I stay close to Your protective grace.

Lord, Paul asked the obvious question, "Have the Jews forever lost any hope of recovery? Or, have they just stumbled temporarily?" Your purpose was to make salvation available to the Gentiles, and then the Jews would be envious of what the Gentiles had, and want it for themselves. If all the world becomes rich in Your blessing because the Jews stumble, think of how much greater will be Your blessing when Jews come back to You and join the Gentiles in Christ.

Lord, You had a special message to the Gentiles and Paul constantly told this to the Jews to make them want what the Gentiles have, and thus some Jews will be saved. For if their rejection means the world is reconciled to You, how much more wonderful will be the return of Israel to You and Christ. It will be like the Jewish nation being resurrected from the dead. If the flour is good, then the bread it makes will be good, and if the root of a tree is good, then it will give good fruit. Since Abraham—the original root—was good, so eventually the nation of Israel will be children of Abraham's faith.

Lord, Paul realized the branches of the olive tree called Israel were cut off, and the Gentiles—like wild olive branches—have been grafted into Your tree. The Gentiles now enjoy the life of Your tree that gives blessing. But Gentiles should not think themselves superior, for the branches do not support the root, but the root supports the branches. Those branches—Israel—were cut off because of their unbelief.

Lord, Paul warns the Gentiles not to brag about their new superiority over Israel because they replaced the branches that were broken off. Gentiles are important because they are part of Your plan, they are branches, not the root. Gentiles may say, "Those branches were broken off so I could be grafted in," and that is true. Israel was cut off because of unbelief. But that fact should not make Gentiles proud, but fearful. If You didn't spare the natural branches—the Jews—You will not spare the Gentiles when they reject You. I won't forget, You can be severe as well as gracious. You are severe to those who reject You, and You are gracious to those who fear You, for the Jews can repent of their unbelief and be grafted back into the place of Gentiles.

Lord, you are eminently able to graft Your people—the Jews—back again. For if Your great power were able to graft wild olive branches into Your eternal plan, then it will be much easier to graft a cultivated olive branch back into its original place.

Lord, when I see Your original love for Israel,
    And I understand Your plan for Your people,
Do not forget we who are Gentiles
    And remember me, because I love You.

Lord, Paul wanted his readers to know the mystery of Your dealing with Israel, so they wouldn't be conceited. Israel is now spiritually blinded, but this will last only until the fullness of the Gentiles comes in. Then all Israel will be saved, as it is written, "The

deliverer will come from Zion, He will turn the Jews from
ungodliness, He will take away their sin."

Lord, I look forward to all Israel being saved,
      I don't know when, where or how it will happen,
But I believe You will fulfill Your promise to the Jews;
      Just remember me in your total plans for this universe.

Lord, the Jews are now enemies of the Gospel, but they are beloved as far as
      Your eternal covenant with them is concerned, because You will
      never withdraw Your gifts and calling. Remember, Gentiles were
      once rebels against You, but when the Jews rejected Jesus Christ,
      You were merciful to the Gentiles, and in the future, You will be
      merciful unto the Jews. For You have given up on all those who are
      habitually sinning, but You will also have mercy on any You choose
      to show mercy.

Lord, how rich are the depths of Your mystery,
      How deep is Your wisdom and knowledge.
I can't possibly trace Your motives
      I don't understand all that You do.
Who could ever know Your mind?
      Who could ever try to tell You what to do?
Who could ever give You anything?
      No one, for You are the Supreme God.
All that exists comes from You, and is for You;
      To You be glory forever.
                Amen.

A Living Sacrifice to Serve God

Romans 12:1-21

Lord, I will dedicate my body to You,
      As Paul pleaded with all believers to do.

Because of Your Mercy, I offer myself
>As a living sacrifice, holy and pleasing to You;
>This is the first and best spiritual worship to You.

I will not allow myself to be conformed
>To the principles of this world.

But I will let my thinking be transformed
>By the power of the Holy Spirit.

Then, I will discover Your will for my life,
>Which will glorify You, and satisfy my desires.

Lord, because I have received grace from You,
>I will not exaggerate my value or importance.

I will honestly estimate the gifts you've given me
>By the standards of faith You've given me.

Just as each body has many parts,
>And each part has a separate function,

So I am one part of Christ's body
>Who serves in harmonious union with other believers
>Because we belong to each other.

My spiritual gifts are different than other believers;
>I belong to the body, i.e., to other believers
>And I need all of them to help me serve You.

Lord, You've given to each one of us a spiritual gift;
>This is an ability to do certain things well.

Those with the gift of prophesy, i.e., speaking for You,
>Should use their gift according to their faith.

Those with the gift of helping others should serve people well,
>Those with the gift of teaching should teach well.

Those with the gift of preaching,
>Should do a good job delivering sermons.

Those who have been given money,
>Should use it generously for spiritual projects.

Those who have the gift of administration,

Should manage everything to Your glory.
Finally, let those with the gift of mercy-showing,
    Show compassion and sympathy to the needy.

Lord, I will love everyone as You loved me,
    I will not pretend to love people when I don't.
I will seek the good things of life,
    And I will turn my back on evil things.
I will love others as your children should,
    And have deep respect for others.
I will serve You with untiring effort,
    And will be enthusiastic in all I do.
I will gladly accept all You plan for me
    And I will be patient in trouble,
    But always praying to do Your will.

Lord, when Your saints are in need,
    I will share with them the things I have
    And open my home to them.

Lord, I will always bless those who persecute me,
    And will never curse them.
I will share the happiness of those who are happy,
    And I will empathize with those who are sad.
I will treat everyone with equal kindness,
    And will not condescend to the poor.
I will not allow myself to be self-satisfied,
    But will show Christ to the world.

Lord, I will never pay back evil for evil,
    I want everyone to see my integrity.
I will try to get along with everyone,
    And be at peace with them.
I will not try to get even when someone wrongs me,
    I will leave revenge to You.

Because the Scripture teach, "Vengeance belongs to You,
      You will pay them back for their evil."
Also the Scriptures teach, "If your enemy is hungry,
      You must give him food,
And if Your enemy is thirsty,
      You must give him water to drink,
      And thus, heap hot coals on his head."
I will resist evil and conquer it by doing good.
                              Amen.

Respect for Government

Romans 13:1-14

Lord, I will submit to government authorities,
      Since You have put them into office
      And all civil authority comes from You.
Those who resist the laws of the land
      Are rebelling against Your authority over them
      And You will punish them.
Those who behave rightly according to Your commandments,
      Should not be afraid of judges,
      Only criminals have anything to fear.
I will live honestly and correctly
      So I won't be afraid of punishment.
You put government in place to serve its citizens
      And to carry out Your revenge on criminals,
      Punishing them when they break the law.
I will obey the laws for my conscience sake
      Also because I'm afraid of being punished.
This is the reason I will pay my taxes,
      Since all officials are your officers.
I will give everyone what I owe them,

And if I owe taxes, I will pay them.
When I'm required to respect officials
>I will respect them and honor them.
I will avoid getting into debt,
>Except the debt of love I owe to all;
>When I love others, I fulfill my debt.

Lord, all the commands such as, "You shall not commit adultery," "You shall not kill," "You shall not steal," "You shall not covet," are summed up in one command, "You must love your neighbors as yourself." Love is the one act that will not hurt my neighbor, it's the only law I need.

Lord, the time has come for me to wake up
>Because the coming of the Lord Jesus is closer,
>Than when I was saved.
The night is almost over
>It will soon be daylight.
I will repent of anything
>Done under the cover of darkness,
>And put on the armor of light.
I will behave because I live in the light,
>I will not attend wild parties, nor
>Get drunk, nor commit adultery, nor get into fights.

Lord, I want you to help me live as I should,
>I will not plan to do anything evil.
>>Amen.

Handling Questionable Things

Romans 14:1-23

Lord, I will give a warm welcome
>To those who are weak in the faith.

I realize there are degrees of Christian obedience
>> So I won't argue with any,
>> Whether or not they eat meat offered to idols.
Some believe eating meat offered to idols is all right,
>> Others who are weak in faith think it is wrong,
>> So they won't eat meat at all, just vegetables.
Those who think it is all right to eat meat,
>> Should not look down on those who don't.
And those who don't eat meat
>> Should not find fault with those who do.
You have accepted all believers as Your children,
>> They are Your servants to command.
Everyone is responsible to please You,
>> They are not accountable to other believers.
I will let You tell them what is right or wrong,
>> You have the power to straighten out believers.
Some treat certain days holier than other days,
>> Others treat all days the same,
>> Each believer is free to hold his own convictions.
Those who observe special days
>> Do so to honor You.
The one who eats meat
>> Does so to honor You,
>> If he gives thanks first.
The one who does not eat meat,
>> Also is honoring You,
>> If he gives thanks first.

I am not my own boss
>> To do anything I please.
When I live, I live for You.
>> When I die, I go to be with You,
>> Whether alive or dead, I belong to You.
Christ died and was resurrected,

So that He might be the Lord of the living and the dead.
This is why I will not pass judgment on any,
>As some have done,
>Because we'll all stand before the judgment seat of Christ.

Because of this I realize that each of us
>Must give an account of ourselves to You.
For it is written in Scripture, "As I live says the Lord,
>Every knee will bow before me,
>And every tongue will confess Me."
So then, every one of us must give an account of ourselves to You.

Lord, I will not pass judgment on other believers,
>Therefore, I've made up my mind
>Never to cause my brother to stumble.
I know that food is all right to eat,
>For the Lord Jesus said, "No food is ceremonially unclean in itself."
If some think certain food is unclean,
>Then it is unclean to them.
If my attitude toward food is upsetting other believers,
>Then I will be guided by love.
I will not eat anything I choose,
>If that means the downfall of a believer
>For whom Christ has died.

Lord, I will not flaunt my spiritual privileges,
>To bring harm on another believer.
For Your Kingdom is not a matter of eating and drinking,
>But righteousness, peace, and joy in the Holy Spirit.

Lord, I will serve Christ with a respectful
>Attitude toward both eating or abstaining from food.
>Then I will please You and be respected by others.
I will adopt any custom that leads to peace,
>And the mutual respect by all believers.

I will not destroy Your work in believer's lives
      Over the question of eating and drinking,
Now all food is ceremonially clean,
      It becomes evil when I eat to make someone fall.
Therefore, my best course is to abstain from meat and wine,
      So I won't trip up a believer or weaken them.

Lord, I will hold on to my convictions,
      They are between You and me.
I will be careful when I make decisions,
      To not go against my conscience.
But any who have doubts, but eats anyway,
      Is condemned because they violate their conscience.
Anything is sin that
      Violates my faith.
                        Amen.

A Believer's Relationship to Others

Romans 15:1-33

Lord, I believe I am a strong Christian,
      So I have a duty to bear the burdens
      Of weak Christians, lest they fall.
I will be considerate of others
      And help them become stronger Christians.
Christ didn't think only of Himself,
      Christ came to suffer from the insults
      Of those who oppose You.
I can learn from everything written in Scripture,
      For it gives me hope and an example how to live.

Lord, help me keep serving You in many ways;
      I refuse to give up.

Help me tolerate other believers
> By following the example of Christ
> Who never stopped doing good.

May I have one mind and voice,
> To give glory to the Lord Jesus Christ,
> And to praise You, the God and Father of us all.

Lord, help me glorify You by treating others
> The same way Christ treated other people.

Christ became the servant of the circumcised Jews,
> So You could carry out the promises
> You made to the patriarchs.

It was also to get Gentiles saved,
> Thus bringing glory to You.

Because the Scriptures teach, "I will worship you among
> The Gentiles, and sing praises to Your name."

In another place the Scriptures teach,
> "Rejoice ye Gentiles with His people."

And yet in another place,
> "Praise the Lord, all you Gentiles,
> And let all people praise Him."

And then Isaiah said,
> "The rest of Jesse shall appear,
> Rising up to rule the Gentiles,
> And in Him the Gentiles will hope."

Lord, may Your hope give me such power and peace,
> That the Holy Spirit will overflow me
> To remove all the barriers that hold me back.

Lord, Paul told the readers, I feel certain you have real
> Christian character and experience and that you can
> keep each other on the straight and narrow path.
> Nevertheless, Paul wrote with frankness,
> to remind them to obey truths they already knew.

Lord, Paul reminded his readers he was given a commission by You to be a minister to the Gentiles. This gave Paul a ministerial duty to tell them Your Gospel, and thus to present them as an offering to You because they are made a sweet smelling offering that You will accept.

Lord, Paul said he had a right to be proud of his work of spreading the message of Jesus Christ. Paul does not know how successful others have been but he says, "I know that I have been used by God to win the Gentiles to Christ, by the power of signs, and wonders, and by the power of the Holy Spirit." Paul tells of preaching the Good News with all his strength from Jerusalem to Illyricum.

Lord, Paul said he had a rule to never preach anywhere Christ's name was already known, lest he build on another man's foundation. Paul's chief purpose was to fulfill Scripture, "Those who have never been told about Him, will see Him; and those who have never heard will understand."

Lord, Paul explained this is why he has been prevented from coming to Rome. But since he is no longer needed in Greece, and since he has always wanted to see the believers in Rome, he planned to see them on his way to Spain. He hoped to spend some time with them, and hoped they would speed him on his journey.

Lord, Paul explained his next destination was Jerusalem to look after the Christians there. Paul was carrying money to the needy Christians there that he had collected in Northern Greece and Achaia. There Gentile Christians, took up a willing offering, even though they owed it to those in Jerusalem for sending the Gospel to them in Greece. For since the Gentiles have benefited from the Jews, it is only right that now Gentiles should look after the Jews with material things.

Lord, Paul explained he would come to them when the gift was safely
delivered to Jerusalem. Then he would come see them on his way to
Spain.

Lord, help me be generous to all needy Christians
    As the Christians of Greece were to those in Jerusalem.
Help me follow the example of Christ,
    Who gave up everything for those most in need.

Lord, Paul asked his readers to stand behind him in earnest prayer that he
would not fall into the hands of unbelieving Jews in Jerusalem, and
that the Jerusalem Christians will welcome his gift to them. Paul
asked these requests for the sake of the Lord Jesus Christ, and for
the love that they had for each other in the Spirit.

Lord, I pray for my life what Paul asked,
    "That the God of peace be with me, Amen!"

Greetings to Paul's Friends

Romans 16:1-27

Lord, Paul commended Phoebe who was coming to visit the church at
Rome. She worked diligently in the Church at Cenchrea, Greece.
Paul asked them to receive her as a sister in the Lord and to help her
because she had helped many, including Paul.

Paul sent greetings to Pricilla and Aquila who had been his fellow
workers, in fact they had risked their lives for Paul. Not only is Paul
grateful for them, he says all the Gentile churches appreciate them.
Paul then greets all who worship in their home.

Paul sends greetings to Epaenetus, the first to become a Christian
in Achaia. Next Paul greets Mary, plus Andronicus and Junia his

relatives who were in prison with him. They are respected by the apostles and were saved before Paul's conversion.

Paul next greets Amplias, Urbanus and Stachys. Then Paul greeted Apelles who is approved by Christ and to those who work in the home of Aristobulus. Paul sends greetings to Herodion, a relative of his, and to the servants in Narcissus' home. He also greets Tryphena and Tryphosa who labor in the Lord, and also to Persis.

Paul sends greets to Rufus, chosen by the Lord, and his mother who had also been a mother to Paul. Paul also greets Asyncritus, Phlegon, Hermas, Patrobas and the other Christians who live with them. Paul sends greeting to Philologus, Julia, Nereus, and his sister, plus Olympas and all the Christians who live with them.

Paul tells them to greet one another warmly because all the churches with Paul send them greetings.

Lord, I will be on guard against anyone
    Who causes divisions in the church,
        And I will avoid them in all possible ways.
I will not be like divisive people
    Because they are a slave to their own desires.
They are not slaves to Jesus Christ,
    Because they confuse people with their arguments.

Paul wants everyone to know of the Roman believers loyal to him;
    Paul wants them to remain very loyal to the good
    And refrain from that which is evil.

Lord, You are the God of peace and harmony,
    You will soon crush satan under Your feet;
    May the grace of the Lord Jesus Christ rest on me.

Lord, Paul sent his readers greetings from Timothy, as well as
    Greetings from Jason and Sosipater. Tertius, Paul's secretary also

sends greetings. Gaius and the church that meets in his house send greetings, Erastus the treasurer of the city of Corinth and Quartus also send greetings.

Lord, I want to be strong and continually steady in my life,
    So that I give all glory to You.
I will rest in the Gospel that I heard preached,
    Because I understood the message of Jesus Christ.

This mystery of Christ and the church is now revealed to all
    But was kept secret in past ages.
Now I glory in the preaching of Jesus Christ that
    Brings all nations to obedience of faith.
Now may You the only wise God be glorified
    Through the Lord Jesus Christ, my Savior.
                    Amen.

1 CORINTHIANS

Chapter 28

THE STORY OF WRITING THE BOOK OF FIRST CORINTHIANS

Date: A.D. 59 ⟲ Written from: Ephesus, Turkey ⟲ Written by: Paul

The sun had burst forth in her glory early in the morning and I had just finishing teaching in the school of Tyrannus. I love teaching when only believers are present.

When I first came to Ephesus, Turkey, the church met in the synagogue where Judaizers always had their negative questions because they rejected the Gospel of Jesus Christ.

But it's different in the school of Tyrannus where only believers are present. We meet in the inner courtyard of a large villa surrounded by lush gardens. When believers have questions about doctrine, I can go deeper to answer their problems. But I couldn't do it in the synagogue because I was always defending the faith.

Then came the letter from Corinth. It told of all the problems of the church in Corinth, the exact opposite of what was happening in Ephesus. The letter told of heated debates in the Corinthian church over divorce, those who never got married. The letter had concerns over speaking in tongues, eating meat offered to idols, and drunkenness at the Lord's table and theological issues at the Lord's table. I was so busy with the revival going on at Ephesus, that I didn't want to deal with a problem-driven church. But the debates were ripping apart the church at Corinth, and I had to do something.

Ephesus was having revival; people were being saved every day in this large capital city. I couldn't leave a revival to go to Corinth. I had to ask myself, *"If I left Ephesus would the Gospel continue to be spread to outlying areas?"*

There are dozens of small outlying villages where the Gospel has been aggressively preached and new churches have been established: Smyrna, Pergamus, Thyatira, Sardis, Philadelphia, and Laodicea. I rejoiced when I got word how these new churches were evangelizing other areas.

But I needed to do something for Corinth. The letter from Corinth asked about meat offered to idols. The temple of Zeus was still dominant in the city of Corinth and every butcher shop in town offered its meat to Zeus before it was sold to his customers. Christians were asking if they could eat the meat offered to Zeus, even if they didn't worship Zeus, or believe there was anything to an idol. Christians were rejecting one another—those who would not eat meat offered to idols didn't want believers in their assembly who ate meat offered to Zeus.

I shook my head as I read the letter. I began formulating a letter of response to them.

Later that day, I talked to Stephanas, Fortunatus, and Achaichus, the ones who brought the letter to me from Corinth.

Stephanas gave me an eyewitness testimony of other problems in Corinth. First, the various house churches were fussing with one another. One house church claimed superiority because they were of Paul, another claimed to be of Apollos, and a third claimed to be of Peter. Then there was an exclusive group that claimed to be the only true followers of Jesus Christ. They rejected the other house churches. I realized I needed to write on unity to the Corinthians.

Next, Fortunatus told me about the problem of human reason and philosophy. Various leaders were arguing over who was the smartest...who was right...who was wrong.... They used human reason to prove what they taught. I will write to them that wisdom comes from the Holy Spirit and that unsaved people don't have the Holy Spirit, so they don't have spiritual understanding. Even carnal Christians have difficulty understanding Christian things. Only those who were completely yielded to the Holy Spirit understand the mind of God.

Achaichus told me of another problem. There was incest in the church at Corinth that upset the people. The problem was not a clear case of incest—parent and child—but rather a man had married his father's second wife. The problem was complicated by the elders doing nothing.

And then there was another problem in the church according to Stephanas. When the various house churches argued with each other over positions of leadership, they took the issue to a secular Gentile court, "Can you imagine Christians allowing an unsaved heathen judge solving their problem of oversight in the church?"

I had to quit listening to write down the list of sins so my letter to them wouldn't omit anything. Each time I heard of another problem, I began to make some notes of what my answer would be.

Then Fortunatus told me about the problem of mass confusion at the Lord's Table. Everyone was bringing their lunch basket for a love feast, and some were even bringing alcoholic beverages and getting drunk before they came to celebrate communion. The rich had big baskets of food that they selfishly kept to themselves, while the poor had their meager rations. Then there were some who had nothing at all, and no one was sharing with them.

I again shook my head in unbelief. The Lord's Table should reflect unity in the Body of Christ when everyone breaks bread together, and when they take the cup together.

And then Achaichus told about another problem in the church. Some leaders quoted me when they spoke to the whole assembly, others would use their wisdom or quote Apollos or Peter. Then there were those who spoke in tongues claiming to have a message directly from God. I knew that tongues were necessary to validate the message of God. The New Testament Scriptures were not yet written as our authority. I wanted everyone to hear the Word of God carefully so I determined to lay down rules for the use of tongues.

And finally, Stephanas told me about the false teaching concerning the resurrection. Some were teaching there would be no resurrection in the future, but death ended it all. When I heard this, I planned to answer their question, "How can a Christian believe there will be no resurrection of their loved ones from the dead?" If they believe the Gospel, that includes the resurrection of Christ.

The day is coming to an end, and I am too tired to write. I'll be fresh to write a letter to the believers in Corinth the first thing in the morning.

Tomorrow, I will write a letter to the Corinthians, but I must be careful to show both sides of my heart. They must feel my grief and disappointment because of their quarrellings and problems; yet, they must feel my holy indignation against their sin. I will tell them to kick the sinning Christians out of the church. Yet, I must plead for their repentance. These young Christians in Corinth need to grow in Jesus Christ.

Sincerely yours in Christ,
Paul the apostle

Chapter 29

PRAYING THE BOOK OF FIRST CORINTHIANS

Divisions in the Church

1 Corinthians 1:1-31

Lord, Paul introduced himself as an apostle,
Called by the will of God
And Sosthenes, a brother in Christ.
He wrote to Your church in Corinth
And to all Christians everywhere.
He wrote to those Christ Jesus sanctified,
Who pray in the name of Jesus Christ.
Paul prays for grace to all who read this letter,
From You and from the Lord Jesus Christ.

Lord, Paul gave thanks to You for the Corinthian Christians
Because they had been saved by grace
And they were established by knowing Christ,
And witnessing for Him;
And they had a full understanding of truth.
Now they were anointed by the Holy Spirit
And had all the spiritual gifts
As they were waiting for the return of Christ.
Paul knew You would keep them firm in faith
And their lives would be blameless
As they waited for the Day of the Lord Jesus Christ,

Because You are faithful to keep those
    You have called to salvation in Christ.

Lord, Paul appealed to them in the name of the Lord Jesus Christ
    To quit fussing among themselves,
But live in harmony so the Body of Christ wouldn't be ruptured,
    And there would be one unified mind in the church.
Paul had been told by those living in Chloe's house
    That the church had serious divisions.
Some are saying, "I follow Paul,"
    Others say, "I follow Apollos."
Still others maintain, "I follow Peter,"
    And some "super" spiritual claim, "I follow Christ."
Paul asked, "Have you divided Christ into many pieces?"
    Also, "Was Paul crucified for you
    So that you were baptized in Paul's name?"
Then Paul declared, "I'm glad I never baptized any of you,
    Except Crispus and Gaius;
    So none of you were baptized in my name."
Paul remembers he baptized the family of Stephanas
    But that's all he could remember.

Lord, You did not primarily send me or others to baptize people
    But to give out the Gospel to everyone.
You did not tell me to preach philosophy
    Or use "deep" words to explain Christ's death.

Lord, I know the language of the Cross is foolishness
    To those who are perishing in sin.
But I know it is Your power to save,
    Because You have saved me from a purposeless life
    And gave me understanding of spiritual matters.

Lord, Paul quoted the Scriptures that told what You said,
    "I will destroy the plans of the wise,

Even when everyone thinks they are smart.
I will confound the intellectuals,
>Then where will the earthly philosophers be?
>What will happen to those who write books?"

Lord, Paul explained how average people are blinded spiritually,
>So they can't find You with their wisdom.
Your plan is to save those who believe the Gospel,
>Which is a "foolish" message to those who are lost.
The Jews demand miracles before they will believe;
>Gentiles are looking for rational answers,
But I will preach Christ crucified,
>He is a stumbling block to the Jews;
>And the Gospel is foolishness to the unsaved Gentiles.
Now God has opened my eyes,
>And all who are saved, whether Jew or Gentile,
>Must see Christ as the catalyst of Your plan for salvation.

Lord, Your "foolishness" is wiser than all human wisdom,
>Your weakness is stronger than all human strength.
When You called me I was not spiritually wise,
>I thought after the pattern of ordinary people.
You did not call many influential rich,
>Or highly educated people of the world,
Instead, You chose people whom the world thinks are "foolish"
>To confound those the world considers smart.
Also, You chose people without influence
>And those whom the world calls "low class."
You chose people hated by the world
>To show up those the world thinks are brilliant
So no one can ever boast of their accomplishments,
>That they had something to do with their salvation.

Lord, from You I have salvation in Christ alone
>Because You have made me a member of His Body.

And by Your enablement, Christ is my wisdom,
>My righteousness, my holiness, and my freedom.
As the Scriptures teach, "If any wants to boast,
>Let him boast about what the Lord has done."
>>Amen.

Understanding Spiritual Things

1 Corinthians 2:1-16

Lord, I will not use impressive words or philosophy
>To give the Gospel to others.
I want everyone to know the simple message of Jesus
>And what His death can do for them.
I will not rely on my ability to convince people
>Because I realize how weak I am.
My speeches or sermons will not be based
>On debate techniques or philosophy.
I want the Holy Spirit to demonstrate His power
>In transforming the lives of those who hear the Gospel.
I don't want anyone's faith relying on human reasoning,
>But on the power of God.
Yet, among those who know the Bible
>I will speak with great wisdom.
Not the type of wisdom that comes from philosophers,
>Nor the kind that appeals to "logical thinkers"
>Whose thinking dooms them to failure,
My wisdom comes from You,
>Telling Your plan for all people throughout the ages.
My wisdom is not understood by the great thinkers
>For if "great men" understood Your wisdom,
>They would never have crucified the Lord of glory.
The Scriptures explain, "No man has seen this wisdom

Nor have they understood God's wonderful plan
That He has for those who believe and love Him."

Lord, I understand Your plan for all people
      Because You sent the Holy Spirit to teach it to me.
Now the Spirit reaches into the depths of Your purpose
      To show me the things
      You hide from the world.
A person is the only one who knows for sure
      What he is thinking,
      Or what he is really like.
No one can know what You are thinking,
      Or what You are really like,
      Except the Holy Spirit reveals it to him.

Lord, You have given me the Holy Spirit
      Who is different from the spirit of this world,
      So I can understand Your gifts and plans for me.
Now I want to tell others about Your plans,
      Not using the phrases of philosophy or logic,
      But using the Holy Spirit's own words,
So those in proper fellowship with the Holy Spirit
      Can understand the spiritual meaning of Your message.

Lord, the average unsaved person can't understand Your plans,
      They sound foolish to him.
Nor can the unsaved know what the Holy Spirit is saying
      For the unsaved are spiritually blinded.

Lord, I understand Your plans for the world,
      But the unsaved person can't understand it at all.
How could they know Your plans or thoughts,
      For they can't properly pray or correctly read Scriptures;
      They are blinded to spiritual truth.
But I actually know Your purposes and plans

Because I have Christ living in me.
Amen.

Carnal Christians

1 Corinthians 3:1-23

Lord, Paul said he couldn't treat the Corinthians
    Like they were spiritual Christians,
    Because they were worldly and babes in Christ.
Paul didn't feed them solid food,
    Because babies can't digest solid food.
He fed them the milk of the Word—the essentials,
    Not the meat of the Word to make them strong.
Paul pointed out when they wrangled over leaders that
    They were acting like average unsaved people,
    They were motivated by the desires of the flesh.
Some in the church were proclaiming, "I am for Paul,"
    Others were yelling, "I am for Apollos."

Lord, who is Paul and who is Apollos, but Your servants
    Who preach Your Word and motivate people to faith.
They use different ways of ministering,
    Because different spiritual gifts were given them.
Paul planted and Apollos watered, but You produced growth;
    Neither the planter nor the waterer counts,
    Only You matter.
Whether they plant or water, they are a team;
    Each will be rewarded for what they do,
    We are all Your co-workers.

Lord, Paul was just the builder who laid the foundation
    On which someone else constructed the building.
That means I am building on the original foundation

Of the Gospel and doctrine that was laid by Paul;
Therefore, I must be careful how I work.
For no one can lay the foundation
Because it has already been laid;
The foundation is Jesus Christ.
I will build on the foundation of Jesus Christ,
I will use various materials of gold, silver, and jewels;
Some will use sticks, hay, and trash.
But Judgment Day is coming
Where our good works will be revealed.
God will use fire to judge our efforts,
If our good works are burned up, we will be losers;
If they stand the test, we will be rewarded.
A few Christians will have everything burned up,
The only thing left will be their salvation.

Lord, I am Your temple, the Holy Spirit lives in me;
I want to be holy to glorify You.
You will destroy anyone who defiles Your temple
Because Your temple is sacred;
My body is the temple where You desire to dwell.

Lord, don't let me deceive myself about spirituality,
Those who think they are wise by worldly standards
Have fooled themselves
Because the world's wisdom is folly in Your sight.
The Scriptures say, "You know men's thoughts,
You know how futile their thoughts,"
So, I will not boast in human thinking,
I will boast in what You've given me.
Everything You have has been given to me,
Paul, Apollos, Peter, life, death, everything;
The present, and the future belong to You

And I belong to Christ, and He belongs to You.
Amen.

Judging Christians

1 Corinthians 4:1-21

Lord, I want people to think of me as Christ's servant,
   One entrusted with knowledge of You.
Now the most important thing about a servant
   Is that I, as Your servant, be found faithful.
I won't worry about what anyone thinks,
   I won't even trust my own thinking.
I have a clear conscience,
      But that is not enough to prove I'm right;
      You, Lord, alone will tell us what's right.
So, I'll not prematurely judge if anyone is good,
   I'll leave that until Christ returns,
Then all hidden things will be revealed
      And we'll know what each of us is like
      And everyone will get the reward he deserves.

Lord, Paul used himself and Apollos as an example
   So no one would play favorites;
   We must not choose one teacher over another.
The Scriptures teach, "Live by the rules,"
   Don't elevate one servant above another.
You didn't make any of us superior to another,
   You gave us the gifts we have
So no one can brag about their gifts
   As if they were superior to anyone else.

Lord, Paul rebuked the Corinthians because they wrongly thought
   They had all the spiritual things they needed.

They were acting like rich kings
> Who sit contented on their thrones.

Paul told them he wished they in fact were reigning,
> And he was reigning with them,
> But that was not the fact.

Paul told them he has been appointed an apostle
> And that apostles will die for the cause of Christ.

Like prisoners on death row,
> Apostles are under the sentence of death
> And the unsaved world will rejoice in their execution.

Lord, Paul said he is foolish by the world's standards,
> But the Corinthians are claiming to be wise.

Paul said he is weak in the sight of the world,
> While the Corinthians are claiming to be strong.

Paul said the world laughs at him,
> Even as the Corinthians act like celebrities.

Lord, Paul said he goes hungry and thirsty,
> He wears rags, is brutally treated, and homeless,
> All for the cause of Christ.

Paul says he has to work hard to make money,
> Yet when he is cursed, he blesses his attackers.
> He is patient with those who injure him.

Paul said he answers quietly when insulted,
> Even when people treat him like dirt.

Lord, Paul explained he is not writing to embarrass them,
> But to warn them because they are like children.

They may have a thousand who try to teach them
> But Paul is their father in the faith,
> They were saved when he preached the Gospel to them.

That is why Paul wanted them to copy his example
> And assume the attitudes he has.

Paul plans to send Timothy to help them

Because Paul won Timothy to Christ,
Just as he won the Corinthians to Christ.
Timothy will teach them what Paul wants them to know,
It's the same thing Paul taught in all the churches.

Lord, Paul realized some seized church leadership
When he did not come to them.
So, he promised to come as soon as
The Lord allows him.
Then Paul promised to examine the pretentious leaders
To see if they measured up to God's standards,
Because the Kingdom of God is not talking,
But it is power, and holiness, and obedience.
So Paul told them to decide if they want
Him to come to punish them,
Or to come with love and gentleness.
Amen.

Influence of Evil in the Church

1 Corinthians 5:1-13

Lord, Paul heard reports of sexual immorality in the church
So bad that even the unsaved won't tolerate it.
A man was living with his father's wife
In sexual immorality.
Paul asked, "Are you so proud and blind
That you can't see this terrible sin?"
"Shouldn't you be overwhelmed with guilt?
You should have cast the man out of the church."

Lord, Paul said even though he was not present,
He already knew what he would do
Just as if he were there with them.

Call the church together to vote on this matter,
  And remember the Lord is present when you gather together.
Vote the man out of your fellowship,
  Place him in satan's hands for punishment
In the hopes his soul will be saved when Jesus returns,
  Even though he dies prematurely.

Lord, Paul rebuked their pride in their accomplishments,
  Reminding them that only a small amount of yeast
  Would influence all the dough.
Paul told them to get rid of sinful yeast
  And make the church a completely new loaf of bread,
  Remembering Christ is our Passover meal.
Paul said get rid of the sinful man,
  So they could be the unleavened bread of Passover,
  Known for sincerity and truth.

Paul reminded them he wrote a previous letter
  Telling then not to associate
  With those living immoral lives.
He explains that he didn't mean unsaved people
  Who are sexually immoral, greedy,
  Liars, thieves, and idol worshipers.
A Christian can't live in this world
  Without doing business with people like that.
What Paul meant was to disassociate
  With those claiming to be Christian
But indulge in sexual sins, including
  All the sins he just mentioned;
  Don't even eat a fellowship meal with them.

Lord, I know it's not my task to judge those outside the church,
  But it certainly is the job of believers
To hold members of the church accountable
  When they sin in the above mentioned ways.

You alone are the judge of those on the outside of the church,
    But the Corinthian Christians must deal
    With the sinning brother who disgraces Christianity,
    And put him out of the church.
                Amen.

Believers Forbidden to Go to Court Against One Another

1 Corinthians 6:1-20

Lord, Paul was distraught that a Corinthian believer
    Was taking a Christian matter
    Before a secular court and not before the church.
Christians will judge the world in the future
    And if the world will be judged by us,
    Why are we Christians taking cases to them?
Since Christians will one day judge angels,
    It follows we can judge one another on earth
    So why go to a judge who isn't a Christian?
You should be ashamed of yourselves,
    Isn't there someone in the church who is wise enough
    To decide these arguments?
But the Corinthian church had one brother
    Suing another in front of unbelievers.
It is embarrassing for Christians to file law suits;
    You ought to let yourselves be cheated.
Christians are wrong when they file law suits
    Because they cheat themselves out of being right.

Lord, Paul told the Corinthian believers that immoral people
    Have no share in the Kingdom of God.
This includes idol worshipers, adulterers, homosexuals,
    Thieves, greedy people, drunkards, slanderers, and swindlers.
The Corinthians committed all these sins,

But now they are washed, cleansed, sanctified,
And saved through the name of the Lord Jesus Christ,
    And through Your Holy Spirit.

Lord, Paul said, "I can do anything I want,
    But these things are not good for me.
Even if I am allowed to do them,
    · I will not become an addict to sin.
I can eat food that is meant for the stomach,
    And the stomach is created to eat food.
Don't let eating food dominate your life
    Because one day God will do away with food and the stomach."

Lord, Paul said sexual sin is never right,
    Our bodies were not created for sexual sin;
They were created as Your dwelling place;
    You, Lord, must dwell in the temple of our bodies.

Lord, I know that my body is only one member
    That makes up the Body of Christ.
That means I can't take the Body of Christ
    And join it to a prostitute. Never!
A man who has sex with a prostitute,
    Has become one body with her
Because the Scripture has stated,
    "The two shall be one flesh."
Anyone who is joined to You,
    Is one Spirit with You.

Lord, Paul warned, "Keep away from sexual sins";
    Other sins are outside the body,
    But our sexual sins are against our own body.

Lord, I will make my body the temple of the Holy Spirit
    And let Him be manifested through my body because

I received the Holy Spirit from You.
My body does not belong to me,
    It belongs to You, Lord.
You have bought me from sin
        And You paid for me with the blood of Christ,
        Therefore, I will use my body to glorify You.
                    Amen.

Instructions About Marriage

1 Corinthians 7:1-40

Lord, Paul answered the question written to him
        About relationships between men and women.
"It is good for men to have
        No physical contact with women."
Since immoral sex is always a temptation,
        Each man should have his own wife
        And each woman should have her own husband.
The husband must attend to the sexual needs of his wife,
        And the wife must do the same for her husband.
The wife does not have sexual rights over her body,
        The husband has those privileges.
In the same way, the husband has no sexual rights
        Over his body; his wife has them.
Do not refuse sexual privileges to each other
        Except for a limited time by mutual consent.
Then have the same relations as before,
        So satan doesn't get an advantage over one another.

Lord, Paul said no one had to marry, but they could if they wished;
        Paul wanted all men to live like him.
But each person is different in needs and desires,

God gives some the ability to be a husband or a wife,
Others have the gift of remaining single, yet being happy.

Lord, Paul told those unmarried and widows, to stay unmarried
As he is unmarried;
But if a person can't discipline himself,
It is better to get married than suffer.

Lord, Paul had principles for the married
That were not just his advice, but were Your rules.
A wife must not leave her husband;
If she does,
She must remain unmarried.
The wife must be reconciled to her husband if possible,
And the husband must not divorce his wife.

Lord, Paul gave the following suggestions that weren't Your commands;
If a Christian has an unbelieving wife,
And she lives peacefully with him,
Then he must not send her away.
If a Christian wife has an unbelieving husband,
And he lives peacefully with her,
Then she must not send him away;
Because the unbelieving husband may become a Christian
Through the influence of his wife,
And the same thing may happen to the unbelieving wife.
If there were no Christian influences from a parent
Then perhaps the children would not be saved,
But they can be saved by the influence of a believing parent.
But if an unbelieving spouse wants to separate,
Then the believer is not obligated to the marriage.
However, if a member of the marriage is a Christian spouse,
A believing wife may lead her husband to Christ,
And the Christian husband may lead his unbelieving wife to salvation.

Paul said his rule for all believers in the churches
      Is to accept the situation in which God puts them.
Make sure in deciding matters about getting married
      That they are living according to God's direction.
If a man was circumcised before he was saved,
      He shouldn't disguise it.
And if anyone was uncircumcised when he was saved,
      He need not be circumcised;
Because circumcision or uncircumcision means nothing to God,
      Obeying God's commandments is what counts.

Paul told Christians to keep on doing the work
      To which God has called them.

Paul said he had no command from God
      Whether young unmarried women
      Should marry,
But Paul had an opinion
      Based on the wisdom God had given him;
Because Christians faced great danger in Paul's day,
      He felt it was best for them to remain unmarried.
Of course if a person was already married,
      They should not separate.
But if they are unmarried,
      Paul did not want them rushing into marriage.
However, if a Christian was going to get married anyway,
      They should go ahead and do it
Because marriage will bring extra problems
      That Paul didn't want them to face at the time.

Lord, I know our remaining time is short,
      So those with wives should remain
      As free as possible to serve God.
Marriage happiness or marriage disappointment
      Should not keep anyone from serving You.

Live as though there is no happiness or sadness,
    And those who live to buy things
    Should live as though they possessed nothing.
Those who have to do business in the world
    Should not become attached to it
    Because this world is passing away.

Lord, Paul wanted the Corinthians free from all worry
    Because the unmarried person can devote
    All his time to pleasing the Lord,
But the married person has to be concerned with
    The affairs and business of this life.
They are torn in two directions—
    Between pleasing the Lord and their spouse.
The unmarried woman can devote herself to You,
    She is concerned about being holy in body and spirit.
The married woman has to be concerned about
    Pleasing You and pleasing her husband.

Lord, Paul said these things to help believers be strong,
    Not to keep them from marrying.
He wanted them to serve You as best possible
    Without being distracted by their marriage.
If anyone feels they must marry,
    Because they have trouble disciplining their desires,
    They should marry; it is not a sin..
If a person has self-control, and decides not to marry,
    Paul says they have made a wise choice.
So the one who marries is living in God's will,
    And the one who doesn't marry can serve God better.
The wife is one with the husband, as long as he lives;
    If he dies, she is free to marry again,
    Only she must marry in the Lord.
In Paul's opinion, he is happier because he's not married

And he thinks this is God's will.

Amen.

Questionable Things

1 Corinthians 8:1-13

Lord, Paul addressed their questions about eating food
 That was offered to idols.
Everyone thinks they have the right answer
 Because their knowledge makes them feel self-important,
 But love for others will make the church grow.
If anyone says he has all the answers,
 He is just showing how little he knows.
But the one who loves God and does His will,
 Is the one God knows.

Lord, Paul told the Corinthians that idols are just carved images,
 They are not really a god;
You are the only true God
 And nothing else is god.
Some people think there are a great number of gods
 Both in Heaven and on earth,
But I know You are the Father, the only One God,
 And that Jesus Christ created everything
 And He gives life to us.

Lord, some people don't realize that an image is not god,
 They think food offered to idols
 Is really offered to a god that lives.
So when they eat food that's been offered,
 They think they are actually worshiping that god.
But You don't care if people eat food
 That's been offered to an idol;

You know the idol is not real or alive.
We do not sin if we eat that food,
    Nor are we better off if we refuse that food;
    Hamburger meat is nothing more than hamburger meat!
But there are some Christians whose consciences are weaker,
    They think they are recognizing or worshiping an idol
    If they eat hamburger meat that's been offered to an idol.
Here's the problem, the Christian with the weaker conscience
    May see you eat hamburger that was offered to an idol,
Then they go against their conscience to eat hamburger offered to idols,
    And they weaken their faith
    Because they think they have sinned.
So the Christian with the stronger conscience
    Who knows that hamburger is just hamburger,
    Causes the weaker Christian to damage himself.

It is a sin against Christ
    To cause a fellow Christian to stumble.
Therefore, if food offered to idols can cause a brother to sin,
    I'll not eat another hamburger for the rest of my life;
    I don't want to cause any Christian to sin against his conscience.
        Amen.

Paul Defends His Apostleship

1 Corinthians 9:1-27

Lord, Paul told the Corinthians, "I am an apostle,"
    When detractors were claiming Paul wasn't an apostle,
Paul said he was not responsible to humans
    And that he actually had seen the resurrected Jesus.
Paul points out that their changed lives
    Are the results of his ministry
    And the certification of his apostolate.

Even though some Christians deny Paul is an apostle,
  Paul claims they are his authentication
  For he had won most of them to Christ.

Lord, Paul claims the right to food that You give,
  And the right to take a believing wife with him
  As do other apostles; i.e. Jesus' brother and Peter.
Then Paul asked a convicting question,
  "Must only Barnabus and I work for a living?"
Paul said he deserved to be paid because
  Soldiers are paid to serve.
Those who plant a vineyard eat of its fruit,
  And shepherds drink milk from their flocks.
While these are only illustrations, the Scriptures teach,
  "Don't put a muzzle on the ox plowing the corn."

The ploughman plows with expectation to get fed,
  And the harvester expects to get his share.
Since Paul has sown spiritual things to them,
  He expects food, shelter, and clothing in return.
The Corinthians have given to other ministers;
  Surely, Paul's rights are greater,
  Even though he hasn't exercised his rights.
Paul says he has never demanded money from them
  Because they might be less interested in the Gospel.
Those serving in the temple got their food from the temple,
  And those ministering at the altar, kept some of the food.
In the same spirit, those who preach the Gospel
  Should be financially supported by Gospel ministry.

Lord, Paul reminded the Corinthians he had not exercised his rights
  And was not writing to get money from them.
Paul said he would rather die
  Than lose the blessings of ministering for free.
But he testified he can't stop preaching the Gospel

Since You have given him that responsibility.
Paul's greatest joy is preaching the Gospel
    Without getting paid by anyone.

Lord, I am not a slave to anyone,
    But I have made myself a slave to everyone
    So I could win as many as possible.
When I am with the Jews, I will live like the Jews
    So I can win the Jews to Christ.
When I am with Gentiles, I subject myself to their laws
    So I can win Gentiles to Christ.
When I am with heathens, who don't have any laws,
    I live among them to win them to Christ.
I don't offend the weaker Christians' conscience
    Who are bothered about meat sacrificed to idols;
    I want to win the weak to Christ.
I try to find a point of identification with all
    So I can present the Gospel message to them.
I do all this to get the Gospel to all people
    So they can come to Christ' salvation.

Lord, every runner in the race tries to win,
    But only one person gets the prize
    So I will always try to win the race for Christ.
Every fighter disciplines himself to win his awards,
    He wins a wreath that will wither;
    I want to win a prize that will never fade.
I run the race of life to win
    But it is not just to win,
    It's how I prepare and how I run.
I train hard so my body will be prepared,
    I don't want to be disqualified;
    Lord, help me win the race of life.
                Amen.

Purity at the Lord's Table

1 Corinthians 10:1-33

Lord, may I never forget that the Jews followed the Shekinah cloud
  As they wandered in the wilderness.
You kept guiding them with the glory cloud
  And they walked safely through the Red Sea.
This is called the "baptism" for they followed Moses into the sea
  And they came out on the other side.
By a daily miracle, You sent manna to feed them
  And they drank from the rock in the desert;
  That rock was a picture of Christ to come.
Yet in spite of what you did for all of them,
  They rebelled against You and died in the wilderness.

Lord, Israel's life in the wilderness is a lesson to me,
  I will not lust after evil things,
  Nor will I worship idols as some did.
The Scriptures said not to follow their example
  For they sat down to eat the food You provided;
  Then they got up to dance and worship the golden calf.
I will never give into sexual immorality
  As some did in the wilderness
  And 23,000 died in one day.
Some of them murmured against You
  And they died of snake bites;
  Others were judged by the destroying angel.

Lord, all the things that happened in the wilderness
  Are warnings for me not to follow their example.
These negative rebellions were written as a lesson
  For me as the end of the world approaches.
When I think that I would never do these things,
  I must take heed lest I fall into their trap.

The temptations and trials that the Corinthians faced
      Are no more than I face each day.
But Lord, I know You will not let me be tempted
      With more pressures that I can overcome.
The evil desires that entice me are not any different
      Than other Christians have faced.

Lord, I know You will not let me be tempted
      Beyond my self-discipline,
But with my temptations, you'll show me how
      To overcome temptation's power.

Lord, I will avoid any idol-worship,
      I will use my common sense to avoid
      Any influence of idols in my life.

Lord, I receive a blessing from You
      When I drink the communion cup
      That represents the blood of Christ.
And I also receive a blessing when I eat the bread
      That represents the Body of Christ that was broken for me.
The single loaf represents the Body of Christ
      That even though I am only one among many,
      We form a single spiritual Body of Christ.
The Jewish people did the same thing in the Old Testament,
      They were one people when they ate together at the altar.
Does that mean when the unsaved sacrifice food to idols
      That the idols are real and alive? No!
      Does their worship have some value? No, not at all!
Those who offer food to idols are really
      Offering sacrifices to demons,
      They positively are not offering to God.
Paul said he didn't want the Corinthians
      Offering anything to demons.
A person cannot drink the communion cup of Christ

And the cup of demons at the same time,
Nor can they eat at the table of the Lord
    And the table of demons;
    Lord, don't be angry with me.

Lord, You permit me to eat all kinds of food
    But not all food is good for me,
    Nor will all kinds of food make me healthy.

Lord, I'll not spend all my time thinking of myself,
    I will be conscious of other people
    And what's best for them.
I will buy what I want in the market
    But I won't ask if it's been offered to idols
    Lest I hurt my conscience or someone else's.
Everything that comes to me from the earth
    Comes from You, and You give it to me.
If a non-Christian invites me to a meal,
    I will go eat what is served;
    I won't ask any questions for conscience's sake.
But if someone tells me that food was offered to idols,
    I won't eat it out of consideration
    For the weaker brother who stumbles at this thing.
The scruples of a weaker Christian are not mine,
    But I won't use my freedom to hurt him,
    And I won't let his conscience bind me up.
I'll eat everything with thankfulness,
    Eating it to the glory of God.
I will not cause anyone to stumble
    Whether they are Jew, Gentile, or Christian.

Lord, I pray I won't hurt anyone at any time,
    I'll do what is best to get lost people saved.
                    Amen.

Instructions About the Lord's Table

1 Corinthians 11:1-34

Lord, my example in all things is Christ,
　　　So others should follow my example as I follow Christ.
The Corinthians had done well by following
　　　The principles Paul taught them,
But there is one matter he wanted to re-emphasize.
　　　The wife is responsible to her husband,
　　　The husband is responsible to Christ,
　　　And Christ is responsible to You, the Father.
Therefore, if a man refuses to remove his hat
　　　When he prays or preaches the Scriptures,
　　　He dishonors his head—Christ.
However, a woman's hair is her honor,
　　　She dishonors her husband
If she prays or speaks the Scriptures without covering her head,
　　　She might as well have shaved her hair.
A man should not wear anything on his head
　　　Since he is made in the image of God,
　　　For a hat is a sign of rebellion to God.
God's glory is the man who is made in His image,
　　　And the woman is the glory of man.
The man didn't come from the woman,
　　　The first woman came from Adam's side.
Man was not created for woman,
　　　But she was created for him.
Because the angels inspect authority in the church,
　　　The woman must cover her head
　　　As a sign of authority.

Lord, I respect Your plan and purpose for men and women,
　　　The man and woman need each other.

515

Although the first woman came from Adam's side,
>> Every man since then has come from a woman,
>> And both men and women come from You.
Paul asked the Corinthians to use their judgment,
>> Is long hair on a woman proper,
>> And shouldn't she have a covering when she prays?
And isn't it foolish when men have long hair?
>> But some people want to argue about this.
All Paul said was that women should be covered when praying,
>> That's the way it's done in all the churches.

Lord, Paul turned his instructions to another topic;
>> When the Corinthians came together for the communion service,
>> They were doing more harm than good.
First, Paul said there were divisions among them
>> When they came together to the Lord's Table,
And their past history of being divisive
>> Made Paul believe what he heard about them.
Because each person thinks he's right,
>> Each thinking they are closer to God than others.
Therefore, the Corinthians ate to honor themselves,
>> Not to honor the Lord Jesus Who instituted this meal.
Some quickly eat all they could eat,
>> They don't wait to share communion with one another.
Some go hungry, they don't get enough to eat,
>> While the others gorge themselves
>> Or they drink so much they get drunk.
Doesn't everyone have a home to eat and drink?
>> They have disgraced the church,
>> And embarrassed those who can't bring a lot of food.
Do you want me to praise the Corinthian church?
>> Paul said, "I will not do it!"

Lord, Paul told the Corinthians You gave
      The following instruction to observe communion,
That on the night Jesus was betrayed,
      He took bread and thanked You for it.
Then He broke it and said,
      "This is My body which is broken for you.
      Eat it in remembrance of Me."
In the same way, Jesus took the cup and said,
      "This cup is the New Covenant made by God to forgive sins.
      Whenever you drink this cup, you remember Me."
Therefore, every time a believer eats this bread,
      And drinks this cup, they re-live the truth of the Gospel;
      The Lord's Table is a memorial until He comes.
Anyone who eats the bread and drinks the cup
      In an unworthily manner,
      Is guilty of sin against the Lord's body and blood.

Lord, I will therefore examine myself thoroughly
      Before eating the bread or drinking from the cup,
Because any who eats or drinks in an unworthily manner,
      Not meditating on the body and blood of Christ,
      Is contributing to his own condemnation.
That is why some Corinthians are weak or ill,
      And some have died prematurely under Your judgment.

Lord, I will carefully examine myself before communion
      So I'll not be punished or judged by You.
Yet, when a Christian is judged or punished,
      It's so he won't be condemned with the unsaved.

Lord, Paul gave them this final exhortation about communion
      That when they gather for the Lord's Table,
      They should wait for one another.
If any one is hungry, let them eat at home,
      Then the communion service will not lead

To anyone's punishment or judgment.
Paul said he would discuss other matters with them
When he arrived in Corinth.
Amen.

Instruction About Spiritual Gifts

1 Corinthians 12:1-31

Lord, Paul wanted the Corinthians to know about their
Spiritual gifts that the Holy Spirit gave to each of them.
Before they were saved, they chose different idols
That couldn't say a single word.
Now there are people in the church who claim
They are speaking messages from the Spirit of God.
How can I know if their messages come from You,
Or are they just making up what they say?
Paul gave the first test—they can't claim
To speak messages from You if they curse Jesus.
The second test is that when they proclaim "Jesus is Lord,"
They are speaking Your message.

Lord, You have given many different spiritual gifts
But they all come from the Spirit of God.
These spiritual gifts are exercised in different ways,
But it's the same Spirit of God working in people.
Also, our spiritual gifts have different influences
On different people, because the Spirit of God
Uses people according to how much they yield to You,
But You are the same God working through each believer.

Lord, You give different spiritual gifts to different people
For Your own divine purposes.
You give to one the ability to preach

518

With great wisdom so people understand Your message.
To another, You give the ability to teach
From great knowledge so people will see many things
In the Word of God.
To another, You give faith to move mountains
And to another, You give the prayer of faith
To heal the sick of their pain and sickness.
To another, you give the ability to do miracles,
And to someone else, the power to preach and teach.
Some have the ability to recognize false spirits,
Another has the spiritual gift of speaking in tongues,
Still someone else can interpret tongues.
The Holy Spirit gives all these different spiritual gifts
To different people, just as He decides;
So believers have the ability to use these gifts
To get results in the lives of others.

Lord, just as a human body has many parts,
But all the parts make up one body,
So is the church—the Body of Christ;
Though it has many different members, it is one Body.
We have all been baptized into the Body of Christ,
Some Jews and some Gentiles; some slaves and some free.
The Holy Spirit baptized us all into Christ
And we all drink of the same salvation.

Lord, I know the body has many parts;
If the foot says "I am not a part of the body
Because I'm not the head," that does not make any difference;
That does not make him less a part of the body.
If the ear were to say, "I am not the eye,
So I'm not a part of the body,"
That would mean nothing.
If the body were all eye,

How could it hear anything?
If the body were all ears,
How could it smell anything?
But You have designed the different parts in the body.
If all the parts were the same,
How could the body function?
As it is, there are many parts of the body,
But it is still one body.
The eye cannot say to the hand,
"I do not need you."
Nor can the head say to the feet,
"I do not need you."

Lord, I know every part of the body is necessary,
But it seems the parts that are the weakest
Are the ones that are the most indispensable,
And the parts that seem to be less admirable,
Their function seems to be among the most necessary.
And the parts that are the most beautiful
Seem to be the least essential in life.
So, You have arranged to give the parts which lack importance
More dignity than the others.
So the body works together as a whole,
All the parts having the same care for others
As they have for themselves.
If one part suffers, all parts suffer with it;
If one part is honored, all parts enjoy it.

Lord, I am a member of Christ's Body,
But I am gifted differently from everyone else.
The first place was given to apostles, second to prophets,
Third to teachers and after them those who do miracles.
Next comes the gift of healing, helps, and leadership,
And last on the list is speaking in tongues.

Is everyone an apostle? Is everyone a prophet?

    Is everyone a teacher, or miracle worker, or a healer?

Can everyone speak in tongues?

    And can everyone interpret them?

    The answer to these questions is "no!"

Lord, I will eagerly seek the best gifts,

    But I know love is the best gift of all.

                Amen.

Love Is Greatest

1 Corinthians 13:1-13

Lord, if I speak with the eloquence of great speakers,

    Or if I speak in the tongues of angels,

But I didn't love others, I'm simply making noise

    Like cymbals clashing or a gong that rings.

If I can predict the future, or understand Your mysteries,

    Or if I know everything, or have faith to move mountains,

    But I didn't love others, I've accomplished nothing in life.

Lord, help me always patiently express love,

    And I will find ways to be kind.

Help me never be jealous of others,

    Nor be conceited or boastful.

Help me not be irritable or resentful,

    I want my love to overlook the mistakes of others;

    I want to rejoice when others do well.

Help me love others no matter the circumstances,

    Keep my hope strong and may my love never wilt.

May my love outlast everything in life

    Because I know true love never fails.

Lord, I know the gift of prophecy will end,
  And the gift of tongues will cease,
  Also, knowledge will pass away,
For my knowledge is finite and imperfect,
  Also, we only prophesy in part on this earth.
But when I am made perfect and complete in Heaven,
  These gifts will no longer be needed.
When I was a child, I thought like a child,
  Talked like a child
  And my world was as small as a child's world.
In the same way, I only see things darkly
  Through a stained-glass window.
But when I see Jesus face to face,
  I shall understand all things fully.
Now my knowledge is partial and imperfect,
  But then I shall know Jesus
  As He perfectly knows me.

Lord, there are only three things
  On this earth that will last:
  Faith, hope, and love, and the greatest is love.
      Amen.

Instructions About Tongues

1 Corinthians 14:1-40

Lord, I want love to be my greatest spiritual gift,
  But I also want the other spiritual gifts,
  Especially the gift of prophecy.
Those with the gift of tongues speak to God,
  But those who prophesy speak to others.
No one understands those who speak in tongues,
  Because they speak the mysterious things of the Spirit.

However, those who prophesy help others grow in Christ
        By motivating and instructing them.
Those with the gift of tongues benefits himself,
        And those who prophecy, benefit the church.
While Paul wanted all the Corinthians
        To have the gift of tongues, but
        He would rather they be able to prophesy.
Unless the gift of interpretation followed tongues
        no one could benefit.

Lord, Paul told the Corinthians that if he only spoke in tongues,
        They would learn nothing new,
        Neither would they be inspired or instructed.
Paul used a musical instrument as an illustration;
        If a harp, or flute could play only one note,
Listeners couldn't appreciate one note from another,
        They couldn't tell what is being played.
If no one can understand a bugle's sound
        Who would be ready for battle?
If tongues do not produce an intelligible message,
        Can anyone know what is being said?
        He might as well be talking to the wind.
There are many different languages in the world
        That are helpful to those who understand them,
        But they didn't help Paul.
He said those speaking in a different language
        Were foreigners to him, and he to them.
Paul wants the same principles for the Corinthians,
        "Concentrate on gifts that will benefit the church."

Lord, Paul told them that if they use tongues,
        Pray for someone to interpret what is being said.
Paul said if he used tongues in his prayers,
        His Spirit was praying to God

But he doesn't know what he is saying.
To solve this problem, Paul said he would pray in tongues
    And he would pray in ordinary languages
    So that everyone understands and prays with him.
Paul worships God in tongues, but also with ordinary languages
    So everyone understands what he is doing.
How can the church join you in worship
    If they do not understand what you are saying?
    No matter how well you speak, the church is not benefited.
Paul thanked God that he had
    A greater gift of tongues than all of them,
But in the church he would rather speak meaningful words
    Than speak ten thousand words that no one understood.
He exhorts them not to be childish,
    But be adults in this matter.

Lord, the Scriptures say, "Through men speaking strange languages,
    And through the lips of foreigners,
    You will talk to the Gentiles
    And still they will not listen to You."
Therefore, strange tongues are a sign for unbelievers,
    Not for the believers.
While prophecy is a sign for the believers,
    Not for the unbelievers;
Otherwise a visitor coming to a church meeting
    Would think everyone was mad,
    Because they were speaking unintelligible words.
But if a visitor heard everyone speaking
    A message he could understand,
    He can be convicted by what he hears.
The visitor will have his secret thoughts exposed,
    Then he will fall on his knees, crying out to You,
    Saying, "God indeed is among the church."

Lord, Paul drew some conclusions from the above explanations:
>When the church comes together, some will sing,
>Another will preach, another will share what God said to them.
Some will use their gift of tongues, others will interpret,
>But they must do what is most beneficial to all
>And build everyone up spiritually,
Some will disagree with what Paul told them;
>He asked, "Do you think the knowledge of God
>Begins and ends with you?" Absolutely not!
Those who claim to have the gift of prophecy
>Or any other special gift from the Holy Spirit,
>Should realize Paul is giving the church Your commandment.
Paul said if anyone disagrees with this conclusion,
>He should not be recognized by the church.

In conclusion on this matter, Paul told the Corinthians to
>Desire the gift of prophecy so they could
>Explain the Word of God carefully.
Do not suppress the gift of tongues,
>Do everything decently and in order.
>>Amen.

The Resurrection of Christ

1 Corinthians 15:1-58

Lord, Paul reminded the Corinthians of the content of the Gospel;
>It is the same good news he preached to them,
>They received it, and became firmly established in it.
This is the Gospel that saved them
>Unless they never originally believed it.
The first aspect of the Gospel is that Christ died for our sins,
>Just as the Scriptures teach.
He was buried and after three days,

He arose just as the Scriptures predicted.
He was seen by Peter, and then by the twelve,
  Next He appeared to 500 at the same time;
  Many are still alive and will attest to having seen Him.
Then He appeared to James, and later to all the apostles;
  Finally, He appeared to Paul.

Lord, Paul said he was the least of the apostles
  Since he persecuted the church,
  He felt unworthy to be called an apostle.
But by God's grace, Paul knew he was an apostle
  And his ministry has been fruitful.
Paul said he had worked harder than the other apostles,
  But it was Your grace, not him doing it.
What was important? Paul preached what the apostles preached,
  He preached the Gospel that saved the Corinthians.

Lord, Paul argued that if Christ were raised from the dead,
  How can any say there is no resurrection?
If there is no resurrection from the dead,
  Then Christ could not have been raised
And if Christ was not raised from the dead,
  Then Paul's preaching accomplished nothing
  And the faith of the Corinthians is useless.
Indeed, Paul has committed perjury against You, and
  The God of Heaven,
  Because he swore that You raised him from the dead.
For if the dead has not been raised,
  Then Christ was not raised from the dead.
And if Christ did not rise,
  The Corinthians are still in their sins
  And those in Christ who previously died, have perished.
If our Christian benefits are in this life only,
  We have a miserable life.

But in fact, Christ *has* been raised from the dead,
>   And is the first of millions who will live again.

Lord, Paul taught death comes through one man
>   And resurrection from the dead came through one man.
Just as all people died in Adam,
>   So, all believers will be brought to life through Christ.
However, there is an order to the resurrection:
>   Christ rose first, then when He returns,
>   All believers who have died will be raised.
After that, the end will come;
>   Christ will abolish all kingdoms, authorities, and rulers,
He will destroy every one of His enemies, of every kind,
>   Including the last enemy, death.
Then the unsaved will be raised
>   To meet their judge, Jesus Christ,
>   Who will punish them according to their sins.
When Christ finally becomes victorious over everything,
>   He will put Himself under Your authority
>   So that You will be supreme over everything.

Lord, if the dead will not be raised in the future,
>   What is the point of our getting
>   The same baptism that they got?
Why would anyone be baptized
>   If they didn't believe they would be raised?

Lord, Paul said he wouldn't continually risk himself
>   If there wasn't a resurrection.
He said he wouldn't face death daily, and fight wild beasts
>   There in Ephesus if all he got
>   Was rewarded down here on earth.
If there is no resurrection,
>   We might as well eat and drink
>   Because eventually we will die.

Lord, Paul warned them against being led astray,
      Paul said, "Bad company corrupts good living."
Paul said some of them are not even Christians
      And they should be ashamed that he had to say it.

Lord, Paul addressed their questions, "How will they be brought
      Back to life?" and "What kind of bodies will they have?"
Paul said the answer is in nature; first a seed
      Must be planted and then die in the ground;
      Then new life shall appear.
The thing that is sown is not what comes up,
      A dry little seed is planted in the ground
      And a new abundant plant comes out of the earth.
The new bush is God's plan,
      The new plant has the same life as the seed that was planted.
Not all flesh is the same kind of flesh;
      There is human flesh, animal flesh,
      Fish have flesh and so do birds.
The angels in Heaven have believed
      But their body is different than ours.
The splendor of their heavenly bodies
      Is vastly different from a human body.
The sun, moon, and stars each has its splendor,
      And each one is different from the others.
These are all illustrations of our earthly body,
      That is planted in the earth to die or decay.
But it will be raised to never decay again;
      What is planted is ugly and sickly,
      But it will be raised in glory and immortality.
Yes, the weak earthly body will be buried,
      But it will be powerful and spiritual when raised.
Just as the soul is embodied in this earthly flesh,
      Your eternal Spirit will live in our new bodies.
The first man—Adam—had a life-giving soul,

The last Adam—Christ—became a living-giving Spirit.
The first one—Adam—had a soul,
    The last one—Christ—made us eternal Spirits.
The first man was made from the dust of the earth,
    The second man came from Heaven.
Every human with a body like Adam's
    Is made of earthly dust.
Every human who is born again by Christ,
    Shall have an eternal body like Christ in Heaven.
Just as we are like Adam,
    One day we will be like Christ.

Lord, I know flesh and blood cannot enter the Kingdom of God
    Because our perishable bodies will not last forever.
It's a wonderful mystery, we shall not all die,
    But all believers will be transformed.
It will happen instantly, in the twinkling of an eye,
    When the last trumpet shall sound,
The dead in Christ will suddenly be raised,
    And the living shall all be transformed.
Our present perishable bodies will become imperishable
    And our mortal nature will be immortal.
Then the Scriptures will be fulfilled:
    "Death is swallowed up in victory.
    Death, where is your victory?
    Death, where is your sting?"

Lord, sin is the sting that causes death,
    And that sting is revealed by Your Law.
So, I thank You for victory over sin
    Through my Lord Jesus Christ.

Lord, I will do what Paul tells the Corinthians,
    I will never give in and never admit defeat.
I will keep on diligently doing Your work,

Knowing my labor is not in vain;
You will keep me safe to the resurrection.
                    Amen.

Personal Greetings and Conclusion

1 Corinthians 16:1-24

Lord, Paul wrote to the Corinthians about needy Christians,
        Telling the readers to take up a collection for them;
        This is the same thing he told the churches in Galatia.
Each Sunday set aside some money
        According to their financial prosperity
        So Paul wouldn't need to take a collection.
Paul plans to send their offering to Jerusalem
        By those the Corinthians approved.
Those taking the offering can travel with Paul,
        If they choose to do so.
Paul told them he will come to Corinth
        And stay with them for the winter
        After he visited Northern Greece.
Paul didn't want to just "pop" in for a visit,
        He wanted to spend time with them,
        If it was "the Lord's will."

Lord, a big door of opportunity was opened to Paul in Ephesus,
        So he planned to stay there until Pentecost,
        But he was also aware of much opposition.

Lord, Paul asked the Corinthians to graciously receive Timothy
        When he visited Corinth
        So he could do Your work.
Paul directed that no one despise Timothy,
        But bless him and send him back to Paul.

Paul begged Apollos to go to Corinth,
>But Apollos adamantly refused to go at the present;
>However, he would go to Corinth in the future.

Lord, I will be aware of dangers to my faith
>And I will courageously face them.
I determine to let love motivate me
>In everything that I do.

Lord, Paul reminded the Corinthians how Stephanas' family,
>Who were the first believers in Corinth,
>Had looked after the Christian brothers.
Paul wants the Corinthians to help families
>Who have this type of ministry.
Paul told that Stephanas, Fortunatus, and Achaicus
>Had arrived in Corinth.
They have encouraged Paul in Ephesus;
>Paul wants them to appreciate these men.

Lord, Paul sends the Corinthians greetings from Aquila and Priscilla
>And the church that meets in their house;
>All the believers in Ephesus send greetings.
Paul sends them his warmest greetings,
>Wishing he could be there to embrace them.
Paul said if any does not love You, the Father,
>A curse should fall on them.
Paul prays, "May you experience the grace of the Lord Jesus";
>"My love to all in Christ Jesus."
"*Maranatha*, come quickly, Lord."
>Amen.

2 Corinthians

Chapter 30

THE STORY OF WRITING
THE BOOK OF SECOND CORINTHIANS

Date: A.D. 60 ~ Written from: Philippi, Northern Greece ~ Written by: Paul

Titus arrived from Corinth bringing me news about the Corinthian church. My previous letters had been blunt and condemning. The Corinthians received my letter as from Christ. Those who were sinning repented. I needed that good news.

When I had written the first letter to the Corinthians, I was in the middle of a revival in Ephesus, Turkey, and couldn't leave—at least that's what I thought. But there was a great riot in Ephesus and the Christians insisted I leave for my own protection. In essence I was run out of Ephesus.

Instead of a calm voyage to Philippi where I could pray and get my thoughts together, my spirit was further upset by a vicious storm. I was shipwrecked but I escaped with my life to Philippi.

Even before reaching Philippi, I was robbed and beaten; no wonder many doubted if I had followed the will of God in this matter.

The church at Philippi was one of my favorites. I had led Lydia to Christ, a woman who sold purple cloth. Also the Philippian jailer and his family were in this church. No matter where I have gone, this church has continued to support me financially.

Titus and I sat in the courtyard of Lydia's villa where he told me what was happening in Corinth. The revival I left in Ephesus seemed to break out in Corinth. My letter had brought repentance—the church had spent whole nights in prayer—constantly begging God to forgive them.

Lord, forgive me for my lack of faith about the Corinthian church. You have done exceedingly abundantly above all I could ask or think for the Christians in Corinth.

Titus and I talked long about Corinth. The servants of Lydia brought us everything we needed, but most importantly, they didn't interrupt us. They could see I was writing—notes for my second letter—or we were praying.

After two days of refreshment and regaining my strength, Timothy arrived. The three of us had wonderful times of prayer.

I wanted to write to the Corinthians to let them know their letter to me was important, but that there is something greater than words on paper. I will remind them, "You are my epistle written in my heart, known and read by all people."

Next, I wanted to write and tell them to receive back the sinning brother because of his repentance. Yes, his sins were great, but when he repented and begged forgiveness, it was the duty of the Corinthians to receive him back into full fellowship.

I decided to begin the second letter to the Corinthians on the topic of comfort. I wanted them to know that the God of all comfort is the One who was comforting me now after I was run out of Ephesus, was shipwrecked, and robbed. He is the same God of comfort who will also comfort them in their problems. I will tell about all of the difficulties I had on this trip, beatings, shipwreck, robberies, and being stranded where there was no food.

I want them to know that I forgive the sinning brother, because it was not clear to me that they had forgiven their brother. I will remind them that satan gets an advantage of us for our lack of forgiveness.

Throughout the letter I will remind the Corinthians that satan is constantly attacking and that they "must be aware of his devices and tricks." I will go on to remind them, "That satan comes into their assembly with teachers denying the Gospel." I will remind them that demons can possess those who claim to be Gospel ministers. I will write, "Be careful of false teachers."

I recognized from their letter to me that the Corinthians still had problems with spiritual understanding. I had written to them in my first letter that unsaved people did not have spiritual discernment. In this letter I will remind them that "the God of this world blinds the minds of those who are not believers."

Then I will tell them that unsaved Jews have a double blindness. Their first is spiritual blindness whereby they can't understand the message of the Gospel of Jesus Christ because they are unsaved. But the Jews have a second judicial blindness because God had judged them.

The Jews told Pilate, "His blood be upon us and our children." By officially rejecting Jesus Christ, God judged them with spiritual blindness. Isaiah predicted this blindness saying, "Having eyes to see, they did not see...." That meant the Jews are blinded when they hear the message of Jesus Christ spoken in their synagogues.

I will write to them, "When the Old Testament is taught in the synagogues, Jews are blinded to teachings of Jesus with a scarf around their eyes, just as Moses had to put a veil around his face after he had seen the Lord on Mt. Sinai."

In this letter, I will again remind the Corinthians about giving money for the collection I am taking for the poor saints in Jerusalem. I will remind them that I worked hard in the shop of Aquila and Priscilla making tents so I wouldn't be a financial burden to them. Therefore, I can say, "Since I worked among you; I have the right to ask money from you to give to the poor saints in Jerusalem."

One last thing the Corinthians need to understand, they must be separated from the lust of the world. I will remind them that their bodies are the temples of God, that God no longer dwells in the temple in Jerusalem, but God dwells in their hearts.

Therefore, I will write to the Corinthians, "Come out from among worldly things and be separate, and don't touch unclean things so God can use you."

This letter must be not only tender, showing my physical weakness, weariness, and pain, but also conciliatory, that they will receive back those who had been ostracized. And if necessary, I want them to know I could still be stern if they were still in their sins when I arrive in Corinth.

I sat in the beautiful garden of Lydia to dictate this letter to the Corinthians. Titus sat at a large banquet table to write. He had stacks of paper, pen, and ink spread out before him. Timothy, who had been a pastor to the people of Corinth, sat next to me as I began. "Paul and Timothy to the believers in Corinth...." My favorite part to write was about encouragement; because God encouraged me, He could encourage them. Why? Because He is a "God of mercy and encouragement."

Sincerely yours in Christ,
The apostle Paul

Chapter 31

PRAYING THE BOOK OF SECOND CORINTHIANS

Greetings to the Church

2 Corinthians 1:1-24

Lord, it was Your will for Paul and Timothy to write
  To the believers in the Corinthian church
  And to all Christians in the surrounding state.
May I experience grace and peace in my life
  From You, heavenly Father, and from the Lord Jesus Christ.

Lord, I bless You for encouraging me
  Because You are the Father of the Lord Jesus Christ,
  And You are the God of mercies and encouragement.
I want to encourage others who are in trouble
  With the same encouragement You gave me.
When I am greatly hurting in every area of life,
  Your promises greatly encourage me.

Lord, Paul said his suffering was for the Corinthians,
  So they could be saved and grow in grace.
Paul was hurting at the same time
  The Corinthians had great pain.
And as God was encouraging Paul to continue in ministry,
  So God would encourage the Corinthians
  To remain strong in their faith.
Paul was confident the Corinthians would remain steadfast,

Even though they were now suffering,
Because they were encouraged by You.

Lord, Paul didn't want to withhold his troubles from them,
So they would not be ignorant of what was happening.
That in Asia, he had intense pressures,
Greater than he ever experienced in his life,
So much that Paul thought he would die.
Paul knew that he might be killed,
But he was not trusting earthly deliverance,
Paul trusted You to raise him if he died.
Paul rejoiced that You delivered him from the threat of death,
And Paul knew that You would deliver the Corinthians.
Paul recognized that the gift of his deliverance
Came through the prayers of many Corinthians
And now they deserve credit for their intercession.

Lord, I will always follow the leading of my conscience
To treat everyone kindly and above board
Without any selfish ulterior motives.
I depend on You to help me,
That's the way Paul acted toward the Corinthians.

Paul's letters have been straight to the point,
He hasn't used worldly wisdom with them;
Paul hasn't written anything they can't understand.
Paul realizes they don't know him well
But he wants them to accept him because
When the Lord Jesus returns, they will be glad they know Christ,
Just as Paul will be glad he knows Him.

Lord, Paul told them his original plan was to visit them
Before going to Northern Greece
And then return to them after leaving Northern Greece.
Paul wanted to bless them with his ministry,

Then go on his way to Judea.
So Paul thought they may doubt his intentions
 Because he did not come to them.
Paul didn't want them to think that
 He can't make up his mind.
Paul reminded them "God means what He says,
 God doesn't say 'Yes' when He means, 'No'";
 Paul knew what You wanted him to do.

Lord, You have a plan for my life;
 You faithfully fulfill Your promises to me,
 No matter how many promises there are.
I will tell everyone that You are faithful,
 Amen, glory to Your name.

Lord, You have helped me be a faithful believer
 And given me the responsibility to spread the Gospel.
You set Your seal—Your brand of ownership—on me,
 And You gave me the indwelling Holy Spirit
 As a pledge of blessings to come.

Lord, Paul swore to You that he did not come to Corinth
 Because he didn't want to rebuke them to their face,
 Or to sadden or embarrass them.
Paul said he is not their dictator
 To tell them what they must do.
Rather, he is their fellow-worker
 To make them happy and firm in the faith.
     Amen.

Forgive the Sinner

2 Corinthians 2:1-17

Lord, Paul told the Corinthians he decided not to visit them
    Because it would be painful to them.
He felt it wasn't smart to make the people miserable
    Who gave him joy;
    And he couldn't be happy if they weren't happy.
Paul explained he hated to write the previous letter,
    It grieved him deeply to expose their sins.
He didn't write to hurt them,
    But he had to deal with their sins
    Because he loved them so much.
The men Paul wrote about caused great sorrow,
    So Paul had to rebuke them all
    Because they allowed sin to exist in their midst.
Paul told them one man's punishment was enough,
    He wanted them to forgive and receive him back,
    Otherwise that man may become bitter and give up.
Paul pleaded with them to show the man that
    They still loved him.

Lord, Paul explained his previous letter tested them
    To see if they were completely obedient.
Paul said he forgave anyone they forgave,
    Based on the authority of Christ's teachings.

    When I forgive, satan doesn't get an advantage of me
        For I am not ignorant of his strategy;
        satan wants to discourage and defeat me.

Lord, Paul told them about the open door
    In Troas to preach the Gospel,
    But Titus was not there with him.

Because Paul was worried about Titus' welfare,
    He went looking for him in Northern Greece.

Lord, I thank You for helping me triumph in Christ,
    And for using me as I spread the Gospel
    Like a sweet fragrance to motivate people to be saved.
I want to be Your fragrance everywhere I go,
    To both those who are being saved,
    And to those who refuse salvation.
Because sin has the smell of death that leads to judgment,
    And the sweet fragrance of the Gospel leads to life,
    Lord, help me spread Your influence everywhere.
Therefore, I will go everywhere to spread the Gospel,
    I will speak with integrity and power.
I won't serve You, Lord, for money,
    As some are in the ministry for a salary;
Because You send me to speak for You,
    I will minister in Your sight.
                            Amen.

Instruction About Ministry

2 Corinthians 3:1-18

Lord, Paul said he didn't need to commend himself
    As other people needed a letter of recommendation
    When they go to meet new people.
The change in the hearts of the Corinthians
    Was Paul's letter of recommendation.
The Corinthian church is a letter written by Christ,
    Not penned with ink, nor engraved on stone,
    But written by the Spirit of the Living God.

Lord, none of us should brag about the results of our ministry,
      But we should have our confidence in Christ
      Because our ability comes from You.
You have made me a minister of the New Testament
      Which is not a written legal contract,
      But it is the inner transformation of the Holy Spirit.
Your written commandment tells me I will die
      If I try to keep the Law to be saved,
      But the Spirit gives me eternal life.
Yet, the face of Moses shone when He was given
      The commandment that led to death.
His face had such a brilliant brightness
      The Israelites couldn't look on him.
I'll experience a far greater brightness
      When I give out the Gospel by the Holy Spirit.
If the gift of the Law was glorious,
      How much more glorious the giving of the grace of God?
Actually, the Law that we thought had such great splendor
      Now seems to have none
      Compared to the splendor of Jesus Christ.
And if the Law that was temporary had some splendor,
      How much more glorious is our heavenly hope
      In Your eternal plan of salvation?
Since I know this new splendor will never cease,
      How much more boldly can I speak for You?

Lord, Moses had to put a veil over his face
      So the Israelites wouldn't see his face shining.
To this day, a veil is over the minds of Jews everywhere
      So that when the Old Testament is read,
      They can't understand what they are reading.
But when any Jew turns to You, the veil is lifted from their hearts
      So they can understand Your message.

Now Lord, Your Holy Spirit is working in hearts,
 And when the Spirit works in my life
 There is freedom to understand Your truth.
Now I, with unveiled face, look at Christ
 To see His brightness reflected
 In the mirror of the Word of God.
And constantly, I am transformed into the image of Jesus Christ
 By the work of the Spirit, Who is the Lord.
      Amen.

Instruction About Ministry (continued)

2 Corinthians 4:1-18

Lord, because you have given me a great ministry
 That I didn't deserve,
I will not falsely represent myself
 Nor will I hide the truth.
I will not use tricks, nor interpret the Bible
 According to my own inclination.
But I will declare Your truth to everyone
 So they can understand Your Word.

Lord, I know lost people are spiritually blinded,
 They cannot understand the Gospel.
Satan has blinded their spiritual understanding
 To prevent them from understanding the glorious Gospel,
They cannot see Jesus Christ in Scripture
 Who is Your image.
I will not advance myself or my reputation,
 I will preach Christ Jesus, the Lord
 And I will serve those I'm trying to help;
For You Who commanded light to shine out of darkness,

Have shined Your light into my heart
So I see Your glory in Jesus Christ.

Lord, I have the treasure of Jesus Christ
 In my frail human body
So that outsiders will see Your power
 And know it doesn't come from my weakness.
I have troubles everywhere I go,
 But I am not distressed;
 And I don't give up.
I am persecuted, but not forsaken by You;
 I am knocked down, but not knocked out.
I face death daily, but I serve Christ Jesus
 Who went to death for sinners like me.
My life is renewed daily so others
 Can see the life of Christ shining through me.
I always faced the threat of death
 So that others can see the life of Jesus in me.
I want the faith that is described in Scripture,
 "I speak what I believe,"
May my life reflect what I speak. May I say what I believe.
 Because as You raised up the Lord Jesus from the dead,
 You'll raise me up in the last days.

Lord, Paul said he suffered so they could be saved,
 And when more are won to Christ,
 Paul will thank You more and glorify You more.
That is why Paul didn't give up
 Even when his outward body was hurting,
 His inward desire was strong to serve You.
Paul said his little troubles will pass away,
 But this short time of suffering
 Will result in Your blessing on him and them.

Lord, I will not look at my present sufferings,
>But I will look forward to being happy in Heaven,
Because things I see on earth last only for a short time,
>But the things I can't see with my physical eyes
>Are eternal—they last forever.
>>Amen.

Our Bodies Now and in Heaven

2 Corinthians 5:1-21

Lord, I know if my earthly body dies
>You have a spiritual body for me in Heaven,
>An eternal body made by You alone.
In this present body I groan
>As I wait for my spiritual body,
For I am not merely a spirit without a body
>Because every person has a physical body.
Yet, I groan and get weary in this body
>But it's better than not having a body at all.
Yet, when I get to Heaven I'll have a new body,
>And I won't lose this present body,
>But it will be transformed into an eternal body.
This is Your plan for me
>And You guarantee it by giving me the Holy Spirit
>To live within this body.
Therefore, I am absolutely confident
>Knowing that while I live in this earthly body,
>I am not yet in Your presence.
In this present body I must live by faith
>Which is obeying Your principles,
>Not living to please the body.

Lord, I am not afraid to die, because when this body dies,
    I'll go immediately to Your presence in Heaven.
Therefore, my aim is to please You in everything,
    Whether I'm in an earthly body or a heavenly body.
I know one day I'll stand before You to be judged
    And everything I've done will be examined,
And I'll get what my actions and thoughts deserve
    For the good or bad deeds I've done.

Lord, because I know You will judge me,
    I work hard to win people to Christ.
You know my intents and actions
    And Paul added that he hoped the Corinthians
    Also correctly knew his motives.
Paul was not making another attempt to commend himself
    To the Corinthians, but giving them reasons
    To support his ministry.
Then they would have an answer to those
    Who constantly criticize Paul.
Paul said if he was "out of place" defending himself,
    It was only to bring You glory.
And if he is making a reasonable case,
    It was for the Corinthians' sake.

Lord, the love of Christ overwhelms me when I think of His death,
    That Christ died for all sinners.
Then if He died for all, then all died with Him,
    So that I should no longer live for myself
    But for Him who died and was raised to new life.
Therefore, I will stop judging Christians
    By what the world thinks of them.
Before Paul's conversion he judged Christ only as a human,
    Now he knows Christ differently.

Because I have received Christ into my life
>> You have created me a new person in Christ,
>> The old life is gone, now I have a new life in Him.
My transformation is Your work,
>> And I am reconciled to You through Christ,
>> Now I must get others reconciled to You.
I know You worked through Christ's death
>> To get the world reconciled back to You,
Now You will not punish people for their sin,
>> But You accept them in Christ.
Now I am Your ambassador
>> To spread the message of reconciliation,
>> Asking people to be "reconciled to God,"
Because You placed my sins on Christ, the Sinless One,
>> And You put His righteousness on me
>> So I stand perfect before You.
>>>> Amen.

Hardship in Ministry

2 Corinthians 6:1-18

Lord, I want to be Your partner in ministry,
>> I want everyone to take advantage
>> Of Your grace that is available to all believers.
The Scriptures teach, "I, the Lord, have listened
>> To my people, when they needed salvation,
>> I came to them and helped them."
Now this is a good time for all people to be saved,
>> Today is the day of salvation.

Lord, I will not do anything to discredit myself
>> So that I make it hard for people to get saved.

Actually, I will do the opposite,
    I will do everything to bring people to Christ.

Lord, I will patiently go through sufferings
    And difficulties and pressures for You.
I am willing to be beaten, imprisoned,
    And will face angry rioters for You.
I am willing to work hard, go without sleep,
    Or go without food for You.

Lord, I want to be pure, patient, and kind,
    Loving and knowledgeable of Your principles.
So, I can minister in the Holy Spirit's power,
    According to the Word of God;
    Clothed in the armor of righteousness.
Therefore, I will stand true on the right hand and on the left,
    Prepared for honor or dishonor,
    Whether good reports or bad reports.
I will continue ministering if I'm accused of lying,
    Or, if people accept my honest presentation.
It doesn't make any difference if I'm ignored,
    Or if I'm well known.
Also, I'll continue in ministry if I narrowly escape death,
    Or if I have a safe environment.

Lord, people think my life is miserable,
    Yet, I always rejoice.
They treat me like I'm poor, and have nothing,
    But compared to all people,
    I'm rich and have everything.

Lord, Paul spoke very frankly to the Corinthians,
    He didn't hide anything from them.
The conviction they felt came from their hearts,
    It didn't come from Paul.

Paul said he spoke to them as children,
>Now he wants them to respond
>With childish enthusiasm and obedience.

Lord, I will not tie my life to the decisions
>Of unsaved people who will lead me astray;
>Good intentions can't tolerate an evil agenda.
There is no common agreement between light and darkness,
>Christ and the devil do not agree on anything.
There is no agreement between Your temple and idols,
>So I won't let unbelievers control my life.
I want You to live in the body of my temple
>Because You said, "I will dwell in my people,
>Just as I dwelt in the Old Testament temple;
I will walk with them
>And they will be my people."

Lord, You want me to separate myself from unsaved people
>And not touch dirty things,
So You can welcome me and be my Father,
>And all believers shall be Your sons and daughters
>As You have promised.
>>Amen.

About the Repentant Sinner

2 Corinthians 7:1-16

Lord, with promises as great as these,
>I will separate myself from evil,
>Whether it touches my body or spirit;
And I will be completely holy unto You,
>Living in reverence to You.

Lord, Paul asked them to keep their minds open about him
      He had not exploited anyone, hurt anyone,
      Or ruined anyone's reputation.
He was not fussing at them or blaming them
      Because they were always on his mind,
      They succeeded or failed together with him.
Paul had the highest confidence in them,
      And was encouraged by them;
      They made Paul happy in spite of his suffering.

Lord, Paul explained that he didn't get any physical rest,
      Even when he got to Northern Greece.
There he found trouble everywhere he turned,
      There were fightings within and fears without.
But You who encourage those who are depressed,
      Encouraged Paul when Titus arrived.
Titus told how the Corinthians received him,
      And were sorry for their sin,
      And their concern for Paul.

Lord, Paul was not sorry he sent them a letter,
      But he was sorry that the letter pained them;
      However, they will hurt only a little while.
Now Paul is glad he sent the letter,
      Not because he hurt them,
      But because their pain drove them back to You.
They had a beneficial sorrow,
      The sorrow sent by You to draw Your people to Yourself.
For godly sorrow leads to repentance for salvation;
      I will never regret this type of sorrow
      That drives me back to You.
But worldly sorrow doesn't lead to repentance
      But to discouragement, despondency, and death.
Paul pointed out how good was their sorrow,

They are now diligent to serve You;
> They were also quick to get rid of sin.
He notes the Corinthians have completely cleaned
> Themselves of their wrongdoings.
Therefore, Paul explains he didn't write to
> Blame the offender, or comfort the offended,
> But make them responsible to You.

Titus encouraged Paul when he arrived
> To tell of their love for Paul,
> And Titus was happy to bring the news.
Before Titus left to bring the letter to them,
> Paul told Titus they would repent of their sin,
> And they did not disappoint Paul.
Paul said he always told the truth,
> And his boastings of them proved true.
Paul told how Titus loved the Corinthians
> Because when he read them the letter,
> The Corinthians willingly received it with deep concern.
This made Paul happy that there was no
> Barrier between them and him;
> Now Paul has great confidence in them.
>> Amen.

Collection for the Saints in Jerusalem

2 Corinthians 8:1-24

Lord, Paul wanted the Corinthians to know
> What Your grace accomplished in Northern Greece.
They in Macedonia have had difficult times
> And they have been tested with disappointments,
But they were extremely generous in giving money
> Even though they didn't have much.

553

Paul assured the Corinthians that the Macedonians
> Gave as much as they possibly could,
> Even more than they should.
They begged Paul to receive their offering
> So they could rejoice in helping
> The poor saints in Jerusalem.
They did more than Paul expected;
> First they gave themselves to God,
> Then they gave money to Paul for Jerusalem,
So Paul encouraged Titus to visit them
> And finish the collection of money
> That he began on a previous visit.

Lord, Paul reminded the Corinthians that they had good leaders
> And they had strong faith, good preaching
> Much knowledge, and enthusiasm.
Plus the Corinthians had a deep love for Paul,
> Now he wanted them to be leaders
> In giving joyfully to the Jerusalem project.
Paul reminded them he was not giving a command,
> But he's reminding them what others have done.

Lord, Paul reminded them of the grace of the Lord Jesus Christ
> That when He had all the riches of Heaven,
He gave up everything to help others
> So all believers could be spiritually rich
> Because of His poverty.
Therefore, Paul only suggested that the Corinthians finish
> The project, because it was they
> Who first suggested it to him.
Having begun so enthusiastically, Paul wanted them
> To finish the financial project with zeal,
> Giving whatever money they could.
Paul reminded them that God wanted them to give

From what resources they had,
    Not from what they didn't have.
Paul also reminded them they shouldn't
    Give so much money that they suffer
    When they give to relieve the suffering of others.
Paul said suffering should be shared by all believers;
    Since the Jerusalem Christians are suffering
    Now the Corinthians can do something about it.
In the future, the Corinthians may have sufferings
    And the Jerusalem Christians will help them.
The Scriptures say, "He who gathered much,
    Had nothing left over,
And he who gathered only a little bit,
    Had enough to meet his needs."

Lord, Paul was thankful that Titus had
    The same concern for the Corinthians as he had.
Titus would visit them again at Paul's suggestion,
    But Titus would have gone anyway
    Because he had deep concern for them.
Paul also sent another brother with Titus,
    Who was recognized as a good preacher
    Of the Gospel among all churches.
Paul told them this brother was elected to
    Travel with Paul to take the money to Jerusalem.
His election would prove to all the churches
    His eagerness to help the Jerusalem Christians
    And that God's grace overcomes difficulties.
By traveling together, the two would overcome
    Any rumor about how this large
    Offering would be used in Jerusalem.
Paul said, "I am trying to do right in the sight
    Of all men and of God."
To accomplish this, Paul sent a third brother

That was well known to Paul,
The brother wanted to visit the Corinthians
    Because Paul had told him about them.

Lord, Paul said, "Tell everyone Titus is my partner
    And he is coming to help you."
"Also tell everyone the other two brothers,
    Are outstanding Christians
    And represent the churches and Paul."
Finally Paul said, "Show Your love to these men,
    And do for them what I promised you would do."
            Amen.

More About the Collection for the Saints in Jerusalem

2 Corinthians 9:1-15

Lord, Paul said he didn't need to write to the Corinthians
    About giving to needy saints,
    Because they were eager to help.
He had been boasting to the believers in Achaia
    That the Corinthians were eager to help.
    That motivated the believers in Achaia to give.
But Paul is sending the three brothers to make sure
    They give as they pledged they would.
Because if the Macedonians came with Paul
    And the Corinthians didn't give what they pledged,
    Both Paul and they would be embarrassed.
So Paul urged the three brothers to visit Corinth
    To make sure the gift is ready and waiting.

Lord, Paul wants the money to be a real gift,
    Not something that is given under pressure.
Remember, "If you give little, God's blessing will be small;

When the farmer plants a few seeds,
> He gets small results."
"When the farmer plants a lot of seeds,
> He gets a big harvest."
Everyone must decide the budget they need to live on,
> So they will always have enough for their needs,
> And some left over to give to others.
As the Scriptures say, "He who gives to the poor,
> His gift will be remembered by God."
God, You Who give seed to the farmers, and bread
> To the hungry, will also give me what
> I need and make my harvest great.
When You make me richer in every way,
> I will be able to give generously
> And cause others to thank You.
As I give money in a Christian way,
> You supply my needs and the needs of the needy
> For this I give thanks to You.
By giving a generous gift, the Corinthians demonstrate
> Their Christian integrity,
> And those receiving the gift praise You.
Then they will pray fervently for the Corinthians
> Because they receive Your grace through them.

Lord, Paul concluded, "Thank You, Lord, for Your gift beyond words,
> The gift of Jesus Christ."
> > Amen.

Paul Defends His Apostolic Authority

2 Corinthians 10:1-18

Lord, Paul appealed gently to the Corinthians about these matters,
> As compassionate as would Christ.

Yet the Corinthians are saying he is timid
    When with them, but bold in his letters.
Paul wants them to do what he asks so he
    Won't have to be harsh when he comes.
Some in Corinth think Paul is an ordinary man,
    So they don't want do what he asks or says.
Paul said, "Yes, I live as an ordinary man
    In the flesh, but I don't use the strength
    Of an ordinary man to win battles."
Paul doesn't use the weapons of the world,
    Paul uses Your power to tear down strongholds
To demolish arguments and every barrier
    Against knowledge about You
    That keeps people from finding You.
With these weapons I can capture people
    And bring them back to You
    So they become obedient to Christ.
Once the Corinthians are fully obedient to Christ,
    Then Paul is ready to punish disobedience.

Lord, Paul said the Corinthians were looking on outward things;
    To them Paul seems weak and powerless,
    But Paul tells them not to just look at the surface.
Yet, if anyone can claim the power of Christ,
    Paul says it's he.
Paul is sorry for talking too much about
    Having the authority of Christ,
But he says the Lord gave it to him,
    Not to pull down, but to build up the saints
    So he'll not apologize for using it.
Paul says he is not trying to frighten them,
    Even though some say his letters are forceful,
    But he is unimpressive in person.
They criticize that Paul's a poor preacher,

And there's nothing authoritative about him.
Paul says those who criticize him should remember that
    What Paul is like in his letters,
    Will be what he is like in person.
Paul said he is not comparing himself
    With people who write their own "brag sheet";
    Their ego is their standard.
Rather, Paul said his standard for achievement
    Is Your divine yardstick for measuring faithfulness,
    Which he followed in Corinth.
Paul said he was not overstepping his commission
    When he brought the Gospel to the Corinthians,
    Or when he exercised authority over them.
Paul said he is not taking credit for ministry
    Others have done in Corinth.
Instead, Paul hopes their faith will grow,
    Then others will appreciate what he has done.
Paul said he will be carrying the Gospel in the future
    To unreached fields; then no one will
    Criticize him for working in someone else's field.
If anyone wants to boast, let him boast in You, our Father.
    Then it's not a matter of self-approval
    But having Your approval.
                Amen.

False Apostles

2 Corinthians 11:1-33

Lord, Paul asked the Corinthians to put up with his foolishness,
    Because he is jealous over them
    With the right kind of jealousy.
Paul said, "I am concerned that the Corinthians

Have a deep love for Christ alone,
    As a virgin bride has for her groom."
But Paul is concerned they will be led away
    From their pure love for Christ,
    As Eve was deceived by satan.
Paul said they were gullible about their faith
    Because if anyone preached another Jesus,
    That was different from the one Paul preached,
They would quickly embrace any false teacher,
    Also they would quickly embrace a false spirit,
    Different from the One they got at salvation,
Paul said those who claimed to be apostles,
    Were no better than he was.
If Paul were a poor speaker, at least he knew
    The message he was presenting; and
    He had preached it many times.

Lord, Paul asked if he did wrong by not taking
    Money from the Corinthians
    When he preached to them.
Paul was taking money from other churches
    To live on, so he could preach to them.
When Paul ran out of money in Corinth
    He didn't take money from them,
    Those who came from Philippi brought him money.
Paul said he was very careful not to burden them,
    And he'd tell everyone the same thing in Greece,
Not to embarrass them but to
    Cut the ground out from under those
    Who say they minister, just as Paul does.
God never sent those false ministers;
    They have fooled the Corinthians
    Into thinking they are Jesus' apostles.
This didn't surprise Paul, because satan can change

Himself into an apostle of light,
So those who serve the devil actually
Appear to be godly ministers.
In the final judgment, they'll get
The punishment their evil deeds deserve.

Lord, Paul asked them not to think he is a fool,
But if the Corinthians take him as a fool
Paul wants to brag as a fool boasts.
Paul said the following bragging is not prompted by God,
But is said because he has something to brag about.
The false teachers have been bragging
Of their worldly achievements,
So Paul will brag about his spiritual achievements.
Paul said the Corinthians had tolerated fools;
They tolerated false teachers who made them slaves.
The false teachers made the Corinthians feed them, obey them,
And give them all their money.
"They were slapping the Corinthians in the face."
Paul never demanded things like that.
Yet, whatever the false teachers brag about,
Paul has more to boast about.
Are they Hebrews, so was Paul.
Are they Israelites, so was Paul.
Are they descendants of Abraham, so was Paul.
Are they ministers of Christ, Paul said
He was foolish to even compare himself
To them, because he was called by Christ himself.
I have served more time in prison,
I have been beaten more times,
I have faced death, time and again.
I have received 39 lashes,
Five times from the Jews.
I have been beaten with rods five times,

I have been stoned once.
I have been shipwrecked three times,
I drifted 24 hours in the sea.
I have been in danger while
  Crossing rivers, from thieves, from Jews,
  And from Gentiles.
I have been in danger in city streets,
  In the desert, on the sea, and by
  False teachers.
I have experienced hard work,
  Exhaustion, sleepless nights, hunger,
  Thirst, fastings, cold, and exposure.
Finally Paul said, "I have had the constant responsibility
  Of the churches. Every time someone sins,
  I have to deal with it."
"When Christians fail, I pick them up.
  When they are hurt, I comfort them."
Paul said, "I'd rather brag about my weaknesses,
  Than my accomplishments."
"God the Father of the Lord Jesus Christ,
  Knows I am telling the truth;
  Let all praise go to Him forever."
Paul told how the governor of King Aretas of Damascus,
  Tried to arrest him at the city gates,
But he was let down by a basket on a rope to escape
  Through a window in the wall.
       Amen.

Paul's Thorn in the Flesh

2 Corinthians 12:1-21

Lord, Paul said it was foolish to boast about accomplishments,
    But he has had visions and revelations from You Lord.
"Fourteen years ago I was taken to Heaven
    Whether it was physically or spiritually,
    I don't know, only God knows.
"All I know is that I was caught up into Paradise,
    (Let me repeat, I don't know if it
    Was in my body or in my spirit).
"I heard things that I cannot repeat,
    I'll not brag of that experience;
    I'll brag only in my weaknesses.
"I have plenty to brag about, but I won't do it
    Because people will think I am a fool.
"I don't want people to think more highly of me
    Than they ought to think."

Lord, because Paul had this extraordinary revelation,
    You gave him a thorn in the flesh
    To keep him from getting puffed up.
Three times Paul pleaded for You to relieve
    Him from that pain,
But You told Paul, "My grace is sufficient for you
    My power will be evident in your weakness."
So Paul said, "I'll be happy to boast of my weakness
    So the power of Christ will rest on me.
"Since it is for the cause of Christ, I am
    Happy to live with my thorn in the flesh.
"I will be happy to suffer insults, hardships,
    Difficulties, and poverty
    For when I am weak, I am strong."

Lord, Paul said the Corinthians were making
    Him look foolish. They should
      Be bragging on him, not Paul bragging on himself.
Paul said he was not behind the first apostles
    In second place.
The things that characterize an apostle
    Are signs, wonders, and miracles
      Which he did among the Corinthians.
These miraculous gifts meant the Corinthians
    Were not inferior to other churches.
The only thing lacking in the Corinthian church
    Was they didn't pay Paul a salary;
      He asks forgiveness in this exception.

Lord, Paul told the Corinthians he was coming
    To them a third time,
And Paul said he will not take money from them,
    It is their love he wants, not their money.
Children don't take care of their parents,
    Parents take care of their children.
Paul said, "I am willing to spend my money on you,
    I will even be spent for you,
      Because I love you more than any other teacher."
Paul notes, "Some of you argue that I didn't
    Receive money from you,
But you think I tricked you,
    You think I made money off you some other way."
Paul asked them, "How did I make money?"
    Titus and the others sent Paul money,
    He didn't take money from them.
Paul noted, "We all live by the Holy Spirit,
    We all live by the same standard."
Paul explained, "You think I'm telling you these things
    To justify myself.

"Actually, I speak the truth in Christ before God,
    I say this so God will know
    I did everything for your spiritual growth."

Lord, Paul was afraid when he got to Corinth
    He would not find what he wanted to find,
And that they would not see in Paul,
    What they expected of him.
Paul was afraid he'd find arguments,
    Jealousy, hatred, divided-allegiance,
    Slander, expressions of ego and disharmony.
Paul asked them, "When I come again, will
    I be embarrassed by your behavior?
"Shall I grieve over any who have sinned,
    And are guilty of impurity,
    Yet have not repented of their evil?"
                Amen.

Final Exhortation and Conclusion

2 Corinthians 13:1-14

Lord, Paul said on this his third trip to Corinth,
    He will tell them the same things
    He said on the second visit.
Now Paul is absent from them
    But he will still tell them the same things.
He repeated his authority, "At the mouth of
    Two or three witnesses
    Every word shall be established.
"I have already warned everyone,
    And especially those who are sinning, that
    I will punish them severely when I come.
"I will give you all proof

That Christ speaks through me
    And He will not be weak in dealing with You.
"His weakened body was crucified,
    But now He has the mighty power of God.
"I am weak in my human body as He,
    But through His power I will be strong."

Lord, Paul told everyone, "Examine yourselves,
    Are you actually a Christian?
    Test yourself with this question.
"'Do you have the presence of Jesus Christ
    Living in Your lives?'
"I have not failed the test,
    But I have passed the test,
    And I belong to Jesus Christ."

Lord, Paul prayed they would live godly lives,
    Not to make him look successful,
    But that God may be glorified.
Paul said his responsibility is to encourage
    Them to live right at all times
    And not do evil.
He was glad to be weak and despised,
    If it meant they would become strong.

Lord, Paul said he hoped he wouldn't need to
    Use his apostolic authority to break them,
    But to lift them up.

Lord, Paul concluded, "Rejoice, grow in Christ
    Live in unity, and peace, and may
    The God of love and peace be with you.
"Greet one another warmly, as you should,
    All the saints greet you.
"May the grace of the Lord Jesus Christ

The love of God, and presence of the Holy Spirit
Be with all of you, always."

Amen.

GALATIANS

Chapter 32

THE STORY OF WRITING THE BOOK OF GALATIANS

Date: A.D. 45 ⌐ Written from: Antioch, Syria ⌐ Written by: Paul

It had been almost a year since Barnabas and I had completed our first missionary journey through the regions of Galatia in Turkey. Because Barnabas was the one with the strong personal relationships, he got word first of what was happening in the churches of Turkey.

Originally the Jews tried to destroy Christianity by attacking Barnabas and me physically. But now the Jews had a different strategy.

The new counter attack by the Judaizers was subtle. They wanted to undermine the foundation of Christian churches that they called a "sect." Judaizers were now infiltrating the churches to dilute the message by saying, "You must be circumcised to be saved."

I was sitting on the back patio praying when Barnabas told me about the new assault on Christians in Turkey.

"Also they deny you are an apostle," said Barnabas. "They say you may call yourself an apostle but you are not on the level of Peter and those who followed Jesus on earth."

By downgrading my authority, the Judaizers were downplaying the message of the grace of God. This way they could keep the Mosaic law and add the new teaching of Christianity. But this new Gospel is not the true gospel.

"I will write them a letter," I said, "I will set the matter straight."

"But you cannot see well enough to write," Barnabas argued with me. "You have had trouble with your eyes ever since the stoning at Lystra."

I was determined to correct the Judaizers and protect the church, so I said, "When a man must do something, God will help him." I answered, "I will squint, I will write big letters, I will write slowly and focus on each letter...but I will write."

Then I told Barnabas that the first part of my letter will justify my apostleship. I will tell them how Jesus called me, and how Jesus gave me the revelation and mysteries of God when I went into the desert.

I told Barnabas that I would add personal things that had happened to me since I saw Jesus on the Damascus Road, including the threats on my life. I will also include the fact I went to Jerusalem, but saw none of the apostles but James the Lord's brother. I will write to them that I conferred not with flesh and blood, and that I did not get my Gospel from other apostles, but from Jesus Himself.

I told Barnabas about the second part of my letter. I will tell them that both Jews and Gentiles are justified before God by faith alone. I will show how that was God's plan from the very beginning when Abraham "believed God, and it was accounted to him for righteousness."[1]

I will show that the law did not come until 430 years after Abraham was justified by faith[2] and that the Law was never intended to replace justification. I believe in the Law because it teaches us our need for Christ.[3]

Barnabas agreed with me and asked, "What about Christian living, how will you instruct them to live?"

I had already thought of the conclusion, "The result of justification by grace is spiritual freedom," I told Barnabas, no one should use their Christian freedom from the Law as an excuse to satisfy their old nature, rather freedom is an opportunity to love.[4]

Then I went on to indicate that being justified by faith does not insulate one from the struggles of life. "I will talk about the contrast between the fruits of the flesh and the fruits of the Spirit and I will show that the

Christian life is a struggle indeed, but that the Holy Spirit struggles with our old nature so that we might serve God victoriously."

The next afternoon I sat down at a table to begin writing the epistle to the Galatians. I was still agitated that the Judaizers would not recognize me so I wrote, "Paul, an apostle, not appointed by any human council, nor by any individual man, but called by Jesus Christ and God the Father."

I then said to myself, "*I am going to pray that the readers will recognize my apostleship when they read this first sentence; if they do that, they will understand what God is saying in the rest of this letter.*"

I knew the Galatians were hard headed. Ethnically, the people of Galatia were from Celtic stock living in central Turkey. They were known for fierce determination, and self-discipline. They were a heady people. Politically Galatia was made a province by Rome in 25 B.C. including people from southern Turkey who were not Celtic. I knew the people well, for I was born in Tarsus in southeast Turkey. Growing up I often heard about the strong-headed Galatians across the foreboding mountains.

Barnabas and I had gone to the area on our first journey. Every time I preached in a synagogue, the Jews ran me out of town until finally in Lystra they stoned me. Whether I died is not clear, but most people who read the story say this was the occasion that I later described, "Fourteen years ago I was taken up to heaven for a visit. Don't ask me whether my body was there or just my spirit, for I don't know; only God can answer that. But anyways, while I was in paradise, I heard things so astounding that they are beyond a man's power to describe or put in words."[5]

I wrote out of white hot fervency telling them that keeping the Law never saved anyone. To the Jews the issue was circumcision, but to me the issue was becoming a "new creation" in Christ.[6] If I do not successfully argue for justification by faith alone, Christianity might become nothing more than a troublesome sect of Judaism and would be lost with the other Jewish sects.

But this commanding letter should not be taken lightly. One must agree with my conclusion that the Law does not save, and that people are saved by justification through faith alone.

Sincerely yours in Christ,
The apostle Paul

Martin Luther, the reformer who "jump started" the Reformation said that Galatians was "his epistle." Luther was so attached to the Book of Galatians in preaching that this book became Luther's "Magna Carta of Christian liberty" as he attacked the "religion of works" taught by the Roman Catholic church of his day.

Endnotes

1. Gal. 3:6; Gen. 15:6.

2. Gal. 3:17.

3. Gal. 3:24-25.

4. Gal. 5:13; 6:7-10.

5. 2 Cor. 12:2-4 LB.

6. Gal. 6:15

Chapter 33

PRAYING THE BOOK OF GALATIANS

The Galatians Have Departed the True Gospel

Galatians 1:1-24

Lord, Paul wrote a letter to the Galatians, reminding them he was an
Apostle by divine commission of Jesus Christ and God the Father.
He was not appointed by any individual or by any group; therefore
they should not reject his clear teaching on salvation by grace
through faith alone.

Paul sent greetings to all the churches of Galatia, from all those
who were with him.

Paul prays for You the Father and the Lord Jesus Christ to give them
grace and peace.

Lord, I want the same grace and peace in my life
That comes only from You and the Lord Jesus Christ.
Thank You for sending Jesus to die for my sins,
To deliver me from this present evil world
According to Your eternal plans.
I give all glory to You, my heavenly Father,
And will continue to do so throughout the eternal ages.

Lord, Paul was startled that the Galatians had turned away so quickly
from the teaching of grace to follow a different gospel of works.
They no longer followed the Gospel of salvation by faith alone. They

were being blinded by those who twisted the truth of Christ into legalism.

Lord, Paul wanted your curse on anyone who preached that salvation comes by works. He said, "Even if an angel preached works, it should be cursed." Then Paul repeated himself, "If anyone preaches a Gospel contrary to what the Galatians received, let him be under a curse forever."

Lord, Paul didn't want to please people. He wanted Your approval. If he catered to people, he'd not be Christ's servant. That's the prayer of my heart; I want to please You.

Lord, the Good News that Paul preached didn't come from human thought or logic. He didn't think it up nor did anyone teach it to him. It came by a direct revelation from Jesus Christ.

Before Paul was saved, he persecuted Christians and tried to destroy Christianity. Paul was more zealous than most Jews his age, and tried as diligently as possible to follow all the Jewish traditions.

But you called Paul before he was born, and chose him to be Your apostle. Your Son was revealed to Paul so that he might preach the Gospel of Jesus Christ to the Gentiles.

When Paul was saved, he didn't consult with anyone, and he didn't go to Jerusalem to consult with the apostles; immediately after Paul was saved, he went to Arabia (the desert) where You revealed to him the doctrine of salvation by grace through faith, apart from works. Then he returned to Damascus. Three years later, Paul went to Jerusalem to meet Peter and stayed there 15 days. The only other apostle that Paul met was James, our Lord's brother.

Then Paul went to minister in the provinces of Southern Turkey and then Antioch of Syria. The churches in the Holy Land didn't even know what Paul looked like. All they knew was, "The One who used to persecute Christians, now preaches the faith he formerly tried to destroy." They praised God for saving Paul.

Amen.

The Out-Living of the In-Dwelling Christ

Galatians 2:1-21

Lord, Paul returned to Jerusalem 14 years later accompanied by Barnabas and Titus with definite orders from God to confront the leaders about their false teaching that a person must be circumcised to be saved. Paul talked privately to the leaders, telling them that in his ministry Gentiles were being saved without circumcision. The leaders agreed with Paul, and did not demand that Titus who was with him be circumcised, even though Titus was a Gentile.

Lord, Paul said the issue of Titus would not have come up, except some false brothers had infiltrated the meeting to spy on what was discussed. They wanted to make everyone a slave to the Old Testament, taking away the freedom we all have in Christ.

Lord, I thank You that I am saved by grace,
And that my faith is not measured by keeping the Law.

Lord, Paul did not give in to those spying on him. He established the truth of the Gospel for all. The leaders didn't add anything to what Paul had said to them, or what Paul was preaching to the Gentiles.

Lord, the apostle who met with Paul accepted him as an equal (their status didn't intimidate Paul for he knew his calling and he knew all were equal before God). In fact, when Peter, James, and John saw the great results Paul had preaching among the Gentiles—just as God had used Peter to evangelize the Jews—they embraced Barnabas and Paul. They encouraged Paul and Barnabas to continue preaching to Gentiles, and they would continue preaching to Jews. The only thing they added was to help the poor, which was what Paul was already doing.

Lord, later when Peter came to Antioch, he ate his meals with Gentile believers. But when a delegation of legalists came from James in Jerusalem, Peter separated himself from the Gentile believers because he was intimated by the Jews. Then some other Jewish believers followed Peter's example by discriminating against Gentile believers. Even Barnabas was caught up in this compromise for a while.

Lord, when Paul realized what was happening, he said to Peter in front of everyone, "If you are a Jew who lives like a Gentile, why do you try to make Gentiles live like Jews?"

Lord, Paul explained: a Jew becomes a Jew by birth. A Christian becomes a child of God by being born again. No one becomes a child of God by keeping the Law, but a person is saved by faith in Jesus Christ. Jews who believe in Christ become a child of God by faith in Christ and not by obeying the Law.

Lord, no one can be saved and justified by keeping the Law;
The Jews who keep the Law are as much sinners
As Gentiles who do not keep the Law.
Does that mean Christ allows us to sin?
No! That is absurd teaching.
Paul did not try to rebuild a new system for Christians to keep the Law,
Because he taught that the legalistic system of the Law
Was done away in the death of Christ.

I died because the Law condemns all to death,
But in Christ I now live with new life.
I was crucified with Christ;
I died when He died on the Cross,

So I no longer try to live for God in the flesh.
Now Christ lives within me to give me new life;
>   The Christian life is the out-living of the in-dwelling Christ.
I live by the faith of the Son of God
>   Who loves me and gave Himself for me.

Lord, if I could be saved by keeping the Law
>   Then there was no need for Christ to die,
>   And the death of Your Son was worthless.
>   Amen.

The Law Condemns but Faith Saves Us

Galatians 3:1-29

Lord, Paul said the Galatians were foolish because someone had blinded
>   them to the truth of the death of Jesus Christ. Paul asked them,
>   "Did you receive the Holy Spirit by obeying the Law?" The obvious
>   answer is "Of course not!" Then he asked, "Are you now trying to
>   live the Christian life by the Law after having been saved by the Holy
>   Spirit?"

Lord, Paul reminded the Galatians that they suffered many things for the
>   Gospel, now they were throwing it out. They were getting nothing in
>   return for legalism.

Lord, I want the power of the Holy Spirit
>   To work miracles in my life.
I know you don't do the supernatural for those living by the Law;
>   You give miraculous power to live for You to those living by faith.

Lord, I know Abraham believed in You,
>   And it was credited to him for righteousness;
>   You looked on Abraham as though he were perfect.
I want to be a child of Abraham,

I want to live by faith;
I want to wholly trust You for everything.

Lord, You predicted the Gentiles would be saved by faith
When you said, "In Abraham all the nations will be Blessed."
So I want the blessing You promised to all;
I want You to enrich my faith.

Lord, I know those who try to keep the Law,
Are under the curse that comes with the Law,
For legalists who don't keep all the Law
Will be judged by the curse promised in Scripture.
No one ever got saved by obeying the Law;
Only those living by faith will be justified.
I remember what the Scriptures teach about the Law;
You must obey every Law without exception,
Otherwise you are cursed by the Law.
But Christ took me out from under the curse of the Law
When He was made a curse for me;
The Scriptures teach, "Cursed is everyone
Who hangs on a tree."

Lord, the blessings You promised Abraham
Come to me through faith in Jesus Christ, and
I receive the promises of the Holy Spirit.
Now in this life a man must do what he promises,
He cannot change his mind after he pledges his word.
God, You promised to save those who exercise faith
So, You cannot change or cancel that promise.
God, You gave this promise to Abraham and to his seed;
One seed—Christ, received Your promise,
So Christ is the One saving me.
Four hundred and thirty years later You gave the Ten Commandments,
But keeping these commandments did not save anyone,
Because You promised Abraham salvation by faith.

Lord, You added the Law to teach us the existence of sin,
Until the Seed came to fulfill Your promise;
Then You forgive the sin of those who exercised faith.
You gave us the Law by angels;
The very fact You used angels proved that the Law
Did not fulfill the promises You made to Abraham,
Because Your promise does not depend on angels,
But it depends on Christ alone who fulfilled that promise
Because Christ alone took away our sin.

Lord, does the Law contradict Your promise?
No, for if the Law gave anyone spiritual life,
Then the Law would produce righteousness.
But, the Scriptures teach all are prisoners of sin,
The only escape is by faith in Jesus Christ
By which I am rescued and made a Son of God.
Before Christ came, we were all prisoners of the Law
Until the coming of Christ who freed us.
The Law was like a strict drill sergeant showing us our weaknesses
Until we went to the school of Christ
And learned to be justified by faith.
Once we have faith in Christ to free us,
We don't need the Law's authority.
Now that we have faith in Christ Jesus,
We are the children of God.
When we were baptized into Christ,
We became a part of His family;
We put on Christ and became like Him.
We are no longer known as a Jew or Gentile,
A slave or free; or even men or women;
We are all the same—we are all equal in Christ.
Since I belong to Christ, I am a descendent of Abraham;
I am a true heir to the promises made to him.
Amen.

Legalism Is an Enemy of Faith

Galatians 4:1-31

Lord, as long as the son of a rich father is a child, he doesn't have the use
of the wealth that his father has left him. When the father dies and
leaves the child an inheritance, the child has to do what his
guardian or manager tells him to do. The child is no better than a
servant in the house.

Lord, I know I am Your child and one day I'll enjoy
The riches of Heaven and perfect fellowship with You.
But, now I'll live as a slave in this present world,
I'll obey every command You give me.

Lord, before Christ came into the world, Your people were slaves to the
Jewish Law that only covered over sins. But in the fullness of time,
You sent Your Son to be born of a woman—born as a Jew—to
purchase freedom for those who were slaves to the Law. Now You
have adopted us as Your children.

Lord, I thank You that Christ Jesus was born as a Jew,
That He perfectly kept the Law,
And He nailed the Law to the Cross,
Satisfying its claims to free me;
So now I am free from its demands.

Lord, because I am Your child, You have sent the Spirit of Christ into my
heart so I can talk to You saying, "Papa, Father." I am no longer a
slave, but Your very own child. And since I am Your child, all
spiritual blessings belong to me.

Lord, before Gentiles were saved, they were slaves to idols and their manmade
gods. When they found You—or You found them—how can they
want to go back to a weak and beggarly religion and try to please
You by obeying laws? They are observing special days, and months,

and seasons to establish favor with You. They are canceling the
preaching of the Gospel that they once believed.

Lord, may I never try to please You by keeping laws
For I am not perfect, nor can I ever be perfect;
My only plea is the blood of Christ
Who has forgiven my sin and given me access to You.

Lord, the legalist should feel as Paul about the Law. They should be as free
from the chains of the Law as was Paul. The Galatians did not
despise Paul when he first preached to them, even though he was
sick at the time. They welcomed Paul as though he were an angel
sent from God, as though he were Christ Jesus Himself. Paul wants
to know what happened to their gracious spirit.

Lord, may I have a good spirit about new converts
As Paul had for the Galatians;
May I love them and pray compassionately for them
So they will be encouraged to grow in Christ.

Lord, because of Paul's illness, the Galatians originally would have given
their eyes to him. Now Paul wants to know why they have become
his enemy. Legalists have taught the Galatians to live by the Law,
but they are wrong. The legalists are attacking Paul so they can win
the Galatians to their point of view. Paul is glad if people take an
interest in the Galatians when their motives are good, but the
legalists would make them slaves again to the Law.

Lord, there are some Christians who live by the Law,
And they try to make others slaves to the Law.
Thank You that Christ has freed me from the Law;
Now, I live free in the Kingdom of Your Son.

Lord, Paul says his children in Christ are hurting him, as though he is going
through childbirth again for them. He is suffering till Christ be
formed in them. Paul tells them if he were with them, he could

change their opinion. He does not like to deal with this issue by a letter. He is perplexed and doesn't know what to do.

Lord, give me grace to understand those who are misguided,
    Teach me how to relate to them.
Keep me as near to the truth as I can be,
    And may Christ always be seen in me.

Lord, Paul asked the Galatians if they really understood what the Law requires of them. They were not able to keep all of the Law, so why should they want to be under it?

Lord, I know I live in the flesh and cannot be perfect,
    I realize I cannot keep the Law.
Thank you for satisfying the demands of the Law in Your death;
    I will now live to please Christ.

Lord, Abraham had two sons, one born of a slave girl, the other born to a free woman. The son born to the slave had a natural birth, the other one was born supernaturally according to Your promise. The first woman—a slave—represented Mount Sinai, being in Arabia, the land of Ishmael, the son of the slave woman. The second woman—a free woman—represented Mount Zion in Jerusalem. This one typifies heavenly Jerusalem and is "spiritually" free from the Law.

Lord, when I was born again by the Spirit of God,
    You gave me a new nature to obey You
Which is a much greater motive to do the right things
    Than trying to keep the Law to please You.

Lord, Paul quoted Isaiah to illustrate his point,
    "Shout for joy, you barren one who bore no children,
Break into shouts of joy and gladness you who were never in labor.
    For there are more sons of the forsaken one
    Than sons of the wedded wife."

Lord, Paul told the Galatians they were like Isaac, children born of the promise. The legalists are like the child born of Hagar. Then Ishmael persecuted Isaac, which is what the Galatians are now doing to him. Paul reminded them of the Scripture, "Drive away the slave girl and her son because she should not have an inheritance with Isaac." Paul exhorts the Galatians to be children born of the free woman and not become children born to the slave woman.

Lord, I will not put myself under the Law,
With all its punishments and curses;
I choose the freedom of living in Christ,
Because the Spirit of God lives in my heart.
Amen.

Characteristics of the Life of Faith

Galatians 5:1-26

Lord, thank You that Christ freed me from the Law,
I won't be chained again to Jewish legalism,
I won't be a slave to the Law.
I won't consent again to religious laws,
I want Christ to be my freedom.
Circumcision will get no one favor with God
For if any think he must keep one law,
Then he must obey every other law.
If any tries to be justified by keeping the Law,
He cuts himself off from the life of Christ;
He has fallen from grace.
For by faith we have the hope of being righteous
And the Holy Spirit works in us to make it happen.
For in Christ—circumcision or uncircumcision—means nothing,
I must have faith which expresses itself in love.

Lord, Paul said the Galatians were growing in Christ until
    someone stopped them from obeying the truth. This wasn't from You
    because You originally called them. The Judaizers had corrupted
    them. It only takes a little leaven to influence the whole lump.

    Paul had confidence the Galatians wouldn't fall to legalism and that
    the Judaizers would be punished.

Lord, some said Paul was preaching that circumcision was necessary for
    salvation. But if that was what Paul was doing, he wouldn't be
    persecuted. The fact that Paul was being persecuted proves he was
    preaching salvation by grace through the Cross alone. Paul wanted
    the Judaizers to be cut off altogether from the Galatians.

Lord, I have been called to freedom in Christ,
    Not freedom to follow my sinful nature
    But free to serve others in love.
The Law is summed up by one commandment,
    You shall love your neighbor as yourself.
Freedom does not mean freedom to attack others
    And tear them down,
    And ruin any fellowship with them.

Lord, I will live in the Spirit
    And not satisfy the lust of my sinful nature.
All the energy of my sinful nature
    Fights against the Spirit's control,
And all the energy of the Spirit
    Fights against being controlled by my sinful nature.
These two forces are constantly fighting to control my life,
    And I feel constant pressure from both of them.
When I am controlled by the Holy Spirit,
    I am no longer a legalist.

Lord, the fruit of the sinful nature is sexual immorality,
>Impure thoughts, sensuality, worship of false gods, spiritism
>(encouraging demons), hating people, attacking people, jealousy of
>others, and anger at everything, drunkenness, wild parties, and
>things like these. Those who indulge in these things will not see the
>Kingdom of God.

Lord, the fruit of the Spirit is love, joy, peace, patience, kindness, a
>generous spirit, faithfulness to one's word, gentleness and self-
>control. This is completely different from trying to live by the Law.

Lord, I will put to death—crucify—the lust that came
>From my sinful nature that tries to control my life.
I will live by the direction of the Spirit
>So I can fulfill the fruit of the Spirit.
I will not be ambitious for my own reputation
>So that I won't be making others jealous,
>But Christ will be the passion of my life.
>>Amen.

The Faith-Life is a Brotherhood

Galatians 6:1-18

Lord, when I see a fellow Christian overtaken by sin,
>I will humbly try to get them back on the right path.
I will not feel superior to them
>But will guard myself against all temptations.
I will bear the burden of other believers
>So I can obey Your commands.

Lord, when people think they are important,
>But they are really nobody,
>They end up deceiving themselves.
May every one of us do our very best in all things,

So we can have personal satisfaction.
When we do something worth doing, then
    We won't have to depend on the approval of others.
Each of us is responsible for our faults and sins,
    For none of us is perfect.

Lord, those who teach the Word of God
    Should be paid by those who learn from them.

Lord, no one should be deceived
    By ignoring what You want them to do;
    Everyone will reap the kind of crop they sow.
When someone sows to their sinful nature,
    Their harvest will be death and destruction;
But when they sow to the Holy Spirit,
    Their harvest will be everlasting life.
I will not get tired of doing good things
    Because I will reap a good harvest
    If I don't give up.
I will do good to all people
    Every opportunity I get,
    Especially to the household of faith.

Lord, Paul wrote with large letters because he had eye problems.
    He warned the Galatians that the legalists were trying to become
    popular by getting them under the Law. The legalists would be
    persecuted if they admitted that salvation comes only by the cross
    of Christ. Even the legalists who teach circumcision don't try to
    keep the rest of the Law. The legalists want to boast that the
    Galatians were their disciples.

Lord, far be it for me to glory
    Except in the cross of our Lord Jesus Christ.
By the Cross I have put to death—crucified—the world's attractions,
    And by the Cross I have crucified my attraction to it.

Now, it doesn't make any difference if I have been circumcised;
    All that matters is my new desire to please You.

Lord, may Your peace and mercy be on all believers
    Who live by the power of the Spirit
    And upon all who belong to You.

Lord, Paul didn't want anyone to bother him with this issue any more. He
    had been persecuted enough with scars to prove it. Paul prayed for
    the grace of the Lord Jesus Christ to be on the Galatian believers.
                    Amen.

EPHESIANS

Chapter 34

THE STORY OF WRITING
THE BOOK OF EPHESIANS

Date: A.D. 64 ~ Written from: Rome, Italy ~ Written by: Paul

I was out for a stroll with my Roman guard; this was a privilege he gave me for the past few days. I had preached to him and he had become a believer.

However, the Roman soldier walked closely by my side and kept a hand on his sword, for if anyone killed me, that soldier might pay with his life.

I went for this walk to think about a letter I wanted to write to the church at Ephesus, so I thought a stroll along the Po River would help me focus on how to form the letter.

I wanted to write a letter to compliment the Christians in Ephesus but I didn't know how to go about it. Ephesus was a strong church that had experienced revival in the past. Of all the churches I had visited, the church in Ephesus was an example in godliness, evangelism, and service to God.

I want to write a letter complimenting them because they had taken advantage of all the benefits of living in Christ. I wanted this letter to be copied and sent to every church in the Mediterranean world. I wanted every Christian to read what a wonderful privilege it is to be a Christian. I didn't want to brag on them, lest they become proud. Also, if I bragged on individuals, the letter wouldn't be effective when read in other churches.

I prayed as I walked, "Lord speak to me, tell me what to write." Then I prayed further, "Lord, guide each word I write so that I write the truth without error."

As I walked under the shadow of the Senate building, this massive government building stood tall in the sky, reflecting the power of Rome. I was deeply impressed with the physical dominance of Rome; both in soldiers and huge government buildings surrounding the Forum. I was impressed with Rome's power, so I decided to remind the Ephesians of the power Christians have in Christ.

I thought, "*Rome is the most dominant military power on earth, but God has all power in the heavenlies.*" I liked that term heavenlies and rolled it around in my mind, "the heavenlies."

So I decided to remind the Ephesians of their privilege to be citizens of Heaven. Being a citizen of Rome has many advantages, but there are more advantages of living in the heavenlies.

Everywhere, I could see the wealth of Rome: the temples...the Coliseum...huge government buildings...gold and silver everywhere. But these shows of power didn't impress me because I thought, "*In the heavenlies, God has all wealth and one day He will share it with every believer.*" I'll write how wealthy Christians are in Christ.

A shopper came pushing people out of the way, and before he could reach me, the Roman soldier stepped in, knocking the rude shopper down. I thought, "*That's a picture of how the Holy Spirit guards every child of God.*" I thought as I continued walking, "*Even when I don't realize danger is around me, the Holy Spirit protects me, and keeps me safe.*" The Ephesians need to know that when they are citizens of the heavenlies, God sends His Holy Spirit to protect them.

As we walked past a huge temple—over 100 new temples in Rome—the soldier began to tell me the differences between the greatness of Herod's temple in Jerusalem in contrast to the greatness of Rome. The soldier had served time in Jerusalem, so he said, "There's never been a rebellion in Rome, but in Jerusalem there are a couple of rebellions by renegade Jews every year."

I laughed and agreed with him, for I knew of those Jewish terrorist cells and I had seen the results of their work. Rome had been very quick to execute those who rebelled against its power.

Looking around as we walked, I saw the results of strong Roman rule. Everyone kept the laws in Rome; there was no theft, no trespassing, no rebellion. The soldier mentioned, "When in Rome, you live as a Roman but you must obey Roman laws." So I began to think of the ways I would tell the Ephesians to live for Jesus Christ. My letter would tell them how to walk as citizens of the heavenlies.

I began to compare this to the duty of a Christian to obey the Father and Jesus Christ. In every part of their life, Christians must submit to the rule of God, whether it be a wife submitting to her husband, servants submitting to their masters, or citizens submitting to their government. Then I paraphrased what the soldier had said, "Christians should live in the presence of God as God expects Christians to live."

The stroll in the sun had been good for me, thoughts crystallized themselves into the *wealth* I have as a Christian, and what God expects of my walk, and every soldier reminded me of *warfare*. By the end of my stroll, I decided that the theme of my letter to the Ephesians will be the *wealth*, *walk*, and *warfare* of believers.

Both Rome and Ephesus were capitols. Rome was capitol of the Empire, while Ephesus was capitol of all Turkey—Asia Minor. I want to point the readers away from Rome and Ephesus, I want them to know what they have in store for them in the heavenlies.

"We live in two worlds," I thought. *"While we must faithfully work in this physical world, we also enjoy our blessings in the heavenly world."*

As I returned to the apartment, I said to Tychicus, "I have a task for you, something that you'll enjoy doing." Then I explained that he would be going to Turkey to deliver letters to Ephesus and Colosse. When he got there, he would read these letters to the congregations. Then the churches would copy the letters and pass them to the outlying churches.

Even though I was in chains, I felt safe in the city of Rome because I was living in the shadow of the strength of the Roman Empire. But that was physical safety. I also know that I am living in the presence of God who protects my soul. Rome only protects my body.

"So I'll write this letter to the Christians in Ephesus, so they will take advantage of their position in Christ, as I take advantage of living in the presence of political Rome."

Sincerely yours in Christ,
The apostle Paul

Chapter 35

Praying the Book of Ephesians

Your New Standing in Grace

Ephesians 1:1-23

Lord, Paul Your ambassador wrote this letter to believers in Ephesus who trusted You to give them spiritual victory in every part of their lives. I also want the same victory in Christ.

Lord, I want grace that comes from You the Father, and from Jesus Christ, my Savior and Lord of my life. Bless me with every spiritual blessing that comes from Heaven.

Lord, thank You for choosing me in love before the creation of the universe so that I can be holy—set aside from sin and imperfection. You chose me to enter Your presence to worship and praise You.

Lord, thank You for choosing me to be Your child according to Your plan of salvation. May I bring praise to You, Father, commensurate with the glory You already have. Christ has made me accepted by You in the grace of Your love.

Lord, my sins are forgiven through the shedding of Christ's blood. This redemption comes by the greatness of Your grace that has been lavished on all believers.

Lord, I praise You for the plan which You designed before Creation to accomplish Your will in my life and the life of every believer, so that

everything in Heaven and earth will come together for the salvation
of the lost.

Lord, I receive the great spiritual inheritance that You planned according
to Your infinite purpose that You have for me and for each one who
puts their trust in Your salvation. May I bring praise to You that is
commensurate with the glory You already have.

Lord, when I heard the message of Your truth—the Gospel—that delivered
me, I put my trust in You and was sealed by the Holy Spirit who
guaranteed my eternal life until I come into possession of it at the
rapture and thus bring You glory.

Lord, ever since I trusted in You, I've had a love for all of Your people. I
have continually given thanks to You in my prayers, asking that You
would give me full wisdom and understanding so I can have full
knowledge of You.

Lord, I ask that You open the eyes of my heart to understand the hope to
which You call me, and to see the glorious riches of my inheritance
that You have given me, and to experience the greatness of Your
power working in me. It's the same mighty power that raised Christ
from the dead and seated Him at Your right hand, my heavenly
Father, far above earthly rulers, authorities, and power in this world
or in the world to come.

Lord, all things were put under Christ's feet and He was given authority
over everything to benefit the church, which is His Body, the full
expression of His life. Christ fills everything and Your presence is
everywhere.

Amen.

Your New Salvation

Ephesians 2:1-22

Lord, even when I was dead in my sins, You gave me spiritual life in Christ. Before I was a Christian, my life was influenced by the world, and I was tempted by satanic powers, and I was jerked around by the rebellious spirit of people around me.

Lord, I confess I lived to fulfill the lust of the flesh, and self-advancement, and I was as rebellious as other people who are angry against You.

By You, Lord, I am rich in mercy because of Your great love for me. When I was dead in sins, You made me alive with Christ—this is Your grace that saved me—and You raised me up together with Christ, and You made me sit together with Christ in heavenly places. Then in ages to come, You will continually show me the exceeding riches of Your grace through Christ Jesus.

Lord, I am saved by grace because I put my faith in You; it was not my own doing, but Your gift to me. I cannot boast that I had anything to do with it. You have made me what I am, a new person created in Christ Jesus to serve You by doing good works, which You planned for me to do.

Lord, I remember that at one time I was a slave to my fleshly desires—the Jews who circumcised their outward flesh were no better—because we were both separated from You, heavenly Father. I was not a part of Your family, and I was not an heir to Your covenants but addicted to worldly pleasures, without hope and without Your salvation.

But now, Lord, I am united with the Lord Jesus Christ. I was far away but now I am one with Christ by His death which gave me Your peace which brought me along with all other believers into His Body. It was Christ's physical death that tore down the wall that separated people from You, the heavenly Father.

Christ, Your death satisfied the legal charges against me, and brought all believers into union with Yourself, giving me the peace of God.

Christ, by Your death on the Cross, You united everyone into one Body and brought us all back to the Father. Christ, You brought peace to those who were far away in rebellion and to those who were close but in self-righteous works. Only through You are we all able to come into the Father's presence by the Holy Spirit.

Christ, those who once were rebellious in sin are no longer foreigners or strangers, but are fellow members of Your Body with those who previously tried to save themselves by keeping the law. Both are now one building built on the foundation of the apostles and prophets, the cornerstone being You Yourself.

Christ, You hold the building together and make it grow. It is a sanctuary where Your presence dwells. Those who are Your followers are being built with other believers into a building—a sanctuary—where the Father lives by the Holy Spirit.

Amen.

Your New Place in the Church

Ephesians 3:1-21

Lord, Paul became a prisoner of Rome because he was first captured by Christ, the Messiah of the Jews. Paul was given this special task of evangelizing the Gentiles, and he was arrested because he persisted in preaching to Gentiles.

Lord, You gave Paul a revelation of his ministry to the Gentiles. You did not reveal the truth of preaching to Gentiles in previous generations, but now by the Holy Spirit You have revealed this task to Paul and to Your apostles and prophets.

Lord, in Your mysterious secret plan, You intended the Gentiles to share equally with the Jews in all spiritual riches that are available to Your children. The Jews and Gentiles are now one Body in Christ. Now because of what You accomplished in Your sacrificial death, both are joint heirs and joint partakers of the same body—the Church— because of their belief in the Gospel. This is the message of grace that You gave to Paul to give to the world.

Lord, Your message was given to Paul, the least deserving person in the world. Before Paul was saved, he blindly caused people to be put to death in his zeal to keep the Old Testament law. But You chose Paul to tell Gentiles about the spiritual treasures now available to them. Paul was chosen to tell everyone Your mysterious secret plan that You the Creator had hidden from the beginning. Now the riches of Your plan are seen by all, that Jews and Gentiles are joined together in Your Body, the Church. This plan was carried out through Your grace and how redemption is offered for all.

Lord, Paul has suffered because of this truth. I am not discouraged when I have to go through troubles and persecutions. Rather I am honored and encouraged that I can be a testimony to the truth.

Lord, because of my faith in You, I can come fearlessly into Your presence, knowing You will receive me and listen to my request.

Lord, because everyone is accepted in You because of Christ, I fall on my knees before You, the Father, the Creator of Heaven and earth, praying that Your power will give me inner strength through the Holy Spirit so that Christ can make His home in my heart by faith and that I'll be rooted and grounded in His love.

Lord, I also pray for the ability to understand—as all of Your children should understand—how broad, how long, how high, and how deep is Your love.

Lord, I again pray to fully experience Your love—even though it is beyond
understanding—so that I can be filled with all the fullness
that comes only from You.

Lord, I pray for You to work Your mighty power in me to do exceeding
abundantly above all I dare to ask or think. Now to You be all glory
from ages to ages and forever!

Amen.

Walk Worthy of Your New Position

Ephesians 4:1-32

Lord, I want to be Your prisoner, just as was Paul. Help me live a life worthy
of the calling You have given me.

Lord, I want to be humble, gentle, and patient with people, tolerating their
faults; because of Your love for them and acceptance of them.
Help me preserve the unity of the Holy Spirit and live peaceably with
other believers.

Lord, I recognize all believers are in one body, placed there by one baptism
and we all have the same calling to the one same hope.
You are the One Lord over us, we share the same one faith, one
baptism, and You are the only one God and Father who is in each of
us, and lives through each of us.

Lord, You have given a spiritual gift to each of us according to Your
generous Spirit. This is why the Scriptures say,

After You ascended up into the heights of Heaven,
You led those You captured,
And gave spiritual gifts to all Your followers.

The phrase, "You ascended up" means You returned to Heaven after
You first came down to live and die on earth. Then You descended

into the lower parts of the earth—hell—to lead Old Testament saints to Heaven. Now You rule Heaven and the entire universe.

Lord, You gave spiritual gifts to Your followers; some apostles, some prophets, some evangelists, and some shepherd-teachers. Their duty is to equip Your people to do Your work and build up the Body, Your Church, until we all become united in faith and knowledge of Your will, so that each of us grows to full maturity, according to the standard You have set up.

Lord, I know my standard is to become like Christ.

Lord, I don't want to be like a child, always changing my mind about what I believe because someone tells me different things, or because someone misleads me. Instead, help me hold on to the truth in love, growing more like You every day, because You are the head of all of us, You are over the Body where we are members. Under Your direction, each part of the Body will help others grow so that all of us become mature believers, and the whole Body becomes mature in love for one another.

Lord, I will no longer live the way the ungodly live, because they do not understand Your ways. Their minds are spiritually blinded and they are far away from You the Father because they have shut their minds to the truth and resisted Your will. They don't care about doing right but have given themselves to immorality. Their lives are filled with filthiness and greed.

Lord, that is not the way You taught me to live. You told me to put off the old evil nature, because it is thoroughly filled with lust and lying. You told me to be spiritually renewed in my thoughts and attitudes so that I put on the new nature which You created to be godly, righteous, and holy.

Lord, I will put away lying, and I will tell everyone the truth because we are related to one another in Your Body. I will stop being angry and sinning against others, and I will not let the sun go down on my wrath because anger gives room for the enemy to get into my life.

Lord, the thief must stop stealing and work for an honest living, then give to those who have needs.

Lord, the curser must stop using foul language. He must only allow good words to come from his mouth that are helpful to those who hear him.

Lord, I will not give grief to the Holy Spirit by living a sinful life, because He has sealed me with the authority of His presence that will keep me until the final day of redemption.

Lord, I will get rid of all bitterness, rage, name calling, mean-spirited words and slander, along with spiteful retaliation. Instead, I will be kind to others, tenderhearted, forgiving others as You, Father, forgave me, because of Christ.

Amen.

Walk Worthy as Children of God

Ephesians 5:1-33

Lord, I will follow You as a child follows his parents because I am Your child. I will walk in love to others as Christ loved me and demonstrated it by giving Himself as a sweet and acceptable sacrifice to You, my Father.

Lord, I will not be involved in sexual sins or dirty actions or greediness because those things are contrary to godliness. Also, I will not be known by filthy speech, foolish talking, and jesting, but I will be gracious in all things.

Lord, I know there is no place in Your Kingdom for those who are sexually addicted, nor for the filthy minded, nor for greedy people. No matter how much people excuse these sins, You, Father, will still punish them, as You will all those who are disobedient. Therefore, I will not get involved in those things.

Lord, in the past I walked in darkness, but now I have Your light; I will walk in Your light.

Lord, I want the fruit of the Spirit in my life; I want to be good and do what is right, and tell the truth so I can be acceptable to You.

Lord, I will not have anything to do with the works of darkness, rather I will expose them, remembering it is shameful to speak of the things people do in secret. But when light shines on them, their deeds are clearly revealed for what they are. This is why it is said:

Awake, sleeper, get up from the dead;
And Christ will give you light.

Therefore Lord, I will be careful how I live my life, not as a fool but as a wise person. I will use my time wisely because these are evil days. I will not be foolish, but will try to understand Your will for my life.

Lord, I won't drink wine, because I will lose control of myself. Instead I will let the Holy Spirit continually fill me and control me. Then I'll sing psalms, hymns, and spiritual songs with other believers, making music in my heart to You.

Lord, I will continually give thanks for everything to You, the Father, in the name of my Lord Jesus Christ.

Lord, I will submit myself to other believers out of reverence to You. I know wives should submit to their own husbands, just as they do to You. For the husband is the head of the wife, just as Christ is the head of the Body and is its Savior. Just as the Body submits to Christ as its head, so also wives should submit to their husband in everything.

Lord, husbands should love their wives, just as Christ loved the Church and gave His life to make it holy and clean, through washing of the Word of God. Christ did this to make the Church glorious, without spot, wrinkle, or blemish. Husbands should love their wives as they love their bodies, because a man is actually looking out for himself when he loves his wife. No one hates his body. On the contrary, a man will feed and care for his body, just as Christ cares for His Body, the Church.

Lord, the Scriptures teach that a man should leave his father and mother to be joined to his wife and the two become one. This is a great mystery; but it illustrates the relationship between Christ and the Church. So each man must love his wife the way he loves himself and the wife must respect her husband.
Amen.

Your Spiritual Warfare as a Believer

Ephesians 6:1-24

Lord, children should obey their parents because they belong to You, for this is what You want them to do. One of the Ten Commandments has a promise stating, "Honor your father and mother so that it will go well with you and you will live a long and prosperous life."

Lord, You don't want fathers to irritate their children because it makes them resentful. Rather, You want fathers to bring them up with positive discipline that You approve.

Lord, You want workers to obey and respect their employers, and fear displeasing their bosses, just as they would fear displeasing You. They shouldn't work hard just to "butter up the boss" when he's watching, but they should put passion into their work as though working for You; because You will reward everyone for their good service, whether they're a boss or worker. And bosses must treat their workers right, not threaten them because both bosses and employees work for You, and You have no favorites.

Lord, I will be strong in Your power and put on all the spiritual armor so I can stand against the deceptive strategy of the enemy. I am not fighting against humans who have flesh and blood, but against evil powers, authorities, and demons of the unseen world; and I'm struggling against the mighty powers of darkness and their tricks. I'm fighting against filthy spirits who influence this world from their ethereal realm.

Lord, I'll use every piece of Your armor so that when evil comes, I'll be able to resist and win the battle. With Your help, I'll stand in battle with Your truth buckled around my waist. I'll cover my chest with the armor of righteousness, and I'll wear the shoes of peace that come from the good news of the Gospel. I'll carry the shield of faith to stop all the arrows and fiery darts of the evil one. I'll wear the protective helmet of salvation and I'll protect myself with the sword of the Spirit, which is the Word of God.

Lord, I will pray at all times, with every type of intercession and spiritual warfare. I will pray persistently and boldly for all Christians everywhere.

Lord, I will pray for those who minister for You so they will have boldness and the right words to proclaim the message of the good news of the Gospel. This was Paul's request and the reason why he was in chains in Rome. Just as Paul prayed for strength to keep on sharing the Gospel, that is my prayer for me and for all your ministers.

Lord, Tychicus delivered this letter to the saints on Ephesus and told them all about Paul so they would be encouraged.

Lord, I want Your peace ruling my heart, and so give me a deep love to live for You. I want Your grace in my life and on all those who love You deeply with an enduring love.

Amen.

PHILIPPIANS

Chapter 36

THE STORY OF WRITING
THE BOOK OF PHILIPPIANS

Date: A.D. 64 ⌁ Written from: Rome, Italy ⌁ Written by: Paul

Yesterday, Epaphroditus arrived in Rome bringing a large financial gift to me and the others from the church in Philippi. We needed the money because there are several of us living in this apartment and we feed many soldiers and guest visitors.

Theophilus originally had given a large gift to Luke for the writing of the Book of Acts, but it was beginning to run out. I knew God would take care of our needs and God heard our request before the money arrived from Philippi.

"I must write and thank them for their gift," I told Silas and Timothy.

The day was sunny and a warm breeze found its way between the buildings and into our apartment. The bitter winds of winter were gone, and each day the sun climbed higher in the heavens. That meant each day more of the sun found its way into our apartment. I could smell spring in the air, the plants in the window pots were beginning to sprout new leaves.

"It's a great day to be alive," I told Luke. But one of the realists reminded me,

"Don't forget, you are still one of Nero's prisoners, you're still in chains, and there is a guard at the door who watches everything you do."

"Yes...but we have Christ...and the weather is comfortable...and we're in Rome, the most powerful city in the world...and the Gospel is penetrating this great city."

I was happy for what God had done for me and the additional money only reinforced my spirits.

"I must write the Philippians to tell them what a joyful thing it is to serve God...even if I have these chains." I rattled my shackles for everyone in the apartment to hear. They smiled sheepishly.

The next morning, I was on the balcony ready to dictate a letter to the Philippians. I could hear the merchants in the marketplace pleading with women to buy their merchandise. It was early in the morning and women were out shopping for their daily bread.

I began my letter, "Paul and Timothy, servants of Jesus Christ, to all the saints in Philippi with the elders and deacons..."

I leaned back in my chair and smiled about the introduction. I didn't need to remind anyone of my apostolic authority, especially in Philippi. This was a church that loved me and prayed for me. There was no theological heresy in the church to correct, and the only problem was two elderly women who fuss about everything. I'll write that Euodia and Syntyche honor one another. To be rebuked in front of everyone should correct the problem.

The Philippi church had been established on my first trip into Greece. Not only was it a prosperous church, but they readily received and studied the Word of God. The people are grounded in Scripture.

Philippi is a Roman colony, therefore there is a strong presence of law and order in the streets. But there are not many Jews there, so there is no synagogue. I realize that in places like Thessalonica, Ephesus, and Corinth there were contentious Jews who attacked me because there were synagogues in those cities.

Also, in cities where there are synagogues, Judaizers greatly pressure the Christians in these young churches. But that was not true in Philippi.

A street salesman yelled under the balcony, interrupting my thought about the other church. I came back to my writing to the Philippians. I wrote that even though I had chains, the Gospel is preached in Caesar's palace. Also, these chains remind me that four times each day a Roman soldier comes to guard me. That is four opportunities each day to present the Gospel to a soldier. When they accept Jesus Christ as Savior, these soldiers become more than representation of the Roman Empire, they become God's soldiers in the Kingdom of Grace. When their duties transfer them into the palace, they preach Christ. But most importantly, these soldiers have been transferred to places throughout the entire Roman Empire. God is using them to spread the Gospel of Jesus Christ to the ends of the earth. They have helped fulfill the last command of Jesus to the church.

As I continued writing to the Philippians, I couldn't help using the word *joy* and *rejoice*. The beautiful day made me rejoice in Christ. But also the people in Philippi are good people, they are happy in the Lord. Their joyful reputation made it easy to write this letter of hope.

Epaphroditus will deliver this letter to Philippi. I will tell him to instruct the people of Philippi to let those itinerant preachers who come to their town to make copies of this letter to share with other churches.

Sincerely yours in Christ,
The apostle Paul

Chapter 37

PRAYING THE BOOK OF PHILIPPIANS

Paul's Confidence in Spite of Suffering

Philippians 1:1-30

Lord, Paul and Timothy considered themselves Your slaves,
      I too will be Your slave, You are my Master.
They wrote to all the saints and church leaders at Philippi
      Greeting them with Your grace and peace.
Paul thanked God for their salvation and godly life;
      In the same way, I am grateful for my salvation
      And I rejoice in opportunities to pray for my family and friends
Because of their partnership in helping me proclaim the Good News
      From the very first until now.

Lord, I know that You who began the good work of salvation
      Will continue it in me until the day You return;
You are always on my mind and in my heart,
      So it is only right that I have this confidence.

Lord, You have given me the privilege of serving You
      Both in difficult circumstances and good days;
This deep assurance comes only from
      Your heart, O Christ Jesus, my Savior.

Lord, I pray that my love of family and friends will keep growing
      And that they will grow in true knowledge
      And perfect understanding of You,

So they will always make the best choices
      And live pure and blameless lives.
I want them filled with all the good qualities
      That only You can produce in them;
I pray this for Your glory and praise.

Lord, may my family and friends understand what You
      Have done in my heart
      That makes me share the Gospel with others,
All those about me know that I am Your slave;
      This has given me boldness to serve you
      And to spread Your message without fear.

Lord, I know some preach the message of Christ
      Out of jealousy or competition,
      But others preach out of a pure heart.
They are motivated by Your love
      Because You have given all of us this task.
Still others preach Christ for the wrong motives
      Doing it out of selfish pride.
I don't care what their motives are,
      Just as long as You, Christ, are preached.
Whether You are preached from right or wrong motives,
      I will rejoice and continue rejoicing
Because I know You will use the message
      To set many free.

Lord, it is my earnest desire and hope
      That I will never embarrass You,
But that with all boldness as always
      You will be magnified in my body
      Whether it is by life or death.

Lord, my passion is to live for You, O Christ,
      And if I die, it will be my gain.

If I go on living in this body,
    I will still continue serving You.
So I am not sure which option I want,
    I want to leave this body to be with You
    Which seems the best choice for me.
But if I stay in this body to serve You,
    I can still accomplish much for You.
So, I am sure that if I stay and continue my ministry,
    I can further Your work in many believers.

Lord, I pray that my family and friends will continue living for You,
    that whether I remain on this earth or die,
    they remain firm in their faith in the Gospel.

Lord, I pray they will not be afraid of their enemies,
    But be courageous in Your care;
Because the testimony of my family and friends
    Will convict their enemies of their sin
    And make them aware of perdition.

Lord, You have given all of us the privilege of believing in You,
    But also, suffering on Your behalf;
My family and friends are both in the same struggle—
    What I fight, they also fight.
                Amen.

Christ, the Pattern for Believers

Philippians 2:1-30

Lord, I want the same harmony for believers today that Paul wanted for the
    Philippians;
Many believers have one purpose in life
    Because we all belong to Christ,
    And we are encouraged by His love,

And we have fellowship with the Holy Spirit.
You have made our hearts tender and compassionate,
As we have a common purpose to glorify Jesus Christ,
And to love one another and work together to serve Him.

Lord, help me keep egotistical desires out of the picture,
And keep me from selfishness.
Help me regard others as better than myself,
And keep me from thinking only of my agenda.
Help me be interested in others
And not just my own affairs.

Lord, I want the same attitude toward others,
As Jesus showed by His example of humility.
Even though Jesus was God
He did not make exceptions for Himself because of His deity.
On the contrary, Jesus emptied Himself
And took on human flesh and became a servant.
He humbled Himself even more;
Jesus became obedient to death
And died as a criminal on the Cross.
Therefore, You raised Jesus to the highest possible position
And gave Him a name above every name.
So that at the name of Jesus,
Every knee will bow in Heaven, earth, and under the earth,
And every tongue will declare that Jesus Christ is Lord,
To Your glory, O Father.

Lord, Paul reminded the Philippians that they followed his instructions
when he was with them. Now he wants them to be just as obedient
while he is away from them, because their reverence and fear
demonstrates to everyone their salvation.

Lord, give me a deeper desire to serve You, just as You gave the Philippians
the power to please You.

Help me do everything without griping or complaining
    So that I have a blameless and faultless testimony to all.
Help me live a clean life as Your child
    So I'm a light in a dark and lawless world.

Lord, help me grab tightly to the Word of life
    so that I'll be faithful until Christ returns.

Lord, help me run my race victoriously
    so that my works will not become useless.
    Even if I die a martyr's death like Paul,
    I will rejoice in this opportunity.

Lord, Paul wanted to send Timothy to the Philippians to find out how they
    were getting along. That would encourage Paul. Because Timothy
    was Paul's trusted helper who put other people's interests
    ahead of his own.

Lord, Paul was grateful for Timothy who was like a son to him.
    Timothy also sacrificed with Paul for the Gospel. Paul told them as
    soon as his affairs in Rome were settled, he planned to visit them in
    Philippi.

Lord, Paul also wanted to send Epaphroditus back to the Philippians. He
    had brought money to Paul from them. Paul was concerned
    because the Philippines heard Epaphroditus was sick and had
    almost died. But God had mercy and he lived. Paul said that his
    death would have been an unthinkable burden.

Lord, Paul was eager to send Epaphroditus back to see them because the
    Philippians wanted to see him. "Welcome him with Christian love,"
    Paul said. Epaphroditus had almost died doing for Paul the things
    the Philippians couldn't do for Paul because they were so far away.
    Amen.

Christic, the Object of Believers' Desire

Philippians 3:1-21

Lord, whatever happens in my life—whether good or bad—
  I want to rejoice in Your provision for me,
  just as Paul never got tired of rejoicing in Your provision for him.

Lord, keep me safe from the pressures of mean-spirited legalists
  Who bite at me like a dog.
  They want everyone to keep the Law to be saved.

Lord, I have the true circumcision of the heart and I worship You
  in the Holy Spirit, and I rejoice in Christ Jesus.

Lord, Paul had better qualifications than all the legalists, so Paul could
  have been the best of all strict legalists. But Paul didn't put
  confidence in the flesh, but in Your grace.

Lord, Paul was born a Jew into the tribe of Benjamin, circumcised on the
  eighth day. Paul spoke Hebrew, kept the Law as a Pharisee, and he
  persecuted the church. Everyone considered Paul blameless.

Lord, just as Paul considered the perfections of his legalism was
  unimportant, help me realize the Law is useless to give me intimate
  fellowship with Christ.

Lord, just as Paul gave up everything for Christ, I also count everything loss
  to have an intimate fellowship with Christ.

Yes, Lord, I give up everything for the knowledge of Christ and I no longer
  treasure them because Christ has become my treasure.

Lord, I am now united in Christ, not having my righteousness based on
  legalism, but based on faith to receive Christ's righteousness.

Lord, I want to experience Christ and the power of His resurrection;
  I want to know what it means to suffer with Christ,

And to share spiritually in His death;
    And eventually be resurrected from the dead.

Lord, I have not yet reached the goal of Christ,
    But I keep pursuing it,
So I can become the Christ-dominated person
    For which You originally pursued me.

Lord, I know I have not attained the goal;
    I do not consider my life perfect,
But, I focus my entire energies on this one thing,
    I daily forget past accomplishments and failures
    And look forward to what lies ahead.
I keep giving all my energy to win the prize
    Of Your upward calling to me in Christ Jesus.

Lord, all spiritual believers should be doing the same thing;
    But many are not pursuing Christ.
Show them what they should do.
    Everyone must live at the level they've learned
    And obey the truth they know.

Lord, help me follow the example of Paul
    And learn from the pattern he set for all believers.
There are many who live as enemies of Christ;
    Paul told us about these people.
They are walking toward destruction,
    Their belly is their god.
They are proud of their sin
    When they should be ashamed of it;
    They live for things in this earth.

Lord, I am a citizen of Heaven
    And I wait for my Savior, Jesus Christ
    To come to take me there.

Then He will transform my finite body
    To be like His glorious body
With the same power He will use
    To conquer everything on earth.
              Amen.

Christ, the Believers' Strength

Philippians 4:1-23

Lord, Paul wanted to see his friends in Philippi that he had won to Christ
    because they were the fruit of his work.

Lord, just as Paul prayed for the Philippians to remain loyal
    to You, may I stay true to You in my faith.

Lord, Paul begged Euodia and Syntyche to settle their
    disagreement and have one focus in serving You.
    Then Paul asked the church to work with these women and with
    Clement to spread the Gospel.

Lord, I rejoice gladly in all Your goodness,
    So always keep me filled with Your joy.
Let my gentleness and goodness be evident to all
    Because Christ may come at any moment.

Lord, I won't worry about anything,
    But I'll pray to You about everything,
    And I'll be thankful for all things that happen.
Then, Your peace will guard my heart and mind
    Because the presence of Christ Jesus in my life
    Surpasses anything that I could ever understand.

Lord, I'll constantly meditate on;
    Whatever things are true,

Whatever things are honorable,
Whatever things are right,
Whatever things are pure,
Whatever things are lovely,
Whatever things contribute to my having a good reputation for You.

Lord, I'll keep doing in my daily life
   the things that Paul does in his life,
   then You, the God of peace, will be with me.

Lord, Paul was thankful the Philippians had not quit
   expressing concern for him and sending money for his ministry.
   Paul did not say this to ask for more money,
   but to let them know his appreciation.

Lord, I'm like Paul, satisfied with what I have; I have experienced poverty,
   and on other occasions, I've had more than enough. I've learned in
   every way and in every place, to be satisfied with what I have,
   whether I am full or hungry, whether I have abundance or poverty.

Lord, I can do all things through Christ
   Who gives me the help to get it done.

Lord, Paul thanked the Philippians for sharing in his ministry,
   reminding them that they were the only ones who sent money in his
   early ministry. Even in Thessalonica they sent money more than once.

Lord, Paul reminded them again he was not asking
   for more money, but telling them that their gift will bring them
   rewards through his ministry he does for Christ. Paul told them he
   had no needs because of the gifts they sent by Epaphroditus. It is a
   sweet-smelling aroma that pleased God.

Lord, I want You to care for my financial needs,
   The same way you took care of Paul,
   From your glorious riches in Christ Jesus.

Glory be to You, my God
>My heavenly Father, forever and ever.

Lord, Paul sent greetings to all the Philippians from all the fellow workers with him. Then he sent greetings from all the Christians in Rome, especially those who had been saved in the emperor's household.

>*Lord, I want the grace of the Lord Jesus Christ*
>*To rest on me.*
>>>Amen.

COLOSSIANS

Chapter 38

THE STORY OF WRITING
THE BOOK OF COLOSSIANS

Date: A.D. 64 ∼ Written from: Rome, Italy ∼ Written by: Paul

I was taking a stroll along the Po River with Epaphras, a fellow disciple of Jesus. My ever-present curious Roman guard was listening to every word I said. This Roman guard had shown great interest in Christianity, but had not yet committed his heart to believe in Christ.

The day was chilly and I had wrapped my tunic tighter with a shawl to ward off the biting wind. A hood over my head kept my body heat from escaping.

Epaphras had heard through friends of some of the problems in the church at Colosse. Epaphras was more than just an idle listener, he was extremely concerned about the church in Colosse. Epaphras knew the rich business man Philemon, and had preached in the church that met in Philemon's home. When Epaphras left Colosse to join me in Rome, he left Archippus with the responsibility of preaching the Word each Lord's day.

"There are two problems in the church at Colosse," Epaphras explained to me. "First, a preacher from Alexandria, Egypt, came with a strong emphasis on asceticism. He kept telling the Colossians, "Touch not, taste not, handle not.""

Since the people at Colosse were hardworking and disciplined, they listened to the message of self-discipline and took it to heart. I know the heart is committed to fanaticism when it is not tempered by the head. Some people in Colosse had become fanatical in mortification in the body.

There was another problem. Certain Judaic elements in the church wanted everyone to observe the Law and observe Jewish holy days with super-legalistic fervor.

Even as I listened carefully to the things that Epaphras was telling me, I was beginning to form a letter in my mind I could write to the Colossians. I knew Epaphras was the perfect one to take the letter. The people would listen to him because he had been their pastor, and they would receive the letter I planned to write.

I planned to write a letter similar to the one I sent to the church at Ephesus. I wanted them to exchange letters to get the full exposure of truth in each of them.

Epaphras explained to me there was another problem in Colosse, "There was the error of false mysticism," which Epaphras described as Christians embrace philosophical thought. He also explained, "Christians speak so often about angels that they seem to worship angels."

Epaphras explained the problem to me. "These Christians are so proud of their deep mystical thoughts, that they use them when they preach the Gospel and they embrace logic as a foundation for the Gospel."

Epaphras threw up his hands in disgust, "They are proud of learning, they don't hold to Jesus Christ the head of all things and they don't use the Scriptures to gain wisdom."

As I heard Epaphras explain the problems in the church, I began to write a letter to the Colossians including many of the things I had previously said to the Ephesians. The Colossians needed to know they were wealthy in Jesus Christ, so I planned to write a letter showing that Christ is everything.

I whispered a prayer, "Lord, help me write a statement about Jesus Christ that will make the Colossians realize His superiority and His preeminence."

I also decided to write that they have been raised together with Christ and they sit with Christ at the right hand of God, the Father.

Again, I shook my head in disgust over the philosophical leanings of the Colossians. I plan to write, "Let the Word of Christ dwell in you richly as your wisdom. Teach and admonish everyone according to the Scriptures. Let the people sing the great songs of the Old Testament, also singing the new hymns and spiritual songs when they come together to worship."

I wanted the Colossians to be absolutely committed to Christ, so I wrote, "Whatever you do in speech or action, do all wholeheartedly to God." In case they missed it, I repeated myself, "Whatever you do, do it heartedly to the Lord, and not to men."

Paul and Epaphras decided to sit for awhile in the sun. It was then when Paul explained that Epaphras would take this letter to the Colossians. He would also take the runaway slave, Onesimus, and a letter to Philemon asking this wealthy brother to receive back the escaped slave who had been taking care of household chores for Paul. Epaphras would deliver that letter. Also on his way to Colosse, Paul asked Epaphras to stop by Ephesus and deliver the letter to them.

"This is a strategic job," Paul explained to Epaphras, "I pray that God would speed you on your way so we may strengthen the church at Ephesus and Colosse. Also, I want to help reconcile Onesimus with his master, Philemon."

Sincerely yours in Christ,
The apostle Paul

Chapter 39

Praying the Book of Colossians

The Prayer for Believers and the Pre-eminence of Christ

Colossians 1:1-29

Lord, Paul was led by God to write to the Colossian believers using his
authority as an apostle to remind them of the greatness of
the indwelling Christ and to warn them of some new doctrinal
problems springing up among them.

Lord, may You always deal with me in grace
as Paul prayed for Your grace on the Colossians.
And may You give me peace that comes from
You my God and Father, and from the Lord Jesus Christ.

Lord, Paul gave thanks for the Colossian believers
from the first time he heard about their salvation,
and for their new expressions of love for all saints.

Lord, use the testimony of my salvation to encourage others,
Just as you used the testimony of the Colossians
To bless others.

Lord, I am looking forward to the promise of Heaven;
This pledge was mine the moment I first believed,
Just as it guarantees the same hope to others who believe.

Lord, the Gospel is the power that is transforming my life
And all other lives everywhere.

This good news is given out all over the world,
      Changing lives, just as it transformed the Colossians.

Lord, Paul reminded the Colossians that Epaphras faithfully
      brought the Gospel to them. Now Epaphras was their
      representative helping Paul in Rome. As a matter of fact,
      Epaphras was the one who told Paul about the strengths and
      problems of the new church at Colosse.

Lord, raise up intercessors to pray for me
      As Paul continually prayed for the Colossians.

Lord, I pray for a total understanding of Your will
      And what You want me to do with my life.
I pray for spiritual wisdom to make decisions
      That will honor and please You.
I pray to continually do good things for others,
      For this is Your command to me.
I pray to know You more intimately
      So I can enjoy fellowship with You.
I pray to be strengthened with spiritual power,
      So I can endure with Your patience;
I pray to be filled with joy so I'll always be thankful
      For the spiritual inheritance You've given me.
I praise You for the freeing power of Christ's blood
      That has forgiven me all my sins.
I'm grateful You have rescued me
      From the kingdom of satanic darkness
      And delivered me into the Kingdom of Christ.

The Pre-eminence of Christ

Christ, I see You as the perfect reflection
      Of the Father who cannot be seen.

Christ, You existed before the Father created all things;
    And Christ, You are supreme over all things.
Christ, You created everything in Heaven and earth;
    You created the things we can see,
    You created the things we can't see.
Christ, everything has been created by You and for You,
    Including kings, kingdoms, rulers, and authorities.
Christ, You existed before all things were created,
    Now Your power holds creation together.

Christ, You are the head of the church
    Which is Your living spiritual Body.
Christ, You were the first to rise from the dead;
    You are first in everything.
Christ, all the fullness of God the Trinity Who
    Lives and dwells in You.
Christ, by You, did God the Father reconcile
    All the things to Himself.
Christ, by the blood of Your Cross
    God the Father in Heaven made peace with everything
    In Heaven and on earth.
Christ, You brought me back as a friend
    When I was far, far away as Your enemy
    By my evil thoughts and sinful actions.
Christ, You brought me into the very presence of the Father
    By the sacrifice of Your body on the Cross.
Christ, I now have access to the Father's presence
    Because I am standing there in You,
    Holy, blameless, and pure.
Christ, I completely believe this truth about You
    And I base my faith on it.
Christ, I will not drift away from this assurance
    For this Good News that has saved me
    Has also been preached all over the world.

Paul was happy to suffer for the believers in Colosse,
>   because he identified with Christ's sufferings, and through
>   Christ's sufferings others are brought to saving faith.

Paul was given the commission to spread the Gospel to all Gentiles, a
>   message that was not known by them in past generations and
>   centuries, but now it has been revealed to them that the riches
>   and blessings of Christ is for them also.

Christ, I rejoice greatly in the truth,
>   That Christ lives in me, my hope of glory.
I share this message of You with all people
>   So that all believers may become perfect in You.
Christ, I am motivated with serving You
>   Because You energize the Father's work within me.
>   >   Amen.

Warning Against False Wisdom and Legalism

Colossians 2:1-23

Lord, Paul interceded for believers in other churches, even though he
>   had not seen them.
>   Paul prayed the following request for them. This is the same
>   that I pray for those I know and for the larger Body of Christ.

Lord, I pray that they may be encouraged,
>   And that they experience strong ties of love to one another.
>   I pray that they may have a full understanding of how Your mystery
>   will work in their lives so they can live confidently for Christ. I pray
>   that they may understand the hidden treasures of wisdom that are
>   hidden only in Christ.

Lord, may no one deceive me with cunning arguments
    That anyone is the wisdom of God;
    I know that only Christ is the wisdom of God.

Lord, Paul was happy that the Colossian believers were living as they
    should and their faith was steadfastly rooted in Christ.

Lord, may I always continue to obey Christ Jesus, my Lord,
    Just as I did when I first believed in Him.
    May I be rooted in the faith, and nourished by Christ
    so I'll grow strong in my Christian life,
    and may I always be thankful for what Christ has done for me.

Lord, Paul warned the Colossians against those who would lead them
    astray by human logic or deceitful theories that come from
    depraved thinking or evil principles of the world.
    Paul reminded them such "teaching" didn't come from Christ.

Lord, Paul reminded the Colossians that Your fullness—the fullness of
    the Godhead—lived in Christ's human body, and that only when
    a believer was indwelt by Christ could he experience Your full
    understanding and leadership.

    Lord, I yield to Your will and I seek Your wisdom,
        For only through Your Lordship in my life
        can I understand Your plan and accomplish
        Your will for my life.

Lord, when I came to salvation in Christ,
    I was circumcised—set apart—in my heart; this was not a
    physical procedure. I was spiritually set apart from satisfying
    my sinful nature so that I might please Christ Jesus. I was
    identified with Christ's death, when I was spiritually baptized
    into Christ; and I was raised with Christ to new life, by the same
    power that brought Him from the dead.

Lord, I was dead in my rebellious sins against You,
  being controlled by my sinful nature; but You forgave all my sins.
  You wiped my record clean of all the charges against me,
  and forgave them by nailing them to Christ's cross.
  Now evil powers have no authority over me, because Christ publicly
  triumphed over sin by His victory on the Cross.

Lord, because I am completely forgiven, no one can condemn me
  for what I eat or drink, or for not celebrating holy days or
  Sabbaths. These Old Testament rules were only a shadow of
  coming things; they pointed us to Christ who fulfilled these rules.

Lord, I'll not let anyone cheat me of my relationship with Christ,
  even when they insist on self-denial or worship of angels;
  for they are puffed up by their deceitful insight. They are not united
  with Christ, the head of the Body, for He nourishes all believers
  into a vital union that grows together by Your nourishment.

Lord, since I have died together with Christ to be separated from this
  sinful world, why would I subject myself to worldly regulations,
  claiming "do not taste, touch, or handle"?

These are merely human rules that mean nothing, even though
these rules seem "right" because they demand self-denial and
humility.

But they never help me triumph over my evil thoughts and desires;
victory comes only through the Person of Christ.
  Amen.

Our Heavenly Union With Christ
Determines Our Daily Walk

Colossians 3:1-25

Lord, since I have been raised to new life in Christ,
      I will control my thinking by the principles of Heaven
Where Christ is sitting at Your right hand
      In the seat of honor and influence.
I will think on things in Heaven and
      Not be controlled by things on this earth,
Because I died when Christ died
      And my new life is hidden by You in Christ.
Then when Christ appears to the whole world,
      I will appear with Him in glory.

Lord, I will put to death any sinful desire—
      My sexual lust, filthiness, evil desires,
      And greed which is idolatry.
These are the vices You punish
      In those who are rebellious to You.
I used to be guilty of these things
      When my life was controlled by the world.
But now that I have Christ dwelling in my life,
      I will get rid of anger, rebellious behavior,
      Slander, and filthy language.
I will not lie to anyone, for I have turned away from
      My old nature with its sinful urges.
I have turned to my new nature
      That You continually renew within me,
      As I learn more and more about Christ.

Lord, all new believers in Christ can be controlled by their
      new nature, whether they are a Jew or Gentile,
      whether they are circumcised or not, whether they

are barbarian, civilized, slave, or free.
Christ is the only power that can control a life,
because He lives in all believers.

Lord, since You chose me to live a holy life,
    I will clothe myself with mercy, kindness,
    Humility, gentleness, and patience.
I recognize that some believers let these sins disrupt their lives
    So, I will forgive their trespasses, as You forgave me.

Lord, love is the most important attitude I can put on
    Because love makes me one with all other believers.
Also, I want Your peace to control my heart
    Because all believers are called to live in peace.

Lord, I want the rich words of Christ to live in my heart
    so that I have His wisdom
    to teach and correct other believers.

    I want to sing palms, hymns, and spiritual songs
    to you with a thankful heart.

    May everything I say and everything I do
    be expressed in the name of the Lord Jesus Christ,
    giving thanks to You my heavenly Father.

Lord, wives must submit to their husbands
    Because this is what You desire of them.
Husbands must love their wives
    And never be mean to them.
Children must always obey their parents,
    For this pleases You.
Fathers must not provoke their children to anger,
    Because they will become discouraged and give up.
Servants must obey their earthly bosses in everything,

Not just when they are watching,

But do it from the heart to please You.

Lord, I will do everything with my whole heart,

Because I am working to please You, and not men.

Then You will give me an inheritance as a reward,

And those who do wrong will be repaid for their rebellion,

Because You will not let anyone get away with sin.

Amen.

Earnest Prayer

Colossians 4:1-18

Lord, masters who direct servants must be kind and fair

Just as You our Master in Heaven treat us.

Lord, I will give myself continually to prayer,

Always remembering to be thankful.

I will pray for Your ministers to have opportunities

To preach the message of Christ

(This is the reason Paul was in chains).

I will pray that ministers preach the Gospel

As clearly as they can.

Lord, I will live a good testimony among non-Christians

And will use every opportunity to share Christ with them.

I will make sure my words are gracious and useful

With the right answer for everyone.

Lord, Paul told the Colossians that Tychicus will tell them how he was

doing. Tychicus had been faithfully serving the Lord with Paul.

Paul also told how he was sending Onesimus back to them in Colosse. Onesimus had recently been saved and now he was a brother in Christ.

Paul gave the Colossians greetings from Aristarchus who is a prisoner with Paul. He also sent greetings from Mark, Barnabas' cousin. Then Paul told his readers to receive Mark when he comes their way. Finally, Paul sent greetings from Justis. He notes they are his Jewish-Christian co-workers.

Paul sent greetings from Epaphrus, who is from Colosse. Epaphrus continually prayed for the Colossians, asking God to make them strong and mature in their Christian faith. Paul reminds them that Epaphrus is a prayer warrior for all believers.

Paul included greetings from Luke the physician, and Demas; then Paul asked that his greetings be passed on to other believers.

Paul asked the Colossians to pass this letter to the church in Laodicea, and that they should read the letter he wrote to them.

Lord, may I always be as faithful to carry out Your work
as Paul faithfully served You.

Paul signed this letter with his own signature, asking people "Remember my chains" and "May the grace of God be with you."
Amen.

1 Thessalonians

Chapter 40

THE STORY OF WRITING
THE BOOK OF FIRST THESSALONIANS

Date: A.D. 54 ∼ Written from: Athens, Greece ∼ Written by: Paul

I have only been in Athens a short time. I was frustrated that the Judaizers had created a riot in Thessalonica; in essence, running me out of the city. I then went to Berea, and the Judaizers followed me there, but the Christians in Berea had a hunger to know the Scriptures. The Christians at Berea were good people. They came with me to Athens to assure my safety.

Then Silas and Timothy arrived in Athens bringing me news of the Christians in Thessalonica. I had only preached in Thessalonica three Sabbaths, but even in that short period of time, I had covered all the foundational doctrines of Christianity. But Silas and Timothy were concerned about doctrinal problems in the church.

I had a tumultuous ministry in Thessalonica, the second city in Greece I visited. I had gone into the synagogue of Thessalonica to reason with them from the Word of God. I had only stayed about a month in Thessalonica, at least I was there for three weekends of ministry from the Scriptures. Many Jews were converted in Thessalonica, including a good number of Greeks.

But the unsaved Jews refused to hear me. When I went into the homes of the leading men and women to teach them the way of God more clearly, the unsaved Jews couldn't stand it. They felt I was teaching a "deplorable sect" because I didn't insist that the Law be kept by new converts.

The unsaved Jews followed me everywhere, attacking me verbally and wanting to debate with me in the marketplace, in the Forum, and in the streets of the city. When the unsaved Jews saw their tactics were not getting anywhere, they turned to a strategy that denied all their Jewish ancestry. They gathered together a group of hooligans—drunks, petty thieves, and rebels. They instigated a riot in the marketplace and accused me of lawless acts. The riot spread through the streets of the city and reached to the Forum.

Since I had been staying in the house of Jason, they surrounded the house and demanded Jason hand me over to them. Fortunately, I was not there at the time. The mob dragged Jason and other Christians to city courts with the accusation, "These men have turned the world upside down and have come here to create a riot."

"What is their crime?" one of the city rulers asked.

"These men say that Jesus is the King, not Caesar." And the rioters began to chant, "These men teach our citizens to break the Roman laws."

The riot continued getting louder so the city rulers demanded that Jason produce a security bond. The magistrate told him, "If this riot breaks out again, we will keep the security bond, and if we have to, we'll take your home."

It was then when the brethren decided that I and Silas would leave the city. No one was in the city streets at night, so they accompanied Silas and me a short way to the city of Berea.

The unsaved Jews chased me to Berea. It was then I came to Athens, the capital city of all of Greece. This is the center of the intellectual world; it is also the center of idolatry in the Greek world. Everywhere I look I see an idol—all types of mythological men and women are worshiped as well as idols portrayed by animals, birds, and fish. If the Gospel can flourish here, it can influence any city in the world.

Silas and Timothy told me, "You must write to the church in Thessalonica, they are gravely concerned about some who died in the last few months. They want to know what will happen to their dead loved ones when Jesus returns to earth."

I told Silas and Timothy I will write them concerning our great hope, that the next great event on God's calendar will be Jesus appearing in the sky for Christians. I will tell them that those who have died will be resurrected first and *caught up* (meaning "rapture") to be with the Lord. Then we who are alive and walking about will instantly follow them to meet the Lord in the air. Then we will ever live with the Lord.

I can have the letter written in two days, I said to Silas and Timothy. "Then you, Timothy, can take this letter to them and encourage them in the faith."

Sincerely yours in Christ,
The apostle Paul

Chapter 41

PRAYING THE BOOK OF FIRST THESSALONIANS

Characteristics of a Model Church

1 Thessalonians 1:1-10

Lord, Paul along with Silas and Timothy, wrote to the church in
Thessalonica, Greece, reminding them that You, our heavenly Father
and the Lord Jesus Christ, founded the church.
Paul prayed grace and peace on the Thessalonians;
I want that grace on my life.

Lord, I am thankful that I can pray for others,
Never forgetting what their faith meant to me,
And how their love strengthened me.
I look forward to the return of the Lord Jesus Christ,
This hope preserves me in difficulties.

Lord, Paul reminded his readers how the Gospel came to them by his
explanation and by the demonstrated power of the Holy Spirit.
Paul reminded them that his life was a demonstration of the truth of
his preaching, and that they received his message with joy, in spite
of the persecution that came on the young church.

Lord, may I be an example to all others
Just as the believers in Thessalonica were to those in Greece.
May I spread the message of the Gospel out to others,
Just as the Gospel reached many because of the Thessalonians.

Lord, everyone was telling Paul of the strong faith of the Thessalonians, how they welcomed the Gospel, and they turned to Christ from idols to serve You, the Living and True God.

Lord, I look forward to the return of Your Son from Heaven
Whom You brought back from the dead.
For He is coming back to deliver us
From the terrible wrath and tribulation
You will pour out on the world in the future.
Amen.

Characteristics of a Model Servant

1 Thessalonians 2:1-20

Lord, Paul reminded the Thessalonians about his visit to them and how badly he was beaten in Philippi before coming to them. Paul reminds them of his strong ministry in spite of vicious opposition.

Lord, Paul reminded his readers that he didn't use ulterior motives or impure desires, nor was he trying to trick them. Paul preached as a messenger from God who gave them the message of salvation. He did not preach to please people, but to please God (who knows the motives of people). Paul says that he never used flattery to get them to believe, nor did he pretend to be their friends just to get their support. He also didn't preach to build up a reputation or get human praise. Then Paul reminded them he could have asked for money because he is an apostle of Jesus Christ, but he didn't.

Lord, help me to be gentle among new believers
As Paul was unassuming and kind to the Thessalonians.
Help me be loving to new Christians,
Willing not only to give them the Gospel,
But to give them my own soul as well.
Help me care for young followers of Christ

To feed and protect them
As a mother cares for her baby.

Paul loved the Thessalonians dearly
 Not only giving them the Gospel,
 But his own life also.

Lord, Paul reminded the Thessalonians that he worked with his hands,
 Slaving day and night,
 So he wouldn't be a burden to them.
Paul reminded them that God was his witness,
 That his treatment of them was fair.
He treated them as a father would treat a son,
 Teaching them what is truthful,
Encouraging them to live worthy of their divine calling,
 Inviting them to share in Your Kingdom of glory.

Lord, Paul was thankful that they received his preaching
 Not as though it were human words,
But as though his message was the very Word of God,
 Which it was; Your living power to transform lives.

Lord, Paul reminded the Thessalonians that they are like the churches in
 Judea, in that they suffer from their countrymen, just as the
 Christians in the Holy Land suffered from the Jews, the ones who
 killed the Lord Jesus and the prophets.

 Those who persecute the church are against both the Gentiles and
 God, because they don't want anyone outside the Jews to be saved.
 Their punishment is adding up in God's records, and one day God's
 punishment will fall on them.

Lord, Paul tells the Thessalonians, "I want to see you,
 Even though you are separated from me physically,
 I still have you in my heart.
"I have longed to come see you

But satan has prevented my coming.
"I live to see my young children in Christ,
    You are my joy, my hope, and my reward.
"You will bring me much joy at the coming of Christ
    For when I stand before God for judgment,
    You will be my glory and reward."

                                    Amen.

Characteristics of a Model Brother

1 Thessalonians 3:1-13

Lord, Paul reminds the Thessalonians that when he went to Athens, he sent Timothy to minister to them, even though he was left alone at Athens. Paul wanted Timothy to keep them strong in the faith and prevent anyone from dropping out.

Lord, Paul reminds them that troubles are part of God's plan for the believers. He told them when he was with them that some persecution would come, as they have recently experienced. Paul was so concerned for them that he sent Timothy to find out if the Thessalonians were standing firm in their faith. Paul was afraid the Tempter would have tripped them up, and his efforts were destroyed.

Lord, Paul was encouraged because Timothy had just returned to bring the good news that the Thessalonians were standing firm. Paul also learned the Thessalonians wanted to see him. This news gave Paul a lot of confidence in his present trials, and that his ministry of planting new churches would succeed, even when trials hit new churches. Now Paul was ready to really throw himself in ministry because of the positive news that the Thessalonians were standing true.

Lord, I cannot thank You enough
    For all the joy I have in Your presence,

That Your work prospers in spite of trials.
I will pray continually for those in trials
    That You will supply what is lacking in their faith.
Now may You, the Father of our Lord Jesus Christ,
    Help me stand in the face of trials.
May You make my love grow
    And overflow to those suffering persecution.
Make my heart strong, blameless, and holy
    Before You, the Father of us all.
And may I live a guiltless life,
    Because the Lord Jesus Christ is returning
    With all those saints who are His.
              Amen.

The Hope for All Believers

1 Thessalonians 4:1-18

Lord, I know the Scriptures teach that I should
    Please You with my daily life.
And that Scriptures command me to live
    As close as possible to the biblical standards.
You want me to be separate from sin,
    And especially keep away from sexual immorality.
You want me to marry in holiness and purity
    And not in sexual lust as do the heathen,
    For this is a sign they know not God.
I will never sin by having sex with another's spouse
    For You have promised to punish this sin.

Lord, You have not called me to be filthy-minded
    But You want me to think pure thoughts.
If anyone rebels against the rule of purity,
    He is not disobeying man's laws,

He is disobeying Your law
    And rebelling against the Holy Spirit Who indwells him.

Lord, Paul didn't need to tell them to love their brothers,
    Since You already taught that in Scripture.
My love is growing toward other Christians
    And I want to love them more in the future.
My goal is to live a quiet life,
    To work diligently at my task,
    And do faithfully all I am required to do.
This way I will influence those who are not Christians,
    And have enough money to live on.

Lord, Paul didn't want the Thessalonians to be ignorant
    Of what happens to believers when they die.
So they wouldn't grieve like the world
    Who has no hope beyond the grave.
Since we believe that Jesus died for us
    And rose again from the dead,
Those who have died and sleep in Jesus
    Will He bring with Him at His return.
The Bible teaches that we who are alive
    at His second coming,
Will not be raptured before these in graves,
    But they will be raptured first.
For the Lord Jesus will come down from Heaven
    With a shout as loud as an archangel,
    And as a blast from a trumpet.
Then the dead in Christ will be the first
    To rise to meet the Lord in the air.
Then we who are alive and remain on earth
    Will be caught up with them in the clouds,
To meet the Lord Jesus in the air,
    To ever live with Him.

Lord, this promise assures me that I'll live with You forever;
I want everyone to know about this prospect
So they'll face death with courage and hope.
Amen.

Characteristics of a Model Life

1 Thessalonians 5:1-28

Lord, I don't expect you to give me dates,
Because You said "no one knows the
Exact time of Your return to earth."
All I need to know is that
"The day of the Lord will come unexpectedly
Like a thief in the night."
When everyone is saying, "We have peace on earth,"
Sudden disaster will come
Like labor pains on a pregnant woman,
And no one can hide from it;
Everyone, everywhere will be punished.
I have known about Jesus' return,
I am not in the dark about coming judgment.
I will not sleep spiritually
But I will watch for Jesus' return.
Night is the time when the unsaved sleep and get drunk,
But I will live in the light and be sober.
I will be protected by the armor of faith,
And I will nurture my love
And I will wear the helmet of hope.

Lord, I know You never meant for believers
To experience the wrath and tribulation that is coming,
You meant to save us though the Lord Jesus Christ.
He died for me so that whether

I am alive or in the grave,
    I will be protected by Him and live with Him.
So I will be encouraged by this fact
    And I will encourage others.

Lord, I will be considerate of those who minister
    Among us as teachers in the Lord.
I will honor them and obey them,
    And I'll not fuss with other believers.

Lord, I will warn those not working for You,
    And give courage to those who are frightened,
And will give watchcare to the weak,
    And will be patient with all.

Lord, I pray that no one will pay back evil for evil,
    But will always do good
    To believers and unbelievers alike.
I will rejoice at all times,
    And I'll pray constantly,
I'll give thinks always to You for everything,
    Because this is what You expect me to do.
I'll not suppress the Holy Spirit's
    Working in my life,
    But will listen to the preaching of Your Word.
I'll not be gullible, but will analyze everything
    By the Word of God
    To determine what is true.
I'll stay away from every form of evil
    And anything that tempts me to sin.

Lord, may I grow in the abundance of Your peace,
    Keep my body, soul, and spirit strong and blameless
    Until You return to receive me.

I know You're faithful to all You call
   To accomplish Your purpose in their lives.

Lord, Paul ended his letter asking the Thessalonians to pray for him and greet one another with a holy kiss. He wanted this letter read to all Christians. Then Paul prayed, "The grace of our Lord Jesus Christ be with you."

Amen.

2 Thessalonians

Chapter 42

THE STORY OF WRITING THE BOOK OF SECOND THESSALONIANS

Date: A.D. 54 ☙ Written from: Athens, Greece ☙ Written by: Paul

It was less than a month after Timothy took my first letter to the Thessalonians that I heard back from them that there were other problems in the church. When Timothy returned with news from the Thessalonians, he told me they had received a forged letter from me that had shaken their faith concerning the Second Coming.

Obviously, the letter was meant to destroy the young church. There were unbelieving Jewish spies in the church who saw the positive effects of my first letter. So, they had a second letter written and forged my signature saying that the persecution of Christians in Thessalonica was really the persecution of the tribulation—the great, and terrible day of the Lord. The poison letter claimed the Christians in Thessalonica had missed the rapture.

While Timothy was away, I had gone into the synagogue to debate with the Jews concerning Jesus Christ. There was little response from the Jews for they were absorbed by the secular city around them and didn't have a heart for the Scriptures nor for God.

Every day I had gone into the marketplace to debate with the Greek philosophers. Some were Epicureans who justified their selfish lifestyle of eating and drinking and making merry. There are also Stoics who believe in self-discipline of every aspect of their life. The philosophers called me a "babbler" and the rumor went about the city that I was proclaiming "some strange god."

I had been busy teaching in the city of Athens. The tall hill in the middle of the city called the Acropolis is topped by the Parthenon. This was a temple built to Athena, the primary goddess of the people in Athens. The Parthenon could be seen from every corner of the city and reminded the people constantly of their idol worship.

Finally, they invited me to Mars Hill, a small hill right below the Parthenon where people gathered to debate and discuss religion. It was there on Mars Hill where I preached,

"I see the men of Athens are very religious, and they have idols to every god known to man. However, when I saw the idol to the "unknown God," this is the one that I want to tell you about. This is the God who created the world and everything in it. He is the Lord of Heaven and earth and He does not dwell in the temple like this Parthenon. It is this God in whom we live and move and have our being. God sent His Son to earth to live without sin and died on a cross for our sins. It was then when God raised Him from the dead...."

When these philosophers heard me preach on the resurrection, they mocked me and refused to listen to me. I couldn't continue my sermon.

Shortly after this, Timothy came back from delivering the first letter. So, I sat down to address the Thessalonians a second time, "Paul, Silas, and Timothy, to the church of the Thessalonians in God the Father and the Lord Jesus Christ...."

I told them, "Do not be shaken in your minds or troubled by a letter." I explained that the day of the Lord, which is the tribulation would not come except first there would be a great falling away from the faith by hypocrites and false teachers, then the antichrist would be revealed, who would go into the temple, receiving worship from those he had blinded. The Holy Spirit who restrains sin will be taken out of the world and when the rapture comes there would be a flood of iniquity in the world. I called the work of antichrist, "the mystery of iniquity." Antichrist will come after Christians are raptured with Christ to do lying miracles to deceive everyone in the entire world.

Of course, many in the world will have questions when thousands of believers are raptured out of the world. They would be asking, "What happened to them?" I wrote that God would send the unsaved a strong delusion because of their rebellion, and they would believe the lie told by antichrist. Because antichrist will have an explanation for their disappearance and because of the spiritual blindness of the unsaved; everyone would believe antichrist.

Timothy told me about another problem in the church. A few people were absolutely convinced that Jesus was coming at any moment, so they had quit working and had gone into the mountains to pray and wait His return. Since they were not working, the rest of the Christians were providing food for them. I wrote the church to not feed them, saying, "Those who don't work, shouldn't eat."

Timothy asked me, "How will the Christians in Thessalonica know you've written this letter?" He explained, "If the Thessalonians were deceived by the previous letter, won't they be skeptical of this letter?"

I smiled and said, "I will sign it with my own name. They have my first letter and they can compare the signatures, they will know I've written it."

Sincerely yours in Christ,
The apostle Paul

Chapter 43

PRAYING THE BOOK OF SECOND THESSALONIANS

Comfort Because They Are Being Persecuted

2 Thessalonians 1:1-12

Lord, Paul, Silas, and Timothy sent greetings to the church in
Thessalonica which
belonged to You the Father and the Lord Jesus Christ. They prayed for
grace and peace from You and the Lord Jesus Christ.

Lord, I continually thank You that my faith is growing,
And my love for others is growing.
May I have patience and faith,
When I face trials and troubles.
My constant determination will demonstrate that
Your care of me is correct
And that I am worthy of the Kingdom of God,
For which I am now suffering.

Lord, I know You will repay
Those who persecute Your believers,
And reward those who are suffering
With the same inner confidence and peace,
We'll all receive when Jesus appears
From Heaven with His powerful angels.

Lord, I know You will come in flaming fire
    To punish those who reject You,
    And refuse to accept the Good News of the Lord Jesus.
They will be punished in everlasting hell,
    Forever separated from Your presence,
    Never to see the glory of Your Kingdom.

Lord, thank You that Jesus is coming to be glorified
    And be seen by His saints,
    Who are those believing in Him.

Lord, I pray continually that I'll be worthy of Your calling,
    And be the kind of follower You want me to be.
Because this way the name of my Lord Jesus Christ
    Will be glorified
    When others see the kind of life I live.
                        Amen.

Antichrist and the Coming of Christ

2 Thessalonians 2:1-17

Lord, Paul explained to the Thessalonians about the coming of our Lord Jesus Christ and how we will be gathered to Him. He did not want them alarmed by a false prediction, or rumor, or any letters that claimed to come from him. They had heard that the tribulation of the Day of the Lord had already begun. They were confused because they were suffering more persecution then ever before, and thought the tribulation had begun and Christ had come, but they had missed the rapture.

Lord, Paul told them the Tribulation could not begin until the man of sin— the antichrist—was revealed and Christians in name only fall away from the faith. The antichrist will oppose everything about God, and exalt himself so that he is worshiped as God, and he will sit in the temple of God claiming that he is God.

Lord, Paul told these things to the Thessalonians while he was there, now
    he reminds them that the antichrist cannot come until the Holy
    Spirit is taken out of the way, because the Spirit holds back a full
    onslaught of evil in the world. But the One restraining sin—the Holy
    Spirit—will be removed when believers are raptured.

Lord, Paul told the Thessalonians that the antichrist will be fully revealed
    after the rapture, but the Lord Jesus Christ will eventually destroy
    him with the breath of His mouth and with the glorious appearance
    of His coming.

Lord, Paul reminded them that the antichrist will be satan's representative
    full of demonic power, and lying tricks. He will deceive all the lost
    people who don't have spiritual insight because they have already
    rejected the truth, and have chosen not to believe it. You will send a
    strong delusion so that they will believe satan's lie. They will all be
    punished who refused to believe Your truth and who chose willingly
    to sin.

Lord, I will forever give You thanks
    Because You loved me and
Chose me from the beginning to be saved,
    And You set me apart to the Holy Spirit and truth.
I thank You for the Good News that came to me,
    And I obtained eternal life through the Lord Jesus Christ.
Therefore, I will stand fast and hold on to the message
    That Paul delivered to the churches, by word and by letters.

Lord, I pray that my heart will be comforted and
    Be established to do every good work,
By You, the heavenly Father, and the Lord Jesus Christ,

Who loves me and gives me the hope of His return.
Amen.

How To Live While Waiting for Christ's Return

2 Thessalonians 3:1-18

Lord, Paul asked for the Thessalonians to pray for him,
As he prayed for them.
I pray that the Word of the Lord
May spread quickly,
And be effective in winning many to Christ.
I ask that I'll be delivered from people
Who are evil and bigoted because they have no faith.

Lord, I know You are faithful to give me strength
And will guard me from the evil one.
I have believed that Your Word,
Will continue to be successful.
May You turn many hearts to Your love
And that they may wait patiently for Christ's return.

Lord, Paul gave the Thessalonians a command
To avoid a believer who is lazy
And avoids work that he should be doing.
Paul wanted his example to be imitated
Because he was not idle but worked hard
And paid for his own meals.
Paul worked constantly and he worked diligently
So he wouldn't be a financial burden on them.
He wanted to be an example for them to follow,
Even though he had the right to expect a salary.

Lord, Paul gave them a rule when he was there,
"Don't give food to anyone who refuses to work."

Paul heard that some Christians were lazy,
    Refusing to hold a job,
    And trying to live off those who were working.
Paul ordered them by the authority of the Lord Jesus Christ
To begin working and earning the food they eat.

Lord, I have learned from Paul and the Thessalonians
    To never tire of doing the right thing.
If any refuse to obey the command of Paul
    I'll have nothing to do with them,
      So they'll be convicted of their wrong ways.
However, he is not an enemy to Christ;
    He is a brother who needs correction.

Lord, I pray to receive the peace that is Yours,
    May I receive it in every day, in every way;
    Lord, be with me!

Lord, Paul finally greeted all the Thessalonians in his own handwriting; that
    gave genuineness to this letter. Finally, Paul prayed for the grace of
    the Lord Jesus Christ to be on them.
                    Amen.

1 Timothy

Chapter 44

THE STORY OF WRITING THE BOOK OF FIRST TIMOTHY

Date: A.D. 65 ⌐ Written from: Northern Greece ⌐ Written by: Paul

I felt good to be out of prison. Yet, I constantly rubbed the wounds on my wrists from those four years of chains. These scars are a visible reminder of my prison experience in Caesarea and Rome. While physical freedom felt good, it was nothing like the freedom Jesus Christ gives me from the Jewish Law.

I have had good memories about that second story apartment overlooking the street in Rome. It was there where I wrote some of my greatest letters—letters to Ephesus, Colosse, and Philippi. I wish every church could read those letters to discover and enjoy the riches they have in Christ Jesus.

I feel good about the church in Ephesus. Because it is a church of spiritual riches, they know the Scriptures plus they have experienced revival. They know the power of God. I am glad that Timothy is now preaching in that church.

It was only a few days ago when I received word that there were some problems in Ephesus. These were not problems of outward sin, as was the case in Corinth. There were no doctrinal problems, as was the case in Thessalonica. Nor were there any tendencies to observe Jewish ordinances and holy days, as with the church in Colosse. No...the church at Ephesus is a great testimony because of their love of God and love for one another.

However, there is some tension between young Timothy who pastors the church and the elders of the church. The elders had not been outwardly criticizing Timothy, it's just that Timothy did things differently from the way I did when I was their pastor. I need to write to them to explain some of the differences between different leaders.

And then there's Timothy's side of the story, the elders in Ephesus do things differently from the way Timothy experienced when he pastored the church at Philippi and Berea.

I will write a letter to Timothy to describe how a pastor and elders should relate to one another.

As I picked up a pen to write to Timothy, I thought to remind him that he is my son in the faith. I will remind Timothy that he is a pastor by God's command. I will pray grace, mercy, and peace for Timothy from God the Father and from Jesus Christ.

I will remind Timothy that he must stay in Ephesus to stop certain false teachers from spreading false doctrine. They must stop basing their message on myths and genealogies that create controversy in the church; rather they must build up one another in the Word.

Then I realized, *"The problem with Timothy is that he thinks he is too young for this church."* Even so, I must realize that the church in Ephesus has had great preaching; Apollos, the golden-tongued orator from Alexander. They've also had John, the beloved disciple who leaned on the breast of Jesus. Also, *"they've had me as a preacher."* Then I realized, *"It would be hard for anyone to follow this lineup of preachers, so I have to put myself in Timothy's shoes and advise him accordingly."*

One of the first things I want to write Timothy is, "Let no man despise your youth." I will remind Timothy that even though he is a young man, his authority in ministry is not based on his experience; but, his authority is based on Scripture and God Himself.

And then I know some outward weaknesses of Timothy. He is spending too much time on developing bodily strength and physical exercise, so I'll write to him, "Bodily exercise profits little." But at the same time Timothy's stomach ulcer prohibits him from doing everything he ought to do. So I'll write, "Take a little wine for your stomach's sake." I think I'll underline the world *little* because wine can lead to intoxication. But I know Timothy has good self-control, so I'll not do that.

In Ephesus I hear some of the elders were pushing their friends to become elders. I hear some of the new candidates do not measure up to the qualifications for elders. So I'll write, "If a man desires the office of elder, he desires a good thing...." And then I'll add the set of standards for both elders and deacons in the Ephesus church.

There are also questions about what women could do in the church. Of course in the synagogue, women don't even sit on the main floor with the elders and men of the congregation. Women sit in the loft with the children. I wrote to the Christians at Colosse, "In Jesus Christ, there is no male or female...." Now I'll have to spell out what women should and should not do. This is very touchy because I don't want to exclude women from ministry, but I don't want to go to the other extreme and let them take over authority in the church.

> *If women had not done what women have done,*
> *Where would the church be?*
> *If men would have done what men should have done,*
> *Where could the church be?*

Apparently, some of the elders in the church at Ephesus were not looking after Timothy's financial needs. So I'll write, "Let the elders who rule well be counted worthy of double honor, especially those who labor in the word and doctrine." When I dot the "i" on that sentence, I'll smile because I know the elders won't pay a pastor double salary, they'll just realize Timothy is *worth* a double salary.

Money seemed to be a problem in the church at Ephesus. Not their lack of money, probably, they had *too* much money and didn't use it properly. So I'll remind the church, "The love of money is a root of all kinds of evil." Then I'll outline various principles about how money should be used in the service of the church and for the glory of God.

I'll have a courier take this letter to Timothy as soon as it's finished. I'll sign my name so Timothy will know it's from me. Then copies can be made and sent to every church so pastors and elders will serve God harmoniously.

Sincerely yours in Christ,
The apostle Paul

Chapter 45

PRAYING THE BOOK OF FIRST TIMOTHY

Paul's Relationship to Timothy and Warning About Heresy

1 Timothy 1:1-20

Lord, Paul wrote to Timothy, his son in the faith, reminding Timothy that
Paul was an apostle by Your command and that the Lord Jesus
Christ was his Savior and hope. Paul prays grace, mercy, and peace
for Timothy from You, the Father and from Jesus Christ.

Lord, Paul reminded Timothy that he was to stay in Ephesus to stop certain
false teachers from spreading false doctrine, and to stop the spread
of myths and genealogies that create controversy in the church.
Rather Timothy should build up Your work.

Lord, I know that love comes from a sincere heart,
A pure conscience, and believing faith.
Some have drifted from these qualities
And spend their time arguing about nothing;
So they don't know what they're saying.
I know the Law is good
When we apply it properly to our lives.
I also know the Law is not given to keep
Good people in line,
But the Law is aimed at rebellious people
To teach them the truth,
And point them to salvation.
The Law is aimed at murderers and

Adulterers, and perverts, and slave traders,
And liars, and perjurers.
The Law was written for those who
Deny the Gospel and sound doctrine
And the truth that was committed to Paul.

Lord, I thank You for giving me strength to serve You
And You found me faithful
So that you called me into Your service.
Before I was saved, I was a liar and curser,
And I was against the faith;
I did all this in ignorance.
You showed me mercy,
So that I became a believer.
Your grace filled me with faith
And with love that comes from Jesus Christ.

Lord, this is a faithful saying,
That no one can deny,
Christ Jesus came into the world to save sinners
And I myself was the greatest of them.
Your mercy was shown to me,
Because Jesus Christ meant to make me
A great example of His inexhaustible patience.
As a result, other people have come to trust Jesus
And gain eternal life.

Lord, I give glory and honor to You, the only God;
You are immortal and invisible, forever and ever. Amen.

Lord, again Paul reminded Timothy, his son,
To do these things he is telling him.
These are the truths spoken by prophets,
So he should fight for them like a good soldier.
His weapons are faith, a pure conscience;

Because some have denied their conscience
They have wrecked their faith.
Such are Hymenaeus and Alexander who are enemies,
Thus Paul has given them to satan to punish them
So they won't bring shame on the name of Christ.
Amen.

Instructions About Prayer and the Role of Women in Church

1 Timothy 2:1-15

Lord, Paul directed Timothy to pray
In every way for all types of people.
I will pray for all people,
Interceding for Your mercy in their lives,
I will give thanks for Your work
In every area of people's lives.
I will pray for political leaders and government supervisors,
So I can live peaceably
And follow holiness and honesty in my life.
In this way, I fulfill my prayer obligation
And will please You, my God and Savior.

Lord, I know you want everyone saved
And learn the full scope of biblical truth.
You are the only God and Christ Jesus—the Man—is the only Mediator
Between You and all people
Because Jesus sacrificed Himself as a ransom
For all the people in the world;
This is the message of truth everyone must hear and believe.
Lord, You appointed Paul as a preacher and apostle,
No one can deny this,
Paul was appointed to teach faith and truth to all.

Lord, because of the way You changed Paul and me
      I will lift freely my hands in prayer to You,
      Free from anger or jealousy.

Lord, Paul wanted women to dress modestly,
      Without being indecent or
      Calling undue attention to themselves,
Paul wanted Christian women to be noticed
      For their inner godly personality
      Not for their outward dress or fixing their hair,
      Or gaudy jewels, or indiscreet clothing.
Paul wanted women to do good works and
      Listen to good Christian women so they could be godly.
Paul didn't want women teaching men
      So that they were in authority over men,
      He wanted them to quietly listen in church.
Paul used the illustration of Adam being created before Eve
      So You created men to be leaders.
But Eve was blinded and deceived by satan,
      Then Adam sinned with his eyes wide open;
      Thus he was guilty and plunged the race into sin.
And women were punished with pain and suffering
      In giving birth to children.
But they will be saved by trusting Jesus the Savior
      And then living quiet lives before You.
                      Amen.

Qualifications for Pastors and Deacons

1 Timothy 3:1-16

Lord, Paul said any man who wants to be a pastor/leader,
      Wants to do a noble work for You.
But he must be a good man; blameless,

The husband of one wife.
He must be self-disciplined, work hard, and obedient;
    Also, he must be courteous, a good teacher,
    And open his home to visitors and guests.
A pastor can't drink alcohol, be hot-tempered,
    But be courteous with people and gentle.
He must not be greedy for money, but must
    Manage his family well.
Because if a man can't make his family behave,
    He shouldn't be responsible for church behavior.
A pastor must not be a new convert,
    Because he may become proud and arrogant.
Then God would condemn him,
    As God condemned satan for his pride.

Lord, Paul said deacons should live by the same standard
    As the pastor of the church.
They should be respected by the church
    And do what they promise.
Deacons should not drink alcohol,
    Or be greedy for money.
They must be conscientious Christians
    Believing and walking in faith.
The church must examine them before
    Putting them into the office of deacon.

Deacons should be the husband of one wife,
    With happy obedient families.
Those who do a good job as deacons,
    Should be respected by all in the church.
God will reward them with His blessings,
    For their faithful walk in Christ Jesus.
In the same way, the wives of pastors and deacons

Must be respectable, not gossipers,
　　But faithful in every area of life.

Lord, Paul told Timothy he wanted to be with him soon,
　　But in case he was delayed,
Paul wanted Timothy to know how people should behave
　　In God's family—the church of the living God—
　　Because it teaches and protects the truth of God.
Paul gave Timothy the doctrinal statement
　　For all of the church to learn and believe.

　　Jesus appeared in a human body,
　　He was anointed by the Holy Spirit,
　　Seen by angels,
　　Preached among the Gentiles,
　　Believed by many in the world,
　　And taken up into glory.
　　　　　　　　　　　Amen.

How a Good Minister Should Live

1 Timothy 4:1-16

Lord, Your Holy Spirit told us that in the last days
　　Some will turn away from Christ.
They will follow seductive spirits
　　And will believe false doctrine that comes from demons.
These false teachers will lie about the truth,
　　They are hypocrites whose consciences are seared
　　As though they were branded with a red-hot iron.
They will forbid marriage
　　And demand that people abstain from food.

Lord, You've created every good food to eat,
　　And I should reject no food

But we must thankfully enjoy it all.
Provided I've blessed it and given thanks,
>Your Scripture and prayer make it holy.
Paul told Timothy to explain this to the church,
>As a good pastor who knows the Word of God.
Paul also told him not to waste time
>Arguing with those deceived by
>Godless myths and old wives tales.
Paul told Timothy to develop his spirituality;
>I also will follow this advice.

Lord, Paul told Timothy physical exercise is all right,
>But don't go to extremes with it.
Spiritual exercise is unlimited,
>It rewards us with a good life here on earth
>And will reward us in Heaven.

Lord, I will give myself diligently to ministry
>And will take whatever suffering comes,
>So that people will believe in Christ.

Because I believe Christ died for me and lives forever,
>My hope is in Him, along with all who put their trust in You.
Help me teach these things to everyone,
>And let no one ignore me because of my age.
Help me be an example to all believers,
>In my speech, behavior, love, faith, and purity.
Help me discipline my time by reading
>The Word of God to people,
>Then preaching and teaching it to them.
I will use the spiritual gifts You gave me,
>That came to me through the Scriptures
>And have been recognized by the church.
I will put all my energy into my work,
>I want everyone to see what You are doing through me.

Therefore, I will be careful of what I do and teach
>So that people will be saved who hear me,
>And I will fulfill Your calling for my life.
>>Amen.

The Good Work of a Minister

1 Timothy 5:1:25

Lord, You told me never to speak harshly to elderly men,
>But to speak to them respectfully as to a father.
You told me to speak lovingly to younger people
>As I would speak to those in my family.
You told me to treat elderly women
>As I would treat my own mother.

Lord, You have instructed the church to take care of widows
>If they don't have anyone else to care for them.
Their children or grandchildren are the ones
>Who should take responsibility for them
To repay the debt they owe to their elders
>For a grateful heart pleases You very much.
But the church should especially care for widows
>When they have no one in this world to care for them.
Then let them spend their nights and days in prayer,
>Nor running around looking for pleasure and entertainment.

Lord, Paul gave Timothy the church principles
>To care for people and do what is right.
The ones who won't care for their needy relatives,
>Especially those in their immediate family,
Have no right to call themselves Christians;
>They are worse than non-believers.
Widows should be involved as a special church worker

When she is 60 years old,
    Having been the wife of one husband.
She must have been hospitable to others
    And helped those in trouble.

The church is not to accept young widows,
    Because they will want to get married again.
And people will condemn them for not keeping their promise
    To be a special committed church worker.
Besides, young widows can become lazy,
    Going from house to house gossiping
    And meddling in others' affairs.
Paul thought young widows should re-marry,
    Have children and look after a home,
    Then no one can accuse them of anything.
Some young widows have already turned from Christ,
    Having been led astray to follow satan.
The relatives of a widow must take care of her,
    And not expect the church to do it.
Then the church can use its money
    To care for needy widows
    Who fit the qualifications of genuine widows.

Lord, Paul taught the church to give worthy pastors
    Double consideration in paying them,
    Especially those who preach and teach well.
The Scripture says, "Never put a muzzle on the ox
    To keep them from eating.
When they work to bring in the crop,
    Let them eat as they work in the fields."
In another place the Scriptures teach,
    "Those who work deserve their pay."

Lord, Paul taught the church not to listen to complaints
    Against the church leaders,

Unless there are two or three witnesses.
If the church leaders are wrong,
Rebuke them in front of the church
As a warning to all believers.
Paul said before God, the Lord Jesus Christ, and the holy angels
To rebuke sinning pastors impartially,
Whether they are friends or not.
Treat all people equally without favoritism,
For we are all equal in Christ.

Lord, Paul taught never to choose a pastor too quickly,
Because some faults may be overlooked.
Therefore, I will learn from the example of my leaders
To keep myself pure from all sin.

Lord, Paul told Timothy to quit drinking only water,
But to take some grape juice for digestion
Because he was frequently sick.

Lord, some people's sins are obvious to all,
Long before a formal complaint is made against them.
Others have sins that are not easily discovered
Until they actually come to light.
In other cases, the sins of some
Will not be discovered until Judgment Day.
The same truth applies to the good deeds that some do,
They will not be hidden forever.
Amen.

Warnings to a Minister

1 Timothy 6:1-21

Lord, workers should work hard for their bosses,
And respect them in all ways.

May Your name and Christian expectations
    Not be laughed at by the world
    Because Christians are lazy workers.
A worker must not take advantage of his boss
    Because he is a Christian.
On the contrary, Christian workers must do better
    Since they are helping their boss
    To make their business effective and successful.
Paul told Timothy to teach these principles
    And those who have a different interpretation
    Are both selfish and ignorant
Because these truths are biblical and effective,
    Based on the words of the Lord Jesus Christ.
Those who question these truths stir up arguments,
    That lead to anger and jealousy and abuse;
    They do it to make a profit from religion.

Lord, Paul told us we are truly rich
    When we are happy and satisfied with what You give.
We have brought nothing into this world
    And we will take away nothing when we die.
So, as long as we have food and clothing,
    We should be content.
Those who are passionate about being rich,
    Are open to all types of temptations
    And get-rich-quickly schemes.
Their financial lust will hurt their walk with Christ
    And eventually destroy their life,
Because the love of money opens people up
    To all kinds of sin.
Those who spend their life chasing wealth,
    Have wandered away from Your standards for living
    And opened up their souls to fatal wounds.

Lord, because I am dedicated to You,
>   I will avoid the evils associated with money.
I purpose to live a saintly life
>   And I will seek to be filled with faith, love, and gentleness.
I will fight to put You first in all my life,
>   I will hold tightly to eternal life that You give.
This is my calling and my commitment,
>   And I have confessed this to the church.
Now before You—the source of life—and before Jesus Christ,
>   I promised to do all that I say I will do,
So that no one can find any fault in me
>   Both now and in the future till Christ returns.

Paul told Timothy to warn those who are rich in this world
>   That they don't look down on others,
>   Or trust in their money,
But trust in God, who out of His riches
>   Gives us all we need to be happy.
Timothy was instructed to tell rich people
>   To use their money to do good.
They are to be rich in good works,
>   Generous and willing to share with those in need.
This way rich people can store up real wealth
>   For themselves in Heaven;
>   This is the only safe investment in life.
Paul told Timothy to guard carefully the commission
>   That God had entrusted him.
Keep out of pointless arguments
>   Of those who show off their knowledge
>   Because they are not really that smart.
They have missed the most important thing in life,
>   They don't know You at all;
>   May they continually experience Your grace.

Lord, I believe the teaching of Scripture that states;
  Christ will come soon to rapture His believers,
Christ is blessed by You, and He is the only ruler of all things.
  He is the King of Kings, and Lord of Lords.
Christ alone is immortal, He is eternal;
  He now lives in light so pure and blinding
  That no one can approach Him,
  No natural person has seen Him.
Now, unto Christ be honor, power, and eternal rulership,
  For ever and ever; Amen!
      Amen.

2 TIMOTHY

Chapter 46

THE STORY OF WRITING SECOND TIMOTHY[1]

Date: A.D. 66 ~ Written from: Rome, Italy ~ Written by: Paul

I knew both sounds clearly. The heavy *clanking* sound—like the dropping of heavy metal bars—is the sound of the gate with steel bars at the end of the hall. The large iron bars are so big that even the strongest of men couldn't bend them. If every evil man in this jail put his weight against that iron door, it wouldn't budge.

Then there is a second sound, the heavy *thud* of the door to my cell. It sounds like a wooden bench dropping on a stone floor. When slammed, the heavy door has a finality of distant thunder. The room is then pitched into darkness. And this hole in the ground called a jail cell is cold—frigid like a wintery night.

With every *clang* of the outer door, my heart jumps. I can't see but I want to know who's there. I listen for a voice, the lonely cell seems more isolated when all my friends are gone.

My heart keeps looking for an escape from this cold, damp prison. With every *clang*, I expect a message of pardon from the Caesar or one of my faithful friends bringing me a warm coat...or books to read...or good news from one of the churches.

But no one comes to see me. Each *clang* is like another nail in the coffin...nothing!

This morning I woke up with a phrase on my mind that I had written to the Philippians, "For me to live is Christ...but to die is gain." Yes, it is hard to live in this damp hole in the ground, but it's easy when Christ dwells in my heart. Sometimes a breeze finds its way down the staircase through the iron bars. I wonder if I'll feel its freshness today.

The worst part of being in isolation is there's nothing to do, nothing to read, there's just nothing...but my thoughts, and they're good thoughts. Just think of all God has allowed me to do.

This morning as I prayed for all of my helpers, I was encouraged by their freedom and what they could do for Christ. Each time I prayed for Barnabas...or for Titus...or for Sosthenes...I got vicarious strength from what they could do for God.

Today I prayed again for Demas, a young man with great potential...I thought that I must tell Timothy about Demas, I will write, "Demas has forsaken me for present worldly attractions." The thought of those pleasures making Demas happy took the air out of my sails. How can I pray for Demas who at one time prayed so zealously? How could I pray for Demas' prosperity when I remember the great sermon he preached from the Scriptures? *"Yes,"* I thought, *"Demas has forsaken me because he loves the pleasures of this world."* I squeezed my eyes to shut out the pain.

I thought I would write to Timothy, "Come to me quickly." I want Timothy here if I should die. I can trust Timothy to tell everyone my last thoughts and words.

And then I thought, *"I'll ask Timothy to bring the books for me to read...."* And as I shiver in this cold, I'll add, *"Bring my cloak."*

The afternoon sun didn't reach my prison cell till after lunch—if you call those starvation rations lunch. I hadn't sat in the warming rays of the sun for two weeks. I know when the afternoons came because the sun filters through the iron bars for about an hour. However, the last two weeks have been cloudy. "Lord, I need sun today." As soon as I prayed, the prison got a little lighter—light enough for me to see with my infected eyes—light enough for me to write a few large letters.

I told myself, *"Rush to take advantage of the sunlight,"* I sat at a feeble table, squeezed the feather into the small bowl of ink, and began to scratch on the pages. "Paul, an apostle of Jesus Christ by the will of God..." It never crossed my mind that prison was a mistake, I knew God had ordained chains for me and shortly I would die. I thought, *"I must include the phrase—'I am now ready to be offered as a sacrifice to God, and I am ready to become a martyr, my departure from this life is at hand.'"*

I didn't want this letter to be too gruesome, I didn't want to discourage Timothy.

I smell some smoke drifting through my cell, so I realize the guard was also cold. The guard was stirring the black ashes in the small fire at the end of the hall. As the guard blew on the black ashes, the embers turned red with fire, and a few seconds later, a flame jumps from the midst of the coals. *"I'll write that...."*

I'll write for Timothy to *"stir up the gift of God as one stirs up a fire."* Paul remembers that Timothy is meek and quite often needs his fires stoked. Timothy needs to feed the fire again.

Timothy has a very prestigious position. He is now the preacher of the church in Ephesus, the largest city in Turkey, the Roman capital of Asia Minor. The church at Ephesus includes the wealthy, as well as the extremely poor. In my mind, the church at Ephesus is one of the most important churches for the continuation of the Gospel and Timothy has the awesome responsibility of leading this church of Ephesus.

So I'll write to Timothy, "Be strong in the grace that is in Christ Jesus," reminding Timothy not to bow to the pressures of politicians, rich men or those with great family inheritance. "Rather," I'll write, "endure hardness as a good soldier of Jesus Christ." I want to remind Timothy that a soldier obeys only his commander, no one else. And so, I want Timothy to obey only the Lord Jesus Christ, not elders, not other itinerant preachers, no one else but Jesus.

Then I thought again about the youthful lusts that had enticed Demas, so I write to Timothy, "Flee youthful lust and follow righteousness." This is my deepest prayer for my young preacher in Ephesus.

Day after day I add to the letter that would be sent to Timothy. I write slowly because of weak eyes, I write until it becomes too dark to see the paper. No one provides me with even the smallest candle. When the sun goes down outside, the prison hole in the ground becomes night.

Each night I fluff what is left of the straw on the stone ledge where I sleep. Even in sleep the hard cold stone punishes my flesh. After prayers, I turn on my side to sleep. I dream of being led outside the main gate called the People's Gate to the city of Rome. It's there I'll probably die.

When the soldiers led me into the city, I had seen the crosses on both sides of the road, stretching over the horizon. On each cross was a martyr whose life was "hid in God" because they had given everything for Christ. I wondered if I would be crucified, and if so, "*I am crucified with Christ, nevertheless, I live. But it is not I who will live or die, it is Christ who lives in me.*"

Later my dream turns to the sharp end of a sword. I remember James the fisherman from Capernaum, the brother of the apostle John. His head was cut off by Herod. I wonder if there was a sword in my future. I had written earlier to the Galatians, "*I die daily.*" One day I will die and that will be the last time I die and then I'll receive eternal life.

I had heard the stories of Christians being hung on a tall spike in Nero's garden. I heard the stories of oil being poured on them and their bodies burned to illuminate the parties of the insane Caesar, Nero. "*Will that be my end?*" I wondered. Then I smile, "*What better way to end my life after I've been ablaze for God all over the world?*"

I have one more thought, "*It doesn't make any difference how I die, because I've written, 'To be absent from the body is to be present with the Lord.' So it's much better to die and be with the Lord, than it is to remain in this life.*"

Before going to sleep, I pray, "*Lord, may I glorify You in my death as I have in my life.*"

And right before sleep coverers my mind, I think, "*Maybe Jesus Christ will come with the dawn, which would be nice.*" So my last prayer before going to sleep, "*Even so come, Lord Jesus.*"

Sincerely yours in Christ,
The apostle Paul

Endnote

1. Paul's second imprisonment in Rome.

Chapter 47

PRAYING THE BOOK OF SECOND TIMOTHY

Paul's Charge to Timothy

2 Timothy 1:1-18

Lord, Paul told Timothy he was appointed by Jesus Christ to be an apostle
> to tell everyone that eternal life is promised to those who believe.
Timothy was a son to Paul in the faith;
>> Paul prayed for Timothy to have grace, mercy, and peace
>> From You the Father, and from Christ Jesus, our Lord.

Lord, Paul remembered Timothy in prayer night and day
>> And he longed to see him,
>> Because Timothy cried when they left each other.
Paul remembered Timothy's genuine faith
>> Which was first in his grandmother Lois,
>> And in his mother Eunice.
Paul said to stir up the inner fire You gave Timothy,
>> Which was evident at his ordination
>> When Paul laid hands on him.

Lord, You have not given me a spirit of cowardice
>> But a spirit of power, love, and self-control.
So, I will never be ashamed of witnessing for Christ,
>> Or ashamed of other Christians.
I will accept my share of hardships as I share the Gospel,
>> Relying on Your power to accomplish Your will.

Lord, You have saved me and called me to holiness,
>   Not because of anything I've done
>   But for Your purpose and by Your grace.
Your kindness and love was shed on me
>   Before the beginning of the world,
But was revealed when our Savior, Christ Jesus,
>   Abolished sin and proclaimed life by His death;
>   Lord, I believed it and received it.

Lord, Paul again reminded Timothy he was a preacher
>   And because he was an apostle to the Gentiles,
>   He is also suffering hardships.

Lord, I am not ashamed of the Gospel
>   Because I know I've put my trust in Christ.
And I have no doubt You, Father, are able to care
>   For all I've entrusted to You until that Day
>   When Jesus Christ will return to earth for me.

Lord, I will continue to believe and live
>   By the sound teaching I've learned from Scripture.
I will guard Your special calling for my life
>   By the help of the Holy Spirit who lives in me.

Lord, Paul reminded Timothy that Phygellus and Hermogenes
>   Have refused to have anything to do with Paul.
Paul prayed blessings on Onesiphorus' home
>   Because he was not ashamed of Paul's chains.
Onesiphorus came to see Paul in jail
>   And helped him when he was in Ephesus.
Onesiphorus went to a lot of trouble to find Paul
>   When he was in Rome.
Paul prayed a blessing on him,
>   Knowing he would be rewarded at the Judgment Seat of Christ.
>   Amen.

How to Minister in the Day of Apostasy

2 Timothy 2:1-26

Lord, I will be strong in the grace
    That comes from Jesus Christ.
All the truth I heard from my teachers,
    I will communicate to trustworthy people
    Who in turn, will be able to teach others.
I will take my share of difficulties
    As a good soldier of Christ Jesus.
No soldier gets bound up with worldly things
    Because he must always obey his commanding officer;
    Therefore, I will separate myself from sinful things.
An athlete cannot win a contest
    Unless he keeps all the rules;
    Therefore, I will discipline myself to obey Christ.
And a farmer gets first claim on the harvest
    Over any crops growing in his field;
    So, I will work hard to get Your reward.

Lord, I will remember the Gospel of Jesus Christ;
    He was a descendent of David,
    He died for me and was raised from the dead.
This is the Gospel for which Paul was being persecuted;
    Paul was chained like a criminal,
    But Your Gospel is not chained.
Paul suffered all his persecutions for the sake
    Of those who have believed the Gospel,
That they may be saved by Jesus Christ and obtain
    Eternal glory that comes to those who are saved.

Lord, Paul gave Timothy a faithful saying
    That he could rely on and share with others.
If I have died with Christ on the Cross,

I will live with Him in Heaven.
If I hold firm in my profession of faith,
>I will reign with Him in glory.
If I deny Christ, He will deny me;
>If I become faithless, Christ is always faithful.

Lord, Paul told Timothy to remind the church about this truth
>And not argue with anyone over this statement of faith,
>Because it will only destroy those who are listening.
I will study to know everything about Christianity,
>So I can be Your approved workman.
I will not be ashamed of my ministry,
>But will rightly handle the word of truth.
I will avoid foolish discussions
>Which make people get angry and sin against one another,
>As it destroyed Humenaeus and Philetus.
They claimed the resurrection of the dead had passed,
>Departing from the truth of God; then
>They dragged others down with their self-destruction.

Lord, even though there are false teachers,
>I know Your truth is as solid as a rock.
You know all who belong to You,
>And all who call on Your name,
>Must avoid doing wrong things.

Lord, in a large home there are all kinds of dishes,
>Some are made of gold and silver, others of wood and clay.
Some dishes are used for special people,
>Other dishes are used for ordinary things.
I want to be a special dish used by my Master, Jesus Christ,
>And kept ready for His good work.
Instead of giving into the lust of youth,
>I will seek holiness, faith, love, and peace
>In fellowship with all who call on the Lord.

I will avoid foolish arguments which upset people,
>   And lead to quarrels.
So, I will not quarrel with anyone, but will be kind,
>   A good teacher and patient with all.
I will be gentle when I correct people who disagree with me,
>   Remembering You can change their mind;
So that they will recognize the truth,
>   And escape satan's grip on them,
>   And be free of his trap.
>   Amen.

The Prediction of Apostasy and God's Answer in Scripture

2 Timothy 3:1-17

Lord, I know that in the last days before Christ comes,
>   There will be dangerous times.
People will be aggressively self-centered and greedy for money,
>   Boastful, arrogant, and scoff at You.
They will be contentious and ungrateful to their parents,
>   And lack any sensitivity for people.
They will be inhumane, without love and without forgiveness;
>   Plus they will be sarcastic, violent, and rebellious.
They will hate anything good, but they will be treacherous,
>   Rash, conceited, and addicted to pleasure,
>   Rather than lovers of God.
They will say they're a Christian and attend church,
>   But their life will deny what they profess.
I won't have anything to do with these people,
>   I'll keep away from them.

Lord, these types of people break up homes,
>   Having sex with stupid people who are obsessed with sex,
>   Trying one fantasy after another.

701

They continually try to educate themselves,
    But they never come to the truth.
Men like this defy the truth just as Jannes and Jambres defied Moses,
    They have polluted minds and
    They have turned against the Christian faith.
And in the long run they won't be very influential;
    Their folly will be their downfall,
    And everyone will see their rebellion.

Lord, I know that Paul taught that we who believe in God
    Should also live godly lives.
Just as Paul demonstrated faith, patience, and love
    In a consistent life-long way,
Paul was persecuted in Antioch, Iconium, and Lystra,
    But You Lord, rescued him from all of them.
Therefore, anyone who tries to live a life
    Dedicated to Christ will be attacked.
These wicked imposters of Christianity
    Will go from bad to worse,
    Deceiving themselves as they deceive others.

Lord, I will be true to the teachings of Scripture,
    Remembering who my teachers were and what they taught me,
Just as Timothy remembered his teachers from childhood,
    Making him wise in the Scriptures
    So that he accepted Christ and was saved.
The whole Bible was written by Your inspiration,
    And is useful to teach me the truth,
And points out what is wrong in my life,
    Helping me to do what is right.
The Bible is Your tool to prepare me
    In every area of my life,
    So I can do Your work.
        Amen.

Paul, a Faith Servant

2 Timothy 4:1-22

Lord, Paul reminded Timothy that he stood before You
> And before Christ Jesus, who will judge the living and the dead
> At His appearing when He sets up His Kingdom.

I will preach Your Word continually,
> At every place, at all times,
> When it is suitable and when it is not.

I will correct all false teaching and rebuke
> Those who believe and spread it around.

I will encourage all people to do the right thing all the time,
> Based on what Your Word teaches.

Lord, the time is coming when people won't listen to the truth,
> But will seek out teachers who reinforce their sin.

They won't listen to Your Word,
> But will live by their misguided rebellious ways.

I will be careful to always follow Your principles,
> I will always be ready to suffer for Christ.

I will try to win others to Christ,
> And do the things I should do.

Lord, Paul testified it was time for him to die,
> His life was being poured out
> As a sacrifice to You.

Paul said, "I have fought a good fight to the end,
> I have run the race to the finish line,
> I have kept true to the faith."

Now Paul expects the crown of righteousness
> That You have for faithful witnesses
> That will be given to all who look for Christ's' appearing.

Lord, Paul asked Timothy to come to him as soon as possible,
Demas had forsaken him, Crescens went to Galatia and
Titus to Dalmatia. Only Luke is with Paul. Paul wants Timothy to
bring Mark when he comes, and to bring his coat from Troas, also
his books and parchments. Paul has sent Tychicus to Ephesus.

Lord, Paul warned Timothy about Alexander the coppersmith because he
bitterly contested what Paul was teaching. Then Paul prays, "Lord,
repay him for the evil he has done."

Lord, Paul said, there was no one with him when he made his first defense
before the judge. He prayed for those who deserted him, "May they
not be judged for what they did." Paul testified the Lord Jesus stood
by me, and gave me power so that the message of grace was
proclaimed for all the unsaved to hear it." On that occasion You
delivered him from being thrown to the lions. Paul stated, "The Lord
will always deliver us from danger, until it's time to go to Heaven."
Paul glorifies You for his deliverance thus far.

Lord, Paul told Timothy to greet Prisca and Aquila and the household of
Onesiphorus. Erastus is in Corinth, and he left Trophimus sick in
Miletus. He sends greetings from Eubulus, Pudens, Linus, Claudia
and the brethren. Paul wants Timothy to come before winter. Then
he prays, "May the Lord Jesus Christ be with you, and may you have
His grace."

Amen.

TITUS

Chapter 48

THE STORY OF WRITING
THE BOOK OF TITUS

Date: A.D. 65 ⁀ Written from: Northern Greece ⁀ Written by: Paul

I t has been a few months since I was released from my imprisonment in Rome. My time in prison was not physically restrictive. Rome allowed me to rent a second floor apartment so I could be with my friends—Luke, Timothy, and the others.

But no one showed up at my trial, so I was released. I had been imprisoned for four years and some thought it was wasted years, but they're wrong. It was then when I wrote the prison epistles to Ephesus, Philippi, and Colosse. I was able to win to Christ many Roman soldiers, some were transferred to Caesar's palace and others were sent around the world. They were employed by Rome but they were soldiers of Christ. They carried out the Great Commission given by Jesus Christ, carrying the Gospel to the ends of the earth.

It felt good to leave Rome and not have a Roman soldier constantly with me. But I still have scars on my wrist from the chains. Physical freedom felt almost as good as freedom in Christ from the law.

When I left Rome I visited Ephesus, then several places throughout Turkey. I visited the Island of Crete and planted some new churches there, to join the older churches already on the island. Because Titus was from Crete, I left him there to strengthen all the churches.

I trust Titus will have an excellent ministry in Crete. He's been with me since the Jerusalem Conference when we settled the controversy about circumcising Gentiles. Remember, Titus is a Gentile believer in Christ who has never been circumcised.

I wrote to Titus from the West Coast of Greece after I got word that Titus was having difficulty with the churches of Crete. Some of the older

Christians from the synagogues felt they knew more about organizing a church than Titus. I heard that some elders were using Jewish fables in their sermons, others were resorting to legalism, and still others were disputing over genealogies.[1]

When I heard of the problems, I immediately sat down to write a letter to Titus, my faithful associate. I had great faith in Titus but I did not trust the elders of the churches. Titus was a young man capable of tough tasks; I once sent him to settle problems in Corinth because I knew he was dependable and diligent.[2] Even though Titus had strength of character, he also had great tact and love.[3]

I had led Titus to Christ and I will write to him about our common faith.

The churches in Crete are struggling with false teaching and they are resisting the leadership of Titus; so I decided to write to Titus noting, "For this cause I left you in Crete, so you could set in order the things that are lacking in the churches and ordain elders in every church."

Then I thought, *"When this letter is copied and sent to all of the churches in Crete, they will allow Titus to organize the churches, appoint elders, and teach them the truth of the Gospel of Jesus Christ."*

Again I thought what I should include in the letter, and then I remembered the words that I had written to the Corinthians, "Titus is my partner and fellow worker."[4] This is the emphasis that I want the Christians in Crete to know. I want them to follow Titus, as they would follow me.

Sincerely yours in Christ,
The apostle Paul

Endnotes

1. Titus 1:10; 14; 3:9-10.

2. 2 Cor. 8:17; 2 Cor. 7:6; 2 Cor. 8:17.

3. 2 Cor. 7:13-15.

4. 2 Cor. 8:23.

Chapter 49

Praying the Book of Titus

Qualifications for Pastors

Titus 1:1-16

Lord, Paul wrote to Titus, calling himself Your slave
    And a messenger of Jesus Christ.
Paul was commissioned to preach to the elect
    So they would have faith in the Word of God,
    And be transformed in this life and gain eternal life.
You cannot lie, You promised eternal life
    Before the world was created.
In Your plan, You revealed the Gospel to Paul,
    So he could share it with everyone.
Paul wrote to Titus who shared his ministry,
    Because Paul led Titus to Christ.
Paul prayed for Titus to experience grace and peace
    From You, the Father, and Christ Jesus, the Savior.

Lord, Paul left Titus in Crete to organize churches
    And appoint pastors in every town.
A pastor must have unquestioned character
    And be the husband of one wife.
His children must be believers
    And he must not be charged with disorderly conduct.
A pastor will be Your representative to the people;
    A pastor must be blameless, never arrogant,
    Short-tempered, violent, greedy, or a brawler.

A pastor must be hospitable, friendly,
>   Self-disciplined, fair-minded, and dedicated.
He must have a firm grip on the message of salvation,
>   And must agree with the doctrine Paul taught,
So that he can teach sound doctrine to all,
>   And refute those who oppose it.

Paul said there were many rebellious Christians in Crete who must be
>   dealt with because they say all Christians must keep the Jewish
>   ceremonial Law. Paul told Titus to silence them because they
>   were ruining whole families just to make money. Then Paul
>   quoted a Cretian poet who said, "Cretians are nothing but liars,
>   dangerous beasts who live to fill their bellies." Therefore, Paul
>   wanted Titus to correct them harshly and point them to sound
>   doctrine, so they will stop doing what the legalists tell them to do.

Lord, those who are committed to purity
>   Will find purity in their search for truth.
Those who are rebellious and evil thinking
>   Will find the corruption they seek.
They claim to know God personally,
>   But their actions deny their search for truth.
They are outrageously rebellious toward You,
>   And everything they do is evil.
>   Amen.

The Work of a Pastor

Titus 2:1-15

Lord, Paul told Titus to teach sound doctrine,
>   Tell the older men to be serious about the truth,
Self-disciplined, dignified, and do everything patiently and quietly;
>   But most of all, they must be men of faith.

Lord, Paul told Titus to teach the older women
    That they must be holy in behavior,
    And that they must not gossip nor get drunk,
    And be the teachers of godliness.
Older women must teach the younger women,
    To behave rightly, love their husbands,
    And love their children.
Younger women must be sexually pure, gentle,
    Keep their houses clean and obey their husbands
    So they don't disgrace the Gospel with their lifestyle.

Lord, Paul told the younger men to behave,
    And be serious about their duties in life.
They should be an example of sincerity and honesty,
    And keep their promises,
So no one can accuse them of lying,
    And they must not take advantage of others financially.

Lord, Paul told the workers to be obedient to their bosses,
    And obey the orders given to them,
And never steal anything from them
    But be completely honest at all times.
Slaves must strive to be an example of Christianity
    In everything they do.

Lord, You revealed Your grace to us,
    And made it available to the entire human race.
You have taught us to deny ourselves of everything
    That does not lead us to godliness.
You have taught us to deny our pride and sinful ambitions,
    To discipline ourselves, and live good lives,
    Here and now in this present world.

Lord, I am looking for the blessed hope and glorious appearing
    Of Jesus Christ my Savior and God.

He sacrificed Himself for me
>To set me free from all contamination and wickedness.

Jesus has purified His people to be His very own,
>And He always wants them to do the right thing.

Paul told Titus to teach these truths
>Then rebuke any who would not listen to him,
>And finally don't let anyone despise him personally.

Amen.

Command to Godly Living

Titus 3:1-15

Lord, I will be obedient to government officials,
>And will obey all civic laws,
>And I'll work honestly for a living.

I will not slander government rulers,
>Nor will I pick fights with them.

But I will be courteous to them
>And be kind to all people.

I remember I was once foolish
>And rebellious to laws, and rude to people
>Because I was a slave to my lust.

I lived for sinful pleasures, hating people,
>And being hated by them.

Lord, then You revealed Your kindness and love to save me;
>I was not saved by my works of righteousness,
>But was saved by your mercy.

You washed my sins way, and I was born again
>By the working of the Holy Spirit in my life

Which you abundantly poured out to me
>Through Jesus Christ my Savior.

Jesus did this so I might be justified in Your sight,

And became Your heir,
Looking forward to inheriting eternal life with You.

Lord, this is Your truth that I rely on,
And will affirm it constantly,
That they who believe in You for salvation
Must be careful to maintain good works.
This truth is good and it works for me,
And will work for all who believe it.

Lord, Paul told Titus not to argue over pointless questions,
And genealogies, and controversies over the Jewish Law.
They are useless and cannot help anyone.
If anyone quarrels about this truth after the first and second rebuke,
Put him out of the Church.
That type of person has already condemned himself,
And has rejected the truth.

Lord, Paul promised to send Artemas or Tychicus to Titus, and then he
was to join him at Nicopolis when Paul decided to spend the
winter. He told Titus to make travel plans for Zenas the lawyer
and Apollos. Paul wanted all believers to help others who have
need, this makes their lives productive. Everyone with Paul sent
greetings to Titus, and he finally prays, "Grace be with you."
Amen.

PHILEMON

Chapter 50

THE STORY OF WRITING
THE BOOK OF PHILEMON

Date: A.D. 64 ☞ Written from: Rome, Italy ☞ Written by: Paul

When I came to Rome as a prisoner, I was scheduled to be sequestered in the Mamertine prison. All the cells are below ground—dark and dreary. But because I'm a political prisoner, I was allowed to rent a room if I had the money. But of course I had to pay all expenses, including the cost of Roman soldiers to guard me 24 hours a day. But God was merciful to me, I rented a second floor apartment with a balcony overlooking the street and the agora (marketplace).

The early morning sun poured between the tall buildings on either side of the street onto my balcony, making it a wonderful place for prayer and relaxation. When I go there to pray, no one disturbs me. The Roman guard—one of four stationed in the apartment 24 hours a day—gave me freedom. He knew I would not jump from the balcony, nor would I try to escape.

Everyone in the apartment heard the rattle of chains when I lifted my hands to pray. It reminded them that even though I was free in Christ, I was a prisoner of Rome. I had been sent to Rome to be tried by Caesar. But when my name was added to the docket of Caesar, I was told it would be two years until my hearing before Caesar.

My apartment was paid for by a rich Christian who pastored a church way up in the mountains. This church leader—Theophilus—had given Luke ten thousand pieces of silver to pay for my needs and the needs of my friends in Rome. But Theophilus was a crafty businessman, in return for the ten thousand pieces of silver, he asked Luke to write an accurate account of the growth of the early church—the Acts of the Apostles. While I was praying on the balcony, Luke was sequestered in a small room, writing the history of Christianity. Each morning Luke interviewed individuals to get the history of the early church, and in the afternoons, he wrote what he learned.

Just as Luke had previously written the life of Christ from his careful research all over the Holy Land, so he wrote the Acts of the Apostles following the same model. He had gathered notes from everyone he interviewed over the years. Just as the Holy Spirit had guided Luke *anothen* (from above) to guarantee the accuracy of the gospel of Luke, so the Holy Spirit was guaranteeing the words of Acts.

One morning I was praying for the little church in Colosse of Turkey, a small village not too far from the capital city of Turkey, Ephesus. I prayed for each person in the church, then I prayed for the slaves in the villa where the church met.

Then a providential thing happened. As I looked on the street, I suddenly saw a face that reminded me of one of the servants in Colosse for whom I just prayed. I cupped my hands to yell out over the balcony railing, "**Hey**,…Onesimus,…up here…**look this way**…I remember you."

Onesimus was shocked that someone in the city of Rome knew him by name. He had been a slave in the villa of Philemon. Later I learned Onesimus was an escaped slave.

Onesimus had known where his master's money was kept. He worked in the house, as opposed to a field slave. Onesimus waited for his opportunity. It came when he learned of a ship leaving on a certain night from Ephesus to Rome. This was Onesimus' lifetime opportunity for freedom. He had his escape plotted out. He stole the money, ran through the back wood paths over the hills to Ephesus, so no one would see him on the main road. He boarded the ship right before it sailed, paid for his ticket, and by the time Philemon missed him, Onesimus was gone from Turkey.

Now…here in Rome…a familiar voice called his name. Onesimus looked up to recognize me calling to him from the balcony. He realized, *"That's the preacher who came to my master's house to tell us the Gospel."* Onesimus thought, *"this preacher will turn me over to the Roman soldiers."*

I yelled down from the balcony, "**Wait**...I am sending Timothy down to get you. We want you to have lunch with us."

Onesimus first looked down the street one way, then the other way. A soldier was standing at both corners. He thought, *"If Paul yells out, the soldiers will arrest me."*

So Onesimus yelled back up to me to say he would enjoy having lunch with me and the other followers of Jesus Christ.

At the lunch table, it was then I found out that Onesimus had run away, and stolen money. I knew immediately that if Onesimus was turned over to the soldiers, they may imprison him or even kill him. Even if Onesimus were returned to Colosse and Philemon, his master had the right to execute Onesimus. If not death, surely Philemon would punish him severely.

I presented the Gospel to Onesimus, preaching to one man as passionately as I had preached on Mars Hill, or before many Jewish synagogues. As Onesimus listened carefully, he became convicted of his sin and was sorry for his crime. But there was another feeling; Onesimus felt the love of God flowing to him. Suddenly, in the middle of our conversation Onesimus had a great desire to know Jesus Christ intimately as Savior. When I bowed my head and led him in prayer, Onesimus offered the sinner's prayer,

"Lord Jesus, come into my heart and save me for I am great sinner...."

For the next six months Onesimus slept on a cot near the back door. He was happier than he had ever been in is life, for he was serving the Lord by doing what he was trained to do. Onesimus was serving me as a house servant. He immediately began keeping the apartment clean, sweeping the floors each day, and preparing meals.

After six months, I planned to send Tychicus to Turkey to carry a letter to the church at Ephesus and Colosse. These letters would circulate to other churches explaining the riches they had in Christ Jesus.

Then one morning I announced, "Onesimus...I am sending you with Tychicus back to Philemon...."

All of the believers with me looked from one set of eyes to the other. They were not sure this was the wise thing to do. Yes, they appreciated the house work done by Onesimus, but they were more concerned about his safety if he went back to Philemon.

Onesimus also had the greatest concern. He dropped his eyes to the floor and wouldn't look at anyone. Even though there was no eye contact, the men in the room could see terror in Onesimus' facial expression.

"Don't worry," I said, "God will go with Onesimus as he returns home to Colosse." Then I explained, "This is the right thing to do, Onesimus must go back to rectify the situation."

I told the men, "I have prayed about this and I plan to write a letter to Philemon telling him how he should deal with this issue. I believe God will hear my prayer and Philemon will receive our brother Onesimus back with open arms."

I told the men sitting around the table that Philemon would do what I asked because I had led Philemon to faith in Christ, just as I had done for Onesimus. "I will write to praise Philemon for all of his love and faith in following Jesus Christ, I will give him our appreciation for the financial gift that he had sent."

Then I explained that I would write of my affection for Onesimus and how he had done the house work for us in Rome. I said to them, "I will ask Philemon to receive him back, not as a slave, but as 'beloved brother.' I am so sure that Philemon will take him back," I assured my followers, "I will offer to pay any expenses that Onesimus has incurred."

Then I laughed and said, "I will tell Philemon that I am coming to visit Colosse and that he should prepare my favorite room."

Everyone around the table laughed and agreed that the letter should be sent in the hands of Onesimus and Tychicus, and that Philemon would do the right thing.

Sincerely yours in Christ,
The apostle Paul

Chapter 51

PRAYING THE BOOK OF PHILEMON

A Prayer for Forgiveness and Restoration

Philemon 1–25

Lord, Paul wrote a letter with Timothy from his prison in Rome to Philemon,
a rich Christian in Colosse. The letter was also addressed to
Philemon's wife Apphia, and to his son Archippus, a church leader
in the Colossian church.

Lord, I pray for grace and peace in my life
The same as Paul prayed for Philemon's life.
Give me that grace and peace
From You, my heavenly Father and the Lord Jesus Christ.

Lord, Paul thanked You for Philemon
And continued praying for him.
That Philemon would keep trusting the Lord Jesus
And develop deep love for Your children.

Lord, I thank You for men like Philemon
Who have influenced my life of service for You.
Thank You that they enriched my life.

Lord, Paul said Philemon had fully committed
Himself to the work of God,
And as Philemon put his generosity to work,
He would understand what he could really accomplish;

Philemon's generosity had given Paul joy and comfort,
    And refreshed Paul's heart in serving God.

    Lord, may I use my resource generously in Your service
        To bless and minister to others.

Lord, Paul boldly asked a favor from Philemon,
    Even though Paul could have demanded it
    Because of all he had done for Philemon.
Paul asked that his request be received from a friend,
    Now an old man in prison for the sake of Christ.

Lord, Paul requested kindness be shown to Onesimus,
    A runaway slave from Philemon,
    That Paul had led to Christ;
Onesimus was not much use to Philemon in the past,
    But now Onesimus is useful to both of them
    Because he had been serving Paul in prison.

Paul says, I am sending Onesimus back to you
    And part of my heart comes back with him.

    Lord, just as the name Onesimus means useful,
        May I be useful to You and to others.

Lord, Paul really wanted to keep Onesimus in Rome
    To do things for him that he couldn't do,
    Because his chains restricted him.
Onesimus could have helped Paul's ministry
    And that would be Philemon's contribution to Paul,
But Paul didn't want to make Onesimus stay in Rome
    Without Philemon's consent;
And Paul didn't want to force Philemon
    To let Onesimus stay in Rome with him.

Lord, Onesimus ran away for a little while,
    So Philemon could have him permanently.
But not taken back just as a slave,
    But received as a beloved brother in Christ.
Onesimus will do more for Philemon now as a brother
    Than he previously did as a slave because
    Now he belongs to You.

Lord, Paul asked Philemon to receive Onesimus
    As he would receive Paul.
If Onesimus has stolen anything
    Or cost Philemon any money,
Paul says, "Put that on my account
    And I will repay it to you"
    (Paul won't mention Philemon owes him his very life.)

Lord, this letter is a wonderful picture of Christianity;
    Just as Onesimus ran away from his master,
    So I was straying away from You.

Just as Paul promised to pray for Onesimus' damages,
    So Christ paid for all the damages
    That sin did to my relationship with You.
Just as Paul prays for Philemon to receive Onesimus,
    So Christ prays for You to receive me.

Lord, Paul trusted Philemon to respond positively,
    Then added Philemon would do more than he asked.
Lord, Paul added one more request, "Get a room ready,
    I'm praying God will send me to see you."
Paul sent greetings from Epaphras, Mark,
    Aristarchus, Demas, and Luke, his co-laborers.

Lord, as Paul prayed for the grace of the Lord Jesus Christ
    To be on his friend, Philemon,

I pray for the same grace in my life.
Amen.

PRAYING THE GENERAL EPISTLES

Hebrews

Praying the Book of Hebrews
1:1–13:25

Chapter 52

THE STORY OF WRITING THE BOOK OF HEBREWS

It was late at night and the candle on the small table reflected the faces of two aged travelers who followed Jesus Christ. Paul, closest to the light, was telling his physician friend, Luke, some of the problems in Jerusalem, "Christians in Jerusalem are going back into the Temple to make blood sacrifices, this is wrong; Jesus is the final sacrifice for sin! Jesus is the Lamb of God Who took away the sins of the world, how can they sacrifice the blood of an animal to forgive their sins?"

Paul explained it was all right for Christians to go back into the Temple to pray, but some Christians didn't like the simplicity of worshiping Jesus in a house church, they wanted the elegance of the Temple. They liked the pomp and ceremony of observing holy days, the Jewish feasts and the Levitical choirs.

Paul reasoned to his friend Luke that the Christians in Jerusalem were comprising by returning to the Temple worship. Gone were the early days when Christians witnessed from house to house. Gone were the early days when they prayed all night for the power of God. Gone were the early days when the leaders of the Sanhedrin persecuted Christians for the miracles done in the name of Jesus Christ.

Luke said to Paul, "Why don't you write a letter to the church in Jerusalem warning them about going back to Temple worship?"

Paul thought about it for a moment and then shook his head, "No!" he explained, "The church in Jerusalem will have nothing to do with me because I am the apostle to the Gentiles." Then Paul added, "The Jewish Christians in Jerusalem would not listen to me, they are so bound up in their traditions that they hate me!"

Then Paul concluded, "Jewish Christians in Jerusalem still will have nothing to do with Gentiles."

Paul thought again about writing a letter to them for a few minutes, then summarized, "No...the church in Jerusalem would not listen to a letter from Paul."

Luke agreed with Paul but he knew something had to be done. Then Luke remembered a sermon that he had heard many times preached by Paul. It was a sermon on the theme *Better*. Luke said, "Your sermon that Christ is *Better* should be written out and sent to the church at Jerusalem."

Because Luke had heard Paul preach the sermon so many times, he began to repeat the sermon to Paul. He had almost memorized it *word for word*. Luke said, "Christ is better than angels...Christ is better than Moses...Christ is better than the high priest...Christ is better than Melchizedek...Christ is better than the sacrifices...Christ is better than the Old Testament tabernacle...Christ is better than the priest who enters into the holy of holies."

Paul laughed! He hadn't realized Luke paid that close attention to his sermon. But when Paul heard Luke repeat his sermon—word for word—an idea crossed Paul's mind. Then the wise apostle said,

"Luke, you write the sermon in your words and in your style, then the Christians in Jerusalem won't know that I have written it. That way, they won't reject the message."

Paul went on to explain that even though the sermon was his idea, it was not important for him to get the credit for writing the letter. Paul wanted the Christians in Jerusalem to get the message that Christ is *Better* than anything the Old Testament had to offer.

Then Luke suggested, "Don't forget about the warnings in your sermon. Several times in the sermon you stop to warn the people what will happen if they go back to their Temple sacrifices."

"Yes," Paul agreed, "add the warnings."

"But one more thing," Paul added. "Don't put your name on the letter—you're a Gentile. The Jerusalem church will reject the letter if it has your name on it."

"That's good," Luke thought.

"I'll begin tonight," Luke replied.

After getting paper and quill, Luke sat at the table and dipped his quill into the black olive oil ink and began to write, "God, who at various times and in various ways spoke in time past to the fathers by the prophets, has in these last days spoken to us by *His* Son...."

Who wrote Hebrews? As a matter of fact, Paul and Luke did such a good job hiding their contribution to the letter, no one in the early church knew for sure who wrote the letter. Some thought Paul, a few thought Luke, some thought Apollos, and a few thought Barnabas. Two hundred years after its writing, Tertullian the Church Father said, "Only God knows for sure who wrote Hebrews."[1]

Endnote

1. See Bible.org, <http://www.bible.org/page.asp?page_id=1360,> (accessed 18 August 2006).

Praying the Book of Hebrews

Jesus Is Better Than the Prophets

Hebrews 1:1-3

Lord, long ago You spoke in many different ways at many different times
    To past believers, by the prophets,
       Giving them a partial picture of Your eternal plan.
But You spoke completely and finally through Your Son
    To Whom You have given everything,
       And through Whom You created the universe.

Your Son is the radiance of Your glory
      And the exact representation of Your nature,
      His power sustains all things.
After the Son provided forgiveness of sins,
      He sat down at Your right hand in glory.

Lord, I bow at the feet of Your son Jesus
      To worship Him with my whole heart
For all that He is and for all
      That He has accomplished for me.

Jesus Is Better Than Angels

Hebrews 1:4-14

Your Son is much greater in superiority over the angels,
      His name—Jesus Savior—is much greater than theirs.
You never said to the angels, "You are my son,
      In eternal day I have become Your Father."
You never said about the angels, "I am His Father,
      He will be My son."
You said, "When I bring the First Born
      Into the world, let all the angels worship Him."
You said, "I make the angels swift as the wind,
      And my servants will punish with fire."
But about the Son You said, "Your kingdom, O God, will
      Last forever and ever, and You will rule in righteousness;
      You love righteousness and hate iniquity."
"Therefore, Your throne—Jesus—is set above all others,
      And I—the Father—will pour out the oil of righteousness on You."
You called Your Son—Lord—when you said, "In the beginning,
      O Lord, You laid the foundation of the earth;
      The heavens were the work of Your hand."
"The heavens will vanish, but You—My Son—remain;

They will wear out like old clothes
But You—My Son—will remain forever
And Your years will never end."
You never said to any angel, "Sit at My right hand
    Until I humble your enemies under your feet."
No, You didn't exalt any angel because they are spirits
    Who minister to You in worship,
    And they minister service to those who will receive salvation.

Amen.

First Warning Against Neglect

Hebrews 2:1-4

Lord, I will pay careful attention to the biblical things I've heard
    So that I don't drift away from You.
Because the message spoken by angels was true,
    And every disobedience has its own judgment,
No one will go unpunished if they neglect
    Your salvation that is promised to them.
The promise was first announced by Jesus Himself
    And passed on to us by them who heard him speak.
God confirmed this message with signs, miracles
    And gifts of the Holy Spirit distributed to them.

Christ Is Better Than Created Man

Hebrews 2:5-18

Lord, You did not make angels rulers of the world to come;
    But You made Your Son ruler of everything.
David said in Psalms, "What is man that You are concerned about Him,
    But you honor the Son of Man?"

"You made him a little lower than angels,

>So You could crown Him with glory and honor

>And You put everything under His feet."

"You left nothing that was not put under Your Son,

>Yet at the present time, everything is not subject to Him."

We see Jesus who for a short time was made lower than the angels,

>Now He is crowned with glory and splendor in Heaven,

Because by Your grace He submitted to death for all mankind.

Lord, it was Your purpose to allow Christ to suffer,

>Because through His death Jesus brought many to Heaven

>Becoming the leader of their salvation by His sufferings.

We have been made holy by Jesus, we have the same Father,

>And Jesus is not ashamed to call me His brother.

For Jesus predicted in Psalms, "I will tell my brothers

>About the Father and in their presence I will praise Him."

At another place Jesus predicatively said, "I will trust my Father;"

>And again He said, "Here I am with Your children

>You have given me."

Since all your human children have flesh and blood,

>Jesus shared this same humanity, so that by death,

He could destroy the one who holds the power of death

>That is the devil, and free all those held captive

>By the fear of death for their entire life.

Lord, Jesus didn't come to free angels, but to free humanity;

>*For this reason Jesus became flesh like His brethren*

>*So He could become my merciful and faithful High Priest.*

Now Jesus has made atonement for my sins,

>*Because He Himself was tempted and suffered,*

>*Now He is wonderfully able to help me when I am tempted.*

Amen.

Jesus Is Better Than Moses

Hebrews 3:1-6

Lord, because You have set me apart for Christ,
>And because You have chosen me by a heavenly calling,
You want me to fix my thoughts on Jesus
>The Apostle and High Priest of my faith.
Jesus faithfully served You as a priest
>Just as Moses faithfully served You in the Holy Sanctuary;
But Jesus was worthy of greater honor than Moses,
>Just as the builder has greater honor than the house he built.
Every house is built by someone,
>But You are the builder of everything.
Moses was faithful to serve in Your House,
>His work was a type—illustration—of Christ's work that was coming,
But Christ has complete authority over Your House,
>And as a Christian, I am part of Your House
>So I will cling with confidence to that hope to the end.

Second Warning Against Unbelief

Hebrews 3:7-19

Lord, when I hear Your voice speaking to me,
>I will not stubbornly resist You as Israel rebelled against You and
>Wandered 40 years in the desert.
In the desert Israel constantly tested You and disobeyed You,
>Even though they knew what You did in the past for them.
That is why You were angry with them and said,
>"Their hearts are hardened and they refuse to obey Me,
>They shall never enter in the rest I have for them."
Lord, I do not have a disobedient heart that rejects You,
>I will listen to Your Word today so I won't develop

An unbelieving stubborn heart.
I will faithfully trust You to the end,
    Just as when I was first saved
    So I can share all the blessings You have planned for me.
But now, I will not harden my heart
    As Israel did in the desert.

The Jews were the people who heard Your voice and rebelled?
    They were the ones Moses delivered out of Egypt.
They were those who made You angry
    So You made them wander in the desert 40 years
    Because of their sin. Their bodies were buried in the wilderness.
Those were the ones You swore would never enter Your rest;
    Why couldn't they enter the promised land?
    It was because of their unbelief.

Amen.

Jesus Is Better Than the Sabbath

Hebrews 4:1-16

Lord, since Your promise of entering Your rest still stands
    I will be careful not to neglect entering Your rest.
You had the Gospel preached to me just as it was preached to Israel
    But they couldn't take advantage of it because of unbelief.
Now, I can enter Your rest by faith, because You said,
    "I made an oath that those who will not believe Me,
    Cannot enter My rest."
I know Your rest is waiting for me because I will finish my work;
    After You worked six days, You rested on the seventh day
    Because You finished all Your work.
The promise remains for some to enter your rest today, even though
    Those who heard the Gospel preached to them rejected it.

God still warns through the words of David, "Today,
> If you hear God's voice, do not harden Your hearts against Him."

If the promised rest was the land into which Joshua led them,
> God would not have later promised a different rest;
> Therefore, there remains a Sabbath-rest for You who read this letter.
When you enter your rest, you cease from your labor,
> Just as You—the Father—ceased from Your labor.
Therefore, I will make every effort to enter Your rest
> Being careful not to disobey You
> As the children of Israel did in the wilderness.

Lord, Your Word is alive and active, sharper than a two-edged sword,
> Piercing the unseen things such as my soul and spirit,
> Exposing my thoughts and attitudes for what they are.
Lord, You know everything about everyone,
> Nothing is hidden to You who will judge everyone,
> So You know who will enter Your rest.

Lord, Jesus Your Son has gone to Heaven as my great High Priest,
> So I will hold fast to my faith.
My High Priest understands me and sympathizes with my weaknesses
> Because He was tempted in all parts of His being, just as I am,
> Yet He did not commit sin.
So, I will come boldly to Your throne;
> So I will receive mercy and find grace in my hour of need.

Amen.

Jesus Is Better Than Human Priest

Hebrews 5:1-10

Lord, the human High Priest was selected from among human men,
> And was chosen to represent Your people before You.

He sympathized with the ignorant and those who make mistakes
> Because as a mortal, the High Priest was subject to weaknesses.

This is why the High Priest offered sacrifices for his own sins
> Before he offered for anyone else.

No one makes a choice to be a High Priest,
> He must be chosen by God, just as Aaron was chosen.

So Christ did not make the choice to be the High Priest
> But the Father chose Him saying, "You are My Son,
> Today I have become Your Father."

Again the Father said, "You are a priest forever
> In the priestly order of Melchizedek."

In His earthly days Jesus prayed with loud cries and tears
> To God who could save Him from death;
> He was heard because of His obedience.

Although Jesus was Your Son, He learned what obedience was like,
> When he experienced suffering.

It was after this experience that Jesus became
> The giver of eternal life to those who obey Him.

Then You declared Jesus to be the High Priest
> After the order of Melchizedek.

Amen.

Third Warning Against Disobedience

Hebrews 5:11–6:12

The author had a lot more to say about the priesthood of Melchizedek,
> But the readers didn't fully understand what he wrote.

When they ought to be teachers, they were still students;
> Needing someone to teach them the elementary truths of Christianity
> They needed milk, not solid food!

Spiritual babies still live on milk, not knowing how to live right because

Solid food is for mature Christians
Who by training can distinguish between good and evil.

Amen.

Third Warning About Disobedience (Continued)

Hebrews 6:1-12

Lord, I won't stay with the elementary teachings about salvation,
　　　But I'll go on to maturity in Christ.
I won't go back to my original repentance from sin,
　　　Nor will I keep studying my baptism, or my spiritual gifts,
　　　Or the resurrection from the dead, or eternal judgment.
Lord, I will build my life on these foundational truths
　　　And grow to maturity in my daily walk with You.

It's impossible for those who are saved to go back to
　　　The Temple to have their sins forgiven by a blood sacrifice.
If a person knew Jesus Christ, and tasted the heavenly gift,
　　　And been filled with the Holy Spirit, and understood the Scriptures,
　　　And felt the assurance of Heaven, and they turn against You,
It's impossible to be spiritually renewed in the Temple;
　　　When they sacrifice a lamb, it's like crucifying again
　　　The Son of God and torturing Him anew.

When farmland drinks in the rain from Heaven,
　　　It grows a good crop because it experiences Your blessing;
　　　That's a picture of our spiritual prosperity from You.
But if farmland keeps growing weeds and briers,
　　　The land is worthless, and it might as well be cursed;
　　　That's a picture of a person who doesn't produce spiritual fruit.
Even though the writer warns the readers
　　　He thinks they will do better things for You.
Lord, You are not unjust, You'll not forget a person's faith,

Nor his love, nor their good works.
I will show the same diligence to the very end of life,
So I will get my full reward when I get to Heaven.
I will not become lazy, but will follow the example of those
Who through faith and patience received the prize.

Amen.

Jesus Is Better Than Abraham

Hebrews 6:13-20

I know You will do what You promised.
When you made a promise to Abraham,
Since You couldn't swear by any other, You swore by Yourself.
You promised to bless Abraham and give him many descendants;
So Abraham received a son after waiting patiently for many years.
People today swear an oath by someone greater than themselves
To guarantee what they promise and end all arguments.
Because You wanted to make it very clear to Your children
What You would do, You guaranteed it with Your oath.
Lord, You have given me two things: Your promise and Your oath;
Since it's impossible for You to lie, I know
Without a doubt that I'll receive eternal life that You've promised.
I have this certain hope of Heaven as an anchor of the soul
For I'm connected to Christ who has gone before me,
To enter the Holy of Holies in Heaven, where
He intercedes for me as my High Priest.

Amen.

Jesus Is Better Than Melchizedek

Hebrews 7:1-10

Lord, Jesus became a priest after the order of Melchizedek,
>Who was King of Salem and Your priest;
>He called You by the name El Elyon, Possessor of Heaven and earth.
When Abraham returned home after defeating the Kings,
>Melchizedek interceded for him. Then Abraham gave
>Melchizedek a tenth of everything he gained.
The name Melchizedek means King of Righteousness, and
>The title King of Salem means King of Peace.
There is no record he had any previous ancestors, or that he died;
>He is like the Son of God, a priest forever.

Lord, Melchizedek was great, even Abraham, the Father of the Jews,
>Gave him a tenth of all he had.
The Old Testament required the descendents of Levi who became priests
>To collect a tenth from all the people, i.e., their brothers.
However, Melchizedek did not trace his heritage to Levi, yet
>He collected a tenth from Abraham and blessed him;
>The one who has power to bless is the greater.
In the case of Levi, ordinary mortals received tithes
>But Melchizedek who received tithes, lives forever.
Levi who was in the body of Abraham paid tithes
>To Melchizedek who lives forever.
Therefore the Jewish priests who came from the rank of Levi
>Couldn't save us, God sent us Christ as a priest
>From the rank of Melchizedek to save us.

Amen.

Jesus Is Better Than Aaron

Hebrews 7:11–8:5

For there to be a change of priesthood, there also
      Needed to be a change of law. Jesus who became a Priest,
      Was from the tribe of Judah, not from the tribe of Levi.
Moses didn't write anything about a person from Judah
      To serve as a priest at the altar. So God's method
      Changed because Christ new position as High Priest
      Came from Melchizedek.
Christ didn't become a priest based on the requirements of Levi,
      Christ became a priest by the power of a life lived forever.
The Psalmist proved this about Christ, "You are a priest forever,
      After the rank of Melchizedek."
The former laws of priesthood were set aside because
      They were weak and useless. The law never saved anyone
      But now we approach God with a better hope.
God promised that Christ would be an eternal priest; remember,
      God never promised this about the Levitical priest.
Only to Christ did the Father swear, "You are a Priest forever
      After the rank of Melchizedek." Because of this oath
      Jesus now guarantees us a new and better covenant with God.
Under the old system, there were many new priests who took the place
      Of the older ones who died off.
But Jesus lives forever, and has a continuous priesthood,
      So I can come to You anytime through Jesus my intercessor.
Now Jesus is able to completely save me when I come to You,
      Since He lives forever to make intercession for me.
Lord, Jesus is the kind of High Priest I need,
      One who is holy, blameless and without sin
      And He has access to You in Heaven.
Jesus is not like human priests who need to sacrifice for their sins,
      First for Himself, then for others.

Jesus sacrificed only once for all the sins of the world
     When He once and for all offered Himself on the Cross.
The old law brought sinful men into the priesthood
     But your oath brought Jesus into His priesthood;
     He is my eternally perfect priest.

        Amen.

Jesus Is Better Than Aaron (Continued)

Hebrews 8:1-5

Lord, the writer makes the point that I have a High Priest
     Who sat down at Your right hand in Heaven,
     Who now serves in the heavenly Tabernacle that You set up.
Since earthly priests appointed by You offer gifts and sacrifices,
     Christ also must make offerings for sin,
     But His sacrifices are far better than the Levitical sacrifices.
Earthly priests serve in an earthly Tabernacle
     That is a reflection of the one in Heaven,
Because when Moses built the Tabernacle, You told him
     To build it after the pattern You showed him on the Mount.

        Amen.

Jesus Is Better Than the Old Covenant

Hebrews 8:6-13

But the ministry of Christ is far better than the former priest
     Because the new covenant is far better than the old one,
     Because the new covenant is based on better promises.
If there was nothing wrong with the old covenant,
     There wouldn't have been a need for a new one.

But You realized the old covenant was limited, so You said,
　　"The day will come when I will make a new covenant
　　With the people of Israel and Judah."
"It will not be like the old covenant I made with them
　　When I led them out of Egypt."
"Israel did not keep their part of the covenant, so You cancelled it;
　　You promised to write the new covenant in their hearts
　　So they will know what You want them to do as Your people."
"No longer will people evangelize others saying, 'Know the Lord,'
　　For all will know You, from the influential to the least important.
You promised to forgive their transgressions
　　And no longer remember their sins."
Because You called this covenant "new," You made the old covenant obsolete;
　　And what is old becomes antiquated and disappears.

　　　　　　Amen.

Jesus Is Better Than the Old Sanctuary

Hebrews 9:1-10

Lord, the old covenant had laws about how to worship
　　And its place to worship was a tent.
Inside this sanctuary were two rooms. The first room, called the Holy Place,
　　Had the golden candlestick and a table of sacred loaves of bread.
Then there was the golden altar of incense
　　That represents prayer, and a curtain that separates the two rooms.
The second room was called the Holy of Holies
　　With the Ark of the Covenant, a gold covered chest,
　　Which contained a jar with some manna, Aaron's rod that budded,
　　And a stone engraved with the Ten Commandments.
On each end of the Ark were carved gold cherubim
　　With their wings stretched out over the lid of the Ark
　　Called the mercy seat, the place atonement was made.

Many priests followed certain regulations, going into the
        Outer room—the Holy Place—to carry out worship.
Only the High Priest entered the Holy of Holies, only once a year;
        He took blood with him for his and others' sins.
The Holy Spirit tells us by this illustration that the average person
        Could not enter the Holy of Holies
        As long as the old system of law was in place.
Lord, this illustration is important, because under the old system of law
        The sacrifices and gifts had to be continually given,
Because they never permanently cleansed
        The hearts of the worshipers.
The old system of laws dealt with what foods to eat,
        How to wash, rules about a lot of little things
        That people had to obey until Christ brought in a better covenant.

Jesus Is Better Than the Old Sacrifices

Hebrews 9:11–10:25

Christ came as the High Priest of a new and better covenant;
        He took blood into the Holy of Holies in Heaven and
        Sprinkled blood on the mercy seat to permanently forgive all sins.
Christ did not take the blood of bulls and calves into Heaven's
        Holy of Holies, but with His own blood He entered once and for all,
        To obtain eternal redemption for all who believe.
If the blood of bulls and calves could temporarily and outwardly cleanse
        Those who were unclean, thus sanctifying them,
How much more will the blood of Christ offered by the Holy Spirit
        Cleanse us, so we can serve the living God?
Therefore, Christ offered this new covenant to all, so that
        They may receive the promise of an eternal inheritance.
And don't forget Christ's death took away all the sins committed
        Under the old system of law.

When a person dies and leaves a will that is in question,
> The death of the one who wrote the will must be established;
> Then people receive the things that were promised in the will.
Therefore, the first system of law became operational when Moses
> Took blood and sprinkled everything having to do with the old law
> Saying, "This blood seals the agreement between You and God."
Moses then sprinkled blood on the Tabernacle and all
> The instruments of worship. All things were sanctified by blood,
> And without the shedding of blood, there was no redemption.
The tabernacle and instruments of worship are copies
> Of the true Tabernacle in Heaven. They were purified
> With the blood of animals.
But the Tabernacle in Heaven was purified with a better sacrifice;
> For Christ did not go into the earthly Tabernacle which is
> A copy of the heavenly one; He appeared before the Father for us.
Christ did not offer Himself repeatedly as the earthly
> High Priest does for himself and others. No!
Christ offered Himself once for all to do away with all our sin,
> And He did away with the existence of the first system of law.

Lord, I know it is appointed unto all people to die once,
> *Then comes the judgment.*
So Christ came once and took the sins of many;
> *The next time He comes to all those who wait for Him.*

Amen.

Jesus Is Better Than the Old Sacrifices (Continued)

Hebrews 10:1-25

Lord, I know the old system of law was only a reflection
> Of coming spiritual realities, not the realities themselves.
The law could never bring the worshiper to spiritual maturity,

Even though repeated endlessly, year after year.
If the sacrifices sanctified the worshiper, or made him mature;
> Then they would have stopped bringing their sacrifices
> When they reached perfection.
Instead, the worshiper had to recall their sin yearly,
> Every time they brought a sacrifice, because
> The blood of bulls and goats never took away sin.
Lord, when Christ came into the world, He said,
> "Sacrifices and offerings didn't do away with sin,
> So You Lord, prepared a body for Me."
It is written in Scripture, "Christ has come
> To lay down His body as a sacrifice for sin."
And the Scriptures said of Christ, "I am here,
> I have come to do the Father's will."
By His death the Father cancelled the old system of law
> To establish a new covenant, a new system of law;
Under the new, we have been made pure and clean
> By the death of Christ, Who died for all, once and for all.
Under the old law, the priest had to offer the same kind of sacrifice
> Day after day, which never took away sin.
But Christ our priest offered one sacrifice for all time,
> To take away all sin,
> Then sat down at Your right hand in Heaven.
Now Christ is waiting for His enemies
> To become His footstool.
For by one sacrifice, Christ made those perfect
> Who claim the power of the Holy Spirit to live holy lives.
You said, "This is the new arrangement I will make
> After they have not kept the old system of law;
I will put My laws in their hearts
> So they will want to obey Me."
Then You said, "I will no longer remember their sins and lawlessness
> Because I have forgiven all sin,

There is no longer need of daily animal sacrifice."
Therefore, children of God, let us walk right into
    The Holy of Holies into the presence of the Father
    By the blood of Jesus Christ.
We have a new and living way into the Father's presence,
    Through the offering of Christ's body
    Which tore the curtain down.

Lord, I will come to You with a sincere heart,
    In full assurance of faith, having my life
    Sprinkled clean from a guilty conscience,
    And having been washed clean from sin.
Now I look forward with confidence
    To the hope of Heaven that You have promised me.
I will motivate others to a response of love and good works
    And I will meet regularly in the church,
    And encourage others who don't come, to be faithful in attendance
    Because the day of judgment is coming.

Amen.

Fourth Warning Against Rejection

Hebrews 10:26-39

Lord, if anyone sin after they have been given knowledge
    Of the truth of the new covenant,
    There is no forgiveness in the animal sacrifice of the Temple.
They have only the terrible judgment of God to face
    And His raging fire that will punish rebels.
If those who rejected the law of Moses were killed without mercy,
    How much more severely will those be punished
    Who trample under foot the Son of God,
And considered His blood of the new covenant as unworthy

And insulted the Spirit of God who worked in their hearts.
Lord, You said, "Punishment belongs to Me,"
So I know, "You will repay."
Also the Scripture said, "Because the Lord will judge His people;
It is a fearful thing
To fall into the hands of the living God."

Lord, I know many have suffered when they first believed;
They stood for You in the face of insults and violence.
And sometimes they suffered because they stood with other believers
Who were being persecuted.
They not only were persecuted because they stood with those in prison,
But their goods were confiscated,
Yet they knew they had better possessions in Heaven.
Lord, I will not let my confidence die away,
Knowing I will be richly rewarded.
I will persevere, so that when I have done Your will,
I will receive what You have promised.
Lord, I know in a little while, You will come
And not be delayed.
I will do what the Scripture says, "The just will live by faith
And if he shrinks back, I will have no pleasure in him."
Lord, I have never turned back from following You;
No, my faith assures me that my soul will be saved.

Amen.

The Superiority of Faith in Jesus

Hebrews 11:1–12:2

Lord, because of my faith I am sure You will answer my request,
And my faith makes me certain about the things I can't see.
Because of my faith, I know the world was created by You

So that things seen came from things not seen.
Because of Abel's faith he brought a better offering
  Than did his brother Cain, and Abel pleased You.
You accepted Abel by receiving his sacrifice,
  And I can learn lessons of faith from Abel,
  Even though he is dead.
Because of Enoch's faith, You took him to Heaven without dying;
  No one could find him for You took him away
  Because You were pleased with him.

Lord, I know I can't please You without faith,
  So I come to You because I know You exist
  And I know You reward those who earnestly seek You.
Because of Noah's faith, he warned people about a flood
  He had never seen. Then he built a boat to save his family.
The faith of Noah condemned the world,
  And his faith gave him a basis to claim Your righteousness.
Because of Abraham's faith, he obeyed Your call
  When he left his home to go where You led him,
  Even though he didn't know where he was going.
Because of his faith, Abraham settled down in the Promised Land
  Like a stranger in a foreign country,
  Living in tents as did Isaac and Jacob who were heirs with him.
Because of his faith, Abraham confidently looked forward
  To living in a heavenly city that would be built by You.
Because of his faith, Abraham was able to become a father
  When he was too old to have children.
And Sarah, who was barren, had faith to bear a child,
  Because she realized that when You promised a son,
  You were certainly able to do what You said.
So the whole nation of Israel came from Abraham,
  When he was too old to have a child.
The nation of Israel had so many children
  That like the stars of Heaven, and the sands of the seashore,

They can't be counted.
Because of the faith of these people, they continued to look forward to
The home You would provide for them,
Even though they never received it down on this earth;
They confessed they were only visitors and strangers in this world.

Lord, when I agree with their faith, it means
I too am looking for a heavenly city prepared for me.

Because of Abraham's faith, when he was tested,
He offered up Isaac as a sacrifice to You.
Abraham believed Your promise that if he offered
His only son as a sacrifice, You would
Raise him from the dead,
Because You had promised, that from Isaac
Would come the whole nation of Israel.
Because of Isaac's faith, he knew You would bless
His two sons Jacob and Esau after his death.
Because of Jacob's faith, he blessed Joseph's two sons
As he steadied himself with his staff to worship You.
Because of Joseph's faith, when he was about to die,
He predicted the exodus of Israel from Egypt
And instructed that his body be buried in the Promised Land.
Because of Moses' parent's faith, they hid him
For three months after he was born
Because they realized he was an extraordinary child.
Because of Moses' faith, he refused to be known as
The son of Pharaoh's daughter.
Moses chose to suffer the affliction of Your people
Rather than enjoy the pleasure of sin for a short time.
Moses considered that the "reproach of Christ"
Was better than inheriting the riches of Egypt,
Because he looked forward to the reward You would give him.
Because of Moses' faith, he left Egypt

And wasn't afraid of the King's anger;
 He would not turn back, because Moses saw You who are invisible.
Because of Moses' faith, he began the Passover,
 And sprinkled blood on the door post,
So the destroyer wouldn't touch the first born of Israel
 As the first born of Egypt died that night.
Because of faith, Israel walked through the Red Sea on dry ground
 But the Egyptians drowned when they tried to follow them.
Because of faith, Israel walked around the city of Jericho,
 And the walls fell down.
Because of the prostitute Rahab's faith, she received the spies
 And was not killed with the rest of the inhabitants.
There's more to be said about the faith of Gideon,
 Barak, Samson, Jephihah, Samuel, or David, or the prophets.
Because of the faith of these men, they conquered kingdoms,
 Did what was right, and received what You promised.
They were not harmed by lions, or the fiery furnace,
 And were protected in battle.
Some were given strength, to be brave in battle;
 They defeated foreign armies, and women received back their dead.
Others were tortured to death knowing they would
 Rise again from the dead to a better life.
Others were mocked, beaten with whips, chained in dungeons,
 Died by stoning, sawed in two, and put to death by the sword.
Some were homeless and wore skins of sheep and goats;
 They were destitute, and ill-treated,
 Living in deserts, caves, and ravines.
These were all heroes of faith, yet none of them
 Received their reward in this life.
God has something better for them,
 But they had to wait to share something even better with us.

    Amen.

The Superiority of Faith in Jesus (Continued)

Hebrews 12:1-2

Lord, I have this large crowd of witnesses watching me
    Therefore I will strip off everything that's in the way,
    Especially any sin that would trip me up.
And I will run steadily the race that I have begun
    Without losing sight of Jesus my leader
Who was willing to die a shameful death on the Cross
    Because He knew the joy that was coming in the future,
    And now He sits at Your right hand in Heaven.

Fifth Warning of Coming Punishment

Hebrews 12:3-17

When I think of the way Jesus endured such torture
    By sinful men for me, I will not give up.
After all, I've never had to take a stand for Christ
    To the point of shedding my blood.
I've not forgotten Your words of encouragement to me,
    "Do not be discouraged when the Lord rebukes you
    Or at His light chastening
Because the Lord disciplines those He loves,
    And punishes everyone He acknowledges as His child."
Lord, I know suffering is part of my training,
    Because You're treating me as Your child;
    What child is not corrected by their Father?
If anyone is not corrected by You, then they are not Your child,
    They are illegitimate children, and not Your true children.
Moreover, many have had wicked human fathers who corrected them,
    Therefore, I ought to be willing to submit to You—my
        heavenly Father.

My human father's punishment prepared me for life on earth,
>But You are preparing me to live a holy life and for Heaven itself.

Punishment isn't enjoyable at the time I get it,
>But it makes me live right and submit to the laws of men
>So I will live in peace and develop character.

Therefore, I'll hold up under Your discipline,
>So I'll not be weak, but strong.

Lord, I'll do everything possible to live peaceably with everyone,
>And I'll live a holy life, because without it no one will see You.

I will make sure other believers don't miss Your grace,
>And that no bitterness grows in the church
>That causes trouble and poisons the assembly.

I will make sure no one is sexually immoral or ungodly
>Like Esau who sold his inheritance for one meal.

Afterward Esau wanted his inheritance but was rejected
>Even though he begged for it with tears.

Amen.

The Presence of Jesus Is Better

Hebrews 12:18-24

Lord, we don't come to a mountain that burned with fire
>To a religion that is dark and gloomy
>To receive the first system of law, i.e., the old covenant.

We don't listen to a trumpet blast that was so scary
>That the people begged it to stop.

We don't stay away from a mountain, "So that even if an animal
>Touched the mountain, it had to be stoned."

The experience was so terrifying that Moses said,
>"I am afraid" and he trembled with fear.

Lord, I come to Mount Zion, Your city, and the heavenly Jerusalem,
    I come into Your holy presence
    Where millions of angels gather to worship You.
I come with the church, right into Your city-heaven itself,
    Where everyone is a first-class citizen.
I come to You—Father—the judge of all people;
    I join the spirits of all the redeemed who possess their inheritance.
I come to Jesus, the Mediator of the new covenant,
    Whose blood intercedes better than Abel's sacrifice.

Sixth Warning of Future Judgment

Hebrews 12:25-29

Lord, I will never refuse to listen to You when You speak
    As those who refused to listen to You and were punished.
How much more will those be punished
    Who go back to Temple worship?
In the future You will send an earthquake to shake the earth;
    You promised, "Once more I will send an earthquake,
    Not to shake the earth only, but Heaven also."
Lord, this means at the final earthquake,
    Everything will be removed that is not permanent;
    Only the things made by You will remain.
Lord, I am part of the Kingdom that is unshakeable
    Therefore, I will serve You with thankfulness.
I will worship You, but always with reverence and fear,
    Because the fire of Your judgment always burns.

Amen.

Faith in Jesus Is the Better Way

Hebrews 13:1-25

Lord, I will love Christians with brotherly love
    And I will be hospitable to strangers because
    Some have entertained angels without realizing it.
I will be concerned for those in prison, as though I were there,
    And I will remember those who are ill-treated
    Because I know how they feel.
I will honor the sanctity of the marriage vows
    Because the marriage bed should be kept pure;
    You will punish the adulterer and sexually immoral people.
I will live free from greedy lust for money,
    And be content with what I have. Because You promise,
"You will be my helper, I will not be afraid
    Of what anyone can do to me."

I will respect church leaders who teach the Word of God,
    I will remember their example and will imitate their godliness.
Lord, I rejoice that Jesus Christ is always the same,
    Yesterday, today and will continue forever.
I will not be side-tracked by strange new doctrines,
    I realize my spiritual strength comes from You, and
    I will not become godly by any rules I keep.
I am fed by the food that Christ gives me,
    No one can get spiritual strength by going back to the Temple;
    Those who do, won't be fed by Christ.
The bodies of animals whose blood is still used for sacrifice
    Were burned outside the city of Jerusalem,
So Jesus suffered outside the gate of Jerusalem
    To offer His blood for me and all who come to Him for salvation.
I will go to Him outside the Temple and outside the city walls,
    There to identify with Him, and bear His shame.

I realize there is no permanent city for me in this life,
      I look for an eternal city that will come in the future.
Therefore, I will offer my worship to You through Jesus;
      May my worship magnify Your name.
Also, I will continue to do good deeds and share with others
      Because You are pleased with that sacrifice.

Lord, I will continue to obey my church leaders and follow their directions
      Because they give an account to You
      Of how well they watch over my soul and others.
I will obey them so they will enjoy their ministry
      Because I would be the loser if I caused them grief.
I know that my conscience is clear in this matter,
      And I will act honorably in every way.

The writer asked for prayer that he could visit the readers,
      Now may You—the God of Peace—the One
      Who brought the Lord Jesus back from the dead,
      To become the Great Shepherd of the sheep,
Equip me thoroughly to do Your perfect will,
      By the blood of the everlasting covenant.
Lord, work in me everything that will please You;
      To Jesus Christ be glory forever and ever, Amen.

The writer asked the readers to listen patiently to this letter
      Because it is a short one.
He tells them Timothy has been released from prison
      And will come to see them;
      Also, he the writer will come with Timothy.
The Christians in Italy who are with the writer
      Send greetings to the readers.
Lord, I ask for Your grace and receive it by faith.

          Amen.

JAMES

PRAYING THE BOOK OF JAMES
1:1–5:20

Chapter 53

THE STORY OF WRITING THE BOOK OF JAMES

James was a tall man with broad shoulders and big bones. His beard was now grey with age because he had endured many pressures as the elder of the church in Jerusalem. Beyond that he had seen much suffering by Christians in Jerusalem for the cause of Christ.

After Jesus was born to Mary, James was the next born to Mary; he was the legitimate son of Joseph, having been conceived by them and born a natural birth.

There came a time when Jesus left his boyhood home to begin his ministry by gathering disciples. James assumed the head of the household and gave direction to his brothers and sisters. Because James led the family, church leadership came natural to him.

After Jesus was raised from the dead, He appeared to James with a special message. No one knows what Jesus told His half-brother James, but James did become leader of the church in Jerusalem after that. It was that appearance that solidified James' fate so that he became unshakeable in all that he did. He was called "the just" and was an austere man with great legal understanding and a reverence for history.

James didn't spend a lot of time chatting with Christians and he was known as a man of few words. But he spent much time in prayer, so much time on his knees they developed huge calluses. He was nicknamed "old camel knees."

One thing James knew for sure, Christians were being persecuted all over the world. He heard quickly about the stoning death of Stephen and that he could be next. James knew that the head of the apostle James had been cut off and he could be next. He also knew that Saul, a young Pharisee from the Sanhedrin, had gone house to house arresting Christians, charging them before the Sanhedrin with crimes punishable by death. (That was before Paul's conversion.) Would he be imprisoned?

Because James had faced all types of persecution—real and imagined—he was qualified to encourage other believers who were facing sufferings. So James picked up a quill to write to Christians who were being persecuted for the cause of Christ, "Friends, don't be surprised if you suffer, as a matter of fact, rejoice in trials...."

Praying the Book of James

Preparing for Trials
James 1:1-27

Lord, James wrote a letter to Jews who were being persecuted
    And were scattered abroad outside the Holy Land;
    James wanted to prepare Christians everywhere for suffering.

Lord, I will rejoice when I suffer for You
    Even when I fall into every type of trial
    Because I know trials will build patience in me.
Lord, let patience have its perfect work in me
    That I may have complete faith, wanting nothing.
Lord, when I lack wisdom, I will ask You for it
    Because You liberally give us spiritual understanding
    And I know I will receive it from You.
But, I must ask with unwavering faith
    Because those who are unstable are like the
    Unpredictable waves of the ocean, driven by the wind.
The vacillating man will not receive anything from You
    Because a double-minded person is unstable in everything.

Lord, when I humble myself and take the low position,
    You will lift me up for Your purpose.

Those who exalt themselves as the rich shall be like
      The flower that is temporality here, then dies and is gone;
Because the sun burns them and they wither with the grass,
      Their beauty is destroyed in the same scorching heat.
      In the same way the proud will be destroyed.

Lord, bless me as I endure the trials that try me
      Because I will receive the crown of life for enduring persecution
      Which You have promised to those who continually love You.
When I am tempted to give up, I can't say You tempt me.
      For You do not tempt anyone to evil actions.
People are tempted by their own sinful desires
      That drag them away and entice them to sin.
When evil lust is planted and grown, it brings forth sin;
      And when sin is fully grown, it brings death.

Lord, I don't want to be deceived. I know every good gift
      Is from above; coming down from You, the Father of Light.
Lord, You give me spiritual birth through the word of truth
      That I might be a firstfruit of praise to Your glory.

Lord, I will be quick to listen, slow to speak,
      And even slower to become angry, because anger
      Does not produce a righteous life.
Therefore, I will get rid of all moral filth and
      Evil intent that is prevalent everywhere. I will
      Humbly accept the implanted Word which saves me.
I will not merely listen to the Word because that
      Is not enough. I will do what it says.
Those who merely listen to the Word and don't obey it
      Are like people who look at themselves in a mirror
      And forget what they see.
Lord, I want to look intently into the perfect law of liberty;
      I know You will bless me if I don't forget what I see there
      And I continue to obey what I learn there.

Lord, those who appear to be religious, but can't control their speech,
> Their religion is empty.
To have pure religion and be clean before You,
> I must minister to the needs of orphans and widows
> And keep myself unspotted from the world.

Lord, I've only had soft persecution in my life
> *And I realize it's nothing compared to those who suffer terribly.*
Help me to see Your presence and will in every uncomfortable situation;
> *I will look for Your guiding hand in the sufferings of life.*

Amen.

Our Good Works Demonstrate Our Faith

James 2:1-26

My Lord Jesus Christ, I will not segregate myself for any person
> But will accept all people equally before You.
I will not show partiality to those who are rich, or finely dressed,
> Nor will I look down on those who are poor and dirty.
Lord, You will not bless those who accept only people in rich apparel
> And reject the poor by making them sit in a segregated place
> Or stand in the back of the crowd.
Those who show partiality are judged by their evil thoughts;
> I will accept all people equally, and
> I reject those who segregate themselves against any.
Lord, I know you love the poor of this world,
> Many of whom are rich in faith and heirs of Your Kingdom,
> Which you promise to all who love Jesus.
Those who despise the poor will eventually have some rich man
> Oppress them and deliver them to judgment.
These rich men blaspheme the very name of Christ,
> By whom all believers are called.

Lord, I will obey the second part of the royal law found in Scripture;
  I will love my neighbors as I love myself.
But if I reject anyone I am guilty of sin,
  And I have broken the Law.
If I keep the whole Law, but break just one point,
  I have broken all the Law.
Lord, you said "Do not commit adultery," and "Do not kill;"
  If I do not commit adultery, but I kill,
  Then I am a transgressor of the whole Law.
I will live by the Law, and speak it;
  Because I know I will be judged by it.
Lord, I know you will judge without mercy
  Those who have shown no mercy;
  But those who show mercy will persevere in judgment.

Lord, I know it is not good to minister by faith
  If I don't have good works to go with my faith.
If a brother or sister doesn't have bread and is naked,
  And I say go in peace be fed and be clothed,
But I do not give them what they need,
  What good is my faith?
Lord, if my faith doesn't result in good works,
  It is dead because it has no fruit.
If I tell anyone you have faith, and I have works,
  You will try to show me your faith without works
  And I will show you my faith by my works.
You can say that you have faith because you believe in God,
  That's all right, the devils believe in God but they tremble;
  You can't prove you have faith without works.

Lord, I realize our father Abraham was justified by works
  Which he demonstrated when he offered his son on an altar;
  Therefore, he demonstrated perfect faith by works.
Then the Scripture was fulfilled which said,

Abraham believed in God and it was counted to him as righteousness
Therefore, he was called a friend of God.
Now, I see how a person is justified by works,
Not by faith only.
Lord, I realize Rehab the harlot was justified by works,
Because she protected the Jewish messengers
And directed them away from the soldiers of Jericho.
Therefore, just as a body without a soul is dead,
So faith without works is also dead.

Lord, thank You for the deep faith You've put within me;
I'll serve You with all my heart
For I realize my deep faith is nothing
If good works don't automatically flow from my faith.

Amen.

We Must Control Our Tongue

James 3:1-18

Lord, I don't want to be a teacher in position only
Because teachers are judged by a higher standard.
I know that I offend in many ways;
If anyone doesn't offend by their speech
They are perfect because when they control their mouth,
They control their whole body.
People put bits in horse's mouths to control them,
This is the way to turn around a horse.
A great ship is driven through the sea by fierce winds,
Yet they are turned around with a small rudder;
The ship goes wherever the captain decides.
In the same way, the tongue is a little thing
But it can boast great things and cause great trouble;

It's like a little flame that can start a great fire.
Therefore, my tongue can spread sin throughout my body
    Just like a little flame can start a forest fire.
So my tongue can defile my entire life,
    Not realizing it is a fire from hell.
People have been able to tame every kind of animal,
    And birds and snakes, and things in the sea,
But no one is able to tame the tongue;
    It is uncontrollably evil and deadly poison.
With my tongue I can bless You, even the Father,
    Or I can curse people who are made in Your image.
Out of the same mouth comes blessings and curses, this is wrong;
    Can a fountain give salt water and fresh water? Obviously not!
    Can a fig tree produce olives? Obviously not!
    Can an olive branch produce figs? Again no!
    So I will not bless God and curse men!
If there is a wise man, I want to see his wisdom
    In his conversation with other people;
    I want to see his meekness and wisdom by the things he says.
Lord, those who are bitter, and envious and start arguments
    Are full of self glory and they lie against the truth.
Their wisdom doesn't come from Heaven,
    But comes from the earth, it is fleshly and devilish
    Because they produce arguments, and confusion and evil.
Lord, give me the wisdom that is from above, it is pure,
    Then peaceable, genteel, and will listen to others.
I want wisdom that is full of mercy and good fruits;
    It doesn't have partiality to anyone
    And it is not hypocritical.
Lord, I want the fruit of righteousness that is sown in peace;
    I want to be a peacemaker.

Lord, I can discipline many areas of my life
    But the most difficult to control is my tongue.

I know it's not the physical tongue itself, but my deceitful old nature;
Strengthen me to discipline my old nature so my tongue will
glorify You.

Amen.

The Danger of Worldliness

James 4:1-17

Lord, I will not fight other believers, because these battles
Come from our old nature that makes Christians fight one another.
When I lust, I don't get what I want. People destroy others
And don't get what they want. People fight and argue
And still don't get the things they want.
I do not have what I pray for because I don't ask rightly,
Sometimes I ask and don't get what I request
Because I ask wrongly to satisfy my lust.

Lord, teach me the right things in life that I need,
Then help me to ask You for them in the right way.

Lord, you've told us that people who commit adultery
Are friends of the world and they hate You;
Help me realize those who are friends of the world are Your enemies.
Lord, I know the Holy Spirit in me has a strong desire
That I live a holy and godly life;
So let the Spirit give me more grace to repent of evil.
I know You said You give grace to those who humble themselves
But You resist the proud.
Lord, I will submit myself to You, I will resist the devil
So that he will flee from me and I'll have power from You.

Lord, I will not speak evil of other believers,
Those who say evil things about a believer

And judge a believer, actually hate the Law.
The Law prohibits me from judging one another
    And those who don't obey the Law actually hate the Law.

Lord, You are the only Lawgiver and I am accountable to You,
    You are able to free or judge, and You judge correctly;
    Take away all bitterness and give me love for all.

Lord, I will not say that tomorrow I'll go to a certain city
    And live there a year, buying and selling different things;
    That's because I don't know what will happen tomorrow.
What is my life? It is like steam from a kettle that's seen for
    A short time then it disappears.
Therefore, here is what I'll say, "If You will, I will live;
    And I'll do certain things within Your plan for my life."
"I will not take confidence in my boasting,
    Because boasting is evil;
    Since I know what good You want me to do, it's evil if I don't do it."

Amen.

Because the Lord Is Coming—Pray

James 5:1-20

Lord, I know that all proud people will soon suffer misery,
    Therefore, they ought to weep and moan for coming judgment.
The riches they trusted in are corrupt
    And their fancy clothes are moth-eaten.
The tarnish on their gold is a witness against them;
    Their treasures will condemn them
    And their flesh shall be eaten with fire.
Lord, you hear the weeping of the workers who
    Harvest the field of the rich who defraud them.
The rich live in pleasure and fulfill their lust,

The rich condemn and "eat up" just people who do not resist them
But the rich have only fattened themselves for slaughter.
Lord, at the same time, the poor must be patient until You come,
Just as the farmer waits for his fruit to grow,
Waiting through the spring and fall rain,
So the poor must wait for Your coming judgment.
Lord, I'll not envy what other people have
Because You are the Judge standing at the door.
I will learn from the prophets who have spoken Your word;
They were blessed because they endured trials,
They are my example to teach me patience in suffering.

Lord, I have heard of the patience of Job and I know
What You do for those who endure suffering.
You are very tender and kind to them;
Lord, when I'm not patient, help me endure all my circumstances.

Lord, I will not swear in trials or pain
Neither by Heaven or earth;
I will let my *yes* be *yes* and my *no* mean *no*!
Because I don't want to be condemned by my speech.

Lord, I will pray when I am afflicted, and if I'm wrongly merry,
I'll read the Psalms to understand the severity of life.

When I am sick, I will call for the elders of the church
So they can pray over me and anoint me with oil in Your name.
I know the prayer of faith will save the sick
And You will raise them up.
If the sick will confess their sins, and pray one for another,
The sick will be healed and when they have committed sins,
They will be forgiven.

Lord, I know the continuous sincere prayer
Of a righteous man will accomplish much.

Elijah was a man subject to the same weakness as me,
      But he prayed continually that it might not rain
      And it didn't rain for three and a half years.
Elijah prayed again and You gave rain from Heaven
      And the earth brought forth fruit.
Lord, if any believer strays from the truth and You restore him,
      You not only turn around a sinner from his error
You save a soul from death
      And hide a multitude of sins.

Lord, I try to pray but I'm not very effective;
      I want to know the secret of power in prayer.
I know the secret is not in the mechanics of how I say it,
      Nor is there power in my actual words I say,
      Power is in You, and prayer is relationship with You.

Amen.

First Peter

Praying the Book of First Peter 1:1–5:14

Chapter 54

THE STORY OF WRITING THE BOOK OF FIRST PETER

The shackles cut Peter's wrists as the Roman soldiers jerked him by the chains through the city gate leading away from Rome. It was then when Peter saw the terrible holocaust before his eyes. He saw hundreds of crosses and he heard the moans and cries of those being tortured, so Peter knew his fate. There were crosses on both sides of the road, stretching all the way to the top of the hill, almost a mile away. Hundreds of crosses...and on most of them were dead Christians left to rot in the Mediterranean sun with others still suffering. This was Rome's way of warning anyone not to become a Christian.

Peter knew his fate; he would be crucified like His Lord. He yelled back to his wife, also in shackles being pulled through the gate, "Keep the faith." But she couldn't hear him because of her torment.

Peter hoped that when they would crucify him their vengeance would be satisfied and somehow they would let his wife go. But the Romans had more torment for Peter than he imagined. Right there before his eyes he saw the soldiers slam his wife's body onto a cross, then callously nail her hands and feet in place. Peter had not seen the Roman soldiers nail the Lord to the cross, but he saw it in his heart. Peter closed his eyes as he heard,

"TWANG...TWANG...TWANG..."

As bad as this torture was, it was not the worse moment of his life. Peter thought back over 35 years ago on the night when he denied Jesus three times. Peter remembered the third time denying the Lord with curses. Just as he denied Him, the soldiers brought Jesus by. When Peter's eyes caught the eyes of Jesus, he was devastated. The worse moment in his life was failing the Lord.

And then Peter remembered that morning breakfast on the shore of Galilee. Jesus asked him three times, "Do you love Me more than these ...?"[1] Peter had to confess that he hadn't loved the Lord with all his heart—again that was an embarrassing moment.

"Up she goes," the gruff Roman soldier grunted and the cross bearing Peter's wife was lifted high and dropped into its place. Another soldier grabbed Peter's head and forced him to watch. He knew that his wife would die shortly, she was a frail woman. He knew that she would go to be with Jesus. Even though his heart ached for his wife, Peter's soul was at peace.

"You, next," the Roman leader pointed to Peter with his whip, and to add to the pain, slapped him across the face.

"Not like my Lord," Peter appealed to the soldiers. "I don't want to die like Jesus died."

"Ha-ha," the Roman soldier laughed at him, "but you're gonna die."

"I'm not worthy to die like Jesus," Peter pleaded with the men, and then requested, "Crucify me upside down."

The soldiers laughed and then the leader said, "What an ingenious idea, you'll be tortured all the more." Immediately the soldiers began to make preparation to crucify Peter upside down. Peter was numb from all the torture he had endured, so he didn't feel the spikes; but he heard the sound.

"TWANG...TWANG...TWANG..."

It's as though Peter didn't feel the spikes tearing through his veins, and as though his feet were untouched. His mind was elsewhere. He was going to see Jesus.

"UP HE GOES," the leading soldiers yelled to the others, Peter was much heavier to lift into place than his wife. "This is it," Peter thought, "I'm going to finally die." Peter reviewed his service for Jesus Christ.

He remembered preaching the great sermon on the day of Pentecost. Peter boldly accused the Jews of crucifying his Lord and Savior. It was then when 3,000 were converted and baptized in one day.

Peter thought about the days he spent in Antioch, that great missionary church. It was there where he had great ministry with Paul; those were glorious days of usefulness.

And then Peter remembered preaching to the Jewish Christians throughout Asia Minor—today Turkey—where Christians were suffering for their faith. He was able to encourage them in persecution to remain faithful until death. Now on the cross, Peter was practicing what he preached to believers in trials.

And then Peter remembered the glorious days he preached in Babylon to the great groups of Christians in that city on the Euphrates River—what is today called modern Iraq. In Babylon there was a Synagogue where 10,000 Jews would gather, and Christians could fill it up when they came to worship the Lord Jesus Christ.

Young John Mark was with Peter in Babylon; it was there where the young disciple began writing the Gospel of Mark. Peter kept telling Mark things that he remembered that Jesus did, and said. Mark was writing the story of Jesus through Peter's eyes.

The agony of the crucifixion tore away at Peter's conscience. The sun was unrelenting, soon he would pass out. "Come, Jesus," Peter breathed an inward prayer, "come back to earth to establish Your Kingdom now…if not, Lord, receive my soul into Paradise." And with that prayer, Peter died.

As Peter stepped from the world of consciousness into the valley of the shadow of death, Jesus met him. The Twenty-third Psalm had promised, "Yea, though I walk through the valley of the shadow of death…You are with me" (Ps. 23:4). So Peter passed from earthly life into eternal life to be with the Lord forever.

Endnote

1. John 21:15.

Your Full Salvation

1 Peter 1:1-25

Lord, Peter the apostle of Jesus Christ wrote a letter
> To Jewish Christians who were scattered throughout Turkey
> And to me who was chosen by Your foreknowledge.

Lord, I have also been sanctified by the Holy Spirit,
> And cleansed by the blood of Jesus Christ.

May I obey You in every thought and action,
> And enjoy Your grace and peace more and more.

Lord, I praise You, the God and Father of my Lord Jesus Christ,
> Because in Your great mercy I was born again into your family;
> I was given life by the resurrection of Jesus Christ.

Now may I have confidence in my perfect inheritance,
> Reserved in Heaven for me that will not decay or change.

Through faith I am guarded by Your power
> Until the coming of Your complete salvation
> That will be revealed by Jesus Christ in the last day.

So I am truly glad this wonderful hope is ahead
> Because I may have to suffer all kinds of trials on earth.

I know that when Jesus Christ is revealed, my faith, though tested,
> Will be genuine like gold, and bring praise, and glory to You
> When Jesus Christ returns to earth.

I love Christ even though I have never seen Him with my eyes;
> Though not seeing Him I trust Him more because
> He has filled me with joy that can only come from You.

I know my future reward for trusting Christ
> Will be the salvation of my soul in the final day.

Lord, even the prophets didn't fully understand this salvation
    Even though they wrote about it;
    They had many questions about the meaning of Scripture.
They didn't understand what Your Spirit within them was saying
    When they wrote the prediction of the coming suffering of Christ,
    And they wrote of the glory that He would have afterward.
The prophets were told these events would not happen in their lifetime,
    But would occur many years later.
Now Lord, these events have happened and have been communicated to all of us
    By those who have preached the Gospel to us;
    Now the angels, like us, have studied these predictions to know Your plan.
Therefore, I will not let my thinking be sidetracked,
    Nor will I live in the future and ignore the present.
I will obey Your truth, and will not be conformed
    To the evil desires that controlled my life before I was saved.
I will live a holy life, just as You who called me to salvation is holy,
    Because the Bible says, "Be holy because God is holy."

Lord, I know that You—my Heavenly Father—have no favorites,
    Therefore, I will pray boldly with reverence,
    Knowing You will judge all people fairly.
I know I was not redeemed with gold and silver that perishes,
    From my meaningless life before I was saved.
But I was redeemed with the precious blood of Christ
    Who was a sacrificial lamb without blemish or spot.
Lord, You chose Him before creation for this purpose,
    But only in time did You reveal Him to us.
Now I have new life because You raised Christ from the dead,
    And glorified Him. Now I have hope beyond the grave.
Therefore, I will separate myself from sin and obey Your truth,
    And I will love believers with all my heart.
I was born again to new life, not from earthly parents,

Who give physical life that will eventually die.
But I was born again to new life that will last for eternity,
    That comes from the Word of God.
Yes, I know our physical life will pass away as the grass;
    Grass withers, flowers die, but Your Word of God stands forever,
    I put my trust in this Word that was preached to me.

Lord, Peter tells me about the greatness of Your salvation;
    Take away my spiritual blindness; help me see all You've done for me,
    Then help me live daily for Your glory.

Amen.

Live Holy Because of Christ's Death

1 Peter 2:1-25

Lord, I repent of all known sin in my life,
    I will not lie, slander anyone, or be jealous of them.
Like a newborn baby, I thirst for Your pure Word;
    I want to taste Your goodness
So I can grow to the fullness of salvation.
Indeed, I come daily to Christ for spiritual strength,
    He's the Rock rejected by unsaved people,
    But chosen because He is precious to You, the Father.
Now I am a living stone that's building Your house,
    But I'm also a holy priest offering worship to You.
As You said in Scripture, "Behold, I lay in Zion,
    Christ as My precious cornerstone."
But Christ the primary cornerstone is a stumbling block to the unsaved,
    And a stone used in execution to those who reject Him,
    But I am not disappointed in the One whom I believe.
Now Lord, I am part of a chosen people, a royal priesthood,
    A dedicated citizen of Heaven, and one claimed by You.

You have set me apart to proclaim the triumphs of Christ
        Who has called me out of darkness into marvelous light.
I am part of the people of God—a saved Gentile—
        Who once was not Your particular people, but now I belong to You,
        Who was outside of Your mercy, but now I have mercy.

Lord, I will keep myself free from self-destructive passions
        Because I am a pilgrim in a foreign land.
I will behave honorably among unsaved people
        So they can see for themselves my good works;
So that when the day of judgment comes,
        They will remember the things they now criticize.

I will submit myself to human institutions for Your sake,
        And especially to the government
        Because they are Your representatives to punish lawbreakers.
Lord, it is Your will that my good testimony
        Silence what fools have said about You in ignorance.
I am a slave to no one except You; I'll live free
        And I'll never use my freedom as an excuse to sin.
I will respect everyone, and I love the church, and fear You,
        And I keep the laws of my government.

Lord, I realize Christian employees must be respectful and obedient
        To their bosses, not only when the bosses are kind to them,
        But also when the bosses are cruel and demanding.

There is a reward for putting up with undeserved punishment
        When it is done for Christ's sake.
But there is no Christian reward when I'm punished
        Because I've done something wrong and deserve punishment.
My reward comes when I accept punishment patiently
        And do my duty, even when I don't deserve punishment.
Because when Christ suffered undeservedly for me,
        He left me an example that I should follow His steps.

Christ did not threaten to get even when He was tortured,
    But committed Himself to You, the Father, who will judge rightly.
Christ suffered for my sins on the Cross
    So I could repent of my sins and live a godly life;
    Through His wounds, I have been healed.
I was straying like a lost sheep, but now
    I have come back to the Shepherd and Protector of my soul.

Lord, Christ has provided a great salvation for me,
    He makes me live holy as a saved person should live.

Amen.

The Sufferings of Christ

1 Peter 3:1-22

Lord, You tell a married woman to be obedient to her husband
    So that if he refuses to obey the Word of God,
He may be won to Christ by his wife's godly behavior
    Because her holy life speaks louder than her words.
You tell women not to dress up to show off,
    And they should not try to be spiritual,
    Depending on jewelry, lovely clothes and hair arrangement.
They must be beautiful inwardly, with a gentile spirit
    And a quiet appearance, which is what You want.
That kind of inward beauty was seen in women of the past
    Who trusted You and submitted to their husbands.
Sarah is an example who obeyed Abraham, calling him Lord;
    Women today can become her descendent by doing what is right
    And not worrying their husbands or giving them anxiety.

Lord, you tell husbands to treat their wives with respect
    And honor them as the weaker vessel,

Because husband and wife are heirs together of the grace of life;
      When the husband does this, his prayers will not be hindered.

Lord, I will live in harmony with other believers,
      I will be sympathetic, love all believers, be compassionate and
      humble.
Lord, I will never repay wrong with wrong, or a curse with a curse,
      Instead, I will repay a curse with a blessing;
      That is what You call me to do, and I will be blessed by You.
Lord, because I want a happy life and enjoy prosperity,
      I will not let my tongue lie, and become deceitful.
I will turn away from evil and will do good;
      I will try to live peaceably and hold on to it when I catch it,
Because You are watching me and listening to my prayers,
      But You frown on those who do evil.

Usually no one tries to hurt me when I do good,
      But if they do try to hurt me, You will reward me;
      I will not be afraid of them or their threats.
I will hold the Lord Jesus reverently in my heart
      And when someone asks why I believe as I do,
      I'll tell them a reason for the hope I have in Christ.
But I'll give my answer with courtesy and respect
      So that when attackers curse me, they will become ashamed
      When they see my exemplary life and conduct.
If it is Your will that I suffer,
      It is better that I suffer for doing right instead of wrong.

Lord, thank You that Christ once suffered for my sins,
      The just for the unjust, that He might bring me to You,
      Being put to death in the flesh, but raised by the Spirit.
Christ descended into hell to preach to people in prison
      Because they were disobedient to You and refused to repent,
Like those who rejected Noah's preaching, even when
      You waited patiently while Noah was building the ark.

But only eight persons were saved from that terrible flood;
> The flood was a symbol of baptism; the water is a picture of
> > judgment;

It is a picture of the judgment for sin that Christ suffered on the Cross,
> Whereby we received cleansing for our sins by His death.

And we received the promise of eternal life because Christ was resurrected;
> Then He entered Heaven to sit at God's right hand,
> And now angels and Heaven are subject to Him.

Lord, my suffering is nothing compared to what Christ suffered;
> *Now I have access to all spiritual blessing because of His death.*

Amen.

Attitudes About Suffering

1 Peter 4:1-19

Lord, I know Christ suffered when He was tortured,
> Therefore I will also be ready to suffer for my faith;
> I will have the same attitude as Christ.

I will not suffer in my body because of personal sin,
> Therefore I won't let sin have domination over me;
> I will always do Your will.

I have lived too long to go back to my unsaved ways, giving myself to
> Sex, debauchery, drunkenness, orgies, and worshiping idols.

My unsaved friends think I'm strange for not indulging myself
> In the same evil activities that they do,
> They laugh at me in scorn.

But they will have to give account to You who judges the living and dead,
> Then they will be punished for the way they lived.

This is why the Gospel was preached to those who died in the flood;
> Their physical life suffered in the flood,
> But their spirits live so they will appear before You in judgment.

The world will soon come to an end, and

I will be clear-minded and self-disciplined so I can pray
> For all who don't know You and do Your will.
I will love everyone because love makes up for my faults;
> I will feed and give hospitality to those who need it.
You have given me special abilities; I will use them to help others,
> Being careful to pass on Your kindness.
If You call me to preach, I will allow You to speak though me;
> If You lead me to help others, I will do it in Your strength.
Lord, I want You to be glorified in my life through Jesus Christ;
> To Christ be glory and power, forever and ever, Amen.

I will not be surprised when painful trials come,
> Because trials are not an unusual thing for Christians.
I will be glad that I can suffer as did Christ,
> Then I will rejoice when His glory is revealed.
When people curse and blaspheme me as a Christian,
> I will have Your blessing resting on me.
My suffering will not be for crimes such as murder or theft,
> Or even for sins, such as hurting people or gossiping.
When I suffer as a Christian, I will not be ashamed
> But will praise You that I bear Christ's name.
Time will come when judgment begins among God's followers,
> If I will be judged for my failures,
> How much more will the unsaved be judged?
If the righteous will barely make it through judgment,
> How much more punishment will the ungodly have?
So, when I suffer for doing Your will, I will keep doing right;
> I will trust my soul to You, the faithful Creator,
> For You will never fail me.

Lord, I'm not good with suffering,
> *And I don't like to be hurt physically or emotionally;*
> *But if I have to suffer for You, I will count it a privilege.*

Amen.

Serving Christ in View of His Return

1 Peter 5:1-14

Lord, Peter spoke to church elders, because he was an elder,
     A witness of Christ's suffering, and one who will share in His glory.
Peter told elders to feed the flock that God has entrusted to them,
     Ministering as overseers, not because they must,
     But because they are willing to do what You want them to do.
Peter told them, "Don't do it for money, but serve eagerly;
     Don't be dictators over God's people, but be an example
     That everyone in the flock can follow."
"When the Chief Shepherd shall appear,
     They'll receive a Crown of Glory that will never tarnish."

Peter told the younger men to follow the leadership of the older men;
     The rest were to clothe themselves in humility but serve one
          another;
Because You oppose the proud but give grace to the humble,
     Therefore, I will bow before You, so You can lift me up.

I will put the weight of all my problems on You,
     I will be watchful for attacks from my enemy, satan;
     He prowls as a hungry lion, looking for prey to feed upon.
I will stand firm against satan, knowing Christians throughout the world
     Are undergoing all types of suffering.
After I suffer for a while on this earth,
     You who have grace, will call me to an eternal glory of Christ.
But now You can protect me, make me stronger, and confirm me;
     To You be all power, forever and ever. Amen.

I am encouraged to learn how you bless believers
     Who are going through the same kind of sufferings that try me;
     Therefore I will stand firm.
Peter sent this letter by Silas, whom he trusted;

The church in Babylon sent greetings along with Mark,
Greeting all believers in all peace;
Peace to all in Christ.

Lord, I never like to think about suffering,
    But Peter reminds me that all Christians will have some suffering;
    Help me suffer in Your will, to Your glory.

Amen.

SECOND PETER

PRAYING THE BOOK OF SECOND PETER
1:1–3:18

Chapter 55

THE STORY OF WRITING THE BOOK OF SECOND PETER

Simon Peter sat with several of his students as he taught them about Jesus Christ. He was describing the sermons of Jesus when a student spoke up, "There are teachers in the church that claim Jesus was not fully God." The student wanted to know how to answer those who said, "Jesus was a spirit from God, but not God Himself."

Then to prove to the students that Jesus was God, Peter described the transfiguration of Jesus on the mount, "No other person has ever been supernaturally changed so that His face shone like the sun and His garment sparkled."

Then Peter reinforced the point by adding he heard the Father speak from Heaven, "This is My beloved Son in whom I am well pleased."

The student answered Peter, "You must write that story in a book so we can answer those who teach false doctrine."

Peter nodded his head in agreement. The spreading grey covered his previous red hair. The twinkle in his eye told his students Peter was thinking how to answer them. Then Peter blurted out,

"I'll do it—I'll write a second epistle." Peter let his thoughts gush out, "I'll begin my second letter, 'Peter, a servant and apostle of Jesus Christ,' that way false teachers can't deny what I write. They must believe what I write."

Peter explained many of the false teachers were not children of God, "So I'll begin by explaining God has given us many precious promises in Scripture so we can receive a new divine nature—false teachers haven't been born again."

Then the eyes of Peter narrowed and the lines in his face hardened—not deep lines from fishing in stormy weather—but deep furrows that reflected his explosive temper. Peter's anger could erupt and boil over. "Those false teachers bring damnable heresies into the church. They're as despicable as the angels who were cast into hell, and as sexually corrupt as the homosexuals of Sodom and Gomorrah." Peter was angry because false teachers used false doctrine as an excuse for their shocking immorality. "I'll expose them," Peter's voice rose to emphasize his passion.

"And they don't think Jesus is coming back!" Peter told his students. "They mockingly asked—when is He coming?" Peter explained that his next epistle would show how false teachers would be punished at the second coming of Jesus Christ. Peter let a quiet smile overcome his anger, he reminded his students, "The Lord is not slack concerning His promises...."

Peter rose to leave his students, announcing, "I must begin immediately. I'll write a second epistle so each one of you will have an authoritative answer when false teachers raise foolish questions in the church."

With that, Peter abruptly left the room to begin writing. It fit his impetuous nature; every thought became an immediate action.

The students knew their teacher well. They knew that shortly Peter would emerge with a letter to protect the churches from heresy. Whereas Luke wrote from research, and Matthew wrote from a daily journal he kept of Jesus' action, Peter would pour out words from his fiery temperament, and his letter would rip the backs of false teachers like the punishing thongs of an executioner's whip.

Then Peter reminded his students that Jesus once asked him, "Who do you say that I am?" Peter's eyes twinkled, "It's the same answer—Jesus is our Messiah, the Son of the living God."

Praying the Book of Second Peter

Learning Virtue From the Scriptures

2 Peter 1:1-21

Lord, teach me to be as bold as Simon Peter
    Who wrote a letter addressed to Christians who
    Had obtained the same precious faith as he received.
Lord, I too have that precious faith and I stand
    In Your righteousness and of my Savior, Jesus Christ.
May Your grace and peace be multiplied in my life
    As I grow in knowing You and the Lord Jesus.
Your divine power has given me all things that relate
    To life and godliness, so I will grow as I
    Know You who called me to a life of excellence and goodness.

You have given me Your precious promises that
    Through the Word of God I have received a divine nature
    Which is the new man with new desires to obey You.
Therefore, I will add character to my faith
    So I will do the right thing in the right way.
I will add Bible knowledge to my character
    So I will always know what to do to please You.
I will add self-control to my biblical knowledge
    So I will be steadfast in knowing and doing right.
I will add godliness to my biblical knowledge
    So that I'll have a basis to become more godly.
Finally, I will add brotherly love to my godliness
    So that my godly life results in a loving relationship to all.
When I abound in these traits, I will not be
    Ineffective or unfruitful in my walk on this earth.
Those Christians who don't have these godly traits are blind,
    They have forgotten that their former sins are forgiven.

I have been called to salvation and chosen by You;
> I will give diligence to demonstrate Your call in my life.

If I do all these things, there is no danger
> That I will ever fall away into sin,
>
> Then I will eventually be given admission to Your eternal Kingdom
> To live forever with my Lord and Savior, Jesus Christ.

Throughout eternity, You'll continually re-tell these truths to me,
> Even though I know them now and hold them firmly.

Peter said it is his duty to remind every one of these truths
> As long as he is in the body, i.e., the tent.

Peter knew his time to leave the tent was coming soon
> Just as the Lord Jesus predicted His death.

Therefore, Peter wrote these things so that after his departure,
> Believers everywhere would be able to recall these things.

Peter did not make up a myth when he
> Went preaching the power of the coming of the Lord Jesus Christ;
> Peter saw with his eyes the majesty of Jesus for himself.

Peter was on the Mount of Transfiguration when the Father spoke,
> "This is my beloved son, in whom I am well pleased;"
> Peter actually heard that voice with his ears.

Therefore, I hold more certain than ever the word of prophecy
> And I will give careful attention to that word
> For it shines like a bright light in a dark world.

It will shine until the day of Christ's return
> Which is the morning star arising in our hearts.

I understand and believe that no prophecy of Scripture
> Can be interpreted and understood in isolation,
> But every verse must be interpreted in light of the whole Scripture.

No word of prophecy was written by human initiative,
> Men who wrote the Bible were inspired
> By the Holy Spirit who wrote through them.

Lord, thank You for Your Word of God that saves me;
Help me to master the Scriptures, then meditate on them
And live a godly life that's taught therein.

Amen.

Warning Concerning Apostasy

2 Peter 2:1-22

Lord, there were false prophets living when the Bible was written
Just as there are false prophets today.
These false prophets will subtly introduce dangerous heresies,
They will deny You Who redeemed them
And eventually they will cause their own destruction.
Many will follow their filthy immorality,
And by their lives discredit the truth of God.
In their lust, they will try to make many people their disciples
But their foolish arguments make their judgment inevitable.
I know You didn't spare the angels that sinned
But bound them in chains and threw them in hell,
So they must wait for the judgment day.
And You didn't spare any of the people who lived before the flood;
You completely destroyed the world with a flood
Except Noah who spoke for You and his family of seven.

Later, You reduced the cities of Sodom and Gomorrah
Into a heap of rubble and completely destroyed them
As a fearful example to those who refuse to live by Your laws,
Yet, You saved Lot, and declared him righteous
Even when he was distressed at the sin of his day.
Lot saw and experienced the filthy sins as he lived among sinners,
And these sins tortured his soul day after day
Because You delivered Lot, I know for certain that You can

Rescue the righteous who are surrounded by temptation;
And I know that You reserve Your punishment
For the wicked until the day of judgment comes.

Lord, I know Your judgment is reserved for those
Who indulge in their lust and despise authority.
These are arrogant and presumptuous, they dare to
Scoff at the Glorious One, the Lord Jesus Christ.
Even the angels who are more powerful than they,
Never criticize these evil men before Your presence.
Lord, these evil men are as dumb as animals
Which You gave us to eat and do our work;
These men laugh at the great powers of the unseen world.
But they will be destroyed in their own corruption,
They will be destroyed with satan and the demons in hell.
These men who do their evil in broad daylight are cancerous spots
Who revel in sin even when they come to Your house to eat.
They look everywhere for adultery and seduce the unsuspecting;
They are cursed because they magnify their greed.
They have left the right path to follow
The path of Balaam who tried to profit from his sin.
The donkey rebuked Balaam with the voice of a man
To restrain him from his sin.

False teachers are like wells without water,
They are like storm clouds without rain;
The dark underworld is reserved for them.
With their proud works they tempt new converts
To return to sin, who have just escaped the world.
They use lust to coax new believers back into sin,
They promise freedom, but they are slaves themselves
Because they are dominated by sin.
Anyone who escapes the pollution of this world
And allows themselves to be enslaved again,

His second state is worse than his first one;
>It would have been better if he never learned the way of holiness.
He is like the proverb that says, "The dog returns to his own vomit," and
>"A pig that is washed returns to wallow in the mire."

Lord, thank You for salvation and a new desire to serve You.
>*I never want to return to sin;*
>*I promise I will always follow You and live a godly life.*

Amen.

The Return of Christ

2 Peter 3:1-18

Lord, Peter wrote this second letter, and in both letters
>He tried to motivate people to spiritual thinking
So they would remember the words of the prophets
>And keep the commandments of the apostles of the Lord Jesus Christ.
Peter wanted to remind them that scoffers would come
>In the last days following their own evil lust.
Scoffers will say, "Where is His coming?" They will add,
>"Ever since our fathers died, everything goes on as
>It has since the beginning of creation."
They deliberately close their eyes to the fact
>The earth was formed out of the waters by Your command.
They also forgot that the earth was covered by water
>And that the present Heaven and earth are being maintained by You,
>And that one day You will judge this earth by fire.

Lord, I believe You created all things and that you judged
>*The earth by water. I believe one day you will judge the*
>*World by fire. Help me live godly in light of Your coming.*

Lord, I will never forget that a day with You is a thousand years,
    And a thousand years is only a day.
I realize some people think You are slow about keeping Your promises,
    As some people measure slowness,
    You will keep Your promises in Your time.

Lord, I know You do not want anyone to perish
    But You want all people to repent and trust You for salvation.
Lord, You will come as a thief in the night
    When the heavens will pass away with a thunderous noise,
    And the elements will dissolve with fire,
    And the works on earth will be burned up with fire.
In view of all these things, I will live godly;
    I will live a good life, looking for Your return.
That is the day when the heavens will disintegrate with fire
    And all the elements will melt.
My hope is set on the new Heaven and new earth
    Which you have promised where the righteous will live.
I will wait in hope for these things, and be found in You
    Without blemish or spot at Your coming.
I know why You are waiting to return. You are giving us time
    To get this message of salvation to as many as possible.
    Paul wrote about these same things in his letters
    Yet some of his comments are not easy to understand.
    Some people who are unlearned and rebellious
    Deliberately have twisted his writings to mean
    Something quite different from what he meant,
Just as they do other Scriptures
    Which is disastrous to them.

Peter wrote to us about these false teachers so we can watch for them,
    And not be fooled by them,
    But that we may stand firm on biblical doctrine.

I will grow in grace and in the knowledge of the Lord Jesus Christ,
To Him be all glory
Both now and forever.

Amen.

FIRST JOHN

PRAYING THE BOOK OF FIRST JOHN
1:1–5:21

Chapter 56

THE STORY OF WRITING THE FIRST LETTER OF JOHN

The aged John saw heresy slipping into the early church. It stirred him to the depths of his soul. He decided to write a letter to the churches to warn them of false doctrine. John told his personal attendant Ansel,

"Many younger preachers don't realize that Jesus was fully man, yet fully God."

The old apostle explained that churches were being influenced with the philosophy of Greek gods. Just as their gods from Mount Olympus were half God and half human, some Christians ministers were preaching Jesus was half man and half God—an *eion*—somewhere between god and man, not fully God nor fully man.

John told Ansel, "I want to write a letter to be read to the churches so all believers will know the truth." This letter is what early Christians came to call *First John*.

Ansel said, "You must begin your letter with strong authority, like Paul began his letters." Then Ansel said that Paul began writing, "Paul, an apostle of Jesus Christ...." Ansel reminded that Paul's letters had the authority of an apostle. He suggested this letter should begin, "John, an apostle of Jesus Christ." That way everyone would pay attention to its message and believe it.

Old John shook his head negatively. "No," he said. He didn't want to begin egotistically or call attention to himself by using the introduction, "John, the apostle of Jesus Christ."

The old apostle knew everyone recognized he was an apostle, so he didn't have to say it.

Then Ansel said, "Begin the letter, 'From the apostle whom Jesus loved,' or 'The apostle who leaned his head on the breast of Jesus.'" Those were phrases John used to describe himself in the Gospel of John.

"No," was the simple answer of the beloved apostle. John had learned humility. He was a different man. He was no longer the fiery, young disciple who wanted to pray fire from Heaven on some listeners who would not receive Jesus. Jesus called young John "Son of Thunder" because his hot temper got him into trouble. In aged humility John didn't want to bring unnecessary attention to himself.

But young Ansel still argued, "How will they know this letter is from you?"

"Because I will send it by messenger to the church of Ephesus, and the messenger will tell them that I wrote it."

But Ansel still had a question. "The scribes of Ephesus will copy the letter, and it will be sent to all the other churches. Those reading the letter in other churches won't know it's you."

Old John beamed; his smiling wrinkled eyes reflected his ingenuity. "When people begin to read this letter, it will sound just like the introduction to the Gospel of John and everyone knows that I wrote that. So John began to write, "The Word existed from the beginning, we have heard it, we have seen it with our eyes and our hands have handled the Word of life...."

"There," John looked up from his writing to young Ansel, "doesn't that sound like me?" And then he pointed to the phrase, "From the beginning." "Readers will know this is the same way I began the Gospel of John."

Then John explained that Paul emphasized legal words in his letters, such as justified, adopted, pre-determined, and reconciled. Then John said, "The words I emphasize are different. I talk about family relationships and being children of God. I emphasize words like light, darkness, abide and verily, verily." John smiled, "Everyone will know I wrote this letter by its vocabulary."

Fellowship With the Father Because of the Incarnation of Christ

1 John 1:1-10

Lord, I have heard the message that is from the beginning,
>Which my spiritual eyes have seen and looked upon,
>And my hands have handled—the WORD OF LIFE.
Eternal life was manifested to me, I have seen it;
>And now I witness to others
>And tell them about eternal life
>Which was with You the Father, and manifested to me.
That which I've seen and heard, I tell others
>That they may have fellowship with me
>As I have fellowship with You,
>And with Your Son, Jesus Christ.

Lord, I worship You because You are light
>And there is absolutely no darkness in You;
>So now I declare this message to everyone.

Lord, if I tell people that I have fellowship with You
>Yet walk in darkness, I lie; and deny the truth.
But when I walk in the light as You are the light,
>I have fellowship with other believers, and the blood of Jesus Christ
>Cleanses me of all my sins.

Lord, if I tell people I have no sin in me,
>I deceive myself, and I don't have Your truth.
When I confess my sins, You are faithful
>To forgive my sins, and cleanse me from all unrighteous.
If I were to say I've never sinned one time,
>I make You a liar, and Your Word doesn't control me.

Lord, because of everything
You've done for me,
I'll love You and live for You.

Test of Fellowship With the Father

1 John 2:1-29

Lord, because You told me not to sin, I won't do it;
But when I slip and sin once, Jesus Christ stands
At Your right hand to plead forgiveness for me.
I know Jesus has forgiven all my sin
And He didn't die for me alone, but for the whole world.
I have confidence that I'm Your child
Because I keep Your commandments.
Those who say that they know You, but don't keep Your commandments,
Are liars, and they don't have the truth.
But those who keep Your Word, have Your love in their hearts
That's why I know I'm Your child.

Lord, John didn't write anything new in His letter
He just repeated the original commandments You gave us,
And that commandment is found in Your Word.
Then John added what is new about the old commandments;
Those who claim to be in the light, but hate their brother,
They are in darkness until now.
Those who love their brother live in Your light
These persons will not stumble in darkness.
Lord, those who hate their brothers live in the darkness of sin,
And walk in darkness and they don't know what they're doing,
Because the darkness of sin has blinded their eyes.

Lord, John has written to new children in the faith
To let them know their sins are forgiven.

Lord, John has written to those mature in the faith
    Because they have known You from the beginning.
Lord, John has written to young men because they
    Overcame the evil one.
Lord, John has written to children in the faith
    Because they know You.

Lord, I will not love worldly attractions, or anything else
    That will pull me away from You. Those who
    Love the world, do not love You, the Father.
Because worldly attraction involves the lust of the flesh,
    The lust of the eyes, and the pride of life,
    These are not from You, but are from the evil one.
I know the world will pass away, as well as fleshly lust,
    But I will live forever by doing Your will.

Lord, John has written that we live in the last days
    And that antichrist will come in the future. Because the
    Spirit of antichrist is already here, we know he will come.
Many Christians have stopped fellowshipping with us
    Which demonstrates they have abandoned their faith,
For if they were of us, they'd still fellowship with us;
    Because they went out from us proves they were not believers.
Lord, I have an anointing of the Holy Spirit
    So I can know spiritual things.
John wrote to us because we know the truth,
    And that no lie comes from the truth.
Those who deny that Jesus is the Messiah are liars,
    They have the spirit of antichrist because
    They deny both You the Father and the Son.
Those who deny the Son, don't have Your presence in their lives;
    And those like me, who have the Son,
    We also have You.
If I continue in the message I heard from the beginning,

And I continue fellowshipping with You and the Son,
>   I have the promise of eternal life.
Lord, I still have the anointing you gave me at salvation,
>   So I don't need anyone to explain truth to me.
That anointing gives me basic spiritual understanding
>   So I will abide in the truth that has been taught me.
Lord, I know that Jesus Christ is righteous
>   So all those who obey the truth taught by Him
>   Are born of God.

Lord, thank You for giving me inward confidence
>   *That I have eternal life.*

Amen.

How Believers Relate to Each Other

1 John 3:1-24

I often think about the love of You—the Father—for me
>   And the fact that You call me Your child
>   Because I really belong to You.
When the world refuses to acknowledge You,
>   It also refuses to recognize my salvation.
Yes, I am already Your child, and I can't imagine
>   What our fellowship will be like in Heaven.
I do know this much about my future life,
>   When Jesus comes, I'll be like Him
>   Because I've seen Him in the Word of God.
Everyone who agrees with me about our future relationship
>   Will keep themselves as pure as You are.

Anyone who keeps on sinning breaks Your commandments
>   Because sin is breaking Your law.
I know Jesus became a man to take away sin

And that there is no sin in Him.
So when I stay close to Jesus, I won't be sinning
    And those who sin continually, were not saved
    In the first place and they don't know Him.
I am Your child, so I won't let anyone deceive me;
    I will live holy because You are holy.
Those who constantly sin belong to the devil;
    Sin began with the devil and he constantly keeps sinning.
I know the Son of God has come to undo all that
    The devil has corrupted with sin.
Because I have been born again, I don't constantly sin
    Because I have a new nature that tells me what to do.

This is how you tell the difference between a child of God
    And a child of the devil. Whoever constantly sins
    And doesn't love other Christians, is not in Your family.
I have heard Your message from the beginning
    That I am commanded to love other believers.
I will not be like Cain who killed his brother
    Because he was not your child,
    And I won't be surprised when the world hates me.
When I love other Christians, it proves I have been
    Delivered from death and hell and I have eternal life.
If I refuse to love a believer, it proves I am just the same as
    A murderer, and murderers don't have eternal life.
I know true love from the example of Jesus Christ,
    Because He died for me; I ought to live for others.
If someone has money and professes to know You,
    Yet refuses to give to a needy Christian,
    How could Your love live in Him?
Therefore, I will not love in words only,
    I will show my real love by the things I do.
Only by actions can I be sure that I am Your child,
    And my conscience will be clear when I come to Your presence.

When my conscience makes me feel guilty because I sin,
> I realize You know everything about me
> For You are greater than my conscience.

Therefore, when my conscience doesn't convict me,
> I can come to You with my request in prayer
> To get what I ask, because I am keeping your commandments.

And this is Your commandment that I believe
> In the name of Your son, Jesus Christ,
> And that I love believers as You commanded us.

Because I keep Your commandments, I know I live in You,
> And You live in me. The Holy Spirit gives me this assurance.

Lord, I want to love everyone more and more;
> *Help me love others, as You love me.*

Amen.

Warning Against False Teachers

1 John 4:1-21

Lord, I will not believe every person who claims
> To be a Christian, but I will test their spirit

To see whether they are from You.
> Because many false teachers are going around.

Every spirit that acknowledges that Jesus Christ
> Has come in the flesh is from You;
> Every spirit that denies Jesus had a body is not from You.

Those who deny Jesus was human are antichrists, who
> Were predicted to come, and are now here.

If Jesus didn't come in a body, He couldn't live a perfect life,
> Nor could He have died, nor would He have bled to redeem us,
> Nor could He have been raised in His physical body.

Lord, I will be victorious over false teaching because
  Greater is the Holy Spirit in me, than the spirit of the world.
Those who speak the language of the world
  Get attention from the world;
  They are not from You.
But I am Your child and I know You listen to me
  And those who belong to You, listen to me;
  This is how I tell the Spirit of truth from the spirit of falsehood.

Lord, I pray Your children will love one another
  Since love comes from You, and everyone who is
  Born again has been given the gift of love.
Those who fail to love other people, have never known You
  Because You are love.
Your love for me was revealed when You sent Your Only Son
  Into the world, so that I could have life through Him.
What is love? Not that I loved You, but that You loved us
  And sent Your Son as a sacrifice to take away my sins.
Since You have loved me so much,
  I ought to love other believers.

No one has ever seen You at any time, but as long
  As I love other believers, You will live in me,
  And Your love will be seen through me.
Thank You for putting the Holy Spirit into my heart
  As a proof that You live in me, and I live in You.

Furthermore, John saw with his eyes and writes to tell us
  You sent the Son to save the world.
Those who acknowledge that Jesus is Your Son
  Lives in You, and You in them.
I know You love me deeply because I felt Your love for me;
  You are love, and whoever lives a life of love,
  Lives in You, and You live in them.
Your love will be complete in me when I stand

Perfect before the judgment seat.
There is no fear in love, because perfect love
    Drives out fear.
It is those who do not love who are fearful because they
    Do not know what will happen to them in judgment;
    That proves they are not Your children.
So, my love for You comes because You first loved me;
    Those who say, "I love God" but hate a fellow Christian
    Whom they can see; cannot love You whom they cannot see.
So this is the summary of love: anyone who loves You,
    Must also love their brother or sister.

Lord, I love You with all my heart, mind, and body;
    Keep me always in the center of Your will.

Amen.

You Can Know You Are God's Child

1 John 5:1-21

Lord, I know I am born again, because I believe
    Jesus is the Messiah. And all who love You,
    Love Your children also.
I know I am Your child because I love You, and
    I do what You have commanded me to do.

This is what loving You means—keeping Your commandments
    Because they are not difficult.
I know I am Your child because I have victoriously
    Overcome the lust of the world by faith.
Who else can overcome the world? Only those who believe
    Jesus is the Son of God;
    Jesus came by water and blood,
    His blood was shed to cleanse us from sin,

And water stands for our Spirit baptism into the body.
The Holy Spirit is another witness that I am Your child;
        The Holy Spirit witnesses in me that I am born again.
These three, the blood, water, and Spirit all agree
        That I am Your child.
Many people accept a man's witness to the truth,
        But Your witness is much greater.
I know I am born again because I have Your witness within;
        Everyone who believes in Your Son has life,
        Those who reject Your Son, make You out to be a liar,
But I know I am born again because of Your testimony
        In Your Word that You have given us Your Son;
        Those who have the Son have eternal life;
I know I am born again because I have Your Son in my heart.
        I also have assurance because You said those who have
        The Son, have eternal life.
I also know I am born again because You hear my prayers,
        And I know You will answer my prayers because
        You do not hear and answer the prayers of unsaved people.
Lord, I will pray for those who commit a sin that
        Does not lead to death and You will give them life.
There is a fatal sin which ends in death;
        I will not pray on this occasion,
        All wrong doing is sin, but not all sin is fatal.
I know I am born again because I do not continually practice sin
        Because the Son of God protects me from the evil one.
I know I am born again because I realize all non-Christians are lost;
        Your children have this spiritual insight.
I know the Son of God has come into my heart to give me
        Spiritual understanding to know You;
        I know You are the true God who gives eternal life.
Lord, I will watch out for anything that takes Your place
        In my heart.

Lord, thank You for assurance of salvation;
  Only Your children can live a life full of confidence.

Amen.

Second John

Praying the Book of Second John
1–13

Chapter 57

THE STORY OF WRITING THE SECOND LETTER OF JOHN

John called out to his valet, "Get pen, ink, and paper." Immediately, young Ansel came running into the room where the ancient apostle was waiting. John explained, "I will write immediately to the church."

Young Ansel was only gone for a few minutes, then he returned with a writing box, containing ink, several quills, and writing paper. Even though John was over 90 years of age, his mind was keen and his eyes were sharp. He could see clearly what he wanted to write. Taking the feather in hand, he squeezed the barrel, dipped it into the ink to suck the black olive oil up into the barrel of the feather. Then placing his quill on the paper, he slowly wrote out the words, "The elder unto the elect lady...."

"Sir...," young Ansel interrupted John, "why don't you write 'from the apostle,' that will give the letter more validity?"

"You mean authority like Paul?" John answered. "Do you want me to speak harshly to the church as my good friend Paul sometimes had to do?" John shook his head negatively, "I don't have to exercise my apostolic authority."

Meekly, young Ansel's head bobbed affirmatively.

John continued, "Paul had to use the word 'apostle' because some doubted if he were an apostle." Then the old man explained, "Paul never followed the Lord three and a half years through Galilee like I did. Paul never leaned his head on Jesus' breast as I did. Everyone knows I followed the Lord, so everyone knows I'm an apostle. Because Paul was saved after Jesus went back to Heaven, some doubted his apostleship. No one doubts me."

Ansel shook his head in agreement.

Then the old apostle wrote, "The elder unto the church which is an elect lady and to all the churches she planted, i.e., her children..."[1]

"I could just write from John, that's all I need. But that sounds as though I am exalting myself above the church." John shook his head negatively and thought for a moment. Again he looked down at the blank sheet of paper.

"The elder unto the...elect lady..." John wrote. "I like that, and what I have written shall remain."

Young Ansel said to John, "Who is the lady to whom you are writing?"

John put his pen back, pushed himself back in the chair, and smiled. He didn't say anything for a long time and then remarked, "The lady is the church! Don't you remember the picture of the church as a bride? I think a beautiful bride is a good picture of the church." John smiled and asked a question, "Don't you remember that the church is married to Jesus Christ?"

Ansel nodded in agreement, he did remember.

"So, I'll call the church *elect lady*, is that agreeable to you, Ansel?"

Again he nodded his head in approval.

Several times in the letter John referred to his personal observations about the church. He mentioned the phrase, "I was very glad when I found my children walking in the truth."

As John grew older, he saw more and more false teachings slipping into the church. It was the passion of the elderly John that every person worship the Lord Jesus Christ accurately. He wanted every believer to know that Jesus was fully God, yet He was fully human; he wanted everyone to know that the Word became *flesh*.

So John warned in the letter, "Many deceivers who deny the faith have spread out everywhere telling people that Jesus Christ did not come in the flesh. Anyone who says this is deceived and deceives other people. He is just as bad as the antichrist."

As a matter of fact, John was so concerned about these deceivers he said, "Anyone who doesn't abide in the doctrine of Christ, was never saved in the first place; they don't have the presence of God in their life." Then John smiled, "Those who abide in the true doctrine of Christ, they have the Father and the Son, Jesus Christ."

Endnote

1. 2 John 1:1 (ELT).

Praying the Book of Second John

Live the Truth

2 John 1–13

A letter from the elderly John,
>   To the church who is an Elect Lady
And Her Children whom I love in truth:

"I and everyone in the Body of Christ love you in the faith
>   Because the Word of God dwells in your heart and in ours,
Grace, mercy and peace from God the Father
>   And the Lord Jesus Christ, the Son of the Father."
"I am glad that I found your children—church plants—walking in truth
>   And obeying God's Word."
"Now, I urgently remind you of the Christian principle that you love
>   one another; This is the commandment I wrote to you from
>   the beginning
>   That when we love one another, we keep His words."

Lord, give me a deeper love for the brethren and help me express it;
Help me receive love from others, and in that relationship
> *May our love grow to overcome all our weaknesses.*

"Watch out for false teachers who believe and teach
> That Jesus Christ was born only with a human body,
> And that He was not deity."

"These false teachers are deceivers and antichrists;
> Keep a watchful eye that you do not lose
> The prize for which you and I work."

"Be constant so you receive your full reward
> For being faithful in all things
Because if you wander from the teachings of Christ,
> You will lose God's influence in your life."

"Those who remain true to Christian doctrine,
> Have both the Father and the Son."

"If anyone comes teaching that Jesus Christ
> Is not equal in nature to the Father,
> Do not receive him or give him hospitality,
Nor recommend him to other churches
> Because those who support him,
> Will become partners in his false teaching."

"I have many things to explain, but
> I will not write them with pen and paper."

"We will both be satisfied when I come
> And speak personally with you about these things;
> The children of your 'sister' greet you."

Lord, I believe You inspired every word of the Bible,
> *So it is accurate and I can rely on it to know the truth.*
Keep me from using my opinions to interpret Your Word;
> *I yield to the Holy Spirit to guide me to understand the Bible*
> *So I can accurately know and teach Your will to them.*

Amen.

THIRD JOHN

PRAYING THE BOOK OF THIRD JOHN
1–14

Chapter 58

THE STORY OF WRITING THE THIRD LETTER OF JOHN

The aged John's voice cracked as he called, "Ansel." John's valet came running to his side, "Diotrophes is up to his old tricks," John the apostle of love didn't feel loving today. He snarled when he spit out the words, "Diotrophes is up to his old tricks again."

The church in Ephesus had sent preachers up to a well-known church in the hills. This church body had many wonderful people in it, but Diotrophes was one of the elders in the church who somehow seized control of the pulpit, and no one could preach there without his permission. Diotrophes had gathered control of the money, and nothing was spent without Diotrophes' permission. Diotrophes had made himself boss of the church, and when the apostle John sent a preacher to the church, Diotrophes wouldn't let him preach.

"Diotrophes loves to have the preeminence," John told his young servant, Ansel. Then John added, "I like what my friend the apostle Paul said, "That in all things, Christ shall have the preeminence."[1]

Ansel asked John, "Why doesn't Gaius do something?" Gaius was a good friend of John's and was one of the elders in the church. Gaius had a level head about things. Gaius was a true servant of Christ and opposed all Diotrophes did in the church.

John agreed and said, "I'll write a letter to Gaius to correct the problem. When Gaius reads this letter to the church, people will understand what's going on and do something."

"How about Demetrius?" Ansel asked about another elder in the church. "Demetrius also has a good report of everyone?" the young Ansel added.

"Demetrius will support Gaius," John answered. Then added to his letter, "The two of them—Demetrius and Gaius—will stop Diotrophes."

John shook his head in disgust as he explained that Diotrophes had rejected letters from the apostles and even rejected the authority of the apostles themselves. Diotrophes acted like he was an apostle, but he never followed Christ, he never saw Christ in His resurrected body, and he sure did not act like Christ.

John told his young servant, "I shall write a letter to the church before I go there." John explained that the church body was the final seat of authority and when the people of the church don't follow Diotrophes, he would lose his authority. John wanted the church to know why he was coming and what he would do when he got there.

"Yes...that's what I'll do. I'll explain to the church that Diotrophes is wrong. If no one in the church follows him, Diotrophes will lose his power."

Endnote

1. Col. 1:18.

Praying the Book of Third John

Watch Out for Church Dictators

3 John 1–14

This letter is from the elder John
 To the well-beloved Gaius, a church leader whom I love:

"I am praying for you to prosper physically
 As you prosper spiritually."
"I rejoiced when I heard from different traveling ministers;
 They told me you are standing for the truth,

And you are living by the truth."
"Nothing could make me happier than to hear
That those I led to Christ are faithful to the Word of God."

Dear Friend, thank you for giving hospitality to the traveling
Preachers and missionaries who came through your town;
They told the church in Ephesus of your friendship and help."
"Thank you for sending them on their way with a financial gift
Because they travel for the Lord without a salary,
And they refuse to take money from the unsaved,
Even though they attended their meetings and received their ministry."
"Remember, the churches have the responsibility to care for them
financially,
Thus becoming fellow-workers with them in the truth."

Lord, thank You for those men of God who teach me the Word of God;
May I grow spiritually because of their ministry.
Use their ministry to edify the whole Body of Christ,
And supply all their temporal needs.

"I previously wrote to the church to take care of them
But Diotrephes, who loves to boss the church, refused to listen
to my advice."
"If I am able to come, I will show you the evil things
He is saying against the Ephesian church."
He refuses to allow the preachers we sent to carry out their ministry,
Nor will he allow others in the church to listen to them;
He kicks them out of the church."
"Dear Friend, do not follow his terrible example,
Pattern your life after a good example;
When the believers in your church do what is right,
They prove they are God's children."
"Everyone recognizes Demetrius does the right things,
So receive him when he delivers this letter to you;
I know he will tell you the truth and answer your questions."

"I have many things to tell you but I can't write them
      Because I hope to see you soon,
      Then we can talk about them; Peace to you."
"Friends here send their love;
      Give everyone a special greeting from me."

Lord, it's so easy to be blinded by our own self importance;
      Keep me from being egocentric and tyrannical like Diotrephes.
May I humbly see my place in the whole Body of Christ and fit in;
      May believers love to be around me because I build them up.
Lord, may I be sensitive to leaders and followers in the church;
      May I build up Your Body, not tear it apart.

Amen.

JUDE

PRAYING THE BOOK OF JUDE
1: 1–25

Chapter 59

THE STORY OF THE WRITING OF
THE BOOK OF JUDE

The Man With Three Names

A craggy old apostle carefully chose his steps between rounded stones climbing to a mountain village where he was to preach to a small church. They were located in a small valley way up off the main road. The Christians babbled with excitement all week because they had never had an apostle preach to them, especially a "distinguished" preacher like this who actually walked with Jesus on earth.

The apostle's thick grey-white silky smooth beard bounced with the wind as he continued climbing. The climb was difficult. His dark brown face looked like that of a workman who had spent his life in the sun. The dark face made his grey beard and white hair shine all the more.

The apostle was proud of his Hebrew name, Judah, because it meant *praise*. Why was he proud? Judah was the largest tribe in Israel, and Judah was the son of Jacob who was spokesman for the rest. And hadn't Jesus been born of the tribe of Judah? As a matter of fact, this apostle named Judah had always been proud of his distinct name and the position it gave to him. But lately he was not sure. Lately his name caused difficulties.

Judah entered the home of a wealthy businessman whose large dining room was filled with Christians. He had gotten lost on his way to the village, so he was a few minutes late. The Christians were already singing psalms when he arrived. Judah hadn't time to meet the individual believers, so he went straight to the front of the room to introduce himself. He didn't introduce himself with the Hebrew Judah, but with the Greek pro-nunciation, Judas.

"Good evening, my name is Judas, I am a disciple of Jesus Christ."

The room erupted in outrage. "NO ..." some men yelled out threats to cru-cify him. "We won't hear you." Others yelled divine curses at him, think-ing he was Judas, the one who betrayed Jesus Christ. Some called him traitor and Beelzebub.

Judas shook his head and began pleaded for silence, "No, no, no, I am not Judas Iscariot who betrayed Jesus Christ." He explained when the crowd began to soften its rhetoric, "I'm the other Judas who followed Jesus. Remember, I'm the one in the upper room who said, "How can you reveal Yourself to us and not to the world?"[1]

Judas should have known better, this same experience happened at other churches when they didn't know who he was. Many had never memorized the 12 disciples' names so they didn't know there were two named Judas. Obviously, Judas Iscariot was better recognized because he was hated for betraying Jesus.

The following morning, the apostle Judas walked down the mountain from the young church, reflecting on what had happened, "What am I going to do?" Judas asked himself. He didn't want to turn every church meeting into a shouting match. And then someone told him it was dan-gerous because some "hot head" might react swiftly to kill him because of their hatred for Judas Iscariot.

"I'll change my name," Judas thought to himself. "I'll no longer call myself by the Greek Judas, but I'll call myself Thaddeus, because that is the Aramaic name for *Praise*. Thaddeus will remind me of my Hebrew name Judah that also means praise."

Later Thaddeus was called "Lebbaeous" which is the root word for *white*. Everyone knew him by his snow white beard and hair. He became Thaddeus, the man with the flashing white hair.

For several years Judah was called Lebbaeous Thaddeus and by that name was accepted into churches. There were no violent clashes. However, after traveling to churches for several decades he realized he had to always explain his "new" name, Lebbaeous Thaddeus.

A few places still reacted to him, thinking he was not an apostle. A few who had memorized the Jewish names of the 12 apostles didn't recognize the Gentile name, Lebbaeous Thaddeus. Then one day he thought to himself, "I'd like to go back to my original name, but I can't use the Hebrew name Judah, nor could I use the Greek name, Judas; I'll use the Latin name, Jude.

Inasmuch as he no longer was traveling the Holy Land, now he was preaching in churches filled with Romans who spoke Latin. So Jude started using the Latin name, Jude.

Two hundred years after the death of Christ, Jerome, the early church father, called Jude Trinomious, i.e., the man with three names.

Endnote

1. John 14:23.

Praying the Book of Jude

Sinful Living Leads to Doctrinal Heresy

Jude 1–25

Lord, I thank You for Jude, a servant of Jesus Christ;
    Thank You that he wrote to me and
Grace to believers everywhere who have obeyed Your call,
    And You keep them in the faith of Jesus Christ.
May I experience Your daily presence in my daily walk with You;
    Lord, I receive Your mercy, peace, and love.
Jude had planned to write about the wonderful truths
    Of the salvation we share in common,
But he found it necessary to urge us in this letter

To be prepared to defend the complete faith
That You have once for all given to me,
Because some have infiltrated the churches
Who are the ones I have been previously warned about;
These people were condemned for denying Your truth and
Have turned Your freedom into an opportunity to sin,
As a result, they have rejected the authority of my Master, Jesus Christ.

Lord, I rejoice that You delivered Israel from the slavery of Egypt,
Even though You later destroyed those rebels who went back to sin.
I also read about the sinless angels who rebelled against You
That You threw them into hell to be chained until the day of
judgment.

Lord, help me remember that when Christians give into sexual sins
They are blinded by their lust, and they lose their understanding
of truth,
Just as Israel was rebellious of You and became blinded to heresy.
Lord, keep me sexually pure and give me strength to live right,
So I will properly know the truth, and correctly live by it.
Lord, help me remember You created angels sinless and beautiful
Yet you punished them for their sin,
Help me live a holy life.

Finally, I read about those in Sodom and Gomorrah who lusted after
sexual sin,
Including unnatural lust of men with men.
You destroyed those cities with fire as a warning to us
That there is punishment in hell for those who give themselves
to sin.

Lord, today false teachers still rebel against You
By living their sinful immoral lives, defiling their bodies,
Laughing at those in authority over them and despising Your
messengers.

Not even Michael dared to denounce the devil over the corpse of Moses
　　　But said, "The Lord rebuke you."
But these false teachers will mock anything they do not understand
　　　And like animals they do anything they feel like doing;
　　　By giving into their lust, their actions become fatal.
May these false teachers get what they deserve?
　　　May they be punished like Cain who killed his brother;
　　　May they get the same reward as Balaam who cursed Israel.

They have rebelled against spiritual leadership just as Korah,
　　　May they share his same fate of falling into hell.
They are a dangerous threat to our fellowship at the Lord's Table
　　　Because they come just to get a good meal.
They are like rain clouds that are blown over the farm
　　　That bring no rain to give life to the fields.
They are like barren fruit trees that give no fruit,
　　　So let's dig them up in winter like the other fruitless trees.
They are like raging waves that threaten the ship of faith,
　　　Also they are like shooting stars that burn out and give no light.

Lord, help me recognize false teachers
　　　And separate myself from them and their influence.
Stop their spread of evil to religious people
　　　Who follow their lust, not the Word of God.

Enoch, who lived seven generations from Adam
　　　Knew about these false teachers when he preached and predicted,
　　　"You will come with millions of Saints
To pronounce judgment on all those who reject You
　　　And judge the wicked for all the wickedness they have done,
　　　And to punish those who speak defiantly against You."
False teachers are complainers, malcontents, doing only
　　　What their desires—lusts—drive them to do.

They boast and brag about their spirituality, and they give "lip service"
> To leaders in the church, but they do it to their advantage.

Lord, Jude had godly hatred for false teachers who destroy
> *People with their false teaching;*
> *Give me a passion to be true in all I know and believe.*

Lord, I remember our Lord Jesus Christ told the apostles
> That in the last days there would be scoffers
> Who will live according to their sinful lust.

These false teachers will split churches, stir up arguments;
> They do not have the Holy Spirit to teach them truth
> Or to convict them of their evil imagination and sin.

Lord, I commit myself to becoming strong in your faith;
> I will pray in the power of the Holy Spirit.

I will keep myself within the constraints of Your love
> And wait patiently for Jesus Christ to give me eternal life.

I will have mercy on those who have doubts,
> And I will try to help those who argue against you.

I will point them to You by being kind to them;
> Some You will save by snatching them from the flaming hell,
> I will be careful I'm not pulled into their sin and into hell itself.

I will hate everything about their sin,
> Being careful not to be contaminated by their lust.

Lord, even though Jude hated false teaching, he had compassion
> *On those believers who were deceived by false teachers;*
> *Give me that same compassion to help uneducated believers.*

Now I praise You because You can keep me from falling,
> And You can deliver me faultless into Your glorious presence
> So that I am happy and preserved in Christ.

To You, the only God who saves me through our Lord Jesus Christ,

To You be glory, majesty, authority, and power
In the ages past, now, and forever in the future.

Lord, Jude probably hated false teachers because he was
Mistaken for Judas Iscariot. No wonder he hated false teachers so
deeply.
Keep me close to Your truth all my life.

Amen.

PRAYING THE BOOK OF REVELATION

PRAYING THE BOOK OF REVELATION
1:1-22:21

Chapter 60

WORSHIP:
WHEN YOU COME TO THE END

Scripture: Revelation 1:1-20

The old man's tired eyes popped open, but he didn't move his head. There was a faint light at the mouth of the cave. His ancient body had a terminal ache; he knew death was close. He was almost 100 years old. But he was not expecting to leave this life by death—he was expecting Jesus to return. His weary eyes crinkled as his young heart prayed...

"Even so come, Lord Jesus...."

Sleeping on the damp, black, rock floor of the cave chilled his bones, but it was better than sleeping outside where the wet dew of Heaven gave him the flu. The inmates who were his parishioners—those he had won to Christianity—insisted he sleep in the cave.

Today is Sunday, the old man thought while trying to blow the cobwebs out of his mind. *Today, I will preach to my flock.*

The cave was cut out of Mt. Elias, a ragged rock that reaches 800 feet out of the Aegean Sea, the highest peak on the small Isle of Patmos. The Roman Caesar Domitian had chosen this isolated bastion during the 14th year of his reign as the home for political prisoners. Then he sent John the apostle to Patmos in an attempt to destroy Christianity. The arrest papers delivered to the guards along with John charged him with treason, "Testifying that Jesus Christ is King and preaching the Word of God."

Yet, this tiny island—ten miles long and six miles wide—could not imprison a person whom Christ had set free. Consequently, aged John had never feared the island, nor had he ever felt isolated. He was over 90 years of age when he first came to Patmos and had walked with Christ ever since he had left his fishing nets to follow the Master. He was not alone on Patmos—Jesus was with him; the Lord Jesus lived in his heart.

"Don't come to get me for the sermon," John told Ansel, the young assistant who was bringing him a cup of water and morsel of bread. Ansel had a large frame that once had been muscular, but now, his was an emaciated body covered by taut skin. The meager rations on Patmos barely kept life and limb together. He had been chosen by the others to protect John because he was the strongest, and also the meekest with the heart of a servant. The young man quietly put a cup of water on the crude table, then covered a scrap of bread with a clean cloth. Even in the cave there were flies. Old John told his assistant, "God is calling me to pray...don't disturb me. I will come preach when I finish praying...."

Each Sunday, the converts would gather in the amphitheater in front of the cave, waiting for John to emerge. Protected by the rocks from the ocean's wind, John would sit in a chair to preach to his church of prisoners—free from sin, but prisoners of Christ.

And while the church waited patiently for John each Sunday morning, they also knelt in prayer, asking God to give John a message for them. While they waited for a sermon, they were interceding to God. Sometimes their wait was short, and at other times it was long; but no one minded. The longer they waited, the more God had to say to them through the apostle John.

"Don't disturb me," John repeated his instructions to the young Ansel leaving the cave. "When the Lord tells me what to say," there was a twinkle in his eye, "I'll come out of the cave. But don't come for me until the Lord finishes talking to me."

The prisoners revered John, knowing he was the last of the 12 disciples left alive who had followed Jesus. He had also been the youngest of the 12, and the one whom Jesus especially loved—he had leaned on the Lord's breast. When Jesus had been betrayed, all the other disciples had run away—but not John. He had remained faithful during the trials and was standing at the foot of the cross when he had heard Jesus tell him to take care of Mary, His mother. John had also been the first disciple to go to the tomb on Easter Sunday morning.

Interestingly, all the other disciples who had run away from the dangers of the cross and who had been been afraid of dying, eventually died violent martyrs' deaths. The Christians on Patmos believed the tradition that John would die a natural death, however. Christians all over the Mediterranean world believed it. No Roman emperor would kill him.

The young attendant emerged from the cave to inform the praying prisoners, "John is alive and awake!"

"Amen!" they all cried, grateful that John had not died in his sleep. Their beloved pastor would live another Sunday to preach to them.

All week long, John had been fasting and praying for God to give him a message to preach. God had burdened his heart as he waited in the presence of God...worshiping God...fellowshipping with God...waiting for a special message from God.

John, rising earlier than usual and feeling younger than the age of his ancient body, didn't pick up the cup of water awaiting him on the crude wooden table, nor did he lift the clean white cloth covering the bread. He wasn't hungry for food; he hungered for God. He knew departure was near, by death or by the return of Jesus.

This might be the crowning day. John staggered to the mouth of the cave to gaze at the eastern sky, but not too close so that his parishioners could see him. He remained in the shadows, looking east...praying...hoping.

Maybe today... He closed his eyes and again prayed, "Even so come, Lord Jesus...."

A rooster crowed in the distance as John listened to the waves breaking over the rocky coast. On winter days such as this one, the entire sky was overcast and fog covered the island. Yet, even though the day—cold as death—chilled his bones and the sun remained hidden, John knew it was still there, just as knew God was near even though He couldn't be touched.

The brisk morning breeze promised a storm, but John didn't mind angry weather; he anticipated God doing something special today. Dragging his frail body back into the cave, he again bypassed the bread and water and knelt at his usual spot.

Because John's faith expected God to do something special today, the Lord responded. The Spirit of God filled the room—it was the atmospheric presence of God, and John could feel Him, just as he had earlier felt the cold misty breeze whipping through his hair. Was he experiencing another Pentecost, when the Spirit of God had fallen on the disciples in the upper room?

"Are You coming back today?" John asked in prayer. "Why not come back today to deliver Your Church?"

John didn't pray for himself. He didn't mind imprisonment—he had no family left. John didn't have any future hope of more evangelism—he was too old to travel. John didn't have any place he needed to visit—he had seen all he wanted to see. John had come to the end of the road, and it ended on this forsaken island. With no more dreams, an old man could do nothing else than pray...

"Lord Jesus, I worship You...Lord Jesus, I thank You...Lord Jesus, come...."

Your Time to Worship

- Thank You, God, that I'm alive, that I can wake up, and that I have another opportunity to praise You.

- Thank You, God, that my problems are not greater than they are, that my health is not as bad as it could be, and that I have a desire to worship You.

- Lord, I expect You to return any moment. Forgive me for not being ready and for putting off Your tasks, while filling my life with selfish things.

- Lord, thank You for the excitement I get thinking You might return today, that my problems will be over, that my imprisoned body will be free, that I can touch You in worship, and that You will touch me.

- Lord, You are great in power to bring me to this place in life. You are loving in generosity to overlook my past mistakes. You are patient with me, even when I forget Your tasks.

- Lord, I praise You for this moment in time, for the opportunity of today, and that I can worship You now!

Believers on Patmos had no comforts and little food; they were separated from their families and homes. Rome was persecuting believers for their allegiance to another King—throwing them to lions, burning them at the stake, beating them, torturing them, simply because their supreme allegiance was to Jesus Christ.

Again, tears came from his closed eyes...

"Come quickly, Lord Jesus."

With that prayer, John felt an inner urge, almost an inner compulsion. It was the same inner drive he had felt when he wrote the Gospel, the one they call "The Gospel of John." John quickly obeyed, as quickly as a man over 90 years can react. Approaching the table, he pushed aside the bread and cup. Taking papyrus paper the other prisoners had made for him from the reeds found in the small inlet between LaScala and Merika, he dipped a feather quill into ink,

"I will write what the Spirit tells me."

"Write what's on your heart," the Spirit told John.

His first morning thought was…Jesus. His last thought before sleep was…Jesus. More than anything else, John wanted to be with Jesus. John remembered what the Master had promised the night before He died…

"I will come again and receive you to Myself." John wept again at the memory of that Last Supper before He died, because Jesus assured him, "Where I am, there you will be with Me."

"That's it," John spoke out loud, but no one was there to hear him. "I know what I will write. I will write a book about the return of Jesus Christ. I will encourage believers everywhere because the Savior is coming back for them." Then he spoke the words in a dark room.

"Jesus is coming…"

How would he begin? What would be the first word of this final book? John thought about the Apocalypse…about believers going to Heaven…about unbelievers thrown into hell…about tribulations…about vision. But John didn't want to write just the black parts of the coming judgment. He continued to look within his heart for the things to write. John didn't find hatred in his heart for Rome; he didn't pray for wrath on his persecutors. The only desire of his heart was Jesus. The only object of his love was Jesus Christ. He scratched the first phrase on paper…

"The Revelation of Jesus Christ…"

He would write about the coming of Jesus. He repeated the phrase softly.

"The Revelation of Jesus Christ."

John was pleased with his first words—they represented the passion of his life…Jesus Christ. He had written a gospel account of the past life of Jesus; now he would write of Jesus' coming in the future. This book would focus the reader on Jesus—not on judgment, not on tribulation, not on miraculous signs in the sky when stars would fall and battles would be fought all over the world.

John carefully penned the words, "From Jesus Who is…From Jesus Who was…and From Jesus Who is to come."

Again, dipping his feather quill into the black ink that the prisoners had made from soot and olive oil, John wrote, "From Jesus our faithful witness...from Jesus, the First Begotten from the dead...from Jesus, the Prince of all kings on earth."

The Spirit of God came upon John as he wrote the book. He was borne along as his pen etched words on paper. At times, the bony fingers wrote what he knew from the depth of his heart. Then at other times, John wrote about things he didn't know. As the Spirit of God whispered in his ear, John wrote the message on paper.

"Unto Jesus who loved us and washed us from our sins in His own blood."

Every time John wrote the name *Jesus*, he would stop and put down his quill to praise his Master. "Thank You, Jesus!" The aged apostle talked to Jesus, even though His Master was not physically present in the cave. It was the way he had prayed for years. The aged ears of John could still hear Jesus talk to him. Though there were no sounds in the room, John knew what Jesus was saying to him, just as he had heard Jesus whisper to him at the Last Supper when he leaned on the Master's breast. John was fellowshipping with Jesus—communing with Jesus—and John knew he couldn't leave the presence of Jesus. There would be no sermon today; he'd be fellowshipping with Jesus all day...he'd be writing all day...all week...all month, for he was to write a lengthy book. He was writing the Book of Revelation—the last Book of the Bible.

Your Time to Worship

- Jesus, thank You for being my *forgiver* of sins, my *reconciler* to God, my *resurrection* from the dead, and my *eternal life*.

- Jesus, I worship You for being the *Creator* of all things past, the *Baby* of Bethlehem, and the *Returning Judge* of sin.

- Jesus, I praise You for Your constant *love*, Your *purity*, and Your restraining *patience*.

- Jesus, give me *wisdom* to know what to do today. Be my *strength* to overcome problems, and my *guide* to always do right.

Even though John didn't come out of the cave, his small church of prisoners continued to wait...watch...pray. Though raggedly dressed and malnourished, their greatest desire was for John to get a message from God for them. Patiently, they prayed as John wrote...

"Jesus the Alpha and Omega...Jesus the Almighty...Jesus the Beginning and the End...Jesus Who is...Jesus Who was...Jesus Who is to come."

The prisoners waited a long time for John that day as he began a writing project we now call the Book of Revelation. It's the last Book of the Bible, and John thought it was probably the last work he would write before he died or before Jesus returned to earth.

What did John do when He faced the end? He did the same thing you should do. Whether you are coming to the end of physical life or to the conclusion of your failed dreams—a place where you can do nothing else—you should worship.

What I Learned From John's Worship

- I can worship Jesus when I approach death.

- I can worship Jesus when I am a prisoner to my circumstances.

- I can continually draw closer to Jesus even though I've walked with Him all my life.

- My memory is an excellent help to intimate worship.

- I can meet Jesus in worship, even though I'm waiting for His physical return.

Section One

Scripture: Revelation 1:1-20

Lord, I want a revelation from You—speak to me;
　　　Teach me truth—where You've been;
　　　Show me revelation—who You are!
　　Unveil to me the future judgment on this earth,
　　　The events surrounding Your rapture and return.
　　　But most of all, unveil Jesus to me.
　Just as You sent an angel to reveal to John
　　　The things that are to come in the future,
　　　Reveal them to me.
John wrote down everything he heard and saw.
　　　Now, may I read it and learn.
Lord, bless me as I read Your revelation,
　　　And enrich my life with what I learn,
　　　Because the time of Your return is close.

Lord, John wrote to seven churches in Asia Minor,
　　　Praying peace and grace for them
　　　From Jesus Who is, Who was, and Who is coming.

Jesus, I worship You the faithful witness,
　　　The firstborn from the dead,
　　　The Ruler of the kings of the earth.

Jesus, I thank You for loving me,
　　　For freeing me from sin by Your blood,

And giving me the intercessory role of a priest
Forever and ever, Amen.

Lord Jesus is coming with clouds,
    Just as He left the earth with clouds.
  I will see Him, along with every other person;
    Even those who crucified Him will see Him.
  And they along with every other person who rejected Him
Will mourn because they are not ready to meet Him.

Lord, I worship Jesus, my Alpha and Omega.
    He is the Lord God Almighty.
    He was, He is, and He is coming.

Lord, John suffered because of His faith;
    He was patiently Kingdom-bound.
  John was imprisoned on Patmos Island
    Because he preached Jesus and witnessed to lost people.

On a Sunday the Holy Spirit filled him,
    And he heard a voice behind him
    That awakened him like a trumpet.
The voice was Jesus' who told John,
    "Write down everything I show you
And send it to seven churches:
    Ephesus, Smyrna, Pergamos, Thyatira, Sardis,
    Philadelphia, and Laodicea."
Then John turned to see the Person speaking to him.
    He saw seven golden candlesticks in a circle;
    Jesus—the Son of Man—was standing in the middle.
Jesus had on a long robe tied with a golden band (sash).
    John could barely make out His head;
His hair was shining brilliantly,
    Like the sun reflecting off white snow.
The eyes of Jesus were aflame with anger,

Burning through the lies and sins of sinners.
His feet gleamed like polished bronze,
And His voice thundered away every other sound,
Like mighty waves breaking on a rocky shore.
Jesus had seven stars in His right hand.
The words of His mouth cut like the sharpest sword.
His face glistened like the blinding sun.

Lord, John fell at His feet like one dropping dead;
I too fall to worship at His feet.
"Do not be afraid," Jesus tells us,
"For there is no fear to those who worship Me."
Jesus said, "I am the First and the Last,
I am the Living One who lives eternally."
Jesus continued, "I was dead but now I am alive;
I will live forever and ever;
I have the keys to death and hell."

Lord, when I face the threats of dying or judgment,
I will listen for the jingle of the keys,
For I know You're coming to deliver me.

Lord, You told John to write all he saw presently happening,
And what You showed him that was coming.
The seven stars in the hand of Christ
Were the seven pastors of the seven churches.
And the seven golden candlesticks
Were the seven churches to which He is writing.
Amen.

Chapter 61

WORSHIP:
WAITING IN JESUS' PRESENCE FOR HIS MESSAGE

Scripture: Revelation 2:1–3:22

The cave's thick blackness was held back by the tiny flame flickering in the olive oil lamp. The prisoners had insisted that John the apostle always have the lamp lit when he was awake; they wanted him to be able to write down anything the Spirit of God spoke. John carefully squeezed his quill, sucking ink into its tiny cylinder, and then he barely squeezed the feather, squirting a tiny flow of ink from the point of the feather onto the paper. The wet black ink formed words—wonderful words of life—from the mind of John and the heart of the Holy Spirit. He wrote...

"I am Jesus Who walks among the churches to determine their faithfulness and I hold their pastors in my hand. Write letters to the leaders of the seven churches to warn them of the coming tribulation that Christians will face."

John reread the words he had just written, then blew on the paper to dry the ink. He thought, *Will I die in this tribulation...or will Jesus return to transform this frail body into a glorified body like His?* It mattered not to John if he died, for that would be better—he would be with Christ.

John had difficulty keeping his mind focused on writing. When he thought about Jesus walking among the churches, he thought about the spiritual condition of each church. Some were spiritually energetic; but in contrast, some were carnal and dabbling in sin.

All old men often have trouble with their memory, their attention span, and their mental focus. John was old, so his thoughts drifted...but his thoughts drifted to Jesus.

A friend once asked John why he could remember the details of his life for the three and a half years he had spent with Jesus before the cross, but couldn't remember where he left his tunic a few moments ago. John answered, "Jesus is as real to me now as He was back then." He continued, "When I'm sitting on the rocks watching the sea waves, Jesus is with me...I talk to Him...I listen to Him." John explained that it was easy to keep focused when talking to a real person—"Jesus is with me everywhere I go. I see Him with the eyes of my heart, although I can't see Him with my physical eyes."

The flame in the candle on the table almost flickered out. The fingers of darkness leaped momentarily into the cave until the tiny fire in the light caught new life.

"Ansel!" John called to the young prisoner who waited on him. "More oil."

The diligent servant did not want to disturb John's thoughts or break his concentration. He rushed into the cave without speaking...without eye contact...and tried to be as inconspicuous as possible, while quickly replenishing the lamp on the table.

"Can I get you anything else?" Ansel reluctantly asked the question, not wanting to interrupt the old man's communion with the Lord. The other prisoners expected him to take care of John's every need.

"Nothing," John answered. Then he smiled. "I need nothing except new eyes and a steady hand." John knew he had much writing to do. Ansel returned the smile, then assured the apostle of his prayers.

"The prisoners are outside on their knees praying for you," Ansel remarked. "They are praying for the Holy Spirit to give you a message for them today."

"Go tell them to pray harder," John told his associate. "Jesus is giving me a message for them—and all the churches. Pray vigorously. Jesus has a message for all Christians."

Ansel left, and John turned again to his writing. He looked at the half-filled sheet of paper but could not determine what to write next. At first, he had written frivolously, but now his mind was blank. Was this writer's block? An old man's memory lapse? Or had the Spirit stopped speaking to him?

I'll pray, John thought. *I'll let God guide me regarding what to write.* He then knelt beside the table, his bony knees scraping against the rock hard floor that they had grown accustomed to.

Praying, John asked the Lord what to write. Although he didn't receive an immediate answer, a picture came to his mind—it was Jesus. All he could think of was Jesus. The Lord didn't tell John what to write; instead, the Lord's presence entered the room. John felt it, just as a person can tell when someone enters a room behind him. No longer could he remain kneeling. He dropped from his knees to bow prostrate with his face to the ground—the only way to worship.

John had experienced the atmospheric presence of God many times before, but this time he felt different.

Your Time to Worship

- Lord, I know You are everywhere present in Your omnipresence.

- Lord, I know You are around me and indwelling me.

- Lord, I want Your atmospheric presence here now as I worship You.

- Lord, I thank You for dying to forgive my sins, and rising from the dead to give me new life.

- Lord, I am grateful for my conversion from my old life and for the new desires You create within me.

- Lord, I thank You for all I've received in salvation, making me a new creature in Christ.

- Lord, I worship You because You are everything I need, and I want to please You in everything I do.

Then hearing something, the ancient apostle's memory was pricked. *Are my ears playing tricks on me?* he thought. What John thought he was hearing made his heart jump; his eyes blinked, and he turned his best ear toward the sound. He had to be sure. It was a voice he had heard 60 years earlier, and it was a voice he could never forget.

The voice was not just a memory, nor was he dreaming, nor was it a vision. The voice was actually speaking. His ears were hearing an audible voice! And it was not the voice of his assistant, nor the voice of any one of the Christian prisoners, nor of a Roman guard.

Slowly, John arose, first to one knee; then he pushed up on the chair to rise to his feet. He heard the voice echoing off the granite walls of the cave from the shadows behind him; but the apostle didn't need to call out, "Who is it?" nor did he need to turn to see who it was who had spoken to him. He knew.

John recognized the voice—one that he could never forget. It was the same voice that first called to him, and now, Jesus was audibly commanding him what to write:

"I walk among the churches to determine their faithfulness. These seven will represent all churches that are scattered around the Mediterranean world, and they will represent future churches scattered throughout time—till I come. These seven letters will represent the strengths of some churches, but also, I will tell you of the complacency and sins of other churches. Write so that all churches will know how to prepare for the coming tribulation and My second return to earth."

Even before Jesus told John what seven churches to include, John's mind began to wander and consider various churches he knew. He first thought of the church in Ephesus, the church he had been pastoring when arrested. The Ephesian church was a good church, but with time they had lost some of their fire for evangelism.

This church, in turn, had planted many other churches surrounding Ephesus. Some were great missionary churches, such as Philadelphia. However, another one had been infected with sexual sins and idolatry—Thyatira. Then there was the lazy church—Laodicea…

Deciding to put a hold on his roaming thoughts, John determined, *I will wait for Jesus to tell me what churches to include in my manuscripts.*

In the meantime, the fading light of the small candle was overwhelmed by the magnificent light of Jesus Christ. His light glistened off the walls of the cave as His presence filled the room. John was no longer experiencing the cave, as God's blazing glory had now transformed it into a sanctuary. His heart soared as he entered the presence of God.

It was no longer another Sunday to worship the Lord. Today was truly the Lord's Day, for the Lord had come to John. Jesus was here!

What I Learned About Prayer
From This Account of John Seeing Jesus

- I can pray to meet Jesus even when I think I'm far from Him, even when stuck in the "caves" of this life.

- I don't think of food or other physical comforts when I meet Jesus.

- I will worship Jesus better when I remember what He has done for me.

- I have difficulty describing Jesus because of His divine perfection and my human limitation.

- I respond in speechless admiration when I'm in His presence.

- I am touched by Jesus for a task when He comes to me.

Section Two

Scripture: Revelation 2:1–3:22

To Ephesus: The Good Church (2:2-7)

Lord, John wrote to the leaders of the church at Ephesus,
      "This is the message of the One holding the seven stars,
      Who is walking in the middle of the churches."
Jesus knows everything that the Ephesian Christians do,
      Realizing their hard work and patience in trials.
Jesus knows they don't tolerate sin among their members,
      And they test imposters claiming to be preachers,
      Revealing their false teaching.
Jesus knows they have patiently suffered for Him,
      Without giving up and quitting.
Jesus has some complaints about the Ephesians—
      They have lost their first love for Him.

Lord, when I lose my first love for You,
      I will remember those times when I was first saved
      And go back to doing what I originally did.

Lord, Jesus said He will come and remove their testimony
      If they do not repent;
      Their candlestick will no longer stand with other churches.

But Jesus notes some good things about them—
      They hate the deeds of the lustful Nicolaitans,
      Because God hates fleshly sin.
Jesus warns them, "Those who have ears
      To hear spiritual messages,
      Listen to what the Holy Spirit is saying to the churches.

Those who live victorious over sin,
      Will eat from the tree of life in Paradise."

To Smyrna: The Persecuted Church (2:8-11)

Lord, John wrote to the leader of the church at Smyrna,
      "This is the message from the First, and Last,
      The One who died and came back to life."
Jesus knows all their trials and sufferings,
      And He knows their poverty, while they are rich
      In heavenly treasures.
Jesus knows the slanderous accusations against them
      By religious people who claim to know God,
      Whose house of worship is satan's home.
Jesus says, "Don't be afraid of coming sufferings.
      Some of you will be tested by imprisonment;
      You will be persecuted for a time.
Even if you have to die for Me—be faithful;
      You will receive the crown of life.
If you have ears to hear spiritual messages,
      Listen to what the Holy Spirit is saying to the churches.
Those who are victorious
      Have nothing to fear in the second death."

To Pergamum: The Tolerant Church (2:12-17)

Lord, John wrote to the church leader at Pergamum,
      From Jesus who has the sharp sword
      To divide between error and truth.
Jesus knows where you live is the place
      Where satan rules and controls.
Jesus knows they are holding firmly to His name
      And do not deny Him when persecuted.
Jesus knows Antipas who was a faithful witness,

Who was martyred before their eyes
By the followers of satan.

But Jesus has some complaints against them;
Some "Christians" have been following Balaam,
Who taught Balak to compromise.
So, Israel commits adultery and sacrifices to idols.
Jesus also knows that some "Christians" have accepted
The teachings of the Nicolaitans.
Jesus tells them, "Repent, or I will come to
Judge you with the truth of the Word of God.
If you have ears to hear spiritual messages,
Listen to what the Holy Spirit is saying to the churches.
Those who are victorious will receive
Hidden manna from Heaven to strengthen them,
And their new names will be engraved on a white stone.
And no one knows what it is, but those who receive it."

To Thyatira: The Compromising Church (2:18-29)

Lord, John wrote to the leader of the church of Thyatira,
"This is the message of the Son of God,
Who has eyes penetrating like a flaming fire,
Whose feet will judge all sin."
Jesus knows all about them—their good works,
And their love, faith, and patience,
And that they are still growing in grace.

But Jesus has a complaint against them—
They permit a woman like Jezebel
To teach and prophesy among them.
She entices Christians away from the true faith
By getting them to commit adultery
And sacrifice to an idol and eat its food.
Jesus tells her to repent and change her ways,

But she has not given up her adulterous ways.
Jesus will bring suffering to her life,
    And those who commit adultery with her
    Will suffer intently unless they repent.
Her children will die prematurely under judgment,
    So all churches will realize that
Jesus continually searches deeply into hearts
    To give people what their behavior deserves.

Jesus does not condemn faithful Christians in Thyatira
    Who have not followed the teachings of Jezebel,
    Nor learned the "deep secrets" of satan.
Jesus tells the faithful ones to hold firmly to their faith
    Until the second coming.
Those who are victorious
    And continue serving until the end
    Will receive power over the nations.
They will rule by absolute authority like a rod of iron
    In the millennium with Jesus Christ,
And crush all rebellion against righteousness.
    Then Jesus will reward them with the morning star.
"If you have ears to hear spiritual messages,
    Listen to what the Holy Spirit is saying to the churches."

To Sardis: The Sleeping Church (3:1-6)

Lord, John wrote to the leader of the church at Sardis,
    "This is the message from the One holding
    The seven spirits of God and the seven stars."
Jesus knows their reputation as an alive church,
    Yet they are inwardly dead.
"Wake up, revive what little you have left
    Because you are about to die."
Jesus has not seen anything in them
    That is commendable to God.

He tells them to remember what they hear,
    And to hold on to the Gospel.
He tells them to repent and wake up,
    Otherwise, He will come unexpectedly to judge them
    Like a thief in the night.

Jesus says there are a few Christians in Sardis
    Who haven't dirtied their clothes with evil.
They are fit to walk with Him
    Because they are clothed in spotless garments.
Those who are victorious will be dressed in white.
    Their names will not be blotted from the Book of Life,
    And Jesus will acknowledge them to the Father.
"If you have ears to hear spiritual messages,
    Listen to what the Holy Spirit is saying to the churches."

To Philadelphia: The Church of the Open Door (3:7-13)

Lord, John wrote to the leader of the church of Philadelphia,
    "This is a message from Jesus, the Holy and Faithful One,
    Who has the keys of David,
From the One who can open what no one can shut,
    And shut what no one can open."

Jesus knows all about the Philadelphians.
    They have an open door of opportunity
    That no one is able to shut.
Jesus knows they are not a strong church,
    Yet they have kept His commandments,
    And have not denied His name.
Jesus will judge those in the false church,
    Who wrongly claim to be Christians,
Making them bow at His feet at the Great White
Judgment Throne,
    And they will acknowledge that the Philadelphia Church

was right.

Jesus will protect the Philadelphian Christians
  In the hour of the Great Tribulation,
Which will come upon the whole world,
  Testing believers to determine their faithfulness.
Jesus wants them to hold firmly to their faith,
  And not let anyone take away their rewards,
  Because He will be with them.
Jesus will make those who are victorious over sin
  Like a pillar in the Temple of God,
  And they will be tested no more.
Jesus will write God's name on them,
  And they will be inhabitants of the New Jerusalem,
  The city that will come down from God in Heaven.
"If you have ears to hear spiritual messages,
  Listen to what the Holy Spirit is saying to the churches."

To Laodicea: The Self-satisfied Church (3:14-22)

Lord, John wrote to the leader of the church at Laodicea,
  "This is the message of Jesus, the faithful
  and true Witness,
  The One who created worlds."
Jesus knows that they are not hot or cold;
  He wants them to be one or the other.
But because the Christians at Laodicea are lukewarm,
  He will spit them out of His mouth.
The Laodiceans are claiming to be rich,
  That they have everything they need;
But they don't realize they are wretched,
  Miserably poor, blind, and naked.
Jesus warns them to buy from Him,
  Gold purified by fire,
  That will make them truly rich.

Jesus tells them to dress themselves in righteousness,
>Like pure white robes to cover their spiritual nakedness.
Put spiritual ointment on their blinded eyes,
>So they can have spiritual insight.
Jesus says, "I am the One who rebukes and disciplines
>All of My followers whom I love."
Therefore, repent from your indifferences,
>And take a stand for righteousness and diligence.
Jesus says, "I am standing at the door of this opportunity,
>Knocking to see if you will open to Me.
If you hear My voice and open the door,
>I will come in to spiritually feed you."
Those who are victorious will share the throne of Jesus
>Just as He was victorious over death,
>And took His place at the right hand of the Father.
"If you have ears to hear spiritual messages,
>Listen to what the Holy Spirit is saying to the churches."
>Amen.

Chapter 62

WORSHIP:
IMMEDIATELY UPON ENTERING HEAVEN

Scripture: Revelation 4:1-11

The heavy rain cloud passed over Patmos that Sunday morning, taking the threat of a storm away. Toward the middle of the day, the early morning fog evaporated under the warming sun. Like a warm inviting ray of light peering through a crack in a heavy timber door, a few golden beams of sunlight intermittently shown between the slits in the clouds to fall on the backs of the prisoners praying in front of the cave. The warm sun encouraged them to continue praying for John.

But inside the cave, John couldn't see the sunlight, nor could he feel its gentle warmth. He had lost all sense of time, busily writing his book of future events. Each time he finished a sentence he paused to pray, asking God to direct the next phrase...the next idea...the next page. It was not his book he was writing; it was God's book...God's Word...The Revelation of Jesus Christ. He prayed...

"Lord, thank You for speaking to me...thank You for using me to write Your message...thank You for loving me..."

The apostle John was known for his oft repeated phrases, such as, "God is love." Back in Ephesus—at the church he loved—when John sat on the pulpit too feeble to preach a sermon, he'd simply exhort the congregation...

"Children, love one another, because God is love."

That was a sermon in itself.

John wanted to be near the heart of God. He wanted to know God...feel God...touch God...experience God. When a person wants to get as close as possible to God, the Lord reacts in kind, and God reveals Himself to him.

When Enoch walked close to God, there came a day when God took Enoch from this earth to live with Him in Heaven. No one else has since received that privilege. When Moses grew close to God, his face shone. Likewise, Stephen's face glowed when he repudiated the wicked demands of the Sanhedrin. Then they stoned him to death.

John wanted to know God intimately. Would God snatch up John to Heaven as He had Enoch? No!

Would John's face shine as Moses' had? Or would his face glow as Stephen's did when he was stoned? No!

God had another plan for old John. He would do something no other could do. Jesus was revealing Himself to the apostle so that he could write a book about the future. John would see the future; and from henceforth, John would be called the Seer. He would write a book of the revelation of the future, and he would be called John, the Revelator.

In that gruesome cave of black stone and cold damp walls, John would soon see the glorious city of light and bask in the warm light of Heaven. Only ten brisk steps from one wall of the cave to the other, but from that cramped little prison, John would be transposed into eternity to God's dwelling place that has no walls...no limits...no yesterdays...no tomorrows.

Was John's Spirit transported to experience future events while his body remained confined to the small cave? Or was John's whole body taken there? What do you think?

Perhaps John only had "eternity eyes" to see the future as God showed him one vision after another. Or, did he leave the cave? Did he vicariously experience the future from the isle prison? When you get to Heaven, ask God to tell you what really happened to John on Patmos. For now, you the reader can determine for yourself.

Meanwhile, in the cave, John prayed, "I worship You, Lord…I'll do what You tell me to do…I'll be what You want me to be…I'll write what You want me to write."

Your Time to Worship

- Lord, show me what You want me to do for You while I wait for Your return. Holy Spirit, lead me!

- Lord, I'll do what You want me to do. Holy Spirit, empower me!

- Lord, I often fail You, and I'm often too weak to serve You properly. Holy Spirit, help me!

- Lord, I want to improve on the things I do for You. Holy Spirit, teach me!

- Lord, help me not procrastinate with my responsibilities, because You are coming back soon. Holy Spirit, quicken me!

- Lord, because I know You are coming for me, and will receive me to Yourself, I worship You in anticipation. Holy Spirit, receive me.

The Lord knew John would be a trusty instrument. Just as he picked up his quill to write on paper, God picked up John in His divine hand to write the holy Word of God. God would write a book through John, and He said…

"Write the things I will show you…things of the past…things of the present…things of the future."

Bowing, the old apostle nodded his head in obedience and whispered, "I will write what You show me."

When John submitted, the Lord showed him a door…it was the door to Heaven. From deep in the bowels of Mount Elias, John looked up through the ceiling of the cave…past the sun and stars…past the future; John looked into Heaven through a door.

When John blinked his eyes, he didn't lose sight of the door. Even with his eyes shut, he could still see the door. He couldn't get the door out of his sight. John looked into the heart of God through the door into Heaven…the door…the hinges…the latch…all as real as though he stood at the actual entrance to Heaven itself. Then a loud authoritative voice invited him to enter,

"COME UP HITHER!"

The voice told John he would go through that door to enter Heaven and see the future. He would then write the events that he saw in Heaven in a book. The voice explained…

"I WILL SHOW YOU THINGS THAT WILL HAPPEN HEREAFTER."

When the door to Heaven opened, John entered. He remembered 60 years ago hearing Jesus say, "I Am the Door…" All who enter Heaven are followers of Jesus. Those who believe in Jesus enter Heaven through Jesus, the Door.

Immediately, John was whisked away in the Spirit from Patmos through the door into Heaven itself. John's spirit left the cave on Patmos, soaring through the few remaining black clouds over the Aegean Sea, past the flaming sun, past trillions of stars, through Heaven's door, to enter the presence of God.

The first thing John saw was God's throne—its brilliance was like the sun itself, and John could look at nothing else. The penetrating light was so blinding that John was not able to see the One sitting on the throne. Then he remembered the Scriptures…

"No man can see God." The old apostle realized that even in Heaven he couldn't look upon God, for an infinite God is "unseeable" with mere human eyes.

Nothing else commanded John's attention. He did not ask to see Zebedee his father or his mother. He didn't think of Mary, the mother of Jesus—the one whose care was given to him by Jesus from the cross. No thought of Abraham, Moses, or David. John couldn't take his eyes off the throne of God, nor could he think of anything else but the captivating vision of God at the center of Heaven.

Beautiful colors flashed intermittently from the throne—the green sparkle of an emerald, the red glow of a ruby, the blue hue of a sapphire, and the captivating and glistening white of a diamond.

John stood transfixed, staring at the throne of God...afraid to move...afraid to think...afraid the scene would go away. He drank deeply of all he saw, because he wanted to remember what he saw.

Finally, John, still in awe at the sight of God's throne, slowly began to gaze upon other magnificent sights in Heaven. The next objects to attract his attention were 24 smaller thrones surrounding the throne of God. Each throne faced God, and each occupant worshiped Him.

Again, John's response was to drop to his knees to worship God. He remembered that he had been told to write what he saw. Although his memory was not as clear now as it had been when he was a youth, he knew that if he would be obedient to Jesus...if he would give diligence to see, then the Spirit would help him remember when it came time to write. The promise of Jesus at the Last Supper came back to John...

"The Holy Spirit will bring all things to your remembrance."

John carefully counted the 24 thrones. Were these 12 thrones for the Old Testament saints? Were they for the 12 sons of Jacob? He didn't know. Were they for 12 judges...12 prophets...12 chosen leaders? Or did the 12 Old Testament thrones stand for all believers before the cross—12 representing the Jewish number of completion?

John wondered about the remaining 12 thrones. Who were these thrones for? Were they for 12 New Testament leaders? During His earthly life,

Jesus had promised the 12 disciples they would sit on 12 thrones in the Kingdom. Would He sit on one of these thrones? Would Paul be sitting on the 12th, the one abdicated by Judas Iscariot? Or would these 12 thrones be symbolic of believers *after* the cross?

As John turned his eyes away from God's throne, he began to survey Heaven itself. In front of the throne was a large sea, a calm sea without a ripple upon the face of the water. This silent sea in Heaven reminded John of his youth when the early morning Sea of Galilee was like glass as the wind held back its breath. Once, John rowed out early before sunrise upon the motionless water. Each dip of his oar into the still water created a concentric circle of waves; his boat left the only wake on the sea. John remembered that rowing on that lake was one of the most peaceful experiences of his life. It was there on the Sea of Galilee that John as a young man worshiped God. Now, the sea before the throne of God filled his thoughts of peace—perfect peace. Here, John as an old man worshiped God.

At the four corners of God's throne were angels—four Seraphims. Among their other duties, the angelic sentries guarded the throne. Not that God needed guarding, or that anyone could guard God. Nevertheless, they were positioned at the four corners of God's throne, not so much to protect God, but for the protection of the inhabitants of Heaven. Just as on earth no one could approach God, so in Heaven, the glory of God kept all creatures at their distance. Even when God appeared on Mount Sinai to give the Ten Commandment to Moses, the people were warned not to come near the mountain, or even touch it, lest they die.

The Seraphim who stood near God knew certain things about the past, the present, and the future to come. They knew all they needed to know as though they had eyes on every side of their head.

As protectors of God, the Seraphim were enormously powerful, yet only God is omnipotent—only God has all power. The Seraphim were imminently intelligent, yet only God is omniscient—God knows everything past, present, and the future, and everything that might happen, but will not happen. The Seraphim could travel everywhere, yet only God is omnipresent—only God is everywhere present at the same time.

The Seraphim were more than protectors; they were also given the task of singing worship songs and were the worship leaders of Heaven. When they praised God, all people followed their lead. All the time—without stopping—the Seraphim sang praises...

"Holy...Holy...Holy...Lord God Almighty."

Constantly throughout Heaven, the continuous voices of the four Seraphim could be heard praising God. They sang a threefold exaltation:

"Holy to the Father...

Holy to the Son...

Holy to the Spirit..."

John had seen more than he could assimilate; his knowledge exceeded his experience. He could wait no longer and again dropped to his knees and lifted his hands in worship with the angels to the Triune Deity.

"Holy...Holy...Holy...!"

The creaking voice of the ancient disciple echoed off the walls of that cave in Patmos. John was singing, from the bottom of his heart, the threefold Amen with the Seraphim. Any human ears that heard John that day would not have understood his heart for they could hear only his voice. They could hear only the exuberant voice of an old man praising God. But if they could have seen his face, they would have known his deep satisfaction. And if they were filled with the Spirit, they too would have worshiped with John, for John was worshiping in the Spirit.

While John worshiped, he heard the Seraphim sing additional words of praise, and John joined them, "Lord God Almighty, who was in the past...who is now reigning...who will reign forever in the future."

Your Time to Worship

- Lord, Your holiness is a glaring contrast to my unrighteousness and uncleanness. Forgive me; don't look on my sins!

- Lord, Your holiness makes You infinitely superior to anything I am or I do. Forgive my sin and give me a desire to be holy!

- Lord, You stand above and beyond me in holiness, higher than any existence I know or experience. Forgive my failures and lift me to You!

- Lord, Your infinite greatness and power make me realize how small and weak I am. Forgive my weaknesses and give me strength!

- Lord, Your holy standards are so pure I cannot attain them. Forgive me and make me perfect in Christ!

- Lord, You have remained holy and majestic, no matter how much I resist and oppose You. Forgive my doubts and give me a heart to worship You!

As a boy, John had gone to the synagogue in Capernaum where he heard his neighbors sing the Psalms of David. Eventually, the young lad worshiped God with the words of David as he sang them in the congregation with other sinners like himself. He, like they, sought salvation from God. This worship of redeemed sinners had been wonderful in its gratitude; but angelic worship, the worship of the Seraphim in Heaven, was different. The four angels had never sinned, so they had not experienced God's reconciliation.

As a boy, John's singing in the synagogue was different from the four Seraphim who worshiped out of a pure Spirit that never disobeyed God.

John knew he had sinned, while the Seraphim knew they had never once disobeyed. The Seraphim were singing—not better than the redeemed families of Capernaum—and not worse. The angels' perfect voices do not make them perfect, even though they worship with perfect music. Rather, the sincerity of their spirit makes their worship perfect.

Likewise, John's imperfect songs, sung with a scratchy voice in off-pitch harmony along with the Capernaum congregation, did not make his worship less than Heaven's worship. The perfection of worship is judged by its object, not by the human who gives praise. Both the angels and the people of Capernaum focused their worship on God. The extent of worship is judged by its sincerity. Both the angels who never sinned, and the forgiven fishermen of Capernaum who knew they were sinners, poured worship out of unfettered vessels. Perfect worship comes from perfect sincerity.

John sang with the four angels—his raspy voice joining their pristine music—to worship God who always has been...who now reigns...and who will always exist.

The four angels sang loudly, "GLORY TO GOD...FOR GOD IS GREAT!"

John repeated their words, adding "Amen."

The four angels sang loudly again, "HONOR...LET GOD BE EXALTED."

John repeated their words again adding, "Amen."

The four angels repeated loudly a third shout, "THANKS TO GOD FOR ALL HE'S DONE."

John wept for he was grateful for all that God had done for him. He remembered being a hotheaded selfish disciple who had arrogantly asked Jesus to call fire down from Heaven to destroy the Samaritans who had rejected the Master. He prayed...

"Thank You for being patient with me and forgiving me."

John remembered selfishly begging Jesus to appoint him over the other 12 disciples. Now in Heaven he worshiped...

"Thank You for letting me be Your slave."

Many times in Jerusalem, John had heard the best Levitical musicians in all Israel sing in the temple to the glory of God. But even the Levitical singers in Jerusalem had never inspired the awe he was experiencing now. His Spirit was lifted with their voices as they worshiped...

"GLORY TO HIM WHO SITS ON THE THRONE..."

"I agree," John whispered from his cold cave.

"HONOR TO HIM WHO SITS ON THE THRONE..."

"Amen," John again agreed with the worship voices.

"THANKS TO HIM WHO SITS ON THE THRONE."

With silent tears, John offered his human understanding of thanksgiving along with the perfect understanding of those in Heaven. Then the 24 saints arose out of their thrones as one man. They looked not at one another, nor did they wait for a signal. Each responded according to the personal hunger of their heart. Each acting independently, yet with homogeneous unity, they all together fell on their faces to worship God, each praising Him with his total being.

Then each saint took the crown from upon his head, the crown given to them by God as recognition of their faithfulness on earth. Each of them now realized they were not worthy of the reward. If each had exhibited any kind of faithfulness, it was because of God's grace to them. With open hands, the crowns were held out to God.

John recognized their gestures. When a poor landowner appealed to King Caesar, he usually brought a gift—an animal, an offering of food, a sack of gold coins. This gift was designed by the pleading landowner to appease Caesar. When the gift was offered with outstretched hands, Caesar either took it or rejected it according to the pangs of his conscience or the reasonable judgment of his mind.

The crown had been given to each of the 24 saints because of what each had done on earth. The crowns represented their best achievements. When each arrived in Heaven, they were met by God who embraced them, "Well done, thou good and faithful servant." Then God gave them a crown of reward. Each crown represented a different kind of glory that was brought to God. Some received a crown of life for soul-winning. Some didn't have great opportunities for evangelism, but were faithful when persecuted, receiving a crown of life. Some, who in spite of hardships, faithfully watched for the return of Jesus and received a crown of righteousness.

The 24 saints offered their crowns to God. Their crowns were more precious than money, position, fame, or fine clothes. Yet, each elder realized without the grace of God, they would have had no opportunity to serve God or bring glory to God. It was the strength of God in them who gave them any ability to work for Him. Thus, each elder offered his crown back to God in Heaven, just as they had offered everything to God on earth.

John curiously watched the ceremony. He watched to see if God would take the crowns from them. He remembered an occasion when Caesar had given a gift back to the landowner. It was Caesar's gesture of affection and goodwill to his subject. *What will God do?* thought John.

Each of the 24 saints knew they were not worthy to receive any honor from God. They had testified with Paul, "For me to live is Christ and to die is gain." They knew they were not worthy to wear a crown in the presence of their God—even if given to them by God Himself. Then in an act of unified resolve, worshiping independently, yet acting as one, they cast their crowns at the feet of God and fell prostrate to worship Him.

"Amen," John joined them from his Patmos cave. The old apostle fell with his face to the ground, just as the elders bowed in Heaven. John prayed, "I give everything to You again." As a prisoner, John had no worldly possessions to give, yet everything the ancient apostle possessed he once again yielded to God.

He had little—a cave in which he slept; a table on which to write; paper, pen, and ink—tools he needed. These John again gave to God.

"I give You my mind," John whispered to God. It was the rededication of his mental facilities, the same thing he had done when he had first met Jesus on the seashore of Galilee.

"I give You all of my feeble strength," John voiced his re-consecration, just as he had previously given the Master all his youthful strength when he had left the nets to follow Jesus. When the 24 saints gave all to God by casting their crowns at the feet of God in Heaven, John identified with them from his vantage place on earth.

Then music began to swell in Heaven; and similar to surging waters lifting a swimmer in its tide, John was lifted by the music. The four Seraphim around the throne led all Heaven in worship, and the 24 saints joined to sing the same words. The music grew in intensity—both in volume and depth of resonance. Everyone in Heaven joined in singing...

"THOU ART WORTHY, O LORD...FOR THOU HAS CREATED ALL THINGS!"

They sang heartily for they knew God was the source of all they were and had. If God had not first created Adam, they would not have been born. If God had not preserved them on many occasions, they would have perished. If God had not redeemed them, they would have been lost. Each—joined by millions upon millions—sang as one voice...

"THOU ART WORTHY, O LORD, TO RECEIVE ALL GLORY, AND HONOR, AND POWER."

John was only supposed to gaze into Heaven so he could see the future events in order to write them down. He was only supposed to be the observer-reporter, the one who would record future events. But John could not keep silent—he was more than an observing scribe. John became a worshiper; even within the parameters of a vision, John worshiped God. His raspy voice agreed with what he heard and saw in the vision...

"THOU ART WORTHY, O LORD...BECAUSE YOU CREATED ALL THINGS. EVERYTHING WAS CREATED FOR YOUR PLEASURE AND YOUR PURPOSE."

"Yes," John agreed with the multitudes. "God is worthy because God created everything according to His purpose and His pleasure."

From John's vantage point as God's seer into Heaven, he could see all that God had created. The earth was such a small place when viewed from Heaven's perspective. The tiny earth, which had been home to millions who now live in Heaven, was small in comparison to its mammoth sun—1,300,000 times larger than the earth.

In the next galaxy, John saw a larger sun named Antares—named by God who knows all the stars by name. John could see that the burning mass of Antares was 64 million times larger than the sun of his tiny hemisphere.

Looking farther away from the earth, John saw in another constellation a larger burning star called Hercules, 100 million times larger than Antares.

Then as far as the eye could see was the burning star Epsilon, several million times larger than Hercules, flaming so bright it could be seen in all corners of God's creation. To John it seemed the farther away from earth he looked, the larger the flaming stars became—all shining to tell the people on earth the times and the seasons. God created all these things for His people on earth.

How many stars? John's curious mind asked. Then surveying Heaven—from one end to the other end—John could see them all in prophetic sight. The stars were too numerous for his aging mind to count, million times a million. *No*, thought John, *a billion times a billion*. Finally, he concluded, *Probably a trillion times a trillion. ...Why so many stars?*

Because God likes stars, John concluded. *God created them to shine for His pleasure.*

The music of Heaven interrupted John's thoughts about the stars. It was music about creation. Now, John joined the singing...

"THOU ART WORTHY, O LORD. FOR THOU HAS CREATED ALL THINGS FOR THY PLEASURE AND FOR THY PURPOSE."

What I Learned From John's Worship

- God does not need anything because He has everything; the only thing I can give to God that He doesn't already have is my praise.

- I will worship God when I first enter Heaven—not look for family, friends, or anything else.

- I can worship God as perfectly as angels in Heaven, because worship is measured by our sincerity, not by our perfection.

- I don't deserve any rewards for anything I've done for God. All my accomplishments were completed because He motivated me and gave me the strength to do them.

- I must magnify God for the greatness of His creation.

Section Three

Scripture: Revelation 4:1-11

Lord, John looked toward Heaven and his eyes were on an open door;
  His ears heard Your inviting voice say,
  "Come up here."
 Your voice penetrated the air like a trumpet.
  You promised to show John
  The things that will happen in the future.
 John yielded himself to the Holy Spirit,
  Who whisked him through the open door into Heaven.
 John saw a throne in the center of Heaven,
  And You were sitting on the throne.
 Coming from You were white rays like the flashes of a diamond
  And red beams like the glistening of a ruby.
 There was a rainbow circling the throne
  With a backdrop of emerald green light.

Lord, John saw 24 thrones surrounding Your throne,
  With 24 symbolic saints sitting there.
 The saints had golden crowns on their heads,
  And they were all dressed in white.
 John saw flashes of lightning coming from Your throne,
  And he heard the rumble of thunder in the background.
 John saw seven burning lamps giving light,
  Which represented the sevenfold ministry of the
  Holy Spirit.
 John saw a sparkling crystal sea in front of Your throne;
  There was not a ripple on its mirror-like surface.
 John saw four angels on the four corners of Your throne;
  They looked in every direction

As they guarded Your throne.
The first looked like a lion to represent royalty;
  The second looked like an ox to represent work;
The third was like a man to symbolize humanity;
  And the fourth looked like an eagle that soars above all.

The Seraphim could see everything in all directions,
  At all times.
Day and night they worshiped God, crying out,
  "Holy...Holy...Holy, is the LORD GOD ALMIGHTY,
  Who was...Who is...and Who is to come."
Then the angels gave glory, honor, and thanks
  To You Who sits on the throne.
The 24 saints fell on their faces before You,
  Worshiping You Who lives forever.
The saints took the crowns from their heads
  And offered them in worshipful appreciation
  To You who originally rewarded them with the crowns.
The saints cried in praise, "You are worthy,
  Our Lord and God, to receive our glory, honor,
  and power."
  Then they cast their crowns at Your feet,
Because You created the earth and all the heavens;
  By Your will everything exists.
    Amen.

Chapter 63

WORSHIPING THE LAMB

Scripture: Revelation 5:1–6:17

When John looked into Heaven, it was not like looking at a painted picture of Heaven, drawn by an artist. Rather, he entered Heaven in a prophetic presence. Even though he remained in the cave, John saw Heaven by standing on its streets, and as he twisted his ancient neck left and right, he gazed down those streets and all around. He drank in the scene with prophetic eyes. It was beautiful beyond description—the peaceful lake...the four angelic Seraphim guarding the throne...the 24 saints...and he still had to shield his eyes when he stared into the blinding light of the heavenly throne. How could he remember everything? How could he find the appropriate words to write what he saw?

Oh, and now, John was gripped with a new scene he had not previously noticed. Multitudes—not hundreds, not thousands, not millions, not billions...but more! Stretching to the endless horizon of his mind, John saw a multitude of people, almost innumerable.

John was completely unaware that the people of Heaven were not looking at him, nor were they looking at the things he saw. They all were looking at one thing, which John seemed not to notice. With his frantic endeavor to see all of Heaven, John missed a most important item. Just as a person looking at the vast seashore misses a multicolored shell lying at his feet, so John had been so blinded by the enormous number of stars in Heaven that he had missed something that was captivating everyone else.

Then John became aware that the mood in Heaven was changing. Like a classroom slowly becoming quiet because the students realize their teacher is waiting for their attention, a hushed anticipation slowly spread over all of Heaven when everyone became aware that God was waiting. John quieted his breathing as Heaven became still with anticipation. Then John saw it.

There was a scroll in the hand of the One sitting on the throne.

Squinting his weakened eyes, John saw that this was no ordinary scroll. It had seven authoritative seals to shield its message from unauthorized eyes. John had seen seals like that before. Official papers from Caesar or Roman officials always had a series of seals to make sure no unofficial person read its contents. Only the one who was supposed to receive the scroll could break its seals and read its message.

Why hasn't God opened the scroll? John naturally thought to himself. The apostle believed God knew everything. *God must already know what is in the scroll, and because God can do anything, He can also break the seals.*

Why is the scroll not opened? again John wondered.

Looking carefully at the many seals, the old apostle knew that very important papers had more than one seal. A few important Roman papers had two or more seals. The most important Roman papers had one seal for Caesar, a second seal for the Roman Senate, a third seal for the general of the army, and a fourth seal for the governor of the province.

John blinked his eyes to see more perfectly, then counted the seals. One...two...three...four...five...six...seven. The scroll in God's hand had seven seals. Seven—God's number; seven—the number of perfection. John knew the message of the scroll must be the most important message in the universe; nothing was more authoritative, for the scroll was perfectly sealed. Then a loud voice bounced off the walls of Heaven...

"WHO IS WORTHY TO BREAK THE SEALS AND OPEN THE BOOK?"

John turned to see who was speaking. He saw a strong solitary angel flying across Heaven asking the question, "WHO IS WORTHY TO OPEN AND READ THE BOOK?"

Immediately, John knew the strong angel couldn't break the seal, for he was looking for someone more worthy than himself to open the scroll. No other angel stepped forward to volunteer his services, for none of them was worthy.

John turned back to the four Seraphim guarding the throne. None of them offered to open the book. John looked up and down the row of 24 saints—neither did any of them accept the challenge. They all kept their place. No one in Heaven volunteered. Could no one open the book?

The flying angel had not asked, "Who is able?" for that question would have suggested physical ability, meaning that the seals were tough and brute strength would be needed to open the scroll. The angel had asked, "Who is worthy?" questioning if anyone had the authority to break the seals.

John thought, *What authority must a man have to be worthy to open the scroll? Must he fight better...think deep thoughts...possess more wealth...do miracles?*

John scanned the crowds of eternity past, looking for the most victorious warrior to step forth, but none was valiant enough. Not Joshua...not Samson...not David. John again looked for a wise man in history to open the seal. However, none was intelligent enough. Not Moses...not Solomon...not Abraham. Nor were any kings, prophets, priests, or miracle workers worthy to open the scroll.

Disappointedly, John began to weep. He could plainly see that God wanted the scroll opened...and he wanted what God wanted. John didn't know what would happen next, so he continued to weep silently, expecting something unexpected to happen. While it is difficult to wait for something of which you're not sure what you are waiting for, John had no other alternative—he waited. He sat on the crude chair in his cave, pulled his tunic about his chilly body, and quietly wept, in anticipation.

Your Time to Worship

- Lord, I worship You for Your infinite knowledge, for when I am frustrated by my ignorance, teach me to trust You who knows all things.

- Lord, I acknowledge You who knows all things past, present, future, and things potential. Teach me to trust You who knows what is best for me.

- Lord, You know everything about my feelings, desires, and hidden thoughts; teach me to trust Your purging of my ungodly thoughts and desires.

- Lord, You continually know all things; teach me to trust Your plan for my life when I can't understand it, just as I know the sun is shining when I can't see it.

- Lord, You are never surprised by anything; and I am shocked, disappointed, and frustrated. Teach me to trust what You know, not what I can see.

"Weep not." The silence was broken by one saint who spoke. All the eyes of Heaven focused on John's tears, after they heard what was said. They knew that only John wept, for in Heaven there are no tears. John's tears of disappointment were theirs.

All the ears of Heaven listened, for they too wanted to know who was worthy to open the scroll. But even so, there were some who already knew. The one speaking knew what all the 24 saints knew, what the four angelic choir leaders knew, and what God Himself knew. They knew who could open the scroll. The speaker announced…

"THE LION OF THE TRIBE OF JUDAH IS WORTHY." John's heart leaped.

"JESUS IS WORTHY TO BREAK THE SEAL, BECAUSE HE HAS DIED FOR US. JESUS IS WORTHY TO TELL US WHAT IS IN THE SCROLL BECAUSE HE HAS BROKEN THE STRANGLEHOLD OF DEATH."

Amen, everyone in Heaven silently agreed.

"THE ROOT OF DAVID HAS BATTLED THE POWER OF SIN AND HAS PREVAILED," the loud voice proclaimed.

The scroll in the hand of God was the title deed to the universe. The scroll determined who owned the world and what would happen in it. And the seals were authoritative agreements by which the world's affairs were run.

The world had been God's world, because He had created it perfect; it was Paradise. The earth had glorified God, and mankind had fellow-shipped with God by walking with Him in the garden in the cool of the day. But when Adam and Eve had listened to satan, they subsequently sinned against God. Consequently, He had to judge them, and He had to judge the earth on which they lived. They then had to die, and the law of sin took control. All people aged until they died, and all died. Men lied rather than telling the truth; they became tyrants and took pleasure in harming one another; they carved idols from roots or stone, then bowed down to worship the demonic spirits that inhabited the idols.

God's Kingdom of light had been put aside for the kingdom of darkness. Thereafter, God and satan entered a contest for the souls of people, and at times it looked as if satan were prevailing through his use of the lust of the flesh, the lust of the eyes, and the appeal of selfish arrogance.

Caesar took delight in burning the apostle Paul alive on a stake in his garden, and he crucified Peter upside down. Thousands of Christians were thrown to hungry lions to be eaten alive. Why? Because satan hates God's people. But how could God allow the devil to do these things? Because life is choice, and God wants all people to freely choose to love

Him and serve Him. Those who reject God, hate God—and pour their hatred on the people of God.

But now, the end of the world has come. Now, the seals must be broken. Now, it is time for satan's power to be terminated. Now, it is time for God to take back control of the earth. Now is the time for the Kingdom of God to rule the earth.

"This is wonderful news…" John turned from the scene in Heaven to his flickering candle and parchment paper. "I must write down this good news for all who are suffering." John wanted to tell them that satan's persecution wouldn't last forever. He wanted them to know that there was a time coming when God would eliminate satan's control and reassert His own control.

As John wrote what he was hearing in Heaven, he turned again to see what was happening about the throne of God.

There was a holy hush, and those whispering were silenced by the growing stillness of the multitude. Something else was happening.

John looked in every direction to see what had captured the crowd's attention. Then the old eyes rested upon what the eyes of millions of others were observing. John saw Jesus. He knew it was Jesus because he had followed the Master for more than three years in Galilee. He had seen the resurrected Jesus in the flesh. But now John saw Him glorified.

Jesus stepped from the throne. This was not the Jesus who had lived before creation. This was not the Baby Jesus of the Bethlehem manger. This was the Jesus who had suffered as a Lamb, dying on Calvary. Every eye in Heaven saw Him as the suffering Savior; they looked at Jesus as the crucified Lamb of God. Just as each person in Heaven had individually seen Jesus in his or her conversion experience—the One who had forgiven their sin, now they were also seeing Him again in Heaven, as in the day of their salvation.

The Lamb stepped forward to the center of Heaven.

Because Jesus as the Lamb had been victorious over sin, He now in His heavenly role stepped triumphantly toward the throne. Reaching out,

Jesus took the scroll with its seven unopened seals, and because He was worthy, Jesus held the scroll high above His head. In response, the inhabitants of Heaven shouted for joy. Soon He would break the seals...but not just yet.

The four angelic Seraphim fell down in worship of Jesus, as they had worshiped the triune God on the throne. With faces to the ground, these worship leaders magnified the Lord Jesus. Then the 24 saints followed their lead. They too worshiped with their faces to the ground.

The 24 saints saw the vessels that contained all the prayers of worship, of all people, of all time—all the prayers that had ever been directed to Jesus. Taking them all—every hymn that worshiped Jesus...every prayer that exalted Jesus...every act of service that magnified Jesus...everything done in the name of Jesus—the 24 saints poured out the prayers in adoration of the Lord Jesus Christ.

All in Heaven sang a new song...new in time. Up until now, Jesus had been the Lamb who forgave their sins. Now, Jesus was also the Lamb who would terminate sin. The new song of heavenly triumph over sin, which had never been uttered until the rapture of the Church into Heaven, could now be sung. Now, at the end of the age, the new song could be sung because all believers, of all tribes, of all ages, from all the earth were gathered to witness the final victory of God over satan. So they sang a new song...

"THOU ART WORTHY TO TAKE THE BOOK AND TO BREAK THE SEALS BECAUSE YOU ARE THE LAMB WHO DIED TO REDEEM US BY YOUR BLOOD FROM OUR SINS."

John had been sitting on his wooden chair in the cave, but instinctively he dropped to his knees to cry, "Amen." He kept repeating, "Amen," for he knew his sins were many. But now John had a new reason to cry out, "Amen!" Jesus was getting ready to finish sin and the devil forever. "Do so quickly," John prayed.

Your Time to Worship

- Lord, I love to sing about Your mercy, but I'm afraid of Your judgment. Bury my sin in the blood of the Lamb.

- Lord, I would devote myself to sin, if I did not know You punish misbehavior. Lord, make me obey You.

- Lord, there is "straightness" in your expectations, but I am "crooked"! Draw a straight line with this crooked stick that I call life.

- Lord, You have never condemned an innocent person, nor have You overlooked the guilty. Remember, I come to You in the perfection of Jesus Christ; He is all I plead.

- Lord, You never delight in making people miserable for the sake of misery, but You punish because of Your truth. I worship You in the security of Jesus Christ.

Jesus took the book from God and stepped to the center of Heaven. Soon there'd be no more aging...no more persecution...no more tears...no more death. Jesus had the future of the universe in His hand and soon, everything would be light.

John's mind went back to those martyrs torn to bits by lions; soon it would be all right. John remembered his parishioners outside the front of the cave praying for him, separated from loved ones, starving and suffering. Soon it would be all right for them. For all the persecutions that Christians have endured for Christ, soon it would be all right.

As Jesus stood in the center of Heaven with the book in His hand, John looked around to see everyone worshiping Him. John saw multitudes of angels worshiping Jesus the Lamb; those perfect messengers were each crying out, "HOLY, HOLY, HOLY."

How many? he wondered.

In his limited estimate, John thought there must be ten thousand times ten thousand, plus thousands of thousands. So many they staggered his mind.

"I can't count them," he gasped.

Then beyond the angels, John saw every person who ever believed in Jesus up to that date, plus those who would believe in Jesus in the future. John saw them all with his prophetic eye. Even though he was imprisoned in a cave and trapped on a tiny island ten miles by six miles, John saw the future for which he prayed. He saw in a vision all believers of all time surrounding the throne of God.

From the drab limitations of a cave in the rocks, John saw the glories of Heaven. He tried to grasp how many followers of Jesus were there—millions times millions. Black-skinned believers of Africa; brown-skinned believers of India; fair-skinned ones of Greece, Italy, and Spain. They came from the East—Chinese, Japanese, and from the islands of the sea. They all spoke a different language, but together they sang the same words...

"WORTHY...." Their music was awesome as they sang, "WORTHY IS THE LAMB."

From the cave on Patmos, John joined in singing, "Worthy."

The entire host of Heaven sang in unison, "HE IS WORTHY BECAUSE HE WAS SLAIN FOR US." They worshiped the One on the throne and the Lamb, "HE IS WORTHY TO RECEIVE OUR PRAISE...OUR RICHES...OUR ALL."

Then suddenly, Heaven was silent, a silence that demanded attention. John rose from his crude chair in the cave. After standing with those in Heaven, he dared not move. The moment was filled with anticipation. John knew what he wanted to do...he knew what everyone in Heaven wanted to do. Then with no one giving a signal to begin, and no one waiting, John in the cave along with everyone in Heaven, all responded at the same time and sang the timeless hymn that would be written centuries later, "O COME LET US ADORE HIM."

What I Learned About the Lamb

- I must always remember to look past my difficulties to the joy of seeing Jesus in Heaven.

- I must make Jesus the center of my focus on earth, because He will be the center of my focus in Heaven.

- I must constantly worship Jesus for the salvation He accomplished for me on Calvary. If I lose the focus of sins forgiven, I've lost my perspective in life.

- I can endure difficulties on earth, knowing Jesus will one day do away with all evil and its influence in the future.

- I find purpose and meaning in life when I worship Jesus, the One who is worthy to receive my adoration.

Section Four

Scripture: Revelation 5:1–6:17

Lord, John saw a scroll in Your right hand;
>> There was writing on both sides of each page,
>> And it was officially sealed with seven seals.
> John saw a mighty angel who asked with a loud voice,
>> "Who is worthy to open the seal and open the scroll?"
> No one was worthy in Heaven, or on earth, or in hell
>> To open and read what was in the scroll.
> John wept bitterly because no one could open the scroll;
>> But one of the saints on one of the 24 thrones said,
>> "Do not weep; there is One who is worthy."
> Only Jesus, the Lion of the tribe of Judah, and
>> The root of David
>> Is worthy to break the seven seals of the scroll,
> Because Jesus has triumphed over satan
>> Who once ruled the universe of souls.
> John saw Jesus the Lamb, standing next to Your throne,
>> Standing between the Seraphim guarding the throne
>> And the 24 saints sitting on 24 thrones.
> The Lamb, Jesus, had been sacrificed.
>> All Your wrath had been satisfied.
>> The whole work of salvation—"It is finished."
> The Lamb, Jesus, took the scroll out of Your hand.
>> Then the four seraphim bowed to Jesus,
>> Followed by the 24 saints who also bowed.
> Each one sang worship to the Lamb.
>> Then they poured out all the worship praise
>> Of all believers, of all time.
> Then they sang a new song,

"You are worthy to take the scroll
And break the seals to open the scroll,
Because the sacrifice of Your blood,
Purchased salvation for all people,
Of every language, from every tribe, and from every nation.
You have made them priests to intercede
And serve in Your Kingdom."

Lord, in John's vision he heard the music
Of an innumerable choir of angels
Gathered around Your throne.
John said there were ten thousand times ten thousand angels,
Plus thousands upon thousands who were shouting,
"The Lamb who was sacrificed is worthy to open the seals,
For He has power, wisdom, riches,
Strength, honor, blessings, and glory."
Then John heard worship from everything that has breath—
Everything in Heaven, everything that lives on earth,
And in the seas and even hell itself.
They worshiped You sitting on the throne,
And Jesus who had the scroll in His hand,
Saying, "All praise, honor, power, and glory
To You and to the Lamb."
And the four guarding Seraphim and the 24 saints
Also worshiped saying, "Amen!"

The First Seal

Lord, John saw the Lamb break the first seal,
And unroll the scroll.
Then one of the four Seraphim
With a voice sounding like thunder shouted, "Come!"
John saw a white horse, and the rider
Was holding only a bow—no arrows.

The rider was given a victor's crown,
  And he went from one battle to another.

The Second Seal

 When Jesus broke the second seal,
   Another Seraphim shouted, "Come!"
John saw a second horse who was bright red.
   The rider was given a huge sword and commanded,
   "And take peace from the earth and set people
   to slaughter one another."

The Third Seal

 When Jesus broke the third seal,
   Another Seraphim shouted, "Come!"
John saw a black horse, and its rider
   Held a pair of scales to measure things.
The Seraphim cried, "A loaf of bread,
   Or three pounds of barley for forty dollars;
   There is no oil or wine available anywhere."

The Fourth Seal

 When Jesus broke the fourth seal,
   A fourth Seraphim cried, "Come out!"
John saw a sickly pale horse, and its rider
   Was named Plague;
   Hell was snatching up all who died.
A fourth of the earth's population was killed
   By Plague, by war, by famine,
   By disease, and by wild animals.

The Fifth Seal

 When Jesus broke the fifth seal,
   John saw under an altar

All those who had been martyred for witnessing Your Word,
 And being faithful in holy living.
The martyrs cried to You, "How much longer
 Will You wait before taking vengeance
 On those who have killed us?"
Each martyr was given a white robe of righteousness
 And told to rest until the coming judgment,
Because there would continue to be martyrs
 Until the second coming of Christ,
 Who would be killed just as they did.

The Sixth Seal

When Jesus broke the sixth seal,
 There was a violent earthquake and the sun didn't shine;
 Darkness covered the earth.
The stars began to fall like figs dropping from a tree
 When a wind storm shakes it;
 Everything was pitch black.
The mountains and islands of the sea
 Shifted their original locations.
Everyone panicked and hid themselves in caves.
 Kings, government leaders, military commanders,
 Rich and poor—all people tried to hide.
They cried for the rocks to cover and hide them
 From the wrath of the Lamb,
 Because they wouldn't survive Your coming judgment.
  Amen.

Chapter 64

MARTYRS WORSHIP AS THEY ENTER HEAVEN, AND THE SEVEN TRUMPET-JUDGMENTS

Scripture: Revelation 7:1–11:15

The aged John had been so focused on seeing the Lamb standing at the center of Heaven, he forgot everything else. He forgot Rome was persecuting Christians. He forgot he was a prisoner on Patmos. He forgot the damp cave and the aches in his decrepit body. He forgot his flock waiting for him outside the cave. Nothing else matters when you look at Jesus.

As Jesus held high the scroll, the title deed to Heaven that no one else could open, the seals seemed more compelling than the book itself. In the next instant, without effort, Jesus broke the seals. It did not take supernatural ability to break the seals; they were simply wax seals that could be broken with the flip of a small finger. John had sealed many letters in his life with melted wax from a candle. Then to make sure the recipient knew he was the one who had sent the document, John had pressed his signet ring in the warm wax. After the wax hardened, his seal—the family signet—guaranteed his authorship. No one else could reproduce the seal without his signet ring.

Who sealed the book Jesus is holding? John asked himself.

John was so focused on Jesus breaking the seals in Heaven that he missed the judgment that was being poured out on earth in the meantime. The rapture had come, saints were in Heaven, and the Tribulation was being poured out on mankind. Satan had been "the god of this world," but now God would purify the earth from his domination.

From the beginning, satan had tempted the earth's inhabitants to follow him, using the love of money, the pleasure of the flesh, and the pride of life. Satan's dominant power on earth had been the influence of a worldly system that conquered the lives of humans.

When the first seal was broken, John saw an angel leave the presence of God riding a white horse. The rider had been commissioned to take peace from the hearts of the people. As the white horse galloped across the face of the earth, everyone was gripped by fear of war; even rumors of coming war stole peace from the hearts of people far from the battle zones. Because the people of the earth had rejected the peace of God, He was sending them the alternative—agony and misery. Usually punishment does not hurt as much as the anticipation of punishment, just as fear of war is probably worse than war itself.

When the second seal was broken, John saw a second angel on a red horse leave the presence of God. *What judgment will He deliver?* thought John. The rider on the red horse instigated war on earth—brother against brother—nation against nation. Men were hacked to pieces with swords, the ground was soaked with blood, millions of widows were grieving.

Why would God send war? God began cleansing the earth of sin by giving it more sin and its consequences than anyone ever anticipated. The rewards of iniquity cause men to hate iniquity. Men cry out, "My sin is greater than I can bear." God allows unparalleled slaughter on battlefields because hell is punished by hell itself. Wars are the tools of satan used to capture his prey. Wars are fought for the love of money, to gain things that satisfy the flesh, and for the pride of rulers and nations.

There was so much carnage that strong men became weak; they vomited and shook with fear. However, rather than repenting of sin, the bloodied soldiers cursed God with clenched fists. Rather than turn to God for peace, men sought to end violence with more violence.

The punishment from God demonstrates the law of God. Those who reject God in peace, hate God all the more when judged by war. Because they won't turn to God in war or peace, the Lawgiver must demonstrate

His control, punishing the lawbreaker by immersing him in lawless anguish.

When the third seal was broken, John saw a third angel ride out of Heaven on a black horse—another messenger of judgment—on his way to judge the earth. This angel spread hunger, famine, and deathly starvation to the earth.

Corresponding judgments were already taking its toll on the earth itself. Forest fires burning out of control created voluminous black clouds that blocked the rays of life-giving sunlight. Growing things began to die. Then, because there was nothing to eat, animals died. Food disappeared from stores; rationing occurred followed by empty shelves and pantries. Rioting broke out. Malnourished children died first, then the aged, and finally the strong.

John didn't want to witness the next scene. Since the first time he had looked into Heaven, the aged apostle turned away from the vision and looked around his desolate cave. He saw the white cloth covering the morsel of bread on the table. His meager diet on Patmos didn't look so small in comparison to the coming world starvation. John wept for those who would die slowly of hunger.

Then John looked again at the vision to see the fourth seal broken from the scroll. He saw another angel leave Heaven riding on a sickly pale horse—the judgment of death. People died by all means, including starvation. Animals that had once feared man, now starving, were attacking mankind for food. All those who had rejected God to seek "pleasure for a season" and had enjoyed instant gratification, now feared the death predator that stalked them. Their original rejection of God justified His punishment for them, for even in their day of dread, they did not turn to Him.

The breaking of the fifth seal revealed God's people who were suffering along with the unsaved. The judgments of God fell not only on unbelievers, but on many who believed in God. Some believers were killed with guns, others were burned at the stake, some were martyred publicly, and still others just disappeared from the public eye. Because the entire earth was being judged, God's people died along with those who hated Him. God's people suffered just as much as the unsaved. The only difference was the attitude of their hearts. The unsaved hated God for their suffering and cursed God with clenched fists. The believers bowed their heads to pray,

"How long, Oh Lord? How long?"

Those on the earth who were martyred were given white robes. They were told, "Rest from your labors till others join you, for more will be martyred." They were promised that suffering on earth would end shortly.

The goodness of God, which allows rain to fall upon the just and the unjust, also allows His judgment to afflict the saved and unsaved alike. Both are killed in earthquakes, pestilence, and famine. Those who reject God in this life will reject Him in death. Those born with clenched fists will die with clenched fists, defying God who gave them life, cursing God for allowing them to die. Then from eternal flames, their blackened eyes will stare defiantly, only to eternally reject God time and again. A look into the hearts of those judged will vindicate God's judgment. While the unsaved curse God from hell, saved people will continue to pray...

"How long?..."

God does not enjoy punishing anyone, but having established laws in the Garden of Eden, He must do what the law demands. Because life is choice, God allows all to choose the filthiness of sin, if they so desire; then during the Tribulation, God will give them what they have chosen. He will allow them to be filthy still. They will cry out, "I cannot bear the filthiness of my sin." They will not cry for God to save them, for if they repented, God would redeem them. No one in hell will ever cry for God to let them out. The choice they made in life to reject God is the same choice they will continue to make in hell. They will declare, "We will not have this man Jesus rule over us," and they will eternally reject God.

The aged John wept as he saw the collapse of civilization. He loved people, and as "the beloved disciple," love broke his heart. The vision of the future tore his heart apart. God was pouring His retribution out on the earth, beginning to cleanse it for a new day—a new people—a new age to come.

When the sixth seal on the title deed to Heaven was broken, a great earthquake shook the earth, more violent than any previous measurement on the Richter Scale. Buildings fell upon their inhabitants. Rocks tumbled down mountains and crushed villages. Great cracks in the earth swallowed up those running to safety. John thought dying by starvation had been terrible, but now, it seemed as though everyone and everything— bridges, towers, factories, churches—were being destroyed. The stars created by God came hurling to earth, causing forest fires, tidal waves, and toxic vapors, killing thousands more.

Presidents and army generals knew the end was near and that God was judging the earth. Yet, rather than praying to God, they ran to hide in caves from the natural disasters and prayed to the rocks...

"Fall on us to hide us from the face of the Lamb who is coming to judge us."

Your Time to Worship

- Lord, You give the devil and his followers what they continually seek—ruin, disaster, and misery. Thank You for giving me peace.

- Lord, when I see human devastation, You are there working Your plan. Thank You for taking care of me.

- Lord, when it seems satan is controlling everything, You are behind the scenes, directing Your plan. Thank You for working all things for good to us who love You.

- Lord, when I have personal catastrophes, You do not let them overwhelm me. Thank You for protecting me.

• Lord, when the lives of good people are destroyed by satan, You have a greater life and reward for them in Heaven. Thank You for Your faithfulness to each one of us who follow You.

John looked back into Heaven and saw four angels holding back the winds of the earth, refusing to allow the gentle refreshing breezes blow through the meadows. Nor did the storms blow across the face of the ocean that would ultimately bring rain for the farmers. Without the wind, the heat became unbearable on the remaining population already reeling from God's judgment. Without the wind, there was no pollination, and plants couldn't reproduce. Birds didn't fly, nor was there rainfall from Heaven to cool the searing heat. And without rain, the ground cracked, and vegetation died.

Why is it that people never appreciate the wind, until it refuses to blow? Why is it that people never praise God for good things, until they are taken away? When there was no wind to hold things together, life came unglued.

Suddenly, John heard a loud voice from Heaven, "DO NOT HURT THE EARTH BY WITHHOLDING THE WIND." The voice explained, "WHEN YOU WITHHOLD THE WIND, YOU HURT THE SEA, THE TREES, AND ALL LIFE ON EARTH."

As John listened to the voice, he knew there was grace in the judgment of God. The strong voice was heard again…

"DON'T HURT THE EARTH UNTIL GOD HAS SEALED HIS SER-VANTS, FOR SOME BELIEVERS WILL NOT DIE. THEY WILL LIVE THROUGH THE JUDGMENT AS A TESTIMONY TO ME UPON THIS EARTH."

They represented every tribe of Israel who came from every place on earth; they represented God's people who were yet to serve Him upon the face of the earth.

Every unsaved person was branded with a seal on their forehead or hand. It was the number 666, the number of man; and those with the number 666 claimed that they belonged to satan, not to God.

In contrast, God's servants were given the brand sign of God in their foreheads. They were sealed with the name of God, a sign of His ownership. These were those who would live for God but would be martyred during the Tribulation.

Entrance Into Heaven

A visionary light turned John's eyes toward Heaven. He saw a light beam, like a vast swinging bridge, extending upward from the earth through a field of fire. It was a shining path that reached into Heaven. Upon it, a vast throng of saints marched triumphantly toward the city of light. John tried to count the number—too great to determine—entering Heaven. In the parade were aged gray-headed saints...teenagers...entire families...children barely able to walk...and babies in arm. They were the martyrs who had been slaughtered for the cause of Jesus Christ upon the face of the earth. They came from every people group on earth—from Korea, Africa—brown faces, white faces, and those with yellow skin. They spoke every tongue, and yet in their differences they could communicate with one another, both hearing and understanding what others said.

John leaned forward to observe them closer. Did he know them? Were any of the 12 apostles there?

They were marching, one group behind the other...orderly...with great dignity...accountable...respectable. John knew he would not join them because Jesus had said he would die a natural death, not a martyr's death. But regardless, John respected them and wanted to march with them—not because of their violent death, but because of their consecration. They had given all.

Each smiled with the look of contentment, yet their altered faces still shown shock. They had learned from their death experience, and maturity remained even in their glorification. The virtue of their character shone through their countenance. John couldn't forget what they had experienced; he would always remember their dedication.

Each martyr in the parade was wearing a white robe symbolizing purity. These people had not dipped their colors, nor had they compromised their stand for God. They had come out of the Great Tribulation having washed their robes, made pure in the blood of Jesus Christ.

"Awesome!" John exclaimed as he saw them triumphantly entering Heaven. As a lad in Jerusalem, he had seen the Roman legions entering the Eternal City dressed in battle gear—their symbols of victory on parade. But Roman pomp couldn't now compare to this spectacular sight that John was witnessing.

The great multitude continued to come, drawn by an irresistible force that pulled them into the very center of Heaven where the throne of God was located. They all wanted to see the One for whom they had paid the ultimate price. They wanted to see God the Father and the Lamb. They had suffered for Him, now they wanted to worship Him.

Just as on Palm Sunday, the multitudes had gone out from Jerusalem to meet Jesus, waving palm branches in their hands, a symbol of victory, so these people in Heaven waved palm branches shouting the same praise...

"HOSANNA...HOSANNA...HOSANNA...!"

They approached the center of Heaven, the throne of God, shining as the sun; however, it was impossible to see God, just as it is impossible to look into the brightness of the sun.

And at the four corners of the throne of God were the guarding Seraphim, the worship leaders still there, directing everyone in worship and calling all voices to magnify the One who sat upon the throne.

In front of the throne were the 24 saints, some of whom had also died a martyr's death, just like the symbolic crowd of 144,000 who had paid the ultimate price of love to Him who sat upon the throne. Seeing the vast number of martyrs entering Heaven, the 24 saints fell upon their faces to worship God. Then one of the saints asked, "Who are these who are dressed in white clothes, and where have they come from?"

"You know the answer to that," John said to him. "These are the martyrs who have come out of the Great Tribulation. Their sins have been washed away in the blood of Jesus Christ and now they have come to worship God."

As the martyrs faithfully served God by dying on earth, now they would serve God by worshiping Him in Heaven. Then they joined in with the four angelic worship leaders and the 24 saints to sing...

"BLESSING...AND GLORY...AND WISDOM...AND THANKSGIV-ING...AND HONOR...AND POWER...AND MIGHT...TO THE ONE WHO SITS ON THE THRONE."

John remembered the sevenfold blessings when he had first observed Heaven. These martyrs were now repeating the same sevenfold blessings of God. *This worship must come deep from within the heart of the people*, John thought. Then he picked up his pen to write again...

"BLESSING...BE TO GOD FOREVER AND EVER."

John agreed with them, saying, "Amen."

"GLORY...BE TO GOD FOREVER AND EVER."

"Amen," repeated John.

"WISDOM...BE TO GOD FOREVER AND EVER."

"Amen," echoed from the cave.

"THANKSGIVING...BE TO GOD FOREVER AND EVER."

"Amen."

"HONOR...BE TO GOD FOREVER AND EVER."

"Amen."

"POWER...BE TO GOD FOREVER AND EVER."

"Amen."

"MIGHT...BE TO GOD FOREVER AND EVER."

"Amen and Amen."

Those who are martyrs have a special place in the heart of God. Because they have died for Him, the Lamb will dwell among them with His special presence. Never again will they hunger, neither will they thirst. They will not remember suffering from lack of food and water. God will wipe away every painful memory. Never again will they suffer from the scorching heat of the sun, nor will anything hurt them.

The Lamb will constantly feed them and will lead them to living fountains of water. And for every pain—and remembrance of pain—the Lamb shall wipe away every tear.

Your Time to Worship

- Lord, You are so full of surprises; when I fear death, You give me life and a parade. Thank You for caring.

- Lord, Your surprises come unexpectedly; when I expect bad days, You give me a good eternity. Thank You for life.

- Lord, You told me to keep my lamp trimmed because You might come at any hour. Thank You for keeping promises.

- Lord, You surprised the scoffers of Noah's day by sending a flood, but You did what You promised. Thank You for Your faithfulness.

- Lord, You gave talents to Your workers and told them to work faithfully till You returned. When payday came, You rewarded them. Thank You for rewards promised to me in the future.

At length the parade was over, and the last martyr entered the doors of Heaven. The singing—hallelujah singing on key—had faded to John's ear.

Then John turned away from the vision and made his way slowly back to the flickering candle on the table. What time was it?...

Then the cricket choruses of the evening filled his ears. The night approached and urged him to get busy writing what he had seen. But before he wrote...just once more...John had to worship God...

"Thank You for strength against the approaching night...thank You for the serenade of the crickets...thank You for the melodious voices of martyrs climbing through the starry fields to Heaven...thank You for the shouts of hallelujah!"

What I Learned From the Martyrs' Parade

- I will enjoy in Heaven the benefits of the decisions I make on earth.

- I should be happy to identify with God's cause on earth, because I will receive His mark on my forehead in Heaven.

- I should praise God for everything—even sufferings—because God will reward me for them when I get to Heaven.

- I should do all I can to win people to Christ on earth because there will be no second chance of salvation after death.

- I should not blame God for my suffering because tribulation will come to all—both saved and unsaved.

- I know God loves me and will preserve me, while satan's desire is to destroy all people.

Section Five

Scripture: Revelation 7:1–11:15

Lord, John saw four angels holding back the wind
      To prevent it from blowing on land or sea.
  Next, John saw another angel coming from the sunrise,
      Carrying the seals of God.
  A voice cried, "Seal the servants of God first
      Before you do any damage on land or sea."
  Then John heard there were 144,000 sealed
      Jews who came from all the tribes of Israel;
  Twelve thousand came from each tribe—from Judah, Reuben,
      Gad, Asher, Naphtali, Manasseh, Simeon,
      Levi, Issachar, Zebulun, Joseph, and Benjamin.
  In addition to the 144,000, John saw another great multitude
      From every race, language, and nation,
  Standing before You and Jesus, the Lamb,
      Wearing white robes and holding palm branches.
      They cried out in worship,
  "Salvation comes from You who sits upon the throne
      And from the Lamb who died for us."
  Then the angels formed a huge circle around
      The 24 saints and the four Seraphim.
  The angels bowed to the ground and worshiped,
      "Amen...praise and glory and wisdom
      And thanks and power and strength
      Be to You our God forever and ever. Amen!"

Lord, one of the saints asked John, "Who are these
      Dressed in white robes?
      Where did they come from?"

John asked the Lord Jesus to tell him
>Who these people were. Jesus said,
"These are the martyrs who were killed
>In the Great Tribulation;
Therefore, their robes are washed in
>The blood of the Lamb."
Now they stand in front of God's throne to
>Worship Him day and night.
The Lamb will take care of them
>So they will never hunger nor thirst,
>Nor suffer anything, ever again.
The Lamb will satisfy their needs for food,
>And will quench their need for water,
>And You will wipe away any remembrance of pain or suffering.

The Seventh Seal

After this parenthetical view of the martyrs in the Tribulation,
>All eyes in Heaven focused on the Lamb
>As He broke the final seal on the scroll.
There was great silence in Heaven as the Lamb
>Prepared to return to the earth;
>It was time for the Second Coming of Christ.

The seven seals describe events on earth during the coming seven-year Tribulation period. The (last) seventh seal judgment describes the event when Christ returns to judge the world. Next, the seven trumpets will sound. Similar to one leaf of cabbage covering another, the trumpets describe judgmental events during the Tribulation that happen simultaneously with the seven seals, but from a different perspective. The (last) seventh trumpet describes the Second Coming of Christ, including the same events as the seventh seal. Finally, there are seven bowls of judgment (see Rev. 16:1-21). Again, like one leaf of lettuce covers the other leaves, the bowl judgments occur simultaneously with the seals and trumpet judgments. The last bowl judgment describes the battle of Armageddon and the Second Coming of Christ.

Lord, seven angels stood before You,
> And You gave them seven trumpets.
Then You told them to be prepared
> To announce judgments coming to the earth.
Another angel went to the altar in Heaven
> With a large amount of incense
To mix with the prayers of God's people,
> To offer to You who sits upon the throne,
The sweet smelling fragrance of prayers
> That ascends up to worship You.
When the angel threw fire from the altar to the earth,
> Thunder rumbled, lightning crashed,
> And an earthquake shook the earth.
Then the seven angels with seven trumpets
> Prepared to blow their message of coming judgment.

The First Trumpet

Lord, when the first angel blew his trumpet,
> Hail and fire rained down on the earth.
One third of the earth was set on fire where
> One third of the trees and green grass was burnt up.

The Second Trumpet

Lord, when the second angel blew his trumpet,
> Something like a great mountain of fire

Was dropped into the oceans.
One third of the water was polluted as with blood.
One third of the living things in the oceans
And one third of the ships were destroyed.

The Third Trumpet

Lord, when the third angel blew his trumpet,
A huge burning star named Wormwood,
Fell on a third of all the rivers and streams.
The waters became bitter as persimmons
So that many people died who drank the water.

The Fourth Trumpet

Lord, when the fourth angel blew his trumpet,
A third of the sun quit shining,
And light from a third of the stars went out.
Daylight was shortened by one third,
And the night was blacker than usual.

Lord, John saw an angel like an eagle fly over Heaven
Announcing, "Woe...woe...woe to the
Inhabitants of the earth."
The next three trumpet judgments
Will be much worse than the original four.

The Fifth Trumpet

Lord, the fifth angel blew his trumpet;
One of God's servants that came from Heaven to earth
Had the keys to the bottomless pit.
Smoke poured out of it when it was unlocked,
So the sun and sky were darkened.
The smoke spawned locust-demons,
And they spread where the smoke blew.

The locust-demons attacked people
    Who didn't have God's seal on their foreheads.
The sting didn't kill anyone, but
    Gave constant pain like a scorpion's sting.
People wanted to die,
    But death escaped them.
The locust-demons looked like horses armed for battle
    Having faces that looked human,
With crowns on their heads, and women's hair,
    And teeth like lion's teeth.
They wore body armor as strong as steel,
    And the noise of their wings sounded like
    The charge of horses and chariots into battle.
Their tails stung like a scorpion,
    And the sores they left ached for five months.
The king of them was the angel from the bottomless pit,
    Whose Hebrew name is Abaddon,
    And his Greek name is Apollyon.

The Sixth Trumpet

Lord, when the sixth angel blew his trumpet,
    John heard a voice from the altar before the throne,
Saying, "Release the four demons kept captive
    Beyond the Euphrates River for this hour.
    They will kill a third of the remaining population of the Earth."
Then John heard it said,
    There were 200,000 locust-warriors.
John saw the locust-demons like riders on horses.
    Some had red armor, others had blue armor,
    And the color of the rest was yellow.
The horses looked as if they had lion heads.
    Smoke, fire, and brimstone blew from their mouths,
    Killing one third of the remaining population.

Their power was in their mouth and tail,
　　　Their tails were like snakes
　　　That were able to kill with their bite.
The population of the world that escaped their wrath
　　　Did not repent of their evil,
Nor did they stop worshiping demon-idols
　　　Made of gold, silver, bronze, stone, and wood—
　　　Idols that can't see, hear, or walk.
Nor did they quit murdering, stealing,
　　　Committing sexual sins, or practicing witchcraft.

Revelation 10:1–11:14 are a parenthesis in the unfolding drama of the Tribulation. John sees an angel that has seven thunder judgments, but they are so terrible, John is told not to write them in his book. Then John describes some of the events that happen in the first part of the Tribulation in Jerusalem.

Lord, John saw another mighty angel come down from Heaven,
　　　Surrounded by a cloud
　　　With a rainbow about his head.
The angel's face shined like the sun, his feet like fire.
　　　He had in his hand a small open book.
He planted his right foot in the oceans
　　　And his left foot on land.
He shouted louder than a roaring lion.
　　　Then seven thunder-judgments rolled across Heaven.
John was prepared to write what he saw
　　　When a voice stopped him saying,

"Keep secret the message of the seven thunder-judgments;
> Do not write them down."
The angel standing in the oceans and on the land
> Lifted his right hand to Heaven
And swore by You Who lives forever,
> You who created all of Heaven
> And everything on the earth.
The time of waiting is over; Jesus will come
> When the seventh angel blows his trumpet.
> Then Your secret intentions will be fully realized.

Lord, John heard a heavenly voice telling him to get the little book.
> So John asked the angel to give it to him.
The angel said, "Read it as you would devour a meal;
> It will upset your stomach,
> But it will be sweet as you eat it."
As John read the book, the angel's words came true.
> It tasted sweet as honey, but it turned his stomach sour.
The book contained a message for John to preach and write,
> A message of what will happen in the Tribulation
> To rulers, people, ethnic groups, and nations.

Lord, John was given a measuring stick and told to
> Go measure the Temple in Jerusalem, the altar,
> And find out how many people worship there.
John was told not to measure the outer court
> Because Gentiles gather there,
> And they will destroy the Temple after 42 months.

You promised to send two witnesses—Enoch and Elijah—
from Heaven,
> Because they did not die on earth,
> Who preached for 1,260 days in Jerusalem.
They came as the fulfillment of the two olive trees
> And the two lamps which stood before Your throne.[1]

When enemies attacked these two, they were able
    To do judgment-miracles
    To destroy their enemies.
They prayed so that it would not rain,
    And they turned water into blood,
    And sent plagues—as did Moses—on their enemies.
After three and a half years, the Antichrist
    Came from the bottomless pit to fight them
    And finally killed them.

Their corpses were left in the main street of Jerusalem
    So unsaved people could see they were dead
    And put their trust in the Antichrist.
People from every nation, ethnic group, and language
    Saw their bodies for three and a half days.

The unsaved rejoiced thinking their torment was over
    And the suffering caused by the Tribulation was past.
The nonbeliever celebrated and gave presents to everyone,
    Thinking these two who had brought plagues on the world
    Were now dead and their troubles were over.

Lord, after three and a half days
    You breathed life into the two witnesses.
Just as everyone had seen their dead bodies,
    Now everyone saw them being raised from the dead.
Then a loud voice shouted, "COME UP HERE!"
    They went to Heaven as their enemies watched.
Immediately, a violent earthquake shook Jerusalem,
    A tenth of the city was destroyed,
    And seven thousand people died in the earthquake.
Those who lived in Jerusalem—the Jews—were fearful,
    And began praising You, the God of Heaven.

Lord, the seventh angel blew his trumpet
>And Heaven got ready for Christ's return to earth.
>Amen.

Endnote

1. See Zechariah 4:1-14.

Chapter 65

WORSHIP: WHEN WE FIRST SEE THE ARK, AND THE SEVEN PERSONAGES OF THE FUTURE TRIBULATION

Scripture: Revelation 11:15–13:18

Each time John saw another vision, it was as though the drab walls of his cave became a giant painting of future events. And what John witnessed, he described quickly in writing, trusting nothing to memory. Through his tear-filled eyes, he then dutifully took his quill and scratched what he saw into letters. The words became alive on the page, and page after page told the story of judgment on earth. Finally, when John could endure the judgment no longer, God would pull back the curtains of Heaven to reveal the occupants worshiping God. Just as a fresh tiny violet, growing out of the ashes of a blackened forest ravaged by fire, signifies hope and a new beginning, so was John's spirit refreshed each time he saw people worshiping in Heaven.

Six trumpets had sounded, each announcing the next severe judgment. A trumpet was a familiar sound to John. On many occasions, he had heard a trumpet calling Roman soldiers to duty, and as a boy, he had learned the meaning of each different trumpet blast.

John had also been taught the importance of the Jewish trumpets calling Israel to worship in the Temple. He knew the Old Testament story of over a million Israelites wandering 40 years in the wilderness, directed by a trumpet blast. Each trumpet call had indicated a different direction to the people.

Now, during the Tribulation, God sent angels to announce judgments with trumpet sounds. Six times the trumpet had blared out its call of judgment, and John was waiting for the seventh. Would the final trumpet call for the most severe judgment?

Unexpectedly, when the seventh angel sounded his trumpet across the corridors of Heaven, there were no judgments handed down. Rather, the door to Heaven began to open. Similar to a Roman trumpet signaling the opening of the gates to a city, so the seventh trumpet indicated it was time for Heaven to open.

Once more, John was transported from his cave on Patmos into the presence of God, as he looked into Heaven and heard many loud voices crying out...

"THE KINGDOMS OF THIS WORLD ARE BECOME THE KINGDOMS OF OUR LORD AND OF HIS CHRIST, AND JESUS SHALL REIGN FOREVER AND EVER."

Once again. the four angelic worship leaders around the throne led Heaven in praising God. When they fell on their faces to worship the Lord, they motivated all Heaven to join them, including the 24 saints.

While judgments were being poured out on the earth, all those in Heaven were worshiping God. They were not celebrating the punishment of their enemy, nor were there joyous feelings of vindication or revenge. Rather, everyone was focusing on God and the Lamb.

Punishment, however, is necessary for lawbreakers. God's perfect law cannot allow one act of rebellion to go unnoticed, nor can disobedience be overlooked. A rebel cannot break the law of God without it eventually breaking him. Many lawbreakers think that because they are not immediately judged, God is weak or He doesn't care. But God doesn't judge broken laws instantaneously. The patience of God gives all time to repent. The goodness of God gives to everyone a window of opportunity. Payday does not come every time a person sins, but it will come someday...assuredly...convincingly...and deadly.

The worship leaders cried, "WE GIVE YOU THANKS, LORD GOD ALMIGHTY...WHO WAS ALWAYS LORD IN THE PAST...WHO IS

LORD OF THE PRESENT...AND WHO WILL ALWAYS BE LORD IN THE AGES TO COME."

John looked into the faces of the people worshiping God and heard their voices exalting Him as their Lord and Master. Then the people cried...

"WE PRAISE YOU BECAUSE NOW THROUGH YOUR JUDGMENTS, YOUR GREAT POWER REIGNS OVER THE EARTH."

For centuries, satan had enjoyed his limited rebellion on earth. He rejoiced when David sinned with Bathsheba to spoil God's honor. He rejoiced when Peter denied Jesus three times. The demons of hell laughed when churches were burned and missionaries were martyred. They delighted to see godly people suffer persecution, thieves break into the homes of Christians to steal their livelihood, and believers hanging on a cross just as their Lord had done.

Satan rejoiced when Christians were addicted to sin, and he only grudgingly gave up those who became free in Christ.

But where was God when His people had suffered?

Why hadn't He immediately rushed in to stop violence against Christians, or to prevent death, or to protect His people? Because the scroll had been sealed with seven seals; the title deed to the earth had been wrapped up in legal litigation. Satan had his day in court. As "the god of this world," he was allowed limited victories.

At times, God did intervene for His followers in answer to prayer—to protect His children. At other times, satan had been defeated because of the faith of God's servants. But the earth had been satan's domain. Some had even called this planet "the playground of the devil." Now, God was taking it back by purifying the earth through tribulation and judgment.

The four worship leaders around the throne cried out thanksgiving to God. The 24 saints joined them, and millions upon millions of voices flooded Heaven, like a river rushing down a valley to the sea. They all were singing...

"THOU HAS TAKEN BACK THE EARTH TO REIGN. THOU HAS MANIFESTED YOUR POWER OVER THE EARTH!"

Satan would not give up easily, however; rebels would not roll over in submission to God. When the powerful hand of God fell upon the earth during the Tribulation, those in rebellion did not cry out for forgiveness, but intensified their rebellion against God. At the same time, the worshipers of Heaven continued to sing to God...

"WHEN YOU ARE TAKING BACK THE EARTH, THE NATIONS ARE ANGRY BECAUSE OF YOUR WRATH. THE NATIONS ARE ANGRY BECAUSE THEY WILL HAVE TO STAND BEFORE YOUR JUDGMENT THRONE. THE NATIONS ARE ANGRY BECAUSE YOU GIVE REWARDS TO YOUR SAINTS AND THOSE WHO FEAR YOUR NAME. THE NATIONS ARE ANGRY BECAUSE YOU ARE DESTROYING THOSE WHO DESTROY THE EARTH AND HIS PEOPLE."

The angry voices of the damned did not reach Heaven. The open heart of God was now closed to them. Their blasphemies only echoed back to their ears. As they cursed God, they were only reminding themselves why they were lost. In His mercy, God did not allow His children in Heaven to again be vilified by the self-justifying curses of those left on earth. The peaceful silence of Heaven was interrupted only with the intermittent voices of praise to God.

In the meantime, the Tribulation scenes on earth were almost too horrible for John's tired eyes. But to be true to his commission, the Seer, faithfully observed this horrible and devastating time and recorded what he saw.

"I thank You that one day I will be with Jesus in Heaven," was John's responsive prayer. "Thank You for forgiving my sin." Once again, John worshiped God, "I worship You for Your protection of me all these years. Thank You that I still have life to serve You."

Your Time to Worship

- Lord, You created a perfect earth and said, "It is good," but satan brought disorder and corruption. I praise You that one day You will restore order and righteousness to this world.

- Lord, You have given every person a chance to choose Your rule, but many still reject You. I praise You for allowing me to choose You and follow You.

- Lord, the unsaved world does not know when payday will come. Because they continue to commit sins and crimes without suffering consequences, they think they've escaped judgment in hell. But one day, You will judge them. I thank You that Christ took my judgment.

- Lord, those who deny You in life, also reject You in judgment. Thank You for accepting me in life and protecting me against condemnation.

- Lord, all the "pleasures" that now tempt us, will one day be gone. Thank You for victory over sin this day and for separation from sin in eternity.

John's head was bowed in worship, when all of a sudden, his concentration was broken by the announcement of an angel...

"LOOK QUICKLY." John lifted his head. The angel explained, "LOOK NOW, BECAUSE YOU WILL SEE SOMETHING THAT HAS NEVER BEEN SEEN BY HUMAN EYES."

John now gazed at the Temple of God in Heaven. The incomparable beauty of this structure reminded him of the grandeur of Herod's temple on earth. But the inconceivable had happened more than 20 years earlier in

A.D. 70. No one had thought that the temple of Jerusalem could ever be destroyed, but the Roman General Titus had totally decimated the imposing work of architecture because Jewish zealots were using it as a fortress.

As a boy, John had always been overwhelmed when he saw the splendor of Herod's temple with its gold covered walls. However, as much as he had loved the temple, he was not grieved when the Roman soldiers desecrated it by offering a sacrifice to Zeus on its altars and tearing it apart stone by stone. Just as Jesus had predicted, the Romans had not left one stone upon another while searching for the melted gold that ran between the stones after the fires.

To John, the temple simply represented the old covenant where animals were sacrificed for sins. The death of Jesus had replaced the old covenant with a new age—the Church Age. So when the Romans destroyed Herod's temple, they actually eradicated any earthly remembrance that might attract Christians away from Christ.

Wrapped up in the darkness of the cave, John gazed into the city of light and stared at the Temple in the center of the city, as bright as a sun-filled day. John imagined how the original Solomon's temple might have appeared, yet he knew that the Temple splendor he saw in Heaven had to be more beautiful than the original temple built by Solomon.

Then John remembered that the voice had promised to show him something new...

This Temple is not new to me, John reflected. Although he had not seen this exact Temple before, he had seen one like it. *I've seen a temple many times,* he continued to reason within himself. *This is not new.*

John continued to wonder if this Temple he saw was new because it included a different pattern for the sanctuaries of God on earth. He knew Herod's temple and Solomon's temple and even before that—the tabernacle—all followed the same layout or design. God had originally given the blueprint for His sanctuary to Moses as he prayed on Mount Sinai in the wilderness.

Continuing to ponder this sight, John prayed...

"Am I seeing the pattern for God's house on earth?"

As John continued to question why the voice had called this Temple something new, all of a sudden, the veil that had been hiding from sight the Holy of Holies slowly began to open.

"I can see inside," John whispered nervously. "No one has ever been able to see into the Holy of Holies." This was the "thing that had never been seen by human eyes." Now, John—along with all those in Heaven—could see inside the Holy of Holies.

"This is amazing," John gasped out loud. "I'm looking into God's heart!"

True, the death of Jesus on the cross had made it possible for outsiders to look into the Holy of Holies. When Jesus had died, the curtain, which veiled the Holy of Holies from outsiders, had split from top to bottom. John smiled when he remembered that curtain—approximately 18 feet thick. While it was impossible for human hands to tear the massive curtain, the mighty hands of God had ripped it in half as a man might tear a leaf. Then John smiled again. The Jews had claimed that the earthquake had ripped the curtain, and subsequently, they quickly replaced the torn veil with a new one. Man had attempted to hide what God had opened.

But the Temple in Heaven was being opened so that John could see into the Holy of Holies. Like a breeze rushing into a vacuum, the unseeable was now seen. John's eyes rushed quickly back and forth to make sure he did not miss a thing. But there was only one article standing within the Holy of Holies.

John said, "I see the Ark of the Covenant."

Instinctively, shielding his eyes with his arms, John repeated the response of every believer when seeing the majesty of God—"Amen." John again fell on his face, for the Ark was the one place in the Old Testament where God had touched the earth. It was the one place in the Old Testament where the presence of God had manifested Himself when communicating with His people. John remembered what God had told Moses.

I will meet with you, and I will speak with you from above the mercy seat, from between the two cherubim which are on the ark of the Testimony [Covenant]... (Exodus 25:22).

John was sure that the Ark he saw in Heaven was not the actual Ark carried by Israel in the wilderness. Just as the Temple in Heaven was probably a pattern of God's house on earth, so the Ark he was seeing was a pattern of the one built in the wilderness.

John remembered all the rumors about the Ark of the Covenant. Some thought when Nebuchadnezzar had destroyed the temple in A.D. 586, the Ark had been buried in a secret cavern under the temple—in the Dome of the Rock—under the Holy of Holies. Others thought Nebuchadnezzar had given the Ark to Jeremiah the prophet, who buried it on Mt. Nebo, or on a Judean hill; or Jeremiah had taken it to Egypt for the renegade temple the Jews built at Tapaneese, on an island in the Nile delta. But wherever the Ark was, John was now looking into the Temple of Heaven, and he was seeing the real Ark of the Covenant.

Your Time to Worship

- Lord, I come to Your presence because there is no place else to go. I worship You.

- Lord, even though I can't see You with my eyes, I can know You in my heart. I adore You.

- Lord, even though You are everywhere present all the time, I want to get as close to You as I can. I want to be in Your heart because I need You.

- Lord, You are so much greater than my experience, but I want to feel You as real as any person can. I want to touch You and have You touch me.

- Lord, my emotions are so limited, and You are an unlimited God; but I want You to know, I love You.

While looking at the Ark, John felt closer to God than he had ever been before. For the Ark was the place where God dwelt with His people; it was the place God touched man. In the Ark (meaning, "box") were the two stone tablets where Moses had chiseled the Ten Commandments. The Ten Commandments given by God explained how He wanted His people to live. Also in the Ark was a symbolic pot of manna to remind God's people of His loving provision of food. When they had faced starvation, God continually fed them with manna. Finally, Aaron's rod that budded was in the box. When many rebelled against Moses as God's leader, God caused Aaron's rod (a dead stick) to blossom. This act reminded them that God can bring life out of death.

John, from his Patmos cave, continued to look into the Temple and gaze into the Holy of Holies. Then, he became aware that he was not the only one afforded this privilege. He turned his eyes away from the Temple to notice millions upon millions of observers in Heaven. They too were seeing what had never been seen before. All those in Heaven were gazing at the Ark of the Covenant with their actual eyes, and all other believers not yet in Heaven would see it through John's eyes; for the aged apostle would write it down so that future children of God could see into the Holy of Holies when they read the Book of Revelation.

As John gazed at the Ark of the Covenant, lightnings flashed and thunder rumbled down the hallways of Heaven, bouncing off the walls, then rolling towards the outer limits of space; just as lightnings and thunders had surrounded Mt. Sinai when God had met Moses there. Eventually, the pounding reverberations of thunder diminished until they were heard no longer.

All of Heaven worshiped God, for they were closer to seeing God than at any time before. Now, with their eyes, they were as close to God as they had been with their hearts when they had invited Jesus into their lives.

The four Seraphim guarding the throne, worshiped God on their faces. Immediately, the 24 saints followed their example, and next, the multitude of Heaven worshiped God as one person—millions times a million. All of Heaven bowed silently before God—as a servant waiting for a word from his master. All Heaven waited before God with their faces to the floor.

The silence of millions of worshipers times a million was overwhelming.

SILENCE!

How could anyone violate this sacred moment? John felt the weighty importance of the moment—millions upon millions of worshipers... still...quiet...waiting...a holy hush. The Temple of Heaven was reverent. Not knowing what to do or say, they waited for their Lord to give them direction. Likewise, John joined them from his cave. He too waited for God to speak.

What I Learned From Seeing the Ark

- I will enjoy things in Heaven that I can't even imagine while living on earth.

- I will see things and learn things in Heaven that are hidden on earth.

- I should expect phenomenal expressions from God when He reveals Himself.

- I should expect the unsaved to be angry when God punishes them for their sin and rebellion.

- I realize that just because God doesn't immediately judge sin in this life, it doesn't mean He will allow people to continually get away with rebelling against Him. There is judgment in the future.

Section Six

Scripture: Revelation 11:15–13:18

Lord, when the seventh angel blew his trumpet,
      You brought all people into Your presence
      Where they saw the original Temple in Heaven.
There was shouting, telling Heaven and earth,
      "The Kingdoms of this world
Have become the Kingdoms of Christ,
      And He will reign forever and ever."
The 24 saints bowed in worship to You,
      Prostrating themselves on the ground,
Saying, "We give thanks to You, the Almighty Lord God,
      You who are,
      You who were,
      And You who will always exist."
Because You have exercised Your omnipotent power,
      And have begun to reign on the earth.
When You judged the nations, they were angry
      Because You judged them in wrath;
      They were not remorseful or repentant.
Now is the time to punish the wicked
      And reward Your servants and Your prophets,
      And those small and great who revered Your name,
Because You destroyed those who destroyed
      The earth and Your followers.

Lord, then the Temple in Heaven began to open for all to see,
> And behind the veil everyone could see clearly,
> All saw the Ark of the Covenant.
Suddenly, there were flashes of lightning,
> Rumbling thunder, an earthquake,
> And violent hail on earth.

Seven Personages

Revelation chapters 12 and 13 depict seven personages (not called people because some of the individuals represent a group of people). These are seven personages that trace the history of satan's opposition to God's plan through Israel.

1. **Israel** — The women dressed in the sun is the nation Israel; the 12 stars are the 12 tribes of Israel; and the Man-Child is the Messiah-Deliverer (see Rev. 12:1). Throughout the Old Testament, satan tried to prevent the birth of the Messiah—Jesus Christ.

2. **Satan** — The red dragon is satan who uses earthly nations (crowns) to oppose Israel (see Rev. 12:3-4,9).

3. **Jesus** — The Man-Child is Jesus who will rule the world in the coming one thousand years of peace (see Rev. 12:5).

4. **Michael** — He is the archangel who opposes all satan tries to do to Israel and Jesus Christ (see Rev. 12:7).

5. **Saved Jews during the Tribulation** — The remnant of the woman's seed, i.e., Israel. Satan persecutes Israel during the last half of the Tribulation, but Israel flees to the desert (Petra) for protection.

6. **Antichrist** — The beast out of the sea (see Rev. 13:1) is the antichrist, or the false messiah. He will imitate Christ. The

antichrist is raised from the dead (see Rev. 12:3,12), and wants everyone to worship him, in opposition to Christ who wants everyone to worship Him.

7. **The False Prophet** — The beast out of the earth is the false prophet (see Rev. 13:11). He is the third person of the unholy triad. Satan wants to be like the Father (see Isa. 14:14); the antichrist takes the place of Jesus; and the false prophet imitates the works of the Holy Spirit. Just as the Holy Spirit exalts Jesus Christ (see John. 16:14), the false prophet tries to entice the world to worship the antichrist during the Tribulation.

1. Israel

Lord, then John saw a woman in Heaven clothed with the sun,
  With the moon beneath her feet.
The woman was the nation Israel
  From whom God promised the Deliverer would come.
Israel was constantly persecuted by satan,
  Because he wanted to prevent the Deliverer from being born.

2. Satan

Lord, John also saw satan as an enormous dragon,
  Controlling seven nation-rulers,
  With ten horns and a crown on each head.
Satan pulled one third of the fallen angels
  With him when he was banished from Heaven to earth.

3. Jesus

Lord, satan tried to kill those in the line of the Deliverer
  So He wouldn't be born;
  Satan knew the Messiah would one day rule over the earth.
The Deliverer-Jesus completed Your work on earth,
  And You received Him back into Heaven.

4. Michael the Archangel

There was war in Heaven where Michael the Archangel
　　Fought against the devil and his fallen angels.
Satan was cast out of Heaven to earth
　　To complete his evil desire on earth.
Satan is also called the devil, the serpent,
　　Who tries to lead the whole world into sin.

Lord, You shouted with a loud voice,
　　　"Victory, and power, and rulership
　　　Now belong to Me."
You shouted, "Now Jesus Christ can rule; satan is cast down;
　　　He will no longer persecute Christians;
　　　He will no longer accuse the brethren to Me."

Satan is beaten by the blood of the Lamb
　　And by the faithfulness of martyrs
　　　Who did not hold onto life in the face of death.
You said, "Let Heaven and its citizens rejoice,
　　　But to those on earth beware."
Satan is angrily coming to persecute believers,
　　Because he knows his time is short.
When satan found himself cast to the earth,
　　He turned his anger against the Jews,
　　Because Jesus the Messiah came from them.

5. The Remnant of Israel

During the last half of the Tribulation,
　　Israel escaped to the wilderness,
　　Away from the devil who persecuted her.
Israel stayed in the desert fortress of Petra
　　For three and a half years,
　　During the last half of the Tribulation.

Every scheme of satan to destroy Israel
  Was thwarted by the desert.
Then satan determined to punish every
  Follower of Christ left on the earth.

6. The Antichrist

Lord, John saw a terrible animal emerge from the sea.
  It was the antichrist, the false messiah.
The antichrist had in his hand seven nation-rulers,
  And the antichrist had crowns on his ten horns.
  He controlled the ten nations of the revived Roman Empire.
The antichrist was opportunistically like a leopard,
  But ferocious like a bear,
  And wanted to rule like the king of the jungle—the lion.
Satan gave the antichrist the same power he possessed,
  And allowed the antichrist to rule the world for him.
One of the antichrist's seven heads had been killed,
  But the antichrist came back to life,
  So that multitudes marveled and followed him.
The antichrist, in a very persuasive speech, blasphemed You,
  And slandered Your Temple and those who follow You.
Satan gave the antichrist power to fight against Your people,
  To overcome them for three and a half years,
  And to rule every ethnic group, language, and nation.
Everyone worshiped the antichrist except those
  Whose names were in the Lamb's Book of Life,
  And those who the antichrist had killed.

Lord, You said, "Those who have ears
  To hear spiritual messages,
    Listen carefully to what will happen."
Christians will be arrested, taken away, and imprisoned;
  Other believers will be killed.

This will be an opportunity for Your children
>   To demonstrate their endurance and faith.

7. The False Prophet

Lord, John saw another terrible animal emerge from the sea
>   Who tried to look like a lamb,
>   But he had a haunting voice like satan.
The second animal—the false prophet—served the antichrist,
>   And propagated his influence everywhere.
He pointed out the antichrist's fatal wound and told everyone
>   How he had been raised from the dead,
>   Persuading everyone to worship the antichrist.
The antichrist organized his own "church"
>   Bringing down fire from Heaven,
>   Just as You sent fire on Pentecost.
The false prophet did miracles to convince everyone
>   To follow the antichrist.
The false prophet erected a statue (idol) to the antichrist,
>   Showing the wound that killed him,
>   Yet also showing that the antichrist was now alive.
The false prophet breathed in the statue of the antichrist
>   So that it spoke his word.
Those who refused to worship the antichrist's statue
>   Were put to death.
The false prophet ordered everyone to be branded
>   With the brand of the antichrist
>   In their forehead or right hand.
Everyone was branded no matter how young or old,
>   Rich or poor, slave or citizen.
And no one could buy or sell anything,
>   Unless they were branded
>   With the name of the antichrist or his number.
Anyone can calculate the number of the antichrist—

Worship: When We First See the Ark, and
the Seven Personages of the Future Tribulation

It is 666.
Amen.

Chapter 66

THE UNKNOWN SONG OF THE 144,000

Scripture: Revelation 14:1-20

The Sunday sun was falling in the west, the dark fingers of afternoon shadows stretched across the backs of the kneeling worshipers in front of John's cave. The threat of the morning storms had evaporated. Praying deep within the belly of the mountain, the aged apostle had been absorbed by visions for hours, and because the setting sunrays couldn't reach him, he didn't realize the time of day.

John should have been getting tired...after all, he was over 90 years old. But the presence of God invigorated him. He was driven by passion.

Soon, another vision appeared to him. Just as his watery eyes had gazed upon Jesus earlier in the day, so now he saw Him standing in the center of Heaven—standing on Mount Zion...the Eternal City...Jerusalem.

John's heart missed a beat. Mount Zion, called the Upper City of Jerusalem, held many warm memories—he knew every street blindfolded. His father, Zebedee, had made enough money while fishing to purchase a home on Mount Zion, and young John ran through its streets as a teenager. Now in a vision, the aged John was revisiting the beloved city of his adolescence.

The rock covered streets and white plastered homes were as real as John remembered them, except he couldn't touch their tall white walls with his hands, nor could his feet walk its dusty streets. He simply visited with his eyes.

In his vision, Jesus was walking on Mount Zion, just as He had walked there toward the upper room on the evening of the Last Supper. The Master knew His way around Mount Zion, just as John did.

There was also a great multitude with Jesus who were all dressed in white—not the everyday white tunics, but in a pure white linen...a spotless white...the dress of the martyrs. John's ears, while failing, could now hear the shout...

"THESE ARE MADE CLEAN BY THE BLOOD OF THE LAMB."

These martyrs seemed to be the same ones he had seen earlier. John's memory was foggy—he wasn't sure. He knew he had previously seen martyrs; he recognized them by their clothing. He knew those martyrs had come out of the Great Tribulation, but had these martyrs died at different times than the previous ones? John's mind was playing tricks with him—they did look the same.

He then saw the name of the Father branded on the martyrs' foreheads. They had identified with the Father, even to the point of death. But, on the other hand, what about those who had refused the identity of the Father? The number 666 had been engraved in the forehead and hands of the unsaved who lived during the Tribulation. They had submitted themselves to satan in order to buy food, clothes, and anything else.

Seeing the courage of these martyrs bolstered John's faith.

They had made a life-changing decision to follow Jesus. In their conversion experience, they had turned their back on the world's system and sin's temptation. Trusting God had been more than a single event to them; daily, they had recommitted their life to Christ. Every time they had tried to purchase food, they were refused because they had decided to follow Jesus. Without the 666 insignia, their money was useless. So daily, their choice was Jesus or food...Jesus or clothing...Jesus or necessities.

These martyrs had been given a choice—renounce Jesus or die! Somewhere along the line, they could have chosen to live, but that would have included a decision to reject Jesus. These martyrs with the Father's name on their forehead had chosen daily to follow Jesus to death.

A decision to die is contrary to the instincts of the flesh. The human nature yearns to live...as happy as possible...as pain-free as possible...as long as possible. When these martyrs had chosen the name of the Father rather than the number 666, they had chosen to suffer for Jesus. Because their Master had suffered for them on the cross, it was the least they could do.

John watched the martyrs following Jesus and was envious of their experience. Although he was suffering on Patmos, he considered his pain superficial. Their pain had been terminal. John knew he would not die a violent death. Jesus had said that Peter and the other disciples would die for their faith, but not John.

These martyrs whom John was watching gave new meaning to the phrase, "I die daily." Theirs was not just a death to evil impulse, nor was their death a crucifixion of the old nature. They had experienced hunger—a constant, gnawing pain slowly eating away at their life. Daily these martyrs lost strength, until death ended their ordeal. They could have ended their suffering simply by accepting the number 666 on their forehead, but instead, they chose the Father's name and with it, they chose martyrdom and received eternal life.

When John discovered that there were 144,000 standing at Mount Zion with Jesus, he knew they must be the martyrs he saw earlier for they were the same number as before.

"Thank You, Lord, for those willing to die for You," John worshiped from his cave. He paused in reverence for the martyrs. Those who had been burned in fire now stood in their new glorified bodies with Jesus...no smell of smoke, no trace of fire. Those who had been torn apart by wild beasts but now whole in body, stood with Jesus...no tears...no remorse. Those who had been starved, now appeared well fed...healthy...happy.

The martyrs did not pray for revenge upon their enemies; they were only interested in surrounding Jesus the Lamb, and their eyes were fixed on Him. Nothing in Heaven distracted them—not the angels, not the 24 saints, not the four angelic worship leaders around the throne. They had been martyred for the cause of Jesus; now they wanted to worship Him.

The next moment, John was distracted by a growing noise, sounding louder as it moved toward him. He turned to look further into the dark cave, but the sound was not coming from deep within the mountains, nor did it come from outside. The surging noise was coming from his vision. And it was becoming louder, as though he were standing next to a waterfall. Then the sound grew much louder than a waterfall; it bellowed like thunder bouncing across the hills. Yet it was not thunder, for it would eventually quiet as it rolled out of hearing. Instead, this sound grew progressively louder in John's ears. He was hearing the sound of the saved coming toward him.

What had been noise the previous moment now changed to the distinct sound of human voices. John heard voices singing—loud singing. On many occasions, John had heard people cheering so loudly he couldn't understand what they were saying. This time, he could hear human words, yet couldn't understand their meaning. It was not the yell of men fighting in battle; it was a happy sound...it was music...it was a gigantic singing choir.

John had heard the Levitical choirs in the temple many times, their precise trained voices giving glory to God. Because these choirs had been so accurately trained, John could understand every word they sang. And when the choirs in Jerusalem glorified God, John joined them in praise.

But John couldn't understand the triumphant words he now heard in the vision. He cupped his hands behind his ears, but to no avail. He still couldn't understand the music. Cocking his ear to the left...then to the right...he still couldn't understand.

The martyrs were singing new words to a new song John had never heard. They were singing to a new meter—the music was different. The Levitical choir had sung in a minor chord, but this was a new joyous song, completely foreign to John.

He hadn't heard music like this in the churches of Egypt, Cypress, Asia Minor, or Greece. Nor was it the music of the Romans. It was entirely new,...and John the apostle liked it. The new music made him want to praise God. However, he couldn't join them because he didn't know the words, nor did he know the tune. Somewhat perplexed, John began to ask some questions in prayer...

"What is this new song, and why can't I sing this song of praise with the 144,000?"

Anytime John had encountered people worshiping God, he wanted to join them. When he had visited the different churches with their different languages or dialects, and their different music, he had never felt strange or left out. Even when believers had worshiped God in a different language, John had joined them, singing in his own language. The language of the heart knows no boundaries. Worship from the heart crosses linguistic, ethnic, and class barriers. And just as John had worshiped with many language groups before, he now wanted to worship with the 144,000...but couldn't. The circumstances were different.

But the problem was not the distance between the cave on Patmos and Mount Zion in Heaven. God answered...

"THE 144,000 MARTYRS ARE SINGING A NEW SONG. NO ONE CAN KNOW THIS NEW SONG EXCEPT THOSE WHO HAVE DIED FOR ME."

God explained they were singing the martyrs' song. Only those who had tasted death—as Jesus had tasted death—could sing with them. Dying as a martyr had given them a unique experience, assuring their love for Jesus was 100 percent pure, and their commitment to Jesus was total. Many others in the Church had claimed to have totally loved Jesus, but there had been dark pockets of resistance in their hearts. They had held back from total devotion, yet the martyrs had held back nothing.

The new song was lovely to John's ears. The martyrs joyfully sang, unlike any human voices. Their singing sounded as beautiful as the music of a harp.

Your Time to Worship

- Lord, when I hear others worshiping You, I am grateful that You receive us all.

- Lord, when I see others worshiping You, I identify with them and exalt You even higher.

- Lord, when I find myself with others who are worshiping You, they motivate me to deeper expressions of my heart. I am grateful for corporate worship.

- Lord, when I don't receive what others do, thank You for what I have. I praise You for who You are!

- Lord, thank You that martyrs praise You; thank You for remembering them. May I live for You as they died for You.

John left the table where he had written the vision. Kneeling with his face to God on the cold stone floor, he worshiped the Lamb.

Although he couldn't worship with the new song of the martyrs, for only they knew the words, John worshiped God for protecting him from danger...for deliverance from physical suffering...for long life. A moment ago, John had been envious that he was not a martyr; now the old apostle was grateful for a peaceful life.

"Thank You for over 90 years of life," John offered his gratitude to God. Tears forced their way through his squeezed eyelids, and he thought, *What is harder—to die for Jesus...or to live for Jesus?*

The eleven disciples who had followed Jesus—John's friends—all had been martyred for their faith. Peter had been horribly crucified—upside down; Paul had been soaked with tar, then set aflame in Nero's garden to be slowly burned on a stake. Just as he had been a blazing witness for God in life, he likewise died in burning flames.

Why have I been spared? Why haven't I died as a martyr? John wondered and then thanked God for a life free from suffering.

John remembered the night before Jesus had died. It was at the Last Supper that Jesus had told His disciples they would desert Him. Even though barely 20 years old at the time, John remembered his youthful courage and pledge...

"Though everyone else runs away, I won't."

When the Roman soldiers had arrested Jesus, John had followed at a distance. And when Jesus had been taken to Caiphas' house for the religious trial, John had been downstairs in the courtyard. When the soldiers had hoisted the cross into the sky, John had watched in disbelief, not knowing what to do. He then remembered Jesus telling him from the cross...

"Son, behold your mother." Jesus gave him the care of Mary. Then to make sure there was no misunderstanding, Jesus told Mary, "Woman, behold your son."

Because John had followed all the way to the cross—facing the possibility of death—God had promised that he would die a natural death in old age. The other disciples who had run from death would eventually become martyrs. John knew their stories. When given a second chance, none of the other disciples had backed away, and all had died violent deaths for Jesus.

John bowed on the hard stone floor of the cave. He was no longer in a prophetic spirit; John was no longer seeing a vision. He was worshiping God, because although many Christians were suffering across the Roman world, their future was secure. After death, they would be with Jesus, worshiping Him. John was thankful for hope, and even from a cold cave, he worshiped Jesus. Shortly, he would return to his table where he would continue to write the vision—this time relaying how martyrs would worship in the future.

What I Learned From the Lamb on Mount Zion

- I can worship God because of the things I remember about Him from my recessive memory.

- I need to faithfully reflect the Father's name, as martyrs in the past were faithful to proclaim His name.

- I will receive a special message from God when I do special things for Him, as did the martyrs.

- I will have a special place with God if I do not defile myself sexually, or any other way.

- I must commit myself to follow the Lord without hesitation, as did the martyrs.

- I realize that martyrs are closest to the heart of God, because they have given the most for the glory of God.

Section Seven

Scripture: Revelation 14:1-20

Lord, John saw the Lamb—Jesus standing on Mount Zion
       In the city of Jerusalem;
  With Him were 144,000 martyrs.
       They had Your name written on their foreheads.
John heard a growing sound
       Like a roar of a great waterfall,
       Like rolling thunder over the plains.
Yet the sound was pleasing, like the singing of a choir
       Accompanied by harps.
The martyrs were singing a new song

In front of Your throne.
The four Seraphim were worshiping with them,
    So were the 24 saints on their thrones.
Only the 144,000 could learn the new hymn
    Because they had been redeemed
    From the suffering and tribulations of earth.
These had not defiled themselves spiritually;
    They were as pure as virgins.
Because they had followed the Lamb in persecution,
    They were redeemed from tribulation.
    They are a firstfruits offering to You.
They never told a lie,
    And their lives were blameless.

Lord, John saw an angel flying over Heaven,
    Announcing the end was near.
The Good News has been preached to all people—
    To every ethnic group, language, and nation on earth.
The angel shouted, "Fear God and praise Him,
    For His time has come to sit in judgment;
    Everyone worship the Creator of Heaven and earth."

Lord, John saw another angel shouting, "All people
    Who worshiped the antichrist,
    And branded themselves with his brand,
Must drink the wine of judgment that is poured out
    By God who is angry against sin."
They will be tortured in the presence
    Of Your holy angels and the Lamb,
    And the smoke of their torture rises forever and ever.
There will be no relief for them day or night,
    Because they worshiped the beast and his statues,
    And accepted his branding in their right hand and foreheads.

Lord, John wrote, "Christians must remain faithful in persecution
Because the antichrist will be judged,
And the unsaved will be punished."
Then John was told to write, "Happy are those
Who die in the Lord during the Tribulation."
The Holy Spirit said, "They will rest from their trials,
Forever in the Lord,
For their good works will follow them."
Again, John looked to see Jesus—the Son of Man,
Sitting on a cloud
With a golden crown on His head.
He had a sharp sickle in his hand
Ready to go to work.
Another angel came out of the Temple and shouted
To Jesus sitting on the cloud,
"The time has come; use the sickle on earth,
For sin is ripe and ready to be harvested.
The people of the earth have gathered to fight You."
Then He swung His sickle against all unsaved people,
Gathering them for judgment before Your throne.
Another angel who also had a sickle
Came out of the Temple to tell Jesus,
"Put Your sickle to work to cut all the grapes
From the vine of the earth,
Because sin is abundantly ripe."
So the sickle was put to the harvest,
And filled the wine press of God's anger
With the people of the earth.
It was the battle of the valley of Armageddon.
And blood ran in a river 200 miles long,
As high as a horse's bridle.
Amen.

Chapter 67

WORSHIPING THE LAMB

Scripture: Revelation 15:1–18:24

John continued to sit at his crude table, writing down everything he saw in one prophetic vision after another. He had looked into Heaven to see one worship scene after another, each one separated by terrible pictures of judgment on earth. Like a gigantic parenthesis or reprieve, each beautiful vision of people worshiping God made it easier for John to write the next scenes of horrendous judgments. John bowed his head over the many pages of his manuscript and prayed...

"Lord, how much longer will You punish the earth?" The old apostle knew that God would have to cleanse the earth of every taint of sin. Again he asked, "How long?" He listened for the response, and then heard an answer...

"Shortly..."

John lifted his tired head to once more gaze into the vision. There in the center of Heaven, John saw seven angels—busy, preparing to do something, although John wasn't sure what they would do.

What John didn't immediately realize was that God was showing him these angels in answer to his question. These seven angels would pour out the final judgment of God on the earth. Then it would be over.

God had not shown John everything; indeed, Heaven was so large that it was impossible for John to see everything from his cave in Patmos. But God had yet to show something special to John—something he had not seen...

A beautiful, calm, glistening sea.

Without one ripple breaking upon its surface, the sea reflected a beautiful red glow, and John thought he was watching a dazzling sunset. The sea glowed as it if were on fire.

Then John saw a multitude standing on the red sea—not as large as the entire multitude in Heaven, nor as large as the 144,000. They were standing on the sea that glowed like fire, and they were singing.

Who are these? the Seer asked himself. He peered long, looking from face to face, trying to determine the answer.

A voice then interrupted John's thoughts and informed him, "These are the ones who were victorious in the Great Tribulation. They refused to bow down to the image of the antichrist or place idols in their homes." These people standing on the glowing red sea had taken a stand against the evil system of satan and had prevailed. They had not accepted the antichrist's number—666—in their hand or forehead and had refused to let satan control their lives. But this crowd had been victorious over satan, unlike the 144,000 martyrs who were killed when they also refused to submit to the antichrist.

What are they singing? John searched his failing memory for the name of the familiar hymn he heard. He could recall that it was a song that he had sung as a youth in the synagogue of Caperneum, but he couldn't remember its title. He listened to its familiar refrain, and then hummed the words. Suddenly, it came back to him, and he said aloud to no one in particular, "They are singing the song of Moses."

John remembered it was a hymn of victory. When Moses and Israel had triumphed over Pharaoh and Egypt, they had sung a psalm of triumph. They had won a religious battle between the gods of Egypt and the God of Israel. It had been a battle of two opposing wills—would Pharaoh rule God's people or would God rule His people? When Pharaoh's 600 chariots had been ready to attack Israel, God had blown the wind upon the Red Sea, pushing back its waters. Then the children of Israel had crossed over to the other side on dry ground. When Pharaoh had tried to follow Israel, God withdrew His wind that had been holding back the sea, and all the Egyptians drowned along with Pharaoh. On the other side, Moses led Israel in singing...

> *I will sing unto the Lord,*
> > *For He has triumphed gloriously.*
> *Pharaoh's horses and chariots threatened me;*
> > *They were destroyed by the sea.*
> *The Lord is my strength and song;*
> > *He has become my salvation.*
> *The Lord is a man of war;*
> > *His name is the powerful Jehovah.*
> *Pharaoh's army has drowned in the Red Sea;*
> > *His officers sank to the bottom as stones.*
> *The Lord's right hand was gloriously revealed;*
> > *He dashed in pieces the enemy.*
> *In an excellent way God overthrew the Egyptians;*
> > *God's wrath burned them as stubble.*
> *God's breath blew the waters apart,*
> > *And Israel passed over on dry land.*
> *The enemy chased Israel into the bottom of the sea;*
> > *Their lust drove them to their death.*
> *God stopped breathing so the waters flooded the enemy;*
> > *They sank as lead to their destruction.*
> *What God is like unto the Lord?*
> > *He is glorious in holiness and powerful in miracles.*
> *God will bring Israel into the Promised Land;*
> > *God will dwell in the sanctuary among His people.*
> *Sing unto the Lord for He has triumphed gloriously.*
> > *The Lord shall reign forever and ever.*
>
> (Exodus 15:1-18, author's translation)

The words came back to John. He joyfully sang the song of Moses along with those in Heaven. Just as God had given Moses a great victory over Pharaoh, so this multitude had won a great victory over satan and his forces during the Tribulation. And just as Moses and the multitude had sung a victory song, so those in Heaven praised God with the same song.

John bowed his head to thank God for victory. Although he was presently a captive, by faith he knew one day he would be free. Although God's people were now being tormented by Rome throughout the Mediterranean world, by faith, each victim would be victorious. In the black cave, John's feeble voice sang the victory song of Moses, and pure light flooded his soul. The damp cave sparkled, and praise vanquished despair.

Your Time to Worship

- Lord, You are greater than our greatest fear, more powerful than our mighty enemy. I praise You for victory in my life.

- Lord, You are more beautiful than our beauty, and more brilliant than our light. I magnify You for knowledge to see and understand.

- Lord, You are superior to our best, and more mighty than our strength. I am grateful for Your strength to overcome.

- Lord, You are truer than our standard of truth; You are more profound than our wisdom. I worship you with my limited human understanding.

- Lord, You are everything and I am nothing; I cannot compare You with anything, for You are above comparison. You are all in all.

John's eyelids became tired, and he dozed. Had the melody put him to sleep? Or did he sleep because the music had stopped? He was mentally alert for a man over 90 years old, but his active mind was imprisoned by a frail body. Even though he resisted, John needed rest—just a catnap—to keep going. His gray hair spread out over the table as he dozed. Suddenly, the silence startled his subconscious. His head popped up, and he gazed into the darkness...

As John rubbed sleep from his eyes, his ears picked up another melody—a different song. Then in prophetic vision, John again saw the multitude singing in Heaven. They were still standing on the sea that glowed as a red fire. This time they were singing a different song. The multitudes in Heaven were composing their own song of triumph and worship, just as Moses had celebrated and composed his psalm of victory.

> *Great and marvelous are Your works;*
> *You are Lord God Almighty.*
> *Just and true are Your ways;*
> *You are King of the saints.*
> *How can we not fear You?*
> *Your name is glorious.*
> *All nations shall come to worship You.*
> *You only are holy.*
> *You have finally judged the earth;*
> *You are faithful to Your Word.*

As the multitudes praised God for the great victory given them, John again slipped from his table to his knees. It was difficult seeing people worship God without joining them. The praise music of one person often motivates another to join in worship to God.

As John was worshiping God, he sensed something else happening, and lifted his head to look about Heaven. The quietness captured his attention. He wondered what everyone seemed to be waiting for and noticed that they were looking at the Temple in the center of Heaven. Something was happening there. Then John saw movement.

The Temple was opening again. Previously, he had looked inside the Temple to see the Ark of the Covenant. As John anticipated the next event, he wondered what he would see this time. Slowly, the doors opened...

The four Seraphim that surrounded the throne, the ones who did the special work of God, held the bowls of the wrath of God located in the Temple. These bowls contained the final and most severe judgments that God would pour out on the earth. The Seraphim gave one bowl to each of the seven waiting angels.

"This is the final judgment of God," John was told. "When these seven angels deliver their punishments to earth, God will have finished purging the earth."

Even though John knew he couldn't see God, he quickly looked back into the Temple, hoping to find Him. But all that John could see in the Temple of God was His wrath—bowls of wrath to be poured out on the earth.

John had constantly preached to his flock, "God is love," yet he knew in his heart that there was another truth—"God is holy."

As the Lawmaker of the universe, God's passion is driven by His love— He is not willing for any to perish. But God is also ruled by His holiness—He cannot allow any infraction of His law to go unpunished. If God forgives the lawbreaker by an arbitrary decision, God is not faithful to His nature and He ceases to keep His promise to punish sin.

In life, John preached God is love; he invited all to salvation through repentance and faith, because Jesus died to forgive any law they had broken. But after life is over and people have been given their final opportunity to repent, God must punish those who break His law. John looked at the seven bowls of God's judgment, then silently asked, "When will God begin the final judgment?"

"NOW," John was told. "Now, the seven angels will deliver God's final punishment to the earth."

John watched as the seven angels left Heaven to deliver their judgment. Only after they had left was the Temple filled with smoke from the glory of God; and John could no longer see anything in the Temple. He remembered that God spoke out of thick darkness on Mount Sinai to Moses. He remembered that when God gave Moses the Ten Commandments on Sinai that the mountain peak was covered with dark clouds and lightnings. The same things were happening here. Now John understood why the clouds concealed the glory of God. God had revealed Himself in love, but covered His glory with thick clouds to preserve from judgment those who were observing the scene.

As much as John didn't want to describe more judgments in his book, he remained faithful to the commission given him by God. He continued to write how each of the seven angels poured out their bowls of judgment, resulting in death, suffering, and misery.

John carefully observed each angel and dutifully wrote what he saw and what each angel did. Finally, when the seventh angel delivered the last judgment, John heard a loud voice out of the Temple—the Temple filled with clouds—a voice that cried with anguish...

"IT IS FINISHED."

These had been the same words that Jesus had announced from the cross. When Jesus had finished dying for the sins of the world, He had claimed His victory from the cross with the words, "IT IS FINISHED." Over the years, John had wondered exactly what Jesus had meant. John had known that the physical life of Jesus was finished; but had there been a deeper meaning? Had Jesus meant, "The penalty against the sins of the world is finished"? Or perhaps Jesus had meant, "The animal sacrifices are finished." Because Jesus had introduced the "age of grace," perhaps he meant "The law as a way of life is finished."

Now 60 years later, John was hearing the same words again. He wondered what the phrase, "IT IS FINISHED" meant. John knew the last angel was pouring out the final judgment. But did it mean more? Did it mean, "The purification of earth is finished"; or did it mean, "The final wrath of God against rebellion is satisfied"?

As soon as John heard the words, "IT IS FINISHED," there appeared lightnings and thunder unlike he ever heard before. And the earth rumbled with a final earthquake, more mighty than before. If there were any thought that a vestige of civilization remained, this earthquake removed all doubt. God had once told Adam to subdue and have dominion over the earth—now everything accomplished by the sons of Adam in every age had been destroyed.

The earth was now prepared to return to its paradise.

Your Time to Worship

- Lord, I praise You because You bring everything to completion. You pronounced, "It is finished" over my salvation.

- Lord, I thank You for completing Your plan in my life, writing, "It is finished" over Your guidance and protection.

- Lord, I adore You because one day You will finish Your plan for this earth.

- Lord, I worship You because one day You will complete the purpose for which You saved me. You will deliver me to Heaven, and You will make me perfect in Your presence.

John, ever the apostle of love, had looked upon the earth for any sign of worldwide repentance or massive turning to God. There had been none. In its place, men had continued to blaspheme God for His judgment on the earth. To the end, John had searched for people to respond to the love of God. But no! To the last opportunity, they had rebelled against Him even as He loved them. And when the end came, those who had been rebellious in life were rebellious in death.

What I Learned From the Victor's Song

- I can worship God with triumphant songs when God gives me victory over difficulties and persecution.

- I can effectively worship God because of my experience, whether I am a martyr or whether I am victorious.

- I can effectively worship God, singing songs written by others, or singing words from my own heart.

- I will never fully know God because I am finite. (God is hidden by smoke and thick darkness.)

- I should praise God for His goodness to us and for His punishment of sin.

- I should praise God because His judgment of this earth will come to an end—"It is finished."

Section Eight

Scripture: Revelation 15:1–18:24

Lord, John then saw a sea without a ripple on its surface.
　　　　The sea had glowing fire in the water.
　　Standing by the sea were those saints
　　　　Who had triumphed against the antichrist.
　　They had refused to worship his statue;
　　　　They had not been branded with the number 666.
　　They had harps and were singing
　　　　The victorious song of Moses—
　　　　How he defeated the Egyptians.

They also sang the song of the Lamb—Jesus,
  Who had given them victory over the antichrist.
"Great and wonderful is everything You do,
  Lord God Almighty.
Just and true are all Your ways.
  You are the King of the nations.
Who would not reverence and praise Your name,
  For you alone are holy?
All nations will come before You,
  To worship and adore You,
  For the righteous things You've done."

Lord, John saw another awful scene in Heaven.
  An angel was distributing the last seven judgments—
  Last, because they were to exhaust God's anger to sin.
John saw the temple of God opening,
  And he could look into the Holy of Holies.
Out came seven angels each with
  A different judgment from God.
Each angel had a pure white linen robe
  And a golden sash around his waist.
One of the Seraphim around the throne gave the seven angels
  Seven bowls filled with the anger of God.
Smoke from the glory of God filled the Temple,
  So that no one could enter
  Until the seven bowls of judgment were finished.

Lord, John heard a voice shout from the Temple to the seven angels,
  "Go pour Your seven bowls out over the earth."

The First Bowl

The first angel poured his bowl on the earth,
  And ugly painful sores broke out on all people
  Who had the brand 666 and worshiped the antichrist statue.

The Second Bowl

The second angel emptied his bowl on the oceans,
And they turned to blood;
Every living thing in them died.

The Third Bowl

The third angel poured his bowl into the rivers and springs.
They also turned to blood.
Then the angel said, "Lord, You live now,
And You lived in the past.
You are Holy in Your judgments.
Because evil people have shed the blood of Your saints,
So You have given them blood to drink.
This is what they deserve."
The angel at the altar responded, "Yes, Lord, God Almighty,
Your punishments are true and just."

The Fourth Bowl

The fourth angel emptied his bowl on the sun,
So the sun scorched people
As if they were burned with fire.
People cursed You for sending these judgments
Because they were severely burned by the sun,
But they would not repent and turn to You.

The Fifth Bowl

The fifth angel emptied his bowl over
The throne of the antichrist,
And his empire was plunged into darkness.
People bit their tongues in pain.
They continued to curse You,
And they refused to repent of their evil.

The Sixth Bowl

The sixth angel emptied his bowl over the Euphrates River,
    And all the water dried up.
And the armies of the East crossed the dry river bed,
    Heading to invade the Promised Land.
Then came a message from the mouth of satan,
    And the antichrist, and the false prophet,
"To all the kings of the nations of the world,
    Join us in fighting God Almighty.
We will finally do away with the Jews
    And fight the God of the Jews."
Three foul spirits came out of their mouth like frogs;
    They were demons sent to deliver the message
    And convince the kings to wage war.
All the armies of the world came to fight God
    At the battle of Armageddon.
Then God attacked them unexpectedly,
    Like a thief in the night catches victims
    When they do not expect violence.

The Seventh Bowl

The seventh angel emptied his bowl into the air,
    And a voice shouted, "The end has come";
    For the last bowl was the sacred coming of Christ.
Then there were flashes of lightning, rolling thunder,
    And a violent earthquake that shook the earth,
    More violently than ever before.
The city of Jerusalem was split into three parts.
    The cities of the earth crumbled to earth.
The city of Babylon was not forgotten;
    It was punished with the violence of its crimes.
The islands of the ocean disappeared;
    No mountain was left standing.

Storms of hail weighing 100 pounds each fell from the sky.
　　And the more fierce the punishment from God,
　　The more people rebelled and cursed God.

The Fall of Religious Babylon

Then one of the seven angels with bowls spoke to John,
　　"Come, I will show you the punishment
　　For the prostituted church of the antichrist."
The kings of the earth have committed sexual sins,
　　By worshiping in his vile temple.
They have made the whole world sin against God
　　By forcing them to partake of her adultery.
John was taken in the Spirit to see the prostitute,
　　Riding on a scarlet red animal.
It had seven heads who were ruling leaders,
　　And ten horns representing the revived Roman Empire.
　　Blasphemy was written all over her.
The prostitute was dressed in purple and red
　　With gaudy jewelry of gold and pearls.
She was drinking a cup of disgusting filthy fornication.
　　On her forehead was written,
　　"Babylon the Great, mother of all prostitutes."
The prostitute was drunken with the blood of martyrs
　　Whom she had killed.
John stared at the prostitute in alarm.
　　The angel said, "Don't be horrified.
　　I will explain who the prostitute is and the beast she rides.
She is the pseudo-church of the antichrist which was alive,
　　But she died and will come from the bottomless pit
　　To eventually be destroyed.
Those whose names are in the Lamb's Book of Life
　　Will be dumbfounded by this reappearance.
The seven heads represent seven rulers

Who live in a city with seven hills.
Five leaders have already fallen, a sixth now reigns;
    The seventh is yet to come.
The scarlet red animal is the eighth ruler;
    He will come up from hell
    But will be destroyed and return there.
The ten horns are ten kings who don't yet have power;
    They will rule in the future for a short time,
    Providing their strength and authority for the antichrist's use.
They will war against the Lamb at Armageddon.
    But the Lamb is the Lord of lords and King of kings;
    He will defeat them and their followers."

The angel continued his explanation, "The waters
    Beside the prostitute are all the people who follow
    The antichrist from every people group, language,
    and nation.
But the ten rulers and the antichrist will turn against
    The pseudo-church, stripping it of its rituals and power.
God will influence the minds of sinful people
    To do His pleasure with the pseudo-church,
    Until He comes to judge the antichrist and his followers."

The Fall of Commercial Babylon

John saw another angel come from Heaven;
    His brightness shined to all the earth.
He shouted, "Babylon is fallen, Babylon is fallen,
    Which is the den of demons.
Every filthy spirit and every detestable idea
    Also lives there.
All the nations have been intoxicated with
    Her proposition to sin.
All the world leaders have committed adultery
    With her and grown rich from her extravagance."

Then John heard a voice from Heaven,
 "Come out from her, people of God.
 Do not share in her crimes and sins.
God in Heaven knows about her sins.
 She will be treated as she treated others;
 She will be paid back double what punishment she gave out.
Every one of her sinful pleasures and luxuries
 Will give her grief and misery.
She boasts that she is a queen on a throne;
 She is not sorry for anything she's done.
Judgment will fall on her in a single day;
 She'll suffer disease, mourning, and hunger.
You, Lord God, who has great power
 Will burn her up.
The world rulers, who have fornicated with her,
 Will weep and mourn for they lose everything.
When they see the smoke of commercial Babylon burning,
 They will stay away at a safe distance and cry,
'Alas!...Alas! Our great city
 Babylon, a mighty city
 Was destroyed in a single hour.'
All the businesspeople of the earth will
 Weep and mourn over her,
Because no one will any longer buy
 Gold, silver, jewels, pearls, fine cloths,
 Perfumes, costly furniture, and sculptures.
They also cry for lack of oil, flour, wheat,
 Meat, and automobiles.
And no one will work anywhere because
 There is no money to pay anyone
 To do anything.
The expensive things they loved are gone, never to return.
 All the ease and pleasure have ceased.

The businesspeople who made a fortune out of
      Commercial Babylon will stand at a safe distance
      To wring their hands and grieve saying,
'This is terrible; what am I going to do?'
      Everything that was beautiful and fine
      And comfortable was destroyed in a single hour.
All the fashionable clothes, accumulated wealth,
      Exquisite meals, entertainment, and vacations
      Were all destroyed in a single hour.
All the captains of ships and people who
      Made a living from the sea,
      Stayed at a safe distance,
Watching the smoke as commercial Babylon burned, crying,
      'There has never been a civilization like this;
      We will never see anything like this again.
That great city—commercial Babylon—that kept
      Us rich through her excesses,
      Was ruined in a single hour.'"

Yet, there was rejoicing in Heaven, from all
      The saints, apostles, and prophets;
For You judged an economic system that persecuted them.
      You judged a way of life that rebelled against righteousness.

Then a mighty angel lifted a huge mill-stone
      And threw it into the ocean saying,
"So shall this commercial way of life
      Never be heard from again.
Never again will there be the sound of music,
      Dancing, reverie, and the laughter of pleasure seekers.
Never again will there be the sound of machines in factories
      Or the ring of cash registers, or any business ventures.
There will be no electricity; everything will be dark.
      Every machine that runs will shut down.

There'll be no laughing like people in love,
    And no one will achieve their heart's desire.
All your luxuries, entertainment, and pleasures
    Will be gone forever;
For in commercial Babylon is found the blood of martyrs
    Who were destroyed by her way of life."
        Amen.

Chapter 68

WORSHIP AT THE
MARRIAGE SUPPER OF THE LAMB

Scripture: Revelation chapters 19–20

John's tired eyes were closed. His face was bowed to the ground in worship to God—it was his only response to the last vision he had seen. He had not looked up for quite awhile. The Seer was having difficulty coming to terms with the atrocities that had been shown in his vision at the end of the Tribulation. It seemed like the wrath intensified as the end approached.

John believed in God, but he had difficulty understanding the extent of the devastation that unfolded before him. While John had not left his cave, nor had he grown any older, even so he had just experienced seven years—seven horrible years of Tribulation wrath poured out on the earth.

John saw the carnage of war with its ensuing starvation, homelessness, and inflation. He saw the pale horse bringing death to 25 percent of the world. He saw persecution spread to God's servants—ultimately 144,000 were martyred.

Next, John saw lightning plummeting to the earth, burning almost a third of the forests in flames. Giant hail stones killed people in the open fields. Then, John witnessed a meteoric fireball plunging into the ocean, claiming approximately a third of all life in the sea. The stability of the universe came unglued, comets plunged to the earth, poison from the sky contaminated much of the drinking water. Earthquakes rumbled across the continents, creating more fires and blinding smoke that blanketed the sun, blocking out its life-giving rays. Disease and sickness spread unchecked.

John shut his eyes to the destruction caused by a herd of demonic spirits spreading out over the earth to do the work of satan and the antichrist.

With the stench of death everywhere, John wearily asked, "Is that all?" But God was not finished with judgment until every wrong had been righted and every transgression punished. Poison in the atmosphere continued to produce grievous sores; rotting corpses of sea creatures in the ocean produced nauseous fumes. A foul stench turned the stomachs of even the strongest men. With no pure water to quench their thirst, and toxic poisons in the sky burning up the ozone layer, the scorching sun burned the bodies of those dying slowly from starvation and thirst.

With suffering everywhere, no one trusted another. Fathers turned against sons, and mothers against their families. Driven by excruciating thirst for fresh water and food to satisfy their hunger, the earth was filled with rioting and looting, and a once civilized people murdered one another over something as insignificant as a piece of bread.

When it seemed as though nothing worse could happen, the antichrist called for the nations to attack Israel in the Promised Land. They knew that in God's city—Jerusalem—the city of peace, people were smiling because of the blessings of God. There was water to drink and food to eat, and the city had not been influenced by the collapse of the corrupt monetary system of the world leader. None of those who were living under God's protection in Jerusalem had the mark of 666 upon their foreheads or hands.

Because of the peace of God's people, in contrast to the anger of those who hated God's people, the antichrist called the world to a final solution of the Jews. Consequently, they planned to march into the Holy Land, and once and for all slaughter all the Jews—a holocaust to solve the Jewish dilemma.

In the final moments of the Tribulation, God finally retaliated against the antichrist and his worldly system. He destroyed the prostitute Babylon, including all her wealth, beauty, and earthly desires—in one day. Those who saw it gasped; they couldn't believe that their magnificent Babylon could disappear so suddenly.

John saw the entire seven years of carnage through the power of prophetic vision. While it was horrible to witness, John realized it would all happen in the future as God predicted. In the coming seven years of Tribulation, the horror of its experience would be worse than any futuristic dream he saw.

Old John's knees creaked as he bowed in worship and prayer. Humility was a position that suited him. He thanked God again for salvation and for daily protection. He thanked God for the safety of the cold cave and for meager bread on the table waiting for him.

But even though John's spirit was comfortable bowing before God, his ancient knees began to rebel. As his heart sought to remain longer in the presence of God, his aching body needed rest.

Your Time to Worship

- Lord, I don't understand all You've done for me on the cross, but I thank You for salvation.

- Lord, I don't see all You do for me each day, but I praise You for supernatural guidance and protection.

- Lord, I don't know why You let me serve You, because I am so feeble compared to Your power; but I am grateful for the opportunity to be Your slave.

- Lord, I don't know why You hear my prayers, because I am so limited and I don't know how to pray; but I continually lift up Your name in praise.

- Lord, there's much about my faith I don't understand, but I know enough to worship You, and I know enough to trust my future to You.

Deep within the dark cave, John heard an approaching rumble coming from his vision of the endtimes. *Is there yet more?* he inwardly asked. *Does God have more earthquakes for the earth?* The old apostle tilted his ear to listen. At the same time, he looked with his prophetic eyes, waiting for God to show him another scene of the future. This time, however, God didn't show him a scene—just a sound. He lifted his bowed head, and his eyes peered through the darkness to see beyond the stone walls of the cave. Then John's eyes turned upward, looking toward Heaven...

Then he realized the sound was not an earthquake, nor was it the loud banging of crashing buildings. The sound was a word—a pronounced word, though John couldn't tell what was being said. At first he heard it softly, muted...

That's it!

It was a Jewish word, one that he had heard back home as a boy in the synagogue.

John remembered the word and smiled. He had first heard the word from the old rabbis in the synagogue reading the Psalms. Each time those godly fishermen from Capernaum would read the word, they stopped, then pronounced it distinctly. It was attached to no other word—it stood alone. When the old men read the word, all the worshipers in that white-stone synagogue would repeat the word in unison. And John now heard it spiraling down the cave toward him. It was not spoken by one, but by many, simultaneously, their voices like thunder rolling down a valley...bouncing off the mountainsides...growing louder....

"HALLELUJAH."

When the shout finally filled the cave, John repeated the Hebrew meaning to the word, "Praise the Lord." John laughed, nodding his head in approval, for he too was saying in his heart, "HALLELUJAH!" Then John heard a second antiphonal wave sweep down the cave filling the chamber, "HALLELUJAH." Then he heard angels singing...

"SALVATION...AND GLORY...AND HONOR...AND POWER... UNTO THE LORD, OUR GOD."

When the angels sang "SALVATION," John echoed in his heart, "Thank You for salvation...." When the angels sang "GLORY," John prayed, "Be glorified in my life...bring glory to Yourself...You have all power...." John knew that all people in Heaven were worshiping God because He had finished the judgment of seven years of tribulation on the earth. Just as the farmer knows that rain brings life, John knew that with the Tribulation and judgments, God was ushering in life and Heaven.

"HALLELUJAH!"

All Heaven worshiped God saying, "YOU HAVE DONE THE RIGHT THING. YOU HAVE BEEN TRUE TO YOUR PROMISES. YOU HAVE JUDGED BABYLON, THE GREAT PROSTITUTE WHO CORRUPTED THE EARTH WITH HER SIN."

"HALLELUJAH!"

God was worshiped, "YOU HAVE CLEANSED THE EARTH. YOU HAVE PREPARED IT FOR ETERNITY. HALLELUJAH!"

When John heard the voices of Heaven, he again nodded his head. The old man agreed with the people of Heaven that tribulation and judgment of sin had been necessary.

Then John realized that he was still on the Isle of Patmos as a prisoner, and there were thousands of other Christians in the Mediterranean world who remained imprisoned by the Roman Empire. Their tribulation was not over. John's response was to pray for his Roman guards, just as Jesus prayed for the Roman soldiers who had nailed Him to the cross...

"Father, forgive them...."

John prayed for the salvation of Roman oppressors everywhere. But if they wouldn't repent, what would God have to do? John knew the Father would one day judge all those who had persecuted Christians.

Again, John heard the voices deep within the cave echoing from Heaven, "HALLELUJAH...GOD HAS AVENGED THE MURDER OF

HIS SERVANTS." Tears filled John's eyes as he continued to thank God for His goodness.

A silence came across Heaven...a holy hush. John lifted his eyes to see the focus of Heaven on the throne and those who sat about Him. The four Seraphim worship leaders had lifted their hands to command silence. Then before them, the 24 living saints fell to their faces, worshiping God. They broke the silence with a shout,

"HALLELUJAH..."

The four angels at the four corners of the throne of God joined them shouting,

"HALLELUJAH."

Then one of the saints from 24 thrones spoke to the multitude...

"Bow down—worship God. All people—the young—the aged—everyone worship God."

Just when John thought nothing else could be added, he heard the great crowd of Heaven erupt into another worship theme, like a multitude of ocean waves breaking upon the rocks at one time. He heard the crashing sound...

"HALLELUJAH FOR THE LORD GOD ALMIGHTY REIGNS."

John felt in his bones that something terminal was about to happen in Heaven. Even though the old apostle was a stranger to the throne room of God, he felt something awesome was to occur. Not only John, but the 24 saints and the four Seraphim anticipated it as well. The vast multitudes held their breath. All were hoping for something, but didn't know what to expect. Then with a gigantic voice that reached all of Heaven, a great angel announced...

"REJOICE AND WORSHIP GOD BECAUSE THE TIME IS COME FOR THE WEDDING FEAST OF THE LAMB OF GOD. THE BRIDE WILL BE THOSE BLOOD-BOUGHT BELIEVERS WHO HAVE CLOTHED THEMSELVES IN THE FINEST WHITE LINEN ROBES,

WHICH REPRESENT THE RIGHTEOUS DEEDS DONE BY THE PEOPLE OF GOD."

Your Time to Worship

- Because Your power from the beginning stretches into eternity, I shout "Hallelujah" for Your present Almighty protection on me.

- Because Your perfect wisdom is evident from past creation stretching into the future Heaven, I shout "Hallelujah" for Your wise plan for my life right now.

- Because Your accurate judgment punishes only those who should be punished, I shout "Hallelujah" for Your faithfulness to keep Your promise of judgment and reward.

- Because Your presence is everywhere in this world to help and keep me, I shout "Hallelujah" for Your love and care for me.

- Because of Your unswerving promise to return to receive me to Yourself, I shout "Hallelujah."

The angel whose voice had been heard, once again made the announcement that echoed throughout the throne room, down the aisles of the great crowd, and out into eternity…

"BLESSED ARE THOSE WHO ARE INVITED TO THE WEDDING FEAST OF THE LAMB."

When John heard the great invitation, he knew that the time of the end had finally come. He remembered the parable that Jesus had told about ten virgins preparing themselves for the wedding feast. There were five wise bridesmaids and five foolish bridesmaids. John remembered that the five foolish virgins didn't have oil for their lamps, and when the time of the end came, they were shut out.

John knew this was the time for the wedding feast to begin. Christ would fully manifest Himself to His believers, and unbelievers would be shut out. Not knowing what else to do, John fell at the feet of the great angel who had made the announcement. The situation was too tense—what else could he do? Then the angel said...

"Stop...don't worship me; I am just a servant of God like you." John knew that angels were different from humans, but both humans and angels, in their tasks, served God. Angels had also been created by God, just like humans. The great angel said...

"Worship God..."

John continued to precisely write everything that he saw in a book—a book that would give a faithful witness to Jesus Christ, so that all might worship Him.

Then John saw the door to Heaven open. It was the same door that John had seen at the beginning of his vision. When the door opened, John saw a white horse standing there, with Jesus sitting upon it. Because those left on earth might not know Him, the great angel announced the rider of the horse...

"HE IS FAITHFUL AND TRUE...." The eyes of Jesus were bright and scary—they were the eyes of war. They had the intensity of a soldier who takes up his weapon to go into battle. This was not the time for compassion, nor was this the time to show mercy. The writer of Ecclesiastes had said, "There is a time of peace and a time of war, a time to kill and a time to refrain from killing." This was a time of final punishment.

Those on the other side of the battle line had made their choice. Although God loved them, they hated Him in return; and they had made themselves an enemy of God by turning their back on His love. They were more than passive unbelievers; they had clenched their fists to shake them in His face, declaring, "You will not rule my life, You will not have my soul." Those on the other side of the battle line had been hardened in their unbelief. If they could have, they would have done anything to destroy God and His influence in their life. They had rejected His rule over themselves and over the world.

Again, John looked at Jesus prepared for battle, and saw behind Him the armies of Heaven—millions upon millions of soldiers ready for battle, ready to follow Jesus into war. This was a battle they would not lose.

The army waited for the command from their Master. Soon, He would open His mouth, and from it would come the Word of God. All people on earth would be judged by His Word, and they would feel the fierce wrath of Almighty God that had been promised in the Scriptures.

John knew who was riding upon the white horse at the head of the army. It was Jesus, the One who had ridden meekly into Jerusalem on Palm Sunday on a donkey. John knew this was the same Jesus who had come to him on the shore of Lake Galilee, inviting him to "Come, follow Me."

But now, Jesus was called, "KING OF KINGS and LORD OF LORDS." While on earth, Jesus had lived in a nation ruled by a king called Caesar. He had obeyed Caesar's law, stood before Caesar's judgment throne, and was executed by Caesar's soldiers. And as Jesus hung on the cross, it appeared that Caesar was both king and lord. But not on this final day of human history.

Jesus is the King of Caesar...but not just Caesar. Jesus is the King of every king who has ever lived. Jesus is "KING OF KINGS and LORD OF LORDS."

John turned his eyes away; he would not write battle descriptions about the final conflict on earth. He would not list the numbers of those who would die in opposition to Jesus Christ, nor would he describe how they died, nor would he describe the final judgment. He would not describe the blood...gore...squalor...and death. The battle scene would not be written in John's Book of the Revelation. Why glorify war? Why describe corpses and magnify death?

Why did they not believe...why did they not repent...why did they not accept Jesus Christ?

As John thought about the millions who would die under God's judgment, he remembered the words he had penned in his Gospel, "For God so loved the world...." All the people in the world were loved by God. God could say that He loved everyone because He allowed His Son to die in the place of all people, even those rebels who would lie dead on the fields of Armageddon. Jesus had died for them, even though they would not believe, nor would they receive salvation. They would waste their lives needlessly because satan would so effectively blind them that they would refuse to believe in God and His Son. When they would choose the path of least resistance, they would choose death.

Then John again heard echoes deep within the cave, a sound returning that he had heard a few minutes earlier. The voice came like thunder rumbling down the valley, like a tidal wave rushing from the ocean. He heard the refrains louder than ever before...

"HALLELUJAH!"

What I Learned From Jesus' Return

- I will use the same words to praise God in Heaven that I use on earth.

- I will express my worship better with some words, such as the word "HALLELUJAH!"

- I know God will reward me when I live for Him and suffer for Him, just as surely as I know God will judge those who disobey and rebel against Him.

- I know God will not punish people without first giving them an opportunity to respond.

- I can better endure present sufferings when I realize there is a future reward.

Section Nine

Scripture: Revelation chapters 19–20

Lord, John heard the roar of a great multitude,
>Shouting, "Hallelujah...victory and glory and power
>To our God."
>It was all Heaven worshiping You because
>>Christ was getting ready for His return to earth.
>The crowd shouted, "God judges accurately and God punishes fair;
>>He has condemned the religious prostitute
>>Who corrupted mankind with her adultery.
>God has avenged the death of the martyrs
>>That the evil prostitute has killed."

Lord, the crowd sang to You, "Hallelujah...the smoke from
>The judgment of the prostitute goes on forever."

Then the 24 saints before the throne
>And the four Seraphim around the throne
>Fell on their faces to worship You, the God of judgment,
>>Crying, "AMEN, we agree with Your judgment.
>>AMEN...Your will be done forever."

Lord, a voice echoed out over the multitude,
>"Praise our God, all His servants,
>Great and small who reverence Him."
>John heard the immense crowd roar like thunder,
>>"Hallelujah...the reign of God over
>>The earth is about to begin.
>Let us be glad and rejoice because
>>The marriage supper of the Lamb is ready;
>>Jesus will be united with His Bride, the Church.

The Bride is ready because she is made pure
    By the blood of the Lamb.
She is dressed in fine white linen
    Which is made from the good deeds of the saints."
The angel told John to write, "God has said, 'Blessed are the saints
    Who are invited to the wedding supper of the Lord.'"

Lord, John fell at the feet to worship the angel, but he said,
    "No, don't worship me, I am a servant
    Of God like you; worship God."
The angel explained the purpose of the prophetic words
    He had given John;
    It was to tell all about Jesus.

Lord, John then saw Heaven open, and riding a white horse
    Was Jesus, who is called Faithful and True.
Jesus was ready to make war with all the armies
    Gathered in the valley of Armageddon to oppose
    Him and His plan for the Holy Land.
His eyes as blazing fire saw into the hearts
    And rebellion of all people.
He wore a crown, symbolic of His rulership
    Over all the earth.
He had a name embroidered on His garment
    That no one knew but Him.
The name of Jesus was the Word of God,
    And His garments were covered with the blood
    Of those He had defeated.
An enormous army followed Him;
    They wore white symbolizing their purity,
    And they rode white horses.
Jesus held the sharp sword of justice
    To strike down those who rebelled against Him,
    And He will rule them with an iron grip.

On His robe is written, "King of Kings and Lord of Lords."
　　Now He will tread over His enemies
　　As grapes are crushed in the wine press.

Lord, John saw an angel standing in the sun,
　　　　Shouting to all the birds of Heaven,
　　"Come eat the bodies of those
　　　　Who fought against God and His plan."
The dead included all the generals, soldiers,
　　　　Horses, and citizens—great and small.

Lord, John saw the antichrist was taken prisoner
　　　　With the false prophet who had worked miracles,
Deceiving those who were branded with 666,
　　　　And who worshiped the statue of the antichrist.
These two were thrown into the fiery lake
　　　　Burning with brimstone.
All the rest were killed under the judgment of God,
　　　　And the birds had a feast on their flesh.

Lord, next John saw an angel descending from Heaven
　　　　With the key to hell.
He had an enormous chain, and when He
　　　　Overpowered satan, who is also called
　　　　The serpent, the devil, and the dragon,
He chained him and threw him into hell
　　　　To remain there 1,000 years.
Then the angel shut the entrance and sealed it
　　　　To make sure the devil would not
　　　　Deceive people until the 1,000 years were over.
At the end of that time, satan
　　　　Would be released for a short period of time.

Lord, John saw many who had the authority to judge,
　　　　Sitting on judgment thrones.

Then John saw the martyrs resurrected to new life;
    They had been beheaded
    Because of their testimony.
They had not worshiped the beast, or his statue,
    Nor had they been branded in their hearts or forehead
With the brand of the antichrist—666.
    They reigned with Christ 1,000 years.

The unsaved dead were not resurrected yet;
    They were to be judged after the 1,000 years.
The saved are raised in the first resurrection;
    The second death holds no power over them.
They will be priests who worship You for 1,000 years,
    And they will reign with Christ for 1,000 years.
        Amen.

Chapter 69

SEEING THE FUTURE HEAVEN

Scripture: Revelation chapters 21–22

John propped his head in his hands, he was weak. The vision of people being cast into hell was distasteful. He didn't want to write about eternal retribution, but he had to write what God commanded. Strength is sapped from people when doing something they don't want to do. John was the apostle of love. He had always appealed to the love of God. But the other side of God was also to be revealed—His holiness and justice. John wrote about hell because he could be trusted to do anything Christ told him to do.

John wrote how millions of unsaved people appeared before God's eternal bar of justice. Then, it was too late to give them a second chance to be saved. Even if God would give them a second chance, they would continue to rebel to the end. The would never repent.

But God never asked, "What sin did you commit?" Their filthiness was no longer the issue. Instead, each, who appeared before God, was asked...

"What have you done with Jesus Christ?"

The books that recorded what each had done on earth were examined. The first book that was opened was called "The Lamb's Book of Life." It contained the names of everyone who had placed their trust in Jesus Christ for salvation.

During this judgment, when a person appeared before God, a voice rang out...

"Is your name written in the Lamb's Book of Life?"

One after another, they all answered the same, "No!" They could not lie in the presence of God, who is truth. When asked if they believed in Jesus Christ, each answered defiantly…

"NO!"

"Depart from Me," was the only response that God could give. "You never believed in Jesus for salvation." They were then sent to hell, the place prepared for the devil and his angels. The lost didn't plead for a second chance, nor did they weep with remorse. As they had died rejecting eternal life, so they stood defiantly before God continuing their rebellion which had characterized their life. Those who had violently rejected God in life, again violently repudiated God as they stood in judgment. Those who had quietly turned from God in life, again softly turned from God as they stood before the Great White Judgment Throne. Their decision sealed their eternity—they had chosen hell over Heaven.

John's head dropped to the table, his eyelids closed. Although he slept fitfully, dreaming nightmares of the lost, he continued sleeping because he was too weary to fight it off. John had to sleep to regain stamina—he still had another scene to write in his book.

Waking a little while later, John stretched his arms to prepare himself to finish his task. The candle burned low, and he wasn't sure if it was day or night outside his cave. But he would not go to see. He didn't need to know the time of day on Patmos; he was concerned with Heaven. Again, he turned away from the morsel of bread—he would not eat until he finished his book. John looked up to God and asked…

"What happened after the unsaved were judged?"

In answer to his prayer, God gave John a new vision—a vision of Heaven.

John saw the first Heaven and the first earth pass away. All the great building projects were gone…civilizations…libraries…communication marvels…humanitarian efforts—gone.

John wept.

Then John the Seer observed the emergence of a new Heaven, more glorious than the previous. Next he saw a new earth, new in the sense of being transformed and glorified, yet an earth like the former one. This time, however, there was no curse, nor rebellion. The new earth was a city ruled by God. It was prepared for people who would be ruled by God, a place where the renewed beauty of nature was more lovely than the previous earth, for God had transformed the world.

The new heavenly city came down from God—it was a place where God would live with His people. The holy city was the New Jerusalem. John was told the city "was pure like a bride prepared for her husband." Just as the believers were called "the Bride" for Jesus the Bridegroom, so the place they would live was compatible to the purity of the people of God.

John knew that his father and mother were in the new city, for they believed in Jesus. Intuitively, John knew that those of his family and friends who had placed their faith in Jesus would also live there. But thinking of his loved ones also made John remember those who wouldn't be there. John remembered a ruler of the synagogue in Capernaum who had refused to believe Jesus was the Messiah. He wouldn't be in the new city. John remembered some other friends from Jerusalem who also wouldn't be there. In life, they had hardened their hearts to Jesus. Then with hardened faces, they rejected Him in hell, as they had rejected Him on earth.

John wept.

Not only did John cry, but all those in the heavenly city wept when they realized that friends and family were missing. How could they enjoy Heaven with the thought of loved ones not there?

Even in the cave in Patmos, John wept real tears, for the future was as real as the present. But he didn't cry for long, for God came to wipe away tears—all tears. Not just the tears trickling down the deep lines of John's wrinkled face, but God wiped away all tears of all believers in Heaven...for all that caused their sadness.

And with God's eternal handkerchief, He erased from the memories of His people all the thoughts that made them weep. They wouldn't remember their lost friends...that memory was wiped away. They wouldn't remember their sins and failures...those memories were gone. They wouldn't remember sickness...pain...betrayals. Every memory that would destroy their joy and peace was wiped away. All sin was gone, separated from them, as far as the east is from the west. In Heaven there was no sorrow, no sickness, no pain.

Your Time to Worship

- Lord, there were many sins in my life before I was saved, but because You forgave them, I thank You.

- Lord, there have been many times I've failed You since I've been saved, but because You put them under the blood of Christ, I praise You.

- Lord, there have been many people to whom I haven't witnessed, but because You forgive my lethargy, I magnify You.

- Lord, there have been many times I haven't prayed as I should have, but because You wipe away the tears of unfulfilled potential, I worship You.

- Lord, there are things I should do today, but still will not have completed at Your return; I continue to pray, "Come quickly."

"Come," the Spirit said to John, "I will show you the center of Heaven and what people will do in Heaven." The Spirit carried John to a high mountain, and from that vantage point, John could see everything in eternity. He was not viewing Heaven with his human eyes, but John saw things through the eyes of the Spirit.

John saw a river, a sparkling clear river flowing through the middle of Heaven. Every city in the ancient world had been built on a river or well; without water, there would have been no life. Likewise, Heaven would have all the water its inhabitants needed, but they wouldn't need to drink water to live. They had already drank from the water offered to the woman at the well by Jesus. "Whoever drinks of the water that I shall give him will never thirst. But the water that I shall give him will become in him a fountain of water springing up into everlasting life" (John 4:14).

Then the Spirit told John, "The people of Heaven don't need to drink to live, but many in Heaven will drink for enjoyment and refreshment."

John looked up the river to see its source and noticed that it was coming from the throne of God and the Lamb. The water came from God Himself. As the river flowed through Heaven, John observed trees growing near the bank on both sides of the river, just as trees on earth had grown near water so their roots could drink. These trees looked similar to the trees of earth, but their fruit was different. The Spirit explained to John that the trees had 12 different kinds of fruit on each tree, and they produced a crop of ripe fruit for each month, not like earthly trees that had produced a crop only once a year. The inhabitants of Heaven would never be hungry, neither would they become bored eating the same kind of food all the time. Abundant fruit continually!

"Will there be enough fruit?" John asked.

"You do not have to eat in Heaven," the Spirit explained. "Because all believers have eternal bodies, food is not required. But if you choose to eat for enjoyment, there will be enough for all."

"Will we sleep in Heaven?" John asked.

"There is no night in Heaven," the Spirit answered. "You won't need a candle, because the Lord will be your light. Sleep is not required because no one will get tired, nor will they get sick. The night was made for sleeping on earth, but people in Heaven will sleep only if they choose."

"Will we know everyone in Heaven?" John asked.

The Spirit smiled because John in his old age was having trouble remembering some of his friends. John had even forgotten what he wrote in his letter about Heaven, "We shall know as we are known." Then the Spirit explained, "You will recognize people as you remembered them. Those you knew on earth, you will know in Heaven. You will not know everyone. Only God knows all things." The Spirit explained to John that he would know all the people in Heaven he needed to know.

"Will I learn things in Heaven and will I grow wiser?" John asked the Spirit.

"Yes…" the Spirit explained the leaves of the trees were for the growth of believers. "You will continually grow in knowledge as you grew on the earth, but you won't learn everything there is to know. Only God knows all things. You will continue to learn things throughout eternity and still never learn everything there is to know."

"Will I work in Heaven?" The ever-curious John continued asking questions of the Spirit.

"Yes…" the Spirit again answered. "All God's servants will minister to Him in worship." The Spirit explained that just as people were created to glorify and worship God on earth, so their task in Heaven would be to give glory and worship to God.

John remembered there was no sin in Heaven and no one would have a sin nature. No one would hate work in Heaven as people hated working here on earth. Those Christians who didn't want to worship God on earth, or didn't do it very often, will all worship God passionately in Heaven. There would be no temptation to by-pass worship. God's people would instinctively return to worship God again…and again…and again. The Spirit explained…

"You will work, you will desire to work, you will grow in maturity from your work, and you will never reach a plateau where you'll stop growing in character and grace. In Heaven, you will continually grow to be like Jesus."

John viewed Heaven from the top of a high mountain, watching people go about their duties. He saw where people lived—the mansions promised by Jesus, and he saw them fellowshipping together. Heaven was a desirable place. Then he commented...

"Life in Heaven is not unlike life on earth."

The Spirit agreed with John's observation, then added, "Why would God create life in the garden of Eden, then change His plans to give a completely different kind of life in Heaven?" The angel noted that God is the same...angels are the same...people are the same; so why then should life be different in Heaven?

John agreed with the Spirit, but he didn't like waiting for this beautiful place. He prayed, "Lord, come now to end Roman persecution of the Church." He wanted Heaven now. God answered...

"Jesus will come soon, but no one knows the hour that He will come...not the angels...not the elders...not the Seraphim." The Lord explained that Jesus would come when people least expected Him...like a thief in the night.

"What will happen to followers who are suffering at the hand of Rome?" John couldn't forget he was in prison at Patmos. He couldn't forget that his brothers—the other apostles—had been violently killed. "Why can't You come now?"

The Spirit explained that the Great Commission still required them to preach the Gospel to the ends of the earth...they hadn't done that yet. The Spirit explained that as a great harvest of evangelism continued, "The devil will continue to persecute the Church, and those addicted to filthiness will continue to be filthy." The Spirit directed His attention to the Church, "Let the believers who live holy lives, continue to be holy."

Jesus was listening to the conversation between John and the Spirit, because Jesus knows everything, and He whispered in John's ear, "Behold, I come quickly, bringing a reward for every believer according to their faithfulness."

John returned to his crude table to write the things he saw in Heaven. He wrote furiously...as fervently as a man past 90 could write, and littered the floor of the cave with pages of the book. Soon John would finish and gather the pages in order. In his heart, he knew his book would not be destroyed by his Roman guards, nor would it be lost at sea by those who might escape to deliver it to the world.

Because the Lord Jesus Christ had commanded him to write...because the Holy Spirit had inspired its inscription...because the Father had revealed its content to him, John knew his book called The Revelation would be first delivered to the prisoners waiting at the mouth of the cave, then to encourage the Church in persecution all over the Roman Empire, and finally to the future believers who needed to know about the coming events and about Heaven itself.

John looked at the white cloth covering the morsel of bread. "Should I eat now?" John wondered if he were finished writing the book. He would not feed his body until he fed the world with the bread of God.

"The Spirit and the Bride invite all to come to God."

Hearing the invitation, John slipped from the table to the floor. He bowed in humility before God, not to worship this time, but to intercede for lost people to come to God. As he prayed, John heard...

"Let all who hear the Word of God come..."

John continued interceding when he again heard the invitation...

"Let him who is thirsty come to drink of the water of God."

When the Lord stopped speaking to John, the ancient apostle arose from prayer, his knees throbbing. Again John sat at his table. Then the Lord gave John further instructions to write in his book...

"If any one hears the prophecies of this book and adds to them, I will give him more punishment than is written in this book."

John wrote the sentence just as the Lord dictated it. Then God spoke again...

"If anyone takes away any words from this book, I will take away his part out of the Book of Life."

John knew he was coming to the end of the book. He bowed his head at the table to ask, "Is there anything else?" Jesus, who came to John in the cave when he began the book, returned. Jesus understood the heart's passion of John and spoke His final words to him...

"Surely, I come quickly."

John wrote the last words of Jesus, then added his own prayer, "Even so, come, Lord Jesus."

Now, John had come to the end, and added the benediction, "The grace of our Lord Jesus Christ be with you all. Amen."

John finished writing and squeezed the last drop of ink from his quill. He gathered the pages, placing them in order. Uncovering the morsel of bread, John lifted his eyes to Heaven, gave thanks, and ate.

What I Learned About Heaven

- I will go to live with God in Heaven if I have believed in Christ as my personal Savior.

- I should attempt to win as many to salvation as possible, because there will be no second chances after death or the return of Christ.

- I will weep in Heaven for my friends who are lost, but God will wipe away all tears and make me forget.

- I will live a life in Heaven that is not much different from life on earth.

- I will learn, grow, and develop in Heaven.

Section Ten

Chapters 21–22

Lord, You showed the new Heaven and the new Earth
>> To John because the first Heaven and earth
> Were burnt up in the fervent heat.
>> The new earth didn't have any seas.
> John saw the holy city—the new Jerusalem
>> Coming down from Your presence in Heaven,
>> As beautiful as a bride at a wedding.
> Then John heard a loud voice announcing,
>> "God is now making His home among people.
> He will live among them,
>> And they will be His people.
> He will wipe away every tear from their eyes,
>> There will be no more death, sickness, or pain;
>> All sorrows of the past are gone."

Lord, You who sits on the throne announced,
>> "I am making everything new!"
> Then You told John, "Write this down,
>> For this is the way it will happen."
> Just as Christ on the cross said of sin, "It is finished,"
>> So You will say of life on this earth,
>> "It is finished."

Then Jesus said, "I am the Alpha and Omega,
>> I am the beginning of all things, and
>> I am the purpose of all things.
> I will give water from the well of eternal life
>> To anyone who thirsts for Me.
>> This is My gift to those who are victorious.

They will be Your children, O Father in Heaven,
 And You will be their God;
But You reserve the lake of fire for
 Unbelievers, cowards, those speaking
 Obscenities, murderers, sex offenders,
Idolaters, and all liars—
 That will be their second death."

Lord, one of the seven angels with bowls of judgment
 Said to John, "Come, I will show you the Bride,
 The wife of the Lamb."
Then John was carried away in a prophetic vision
 To a high mountain where he saw the new Jerusalem,
 The holy city coming down from God.
It was filled with the Shekinah glory of God,
 And it sparkled like a dish of precious jewels,
 And it was crystal clear.
The walls were very high and very wide,
 And there were 12 gates, guarded by 12 angels.
The names of the 12 tribes of Israel
 Were written on the 12 gates.
There were three gates on each side—
 North, South, East, and West.
The walls were built on 12 foundation stones,
 And the names were written on them
 Of the 12 apostles who had followed Jesus.
The angel held in his hand a golden
 Rod to measure the city and walls.
He measured 1500 miles from side to side
 And from top to bottom.
The city was foursquare, as long
 As it is wide, and it is high.
Next he measured the thickness of the walls;
 They were 216 feet across,

According to his measurement.
The city was constructed of transparent gold;
    One could see through it like glass.
The walls were like jasper;
        The 12 foundations were garnished with jewels.
        The first foundation was like jasper,
        The second foundation was like sapphire,
        The third foundation was like chalcedony,
        The fourth foundation was like emerald,
        The fifth foundation was like sardonyx,
        The sixth foundation was like sardius,
        The seventh foundation was like chrysolite,
        The eighth foundation was like beryl,
        The ninth foundation was like topaz,
        The tenth foundation was like chrysoprase,
        The eleventh foundation was like jacinth,
        The twelfth foundation was like amethyst,

The 12 gates glistened like a pearl,
        And the streets were paved with pure gold,
        As clear as transparent glass.

There was no temple in the city, because people
        Worshiped You and the Lamb everywhere.
The city did not need sun or moon for light,
        Because it was continually lit by
        Your Shekinah glory and the Lamb.
The people who are saved will walk in the light,
        And everyone—including all kings—will glorify You.
The gates will never be shut; they remain open
        For there is no night there.
Nothing sinful will enter the city; no one
        Who is filthy or lies
        Will be allowed in the city.

The only ones there will be true believers
      Whose names are written in the Lamb's Book of Life.

Lord, the angel showed John a sparkling clean river,
      Flowing from Your throne and the Lamb.
   It flowed down the middle of the central street of Heaven.
      Trees of Life grew on each side of the river,
 And a new crop of fruit grew each month
      That could be harvested each month.
The leaves provided growth for all people
      Who will eat from the Trees of Life.

Lord, there is nothing evil in the city,
      Because Your throne and the Lamb are there.
      All Your servants will worship You continually.
Your servants will see the face of the Lamb,
      And His name will be on their forehead.
There will be no night—no need for lights—for You
Will give light to the city.
      And You will rule Your people forever.

Lord, the angel told John, "God's people can trust
      These words and descriptions of Heaven.
      Be prepared, He is coming soon."
You who tell the future to Your prophets
      Sent your angel to tell John these things that will soon occur.
They are blessed who read this book
      And believe what it says.

Lord, when John saw and heard all these things that
      Were about to happen, he lay prostrate
      To worship the angel who showed him these things.
The angel said, "No! I am a servant of Jesus
      Like you are. Obey what prophets say,
   'Worship God!'"

The angel instructed John not to close
 The book he was writing,
  But tell everyone its message
Because the evil person will continue to do evil
 And the filthy will continue to do filthy things.
Also good people will continue to do good,
 And holy people will continue being holy.

Lord, Jesus said, "I am coming soon, and I'll
 Have a reward for everyone,
  According to the deeds they have done."
"I am Alpha and Omega, the Beginning and the End,
 The First and Last of everything.
Those who live by My Word
 Can enter the gates into the city,
  And eat the fruit of the Tree of Life."
Outside the city there will be rebels, and sorcerers,
 And the sexually impure, murderers,
  Idolaters, and those who love to lie.
Jesus sent an angel to tell John
 These messages for the churches.
Jesus was born in the family line of David.
 He is the bright Star of the morning.

Lord, the Holy Spirit and all believers
 Tell the unsaved, "Come!"
  Let all those who are thirsty, "Come!"
All who want the water of eternal life
 May have it free.

Lord, John warned everyone who read this book,
  Don't add anything to this book, or God
  Will add to their punishment.
And if any take away from the things in this book,
  God will take away their part in the Book of Life

And in the holy city.
Jesus who repeated the warnings said,
    "Surely I come quickly!"
John agreed with Jesus and said, "Amen!
    Even so, come, Lord Jesus."
Then John gave the benediction, "The grace
    Of our Lord Jesus Christ be with you."
        Amen.

ABOUT THE AUTHOR

DR. ELMER TOWNS is an author of popular and scholarly works, a seminar lecturer, and dedicated worker in Sunday school. He has written over 125 books including several best sellers. In 1995 he won the coveted Gold Medallion Book Award for *The Names of the Holy Spirit.*

Dr. Elmer Towns also cofounded Liberty University with Jerry Falwell in 1971 and now serves as Dean of the B.R. Lakin School of Religion and as professor of Theology and New Testament.

Liberty University was founded in 1971 and is the fastest growing Christian university in America. Located in Lynchburg, Virginia, Liberty University is a private, coeducational, undergraduate and graduate institution offering 38 undergraduate and 15 graduate programs serving over 25,000 resident and external students (9,600 on campus). Individuals from all 50 states and more than 70 nations comprise the diverse student body. While the faculty and students vary greatly, the common denominator and driving force of Liberty University since its conception is love for Jesus Christ and the desire to make Him known to the entire world.

For more information about Liberty University, contact:

**Liberty University
1971 University Boulevard
Lynchburg, VA 24502
Telephone: 434-582-2000
E-mail: www.Liberty.edu**

ALSO FROM ELMER TOWNS

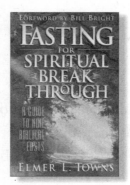

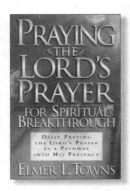

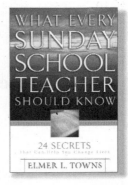